THE CUSTER MYTH

The Passing of the Yellow Hair

THE
CUSTER MYTH

A Source Book of Custeriana

Written and compiled by
COLONEL W. A. GRAHAM
UNITED STATES ARMY, RETIRED

To Which is Added
IMPORTANT ITEMS OF CUSTERIANA
and
A COMPLETE AND COMPREHENSIVE
BIBLIOGRAPHY
by FRED DUSTIN

University of Nebraska Press
Lincoln and London

First Bison printing: 1986
Most recent printing indicated by the first digit below:
2   3   4   5   6   7   8   9   10

Library of Congress Cataloging-in-Publication Data
Graham, W. A. (William Alexander), 1875–1954.
The Custer myth.
Reprint. Originally published: Harrisburg, Pa.:
Stackpole Co., [1953].
Bibliography: P.
Includes index.
1. Little Big Horn, Battle of the, 1876—Sources.
2. Custer, George Armstrong, 1839–1876. I. Dustin,
Fred, 1866–   . II. Title.
E83.876.G7 1986   973.8'2   86-4308
ISBN 0-8032-2124-X
ISBN 0-8032-7016-X (pbk.)

Reprinted by arrangement with Stackpole Books,
Harrisburg, Pennsylvania.

TO THOSE PERSONS

who think that Dis-solution of the Custer Myth

is easy,

and

particularly to those

who are quite sure they have Dis-solved it,

This work is dedicated:

(with malice aforethought, express and implied)

PROLOGUE

THE Battle of the Little Big Horn, in which Major General George Armstrong Custer and five companies of the 7th U.S. Cavalry who rode with him died at the hands of the followers of Sitting Bull, has for over three quarters of a century afforded a rich field for controversial discussion and speculation.

Writers by the score have attempted to explain the events of that sultry June afternoon in 1876, choosing such titles as CUSTER'S LAST STAND, THE CUSTER TRAGEDY, GLORY HUNTER, LEGEND INTO HISTORY, et al.

Of all the authors who have covered the subject, Colonel W. A. Graham, U.S.A. Retired, has gained the deserved reputation of having written the most definitive, factual account of the battle in THE STORY OF THE LITTLE BIG HORN, originally published by The Century Company in 1926 and three times re-published by The Military Service Publishing Company, the most recent edition appearing in 1952.

This latest and most comprehensive of his works, THE CUSTER MYTH, was inevitable. As the arguments between Custerphiles and Custerphobes continued to wax fast and furious, the Colonel, maintaining his admirable neutrality, concluded that the need for "a source book to end all source books" on Custer had become imperative.

In the course of an extended pre-publication correspondence between author and publisher, the latter questioned the appropriateness of the word "myth" as a part of the title, suggesting that The Custer Mystery might possibly come closer to hitting the target. The author's reply, in the clipped, decisive phrases which characterize the 'old Army' Regular, advised that the title was chosen deliberately. So lucid and interesting was his reasoning that it is quoted herewith in full:

"Just what is a Myth? Ever since I began the study of history, many long years ago, I have been making the acquaintance of myths in one form or another. The exploits of the ancient gods of Greece and Rome come to one's mind instantly when one speaks of myths; but each of them, very probably, was founded in greater or less degree upon the accomplishments of some man, whose identity, once known, was lost in the maze of traditions, fictions and inventions that ascribed to him the attributes of a superman; and as the centuries passed, endowed him with the character of a supernatural person.

"We have ourselves created myths in the course of our own short history, which spans less than two hundred years. Washington was in fact a very human person, as contemporary records prove; but the Washington the average American knows is not the real Washington. As "Father of his Country"; the all-wise leader, the military hero, the champion of freedom and foe of tyranny, his human qualities have all but disappeared. He has become a Myth.

"So also with Lincoln, martyred savior of his country; about whom and around whom has been built so fantastic a structure of fictitious tales and absurd stories, that the real Lincoln has been obscured from view; and so, in our own day with Franklin D. Roosevelt, who to millions of Americans was a selfless, immaculate latter-day Messiah, who gave his life on the altar of self sacrifice. Both these men were human beings—very human; but the Lincoln and the Roosevelt known to the average American are Myths.

"And so with Custer, and so with nearly everyone involved in the Custer story. It began in controversy and dispute; but because a devoted wife so skilfully and so forcefully painted her hero as a plumed knight in shining armor—a "chevalier sans peur and sans reproche," that all who stood in the way of her appraisal were made to appear as cowards or scoundrels; and because her hero went out in a blaze of glory that became the setting for propaganda which caught and held, and still holds, the imagination of the American people, what began in controversy and dispute has ended in Myth; a myth built, like other myths, upon actual deeds and events, magnified, distorted and disproportioned by fiction, invention, imagination and speculation. The Custer known to the average American is a Myth; and so is Reno; and so also is Benteen.

"The Source book does not attempt to unravel a mystery—Kuhlman and Dustin did that, each arriving at a different conclusion. What the Source book does is to present the "makings" of the Custer Myth.

"There *is* a Custer mystery, of course; there always will be, because, except for the result, exactly what happened to his battalion can never be known; and out of this very fact grew the fictions, inventions and fantastic tales and legends that together form the Custer Myth."

CLAY MODEL OF CUSTER BATTLEFIELD

A vertical photograph of the terrain model constructed by Artist Gayle P. Hoskins, based on the U.S.G.S. contour map, to assure accuracy in developing his painting of the battle, *Custer's Last Fight.*

The battleridge appears at the top of the photograph, with Calhoun Ridge at the extreme upper right. The loops of the Little Big Horn River are easily identifiable in the lower half of the model.

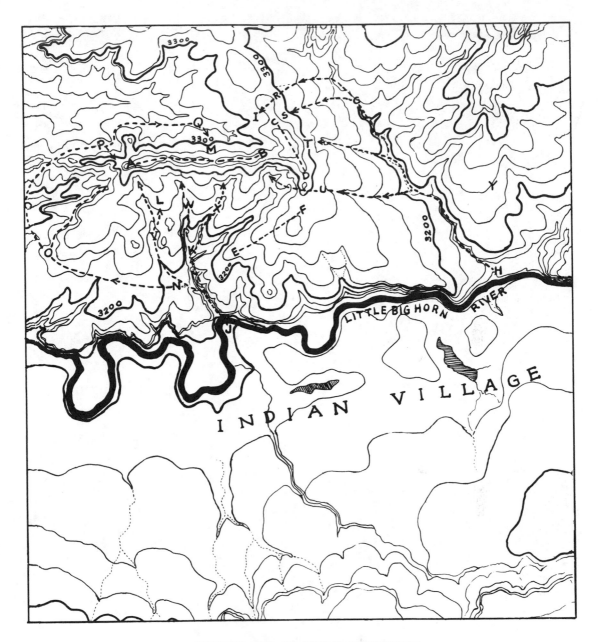

CONTOUR MAP OF CUSTER BATTLEFIELD

Approximate scale, 1 inch = 3350 feet
CONTOUR INTERVAL, 25′

A: Custer Hill	E-F: Greasy Grass Ridge	J: Crazy Horse Crossed	M: "I" Destroyed
A-B: Battle Ridge	G-H: N. Medicine Tail	K: Gray Horse Ambushed	N-O-P-Q: Crazy Horse Strikes
C-D: Calhoun Ridge	I: "I" & "L" Led Horses	L: "C" & "F" Routed	R-S-T-U: Gall's Attack
	V-W-X: Lame White Man's Attack	Y: Sergeant Butler	

This is a reproduction of the U. S. Geological Survey map of the battlefield, upon which the Author has (a) super-imposed the movements of the Indian warriors who played decisive roles in the destruction of Custer's Battalion; and (b) spotted the principal terrain features and the actual locations where the several troops of the 7th Cavalry are presumed to have been overwhelmed.

PREFACE

IN SUBMITTING to the public the within material, which for want of a better title, I have chosen to call "THE CUSTER MYTH: a Source Book of Custeriana," a short preface is considered desirable in order that its purpose may be made clear.

ON JUNE 25, 1876, GENERAL GEORGE A. CUSTER AND FIVE TROOPS OF THE SEVENTH UNITED STATES CAVALRY WERE COMPLETELY WIPED OUT BY INDIANS AT THE BATTLE OF THE LITTLE BIG HORN RIVER IN MONTANA. THE REMAINDER OF THE REGIMENT, UNDER MAJOR RENO, AFTER A SHORT ENGAGEMENT IN THE VALLEY OF THAT RIVER, IN WHICH HIS OWN BATTALION OF THREE TROOPS WAS ROUTED, WAS BESIEGED THROUGHOUT THE LATE AFTERNOON AND EVENING OF THE 25TH AND DURING MOST OF THE 26TH, SUSTAINING VERY HEAVY LOSSES. LATE ON THE 26TH, THE INDIANS WITHDREW AND THE SURVIVORS WERE RELIEVED BY FORCES UNDER GENERALS TERRY AND GIBBON DURING THE MORNING OF JUNE 27TH.

The above are the bare facts, stripped to the bone; devoid of all detail. Under ordinary conditions, so small and insignificant an event might well have received little more notice in the public prints than is contained in the foregoing paragraph. Yet, as "Custer's Last Fight," it has been the subject of more controversy, dissension, dispute and mendacity ever since the year of its occurrence than almost any other event in American history. Even the battle of Gettysburg had less written about it. Artists of every class—good—bad and indifferent—(indeed, even "modernists") have done pictures of "Custer's Last Stand"; at least 105 of these imaginative productions presently exist. Even foreign artists have competed with our own in the effort to make the "Last Stand" graphic. Poets have used alleged incidents of the battle as subjects for the expression of their art. The Custer Myth is a living thing, which refuses to die despite the efforts of careful historians to reduce it to uncontroverted facts. Almost everything about it is in some degree disputed except the skeletonized item capitalized above.

"CUSTERIANA" is a relatively indefinite term, which embraces not alone things pertaining to General Custer, but also events and persons connected with and pertaining to, his last campaign, whether directly or indirectly. The term not only could, but ordinarily *would,* apply to data concerned with his entire career; but it is *not* so applied in this volume. The reason is, that it was the impact upon the minds and imaginations of the American people of the events of his last campaign that made of Custer an almost legendary figure. Nearly everyone has heard of "Custer's last fight" or "Custer's last stand": comparatively few know much about him in any other connection. But for the "blaze of glory" that formed the setting for his dramatically tragic departure from this mundane sphere at the hands of yelling savages, he would probably be just another name of a long list of names in our histories of the Civil War, in which as "The Boy General" he made an outstanding record as a leader of Cavalry, as did also numerous others who have been long since all but forgotten.

There is, I believe, no incident of American history that has been made the subject of more research, investigation, and speculation than the battle of the Little Big Horn, which was the culmination of Custer's career, and in which he and his men reached the end of the trail. Hundreds—indeed thousands—of books, pamphlets, magazine articles and newspaper stories have been written about it; some of them good, more of them bad, and still more, indifferent. And the end is not yet.

One of the few, indeed, the very few things on which competent students of Custer's last campaign are agreed, is that the most important repository of information concerning it is the Official Record of the Court of Inquiry convened at Chicago in 1879 at Major Reno's request to investigate his conduct at the Battle of the Little Big Horn. Had that record been accessible to the public during the seventy-two years it was held "incommunicado" in the files of the War Department and the National Archives, much of the literature above referred to would probably never have been written.

But the Reno Inquiry record was not accessible to the public until 1951, when after long months spent in unraveling governmental red tape, I was permitted to publish it. This I did in an edition limited to 125 copies and it is now available to students in many college and reference libraries, and in the collections of historical societies. "It is the details found in the record" says Dr. Charles Kuhlman, author of that remarkable work "Legend into History," "that make it possible to understand and control other sources emanating from the Indians and the surviving members of the 7th Cavalry."

It is the purpose of this volume to present under one cover, a representative selection of the "other sources" thus alluded to by Dr. Kuhlman. These cover a wide field; so wide that it is manifestly impossible to include them all. I have done my best to bring together, however, narratives of the hostile Sioux and Cheyenne; of the friendly Arikara and Crow; all as translated from their native tongues by interpreters who were for the most part, whites. I have set forth in their original form, statements and letters of white scouts and other non-military participants. I have included the oft alluded to but never published Benteen-Goldin letters, for the editing and expurgation of which I assume responsibility, for they could not be published "in the raw." And I have produced, in his own handwriting, certain statements and letters written by Benteen, in order that readers may know exactly what this stern old soldier actually said, and when, and why. I have reproduced, in large part, General Godfrey's famous "Century" article, and also my own first Cavalry Journal effort, "Come on; be quick; bring packs," the first hand story of Trumpeter Martini, as he told it to me in 1922: and I have added its sequel "The Lost is Found," published by the Journal in 1942. I have presented some hitherto forgotten facts about the first publication of the news of the battle, which explains why the "scoop" did not come from Bozeman July 3rd instead of from Helena two days later. I have set out the military and literary records of Theodore W. Goldin who, if his stories can be believed, took part in almost every important phase of the battle, and I have answered innumerable inquiries received from anxious students as to why I did not credit his tale of a Paul Revere ride to carry a message to—Reno! In short, I have collected here, and offer in this volume, a great many bits of now scarce source material, from which you, the reader, may construct a mosaic of your own, appraising the value and the proper placement of each item, should you wish to write a story of Custer's Last Fight. It will probably be a better one than many heretofore written. And if you want more information, as you very well may, you have only to turn to the appended Bibliography, the product of that master of research, Fred Dustin, author of "The Custer Tragedy," itself an encyclopedic work.

Mr. Dustin is now 86 years old: I am 78. Both of us have exhausted our allotted three score and ten, and in presenting this, our farewell bow to students of Custeriana, we are interested primarily in offering to them a wide selection of hard-to-find source material that will not only whet their appetites for more, but point the way to where that "more" can be found, and in abundance.

The causes of the Sioux War of 1876 are *not* treated in this volume: and the spelling of proper names, which varies greatly, has been left as it was found in the originals of compiled articles and reports.

THE FRONTISPIECE

Pictures by scores have portrayed General Custer and his "Last Stand." Almost without exception, these have shown him immaculately attired, neat, and cleanly shaven; sartorially impeccable even in the buckskins he was wont to wear.

No picture so conceived is realistic, nor remotely approaches his true appearance during the melee and confusion of the Little Big Horn, when an Indian bullet laid him low.

The frontispiece, a reproduction of the figure of Custer during his last moments, done for this work by the famous artist Dwight Franklin, shows him as he really was. His yellow locks had been closely shorn with clippers before he left Ft. Lincoln on the 17th of May, nor had he shaved during the more than five weeks that intervened before the battle. For three long days and at least one night he had led his regiment of horsemen over a rough country, through veritable clouds of alkali dust, with which both men and animals were literally coated when the fight began. The day was very hot, and sweat and dust combined to begrime both face and hands. He was far from being the natty, debonair, well-groomed cavalier of the pictures: he was a weary, dirty, unkempt man who, fighting desperately for life, had reached the limit of vitality and strength, and whose drawn and haggard features made him appear older than his age by many years.

Such was Custer on June 25, 1876, and thus Dwight Franklin has depicted him; hair short, face covered with stubbly auburn beard, smeared and streaked with sweaty dust; blue shirt open at the neck, sleeves rolled up; buckskin breeches tucked into square topped boots, armed with revolvers and a hunting knife suspended from a canvas belt—his once white broad-brimmed hat, swept off in the heat of combat, lying in the sage behind him.

This then was Custer, "The Yellow Hair" at the moment of his passing; before the savages who killed him stripped the body and left it lying stark and bare. When examined, two bullet wounds were found, either of which was fatal. One pierced the left breast at or near the heart; the other crashed through the temple to the brain. The first was slightly blooded, the other not at all, which indicates probable infliction after death, when exultant Sioux and Cheyenne rode among the bodies of the slain, striking again the lifeless clay with bullets and with arrows.

ACKNOWLEDGMENTS

APPRECIATIVE thanks and acknowledgments are made by the author-compiler of this volume, to the many persons and publishers who have graciously authorized the use of copyrighted or otherwise restricted material.

Especial acknowledgment is made to The State Historical Society of North Dakota for permission to include generous excerpts from "The Arikara Narrative," a work of sterling value edited and compiled by the late O. G. Libby, then Secretary of the Society; to Appleton-Century-Croft, Inc., for permission to include extensive excerpts from the article "Custer's Last Battle," by General E. S. Godfrey, as published in the Century Magazine for January 1892; to the Houghton-Mifflin Company, publishers of Major James McLaughlin's great work "My friend the Indian," for permission to quote excerpted passages from the story of Mrs. Spotted Horn Bull; to Rinehart and Company, Inc., publisher of Joseph Mills Hanson's work "The Conquest of the Missouri," for permission to Fred Dustin to quote Sgt. Caddle's description of conditions found on the Little Big Horn battlefield in 1877; and to the Cavalry Journal for permission to reproduce my own articles, "Come on; Be quick; Bring Packs," and "The Lost is Found."

To Anita Benteen Mitchell, representing Colonel F. W. Benteen, Jr., for authorization to edit and publish the "Benteen-Goldin" letters; to Captain E. S. Luce, Ret'd, Pvt. Robert M. Utley, U. S. Army, Dr. Charles Kuhlman, Fred Dustin, Michael Harrison, Hugh Shick, Dr. Lawrence Frost and James S. Hutchins, for aid and research; and for material I could not myself command.

And to my preceptors and friends who, though they have passed on, during their lifetimes granted to me full and free permission to make use in any way I might see fit, of writings, letters, data and material sent or given me. Among these were Generals Edward S. Godfrey and Winfield Scott Edgerly; Generals Hugh L. Scott and Charles King (better known as "Captain King" whose writings picture accurately life in the "Old Army"); and to General Blanton Winship, General Benjamin Poore, and Captain Robert G. Carter. And there were many others, not of the Army, among them Frank Huston, W. A. Falconer, W. J. Ghent, and Dr. Francis Hagner, from each of whom I learned something of a subject whose ramifications, scope and variety seem limitless.

To the heirs of the late Herbert Coffeen, Publisher of the Tepee Book, for permission to make use of certain material in the 1916 issue of that magazine; to Colonel Tim McCoy, for contributing the stories of the Crow Scout 'White Man Runs Him,' and the Arapahoe warriors, 'Waterman' and 'Left Hand', and to the New York *Herald-Tribune* for permission to use a Webster-Roth cartoon.

And last, but by no means least, to my wife Helen Bury Graham, but for whose unselfish aid in typing, comparing, proof reading, assembling, and the multitude of other things that someone *must* do, I could never have collected and put together a compilation such as this, my thanks and deepest gratitude.

TABLE OF CONTENTS

PART I. INDIAN ACCOUNTS

Chapter 1

A WORD TO THE WISE

Chapter 2

"COMING EVENTS CAST THEIR SHADOWS BEFORE"

Chapter 3

Chapter 4

PART II. GODFREY, BENTEEN AND EDGERLY

LIST OF ILLUSTRATIONS

Part I

INDIAN ACCOUNTS

CHAPTER 1

A WORD TO THE WISE

IN CONSIDERING the weight to be given Indian accounts concerned with any event that involved differences with whites, one should be wary. One should make sure, so far as that be possible, that the accounts are authentic; that they are in truth and in fact correct and truthful renderings into English of what the Indians concerned actually said, whether by word of mouth or by the sign language. This admittedly is difficult to do; it is, indeed, quite frequently impossible. Even with the best and most honest of interpreters mistakes did occur. A classic example of erroneous interpretation which, though presumably uninten tional, caused the arrest and led indirectly to the tragic and untimely death of one of the greatest of Indian chiefs, was that made by Frank Grouard in 1877. Notwithstanding he had lived among the Sioux for many years, Grouard reported that the great Ogalalla, Crazy Horse, was ready to go north with his band *against the whites,* whereas his spokesman, Touch-the-Clouds, had in effect, actually said that they were ready to go north *to assist the whites against the Nez Perces.*

Being satisfied as to authenticity, the conditions under which a given statement was made becomes an all important consideration which involves many ingredient considerations. Was the Indian concerned friendly or hostile? Had he been on the warpath? Had he taken part in fighting or depredations against the whites? Had he been in combats in which whites were killed and scalped or otherwise mutilated? Had whites been captured, tortured and burned at the stake? Did he fear that if he told the truth he would be punished? Did he tell a story designed to please rather than to disclose facts? Did he think it the part of wisdom to alibi himself? Such questions are hard to answer as to statements made three quarters of a century ago.

We, at various times, have found it difficult to understand the acts and doings of alien races; and they, no doubt, have found it just as difficult to

understand us. Differences in point of view; in approach; in mental attitude; in psychology—all make it hard to reach a common ground. To truly understand the member of an alien race, one must learn to think as he thinks and thus to know what he means by what he says. Mere ability to speak an alien tongue does not necessarily imply that one understands the native who uses it.

The Indians were an alien race; they still are. We do not understand them even yet; as a nation we never really tried to understand them; and because they are a dying race, we never shall understand them.

When I wrote "The Story of the Little Big Horn," I had before me and had studied a great many Indian accounts, and it was my earnest desire to include as a part of the narrative, a description of the combat from the Indian point of view. I did not succeed, because the Indian accounts contradicted each other to such an extent that I found them irreconcilable. In this dilemma I turned to General Hugh L. Scott, a famous authority on the American Indian, who could reconcile them if anybody could. Scott went over them and threw up his hands. So I did not use them.

The selections that follow are believed to be *representative* and *reasonably authentic,* but none carries a guaranty that its content is true. I believe interpretations made by the Crow Russell White Bear to be reliable, for he translated the language of his own people. I believe those made by Mrs. McLaughlin to be reliable, for she too, dealt with the Lakotah, a language that to all intents and purposes, was her native tongue. I believe the interpretations contained in "The Arikara Narrative" faithfully represent what the Indians said. General Edgerly endorsed the interpretations of the Ft. Yates statements of the Sioux Chiefs in 1881, and I defer to his judgment. I do not know who interpreted the statements of Sitting Bull, of Kill Eagle, or of Horned Horse, who spoke for

Crazy Horse. It was Philo Clark, I believe, who interpreted for Red Horse, and Clark was reputed to be one of the best and ablest of interpreters of the language of the Sioux, as was also Dr. Marquis of the language of the Cheyennes.

The reader will find in these Indian statements discrepancies and contradictions and inconsistencies. He will have to do with them as all who have studied them have done, and reconcile them if and as he can.

After all, one finds quite as many, if not more, contradictions, discrepancies, inconsistencies and even easily identifiable falsehoods in the tales told by white men. The chief difference lies in the ease or difficulty of appraisal. The white man's state-

ments we understand: because English is his native tongue, we know what his language means. One cannot be sure on either score when dealing with the Indian.

However, when appraising the historical value of *any* uncorroborated statement concerned with the battle of the Little Big Horn, it is the part of wisdom to bear always in mind that those diabolical twins, The Great American Faker and The Great American Liar have been celebrating a continuous Field Day ever since the 25th of June 1876, and that General Custer and his Last Fight have furnished the inspiration for some wondrous and fantastic tales, the like of which the late lamented Baron Munchausen never excelled and seldom equalled.

CHAPTER 2

"COMING EVENTS CAST THEIR SHADOWS BEFORE"

Chief Blackfoot's Warning

THE CROW COUNCIL OF 1873
BLACKFOOT, THE CROW ORATOR
*Warns Them Concerning
the Sioux*

WHEN the Commissioners met at the Crow Agency in 1873, for the purpose of making a treaty with the Crows, they were told certain truths by the Chiefs respecting their common enemy the Sioux, which recent events confirm. The leader Chief and orator, Blackfoot, and a firm friend of the whites, (if an Indian can be one,) during the proceedings of the second day made several speeches, from one of which we make the following extract:

* * * "The commissioners told me that we should have plenty of food given us for forty years. They were big men who talked to us; they were not drunk when they told us. I told the commissioners at Laramie that I had seen the Sioux commit a great massacre; they killed many white men. But the Sioux are still there and still kill white men. When you whip the Sioux come and tell us of it. You are afraid of the Sioux. Two years ago I went with the soldiers; they were very brave; they were going through the Sioux country to Powder river and Tongue river. We got to Prior creek, just below here in the Crow country. I wanted to go ahead into the Sioux country, but the soldiers got scared and turned back. I was there and so were others who are here; they know what I say is true. The soldiers said they were going to Tongue river, but they got frightened at the Sioux and turned back. The soldiers were the whirlwind; they went toward the Sioux country, but the whirlwind turned back. Last summer the soldiers went to Prior creek again; again they said they were going through the Sioux country, but they saw a few Sioux; they were afraid of them; they got scared and turned up to the Muscleshell,

and went back again; again the whirlwind was going through the Sioux country, but again the whirlwind turned back. We are not the whirlwind, but we go to the Sioux; we go into their country; we meet them and fight, but we do not turn back; but we are not the whirlwind. You say the railroad is coming up the Yellowstone; that is like the whirlwind and cannot be turned back. I do not think it will come. The Sioux are in the way and you are afraid of them; they will turn the whirlwind back. If you whip the Sioux, and get them out of its way, the railroad may come, and I will say nothing."

On the fifth day he said: "You want to shake hands with them. We want to know whether you are going to fight the Sioux or not; we want to know." At the close of the Council the same Chief said: "You ought not to give the Sioux guns and ammunition; you should wipe them all out; you should throw a disease upon them." This Crow knew of the arming of the Sioux nation by Indian traders; the frontiersmen knew it; the Commission knew it; the Government knew and winked at it, and now we have the bloody fruits of a murderous Peace Policy.

(The *Helena Daily Herald*, Saturday,
July 15, 1876)

SITTING BULL'S G-2 WAS EFFICIENT

SOMETIME during the Spring of 1927, to the best of my recollection, General W. C. Brown, Retired, whom I had met some years before at the Army and Navy Club in Washington, sent me the following memorandum, which speaks for itself:

The following is an extract from an article by Sam O'Connell, who was book-keeper during 1875 at Juneaux's Indian Trading Post at the mouth of Frenchman's Creek on Milk River, Montana. It is interesting to me both because when eight years old I was a refugee during the Sioux War of 1862 in which the Santee Sioux were engaged, and because it shows that in 1875 the Indians knew, from some source, what was planned against them, months before the Army was called in; and their resistance was organized long before the 1876 campaign commenced. Dupré, I think, was a French-Canadian trader who visited the various tribes. Here is the extract:

"Dupré one day paid a visit to a camp of Santee Sioux. The name of the chief, if I remember right, was White Eagle. It will be remembered that the Santees were engaged in 1862 in the never to be forgotten New Ulm, Minn., Massacre. Many of the Santees were hung by the authorities, and the remnants appealed to the Great Father for a new home, which was given them in the Milk River country. While Dupré was at the Santee camp an Indian runner came in from one of the lower agencies and told the Santee Chief that the soldiers were coming out the following spring and were going to kill all the Indians that were found away from the agencies and they wanted help, and the runner also told that the Indians would get together near the mouth of Rosebud River and that the soldiers were coming from many directions and that Sitting Bull wanted Indians enough to kill off all the soldiers. It seems the Indians' appeal as far as the Santees were concerned was not heeded, and not any of the Santees went to the hostile camp.

"The runner had better success with the renegades, as we realized that their camp was growing less near the approach of spring. Dupré would often tell Juneaux and me of the big fight that was coming off and did occur the Centennial year of 1876 when Custer and his troops met their fate on the banks of the Little Big Horn."

The Crow Scout Curley reaches the steamboat Far West—June 28, 1876.

CHAPTER 3

THE CROWS

The Stories of the Crow Scouts

IN PRESENTING the stories of the Crow scouts who stayed with Custer until shortly before he rode to his death, I am in doubt as to what should be said concerning the one about whom the most has been written throughout the years—the scout "Curley," in 1876 a youth of seventeen.

The first recorded mention of Scout Curley as a "raconteur" is contained in a report to Terry's Engineer Officer, Lieut. Maguire, by Sergeant James E. Wilson, who was aboard the Steamer "Far West" at the mouth of the Little Big Horn, 28 June 1876:

"An Indian Scout named 'Curley,' known to have been with General Custer," says the report, "arrived about noon with information of a battle, but there being no interpreter on board very little reliable information was obtained. He wore an exceedingly dejected countenance, but his appetite proved to be in first class order."

But in sharp contrast to the above is the Arikara Narrative, which at page 208, in the course of a sketch of James Coleman, a trader who peddled whiskey to officers and soldiers of the Little Big Horn expedition, states:

"After Custer's defeat, Coleman was on the boat with Terry at the mouth of the Little Big Horn, when Curley appeared on the east bank * * * Curley held up his hand with a rag in it, and they waved him aboard. He wore a cloth about his head, a black shirt, a breech-clout, and moccasins. He came on board by the gang plank. Coleman saw Curley make one sign, the sleep sign, once. Then a crowd of officers and men cut off his view. George Morgan, a squaw-man (he had a Crow wife) * * * translated Curley's signs and speech. He reported that Curley said he had crawled two miles wrapped in a Sioux blanket; that Custer's command was wiped out and that Reno was in great danger."

Union--Extra.

GREAT BATTLE WITH THE INDIANS.

Terrific Slaughter

GEN. CUSTAR'S COMMAND ANNIHILATED.

CUSTAR KILLED!

Three Hundred Dead Left on the Field.

Gen. Custar's Two Brothers, a Nephew, Brother-in-Law, and 17 Commissioned Officers Among the Killed.

Special Dispatch to The San Diego Union.

STILLWATER, Montana Ter., July 2.—Mug. Taylor, scout for General Gibbons, arrived here last night direct from Little Horn river. He brings intelligence that General Custar found an Indian camp, of about two thousand lodges. on the Little Horn, and immediately attacked it. He took five companies, and charged into the thickest portion of the camp. Nothing is known of the operations of this detachment, only as they are traced by the dead. Major Reno commanded seven other companies, and attacked the lower portion of the camp.

The Indians poured in a murderous fire from all directions, and the greatest portion fought on horse-back.

General Custar, his two brothers, nephew and brother-in-law were all killed, and not one of his detachment escaped. Two hundred and seven men were buried in one place, and the number of killed is estimated at three hundred, with only thirty-one wounded.

The Indians surrounded Major Reno's command, and held them for one day in the hills, cut off from water, until General Gibbons' command came in sight, when they broke camp in the night and left.

The Seventh company fought like tigers, but were overcome by brute force. The Indian loss cannot be estimated, as they bore off and *cached* the most of their killed. The remnant of the Seventh Cavalry, together with General Gibbons' command are returning to the mouth of the Little Horn, where a steamer lies, The Indians got all the arms of the killed soldiers.

There were seventeen commissioned officers killed. The whole of the Custar family died at the head of their column. The exact loss was not known. Both the adjutant and sergeant major were killed.

The Indian camp was from three to five miles long, and was twenty miles up the Little Horn from its mouth. The Indians actually pulled men from their horses in some instances.

The above is confirmed by other letters, which say that Custar met a fearful disaster.

The Boyeman (Montana) *Times*, Extra, confirms the report, and says the whole number killed was three hundred and fifteen. Gen. Gibbons joined the command at Reno. When the Indians left the battle field looked like a slaughter-pen, as it really was, being in a narrow ravine. The dead were horribly mutilated. The situation now looks serious.

General Terry arrived at Gibbons' camp on a steamer, and crossed his command over to join General Custar, who knew it was coming before the fight occurred. Lieut. Crittenden, son of Gen. Crittenden, was also among the killed.

This "broadside" was published by the San Diego, California, "Union," 6 July 1876 at 11:30 A M It reproduces, almost verbatim, the 4 July EXTRA of the Helena Herald, and is unquestionably the "Helena Scoop", which might, with the exercise of a little energy, have been sent from Bozeman the afternoon of 3 July, as "Muggins" Taylor arrived at Ft. Ellis that morning. The description of the firing "like the snapping of threads in the tearing of a blanket," does not occur in either extra. That description, attributed to "Curley," first appeared in the Helena Herald of 15 July 1876.

An original copy of this "broadside" is owned by the Los Angeles County Museum, and is reproduced by its courtesy. The size of the original is 6⅞ x 11½".

The Coleman-Morgan "Curley" story, set out above, was probably the genesis of the Curley myth, which despite the statement of Tom Le-Forge (reported by Dr. Marquis in his "Memoirs of a White Crow") that he interpreted Curley's story for Lieut. Bradley shortly after the battle, and that Curley said: "I did nothing wonderful— I was not in the fight," the myth "grew and grew and grew" until the marvelous tales of Curley and his miraculous escape from death with Custer became not only incredible but fantastic; even absurd and ridiculous.

But the "standard" Curley story, as first printed by the *Helena Herald* did not satisfy the disciples of Munchausen, and so, in later versions, we find Curley, wrapped to the eyes in a Sioux blanket, which he had filched from the dead pony of a hostile warrior, pleading with Custer to accept still another Sioux blanket (source not identified), in which to disguise himself and so escape the stricken field. But Custer, of course, declined the offer, as became one of an heroic mold, and nobly chose to perish with his men. The blanket story, however, contained some slight flaws that none seemed to recognize, which were that Custer's fight occurred during the hottest part of a scorching day late in June, and that the Indians had stripped for action, many being naked except for breech-clout and moccasins. Under the circumstances, a blanket would have furnished a disguise about as effective as a plug hat, white tie and tails among a multitude of one piece bathing suits!

Another remarkable variation of the Curley myth, repeated as late as 1950 in *Life* Magazine, has Curley conceal himself inside the carcass of a disembowelled horse, until the murderous Sioux depart; at which time he emerges, hale and hearty, remounts his faithful pony, which has conveniently waited for him, and rides away to the "Far West," where he arrives three days later, though the distance traversed is but 20 miles!

Other Indians, learning of these wondrous tales, said that Curley was a liar. But if he really authored them (which I take the liberty to doubt), he was no mere liar of the common or garden variety, but a Hollywood genius who flourished before his time, and whose talents as a director of "Authentic Westerns" were lost to "meller-drammer" and the moving picture industry long before they were discovered.

As for myself, I am inclined to credit LeForge's statement to Marquis above referred to *as to what Curley said to him*, but I have been unable to discover any statement or report by Bradley of such an interview. As it was the same Bradley whose

Curley as he appeared a few years after the battle. Photo by D. F. Barry. Denver Public Library Western Collection.

letter, dated at Helena 25 July 1876, to the *Helena Herald* (see "The Story of the Little Big Horn, p. 163) and directed to the dispersal of other growing myths, was published by that paper 10 days *after* the first of the sensational Curley stories had appeared in its columns, it is incredible that he did not at any time note LeForge's interpretation, if it in fact ever came to his attention.

My reason for believing that Curley disclaimed having done anything wonderful because he was not in the fight rests upon the description of his meanderings as found in the statement of the Arikara Scout Red Star (see p. 39, this volume); and the official report of Col. M. V. Sheridan of 20 July 1877 (see Part IV, Ch. 4) which clearly indicates that neither Curley nor Half Yellow Face, both of whom accompanied him to the battlefield in 1877, were able to furnish any information of value concerning Custer's fight, Sheridan being convinced that Curley "had run away before the fight really began," and that "the greater portion of his tale was untrustworthy."

Bearing in mind the foregoing, the reader is now introduced to the "standard" Curley story, as it appeared in the *Helena Herald* 15 July 1876.

THE "STANDARD" CURLEY STORY

THE VALLEY OF DEATH
PARTICULARS OF THE MASSACRE OF CUSTER'S COMMAND
* * *
THE UNWRITTEN CHAPTER
* * *
"CURLEY," A CROW SCOUT, THE ONLY SURVIVOR OF THE BATTLE, TELLS THE STORY
* * *
NOT UNTIL THEIR AMMUNITION WAS GONE WERE OUR TROOPS BUTCHERED.
* * *
A LARGE NUMBER OF INDIANS KILLED
* * *

Lieut. Jas. H. Bradley, of the 7th infantry, who commanded the scouts under Gibbon on the recent march from the Yellowstone to the Little Horn and return, arrived in this city last night and left for Fort Shaw this morning. He left the command

A later photograph of Curley—in warbonnet.

one week ago to-day, in camp near Fort Pease, and everything was quiet. Our reporter interviewed Lieut. Bradley, who very kindly gave us a description of the Little Horn disaster, but more particularly the account of Custer's battle and massacre, which has not heretofore been published. It would be in place at this juncture to state that Lieut. Bradley, with his scouts, on the morning of the 27th of June, crossed to the opposite side of the Little Horn from which the command was marching, and deployed out through the hills in skirmish line. (The evening previous three Crow scouts had reported to the Lieutenant that Custer's regiment of cavalry had been cut to pieces. This report was not credited by Terry and Gibbon; yet it was known that they were approaching the Indian village, and the scouts were, if possible, unusually vigilant and active.) About 9 o'clock, a scout reported to Lieut. Bradley that he saw an object which looked like a dead horse. The Lieutenant found it to be a dead cavalry horse, and, going a few yards further on, to the brow of a hill, looking into the valley below, a terrible scene was presented to view. It was literally strewn

Custer's Battlefield

with the dead of the gallant Seventh Cavalry. Lieut. Bradley rode hurriedly over the field, and in a few minutes time counted *one hundred and ninety-seven* dead bodies. Custer fell upon the highest point of the field; and around him, within a space of five rods square, lay forty-two men and thirty-one horses. The dead soldiers all lay within a circle embracing only a few hundred yards square. The Lieutenant immediately reported to Gibbon, which was the first intelligence of the battle received. A few moments later a scout arrived from Reno's command, asking for assistance, and Terry and Gibbon pushed forward to the rescue.

"Curley"

Not a single survivor of Custer's command was found, and even up to the time General Terry made out his official report to General Sheridan it was supposed that the last soul had perished. But when the command returned to the Yellowstone they found there a Crow scout named "Curley," who, as verified by Major Reno, rode out with Custer on that fatal day. He alone escaped, and his account of the battle we give below. It is interesting, as being the only story of the fight ever to be looked for from one who was an actual participant on Custer's side— Curley being, in all human probability the only survivor of his command:

Custer, with his five companies, after separating from Reno and his seven companies, moved to the right around the base of a high hill overlooking the valley of the Little Horn through a ravine just wide enough to admit his column of fours. There were no signs of the presence of Indians in the hills on that side (the right bank) of the Little Horn, and the column moved steadily on until it rounded the hill and came in sight of the village lying in the valley below them. Custer appeared very much elated, and ordered the bugles to sound a charge, and moved on at the head of his column, waving his hat to encourage his men. When they neared the river, the Indians, concealed in the undergrowth on the opposite side of the river, opened fire on the troops, which checked the advance. Here a portion of the command were dismounted and thrown forward to the river, and returned the fire of the Indians. During this time the warriors were seen riding out of the village by hundreds, and deploying across his front to his left, as if with the intention of crossing the stream on his right, while the women and children were seen hastening out of the village in large numbers in the opposite direction.

During the fight at this point Curley saw two of Custer's men killed who fell into the stream. After fighting a few moments here, Custer seemed to be convinced that it was impracticable to cross, as it only could be done in column of fours, exposed during the movement to a heavy fire from the front and both flanks. He, therefore, ordered the head of the column to the right, and bore diagonally into the hills, down stream, his men on foot, leading their horses. In the meantime the Indians had crossed the river (below) in immense numbers, and began to appear on his right flank and in his rear; and he had proceeded but a few hundred yards in the new direction the column had taken, when it became necessary to renew the fight with the Indians who had crossed the stream. At first the command remained together, but after some minutes fighting it was divided, a portion deploying circularly to the left, and the remainder similarly to the right, so that when the line was formed it bore a rude resemblance to a circle, advantage being taken as far as possible of the protection afforded by the ground. The horses were in the rear, the men on the line being dismounted, fighting on foot.

Of the Incidents of the Fight

on other parts of the field than his own, Curley is not well informed, as he was himself concealed in a deep ravine, from which but a small part of the field was visible.

The fight appears to have begun, from Curley's description of the situation of the sun, about 2:30 or 3 o'clock p. m., and continued without intermission until nearly sunset. The Indians had completely surrounded the command, leaving their horses in ravines well to the rear, themselves pressing forward to attack on foot. Confident in the great superiority of their numbers, they made several charges on all points of Custer's line; but the troops held their position firmly, and delivered a heavy fire, and every time drove them back. Curley says the firing was more rapid than anything he had ever conceived of, being a continuous roll, like (as he expressed it)

"The Snapping of the Threads in the Tearing of a Blanket."

The troops expended all the ammunition in their belts, and then sought their horses for the reserve ammunition carried in their saddle pockets.

As long as their ammunition held out, the troops, though losing considerably in the fight, maintained their position in spite of all the efforts of the Sioux. From the weakening of their fire towards the close of the afternoon the Indians appeared to believe that their ammunition was about exhausted, and they made a

Grand Final Charge,

in the course of which the last of the command was destroyed, the men being shot, where they laid in their positions in the line, at such close quarters that many were killed with arrows. Curley says that Custer remained alive through the greater part of the engagement, animating his men to determined resistance; but about an hour before the close of the fight received a mortal wound.

Curley says the field was thickly strewn with the dead bodies of the Sioux who fell in the attack—in number considerably more than the force of soldiers engaged. He is satisfied that their loss will exceed 300 killed, beside an immense number wounded. Curley accomplished his escape by drawing his blanket about him in the manner of the Sioux, and passing through an interval which had been made in their line as they scattered over the field in their final charge. He says they must have seen him, as he was in plain view, but was probably mistaken by the Sioux for one of their own number or one of their allied Arapahoes or Cheyennes.

In most particulars the account given by Curley of the fight is confirmed by the position of the trail made by Custer in his movements, and the general evidence of the battlefield. Only one discrepancy is noted, which relates to the time when the fight came to an end.

Officers of Reno's command, who late in the afternoon, from high points surveyed the country in anxious expectation of Custer's appearance, and commanded a view of the field where he had fought, say that no fighting was going on at that time—between five and six o'clock. It is evident, therefore, that the last of Custer's command was destroyed at an earlier hour in the day than Curley relates.

(The *Helena Daily Herald*, Saturday,
July 15, 1876)

GENERAL HUGH L. SCOTT'S INTERVIEWS WITH THE CROWS "CURLEY" AND "WHITE MAN RUNS HIM," AND THE MINNECONJOU "FEATHER EARRING."

GENERAL HUGH L. SCOTT was not present at the battle of the Little Big Horn, but was assigned to the Seventh Cavalry after his graduation from West Point with the Class of 1876. He enjoyed a long and brilliant career in the Army, rising through all ranks to that of Major General, and before his retirement from the active list, became Chief of Staff. Throughout the earlier years of his service, he was a careful and sympathetic student of the American Indian, and came to be considered the Army's first authority on the sign language.

I met General Scott through General Godfrey, during the year 1921, shortly after I had completed an abstract of the testimony taken at the Reno Court of Inquiry, a copy of which I presented to him.

He told me of his interviews with the Crow Scouts, and with many of the hostile Sioux and Cheyenne, and promised to furnish me with copies. But as he was then living at Princeton, N. J., and most of his personal papers were stored elsewhere, I received only the notes of his interviews on the ground, with "White Man Runs Him" and "Curley," two of Custer's Crow Scouts; and with "Feather Earring," a Minneconjou Sioux. These he sent me with his letter of December 20, 1921, as follows:

My dear Col. Graham:

Since receiving your letter of Nov. 23 I have moved from our house for the winter and have

Curley at age 54, with his favorite pony. E. A. Brininstool Collection.

not been able to put my hands on those Custer papers and expecting from day to day to find them I have not replied to your letter—today I have found two of them and forward them herewith. With best wishes for yourself for the coming year I am

Very Sincerely Yours,

H. L. SCOTT

Dec. 22—Many thanks for Reno transcript received today. It will be read with deepest interest.

H. L. S.

Note by W. A. G.:
    The Crow accounts follow immediately. That of the Minneconjou, "Feather Earring" will be found among the Sioux accounts.

CUSTER FIGHT

Accounts Given to General H. L. Scott by Two Crow Scouts, "White Man Runs Him" and "Curley."

ON THE SOUTH SIDE OF RENO CREEK, ABOUT 1¼ MILES FROM THE MOUTH.

White Man Runs Him

Reno Creek is called by the Indians the Creek of Many Ash trees, or Ash Creek, because the wood is hard.

(In the following account White Man Runs Him first said the 'left wing' referred to was Benteen with his men; later he said he was mistaken, that it was Reno and his men).

Custer came down Reno Creek along the north side to a little flat between the north and south forks of the creek, where he stopped for a short rest. This was about 1¼ miles from the mouth of the creek where it flows into the Little Big Horn river. (He pointed out the flat). He looked down the creek and saw dust rising near the mouth of the creek and he called Half Yellow Face, the leader of the Crows, to him and asked what the dust was. Half Yellow Face said "The Sioux must be running away." Custer then said to them, "I am through with the Scouts, you have brought me to the Sioux. I will throw my left wing (Reno) South in case the Sioux should go south." Then Reno started South and crossed the creek just below the flat. He (Custer) called Half Yellow Face and White Swan and told them to go over to the ridge and see if the Sioux Camp was there. They started, but instead of going over to the ridge, they followed Reno and that was the last we saw of them until the trouble was over. Then Custer started moving toward the ridge. Mitch Boyer noticed the scouts Custer had sent to look over the ridge had followed Reno, so he (Boyer) called me, Curley, Goes Ahead, and Hairy Moccasin and said, "Let us go over to the ridge and look at the lodges." When we reached there we saw that the lodges were over in the valley quite a ways down the river, so we went on ahead, Custer following. This was about 9:15 A. M. (old time). Custer moved slowly and took his time and stopped occasionally. He did not leave that place until Reno had started skirmishing. Reno was fighting long before Custer moved. That was about 1:00 P. M. I went with Custer as far as Custer Creek and then came back with the other Scouts. We met some soldiers (Reno's men) on our way to the pack train. We were up on the hill with Reno all the afternoon.

Curley

"Custer with his men came down Reno Creek. We stopped by some pines for a little while, about 4 miles from the mouth of the creek. Then we came down to the flat over there. (As pointed out by White Man Runs Him). Mitch Boyer talked to the Scouts and told us that Custer wanted Half Yellow Face and White Swan to go over on the hill to the ridge and look over at the camp. The two Scouts were almost to the foot of the hill when the trumpeter sounded a call and the left wing started moving. That was Reno who moved. The scouts turned to the left and joined Reno.

Another outfit went further up the river. (Benteen). Mitch Boyer said, "Come on, we will go up on the hill and look over." So Mitch Boyer and we four Crows started up the hill on a gallop and when we looked back from the top of the hill, Custer had moved on and Reno had crossed the river. Custer and his brother went to the right of us as we were standing on the hill. Custer turned around as he reached the top of the ridge and waved his hat, and his men at the bottom of the hill waved their hats and shouted. Custer kept on going on the ridge and the men followed him. Custer's men were about 100 yards ahead of us. We scouts followed Custer. We galloped our horses and moved fast after Custer and his men. Custer went to a point on the ridge and then turned to the right and followed a coulee down in a northerly direction. When Custer left, Mitch Boyer and we Scouts remained on the point. When we looked down to the camp we noticed there were not many around and Mitch Boyer said he thought the Indians were out campaigning somewhere and suggested we hurry down and fight them. There were 5 of us altogether. We went further north on the high bluffs and came near the Indian camp just below the bluffs. Each of us fired 2 or 3 shots at the camp. Custer had reached the river when we were at this point on the bluffs. The Indians commenced moving as

The Crow Scout White-Man-Runs-Him.

soon as Custer reached the river. There were thousands of them, some going towards Custer and some towards Reno. When Custer reached the river, we turned. By the time Custer reached the river Mitch Boyer said he was going down to Custer and his men, and for the rest of us to go back to the pack outfit. Being on the hill we could see Reno was retreating and was well to the foot of the hills. The Arapahoe scouts of Custer had some of the Sioux horses and brought them across the river just below the ridge on the east side. We also met two groups of soldiers on the ridge just north of where Reno made his stand. We came back past the Arapahoe scouts but do not know what became of them afterwards. The Sioux did not follow Reno across the river at first. Their attention was turned to where some Crow and Arapahoe scouts were surrounded in some woods on the west side of the river. We stopped while they were doing this. Things looked bad, so we thought we had better hunt safety. We then turned and followed the ridge, going east toward the Rosebud. I left the others and travelled toward the mouth of Reno Creek in a Southwest direction. The others yelled to me and asked where I was going. I answered "I am going down to see if I can reach the river and get some water." They said "Come on; do not go that way, it is dangerous there." But I did not listen to them. After travelling as far as where Custer had crossed Reno Creek to go on the ridge, I turned up (east) Reno Creek toward the buttes and met the pack train. The outfit went on thru and that was the last I saw of them. The outfit was about three miles up the creek when I saw them. From the butte above when I saw and met the pack outfit, I went on down to the mouth of the Little Horn. The Arapahoe scouts came from near the Gros Ventres, down on the Little Missouri River.

Note; by the interpreter and stenographer:

While White Man Runs Him was talking, Curley often interrupted him and laughed and said he was telling many lies. Then he became sulky and went back and got in the machine. General Scott told them to talk one at a time. We could not see any real material difference in the stories of the two scouts, although there seemed to be a great deal of feeling between the two.

On being questioned, White Man Runs Him said the 3 scouts Hairy Moccasin, Goes Ahead and himself, stayed and fought with Reno. White Swan and Half Yellow Face were down in the trees near the Little Horn where they were fortifying and fighting.

ON THE NORTH FORK OF UPPER RENO CREEK

White Man Runs Him:

Custer followed down the Lodge Pole Trail which goes down the north fork of Upper Reno Creek, then down Reno Creek to the Little Horn River. The lodge where the dead Sioux was found was near where we saw the pack train. The trail often crossed the creek down the valley. Custer was led into the pocket near the last point north of the Wolf Mountains. It heads up near the lookout. Crook fought the Sioux village on the Rosebud and Custer followed the Sioux from the Rosebud. Custer came in a southwesterly direction through a pass to the head of the north fork of Upper Reno Creek. This pass follows up Davis Creek from the Rosebud and is fairly smooth. *Cha tish!;* Crow word for the Wolf Mountains, or Wolf Hair Mountains.

AT THE POCKET BELOW CUSTER LOOKOUT

White Man Runs Him:

Q. Did Custer come in here himself? Show me where he came in.

A. Custer came up the valley from the other side but did not come in with the horses. The soldiers stopped this side of the creek north of the point. Custer did not climb clear to the top. He came up far enough to see over and down the valley.

(Note: There are 6 pines in the coulee leading to the pocket, which winds right behind the ridge which Custer climbed from the other side)

ON THE RIDGE, THE POINT TO THE RIGHT WHERE THE SCOUTS FIRST CAME

White Man Runs Him:

Q. Who led the horses into the pocket?

A. An Army officer (Varnum), Mitch Boyer and myself.

Q. Who was the guide?

A. I was the guide.

Q. How did you know the place; is it such a good hiding place?

A. I am acquainted with all the country here.

Q. How did you know you could see the Little Horn?

A. The Crows often hid their horses here during the campaigns and I had been here many times before.

Q. There was water here?

A. Not to speak of; just a little.

Q. What did you see when it became light?

A. We could see the smoke from the camp of the Sioux in the Little Horn Valley. We also saw two Sioux out there by the lone tree. (Due west 1½ miles). From this point we moved to a point to the left and by that time the Sioux had gone down Davis Creek toward the soldiers camp. The soldiers and the Sioux met.

Q. Where did Custer come?

A. He came up Davis Creek and stopped opposite the point. We went down and told him about the smoke, and Custer came up part way, far enough to see the smoke.

Q. What time was that?

A. The sun was just up; a little after 6:00.

ON THE POINT TO THE LEFT: CUSTER'S LOOKOUT.

White Man Runs Him:

The officer who led us into the pocket had a large nose and a long moustache.

Q. Could you see any horses?

A. Yes, we could see some white horses on the other side of the Little Horn River. The horses were on the hills.

Q. Was it a clear day?

A. Yes; nice and clear. We also saw 6 Sioux to the northeast over on the other side of Tullocks Creek.

Q. Any buffalo in the country then?

A. Yes; the Sioux were hunting them and they were going ahead of the Sioux.

Q. Where were the buffalo?

A. Over to the north and northeast on Tullocks Creek.

Q. Did you come up on the point with Custer?

A. I went down and reported to Custer what we saw, and Custer came up to see.

Q. What did they call Mitch Boyer?

A. Ca pay.

Q. What did the scouts say to each other up here on the point?

A. I told Mitch Boyer it would be a good thing if they would hide here until night and then surprise the camp. Then the two Sioux appeared over there and I said we had better hurry and get over there just as soon as possible. We did not know whether Custer would listen, but if we hadn't seen the two Sioux we would have suggested to him to stay here all day and make a night march. I was judging from the Indian campaigns and warfare. Custer always advised them not to bother anyone and to keep out of sight if possible, but if the enemy saw them to go ahead and fire into them. If the Indians came up on them here, they could do nothing with them.

Q. What brought them here in the first place?

A. We decided to come here when we were below Busby. We know this place. We knew we could see very far from up here. Night was coming on when we were at Busby. We reached here about 2:00 in the morning.

Q. Were you following any trail?

A. We were trailing the Indians down the Lodge Pole trail and horse trail. This was the regular trail from the Rosebud over on to the Little Horn. On June 24, Hairy Moccasin, Goes Ahead and I rode some soldiers' horses and came to that peak and then rode back. The soldiers were just below Busby.

Q. What did you see?

A. We were not sure whether the Sioux were camping there. It was late and we could not see so well. We knew the trail and the way the Sioux were moving, but were not sure which way they went. Mitch Boyer and the officer and I left Custer at Busby about sundown on the 24th. I was one of the oldest scouts and I did most of the advance scouting. I was very familiar with this country, so I knew the country well and I told Custer he had better go down Reno Creek and then he could wait this side of the divide before going into the Little Horn Valley. The soldiers moved fast down Reno Creek, their horses trotting all the time. Our ponies were loping most of the time. The Sioux tell the story that the soldiers made their first appearance when the laziest were just getting up, about 9 or 10 o'clock in the morning. I do not know how long Custer left with his outfit, but I was with Reno and stayed there quite late; about 7 or 8, near sundown. Then I came toward the east. The first time we stopped on the bluff when Mitch Boyer left us to go to Custer, and before we returned to Reno those nearest began to run. Custer's men did not fire at all on this side. Custer believed that Reno's command was all killed because they were retreating into the bluff and the dust was flying. The scouts believed that Reno's outfit was all killed. It was hard to tell because the dust was flying and they were retreating so fast. I know for sure that Custer went right to the river bank. I saw him go that far. The Sioux were right across the river. Then Custer fired. That was the first firing Custer did. If it wasn't for Mitch Boyer most likely I would be there with Custer buried, but Mitch Boyer told us to go back. There were only three of us, Hairy Moccasin, Goes Ahead and myself. We did not see Curley. Mitch Boyer told us to go back. He said "You go back to the pack train and let the soldiers fight." We went back and met some soldiers and soon after that the pack train was there. If those soldiers hadn't turned back and been reinforced by the pack train they would all have been killed. The Sioux were coming up fast. Curley would have been one of the live ones because he was with the Arikarees and the horses. There were older men with me and they all said my story was true as much as they could remember in all the excitement; but I did not see Curley at all when he went back to the pack train. The Arapahoes said they took the horses and went on to the Rosebud Junction (near Lame Deer). When they left with the horses they hurried and by evening they were where the Rosebud flows into the Yellowstone. They said Curley was with them. After the Sioux had killed all of Custer's men they had better guns and they came back and killed more of us than they did before. Hairy Moccasin and Goes Ahead say the same story as I tell. I tell the story from the scout's standpoint. While there were many things happened during the day, I try to tell a general outline of the campaign, but I cannot remember every detail. When we were fortified with Reno and the soldiers got real thirsty they would volunteer to get water and many were killed while getting the water. I left Reno and went down where the Little Horn flows into the Big Horn. The next morning I was there. It was just daybreak. I could see the soldiers just across there—Terry's outfit. I was on the east side of the river and I saw the soldiers in a boat on this side of the river. We call General Terry, "Man without Hip," or "Lame Hip"; another officer we called "White Whiskers." I told them I had no more clothes and I had done lots and scouted and was going home. The officers said "All right" and I went on. I went to Pryor. They had another fight when I came into camp. The Crows thought I was a Sioux and commenced firing.

Q. When did you see Curley?

A. I did not see Curley until next fall. That fall I saw Curley.

Q. Where?

A. Up the Yellowstone in the camp of the Mountain Crows. Very soon after reaching home others and myself left the Crows again on a scouting trip. That was the reason I did not see Curley until in the fall.

Q. What did the Indians call Custer?

A. They called him "Son of the Morning Star."

Q. How was Custer dressed?

A. His hair was down to his shoulders. His hair was yellow. He wore buckskin.

Q. What would you do if you had the troops and were going to fight the fight?

A. That depends. If I wanted to surprise them I would attack by night, but if anyone saw me I would hurry and get there and get an even fight with them.

Q. Would you go all with Reno or all with Custer; or would you do just as Custer did?

A. I would not split the command. Custer should have held his men together.

Q. You think he could have whipped them that way?

A. He would have had a better chance. Some would have been killed, but not all. Custer was reckless. Instead of Custer going ahead and starting at the same time as Reno, Custer held back and did not start until he saw Reno fighting. That was poor generalship. We do not cut up our command when we fight and say "While you wait I will fight, and while I wait you will fight." If he had gone right down, there were plenty of places to ford just as well as at Reno Junction. I have been with other officers of the Army and they attacked differently than Custer did. It did not look right. It was just as if he said, "Reno, you go ahead and let them whip you and then I will go ahead and they will whip me." Only seven who crossed the river with Reno came out alive.

Q. What did Custer say when he saw the village?

A. He looked over and said, "These people are troublesome and bother the Crows and the white people. I am going to teach them a lesson today. I am going to whip them and I will build a fort at the junction where the Little Horn flows into the Big Horn and you Crows may live in peace." He said he would finish the Sioux trouble.

Q. Did the Scouts think there were too many Indians for Custer to fight?

A. Yes; from Garryowen down the valley were camps and camps and camps. There was a big camp in a circle near the west hills.

Q. How many warriors?

A. I would say between 4000 and 5000, maybe more. You can ask Curley about that if you care to do so.

Q. Why did you leave Reno?

A. Because I could get no water and I wanted to go down and get some water.

Q. Were the Sioux on this side?

A. No; north, west and south. Only a few were on the east and I had a chance to get away.

Q. Who was with you?

A. Hairy Moccasin and Goes Ahead.

Q. Did you walk?

A. No; we were on horseback.

Q. Was it light or dark?

A. It was just about sundown. It must have been about 8:00 o'clock.

Q. Where did Curley go?

"Custer's Last Fight," illustration from Whittaker's "Life of Custer," published in the fall of 1876. The artist was A. K. Waud. This is the first known picture of "Custer's Last Stand."

A. I do not know. The Arapahoes told me Curley went as far as the Junction (Rosebud and Yellowstone).

AT THE SITE OF THE LODGE WHERE THE SIOUX WAS BURIED.

(Note: Located 9 miles down the north fork of Upper Reno from Custer's point. On a flat near where Upper Reno forks into the south and north streams.)

White Man Runs Him: says "the lodge was not burned by the scouts but by the soldiers."

AT RENO'S BATTLEFIELD.

White Man Runs Him:

Q. Where did the Sioux go when General Terry came up?

A. They went up the Little Horn River.

Q. Did you find any dead bodies and evidence?

A. I was not here then.

Q. Where did you last see Custer here?

A. Over there when he was going down the draw where he made his first charge.

Q. Where did Reno go around the flat at the left of the divide?

A. Out across the river at the mouth of Reno Creek near the present Spear Camp.

Q. Where did he dismount first?

A. Just over the divide near the woods in the valley.

Q. Where did he cross coming back?

A. No particular place. The soldiers stampeded and they scattered coming back. They crossed at the foot of the bluffs.

Q. Can you see where he fortified himself?

A. Yes.

CURLEY:

Q. Where was Custer when you saw Reno come across?

A. Over the divide to the right of the first intrenchment. Custer saw the camp from the highest point on the ridge to the right of the first intrenchment. He just saw Reno going down the valley but did not see him come back.

Q. How far down the valley did Reno get?

A. The Sioux met Reno's command where Garryowen now is.

Q. Where did he cross coming back?

A. I do not know. I was not there to see them.

Q. Did you see a negro with them?

A. He was killed on the other side of the river.

White Man Runs Him:

Curley left us up on Reno Creek. I do not like to quarrel with Curley, but that is the truth.

AT THE MOUTH OF CUSTER CREEK OR MEDICINE TAIL CREEK, 4 MILES FROM RENO'S INTRENCHMENT.

White Man Runs Him:

Q. How far down here did Custer get?

A. Right down to the river

Q. How far did they come?

A. They came down the ravine to the river here and started back.

Q. What did the scouts do then? Where was Mitch Boyer?

A. He was on that point there.

Q. Where was Curley?

A. He was back on the ridge.

Q. Where did you go then?

A. I went back.

Q. Why?

A. Mitch Boyer said "You go back; I am going down to Custer."

Q. Did you see Reno go up on the bluffs then?

A. No. I saw him fighting across the river but didn't know he had retreated back to the bluffs.

Q. When Custer came down here could he hear the shooting over there?

A. Didn't pay much attention; everybody around us was shooting and no one could tell the place where most of the firing was done.

Crow Agency, Mont.,
August 25, 1919.

I hereby certify that the foregoing account is correct as told by the two scouts on August 24, 1919.

(Sig.) Russell White Bear

I hereby certify that the foregoing account in sixteen pages is as interpreted by Russell White Bear on August 24, 1919

(Sig.) Angela Buell

NOTE: Wherever the word 'Arapahoes" occurs in the foregoing, it should be read "Arikaras." This was probably a typographical error in the original transcription.

—W. A. G.

RUSSELL WHITE BEAR ON "CURLEY"

RUSSELL WHITE BEAR, a noted Crow Indian, who acted as interpreter for General Hugh L. Scott upon many occasions, and who became an official of the Crow Nation, in a letter written many years ago to a mutual friend, had the following to say concerning the scout Curley, whom he knew intimately:

This is Curley's last story. Curley died about three years ago.

"Custer, after leaving Major Reno's command and on reaching the Medicine Tail Creek, halted his command, and here the men rearranged their saddles. Custer at this point gave a trooper a paper and after a brief conversation, the trooper rode away, heading *north*. This trooper rode a *sorrel-roan horse*. After Custer sent his message away he rode to an officer who seemed to be in command of one of the troops (this troop had gray horses) and gave him an order. Immediately the troop turned its direction toward the Little Horn. Custer with the remainder of his command continued going northward—his trail was about 1½ miles from the river. In the meantime Mitch Bouyer told Curley to leave the command and go to Terry."

Mitch Bouyer's conversation with Curley was:

"Curley, you are very young—you do not know much about fighting. I am going to advise you to leave us and if you can get away by detouring and keeping out of the way of the Sioux, do so, and go to the other soldiers (meaning Terry's men) and tell them that all are killed. That man (pointing to Custer) will stop at nothing. He is going to take us right into the village where there are many more warriors than we have. We have no chance at all."

The two men hastily shook hands and Curley departed. He immediately turned his bay horse around and retraced Custer's trail as he was instructed by Mitch Bouyer. Curley rode back to the creek where Custer and his men halted a few minutes before and then followed its meanderings up until he came to a tributary that took him in a northerly direction. He followed this tributary until he reached the high ridge east of the battlefield. From this place Curley (about 1½ miles from the battlefield) with field glasses could see the battle. He saw how the Indians circled Custer's men. After being satisfied that what Mitch Bouyer said came true, he rode away toward the Pine Hills."

The foregoing shows what Custer did on reaching Medicine Tail Creek.

CURLEY'S LAST STORY

A letter from *Russell White Bear* to Fred Dustin, postmarked Dec. 1, 1938, written in response to his request for information concerning the Crow scouts at their farthest point of advance, is in part as follows:

* * *

"A few days before Curley passed away—I visited him and said 'Curley—I have interpreted for you a number of times—I am not clear yet on your stories—tell me for the last time if you were with Custer up to the time when the gray horse troop separated from the main command.'

Curley replied:

"Mitch Bouyer remained with Custer's men

when Reno separated to go to the valley. We rode to the north fork of Reno Creek and crossed it, going to the hill, turning westward on the ridge—we could see nothing of the valley where the village was located—Custer's troops were not hurrying—they rode at a walk—probably because they were going up a grade. When we reached the ridge the soldiers kept marching on the east side of Reno Hill and going down on the west side of the ridge—down a ravine, running northward. At this point Custer and two other soldiers besides Bouyer and I rode over to a high point that overlooks the Little Big Horn valley to see what was going on—we could see dust rising everywhere down the valley. Reno's men were riding toward the Indians—Custer nor any of us dismounted. Custer made a brief survey of the situation and turned and rode to his command. He did not ask Bouyer or me about the country—we rode following the creek (ravine? F. D.) as you know—we were all the time going away from the valley. We finally came out at the Creek-Medicine Tail Creek—and seeing we were a long ways away from the valley—Custer—turning left, rode down Medicine Tail. After riding awhile, he halted the command—then the gray horse troop left us and started down the creek—when we turned north—crossing Medicine Tail Creek going on the hills north of the creek—here the command halted again—Custer wrote a message and handed to a young man—on a sorrel-roan horse—who galloped away. Bouyer called me to him—he said—'Curley you better leave us here' he said—'You ride back over the trail a ways and then go to one of the high points—' pointing eastward over to the high ridge east of the Custer Hill—'watch awhile and see if the Sioux are besting us and you make your way back to Terry and tell him we are all killed.' Curley immediately turned back—done as he was instructed—He climbed to the high point—with glasses he watched the battle awhile and then rode away. As he was riding alone he came to a horse without a rider, and looking around he found a dead Sioux—he stripped off his equipments and went away. The dead Sioux was killed by Goes Ahead."

NARRATIVE OF THE CROW SCOUT GOES AHEAD

From the Arikara Narrative

THE soldiers were encamped where still water flows into the Yellowstone. * * * They went on to where Powder River joins the Yellowstone. * * * The Crows were on the north side of the Yellowstone and the soldiers wanted to cross

The Crow Scout Goes Ahead.

but it was too high. General Terry had a canoe. * * * Then a steamboat came up the Yellowstone, opposite the mouth of the Rosebud. Some of the Crow scouts got on this boat and went across. * * *

The roll was called at the bank at the boat for these Crow scouts. Six of them were called to go on board, Hairy Moccasin, White-Man-Runs-Him, Goes-Ahead, Curley, Half-Yellow-Face, White Swan. The boat went up a little way and landed the scouts. Their interpreter was Mitch. Bouyer (Ka-pesh), a half-breed Dakota. He told them that when they went down below the mouth of the Rosebud they would see Arikara scouts. When they came to this camp there was a big tent with a flag, and in it they met Custer. He shook hands with them and said, "We are glad to have you, we sent for you and you came right away." Custer * * * told them he was going to fight the Dakotas and Cheyennes and that he understood that the Crows were good scouts. "If we win the fight, everything belonging to the enemy you can take home, for my boys have no use for these things." The next day they broke camp and went up the Rosebud until night. Next day they found where the Dakotas had their first camp, a very big one. They had had a sun dance, they could see the frame of the dance lodge. The third day they camped at what is now Busby School, the second camp on the Rosebud. Just at dawn they reached

Wolf Mountains, the sun was just coming up. Custer always warned them to look out for themselves, for every squad of soldiers had scouts and they might be mistaken for the enemy. Custer said to the six Crow scouts: "If nothing happens to me I will look after you in the future." From Wolf Mountains the Crow scouts were ahead but stopped a moment at the lone tepee. At White Rocks, Mitch Bouyer told them to go with Custer. As Custer swung off from the trail after Reno left him to cross the upper ford there was an Arikara scout and four Crow scouts with him. Custer rode to the edge of the high bank and looked over to the place where Reno's men were, as though planning the next move. When they had arrived at about the point where Lieutenant Hodgson's headstone was placed later, the three Crow scouts saw the soldiers under Reno dismounting in front of the Dakota camp and thought that the enemy were "too many." Close to where Reno and Benteen later in the day were attacked by the Dakotas, on the ridge of hills above the river, the three Crow scouts were left behind and Custer's command went down the draw toward the lower ford on the run. Custer had told the Crow scouts to stay out of the fight and they went to the left along the ridge overlooking the river while he took his command to the right (Goes-Ahead is sure Curley, the Crow scout, was not with him). At this point both Curley and Black Fox, Arikara scout, disappeared. Black Fox rode a bay horse and Curley rode a bald-faced pony with front white stockings and a D brand on the rump. The three Crow scouts rode along the high ridge, keeping back from the view of the Dakotas till they came to the end of the ridge and to the bluff just above the lower ford. There they dismounted and fired across into the Dakota camp, the circle of tents they could see over the tree-tops below them. They heard two volleys fired and saw the soldiers' horses standing back of the line in groups. Then in accordance with orders Custer had given them about staying out of the fight, they rode back along the ridge and met the Arikara scouts and pack-mules. They then rode away around the point of the highest hill, * * * and along the ridge. After riding all night they reached the mouth of the Little Big Horn by daylight. Here Terry met them. He asked about Custer and they told him Custer had been wiped out. He asked them four times.

THE STORY OF WHITE MAN RUNS HIM

1919

The following story of the Crow scout White Man Runs Him, never before published, is contributed by Colonel Tim McCoy (Retired), General Hugh L. Scott's most accomplished pupil in the Indian sign language, who was with Scott at the battlefield in 1919 when the Crow scouts were interrogated. Of this and two other statements made by the Arapahoe warriors Waterman and Left Hand, which appear at pages 109 and 111 herein, Colonel McCoy says: "These three stories I had written into continuity from the questions asked these Indians. The errors of time etc., are just as they told them—such as the Crow's description of Custer. Time played tricks on their memories, I think."

Perhaps so: time does that to all of us. But this story of White Man Runs Him, in all but a few minor details, is easily the most valuable, historically, to come from any of the Crows. The statement follows.

————O————

I am an old man, and soon my spirit must leave this earth to join the spirits of my fathers. There-

An earlier photograph (1889) of White-Man-Runs-Him. E. A. Brininstool Collection.

fore, I shall speak only the truth in telling what I know of the fight on the Little Big Horn where General Custer was killed. Curley, who was with us, will tell you I do not lie.

The scouts with General Custer were all Crows and Arikaras. Mitch Boyer, a half-breed Sioux, was Chief of Scouts. The Crow Scouts were Half Yellow Face, White Swan, Goes Ahead, Hairy Moccasin, Curley and I, White Man Runs Him.

On June 24th we were camped just below Busby, and Hairy Moccasin, Goes Ahead and I took some soldiers' horses and rode to a high point on the Divide between the Rosebud and the Little Horn. This place was used by the Crows as a look-out during campaigns, and from it you could see for miles around. In this hill was a pocket where horses could be hidden. We knew the trail and the way the Sioux were moving, but were not sure which way they went. When we reached the Crow look-out the light was not good and we could not see much, so we returned to camp and reported.

Just after sun-down Mitch Boyer and an army officer with a long mustache and large nose (Captain Varnum) left the camp with me and started back for the look-out. I know this country well, so I acted as guide. We followed down the Lodge Pole trail, which was the regular trail from the Rosebud across to the Little Horn, and reached the look-out about two o'clock in the morning. Our horses were led into the pocket where they were hidden, and we lay down to wait for daylight. As soon as it became light enough to see, we could make out smoke from the Sioux camp down in the Little Horn Valley and could see some white horses on the other side of the Little Horn River. We also saw two Sioux about one mile and a half west moving down Davis Creek toward the soldiers' camp and six other Sioux to the northeast over on Tullock Fork. The soldiers had marched during the night and were now camped a little below us on Davis Creek. We could see the smoke of their camp-fires as they cooked breakfast. In a little while we saw the soldiers marching up Davis Creek, and Custer stopped opposite to our look-out. I went down and told him about the smoke we had seen from the Sioux camp. This was about six o'clock in the morning. Custer came up the hill far enough to see over and down the valley. When he saw the Sioux village, he

The four Crow Scouts who went down-river with Custer. Left to right: White Man Runs Him, Hairy Moccasin, Curley, and Goes Ahead. Photo by Wanamaker. (1916)

The original "Custer's Last Stand," painted by Cassily Adams. It was done on a tent fly, from descriptions by various Indians, including "Curley". It was exhibited in a St. Louis saloon, afterwards purchased by Adolphus Busch of Anheuser-Busch, who had it copied and a different figure (resembling John A. Logan) substituted for the Adams figure of Custer. Busch presented the original to the 7th Cavalry, and it was destroyed by fire at Fort Bliss, Texas, on June 13, 1946, when the Officer's Club burned.

said: "These people are very troublesome and bother the Crows and white people. I am going to teach them a lesson today. I will whip them and will build a fort at the junction where the Little Horn flows into the Big Horn, and you Crows may then live in peace." He said he would finish the Sioux trouble. We scouts thought there were too many Indians for Custer to fight. There were camps and camps and camps. One big camp was in a circle near the west hills. I would say there were between four thousand and five thousand warriors, maybe more, I do not know. It was the biggest Indian camp I have ever seen. If we had not seen the two Sioux scouts earlier in the morning, I would have advised Custer to hide at this point all day, and then surprise the camp at night, but since these scouts had seen the soldiers it was no use to wait longer. I was one of the oldest of the scouts and did most of the advance scouting. I knew this country very well, so I told Custer he had better go down Ash Creek (Reno Creek), then he could wait this side of the Divide before going into the Little Horn Valley. Custer moved forward, the soldiers going at a fast trot down Ash Creek. Our ponies were much smaller than the horses ridden by the soldiers, so we had to gallop most of the time to keep up. Custer followed down the Lodge Pole Trail, which goes down the North Fork of Upper Ash Creek. This trail comes from the Rosebud up Davis Creek through a pass to the North Fork of Upper Ash Creek, then down Ash Creek to the Little Horn River and is fairly smooth.

About nine miles down the Upper Fork of Ash Creek, we found a lodge with a dead Indian inside. He had probably died from wounds received in the battle with General Crook on the Rosebud June 17th. As we passed by, some soldiers set fire to this lodge.

Custer halted his command on a small flat about a mile and a quarter from the mouth of Ash Creek, and ordered Major Reno to swing out to the left, cross the Little Horn and attack the upper end of the Sioux village. He saw some dust rising near the mouth of the Creek and called Half Yellow Face, the leader of the Crows, to him and asked what the dust was. Half Yellow Face said: "The Sioux must be running away." But Custer said: "I will throw my left wing (Reno) south in case the Sioux should go that way." Then Reno moved out and crossed the Creek just below the flat. Custer then called White Swan and told him and Half Yellow Face to go over to the ridge and see what was going on in the Sioux camp. They started, but instead of going over to the ridge as they were told, they followed Reno, and that was the last we saw of them until the trouble was over. Then Custer started moving toward the ridge. Mitch Boyer (Chief of Scouts) noticed the scouts whom Custer had sent to look over the ridge, had followed Reno, so he called Curley, Goes Ahead, Hairy Moccasin and me and said: "Let us go over to the ridge and look at the lodges." When we reached there, we saw that the lodges were over in the valley quite a ways down the river, so we moved on ahead, Custer following. This was about nine o'clock in the morning. Custer moved slowly, taking lots of time and stopping occasionally. He did not leave that place until Reno had started fighting. Before Reno left Custer on the flat, another body of soldiers had been ordered away towards the left, but we were far in advance at that time, so I do not know where they went (This was Captain Benteen). Custer and his brother went to the right of us and halted on a small hill. His troops were moving forward below him. Custer turned around as he reached the top of the hill and waved his hat, and the soldiers at the bottom of the hill waved their hats and shouted. Custer then proceeded on up the ridge and his men followed. They were moving rapidly, and the scouts were forced to gallop their ponies sometimes to keep up with them. At a certain point on the ridge they turned to the right and rode down a coulee in a northern direction. The scouts took up a position on the high bluffs where we could look down into the Sioux camp. As we followed along on the high ground, Custer had come down Medicine Tail Creek and was moving toward the river. The Indians saw him there, and all began running that way. There were thousands of them. Custer tried to cross the river at the mouth of Medicine Tail Creek, but was unable to do so. This was the last we saw Custer. Mitch Boyer said to us: "You scouts need go no farther. You have guided Custer here, and your work is finished, so you had better go back to the pack-train and let the soldiers do the fighting." He (Mitch Boyer) said that he was going down to join Custer, and turning his horse galloped away. That is the last time we saw Mitch Boyer. He was killed with Custer over on the ridge. We went back along the ridge and found Reno's men entrenched there. We stayed there all afternoon. It was very hot and the soldiers had no water. When they got very thirsty, some would volunteer to go to the river and fill the canteens. Many soldiers were killed trying to get water.

After sun-down that night I slipped through the Indian line and swung around towards the north, and the next morning at day-break I was down where the Little Horn flows into the Big Horn

The Crow Scout Hairy Moccasin, about 1915.

I cannot remember every detail of the fight because there were so many things happening during the day and so much excitement that it is hard to remember little things, but I have tried to give a general outline of the campaign, and have told only the things that I saw. I remember Custer well. The Indians called him the "Son of the Morning Star." He had long yellow hair, and at the time of the battle was dressed entirely in buckskin. If it were not for Mitch Boyer, who sent us back, Hairy Moccasin, Goes Ahead, and I too would be buried over on that ridge with Custer and his men. I have told you only the truth without trying to claim any credit myself, and Curley, who was with us, cannot deny the truth of my story.

THE STORY OF THE CROW SCOUT— HAIRY MOCCASIN

From the June 1916 Teepee Book

AT THAT time I was twenty-four years old, and was an enlisted scout under Gen. Custer's command. Mitch Boyer was our interpreter. I was sent ahead. Custer said, "You go and find that village." I went to a butte at the head of Reno Creek, from where I could see the village. I reported the camp to Custer. He asked if any

River. There were some soldiers there (General Terry's) and their leader was an officer whom the Indians called "Man Without Hip" or "Lame Hip" (General Terry) and another officer whom the Indians called "White Whiskers" (General Gibbon). I told them all I knew about the fight, and that my clothes were worn out. I had no moccasins, so I was going home. The officers said all right and I rode on. I went to Pryor where the Crows were camped. When I came into camp, some of the Crows thought I was a Sioux and commenced shooting at me.

I have heard many people say that Curley was the only survivor of this battle, but Curley was not in the battle. Just about the time Reno attacked the village, Curley with some Arikara scouts ran off a big band of Sioux ponies and rode away with them. Some of the Arikaras, whom I met afterwards, told me that Curley went with them as far as the Junction (where the Rosebud joins the Yellowstone River). I did not see Curley again until the next fall, when I met him up on the Yellowstone in the camp of the Mountain Crows, so Curley did not see much of the battle.

The Crow Scout White Swan.

were running about away from the camp. I said "No." We then came on down to the forks of Reno Creek. When we stopped there to divide up I could hear the Indians in camp shouting and whooping.

When we separated Half-Yellow-Face and White Swan were ordered to go with Reno. Goes-Ahead, White-Man-Runs-Him, Curley and myself were ordered with Custer. We came down and crossed Reno Creek. Mitch Boyer was ahead with the four scouts right behind. Custer was ahead of his command a short distance behind us. Custer yelled to us to stop, then told us to go to the high hill ahead (the high point just north of where Reno later entrenched). From here we could see the village and could see Reno fighting. He had crossed the creek. Everything was a scramble with lots of Sioux. The battle was over in a few minutes. We thought they were all killed.

We four scouts turned and charged north to where Custer was headed for. Three of us stopped to fire into the village. We saw no more of Curley after that. I don't know where he went. When we met Custer he asked, "How is it?" I said, "Reno's men are fighting hard." We went with

the command down into a dry gulch where we could not see the village. Custer told Mitch Boyer to tell us to go back to the pack-train, which we did. We met Benteen's command just south of where they afterward entrenched. We said to Benteen, "Do you hear that shooting back where we came from? They're fighting Custer there now."

We started to leave Benteen to join the Ree scouts who were quite a way back up the creek, but Benteen told us to stay, and we did. We went with him and helped dig entrenchments. The firing seemed to stop where Custer was, and the Sioux came toward us. Then Reno's command came back where we were entrenched.

Just before sundown the enemy drew off. We had been fighting quite a while. We three scouts got away and rode till we came to the Big Horn, but did not cross that night. It was dark and raining. The next morning some Crow scouts of Bradley's command came along and followed us, where we had crossed the river. They joined us and we all rode to the main Crow camp, two sleeps away on Pryor Creek. This is the way it happened just as near as I can remember.

Note by W.A.G. The name of Custer's half-breed guide is variously spelled in different accounts. Sometimes it is "Mitch Boyer," sometimes "Mich Bouyer," sometimes "Nuch Bayer"; but all refer to the same man.

RED STAR
BOY CHIEF
RED BEAR

YOUNG HAWK
SOLDIER
STRIKES TWO

LITTLE SIOUX

CHAPTER 4

THE ARIKARA

VARNUM'S ARIKARA DETACHMENT

SCOUTS, both White and Indian, played important roles in all our troubles with the aborigines throughout the quarter of a century that followed the end of the Civil War. White scouts, for the most part, were civilians, employed at an agreed wage by the Quartermaster Department of the Army; but Indian scouts were enlisted men, who, while they were not soldiers, were nevertheless declared by the Attorney General of the United States to be part and parcel of the Army.

The service of Indians was provided for by the Act of Congress approved 22 June 1866, the language of the law as it appears in section 1112 of the Revised Statutes of 1873 being as follows:

"The President is authorized to enlist a force of Indians not exceeding one thousand, who shall act as scouts in the Territories and Indian country. They shall be discharged when the necessity for their service shall cease, or at the discretion of the Department Commander."

It was further provided by the law that Indian scouts, so enlisted or employed by the President, were entitled to receive the same pay and allowances as cavalry soldiers, which at that time, and for many years thereafter were, in the words of the old Army song, "thirteen dollars a month and found, in the Regular Army O!"

The statute did not mean, of course, that the President must exercise *in propria persona* the power to enlist Indians. Its grant of authority merely continued a long established pattern of legislation relating to the Army which, by recognizing in him the proper repository of military administration, followed the Constitutional provision that makes of the President the Commander-in-Chief of the Army and Navy. The actual work of recruiting was done by recruiting officers, to whom the presidential power was delegated, just as it has always been done and is done today.

Indian scouts, however, unlike white soldiers, were enlisted for an indefinite period, being subject to discharge at any time in the discretion of a department commander. They thus formed what was technically described as a "temporary and provisional" part of the Army; but notwithstanding their more or less ephemeral status, many Indian Scouts have been retained on duty for more than thirty years, and were retired from active service in the same manner and under the same rules and conditions as white soldiers.

It was under the legal provisions cited above that Varnum's detachment of Arikara scouts was enlisted for the 1876 campaign; and presumably, the same is true as to the Crow scouts who accompanied the troops to the Little Big Horn. Varnum's detachment of Arikaras numbered forty-one, of whom thirty-nine were enlisted at Ft. Lincoln during April and May, 1876, the remaining two, according to the records having enlisted at the camp on the Little Big Horn, 25 June 1876—the day of the battle.

On 25 June 1876, therefore, Varnum had in his Scout detachment, forty-one Arikara Indians, whose names, as gathered from available authentic sources, were as follows:

1. William Baker
2. Barking Wolf
3. Bear
4. Bear Come Out
5. Bears Eyes
6. Bear Running in the Timber
7. Black Calf
8. Black Fox
9. Black Porcupine
10. Bull
11. Bull in the Water

12. Bush
13. Climbs the Bluff
14. Cross William
15. Curly Head
16. Foolish Bear
17. Forked Horn
18. Good Elk
19. Good Face
20. Goose
21. Horns in Front
22. Howling Wolf
23. William Jackson
24. Laying Down
25. Long Bear
26. One Feather
27. One Horn
28. Owl
29. Rushing Bull
30. Round Wooden Cloud
31. Sioux (Little Sioux?)
32. Soldier
33. Stab (Stabbed?)
34. Strike Bear
35. Strike the Lodge
36. Strikes Two
37. Wagon
38. White Cloud
39. White Eagle
40. Wolf Runs
41. Young Hawk

To the above, however, must be added the names of "Bloody Knife," known as Custer's favorite scout, and of Bobtailed Bull, both of whom were members of a separate detachment, though nominally under Varnum's command on 25 June. These two scouts were killed during Reno's engagement in the valley, as also was the scout "Stab." The records indicate that about half of the detachment disappeared during the battle, but rejoined the command on 28 June 1876, which would appear to disprove a statement frequently made that those who left for parts unknown during the battle were not seen again until months thereafter.

It is noteworthy, and a circumstance for which no explanation is apparent, that several of the Arikara Indians whose stories appear in the "Arikara Narrative," are not identifiable by name as members of Varnum's detachment. These, however, may in 1876 have been known by other and different names, or they may, like Bloody Knife and Bobtailed Bull, have been members of another detachment. It is impossible to say which, if either, explanation is correct.

NARRATIVES OF YOUNG HAWK, RED BEAR, SOLDIER, AND RED STAR, ET AL.

FROM THE ARIKARA NARRATIVE

GENERAL CUSTER had told them that he was going on another expedition and that they might be called upon to serve. After his return Young Hawk decided not to serve any more, but his father insisted that he should go. After a time Son-of-the-Star got a letter from Custer asking for more scouts. It was announced that Son-of-the-Star would call a council in his own house and many came. Son-of-the-Star said: "My boys, I have had a letter from a white man asking for some of you boys to serve as scouts." He told them that they would serve under Long Hair (Custer) and they were not surprised at this, for tl.ey had heard him say he would go on another expedition, and, besides, Son-of-the-Star had been to Washington. His words were heard by all present and all that was necessary to say was: "I will go." Young Hawk's father said, "I will go and my son, too." Those who promised to go at this time and afterwards enlisted were: Bob-tailed Bull, Stabbed, Charging Bull, Horns-in-Front, Young Hawk, Bull-in-the-Water, Little Brave, Bloody Knife, Tall Bear (High Bear), One Feather, Running Wolf, Red Star, Strikes Two, Foolish Bear, Howling Wolf, White Eagle, Crooked Horn, Strikes-the-Lodge, Scabby Wolf, Pretty Face, Curly Head (Hair), Black Fox, and One Horn. Certain scouts had reenlisted at Fort Lincoln and were already in service. Red Bear was asked to remain by Crooked Horn, so that they could return to Fort Lincoln together and he did so.

* * *

Gerard took them all over to the office of the commanding officer and he took in Red Bear's permit and coming out soon told them they were to enlist and get clothes and arms. After medical examination was over, Gerard took them into Custer's office where Custer's brother (Tom, the one with the scar on his face) was. He raised his hand and Gerard told the Indians to raise theirs also. Custer soon came in and told them through Gerard that they were the last scouts to enlist and for that reason, since the expedition was ready, they must remain on duty at Fort Lincoln.

* * *

Soldier and Bob-tailed Bull met Custer at his camp on the river bank, in his own tent, Gerard was interpreter. Custer said: "The man before me, Bob-tailed Bull, is a man of good heart, of good character. I am pleased to have him here.

I am glad he has enlisted. It will be a hard expedition but we will all share the same hardships. I am very well pleased to have him in my party, and I told it at Washington. We are to live and fight together, children of one father and one mother. The great-grandfather has a plan. The Sioux camps have united and you and I must work together for the Great Father and help each other. The Great Father is well pleased that it was so easy (took few words) to get (coax) Son-of-the-Star to furnish me scouts for this work we have to do and he is pleased, too, at his behavior in helping on the plan of the Great Father. I, for one, am willing to help in this all I can, and you must help too. It is this way, my brothers. If I should happen to lose any of the men Son-of-the-Star has furnished, their reward will not be forgotten by the government. Their relations will be saddened by their death but there will be some comfort in the pay that the United States government will provide."

Bob-tailed Bull replied: "It is a good thing you say, my brother, my children and other relatives will receive my pay and other rewards. I am glad you say this for I see there is some gain even though I lose my life."

Custer then said: "No more words need be said. Bob-tailed Bull is to be leader and Soldier second in command of the scouts."

* * *

It was early in the morning when the bugle sounded, and the camp broke up and the march began. The army strung out in order toward the fort. Gerard told the scouts they were to have their own company, and they were the first to parade on the fort grounds.

* * *

The parade ended and the march began, with Custer ahead. There were four Dakota scouts who had been at Fort Lincoln that went along with the Arikara. One of these scouts was Ca-roo, another was Ma-tok-sha, a third was Mach-pe-as-ka (White Cloud), the fourth was Pta-a-te (Buffalo Ancestor). The first camp was on both sides of the Heart River. A drove of cattle went along to furnish beef to the soldiers; he saw them on the first day's march. The white soldiers were paid off at this camp, the scouts did not receive any pay at all for they were just enlisted.

* * *

At one of the earlier camps on Powder River * * *. They were two days in camp here and there was a camp of soldiers just across the river.* Two Arikara scouts were sent out ahead, Stabbed and

*Gen. Gibbon's camp.

Goose, and they were given a letter to take to the camp across the river. Here there were some Crow scouts, and their interpreter, Man-with-a-Calfskin-Vest,** came across the river to tell them about it. When Custer's army came up to Camp 20, Red Star saw the army across the river, it was already on the march up the Yellowstone. Stabbed and Goose came back and reported to Custer's camp. Camp 20 was the base camp for the infantry, the band, all the wagons, and part of the mules. There was an inspection of the horses of the scouts and of the cavalry here. * * * They broke camp and marched on; the band played all the time. Custer and Bloody Knife came by and Bloody Knife said: "The General says we are all marching. There are numerous enemies in the country; if we attack their camp we are beaten, we must retreat in small groups. You scouts must not run away, nor go back to your homes."

The next order was that if our command was broken up into squads or single horsemen that this camp should be the appointed place for reassembling all those that had scattered. For my part my heart was glad to hear the band, as far as we could hear the band played. There were some cannon being brought along. We came to the mouth of the Tongue River and here a camp was made. We marched up on a hill overlooking the Elk River and then down to the mouth of the Tongue River. Right at this point was an abandoned Dakota camp. Here lay the body of a soldier, and all about him were clubs and sticks as though he had been beaten to death, only the bones were left. Custer stood still for some time and looked down at the remains of the soldier.

They found a burial scaffold with the uprights colored alternately black and red. This was the mark of a brave man buried there. Custer had the scaffold taken down and the negro, Isaiah, was told to take the clothing and wrappings off the body. As they turned the body about they saw a wound partly healed just below the right shoulder. On the scaffold were little rawhide bags with horn spoons in them, partly made moccasins, etc. Isaiah threw the body into the river, and as he was fishing there later, they suppose he used this for bait. They camped here, and next day crossed the Tongue River and went through the bad lands and encamped at the mouth of the Rosebud. There was a steamboat here, and the cannon† were taken across the Yellowstone by the steamboat. Here they waited while the scouts went up the river. Two

**Probably Mitch Bouyer.

† Low's gatling guns which had accompanied the 7th from Ft. Lincoln.

The Arikara Scout Bob-tailed Bull (right) with unidentified warrior, possibly Bloody Knife. Bob-tailed Bull was killed on Reno's skirmish line.

days later the scouts returned and reported a big Dakota trail on each side of the Rosebud. Opposite this camp there was another camp on the other side of the Yellowstone. Six of the Crow scouts and one interpreter came across from that camp. They broke camp and went up the Rosebud River. From this camp Howling Wolf, Running Wolf, and Curly Head were sent back with mail to the base camp. At this camp they issued mules for carrying supplies. The scouts were given five mules to carry their supplies. Here Gerard told us he wanted us to sing our death songs. The Dakota trail had been seen and the fight would soon be on. Custer had a heart like an Indian; if we ever left out one thing in our ceremonies he always suggested it to us. We got on our horses and rode around, singing the songs. Then we fell in behind Custer and marched on, and a halt was soon made. Custer then ordered two groups of scouts to go ahead, one on each side of the river. * * * Next morning at breakfast Bloody Knife appeared leading a horse. He had been out all night. Then the bugle sounded and we saddled up, Custer ahead, the scouts following and flanking the army that marched behind. Bob-tailed Bull was in charge, with Strikes Two and others on one side. About nightfall they came to an abandoned Dakota camp where there were signs of a sun dance circle. Here there was evidence of the Dakotas having made medicine, the sand had been arranged and

smoothed, and pictures had been drawn. The Dakota scouts in Custer's army said that this meant the enemy knew the army was coming. In one of the sweat lodges was a long heap or ridge of sand. On this one Red Bear, Red Star, and Soldier saw figures drawn indicating by hoof prints Custer's men on one side and the Dakota on the other. Between them dead men were drawn lying with their heads toward the Dakotas. The Arikara scouts understood this to mean that the Dakota medicine was too strong for them and that they would be defeated by the Dakotas. * * * On the right bank of the Rosebud as they marched they saw Dakota inscriptions on the sandstone of the hills at their left. One of these inscriptions showed two buffalo fighting, and various interpretations were given by the Arikara as to the meaning of these figures. Young Hawk saw in one of the sweat lodges, where they had camped, opposite the entrance, three stones near the middle, all in a row and painted red. This meant in Dakota sign language that the Great Spirit had given them victory, and that if the whites did not come they would seek them. Soldier saw offerings, four sticks standing upright with a buffalo calf-skin tied on with cloth and other articles of value, which was evidence of a great religious service. This was also seen by Strikes Two, Little Sioux, and Boy Chief. All the Arikara knew what this meant, namely, that the Dakotas were sure of winning. Soldier said he heard later that Sitting Bull had performed the ceremonies here in this camp. After they passed this inscription of the two buffaloes charging, they came to the fork of the Rosebud River (about where the Cheyennes are now located). Six of the Crow scouts with their interpreter had been out scouting and they returned at this camp. They reported many abandoned Dakota camps along the Rosebud. The whole army stopped here and ate dinner on a hill. While the scouts were at dinner, Custer came to their camp with his orderly, the one who carried his flag for him. The Arikara were sitting in a half-circle, Stabbed sat at the right of Red Bear. Custer sat down with one knee on the ground and said: "What do you think of this report of the Crow scouts? They say there are large camps of the Sioux. What do you suppose will be the outcome of it all?" * * * The other officers came to the fire and stood around it. Custer said again through Gerard: "My only intention in bringing these people to battle is to have them go into battle and take many horses away from the Sioux." At this Custer extended his arms and said he was glad and pleased to have with him on this expedition familiar faces. "Some of you I see here have been with me on one or two other expeditions, and to see you again makes my heart glad. And on this expedition if we are victorious, when we return home, Bloody Knife, Bob-tailed Bull, Soldier, Strikes Two, and Stabbed will be proud to have following behind them on parade marches those who have shown themselves to be brave young men. When your chief, Son-of-the-Star, sees you on this parade, I am sure he will be proud to see his boys." To Gerard, Custer then said: "I want you to tell these young men, these boys, that if we are successful, when we return, my brother, Bloody Knife, and I will represent you at Washington and perhaps we will take you in person to Washington."

The bugles blew and they went on, Bob tailed Bull ahead. They came upon another abandoned Dakota camp. These camps were large, one-half to one-third of a mile across. It must have rained at this camp for the sod was dug up about the tent circles to carry off the water. At this point they could see, far ahead, the hill called "Custer's Last Look," about twelve miles off. They marched towards these hills for they were to stop merely for supper and then push on all night. This temporary camp was on both sides of the Rosebud and it was very dark after they had eaten supper. From across the Rosebud Crooked Horn called over: "Strikes-the-Lodge, you saddle up and Red Star also with Red Foolish Bear, Black Fox, and Bull." Forked Horn led this party and here Red Bear heard that Bob-tailed Bull was ahead and had been gone since noon. This was the beginning of the night march and they rode all night. At dawn they came to the stopping place for breakfast and they were tired and tumbled off their horses for a little sleep. Bull-in-the-Water and Red Bear had charge of one mule which they were unpacking and the former said: "Let us get breakfast for if we go to the happy hunting grounds we should go with a full belly." In getting water for their breakfast they had to pass through the camp of the soldiers. The soldiers were lying in groups on the ground snoring, for they were very tired, and lay down where they had unsaddled. * * * Camp broke up, the horses trotted, and the army stopped at a hill and Custer came down to join them. His orders were to go ahead riding hard and take the Dakota horses. Stabbed rode around on horseback, back and forth, exhorting the young men to behave well and be brave. He said: "Young men, keep up your courage, don't feel that you are children; today will be a hard battle. We have been told that there is a big Sioux camp ahead. We attack a buffalo bull and wound him, when he is this

way we are afraid of him though he has no bullets to harm us with." He said these things for he saw many of us were young and inexperienced and he wished to prepare them for their first real fight. He was at some distance when he said this and he was rubbing some clay between his hands. Then he prayed: "My Father, I remember this day the promises you have made to me; it is for my young men I speak to you." Then he called up the young men and had them hold up their shirts in front so that he could rub the good medicine on their bodies. They came up one by one, he spat on the clay and then rubbed it on their chests. He had carried this clay with him for this purpose. The mule train with supplies was left behind and Pretty Face was detailed on the duty of looking after it.

* * *

Note:

Here follows a list of the twenty-two Arikara Scouts who crossed the river and went into the fight with Reno's battalion; of the nine who did not cross the river at all, and of the thirteen who were in the fighting line on the hill after Reno's retreat. W.A.G.

NARRATIVE BY RED STAR

WE WERE eating supper at the temporary camp on the Rosebud when, a little after dusk, Crooked Horn was called to Custer's quarters. On coming back he said to us: "Come,

The Arikara Scout Red Star.

Black Fox, Red Foolish Bear, Strikes-the-Lodge, Red Star (Strikes-the-Bear), and Bull." These scouts reported at Custer's headquarters and there they saw four ponies of the Crow scouts standing saddled. At his tent stood Custer with Gerard, and Gerard said to them: "Long Hair wants to tell you that tonight you shall go without sleep. You are to go on ahead, you are to try to locate the Sioux camp. You are to do your best to find this camp. Travel all night, when day comes if you have not found the Sioux camp, keep on going until noon. If your search is useless by this time you are to come back to camp. These Crow Indians will be your guides for they know the country. Just then Charley Reynolds (called by the Arikara, Lucky Man) came along with his horse all saddled, he was to be their interpreter. The four Crow Indians were called by the Arikara, Big Belly, Strikes Enemy, Comes Leading (Man-with-Fur-Belt), Curly Head. Their interpreter was called Man-Wearing-Calf-Skin-Vest, a white man, and he went along, making a party of twelve. Custer said to them: "Soon after you leave we will march on." They started out, their horses trotted on briskly, being used to the broken country. They headed for the Custer Butte, led by the Crows, directly from their camp on the left side of the Rosebud. They stopped to smoke and one of the Crows told them by signs that by daybreak they would reach a high mountain where they could see far, from it all the hills would seem to go down flat. They rode on and on and reached a small grove where they smoked again and a Crow scout told them they were near. They came on to the foot of the mountain and the same Crow scout, the leader, told them they had come to the mountain and they were to climb up. They climbed up and dismounted on the top nearest their camp on the Rosebud and they smoked there together on the hill. As soon as they reached the top they unsaddled and it was just daybreak. "I saw two of the Crow scouts climbing up on the highest peak of the hill. I had carried some coffee on my saddle to give Bob-tailed Bull the night before. I was told to give it to the Crow scouts, and started towards them when I heard the Crows call like an owl, not loud but clear (the Sioux call this way). The scouts were all sitting together when they saw the two Crow scouts coming back from the highest point of the hill. These two scouts touched the Arikara scouts and they got up to sing the song they usually sing, but the two scouts signed to them to keep silent. One of these two Crow scouts then came up to Crooked Horn and told him by signs that they had seen Dakota tepees ahead. Then all the scouts climbed up the

peak to look for signs of the Dakotas. The first two Crow scouts pointed in the direction of the Dakota camp. As Crooked Horn and Red Star looked, the former said: "Look sharp, my boy, you have better eyes than I." Red Star looked and saw a dark object and above it light smoke rising up from the Dakota tepees. It was at the upper end of the village, the tepees were hidden by the high ridge but the smoke was drawing out and up. Beyond the smoke he saw some black specks he thought were horses. Charley Reynolds looked a long time, then took out his field glasses and looked a long time. Then he put them down and nodded his head. He took a note book, sat down and wrote a note and got up, folded the paper, and handed it to Crooked Horn. Crooked Horn took it and turned to Red Star and said: "Boy, saddle up your pony; Bull, saddle up your pony." They had saddled up when Crooked Horn said to them: "Look, you can see the smoke of our camp." Red Star looked and saw a cloud of smoke rising up and their way back was clear, they could follow the smoke. They started down the hill, after they were down he urged his horse on for he had the note and he paid no attention to his companion. Once in a while he looked back to see where Bull was, his horse was bad. As he came up out of the hollow he saw the sentries and he gave the call, as is the custom among Arikara (the Crow scouts use the same call on bringing a message to camp), and he also began turning his horse zig-zag back and forth as a sign that he had found the enemy. When he left camp he had told Stabbed that if he came back with a message that they had found the Dakota camp, he would tie up his horse's tail, as is the custom of the Arikara. The sun was just coming up when he got to camp. The sentries began to come together in groups. Stabbed came up and said: "My Son, this is no small thing you have done." (Meaning it was a great honor, according to Arikara custom, to have brought such a message.) Red Star rode by Stabbed and got off and unsaddled. Stabbed turned and called out to the scout camp: "Why are you sleeping, Strikes-the-Bear (Red Star) has come back." Bloody Knife got up at once and met Red Star and asked him if he had seen anything. He said, yes, they had found the camp. Then he saw Gerard coming up with Custer and they came where he had unsaddled. Tom Custer was there. Custer sat down on his left knee near Red Star who was squatted down with a cup of coffee. Custer signed to Red Star asking him if he had seen the Dakotas, and he answered by a sign that he had. Then Red Star handed the note to Custer, taking it from his coat, and Custer read it at once and nodded his head. By Red Star's side was Bloody Knife and Tom Custer. Custer said to Bloody Knife by signs, referring to Tom, "Your brother, there, is frightened, his heart flutters with fear, his eyes are rolling from fright at this news of the Sioux. When we have beaten the Sioux he will then be a man." Custer then told Red Star, through the interpreter, to saddle up at once. "We are going back to where his party are on the hill," he said. Red Star was not through his breakfast, but he left his coffee, knocking it over with his foot, saddled up, and joined Custer. In the party were Custer, his bugler, Tom, Red Star, Gerard, Bloody Knife, Bob-tailed Bull, and Little Brave. They rode hard toward the hill and Red Star heard a bugle as he left camp, blown by Custer's bugler, who turned backward on his horse to do so. Custer asked by signs of Red Star if the distance was short, and Red Star made signs that it was. When they got to the foot of the hill, Red Star signed that this was the place. They climbed the hill, and came to the scouts. Charley Reynolds came up and he and Custer went ahead leaving the others behind. Charley Reynolds pointed where Custer was to look, and they looked for some time and then Gerard joined them.

Gerard called back to the scouts: "Custer thinks it is no Sioux camp." Custer thought that Charley Reynolds had merely seen the white buttes of the ridge that concealed the lone tepee. Charley Reynolds then pointed again, explaining Custer's mistake, then after another look Custer nodded that he had seen the signs of a camp. Next Charley Reynolds pulled out his field glasses and Custer looked through them at the Dakota camp and nodded his head again. Crooked Horn told Gerard to ask Custer how he would have felt if he had found two dead Dakotas at the hill. The scouts had seen six Dakota Indians after Red Star and Bull had left them. Two of them had gone over the ridge down the dry coulee and four of them had ridden into the timber at the foot of the hill. They thought the two Dakotas were planning to ambush the messengers and they wished to kill them first. They did not do so because they were afraid Custer might not like it. Custer replied that it would have been all right, he would have been pleased to have found two dead Dakotas. Then the scouts sat down and one of the Crow scouts, Big Belly, got up and asked Custer through the Crow interpreter what he thought of the Dakota camp he had seen. Custer said: "This camp has not seen our army, none of their scouts have seen us." Big Belly replied: "You say we have not been seen. These Sioux we have seen at the foot of the hill, two going one way, and four the other, are good scouts, they have seen the smoke of our camp." Custer said, speaking angrily: "I say again we have not been seen. That camp has not seen us, I am going ahead to carry out what I think. I want to wait until it is dark and then we will march, we will place our army around the Sioux camp." Big Belly replied: "That plan is bad, it should not be carried out." Custer said: "I have said what I propose to do, I want to wait until it is dark and then go ahead with my plan."

Red Star as he sat listening first thought that Custer's plan was good. The Crow scouts insisted that the Dakota scouts had already seen the army and would report its coming and that they would attack Custer's army. They wanted him to attack at once, that day, and capture the horses of the Dakotas and leave them unable to move rapidly. Custer replied: "Yes, it shall be done as you say." The army now came up to the foot of the hill and Custer's party rode down and joined the troop.

NARRATIVE OF YOUNG HAWK

THE army was on the little knoll at the foot of the hill, they were met by Custer's party from the high butte. Considerable excitement among the scouts was to be seen. They wondered what Custer would say when he heard that the Dakotas knew of his approach. The scouts from the hill had told them of the six Dakotas. When the scouts saw Custer coming down they began to group themselves according to tribes, Arikara, Crows, etc. The Arikara grouped themselves about the older men who spoke to the younger men as is the custom of the tribe. Stabbed spoke to the young men and Custer gave the instructions here to the scouts through Gerard. He said: "Boys, I want you to take the horses away from the Sioux camp." Then Stabbed told the Arikara scouts to obey Custer's instructions and to try and take away as many horses as possible. Custer continued: "Make up your minds to go straight to their camp and capture their horses. Boys, you are going to have a hard day, you must keep up your courage, you will get experience today." On the top of the ridge the bugle sounded for the unfurling of the flag (this is what Gerard told the scouts). This caused great excitement, all made ready, girths were tightened, loads were made light. Another bugle sounded and Custer ordered the scouts forward. They went down the dry coulee and when about half way to the high ridge at the right, Young Hawk saw a group of scouts at the lower end of the ridge peering over toward the lone tepee. The scouts he was with slowed up as the others came toward them. Then behind them they heard a call from Gerard. He said to them: "The Chief says for you to run." At this Strikes Two gave the war-whoop and called back: "What are we doing?" and rode on. At this we all whooped and Strikes Two reached the lone tepee first and struck it with his whip. Then Young Hawk came. He got off on the north side of the tepee, took a knife from his belt, pierced the tent through and ran the knife down to the ground. Inside of the lone tepee he saw a scaffold, and upon it a dead body wrapped in a buffalo robe.

At the same moment he saw by him on horse-back, Red Star. All of the scouts rode around to the north side of the tent at full speed and turned into the dry coulee just beyond the tepee. A little further down they overtook the white soldiers and all rode on mixed together. The best mounted scouts kept up with the hard riding soldiers, others straggled behind. They crossed at the mouth of a dry coulee through a prairie dog

The Arikara Scout Young Hawk.

village, turned sharp to the right, and Young Hawk saw across the Little Big Horn on the west side, Red Star, Goose, Boy Chief, and Red Bear. Young Hawk had a bunch of loose eagle feathers, he unbraided his hair and brought it forward on his head and tied it in with the eagle feathers. He expected to be killed and scalped by the Dakotas. Turning sharp to the right the battle began at about the spot where the prairie dog village stands. The first fighting began as skirmishing in front of the line. Behind the ridge at the left he could see the Dakotas circling in and swarming about. The soldiers and the scouts dismounted, the horses were held in groups behind the line. The soldiers formed in line toward the right, the scouts at the left out toward the ridge, while far to the left on a slant were scattered scouts. Bob-tailed Bull was farthest at the left and nearest the ridge. In front of the line rode the Dakotas skirmishing back and forth. Young Hawk moved toward the right and took his position there. He saw the following scouts in order: Red Bear, Little Brave, Forked Horn, Red Foolish Bear, Goose, Big Belly (Crow) and Strikes Enemy (Crow). The last scout to the left was Bob-tailed Bull, far out beyond the others. Young Hawk stood between Goose and Big Belly. Behind them all, on the Little Big Horn, there appeared Bloody Knife. "He came right toward me and I looked up and noticed his dress. He had on the black handkerchief with blue stars on it given him by Custer. He wore a bear's claw with a clam shell on it." Bloody Knife spoke to Young Hawk, calling out: "What Custer has ordered about the Sioux horses is being done, the horses are being taken away." Then Bloody Knife passed on back of the line and took his stand by Little Brave. The battle got stronger and the line curved back toward the river. Many of the soldiers were killed and they began to fall back. One Dakota charged the soldiers very closely and was shot about sixteen feet from the line. * * * All this time the Dakotas had been collecting back of the ridge nearest to Bob-tailed Bull. All at once over the middle of the ridge came riding a dense swarm of Dakotas in one mass straight toward Bob-tailed Bull. At the same moment a white soldier standing nearest to Young Hawk turned to him and cried: "John, you go!" The Dakota attack doubled up the line from the left and pushed this line back toward the soldiers. They all retreated back across the river lower down about two miles. They retreated across the flat and up the bluff on a long diagonal up the steep bank, which was hard climbing. The soldiers were the first to retreat across the river. Of the scouts two Crows were ahead, Half-Yellow-Face and Strikes-Enemy, then followed Red Foolish Bear and Forked Horn and then Goose and Young Hawk. When Young Hawk got back to the timber, before crossing the river, he heard Forked Horn call: "Let's get off and make a stand." He did this on account of Bob-tailed Bull who was hard pushed by the pursuing Dakotas and had fallen back nearly to the ford used by the soldiers. Young Hawk thought this was a general signal for the scouts and jumped off his horse and Goose followed him, also, in making the stand. They did not stop their horses, but leaped off as they were running and both shot at the Dakotas. At the crossing where the soldiers forded the river Bob-tailed Bull got over the river. The charging Dakotas turned sharply as the scouts fired at them and rode back. Young Hawk intended to fire again, but as he opened the breech of the gun he dropped his shell. The four scouts, Half-Yellow-Face, Strikes Enemy, Red Foolish Bear, and Forked Horn rode into the brush and over the river still lower down less than one-eighth of a mile. Goose and Young Hawk followed them through the brush and crossed the river where the water was deep and the brush grew very thick on the opposite bank and the horses struggled hard before getting to land. They took refuge in a thick grove of trees just across the river. The Dakotas were riding on all sides of them by this time. Here Young Hawk found the other four scouts who had ridden ahead, he did not know they were there.

All of the scouts had their horses in this grove. The Dakotas saw them ride in and began firing at them through the trees as they crouched there on horseback. He and Goose stood facing each other, then he heard a sound like a sigh and Goose groaned and called to him: "Cousin, I am wounded." Young Hawk said: "When I heard this my heart did not tremble with fear but I made up my mind I would die this day." Goose showed him his wound, his right hand was badly shot. Then Young Hawk took off the cartridge belt belonging to Goose and put it on himself, as he stood by the horse on the ground. He told Goose to get off his horse and he helped him dismount. Then Young Hawk was seized with rage (madness). He took off his coat and army blouse and made ready to fight for his life. Just as Goose dismounted his horse was shot down. Young Hawk put Goose against a tree and told him to hold his horse. Goose had a revolver in his belt. Just then Young Hawk saw Half-Yellow-Face crawling toward him. He said, "My friend is being killed, he is just on the edge of the thicket." Young Hawk went with him crawling on hands and feet to where the Crow scout lay on his back with his hands up. The two scouts took him by his arms and dragged him back to where Goose sat with his back against a tree. He was Strikes Enemy or White Swan (Crow). He told them he was not afraid and that he was glad he was wounded. Young Hawk said: "The sight of the wounded men gave me queer feelings, I did not want to see them mutilated, so I decided to get killed myself at the edge of the timber. Before going out I put my arms about my horse's neck, saying, 'I love you.' I then crawled out and stood up and saw all in front of me Sioux warriors kneeling ready to shoot. I fired at them and received a volley, but was not hit. I was determined to try again and get killed, so I crawled out to the edge of the timber in a new place, jumped up and fired again and received a volley, but I dropped out of sight before I was hit. Then I saw near me a tree with driftwood piled against it, making a very good protection and behind it I found Forked Horn lying face down to avoid being shot." When Forked Horn saw that it was Young Hawk who had drawn the fire of the Dakotas the second time, he scolded him, saying, "Don't you do so again, it is no way to act. This is not the way to fight at all, to show yourself as a mark." The Dakotas tried to burn the scouts out but the grass was too green to burn. Young Hawk sat still for a time after being scolded by Forked Horn and the Dakotas came closer, one on a gray horse came very close indeed. Young Hawk fired and missed him, then he jumped up and shot again, killing him. * * * "Some little time after this the Sioux came closer again and I saw one Sioux coming right toward me and I drew a fine bead on him and dropped him, then I jumped up and gave the death call again." While this was going on several Dakota women rode up an gave the woman's yell urging on the warriors to kill all the Arikara. He heard them in many places about the bushes where he lay hiding, then they went away with the others. Some time before noon he noticed that the Dakota attack was slackening and he saw them begin to ride off down stream, which made him think that Custer's attack had begun at the lower ford. They could see many Dakotas crossing the river farther up and riding down past them to the north. He said: "After the shooting had slackened, I stood up and looked around. On the ridge above me on the highest point I saw a United States flag." Forked Horn then said to Young Hawk: "My grandson, you have shown yourself the bravest. The flag you have seen up there shows where the pack-train is which we were to meet and we must try now and reach it." Custer had instructed them what to do, so as not to be mistaken for the Dakotas. So Young Hawk cut a stick and tied his white handkerchief on it. They tried to put Strikes Enemy on a horse; his leg was pierced by a shot and his right hand also. They were able to put him on his own horse and Goose was mounted on the horse of Red Foolish Bear, who himself went on foot. Young Hawk rode ahead with the white flag. They rode down the stream half way the length of the ridge and as they climbed up the slope they saw the Dakotas riding back on the east side of the ridge toward the white camp. The Custer fight was over and the Dakotas completely covered the hill where the soldiers had made their last stand and were swarming toward him and beginning to fire. The rest of the party turned back down the hill. Goose took Red Foolish Bear up with him and they rode back the entire length of the ridge and up at the other end into the white camp. Young Hawk remained behind and the Dakotas chased him along the ridge. He held to his white flag, waving it in front of him. The soldiers fired over him at the enemy and the Dakotas fired at him. A few rods from the camp his horse was shot down but he scrambled to his feet still carrying his white flag and ran into the camp. The first man he saw was his chief of scouts, Peaked Face (Varnum). The pack-train was there and the survivors from the fight on the Little Big Horn. Then he met the officer in charge and he was glad to see Young Hawk, his face showed it. He signed to Young Hawk that the sergeant (Bob-tailed Bull) was killed and that his horse was in camp there.

* * * Meanwhile the Dakotas were coming up and riding around them. The other scouts who had left him now rode into the camp. Then the whole party retreated into a ravine near by. * * * Here the Dakotas attacked them and the shooting made a continuous roar on both sides, soldiers and horses were killed very fast. Then the Dakotas worked around at the right and began firing into the ravine at one end. The soldiers threw up breastworks across the open end of the ravine, consisting of cracker boxes, bags of bacon, etc. Young Hawk was not one of the party that built these breastworks, but he took a cracker box and put it in front of himself as he lay on the ground. The Dakotas were on every side, firing into the ravine, they came very close, crouching in lines on all sides. The guns made such a noise that nothing else could be heard. The wounded men were dragged up to the breastworks as the safest place. This heavy firing went on without a break until it was dark. When it grew dark they began to take up the wounded and to place the dead at one side. They all stayed up until morning watching for the Dakotas and just at dawn a few shots were fired at them. Then the fight began again with heavy firing as before and this went on until late afternoon. All the scouts were together on the side next to where the Dakotas came from and nearest to the ridge. During the first afternoon an officer came to the scouts, saying a message was to be carried after dark. Forked Horn said, "All right." The officer told Goose he could not go for he was wounded and that each scout was to carry the same message. Later he came again and brought with him a sergeant and told them that this man was to go with them so that in case all the scouts were killed he could tell what the conditions were in the camp. Goose said he would go, too, although his hand was wounded; if they were killed, he wanted all to be killed. The officer told the scouts they were to carry the message out to the President of the United States, in order that all might know what had happened. They were told that they could ride government horses since they were faster than their own. Each one was to ride hard and pay no attention to anyone else who might be shot by the Dakotas. If anyone fell wounded or shot he was to pull out the paper with the message on it and leave it on the ground so that when the soldiers came they could learn what had happened and where the camp was. Then Forked Horn said that the government horses were shod and he wanted the shoes taken off so they could run better. When the messages were written for each of the scouts, the two Crow scouts stayed behind, one was wounded and the other stayed to care for him. The scouts who had the messages to carry were Goose, Forked Horn, Red-Foolish-Bear, Young Hawk, and the white sergeant. When it was dark they followed the ravine out but there the Dakotas fired on them and they all ran back. The officer told them to stay until morning and start again. They stayed there all night and in the morning the Dakotas began firing again as hard as ever, the guns were going

very rapidly (Young Hawk showed how the guns sounded by clapping his hands as fast as possible). Then he heard in the midst of the firing on the farther side of the ravine, the south side, not fifty yards away and very close to the soldiers, a Dakota warrior call out and give the Dakota song for a charge. The words were: "Come on, white man, come on, if you are brave, we are ready for you." As soon as he had done singing, all the Dakotas seemed to disappear suddenly and the firing stopped. Then the soldiers and scouts all got up and in every direction they saw the Dakotas retreating all on horseback toward their camp over the ridge down to the dry coulee. He saw no wounded or dead being carried off. When they climbed the ridge they could see the Dakotas in groups retreating down toward the dry coulee, all on horseback. This was now about noon. The Dakotas got to their village and the tents went down in a hurry. They thought that the Dakotas might camp where they were before. The Dakotas then moved toward the ford and reached the prairie dog village near the ford, only five tents were standing on their camping place. But the Dakotas passed the ford and went into the timber along the Little Big Horn above the ford. Then smoke began to come up as from a camp. They could see the trees above which the smoke rose. As they watched, off past the old Dakota camp to the west was a ridge over two miles away and here they saw a band or body of people moving over the ridge and down toward the Dakota camp. They thought it was a band of Dakotas returning to camp from hunting. Then the party approached the five Dakota tents and they rode about among them. The commanding officer said to Young Hawk and Forked Horn: "They are the white men who were coming to help us. Saddle up and go to them." So these two scouts rode to meet them down the ridge to the west and across the Custer ford until they were quite near to the party. Then they saw that they were whites and they rode back again.

The soldiers in the party were busy stripping off the buckskin shirts from the bodies of the dead Dakotas there and taking their earrings. When the scouts got back they told the officer through the interpreter, Gerard, that the party were white men. The officer, Varnum, said that these were the white men whom they were expecting to come and help us. It was not right that Custer went ahead, he ought to have waited. The officer then said: "Now let us go and look for Custer's body." Then Forked Horn, Red-Foolish-Bear, Goose, Young Hawk, and Gerard, Varnum, and some soldiers (the Dakotas called one of these soldiers Jack Drum Beater, probably a white drummer) went down to look for Custer's body. They went north along the ridge and followed Custer's trail across a low soft place or coulee east of the hill called Custer's last stand. On the other side of the ravine they began to find dead soldiers lying with a few dead horses. When they came to the flat-topped hill where Custer fell, the officer, through Gerard, told the scouts to go off east on the hill and watch for the Dakotas lest they come back to attack them. Lying all over the hill Young Hawk saw dead horses of the Dakotas and of the whites and also many bodies of the soldiers, lying stripped. He also saw the circle breastwork made of dead horses on top of the hill. * * * Varnum told them through the interpreter that when they found Custer's body the bugle would call and Gerard would go and tell the scouts that they had found his body. The scouts had not been long on the hill watching (a little more than half a mile away) when they heard the bugle sound the reveille and Gerard came to tell them that Custer's body had been found. When he told them this they came back to camp, the sun was near the horizon and they were very hungry. The commanding officer said: "Let's go to the village and follow along up the river through where the Sioux camped." The soldiers at the camp had been placing the dead in rows in preparation for the burial. They crossed lower down than where they had first crossed, a good watering place, right below Custer's hill (probably the Custer ford). The body of Bloody Knife lay a little back from the brush near the ford. He saw evidence of fighting from the Custer hill clear to the river by the dead horses, though he saw no bodies of soldiers. The five tepees in the deserted Dakota camp were thrown down and some of the bodies stripped by the soldiers they had seen there. They went on to the Dakota camp and found the body of a dead Dakota lying on a tanned buffalo hide. Young Hawk recognized this warrior as one who had been a scout at Fort Lincoln, Chat-ka. He had on a white shirt, the shoulders were painted green, and on his forehead, painted in red, was the sign of a secret society. In the middle of the camp they found a drum and on one side lying on a blanket was a row of dead Dakotas with their feet toward the drum. Young Hawk supposed that a tent had covered them, with the entrance to the tent at the side opposite where the dead bodies lay, that is, at the holy or back side of the tent. When alive these braves would sit on the other side and drum. This drum was cut up and slashed. Farther on they found three more groups of dead Dakotas lying on canvas, buffalo hides, or blankets at the back side of where the tent had stood, that is, opposite the opening. All the fine buckskin shirts they had worn as well as beads and earrings had been stripped off by the soldiers. These groups of bodies were two, three, or four. In this camp they found evidence of great haste, bedding thrown away, bundles of dried meat dropped, etc. * * *

In the morning they looked after the dead. Young Hawk saw one of the soldiers standing near the bank. He went close and the soldier told him to go into the river and get out the body of the dead soldier there. There were no bushes on the bank here; this was about the place where the soldiers retreated across two days earlier. He took off his clothes and went into the water nearly to his armpits. The dead soldier lay on the water, head down, and his back was out of the water; he had on trousers but no coat or shirt. It seemed to Young Hawk that the Dakotas on the other side had pulled this much of his clothes off and left him there. He and the soldier pulled the body up on the land and left it and went further up the bank. Then Young Hawk met the rest of the scouts and they agreed to go where Bob-tailed Bull was chased by the Dakotas. They found the place where he went over the bank and there they saw four leafy branches of willow sticking up in the stream. The water was shallow here and they wondered to see the willow branches there. Then they went up to a better crossing; the water was up to their hips when they crossed over. They came down on the right bank, seeing two dead soldiers stripped, all the way to the brush and there, in the edge of the brush, was the body of a sergeant (they called him "Sarge"). The soldiers followed and placed the bodies straight. The scouts went into the bushes and found their coats where they had left them on the day of the fight and they put them on. They went on but found no more dead soldiers and crossed back again at a watering place for horses. As they came up the bank they found a soldier standing there and he said: "Here is one scout lying in the bushes." They could not tell who the scout was because his face and head were all pounded to pieces, but they think it was the body of Bloody Knife. Then they all got together and Gerard told them that the soldiers were going to cut poles for horse travois for carrying all the wounded. * * * The march was very slow and wounded suffered very much. Young Hawk led the pony which dragged the travois upon which Goose lay. At last they reached the Elk River and saw the steamboat waiting for them near the shore with soldiers on board. Young Hawk put Goose and his property near the wheel, for the deck was covered. The Crow scout, White Swan, was helped on board by his companions. The soldiers and scouts, who were not wounded, marched down the south side of the Yellowstone and camped there. The next day they saw a soldier-camp across the river. * * *

NARRATIVE BY SOLDIER

Soldier caught up with the scouts at the lone tepee but his horse was behind from the start. They started to go very fast from just beyond the lone tepee. As the charge went on, the poor horses trailed out far behind. As he started on he heard a whistle behind him and he saw Stabbed coming up. He had been detailed to follow up a trail off toward the left and had not gone on with the rest of the scouts. * * * At this point he heard the firing begin, it was about two miles away. Soldier first caught up with White Eagle and the two rode on together until they caught up with Bull. Stabbed rode on ahead to the end of the ridge east of the river and the three scouts followed him. At the ridge they began to see signs of Custer's march off to the east. They could see the trails through the grass. Here they found a white soldier trying to get his horse up, he was cursing and swearing, pounding his horse's head with his fists and kicking him under the belly.* Here the grass was much trodden down and the trails were very plain. Soon a little farther up the ridge, they found another white soldier with his horse down. This soldier indicated by signs that he belonged to Custer's command. From the ridge they saw the whole Dakota camp and the battlefield. At this point Soldier was riding very hard. He saw Bob-tailed Bull far out at the end of the line and many Dakotas riding behind the ridge at the left. He met on the ridge some of the Arikara scouts driving off the Dakota horses from between the ridge and the river. He saw some shooting at the end of the ridge over which the Dakotas were to charge later on down upon Bob-tailed Bull and the rest of the scouts. * * * Just at the point of the ridge where the horses came over, they met Red Wolf and Strikes-the-Lodge. Stabbed now came back and joined the party. Soldier

---

* See page 44.

saw many Dakota tents go down and many of the Dakotas swarming back and forth at the end of the village nearest where the fighting was going on. Now the Arikara scouts, Stabbed, Strikes-the-Lodge, Red Wolf, White Eagle, Soldier, Red Star, and Strikes Two, headed the horses some distance from the ridge. * * *

NARRATIVE BY RED STAR, BOY CHIEF AND STRIKES TWO

Custer's plan was for them to seize the Dakota horses across the river. They crossed the river at a point where there was no regular ford and rode after the horses of the Dakotas. There was very little fighting on the line at this time and the village was just stirring. As they headed the horses into a group, One Feather and Pta-a-te had a bunch nearer the ford and these horses were retaken by the Dakotas who had crossed the river lower down, below the timber where Young Hawk and his party were to hide. They crossed the ridge just ahead of the Dakotas and got away with the horses. Little Sioux and Bull-in-the-Water helped to get the horses over the

A later photograph of Boy Chief.

ridge. Here were all the remaining scouts who did not cross the river. The horses were headed into a ravine east of the ridge and the scouts changed horses. There were twenty-eight of these Dakota horses here. As the scouts turned back to fight and rode up on the ridge, they saw that the line was broken and that the soldiers were coming up the hill. The Dakotas were across the river already and coming right after the soldiers. Down the river they could see the smoke of much firing around the grove where Young Hawk and his party were hiding. At the Dakota camp they noticed that the riders were headed down stream. Red Star saw Varnum, his orderly was with him, wounded in the ankle. * * *

When Custer stood at the bank where Hodgson's stone stands. Curley and Black Fox (Arikara) were there with him (Goes Ahead confirms this). Pretty Face reported that after he had joined the Arikara scouts he saw an Arikara with a white cloth about his head. Black Fox was the only Arikara with this on. When Black Fox reached the mouth of the Rosebud he met the older scouts already there, they came out to meet him, he came on slowly. In answer to their queries he said he and Curley got together near Reno ford. Curley told Black Fox he would take him back to show him where the soldiers left some hard tack. So Curley took Black Fox to the flat below the hills overlooking the present town of Busby north side. Curley told Black Fox that for his part he was going home.

NARRATIVE BY RED BEAR

CUSTER had ordered the charge and he also gave them orders to take the Dakota horses from their camp. The scouts charged down the dry run, and when Red Bear came to the lone tepee, the other scouts were ahead of him and were riding around the lone tepee, striking it with their whips. * * * Just then Custer rode up with Gerard and the latter called out to them: "You were supposed to go right on in to the Sioux village." While the scouts were examining the lone tepee, Custer, who was ahead of his troops, overtook them and said by words and signs: "I told you to dash on and stop for nothing. You have disobeyed me. Move to one side and let the soldiers pass you in the charge. If any man of you is not brave, I will take away his weapons and make a woman of him." One of the scouts cried out: "Tell him if he does the same to all his white soldiers who are not so brave as we are,

A later photograph of Red Bear.

began to go off and we got off our horses and began to shoot." The Dakotas were shooting at them from the bluffs or hills, lying down out of sight. At this time no one was riding around on horseback. They were less than a quarter of a mile off when they dismounted to fire. Forked Horn was at the point of the timber at one side and called out: "Come on this side." At the ford as they crossed down to the Dakota village, the soldiers caught up with the scouts, and the scouts crossed more at the left and Red Bear saw at his right the soldiers stringing across the river. All was excitement and confusion at this point, he recognized no white soldier or officer. When Bloody Knife called out about the horses, the white soldiers had not yet dismounted. But they were all there with the scouts. The soldiers were dismounting at the time Forked Horn called and Red Bear mounted and rode to him. * * * Just then he saw Little Brave riding from the timber and he said that he had heard from the yelling at the Dakota camp (he knew a little of the Dakota language) that they were about to charge. He said: "Let me fire one shot at the camp, and then let's get back to the hill, for they are too much for us." Now as Little Brave went to fire his one shot on foot, Red Bear held his horse for him. He came back at once and said to Red Bear that the Dakotas were about to charge, and that they had better mount and ride back to timber and then across the river. They started to ride back and as they were going through the bushes toward the river, they received a volley from the bushes in front of them just across the Little Big Horn. The Dakotas were in ambush there, without horses. At this the scouts doubled back again to where they started from. When they rode toward the river, they saw a great mass of Dakota horsemen between the ridge and the river, riding toward the ford, yelling and firing,—it was alive with them. * * * He could see nothing on account of the smoke and dust which filled the air, but somewhere ahead he saw dimly someone riding. Just then he saw ten soldiers on horseback in full retreat toward the timber. At this point there was a deep cut and the horses of the soldiers fell into it and he heard the soldiers calling out, "Whoa, whoa." He swung his horse to the left and escaped falling into the cut and he left the soldiers floundering there with their horses. * * * His horse stumbled and fell and threw him off. The horse then ran on toward the river and Red Bear chased him. It was an open place here, a few trees and many rose bushes. A long, dry limb caught in the side of the bridle and dragged behind the horse,

it will take him a very long time indeed." The scouts all laughed at this and said by signs that they were hungry for the battle. They rode on ahead at this, but Red Bear noticed that Custer turned off to the right with his men about fifty yards beyond the lone tepee. Gerard rode on with the scouts here. Young Hawk, Goose, Black Fox, Red Star, Strikes Two, Bloody Knife, Little Sioux, Bob-tailed Bull were with him, also Forked Horn, Red-Foolish-Bear, Boy Chief, Little Brave, and One Feather. They rode hard, charging down to the Little Big Horn and, after crossing it, they were near the camp of the Dakotas. When they got across, they separated again. Six of the scouts turned off to the right sharply, where the Dakotas horses were by the timber. Boy Chief and Red Star were ahead, then followed Strikes Two, Black Fox, Little Sioux, and One Feather. The other party led by Bloody Knife went on toward the point of the Dakota camp. Bloody Knife was far ahead and he brought back three horses toward his party, calling out: "Someone take these horses back to the hill. One of them is for me." Red Bear did not see Bloody Knife because of the dust, but he heard afterwards who it was. In this party were Bloody Knife, Young Hawk, Goose, Forked Horn, Little Brave, Red Bear, Bob-tailed Bull, and the two Crow scouts. "Now we all came to the point of the Sioux camp, the guns and stopped him so that Red Bear could catch him. The hanging rope gave him a hold but the horse was scared and jumped about a good deal. Because he could use only his left hand, he could not stop the horse very well, for he still held his gun in his right hand. Then he saw a Dakota riding toward him up stream on his right, his face was painted, the lower half red and the upper half and forehead yellow as well as the eyes. He shot the Dakota and he fell from his horse, which reared up and wheeled back. By this time he could hear nothing but the steady firing of guns and the shrill whistles of the Dakotas. * * * Just then, up the bank, through the bushes at his left downstream came the horse of Bob-tailed Bull, the reins and rope were flying, and the tail and mane floating in the wind. The horse was much frightened and ran snorting past Red Bear but a few yards away from him and Red Bear saw that the saddle was all bloody in front. Five or six white soldiers were riding through the bushes at his left, having just crossed the river. The horse of Bob-tailed Bull followed after them, * * *. The Dakotas were above them on the hills firing down at them. * * * Finally he * * * mounted his own horse. He did not see Little Brave again and he thought the soldiers were all killed. As he rode up to the end of the ridge, he saw many soldiers retreating. Then at their head he saw Reno, with a white handkerchief tied about his head, his mouth and beard white with foam, which dripped down, and his eyes were wild and rolling. The soldiers with Reno took Red Bear for a Dakota and aimed their guns at him, but he rode in close to Reno and struck him on the chest with his open hand, crying "Scout, scout." Reno called out to him in reply: "The Sioux, the Sioux; where?" Red Bear pointed down over the ridge where the Dakotas were. Just then an officer with three stripes gave him some cartridges for his gun, this officer had cartridges in boxes on his arm and as he opened a box the cartridges tumbled out. As the officer gave Red Bear the cartridges, he called to him, "John, John." They then all fired at the Dakotas higher up on the ridge without taking any aim, merely holding the guns up on a slant and firing. * * * Here Reno made a short halt, but he could not hold his men together, they kept falling back all the time, though quite a group stayed here. Then the Dakotas began to fall back and stop firing. The other remounted scouts now came up and formed a group with Reno's men. Seven scouts were missing: Young Hawk, Bloody Knife, Bob-tailed Bull, Little Brave, Forked Horn, Red-Foolish-

Bear, and Goose. Red Bear had remounted when he could not catch the horse down on the flat, and the last he saw of Little Brave was his horse and the rider coming on a slow trot. Red Bear rode up to the top of the ridge and saw the Dakota scout, White Cloud, riding up from the river, and he told Red Bear that the Arikara scouts had driven off a number of Dakota horses, and they were to return but they had not yet come back. Then White Cloud said to Red Bear: "Let's go where the scouts are with the horses." White Cloud had one horse he was leading and Red Bear had picked up two where Reno had halted, and he led them. They came to a little hill and from there they saw four riders coming toward them, they thought they were Dakotas and turned to ride back to where Reno was. The riders were really Crow scouts and they seemed to recognize Red Bear, and waved to him that they were friends. He stopped and called the Dakota scout back, for he recognized then the dress of the Crow Indian, red shoulders painted on a white shirt. The Crow scouts halted and then they rode together. The Crow scouts said that two of their number had been killed on the ridge and that they were going there and then would come back (the missing Crow scouts were those that escaped with Young Hawk). So the Crow scouts rode on to the ridge and Red Bear and White Cloud waited for them a long time. Then Red Bear said to White Cloud: "The Crow scouts will not return, let us go back to Reno." They went back and found Reno with his soldiers still there. Just then the scouts who had taken fresh horses came back. * * * After awhile the other scouts came in with the herd of captured horses, about forty in number: * * * Where Reno was the soldiers were on higher ground, and the scouts were down the slope about ten rods off. Stabbed was riding about on horseback, making a speech. He said: "What are we doing now, we scouts? We ought to do what Custer told us to do if we were defeated. He told us to fall back to the Powder River where the rest of the scouts are and the wagons and provisions." * * * They followed the old Custer trail very slowly until they were near the Tongue River and then camped on top of the ridge in the timber. In the morning they reached and crossed the Tongue River and found the place where the soldier had been clubbed to death. On the top of a range they went on and reached the Powder River camp. Here they found the party led by Strikes Two and a company of infantry, with a wagon train. The commander was called Wearer-of-the-White-

Hat, he was from Fort Buford. This officer had two interpreters, a half-breed Dakota called The Santee, and a Grosventre called Crow-Bear. They told the officer through these interpreters all that they knew about the fight. The officer called the scouts all together and told them to bring their horses. He picked out two of the best horses for the scouts who were to carry word to the officer who had gone up the Elk River on a steamboat to the mouth of the Big Horn River. * * *.

NARRATIVE BY LITTLE SIOUX

IT was early in the morning, just at sunrise, and there came down from the butte, Red Star and Bull. By this time the army was all together and the mule pack train was with them. Custer told all the scouts to come to him and they made a circle about him. He said to them: "Well, I want to tell you this, the way I want it. We all want to charge together and after we get to the Sioux camp I want you to run off all the horses you can." Then the charge began for the Dakota camp; they went three or four miles and then Custer went up on the high butte and came down again after seeing the Dakota camp. The scouts led on with the charge and reached the lone tepee about noon. It was about as far to the Little Big Horn as it was from the high butte to the lone tepee. It was nearly 3 o'clock when they reached the Dakota camp. They rode at full speed with Custer and Little Sioux about the middle. When he reached the river he saw going up the bank on the other side, Young Hawk, Strikes Two, Boy Chief, and Goose. As he came up the bank he saw before him a curved, flat space covered with sage brush and with timber at the right. The soldiers were forming a line at right angle to the timber and then the firing began. In front of the soldiers, while he was a little way from the bank, Little Sioux saw Black Fox and Forked Horn. Away to the left and in front of the soldiers, near some buttes, he saw Bob-tailed Bull. Some Dakotas were riding in between Bob-tailed Bull and the soldiers. Little Sioux was about half way to the line of soldiers with others all around him, and then he saw Bloody Knife swing in from the timber along which, from the direction of the Dakota camp, he was driving three horses. Bloody Knife was his uncle and he came up to him and said: "Take these horses away back, this is what Custer told us to do." Little Sioux paid no attention and Bloody Knife turned back without

waiting to see what became of the horses. With Little Sioux there were Red Star, Strikes Two, and Boy Chief. As they stood there together looking across the river they saw at the foot of the ridge (about where they were to cross later) three women and two children coming across the flat running and hurrying along as best they could, on a slant toward the river. Little Sioux fired twice at them and so did Red Star. Then all four of the scouts rode through the timber toward the river to kill them. But just at this point they saw across the river on the flat a large herd of about two hundred Dakota horses in the sage brush, so they stopped pursuing the women and children and started after the horses. Little Sioux had no trouble at either bank, he rode his horse swimming. On the opposite side there was much sage brush and willows and the four all crossed together. They started to head the horses upstream. Red Star rode farthest to the left, then Boy Chief, then Strikes Two, and last of all Little Sioux. While they were driving the horses he first saw the tepees of the Dakotas, three-quarters of a mile away across the river, just the tops of the poles and very many of them. They had ridden farther ahead than the battle line of the soldiers, that is, farther down-stream in order to head off and drive the horses back to where they could get them away from the Dakotas. They had hardly headed the horses before the Dakotas came across the river from the village where he had seen the tops of the tepees and from there they carried on a running fight up the valley for over a mile with the pursuing Dakotas chasing and firing at them. They reached and crossed the high bluff, at which point was the hardest fighting, and the Dakotas chased them back on the trail seven or eight miles. This fight for the horses was kept up until nearly dark or until the red blaze from the guns could be seen and there were only five Dakotas left. These seemed to have ridden around in front of the herd and attacked the scouts as they went by. The flat between the ridge and the river was about three-quarters of a mile wide and they drove the horses nearer the river than the ridge. They crossed the ridge because it curved in front of them and they did not turn out of their course. Where they crossed the ridge, was a mile below the first crossing and about three-quarters of a mile from the second crossing. The two places on the river where Little Sioux crossed were about a mile apart. While he was driving off the horses on the flat he heard the battle going on very plainly at his right and on his left also. Slightly behind him he heard sounds of another battle but not quite so plain. As Little Sioux came up the ridge he met the other scouts that had been left behind and they all went on together. From the ridge he saw that the battle was over, dead men and horses lay all the way from where the battle line was to the river, and also on the bank and up to the hill. They rode on and looking back they saw some dismounted soldiers, who had straggled up from the river, fighting the Dakotas back. He saw a dead soldier lying just where he came up over the ridge on the hill. Here Little Sioux's horse played out, the one he had ridden from the first. He was riding ahead of the other scouts when he saw a black horse with a piece of buckskin around his neck from which hung a bell. He threw himself off his horse, caught the Dakota horse, put his own saddle on it, and turned his own horse loose, all of this during his ride up the hill. At the time he looked back to the battle-ground he also looked toward where he had heard the firing at his left. There he saw, about two miles west, near enough to hear the guns, along the ridge, a high sloping hill, the sides of which were covered with Dakota horsemen, thick as ants, riding all about. At the top some soldiers were lying down and were shooting down at the Dakotas, who were firing back. He noticed many little fires on the prairie where the first fighting took place, much smoke but no blaze. He saw also on the hill at the south, groups of Indians moving off here and there. He noticed that these groups scattered as they got up higher and broke up in every direction, this was about three miles off. He saw also on the battleground Dakotas riding about among the dead bodies shooting at them. There were five Dakotas in the last attack which was made on the scouts who were driving off the herd of Dakota horses. Stabbed told some of them to dismount and hold back the enemy. Those who stopped to do this were Little Sioux, Soldier, Strikes Two, Boy Chief, Stabbed, and Strikes-the-Lodge. When the four scouts met the others at the top of the hill some of them stayed behind to fight back the Dakotas. These were: Soldier, Little Sioux, Stabbed, Strikes-the-Lodge, Strikes Two, and Boy Chief. They fought on foot to hold back the Dakotas who had by this time killed all the dismounted soldiers. Their horses were tied to their cartridge belt by a loose slip-knot and when riding this rope hung in a coil on the saddle-horn. This device was used by all the Indians so that they might never be in danger of losing their horses in battle. When this group of scouts had stopped the Dakotas

The Arikara Scout Bloody Knife. Custer's favorite scout; killed with Reno's command.

and driven them back, it was about an hour from sunset and they tried to find the herd but missed the way for a time. In the last fight with the five Dakotas, already referred to, the herd of horses was so close that the firing scared them and in spite of all the other scouts could do the whole herd was lost. Little Sioux fell back now with the other five scouts for they thought all the soldiers were killed and all the horses lost. Stabbed drove his horse and rode a mule taken from the big herd when the scouts first met him. They rode all night long and all the next day till evening without stopping and they came to where the steamboat unloaded. Here were some spoiled crackers and they made camp all night and rested and ate. While they were in camp here they were seen by the party led by Running Wolf, who thought that they were Dakotas. After sunrise the next day Black Fox came up and joined them. After he was seen in distance Little Sioux was sent back to meet him and he called to him that he was an Arikara, but Black Fox could not hear him for the wind blew toward him and he thought it was a party of Dakotas. Black Fox got off of the Dakota horse he was riding, leaving the saddle, and mounted his own bareback. He rode into a blind washout with high banks but here he heard Little Sioux's voice echoing back from the high bank and he recognized him and rode out again. He was glad to see Little Sioux and gave him the horse he had caught. The six scouts slept under the roots of a fallen tree and they had a fire. They were cooking some camp leavings when Black Fox came in sight a long way off, about 8 o'clock. The seven scouts traveled all day and camped at the mouth of Tongue River and slept there. The next day they came to the Powder River base camp just as the bugles were blowing for dinner. Some soldiers came out to meet them and they told them what had happened but the soldiers did not believe them. Then the commanding officer called them in and the scouts told him what they knew. He said nothing when they had finished and sent them out again. In camp they found four scouts, Horns-in-Front, Cha-ra-ta, and two others. About three days later the commanding officer ordered them to bring their horses up for inspection, as mail was to be carried. But the horses were all worn out so two mules were used instead. He sent the mail out by two scouts, Crow Bear and a half breed, to General Terry on the Big Horn River. No other scouts had come in yet. Before they had reached Terry's camp the steamboat came in with the wounded. Until the boat came in seven scouts were missing, the three who were killed and the three with Young Hawk, besides the interpreter, Gerard. The steamboat took the scouts across the river, about twenty-four of them, and they went up the river and met the Crow Indians who had come together too late to help Custer at the mouth of the Rosebud. They recrossed the Elk River by steamboat and it went along with them up the river. They marched on the east side of the river and met some soldiers and later some other soldiers with Arapahoes. All of these were to meet and go with Custer against the Dakotas but it was now too late. As the Arapahoe Indians came near, the soldiers first took them for Dakotas and got ready to fight. The Arapahoes told the scouts that the whole plan had been made for battle after all the soldiers had assembled, but Custer had fought too soon.

STORY OF A "REE" SCOUT
(Not identified)

Extract from a letter of W. M. Camp to Peter Thompson, a Private of "C" Co. at the Little Big Horn. (Compare Narrative by Soldier, Supra.)

"I was riding a slow horse that had become tired out, and this put me behind the command. There were two other Ree scouts with me. We passed the lone tepee and came to the place where the trail of the soldiers separated, one trail keeping on down the creek toward the Little Bighorn, and the other taking off to the right, in a direction down the river. We three Rees took the right-hand trail, which we afterward learned was the way Gen. Custer had gone.

We followed this right-hand trail and came to the bluffs overlooking the Little Bighorn, and after going some farther we came upon a soldier whose horse had given out. He was kicking the horse and striking him with his fist, and saying: "Me go Custer! Me go Custer," at the same time pointing in the direction that Custer and the five companies had gone.

We went up a little dip and came in view of the Sioux camp in the valley, and soon came up to another soldier whose horse was down, overcome by the heat, and he could not get him up. He was kicking the horse and swearing and calling the horse a son of a b——. We went on some distance and then turned back, going along the bluffs in a direction up the river. We again saw the two soldiers whose horses had given out. They were together, and on foot, on the side of the bluffs. Five Sioux came up over the bluff, from the valley, following us. We went on, and the last we saw of the two soldiers they had separated and the five Sioux were circling them. We always supposed that these two soldiers were killed right there, as they were afoot and the Sioux had them where they could not very well get away."

When I told this Ree that at least one of the two soldiers whom he had seen surrounded by the five Sioux was still living he would not believe me.

(The survivor was Peter Thompson. W.A.G.)

A photograph of Sitting Bull by D. F. Barry.

CHAPTER 5

THE SIOUX

A GENERAL REPORT
BY
SEVEN UNIDENTIFIED
WARRIORS

The CHICAGO TRIBUNE *of August 1, 1876, printed the following report from the Commanding Officer at Standing Rock.*

Headquarters U. S. Military Station,
Standing Rock, D. T., July 24, 1876.
To the Assistant Adjutant General
Department of Dakota,
Saint Paul, Minn.
Sir:

I respectfully report the following as having been derived from seven Sioux Indians just returned from the hostile camp (July 21st) some of whom were engaged in the battle of June 25th with the Seventh Cavalry.

The agent of course makes no distinction between them and the other Indians at the agency. He sent *them* word to keep quiet and say nothing. To the other Indians he sent or delivered personally the instruction that they must not tell the military of the return of Indians from the hostile camp, nor circulate reports of operations in the late fight.

The Indian account is as follows: The hostiles were celebrating their greatest of religious festivals —the sun dance—when runners brought news of the approach of cavalry. The dance was suspended and a general rush—mistaken by Custer, perhaps, for a retreat—for horses, equipments and arms followed. Major Reno first attacked the village at the south end and across the Little Big Horn. Their narrative of Reno's operations coincides with the published accounts: how he was quickly confronted, surrounded; how he dismounted, rallied in the timber, remounted and cut his way back over the ford and up the bluffs with considerable loss; and the continuation of the fight for some little time, when runners arrived from the north end of the village, or camp, with the news that the cavalry had attacked the north end of the same—three or four miles distant. The Indians about Reno had not before this the slightest intimation of fighting at any other point. A force large enough to prevent Reno from assuming the offensive was left and the surplus available force flew to the other end of the camp, where, finding the Indians there successfully driving Custer before them, instead of uniting with them, they separated into two parties and moved around the flanks of his cavalry. They report that he crossed the river, but only succeeded in reaching the edge of the Indian camp. After he was driven to the bluffs the fight lasted perhaps an hour. Indians have no hours of the day, and the time cannot be given approximately.

They report that a small number of cavalry broke through the line of Indians in their rear and escaped, but was overtaken, within a distance of five or six miles, and killed. I infer from this that this body of retreating cavalry was probably led by the missing officers, and that they tried to escape only after Custer fell. The last man that was killed, was killed by two sons of a Santee Indian, "Red-top," who was a leader in the Minnesota massacre of '62 and '63.

After the battle the squaws entered the field to plunder and mutilate the dead. A general rejoicing was indulged in, and a distribution of arms and ammunition hurriedly made. Then, the attack on Major Reno was vigorously renewed. Up to this attack, the Indians had lost comparatively few men, but now, they say, their most serious loss took place.

They give no idea of numbers, but say there were a great great many. Sitting Bull was neither killed nor personally engaged in the fight. He remained in the council tent directing operations. Crazy Horse (with a large band) and Black Moon were the principal leaders on the 25th of June.

Kill Eagle, Chief of the Blackfeet, at the head of some twenty lodges left this agency about the last of May. He was prominently engaged in the battle of June 25, and afterwards upbraided Sitting Bull for not taking an active personal part in the engagement. Kill Eagle has sent me word that he was forced into this fight; that he desires to return to the agency; and that he will return to the agency if he is killed for it. He is reported actually on the way back to go to his Ate father the agent and make confession; to receive absolution for his defiant crime against the hand that has gratuitously fed him for three years. He is truly a shrewd chief, who must have discovered that he who fights and runs away may live to fight another day.

The Indians were not all engaged at any one time: heavy reserves were held to repair losses and renew attacks successively. The fight continued until the third day when runners, kept purposely on the lookout, hurried in to camp and reported a great body of troops (General Terry's column) advancing up the river.

Lodges having been previously prepared for a move, a retreat, in a southerly direction, followed, towards and along the base of the Rosebud mountains. They marched about fifty miles, went into camp and held a consultation, where it was determined to send into all the agencies reports of their success and to call upon them to come out and share the glories that were to be expected in the future. Wherefore, we may. expect an influx of overbearing and impudent Indians to urge, by force perhaps, an accession to Sitting Bull's demands.

There is a general gathering in the hostile camp from each of the agencies on the Missouri River, Red Cloud and Spotted Tail's, as also a great many Northern Cheyennes and Arapahoes (lila ota—a great many).

They report, for the especial benefit of their relatives here, that in the three (3) fights they have had with the whites they have captured over 400 stand of arms—carbines and rifles (revolvers not counted)—and ammunition without end; some sugar, coffee, bacon and hard bread. They claim to have captured, from the whites, this summer, over 900 horses and mules. I suppose this includes operations against soldiers, Crow Indians and Black Hills miners.

The general outline of this Indian report coincides with the published reports. The first attack of Reno's began well on in the day, say the Indians. They report about 300 whites killed. They do not say how many Indians were killed.

A report from another source says the Indians obtained from Custer's command 592 carbines and revolvers.

I have, since writing the above, heard the following from the returned hostiles: They communicated, as a secret to their particular friends here, the information that a large party of Sioux and Cheyennes were to leave Rosebud mountains, or the hostile camp, for this agency, to intimidate and compel the Indians here to join Sitting Bull; and if they refused, they are ordered to soldier them (beat them) and steal their ponies. Of course any resistance to their attempts by the military or whites will provoke an attack upon the post, although that secret, or so much of it, has not been revealed to friends of the military.

I shall report any additional news received from reliable Indian sources as soon as obtained.

Very respectfully,
Your obedient servant,
(*Signed*) J. S. Poland,
Captain 6th Infantry,
Brevet Lieut. Col., U.S.A.,
Commanding.

KILL EAGLE'S STORY OF HIS STAY WITH THE HOSTILES

Graphic Description of the Battle of the Little Big Horn.

(From *New York Herald*, September 24, 1876.)
Bismarck, D. T., Sept. 23, 1876.
A Standing Rock letter of the 20th gives the following, of intense interest, in relation to Custer's Battle. Kill Eagle, of whose surrender at this station, last Friday, you have already been

informed, has given quite a lengthy account of Sitting Bull's forces the past season.

He commences with the date at which he left this agency, last spring, with twenty-six lodges, for the purpose of hunting buffalo and trading with hostile Indians. He speaks of having heard reports that troops were going out to punish the hostiles, but thought he would have time to do his hunting and trading and get out of the way before a battle occurred. They were obliged to hunt, as they were starving at the agency, and from his account they were very successful, killing twenty or thirty buffalo some days, and in one herd they killed all but two. He details the progress and incidents of each march.

On the seventh day they arrived at Sitting Bull's village, where a feast and numerous presents of ponies and robes were given them. Efforts were made to induce Kill Eagle and his band to join in the contemplated movements and hostilities, but evidently without much success. They were desirous of getting back again to the protecting arms of the agency, but were unable to escape from the meshes of the wily Sitting Bull. They found, too late, that for them there was no escape; their horses were shot or stolen, and wounds and insults were showered upon them from every side. In the meantime the forces of Crook were approaching, and with his people Kill Eagle succeeded in escaping temporarily from the hostiles. He claims to have been distant some forty or fifty miles at the time of the Rosebud fight, and relates many of the details and incidents which he was able subsequently to gather from the participants. He places the loss of the Indians in the Rosebud fight at four dead, left on the field, and twelve that were brought to camp. He places the wounded besides at as high as 400, and says that they had 180 horses killed, besides those that were captured. He next comes to the fight on the Little Horn, and describes the Indian village, which was six miles long and one wide, and the Indians swarmed there as thick as maggots on a carcass, so numerous were they.

He then goes on and speaks of Custer's approach and fight with its tragic details as an unwilling spectator rather than as a participant, who, during its progress, remained quietly in his lodge in the center of the Indian village. The fight with Reno commenced about noon, the Indians all rushing to oppose his advance, until the approach of Custer from the lower end of the village was announced, when the wildest confusion prevailed throughout the camp. Lodges were struck and preparations made for instant flight. Vast numbers of Indians left Reno's front and hastened to the assistance of their red brethren engaged with Custer, who was steadily forced back and surrounded until all were swept from the field by the repeated charges of the Indians as if they had been carried into eternity by the irresistible.

He described the firing at this point as simply terrific, and illustrated its force by clapping his hands together with great rapidity and regularity. Then came a lull in the fearful storm of iron hail and his hands were still again. The storm beat fast and furious as the thought of some loved one nerved the arm of each contending trooper. Then the movement of his hands gradually slackened and gradually grew more feeble. A few scattering shakes, like rain on a window pane, and then the movement ceased as the last of Custer's band of heroes went down with the setting sun. It was dusk as the successful combatants returned to camp littered with their dead and wounded. It had not been to them a bloodless victory. Fourteen had fallen in front of Reno, thirty-nine went down with Custer and fourteen were dead in camp. Horses and travois were laden with their wounded on every hand, and in countless numbers. One band alone, of Ogalallas, had twenty-seven wounded on travois and thirty-eight thrown across horses. Kill Eagle says it seems as if every one was wounded, and places the number as high as 600.

He is very positive, however, that no prisoners were taken. There were no white men in the fight or on the field. One who had been with them went to Standing Rock Agency. The bugle calls so often spoken of were sounded by an Indian. He speaks of Sitting Bull as a heavy, muscular man, with large head and light hair hanging to his shoulders. He is not white or half-breed. He gives the names of the leading chiefs present in the fight, and reports a chief, High Elk, as being killed in front of Reno. He even goes on to speak of the approach of General Gibbon's column and the immediate flight of the Indians and the subsequent fight with Lieutenant Sibley's party, where a chief of the Cheyennes was shot through the head and instantly killed.

His statement is quite lengthy, but I have endeavored to give you such portions as are of particular interest and have not before been made public.

(From *New York Herald,* October 6, 1876.)

Standing Rock Agency, D.T., Sept. 18, 1876.

Herewith I send you a copy of the official report upon the statement made to the Indian Agent here by Kill Eagle, a chief of the Blackfeet Sioux, and Afraid-of-Eagles, an Uncpapa Sioux warrior, who were with the hostiles during the late campaign.

September 17, 1876.

To the Commissioner of Indian Affairs:—

Sir—I have the honor to submit the following statement made by Wan-bli-kte (Kill Eagle), a Blackfeet Sioux chief, who left this agency last spring with twenty-six lodges, and who has spent the past summer with the hostiles.

I would state that while he was making this statement he surrounded himself by a number of his men, and when he had any doubt as to the correctness of what took place on certain occasions he would call upon them to assist him in remembering all the particulars. I have taken his statement with a great deal of care, and am satisfied from his manner and bearing that he has endeavored to tell the truth. I had two interpreters present, and fully believe that they have given me a correct interpretation. I requested Kill Eagle to make oath to the truthfulness of his statement, and he did so cheerfully and without hesitation. He is fifty-six years of age, has been thirteen years with the whites, and is one of the most intellectual Indians I have met in Dakota.

Q. I have come to see you and have you make a statement for me to send to the Great Father. You will be careful to tell the exact truth?

A. How.

Q. I will commence with you when you left the agency last spring. Let me know why you left and where you have been? Take your time and think, so as to make no mistakes.

A. All right. You two interpreters were here, and there was an agent here, but no one told me to go out, I went in accordance with my own judgment. I had heard that there was an expedition going into the Indian country, but as I had heard the same every summer I did not believe it. I was in want of lodges, robes and skins for making moccasins, and I went to get them. I thought I could get them and get away before any of the soldiers got there.

Q. Before you left here last spring you had a dance in the garrison. After the dance you fired your pistols in the air and told Colonel Poland, "I am tired of this place, I am going away." Why did you do this?

A. I never did so. The man who fired off the pistol did not belong to my band. He was a hostile. He fired off his pistol and said, "This is the way a brave man acts." I did not know he was going to fire. I asked him why he did it. He made no reply. This man was killed in the fight. His name was "The-Man-Whose-Breast-is-Dobbed-With-Mud."

Q. Let me know how you got along every day, where you went and how you lived.

A. I left this agency last April with twelve lodges belonging to my band and fourteen belonging to other bands. One belonging to Running Antelope, named Dog; one belonging to Iron Horn, named Scarlet Thunder; one belonging to Wounded Head, named Eagle Man; one belonging to Bad Hand, named Bull; one belonging to Medicine Man, named Bear King; two belonging to Belly Fat, named Brave Hawk and The-Man-Who-Walks-With-His-Dogs; two belonging to Two Heart, named Strong and Scarlet Bear; one belonging to Sitting Crow, named Scarlet Eagle; one belonging to Plenty Crow, named Little Eagle; two belonging to Bare Ribs, named Afraid-of-Eagles and Bear Ears; one belonging to Gall named Blue Cloud; one belonging to Lone Dog, who has not returned.

Q. Did any other lodges join you in your way out to the hostile camp?

A. That is all that went out with me. Others went out before me. I do not count for them.

Q. How many young men did you have with you who have not come back?

A. One, Little Wound's son; he died out there.

Q. These are all middle aged men. Where are your young men?

A. I do not go around all the lodges, my children are all girls.

Q. Are there any young men here I have not seen?

A. We have no others, only what you have seen.

Q. What other people left here before and after you?

A. I can't say. Some went before and some after me; they were in different parts of the village.

Q. What were the names of the chiefs?

A. I can't say.

Q. Is "Gall" out there?

A. He is; with as big a belly as ever.

Q. Is "Rain-in-the-Face" out there?

A. I don't know. He was there and I think he came to Cheyenne Agency and went back to the hostiles again.

Q. Is "Plenty Crow" out there?

A. "Plenty Crow" has never been away; he is here.

Q. What about his peoples.

A. His son-in-law died out there. There is none of his band out there.

Q. Is "Ball-of-the-Foot" out there?

A. I have not seen him. I think he is at Fort Peck.

Q. Are there any others from here out there?

A. I would tell you if I saw any. I was not allowed to go around and see who was there or learn anything. I was watched all the time. I am in earnest when I say they guarded me closely day and night.

Q. I have got all the people; now tell me about your journey.

A. I went out from here, and camped the other side of the Big Hill.

Q. Did you all have guns when you started?

A. We had only what we turned in.

Q. Did you have plenty of ammunition?

A. The sale of ammunition was stopped here before I went away. I was displeased with that, and I thought I would go out and starve anyway. I thought I could kill some game with arrows.

Q. Did you have plenty of provisions when you started?

A. No, sir. The rations were very scarce; that was the reason I wanted to go out and kill some game.

Q. Where did you go the second day?

A. I camped at Porcupine Hill; third night at Leafey Butte; fourth night, creek unnamed; fifth night at creek that branches off Cedar Creek; sixth night at the place where they hold the enemy; seventh night, Cedar Creek; eighth night, camped at the head of Cedar Creek; ninth night, on Cedar Creek—moving up we struck the White Man's Road, leading to the Black Hills; tenth night, traveled up Cedar Creek and camped on it; eleventh night, camped at the extreme head of Cedar Creek, where there was no timber; near this camp there is a place where we get whetstones. Some of my men who went after whetstones returned, riding in great haste and reported that there were white men coming. I answered, "Very good. I will go and see them." We went to

see if they were white men, and instead of being white men, it was a herd of buffalo. We killed forty-five of them, including two sick calves. This is what we lived on.

I then called my men to a feast of buffalo meat and said, "This is what induced us to leave the agency. Now we have got it we will turn by a round about way, and return to the agency." My brother-in-law (who is dead), said, "No; here is the village over at the place where they get blue earth (meaning Sitting Bull's village). We will go over there and get skins for moccasins, etc., which we need, and then return to the agency," and in doing this he plotted my death, but died himself. From there I went and camped at the White Mountains; from there to Box Elder Creek, where I killed thirty buffalo, only one of the herd getting away from us. We ate our meat and slept there that night. In the morning when we got up horsemen were reported coming toward our camp. These were Indians coming from Sitting Bull's village. From them I heard from Sitting Bull's camp. They told me there were contributions being made in Sitting Bull's camp for me, and that I should make haste and get there, that they would make my heart glad. From there there was nothing worth speaking about for six days and nights. On the evening of the seventh day, as the sun was going down, I came in sight of Sitting Bull's camp. Many of my horses had given out, and I had to leave them on the way. The camp was on Tongue River, just about the mouth of Four Horn River. When I got to the camp I found the Indians starving, but they killed dogs and made a feast for me, and told me, notwithstanding I was tired, I must march again the next day and camp where the buffalo were. In the morning the camp moved to Cottonwood Creek. I was the last to move, and when I got into camp they were bringing in buffalo meat. Now that they had meat, the "Crow Society" of the "Uncpapas" made a feast for me; I went to the feast, and a young man made me a present of a large roan horse and said to the Indians, "Here is a man that lives with the white men, you have invited him to come out here and get robes and skins, now he is here why don't you speak? This is why I have given him the horse, now come forward and give him your robes and skins." They gave me thirty-four robes packed on horses (horses and all), and said, "Here is what you came for; take it and go." These gifts made my heart very glad. The young man who gave me the roan horse was named "Spotted Eagle." The next morning I got on my horse and went to an Indian soldier's lodge, where there were many soldiers assembled, and said to them, "My kindred, I came out here for robes and skins, I have got them, now my heart is glad, and now my friends, be merciful to me and let me go back to the white men." They all answered, "How," but one man jumped up and spoke differently. There were four chiefs of soldiers there, who sat in the back part of the lodge. They said: "you have not spoken well, we are killing buffalo, wait until we have sufficient to send in with you, and when you get it you will have plenty meat to speak with, and then your heart will be glad."

From that day I was to suffer—that evening criers went about the village saying, "A man has come here. You have given him presents and told him to go." The next morning the camp moved, but I remained behind. I pretended not to notice their movements, but the Indian soldiers surrounded my camp and made me move with them, the Indian soldiers marching behind and on both sides of us, so that it was impossible for us to get away. This is when they took us to the Rosebud and went into camp on the Rosebud. At this camp I was called to a grand council and was told they were going to have a sun dance, and such men of mine that did not have horses could get them. They told me this to deceive me. From there we moved up the Rosebud. There was nothing outstanding occurred while we remained on the Rosebud, only that I was watched all the time. On leaving the Rosebud we went to Greasy Grass Creek, camping twice between these two places, and all the time the Indian soldiers were closely watching and guarding us. We camped very close to this creek and all at once there was a great commotion it being reported that white men were coming. I got on my horse and said, "Pity me, my friends, we come from the whites and they want you to listen to me. You are all grown men and must obey me. This nation here fights with the whites (meaning Sitting Bull's and others), but the whites are our friends and we don't bear arms against them." The Indians then went out to battle, but there came a herd of buffalo, and I and my men went after the buffalo and brought back buffalo meat.

When the Indians returned from the battle they denounced me as a traitor because I did not go on to the fight and forced me into camp on Greasy Grass Creek. There was a very large camp here, and I was ordered to go on one side of it, but I camped in the middle and there I was continually surrounded by Indian soldiers, at night the soldiers built fires all around my camp. The next day I could see from my camp in the road a great smoke or dust rising. The ponies belonging to all the bands were a long way from our camp, we went after them, but they stampeded. All of my men that you see here went for our horses but we could not catch them, finally we caught some of them and brought them to camp. I then said to my men, "Take your lodges and everything that is valuable and let us flee back to the whites." At this time Sitting Bull's men set fire to the prairie around my lodges and burnt some of my lodges up. They took some of my horses, killed eight of them, and returned the others. They abused and whipped my men, they can show the marks today (a number of his warriors at this time exhibited wounds made by knives, spears and whips. Kill Eagle exhibited quite a large wound on his left hip). They did this because we did not go into the fight with the whites. After this we moved with them, but were never left alone. We were guarded all the time. In this way they brought us further down, and while moving, Sitting Bull's men were hunting game, and our children were starving, for they would not allow us to kill any game. They said to us, "You have no right or title to these buffalo. The white man's food is food for you, and when you get back you can eat it." We got back to Cottonwood Creek, and there I met my grandson (by name Bad Hip). Here is where I first heard any news, and here again they whipped and abused us. They killed another of our horses, belonging to my father-in-law. I could stand it no longer, and I, in return, shot one of their horses. After this they treated us still worse. I got together nine new blankets and went around and made presents of them to the soldiers, but accomplished nothing by it.

We then went to Beaver Creek. Here I made a feast of wild turnips (a feast for the children) and called the Cheyenne Indians to it. The Cheyenne Indians all came (four societies represented), and I said to them:—"You alone I have before excluded from my councils; this day I take you into my council." Four of the Cheyenne chiefs spoke to me through an interpreter. One chief said:—"Your friend speaks to you and says, these Sioux, who are kindred to you, have abused you, notwithstanding your good treatment of them. Now this day you have honored us with your attention."

Another chief then spoke, as if with one voice, and said:—"You have been mistreated, but hereafter we will protect you. We are 500 lodges strong. Go your way and we will stand between you and Sitting Bull's men."

When I got ready to go an old Cheyenne chief came to me and advised me to move in the night; otherwise there might be trouble.

The following night it was dark and rainy, and under these we struck our lodges and moved, traveling all the night and most of the following day. While stopping for rest a young man came to me from Sitting Bull's camp and told me, "the Indians have been ordered out to stop us." That evening, just at dark, my brother-in-law, who stopped on a hill to watch, reported that a body of Indians were in sight after us. Upon receiving this information, our flight pell-mell, everybody for their own life, was continued all night and all the next day—it was wonderful how the children stood the hardships—and we arrived at Grand River that evening. Now we were back on Grand River and near "Black Horse Butte," and the reason that you now see me alive is that there we found wild fruits and berries. On this side of Grand River seven of my horses gave out and I had to leave them. When I came into camp where I have been so long I found turtle, fish and beaver, and this was our food. I staid there not because I was afraid to come in, but because there was plenty of this kind of food and I was feeding the children on it. When I came to my last camp I wanted to come in very much. I heard some things from the whites while here that frightened me; still I was not afraid. There was an Ogalalla Indian that came into the agency to look for his wife; he came into our camp and told us that we would all be hung, together with our children; but I did not fear it. You have said that I am charged with remaining out in camp, and that my friends from the agency have supplied me with food to enable me to do so. The Ogalalla Indian's name was Ridiculous, he belongs to the hostiles and has gone back to them again. I had heard all these bad reports, but I was still willing to accept whatever was in store for me, and was resigned to my fate. You have asked me to speak truthfully, and I am going to. After hearing this, bad news, I saddled my horse and came in. I came down here and went to the interpreter's house (my grandson). He was asleep when I got there. I told him that I wanted to see the agent and then the other authorities in turn. He came with me then to see the agent. I stood on the other side of the warehouse and he went to the agent's house. The agent's people were asleep; he knocked at the door; the agent opened the door and said

to the interpreter; "What is Kill Eagle afraid of? Why don't he come in? Let him come to me and I will give him advice and then take him to the commanding officer." I went back to the Blackfeet's camp, and at daylight I went to my own camp. When I arrived there I told my own people to move and we would go into the agency. We moved closer in, and here is where I was taken sick with a sore throat and could eat nothing but broth. While lying in this condition the men sent out by the agent arrived in camp. The horses that these men rode out there were tired, and as Little Wound had also slipped away from the hostile camp and was only a little way off, and wishing to have him come in too, I laid over.

This is all.

Q. Did Sitting Bull give you any arms or ammunition before the Rosebud fight?

A. No, sir.

Q. What did you do for ammunition to shoot game on the way?

A. We were brought up to shoot buffalo with arrows and this is what we shot them with.

Q. What time of the day did the fight commence on the Rosebud?

A. We did not get near the fight.

Q. Did you hear the firing?

A. It was too far away, but I heard them tell about it when they came back.

Q. Was Sitting Bull in command at the fight?

A. Sitting Bull started out with them in command.

Q. How far was it from your camp to where the fight was?

A. At least forty or fifty miles.

Q. What did Sitting Bull do with the women and children?

A. After Sitting Bull's party went out to battle, my party went out to hunt buffalo. Having an opportunity when the warriors left we brought in meat and had it cooking, when all at once there was a great commotion in camp and all the lodges were taken down. Here I thought I would have an opportunity to get away, as Sitting Bull's men were greatly confused and at a loss to know which way to go. I said to my men, "We will flee to where we came from." The excitement subsided and the lodges were put up again, near where they were before, and that evening began returning from the fight, some returning the next morning. This is when they cried about the camp that they were going to kill us, as they had lost some of their young men and we did not go to help them in the fight.

Sitting Bull, Chief Medicine Man of the Sioux Nation. Photo by D. F. Barry.

A man who had cut himself all up on account of having lost a son in the fight, came to my lodge and shook hands with me, and told me to go to the centre lodge, where the warriors were assembled. I now expected to be killed. I went to this lodge; people were crying around it, and warriors were assembled in it. When I got there this man came back and shook hands with me again and said:—"This nation of hostile Indians are all fools; this man came out here to trade, and belongs to the whites and is not pleased to stay, but you draw weapons on him and abuse him. You nations of hostiles here made war on the whites. My only son has this day gone to the spirit land; if any of you here undertake to molest this man (Kill Eagle) I will stab you and cut you up."

Q. How many warriors had Sitting Bull in this battle?

A. A great many. I could not tell how many.

Q. How many roads did they take?

A. I could not tell.

Q. Did they cover much country?

A. They went by the file, filing up the creek, a small ravine from the camp.

Q. Were the warriors all on foot?

A. It was a good ways and they would not be able to go on foot.

Q. Did they have plenty of arms and ammuntion?

A. They seemed to have. I could not tell, as I had not opportunity to get about to see them. All the Indian soldiers who were guarding me had splendid arms.

Q. Did they have needle guns?

A. They had all kinds of guns; Henry rifles, Winchester, Sharps, Spencers, muzzle loaders, and many of them two or three revolvers apiece; all had knives and lances.

Q. Did you hear them say where they got these arms?

A. I heard some of them say where they got them. I heard the Cheyenne Indians say they had always been hostiles, and they captured theirs in battle. This is the only way I heard them say they got their arms.

Q. Did you hear anyone say where Sitting Bull got his ammunition?

A. I was not permitted to run about the camp, and did not hear about it.

Q. Did any of your men hear about it?

A. I was not allowed to go around, and my men were used worse, and not allowed to go anywhere. Some of my men proposed to steal a lot of Sitting Bull's horses and flee; but I advised them not to do it, as we would all be killed.

Q. Did the soldiers who were guarding you have plenty of ammunition?

A. Yes, their belts full, and the best kinds of arms, fixed ammunition, metallic cartridges. All of us here had very bad guns. You see what we turned in.

Q. In this fight how many Indians were killed or wounded?

A. Four killed and left on the field, who were mutilated by Crow Indians, and twelve died in the camp. It was impossible to say how many were wounded, there were so many—nearly 400. The four killed fell near the Crow lines, and they cut them up and scalped them. One hundred and eighty Indian horses were killed. They numbered them at the Statemen's lodge after the battle.

Q. What did the Indians report about killing white men?

A. When we were in the council lodge, smoking, a warrior named Black Moccasin (a Cheyenne) brought in a white man's arms; he began beating me and my men over the head and shoulders with it, and said "Here is your husband's hand."

Q. Did they say how many were killed?

A. I did not hear how many.

Q. Did they have any white men's scalps?

A. They brought in Crow Indian's scalps and beat us over the head with them. If ever one of these men comes into the agency, I vow to kill him. I will tell you the way they abused me. My daughter (holy woman) traded a horse for a large, fat dog. She had it out dressing it, and the Indian soldiers came and snatched it away from her, and we were starving and needed it badly. I can never forgive this abuse. The Indian soldiers came to our camp, lariated and stole all our dogs.

Q. What did the Indians say about who won the fight?

A. They said that they had been whipped, and that the white men charged them.

Q. Did they get any horses and mules there?

A. No, sir. The white men captured a good many of their horses that had given out, beside 180 killed.

Q. How long did you remain in the camp after the fight?

A. We moved the next day to where the Indian soldiers took the dog from my daughter.

Q. Where did you go from there?

A. After the Rosebud fight the camp moved on to Greasy Grass Creek, at once.

Q. How long did you stay there?

A. One day.

Q. Where did you go next day?

A. We moved this way.

Q. Tell us about the Custer fight.

A. We were coming down the tributary of Greasy Grass Creek after the battle was fought on the Rosebud. (Here he makes a sketch of the battlefield on the ground.) We crossed the Greasy Grass Creek, went down and camped on it. The troops struck our trail on the tributary, followed it down, swam their horses over Greasy Grass Creek and struck the camp at the upper end, where there was a clump of timber, and opened the fight. When the firing commenced the Indians rushed to the scene of action. I and my men were lower down, about the middle of the camp. The Indians drove the soldiers back out of the timber, and they recrossed the Greasy Grass Creek below the mouth of the tributary, taking their position on the hill, bare without any grass. They were reinforced by the soldiers who had not crossed the creek (Colonel Benteen and Captain McDougall). Before retiring across the creek the soldiers (Colonel Reno) got into camp and set fire to some of the lodges. On re-treating across the creek to take position on the hill, they left their dead behind them. Another party appeared on top of a long hill moving toward the south.

After quitting the party on the hills word came that soldiers were on the left across the creek, and there was great excitement in the camp, the Indian warriors rushed to the left to meet the troops. The Indians crossed the creek and then the firing commenced. It was very fast at times and then slower until it died away. (He describes the firing as follows:—He claps the palms of his hands together very fast for several minutes, stopping suddenly, which denotes the sound of the firing when they (Custer) first began. After a few seconds elapses he repeats the same as above and continues but all the time lessens the quickness of the patting and sound until it suddenly dies out.) The United States troops were all killed on the east side, none crossed the stream.

I got the following information from Sitting Bull himself:—"After crossing the creek with his warriors he met the troops (Custer) about 600 yards east of the river. He drove the soldiers back up the hill. He then made a circuit to the right around the hill and drove off and captured most of the horses. The troops made a stand at the lower end of the hill, and there they were all killed. In going around the hill the Cheyenne Indians killed a warrior, thinking he was a scout who left his agency; but he was not, he was a hostile."

Q. How long did the fight last on the right?

A. It was about noon when they struck the camp and it only lasted a few minutes. The fight at the lower end (under Custer) was not finished until near sunset.

Q. Did all the warriors leave the right to go to the left?

A. They did; the whole thing left.

Q. What did they do after killing all the troops?

A. At first a Cheyenne Indian came in with a war bonnet and proclaimed:— "I have killed three soldiers but they have killed me at last." He was wounded in three places. They kept continually coming in with wounded, thrown over horses, with their heads hanging down and blood running out.

About sundown they all returned and said:— "We have killed them all; put up your lodges where they are." They had just begun to fix their lodges that evening, when a report came that troops were coming from toward the mouth of the creek. When this report came, after dark, the lodges were all taken down and they started up the creek. I told my men to keep together, and we would try to get away. Some one told on me, and they said "let us kill him and his band, we have lost many young men today, and our hearts are bad." We travelled all night and next day after crossing Greasy Grass Creek. We encamped near the foot of the White Mountains. That night, while I was asleep, I heard a man calling. I woke my people up, and this man proved to be a Cheyenne Indian, belonging to a party that had been off on the warpath in the White Mountains. He reported that he had seen a great many soldiers—no end of them—crossing along the base of the mountains. Next morning the warriors left the camp with led horses and started off to meet the troops, who were reported coming, so that the women and children would not be near the fight. This was three days after the Custer fight. Some of the horses got worn out and some of them returned and said they had struck a white man's trail, and were following it into the mountains.

Others came back and said eight Cheyenne Indians had engaged the whites—their horses were better than the others. One Cheyenne, noted for bravery, and who wore a war bonnet, was shot through the head and killed and brought back to camp. The Indians were approaching the soldiers when this one was shot; they dragged him back by the feet. After this a number of other Indians crept up and found the horses tied there, but no one with them; they took the horses and returned to camp. From this camp all went up to the Rosebud; this is the place I escaped from.

Q. How many Indians were killed on the right of the camp, in the fight with Reno?

A. Fourteen were killed on the field with Reno and thirty-nine died on the field with Custer. I know of seven who died of wounds within camp afterward.

Q. How many were wounded?

A. A great many. I would judge about 600—wounded in every way, head, hands, arms, body, etc.—nearly all I saw were wounded more or less. A lot of Ogalalla Sioux ranged in line and called me to look at them, and said:—"Here are the wounded on one hand;" there were twenty-seven on travois and thirty-eight on horseback.

There was a Cheyenne woman who had a revolver strapped on her and went into the fight and got killed.

Q. Did Sitting Bull take any prisoners alive in this fight?

A. He did not; he took no one alive; it was like a hurricane; and swept everything before it.

Q. Did they scalp any white men?

A. I did not see any.

Q. Did they burn or torture any of them after the battle was over?

A. There was one became separated from Reno's command and two Cheyennes gave him chase and overtook him and killed him.

Q. Did they scalp him?

A. I do not know.

Q. After the fight did you have a big dance?

A. No, sir; the soldiers were reported coming from the mouth of the creek, and everyone fled.

Q. What did they do with the arms, ammunition and horses captured?

A. They have them. A great many horses died of wounds and fatigue. Whoever captured them kept them.

Q. How many warriors do you think were in Sitting Bull's camp?

A. I cannot say; they were like maggots on a carcass.

Q. Who were the principal chiefs aside from Sitting Bull?

A. Crazy Horse of the Ogalalla Sioux; Big Man, of the Ogalalla Sioux; High Elk, of the Sans Arc, killed by Reno, and the head chief of the Cheyennes, killed by Lieutenant Sibley's party.

Q. Were there any Indians killed in this fight belonging to this agency?

A. Not that I know of.

Q. Were there any wounded?

A. Yes, one; the Rattler's son. He is out there yet.

Q. Did you have plenty to eat during the fight?

A. No. The Cheyenne Indians ate the horses killed in the battle. I had a little buffalo meat left.

Q. How do the Indians go into battle—does each chief lead his own band?

A. They go without discipline, like bees swarming out of a hive.

Q. Did you have plenty of grass for the ponies?

A. Yes.

Q. Could you kill any game during this time?

A. Now and then an antelope, which the Indians would kill.

Q. Were there any white men among the Indians?

A. There was no white men in the camp that I saw.

Q. Was there not a man who blew a bugle call like a soldier?

A. There was, but it was blown by a Indian.

Q. Has Sitting Bull any white women in his camp?

A. No.

Q. What do you think Sitting Bull is going to do now?

A. I did not hear. I slipped away in the night, but there is a man here—a prisoner—who will probably know—Bear Rib's brother.

Q. Do you think he will fight next summer?

A. I can't say.

Q. Did Rain-in-the-Face cut out the heart of a dead officer and show it around the camp on a stick?

A. Rain-in-the-Face was with me; he did not do it.

Q. Did not some of the young men here take you out some beef and coffee, when you were in camp out in the country, before you came in?

A. No one brought me anything; neither sugar, coffee, flour, tobacco or anything.

Q. What time of the evening was it reported in the hostile camp that soldiers were coming on the left of the camp?

A. The sun was just going down.

Q. When Reno was driven across the creek where was Sitting Bull?

A. I don't know.

Q. What were the families doing when the fighting was going on on the hill?

A. The women fled to the lower end of the camp and left everything.

Q. What did they do when they heard the firing on the left by Custer?

A. The upper end of the camp was at this time all deserted, and at the lower end they took down the lodges and packed them for flight.

Q. In what direction did you hear the troops were coming again?

A. The men who were out after their horses, after the Custer fight, came in and said, "More troops are coming up the creek from the Yellowstone River.

Q. Did you see Sitting Bull that day?

A. I did not.

Q. I heard Sitting Bull stayed in his council tent, away from the battlefield, and urged his men forward.

A. This is probably so, but I don't know.

Q. What time of night did everybody leave the camp?

A. Just at dusk.

Q. Did the women, children and lodges, or did the warriors go first?

A. The women, children and old people went first, the warriors in the rear.

Q. How long was the camp—how many miles?

A. About six miles long.

Q. How wide?

A. About one mile wide.

Q. Were the tepees close together?

A. Just as thick as they could be put up.

Q. What part of the camp was Sitting Bull in?

A. He was camped near where the soldiers, who took their horses in the woods, attacked.

Q. What kind of a lodge has Sitting Bull?

A. He has a very large skin lodge.

Q. How many wives and children has Sitting Bull?

A. Two wives and four children.

Q. Does any one else live with him?

A. His sister did, but she died this summer.

Q. Are Sitting Bull's soldiers camped near him?

A. They are camped about the middle of the camp.

Q. What part of the camp was the council tent?

A. Near the centre; it was painted yellow, and holds a great many when they crowd in.

Q. How old do you think Sitting Bull is?

A. About forty years.

Q. What is the color of his hair; I heard it was light?

A. He has light hair.

Q. Is he light himself?

A. He is not a white man; you can't expect an Indian to be white.

Q. How large a man is he?

A. About five feet ten inches; he is very heavy and muscular and big around in the breast; he has a very large head; his hair is not long, it only comes down to his shoulders.

Q. How does he dress?

A. He changes his dress so often I can't say; the last time I saw him he had on a very dirty cotton shirt.

Q. What does he wear on his hair in battle?

A. I don't know, I did not see him in battle.

Q. Do the Indian soldiers strip off when they go into a fight?

A. Yes. Anybody who has a war bonnet wears it; it is made of long eagle feathers and trails behind him.

Q. I have heard that after the Custer fight, the Indians went back to the other end and attacked there again. How is it?

A. That is correct; the Indian soldiers went back and attacked the troops (Reno) on the hill again.

Q. Did you hear the firing?

A. Yes, I heard the firing while moving away.

Q. How far away were you in the morning?

A. We never stopped; we just crossed Greasy Grass Creek in the morning, the soldiers were in the rear.

Q. Did you hear any firing in the morning when you were crossing the creek?

A. We got out of hearing of the firing long before morning.

Q. What time next day did the Indian soldiers join the party?

A. They were overtaking us all day, coming in in squads.

Q. What did they report?

A. I did not hear what they said.

Q. Did they say they could not drive the troops (Reno) off the hill?

A. A few days after when the excitement died away they said they could not drive the troops off the hill.

Q. Did you see any of the Indians wearing soldier's clothes after the fight?

A. I did not. I saw lots of soldier's horses and arms.

Q. I have heard that there was a Spaniard fighting with the Indians. Did you see him?

A. There was once a white man in camp, but he went to Spotted Tail's before the fight.

his

WAN-BLI-KTE   x   KILL EAGLE

mark

Chief of Blackfeet Sioux

STATEMENT OF AFRAID OF EAGLES

(New York Herald, Sept. 24, 1876)

Q. What is your name?

A. Afraid of Eagles, brother of Bear Rib, a sub-chief of the Uncpapas.

Q. Do you know Sitting Bull?

A. Yes.

Q. Have you been with him this summer and heard him talk?

A. Yes.

Q. Where is he going to camp this winter?

A. I did not hear.

Q. Do you know where he is now?

A. I do not know. I left him on Beaver Creek.

Q. How many warriors has Sitting Bull got?

A. I can't tell, a great, great many.

Q. Were you in the Custer fight?

A. I was with Kill Eagle and what he tells you is just what I would tell you.

Q. Where does Sitting Bull get his arms and ammunition?

A. I could not learn; I am not a chief; I expect they have a good deal of it.

Q. Does Sitting Bull intend to keep up the fight?

A. I heard a little of what Sitting Bull said; the white men sent some word out to Sitting Bull from Spotted Tail Agency, and I heard what Sitting Bull said, "If we hear any time this fall that the white men would make peace he would come in long enough to trade for ammunition."

his

AFRAID OF   x   EAGLES

mark

Witness—E. P. Munn, John L. McCartney.

Sworn and subscribed to before me, this 18th day of September, 1876, at Standing Rock Agency, D. T.

R. E. Johnston
Captain, First Infantry battalion, Brevet Lieutenant Colonel, U.S.A., Acting Assistant Indian Agent.

THE STORY OF THE SIOUX CHIEF "RED HORSE"

Extract from Report of Col. W. H. Wood, Commanding Post, Cheyenne Agency. Dated Feb. 27, 1877.

RED HORSE replied as follows, in answer to the various questions put to him concerning the battle of "Greasy Grass Creek" (Little Big Horn):

"On Greasy Grass Creek was the main camp of

The Sioux Chief Red Horse. Photo by D. F. Barry; Denver Public Library Western Collection.

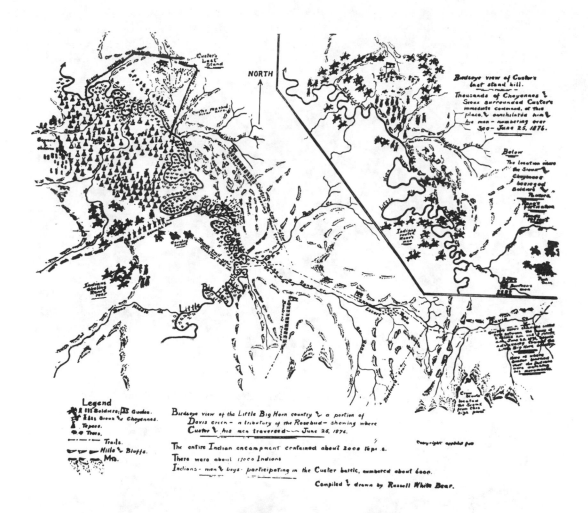

Map of the battlefield drawn by Russell White Bear, General Secretary of the Crow tribe, using data from Indian sources.

the hostiles at that time. I was one of the head council men in that camp. My lodge was situated in the center of the camp. The Uncpapas (Hunkpapas) Yanktonais and Santees were camped northeast of us, on the right, facing the battlefield. The Minneconjous, Sans Arcs, Two Kettles and Brules formed the center. On the left to the west were the Ogalallas and Cheyennes. On the morning ot the attack myself and several women were out about a mile from camp gathering wild turnips. Suddenly one of the women called my attention to a cloud of dust arising in the neighborhood of the camp. I soon discovered that the troops were making an attack. We ran for the camp, and when I got there I was sent for at once to come to the council lodge. I found many of the council men already there when I arrived. We had no time to consult one another as to what action we should take. We gave directions immediately for every

Indian to take his horse and arms; for the women and children to mount their horses and get out of the way, and for the young men to go and meet the troops.

Among the latter was an officer who rode a horse with four white feet. The Indians have fought a great many tribes of people, and very brave ones, too, but they all say that this man was the bravest man they had ever met.

I don't know whether this man was Gen. Custer or not; some say he was. I saw this man in the fight several times, but did not see his body. It is said he was killed by a Santee, who still holds his horse. This officer wore a large-brimmed hat and a buckskin coat. He alone saved his command a number of times by turning on his horse in the rear in the retreat. In speaking of him, the Indians call him "The man who rode the horse with four white feet." There were two men of this descrip-

Pictograph—Sioux Attacking Custer's Soldiers—by Chief Red Horse (1881). From the Tenth Annual Report, Bureau of Ethnology.

Pictograph—Sioux Leaving the Battlefield With Captured Seventh Cavalry Horses—by Chief Red Horse (1881). From the Tenth Annual Report, Bureau of Ethnology.

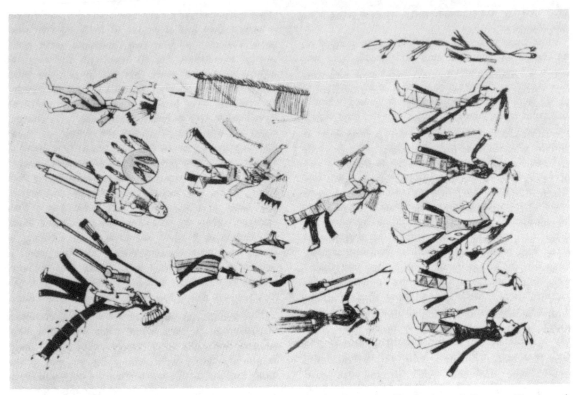

Pictograph—The Sioux Dead—by Chief Red Horse (1881). From the Tenth Annual Report, Bureau of Ethnology.

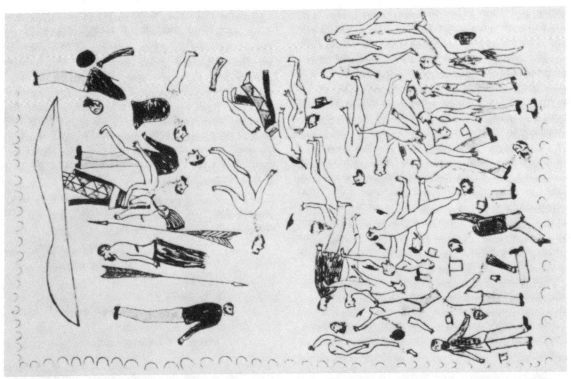

Pictograph—Custer's Soldier Dead—by Chief Red Horse (1881). From the Tenth Annual Report, Bureau of Ethnology.

tion, looking very much alike, both having long yellowish hair.

Some time before this fight, we were camped on the Rosebud, but we moved, crossed over and struck a tributary of Greasy Grass Creek and went into camp on the west bank. An Indian started to go to Red Cloud agency that day, and when a few miles from camp he discovered the dust rising. He turned back and reported that a large herd of buffalo was approaching the camp. The day was very warm, and a short time after he reported this, the camp was attacked by troops, who had followed our trail down the tributary and crossed Greasy Grass Creek a little above where we did, and above the mouth of this tributary. They attacked the upper end of the camp where the Hunkpapas were. The women and children fled immediately down Greasy Grass Creek a little way and crossed over. The troops set fire to the lodges. All the warriors then rallied and attacked this command in an overwhelming force, and drove them in confusion across the creek. They forced them back over a place below where they first crossed. The creek was very high and swift, and several of the troops were drowned. After driving this party back, the Indians corralled them on top of a high hill and held them there until they saw that the women and children were in danger of being taken prisoners by another party of troops (Custer's) which just then made its appearance below. The word passed among the Indians like a whirlwind, and they all started to attack this new party, leaving the troops on the hill. From this hill to the point where the troops were seen below it was open ground all the way, with the exception of the small tributary I spoke of before. While this last fight was going on, we expected all the time to be attacked in the rear by the troops we had just left, and when we found they did not come, we supposed they had used up all their ammunition. As soon as we had finished this fight, we all went back to massacre the troops on the hill. After skirmishing around awhile we saw the walking soldiers coming. These new troops making their appearance was the saving of the others. The Indians can't fight walking soldiers; they are afraid of them, and so we moved away.

The attack was made on the camp about noon. The troops, it appears, were divided, one party charging right into the camp. We drove them across the creek. When we attacked the other party, we swarmed down on them and drove them in confusion. The soldiers became panic-stricken, many of them throwing down their arms and throwing up their hands. No prisoners were taken. All were killed; none left alive even for a few minutes.

These troops used very few of their cartridges. I took a gun and a couple of belts off two dead men. Out of one belt two cartridges were gone; out of the other, five. It was with the captured ammunition and arms that we fought the other body of troops. If they had all remained together they would have hurt us very bad. The party we killed made five different stands. Once we charged right in until we scattered the whole of them, fighting among them hand to hand. One band of soldiers was right in rear of us; when they charged we fell back and stood for one moment facing each other. Then the Indians got courage and started for them in a solid body. We went but a little distance, when we spread out and encircled them. All the time I could see their officers riding in front, and hear them shouting to their men. It was in this charge that most of the Indians were killed. We lost 136 killed and 160 wounded. We finished up this party right there in the ravine.

The troops up the river made the first attack skirmishing. A little while after, the fight commenced with the other troops below the village. While the latter fight was going on, we posted some Indians to prevent the command from forming a junction. Some of the young men took the clothing off the dead and dressed themselves in it.* There were several among them who had citizen clothing. They went up and attacked the other command that way. Both banks of the river were very steep and difficult of ascent. Many of the troops were killed while crossing. When they got on the hill, they made some kind of fighting words, and the fight was then carried on at a distance, the young men sometimes charging close up. The fight continued at long range until the walking soldiers came. There are many little incidents connected with this fight, but I don't recollect them now. I don't like to talk about that fight. If I hear any of my people talking about it, I always move away.

We kept moving all summer, the troops being always after us. They stopped following us near the mouth of Powder River.

Headquarters Military Division
of the Missouri.
A true copy
from the original.
Chicago, Oct. 31, 1877.
(s) George A. Forsyth,
Major 9th Cavalry, A.D.C.

* This statement bears out the story of Lieut. DeRudio, who mistook these Indians for Tom Custer's command, when he was unhorsed in the river bottom and left behind in Reno's retreat.

ANOTHER VERSION OF THE STORY OF "RED HORSE"

IN 1881, Chief Red Horse repeated to Assistant Surgeon McChesney of the Army, the story he had told in 1876, and the later (and I believe more correctly interpreted) version appears in the Tenth Annual Report of the Bureau of Ethnology at pp. 563 foll. Red Horse at that time drew a map which shows the location of the Little Big Horn battlefield and also much adjacent territory in Montana and the Dakotas. The map is unimportant and will not be reproduced. Red Horse also drew a large number of pictographs to illustrate his story, some of which are considered valuable, as showing the old chief's recollections of how the battle was fought. Four of the pictographs are reproduced. They picture the Sioux engaged with Custer's battalion; Custer's dead, and the Indian dead.

These pictographs are especially interesting, showing as they do, the stars and stripes guidons carried by the troops; the type of trumpet used, the headgear and dress of the soldiers, and the manner in which the soldier dead were mutilated and dismembered. The 1881 narrative follows:

"Five springs ago I, with many Sioux Indians, took down and packed up our tipis and moved from Cheyenne River to the Rosebud River, where we camped a few days; then took down and packed up our lodges and moved to the Little Bighorn River and pitched our lodges with the large camp of Sioux.

The Sioux were camped on the Little Bighorn River as follows: The lodges of the Uncpapas were pitched highest up the river under a bluff. The Santee lodges were pitched next. The Ogalalla's lodges were pitched next. The Brule lodges were pitched next. The Minneconjou lodges were pitched next. The Sans Arc's lodges were pitched next. The Blackfeet lodges were pitched next. The Cheyenne lodges were pitched next. A few Arikara * Indians were among the Sioux (being without lodges of their own). Two-Kettles, among the other Sioux (without lodges).

I was a Sioux chief in the council lodge. My lodge was pitched in the center of the camp. The day of the attack I and four women were a short distance from the camp digging wild turnips. Suddenly one of the women attracted my attention to a cloud of dust rising a short distance from camp. I soon saw that the soldiers were charging the camp. To the camp I and the women ran.

When I arrived a person told me to hurry to the council lodge. The soldiers charged so quickly we could not talk (council). We came out of the council lodge and talked in all directions. The Sioux mount horses, take guns, and go fight the soldiers. Women and children mount horses and go, meaning to get out of the way.

Among the soldiers was an officer who rode a horse with four white feet. [From Dr. McChesney's memoranda this officer was Capt. French, Seventh Cavalry.] The Sioux have for a long time fought many brave men of different peoples, but the Sioux say this officer was the bravest man they had ever fought. I don't know whether this was Gen. Custer or not. Many of the Sioux men that I hear talking tell me it was. I saw this officer in the fight many times, but did not see his body. It has been told me that he was killed by a Santee Indian, who took his horse. This officer wore a large-brimmed hat and deerskin coat. This officer saved the lives of many soldiers by turning his horse and covering the retreat . * * * I saw two officers looking alike, both having long yellowish hair.

Before the attack the Sioux were camped on the Rosebud River. Sioux moved down a river running into the Little Bighorn River, crossed the Little Bighorn River, and camped on its west banks.

This day [day of attack] a Sioux man started to go to Red Cloud agency, but when he had gone a short distance from camp he saw a cloud of dust rising and turned back and said he thought a herd of buffalo was coming near the village.

The day was hot. In a short time the soldiers charged the camp. [This was Maj. Reno's battalion of the Seventh Cavalry.] The soldiers came on the trail made by the Sioux camp in moving, and crossed the Little Bighorn River above where the Sioux crossed, and attacked the lodges of the Uncpapas, farthest up the river. The women and children ran down the Little Bighorn River a short distance into a ravine. The soldiers set fire to the lodges. All the Sioux now charged the soldiers and drove them in confusion across the Little Bighorn River, which was very rapid, and several soldiers were drowned in it. On a hill the soldiers stopped and the Sioux surrounded them. A Sioux man came and said that a different party of soldiers had all the women and children prisoners. Like a whirlwind the word went around, and the Sioux all heard it and left the soldiers on the hill and went quickly to save the women and children.

From the hill that the soldiers were on to the place where the different soldiers [by this term Red-Horse always means the battalion immediately commanded by General Custer, his mode of dis-

* This is an obvious error, and should read "Arapahoe."

Comanche, the horse ridden by Capt. Myles Keogh, 7th Cavalry, at the Battle of the Little Big Horn. It had three severe wounds when found—through the neck, fore shoulder, and hind quarter, and several flesh wounds.

tinction being that they were a different body from that first encountered] were seen was level ground with the exception of a creek. Sioux thought the soldiers on the hill [i.e., Reno's battalion] would charge them in rear, but when they did not the Sioux thought the soldiers on the hill were out of cartridges. As soon as we had killed all the different soldiers the Sioux all went back to kill the soldiers on the hill. All the Sioux watched around the hill on which were the soldiers until a Sioux man came and said many walking soldiers were coming near. The coming of the walking soldiers was the saving of the soldiers on the hill. Sioux can not fight the walking soldiers [infantry], being afraid of them, so the Sioux hurriedly left.

The soldiers charged the Sioux camp about noon. The soldiers were divided, one party charging right into the camp. After driving these soldiers across the river, the Sioux charged the different soldiers [i.e., Custer's] below, and drove them in confusion; these soldiers became foolish, many throwing away their guns and raising their hands, saying, "Sioux, pity us; take us prisoners." The Sioux did not take a single soldier prisoner, but killed all of them; none were left alive for even a few minutes. These different soldiers discharged their guns but little. I took a gun and two belts off two dead soldiers; out of one belt two cartridges were gone, out of the other five.

The Sioux took the guns and cartridges off the dead soldiers and went to the hill on which the soldiers were, surrounded and fought them with the guns and cartridges of the dead soldiers. Had the soldiers not divided I think they would have killed many Sioux. The different soldiers [i.e., Custer's battalion] that the Sioux killed made five brave stands. Once the Sioux charged right in the

midst of the different soldiers and scattered them all, fighting among the soldiers hand to hand.

One band of soldiers was in rear of the Sioux. When this band of soldiers charged, the Sioux fell back, and the Sioux and the soldiers stood facing each other. Then all the Sioux became brave and charged the soldiers. The Sioux went but a short distance before they separated and surrounded the soldiers. I could see the officers riding in front of the soldiers and hear them shouting. Now the Sioux had many killed. The soldiers killed 136 and wounded 160 Sioux. The Sioux killed all these different soldiers in the ravine.

The soldiers charged the Sioux camp farthest up the river. A short time after the different soldiers charged the village below. While the different soldiers and Sioux were fighting together the Sioux chiefs said, "Sioux men, go watch the soldiers on the hill and prevent their joining the different soldiers." The Sioux men took the clothing off the dead and dressed themselves in it. Among the soldiers were white men who were not soldiers. The Sioux dressed in the soldiers' and white men's clothing fought the soldiers on the hill.

The banks of the Little Bighorn River were high, and the Sioux killed many of the soldiers while crossing. The soldiers on the hill dug up the ground [i.e., made earthworks], and the soldiers and Sioux fought at long range, sometimes the Sioux charging close up. The fight continued at long range until a Sioux man saw the walking soldiers coming. When the walking soldiers came near the Sioux became afraid and ran away.

CRAZY HORSE SPEAKS
THE CUSTER MASSACRE
AN INDIAN'S DESCRIPTION OF THE BATTLE WITH
CUSTER ON THE BIG HORN, AND ITS TRAGIC ENDING
* * *

Telegram to Chicago *Times* from Camp Robinson, Nebraska.

Your correspondent has obtained some very valuable information in regard to

THE CUSTER MASSACRE

from CRAZY HORSE, through Horned Horse as his spokesman, which is authentic, and confirmed by other principal chiefs. I interviewed these chiefs this afternoon, Lieut. Clark arranging for the meeting, and William Hunter acting as interpreter, a man perfectly reliable and thoroughly conversant with the Indian language. This is the Indian version and the first published: The attack was made on the village by a strong force at 11 o'clock in the morning, at the upper end of the village. This was the force commanded by Maj. Reno, and very shortly afterward the lower end of the village was attacked by another strong force, that commanded by Custer.

The Village Was Divided

into seven different bands of Indians, each commanded by a separate chief and extended in nearly a straight line. The bands were in the order mentioned below, commencing from the lower end where Custer made the attack. First, the Uncpapas, under Sitting Bull; second, the Ogalallas, under Crazy Horse; third, the Minneconjous, under Fast Bull; fourth, the Sansarcs, under Red Bear; fifth, the Cheyennes, under Ice Bear, their two principal chiefs being absent; sixth, the Santees and Yanktonias, under Red Point, of the Santees; seventh, the Blackfeet, under Scabby Head. The village consisted of eighteen hundred lodges, and at least four hundred wickayups, a lodge made of small poles and willows for temporary shelter. Each of the wickayups contained four young bucks, and the estimate made by Crazy Horse is that each lodge had from three to four warriors. Estimating at three made

A Fighting Force

of seven thousand Indians. This is the lowest estimate that can be made, for there were a good many Indians without shelter, hangers-on, who fought when called upon, and the usual number was much above seven thousand. The attack was a surprise and totally unlooked for. When Custer made his charge the women, papooses, children, and in fact all that were not fighters made a stampede in a northerly direction. Custer, seeing so numerous a body, mistook them for the main body of Indians retreating and abandoning their village, and immediately gave pursuit. The warriors in the village, seeing this, divided their forces into two parts, one intercepting Custer between their non-combatants and him, and the other getting in his rear. Outnumbering him as they did, they had him at their mercy, and

The Dreadful Massacre Ensued

Horned Horse says the smoke and dust was so great that foe could not be distinguished from friend. The horses were wild with fright and uncontrollable. The Indians were knocking each other from their steeds, and it is an absolute fact

The above portrait by S. J. Morrow of Yankton, S. D. (circa 1877) was labeled by him CRAZY HORSE. The original is in the Morrow collection at University of South Dakota; and competent judges have expressed opinion that its authenticity is probable. However, no definitely established portrait of the great Ogalalla is known to exist.

that the young bucks in their excitement and fury killed each other, several dead Indians being found killed by arrows. Horned Horse represented this hell of fire and smoke and death by intertwining his fingers and saying: "Just like this, Indians and white men." These chiefs say they suffered a loss of fifty-eight killed, and over sixty wounded. From their way of expressing it, I should judge that about 60 per cent of their wounded died.

While This Butchery Was Going On

Reno was fighting in the upper part of the village, but did not get in so as to get surrounded, and managed to escape. They say had he got in as far, he would have suffered the same fate as Custer, but he retreated to the bluffs, and was held there until the Indians fighting Custer, comprising over half the village, could join the northern portion in besieging him. These Indians claim that but for

The Timely Arrival of Gen. Terry

they would have certainly got Reno. They would have surrounded and stormed him out or would have besieged and eventually captured him. From what I know of Crazy Horse I should say that he no doubt is capable of conducting a siege. In

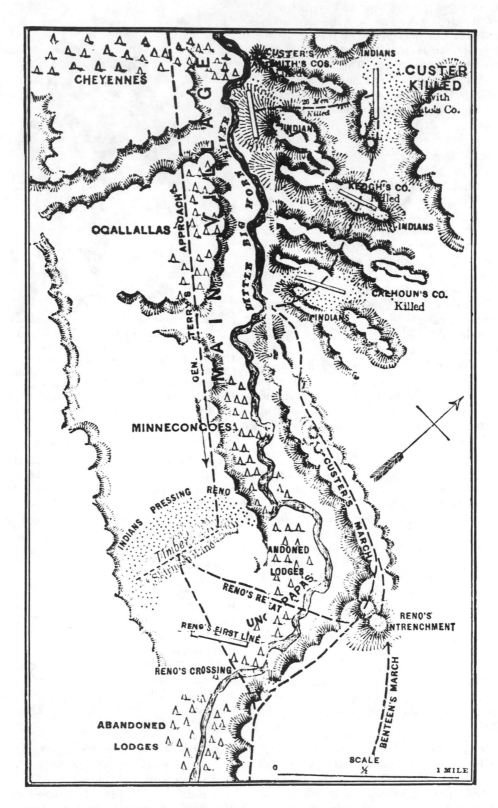

Map of the battlefield, supposedly incorporating changes suggested by Sitting Bull.
(New York Herald, November 16, 1877)

both the Rosebud fight and the Custer massacre the Indians claim he rode unarmed in the thickest of the fight invoking the blessing of the great spirit on him—that if he was right he might be victorious and if wrong that he might be killed.

(St. Paul *Pioneer Press,* May 28, 1877)

INTERVIEW WITH SITTING BULL

(From *New York Herald,* Friday, November 16, 1877.—Triple Sheet)

SITTING BULL TALKS
Valuable Interview with a *Herald*
Correspondent
"I AM NO CHIEF."
*Graphic Description of the
Rosebud Fight*
"HELL—A THOUSAND DEVILS."
"Bullets Were Like Humming Bees—
Soldiers Shook Like Aspen Leaves."

CUSTER NOBLY VINDICATED

*"A Sheaf of Corn with All the Ears
Fallen About Him."*

HE DIED LAUGHING

An Implied Charge Against Major Reno

Fort Walsh, Northwest Territory,
October 17, 1877.

THE conference between Sitting Bull and the United States Commissioners was not, as will presently be seen, the most interesting conference of the day. Sitting Bull and his chiefs so hated the "Americans," especially the American officers, that they had nothing for them but the disdain evinced in the speeches I have reported to you. After the talk with Generals Terry and Lawrence the Indians retired to their quarters.

But through the intercession of Major Walsh, Sitting Bull was persuaded at nightfall to hold a special conference with me. It was explained to him that I was not his enemy, but that I was his good friend. He was told by Major Walsh that I was a great paper chief who talked with a million tongues to all the people in the world. Said the Major: "This man is a man of wonderful medicine; he speaks and the people on this side and across the great water open their ears and hear him. He tells the truth; he does not lie. He wishes to make the world know what a great

tribe is encamped here on the land owned by the White Mother. He wants it to be understood that her guests are mighty warriors. The Long Haired Chief (alluding to General Custer) was his friend. He wants to hear from you how he fought and whether he met death like a brave."

"Agh-howgh!" (It is well) said Sitting Bull.

He finally agreed to come, after dark, to the quarters which had been assigned to me, on the condition that nobody should be present except himself, his interlocutor, Major Walsh, two interpreters and the stenographer I had employed for the occasion.

Sitting Bull As He Appears

At the appointed time, half-past eight, the lamps were lighted, and the most mysterious Indian chieftain who ever flourished in North America was ushered in by Major Walsh, who locked the door behind him. This was the first time that Sitting Bull had condescended, not merely to visit but to address a white man from the United States. During the long years of his domination he had withstood, with his bands, every attempt on the part of the United States government at a compromise of interests. He

Sitting Bull. From a photograph by Goff, of Bismarck (1881).

had refused all proffers, declined any treaty. He had never been beaten in a battle with United States troops: on the contrary, his warriors had been victorious over the pride of our army. Pressed hard, he had retreated, scorning the factions of his bands who accepted the terms offered them with the same bitterness with which he scorned his white enemies.

Here he stood, his blanket rolled back, his head upreared, his right moccasin put forward, his right hand thrown across his chest.

I arose and approached him, holding out both hands. He grasped them cordially.

"How!" said he.

"How!"

And now let me attempt a better portrait of Sitting Bull than I was able to despatch to you at headlong haste by the telegraph. He is about five feet ten inches high. He was clad in a black and white calico shirt, black cloth leggings, and moccasins, magnificently embroidered with beads and porcupine quills. He held in his left hand a foxskin cap, its brush drooping to his feet.

* * * * *

I turned to the interpreter and said:—

"Explain again to Sitting Bull that he is with a friend."

The interpreter explained.

"Banee!" said the chief, holding out his hand again and pressing mine.

Major Walsh here said: "Sitting Bull is in the best mood now that you could possibly wish. Proceed with your questions and make them as logical as you can. I will assist you and trip you up occasionally if you are likely to irritate him."

Then the dialogue went on. I give it literally.

"I Am No Chief."

"You are a great chief," said I to Sitting Bull, "but you live behind a cloud. Your face is dark; my people do not see it. Tell me, do you hate the Americans very much?"

A gleam as of fire shot across his face.

"I am no chief."

This was precisely what I expected. It will dissipate at once the erroneous idea which has prevailed that Sitting Bull is either a chief or a warrior.

"What are you?"

"I am," said he, crossing both hands upon his chest, slightly nodding and smiling satirically, "a man."

"What does he mean?" I inquired, turning to Major Walsh.

"He means," responded the Major, "to keep you in ignorance of his secret if he can. His posi-

tion among his bands is anomalous. His own tribes, the Uncpapas, are not all in fealty to him. Parts of nearly twenty different tribes of Sioux, besides a remnant of the Uncpapas, abide with him. So far as I have learned he rules over these fragments of tribes, which compose his camp of 2,500, including between 800 and 900 warriors, by sheer compelling force of intellect and will. I believe that he understands nothing particularly of war or military tactics, at least not enough to give him the skill or the right to command warriors in battle. He is supposed to have guided the fortunes of several battles, including the fight in which Custer fell. That supposition, as you will presently find, is partially erroneous. His word was always potent in the camp or in the field, but he has usually left to the war chiefs the duties appertaining to engagements. When the crisis came he gave his opinion, which was accepted as law."

"What was he, then?" I inquired, continuing this momentary dialogue with Major Walsh. "Was he, is he, a mere medicine man?"

"Don't for the world," replied the Major, "intimate to him, in the questions you are about to ask him, that you have derived the idea from me, or from any one, that he is a mere medicine man. He would deem that to be a profound insult. In point of fact he is a medicine man, but a far greater, more influential medicine man than any savage I have ever known. * * * He speaks. They listen and they obey. Now let us hear what his explanation will be."

A Savage Companion

"You say you are no chief?"

"No!" with considerable hauteur.

"Are you a head soldier?"

"I am nothing—neither a chief nor a soldier."

"What? Nothing?"

"Nothing."

"What, then, makes the warriors of your camp, the great chiefs who are here along with you, look up to you so? Why do they think so much of you?"

Sitting Bull's lips curled with a proud smile.

"Oh, I used to be a kind of a chief, but the Americans made me go away from my father's hunting ground."

"You do not love the Americans?"

You should have seen this savage's lips.

"I saw to-day that all the warriors around you clapped their hands and cried out when you spoke. What you said appeared to please them. They liked you. They seemed to think that what you said was right for them to say. If you are not a great chief, why do these men think so much of you?"

At this Sitting Bull, who had in the meantime been leaning back against the wall, assumed a posture of mingled toleration and disdain.

"Your people look up to men because they are rich; because they have much land, many lodges, many squaws?"

"Yes."

"Well, I suppose my people look up to me because I am poor. That is the difference."

In this answer was concentrated all the evasiveness natural to an Indian.

"What is your feeling toward the Americans now?"

He did not even deign an answer. He touched his hip where his knife was.

I asked the interpreter to insist on an answer.

"Listen," said Sitting Bull, not changing his posture but putting his right hand out upon my knee. "I told them today what my notions were—that I did not want to go back there. Every time that I had any difficulty ·with them they struck me first. I want to live in peace."

"Have you an implacable enmity to the Americans? Would you live with them in peace if they allowed you to do so; or do you think that you can only obtain peace here?"

"I Bought Them."

"The White Mother is good."

"Better than the Great Father?"

"Howgh!"

And then, after a pause, Sitting Bull continued;—"They asked me to-day to give them my horses. I bought my horses, and they are mine. I bought them from men who came up the Missouri in macinaws. They do not belong to the government; neither do the rifles. The rifles are also mine. I bought them; I paid for them. Why I should give them up I do not know. I will not give them up."

"Do you really think, do your people believe, that it is wise to reject the proffers that have been made to you by the United States Commissioners? Do not some of you feel as if you were destined to lose your old hunting grounds? Don't you see that you will probably have the same difficulty in Canada that you have had in the United States?"

"The White Mother does not lie."

"Do you expect to live here by hunting? Are there buffaloes enough? Can your people subsist on the game here?"

"I don't know; I hope so."

"If not, are any part of your people disposed

to take up agriculture? Would any of them raise steers and go to farming?"

"I don't know."

"What will they do, then?"

"As long as there are buffaloes that is the way we will live."

"But the time will come when there will be no more buffaloes."

"Those are the words of an American."

Poisoned With Blood

"How long do you think the buffaloes will last?"

Sitting Bull arose. "We know," said he, extending his right hand with an impressive gesture, "that on the other side the buffaloes will not last very long. Why? Because the country there is poisoned with blood—a poison that kills all the buffaloes or drives them away. It is strange," he continued, with his peculiar smile, "that the Americans should complain that the Indians kill buffaloes. We kill buffaloes, as we kill other animals, for food and clothing, and to make our lodges warm. They kill buffaloes—for what? Go through your country. See the thousands of carcasses rotting on the Plains. Your young men shoot for pleasure. All they take from dead buffalo is his tail, or his head, or his horns, perhaps, to show they have killed a buffalo. What is this? Is it robbery? You call us savages. What are they? The buffaloes have come North. We have come North to find them, and to get away from a place where people tell lies."

To gain time and not to dwell importunately on a single point, I asked Sitting Bull to tell me something of his early life. In the first place, where he was born?

"I was born on the Missouri River; at least I recollect that somebody told me so—I don't know who told me or where I was told of it."

"Of what tribe are you?"

"I am an Uncpapa."

"Of the Sioux?"

"Yes; of the great Sioux Nation."

"Who was your father?"

"My father is dead."

"Is your mother living?"

"My mother lives with me in my lodge."

"Great lies are told about you. White men say that you lived among them when you were young; that you went to school; that you learned to write and read from books; that you speak English; that you know how to talk French?"

"It is a lie."

"You are an Indian?"

(Proudly) "I am a Sioux."

Another photograph of Sitting Bull. Photo by D. F. Barry.

Then, suddenly relaxing from his hauteur, Sitting Bull began to laugh. "I have heard," he said, "of some of these stories. They are all strange lies. What I am I am," and here he leaned back and resumed his attitude and expression of barbaric grandeur.

Predestination

"I am a man. I see. I know. I began to see when I was not yet born; when I was not in my mother's arms, but inside of my mother's belly. It was there that I began to study about my people."

Here I touched Sitting Bull on the arm.

"Do not interrupt him," said Major Walsh. "He is beginning to talk about his medicine."

"I was," repeated Sitting Bull, "still in my mother's insides when I began to study all about my people. God (waving his hand to express a great protecting Genius) gave me the power to see out of the womb. I studied there, in the womb, about many things. I studied about the smallpox, that was killing my people—the great sickness that was killing the women and children. I was so interested that I turned over on my side. The God Almighty must have told me at that time (and here Sitting Bull unconsciously revealed his secret) that I would be the man to

be the judge of all the other Indians—a big man, to decide for them in all their ways."

"And you have since decided for them?"

"I speak. It is enough."

"Could not your people, whom you love so well, get on with the Americans?"

"No!"

"Why?"

Why He Fought

"I never taught my people to trust Americans. I have told them the truth—that the Americans are great liars. I have never dealt with the Americans. Why should I? The land belonged to my people. I say never dealt with them—I mean I never treated with them in a way to surrender my people's rights. I traded with them, but I always gave full value for what I got. I never asked the United States government to make me presents of blankets or cloth or anything of that kind. The most I did was to ask them to send me an honest trader that I could trade with and I proposed to give him buffalo robes and elk skins and other hides in exchange for what we wanted. I told every trader who came to our camps that I did not want any favors from him— that I wanted to trade with him fairly and equally, giving him full value for what I got— but the traders wanted me to trade with them on no such terms. They wanted to give little and get much. They told me that if I did not accept what they would give me in trade they would get the government to fight me. I told them I did not want to fight."

"But you fought."

"At last, yes; but not until after I had tried hard to prevent a fight. At first my young men, when they began to talk bad, stole five American horses. I took the horses away from them and gave them back to the Americans. It did no good. By and by we had to fight."

The Great Custer Battle Explained

It was at this juncture that I began to question the great savage before me in regard to the most disastrous, most mysterious Indian battle of the century—Custer's encounter with the Sioux on the Big Horn—the Thermopylae of the Plains. Sitting Bull, the chief genius of his bands, has been supposed to have commanded the Sioux forces when Custer fell.

That the reader may understand Sitting Bull's statements, it will be necessary for him to scan the map of the illustrious battle ground, which is herewith presented,* and to read the following preliminary sketch. It should be understood,

* See page 64, supra.

moreover, that, inasmuch as every white man with Custer perished, and no other white man, save one or two scouts, had conferred lately with Sitting Bull or any of his chiefs since the awful day, this is the first authentic story of the conflict which can possibly have appeared out of the lips of a survivor. It has the more historical value since it comes from the chief among Custer's and Reno's foes.

* * * * *

The Indian village, consisting of camps of Cheyennes, Ogalallas, Minneconjous and Uncpapas, was nearly three miles long. The accompanying map will show its exact situation, also the routes pursued by Reno's and Custer's forces. It is seen from this map that Reno crossed the Little Big Horn, formed his first line just south of the crossing and charged. He says:—

"I deployed, and, with the Ree scouts on my left, charged down the valley with great ease for about two and a half miles."

Reno, instead of holding the ground thus gained, retreated, being hard pressed. The map shows the timber in which he made a temporary stand, and it shows, too, his line of retreat back over the valley, and across the Little Big Horn and up the bluffs, on the summit of which he intrenched himself late in the afternoon.

The map expresses the fact that Custer's march to the ford where he attempted to cross the Little Big Horn and attack the Indians in their rear was much longer than Reno's march, consequently Custer's assault was not made until after Reno's.

* * * * *

"We Thought We Were Whipped"

The testimony of Sitting Bull, which I am about to give, is the more convincing and important from the very fact of the one erroneous impression he derived as to the identity of the officer in command of the forces which assailed his camp. He confounds Reno with Custer. He supposes that one and the same general crossed the Little Big Horn where Reno crossed, charged as Reno charged, retreated as Reno retreated back over the river and then pursued the line of Custer's march, attacked as Custer attacked and fell as Custer fell.

"Did you know the Long Haired Chief?" I asked Sitting Bull.

"No."

"What! Had you never seen him?"

"No. Many of the chiefs knew him."

"What did they think of him?"

"He was a great warrior."

"Was he brave?"

"He was a mighty chief."

"Now, tell me. Here is something that I wish to know. Big lies are told about the fight in which the Long Haired Chief was killed. He was my friend. No one has come back to tell the truth about him, or about that fight. You were there; you know. Your chiefs know. I want to hear something that forked tongues do not tell—the truth."

"It is well."

Here I drew forth the map of the battle field and spread it out across Sitting Bull's knees and explained to him the names and situations as represented on it, and he smiled.

"We thought we were whipped," he said.

"Ah! Did you think the soldiers were too many for you?"

"Not at first; but by-and-by, yes. Afterwards, no."

"Tell me about the battle. Where was the Indian camp first attacked?"

"Here" (pointing to Reno's crossing on the map).

"About what time in the day was that?"

"It was some two hours past the time when the sun is in the centre of the sky."

Custer Commanded.

"What white chief was it who came over there against your warriors?"

"The Long Hair."

"Are you sure?"

"The Long Hair commanded."

"But you did not see him?"

"I have said that I never saw him."

"Did any of the chiefs see him?"

"Not here, but there," pointing to the place where Custer charged and was repulsed on the north bank of the Little Big Horn.

"Why do you think it was the Long Hair who crossed first and charged you here at the right side of the map?"

"A chief leads his warriors."

"Was there a good fight here, on the right side of the map? Explain it to me."

"It was so," said Sitting Bull, raising his hands. "I was lying in my lodge. Some young men ran into me and said: 'The Long Hair is in the camp. Get up. They are firing into the camp.' I said, all right. I jumped up and stepped out of my lodge."

"Where was your lodge?"

"Here, with my people," answered Sitting Bull, pointing to the group of Uncpapa lodges, designated as "abandoned lodges" on the map.

"So the first attack was made then, on the

right side of the map, and upon the lodges of the Uncpapas?"

"Yes."

"Here the lodges are said to have been deserted?"

"The old men, the squaws and the children were hurried away."

"Toward the other end of the camp?"

"Yes. Some of the Minneconjou women and children also left their lodges when the attack began."

"Did you retreat at first?"

"Do you mean the warriors?"

"Yes, the fighting men."

Mistaking Reno for Custer

"Oh, we fell back, but it was not what warriors call a retreat; it was to gain time. It was the Long Hair who retreated. My people fought him here in the brush (designating the timber behind which the Indians pressed Reno) and he fell back across here (placing his finger on the line of Reno's retreat to the northern bluffs).

"So you think that was the Long Hair whom your people fought in that timber and who fell back afterward to those heights?"

"Of course."

"What afterward occurred? Was there any heavy fighting after the retreat of the soldiers to the bluffs?"

"Not then; not there."

"Where, then?"

"Why, down here;" and Sitting Bull indicated with his finger the place where Custer approached and touched the river. "That," said he, "was where the big fight was fought, a little later. After the Long Hair was driven back to the bluffs he took this route (tracing with his finger the line of Custer's march on the map), and went down to see if he could not beat us there."

[Here the reader should pause to discern the extent of Sitting Bull's error, and to anticipate what will presently appear to be Reno's misconception or mistake. Sitting Bull, not identifying Reno in the whole of this engagement, makes it seem that it was Custer who attacked, when Reno attacked in the first place and afterward moved down to resume the assault from a new position. He thus involuntarily testified to the fact that Reno's assault was a brief, ineffectual one before his retreat to the bluffs, and that Reno, after his retreat, ceased on the bluffs from aggressive fighting.]

Bull's Description of Hell

"When the fight commenced here," I asked, pointing to the spot where Custer advanced beyond the Little Big Horn, "what happened?"

"Hell!"

"You mean, I suppose, a fierce battle?"

"I mean a thousand devils."

"The village was by this time thoroughly aroused?"

"The squaws were like flying birds; the bullets were like humming bees."

"You say that when the first attack was made, up here on the right of the map, the old men and the squaws and children ran down the valley toward the left. What did they do when this second attack came from up here toward the left?"

"They ran back again to the right, here and here," answered Sitting Bull, placing his swarthy finger on the place where the words "Abandoned Lodges" are.

"And where did the warriors run?"

"They ran to the fight—the big fight."

"So that, in the afternoon, after the fight, on the right hand side of the map was over, and after the big fight toward the left hand side began, you say that the squaws and children all returned to the right hand side, and that the warriors, the fighting men of all the Indian camps, ran to the place where the big fight was going on?"

"Yes."

"Why was that? Were not some of the warriors left in front of these intrenchments on the bluffs, near the right side of the map? Did not you think it necessary—did not your war chiefs think it necessary—to keep some of your young men there to fight the troops who had retreated to those intrenchments?"

"No."

"Why?"

"You have forgotten."

"How?"

A Charge Against Reno

"You forget that only a few soldiers were left by the Long Hair on those bluffs. He took the main body of his soldiers with him to make the big fight down here on the left."

"So there were no soldiers to make a fight left in the intrenchments on the right hand bluffs?"

"I have spoken. It is enough. The squaws could deal with them. There were none but squaws and pappooses in front of them that afternoon." * * *

"Well then," I inquired of Sitting Bull, "Did the cavalry, who came down and made the big fight, fight?"

Again Sitting Bull smiled.

"They fought. Many young men are missing from our lodges. But is there an American squaw

Sitting Bull Receiving The Message "We Have Killed Them All." From an original painting in the Karl May Indian Museum, Dresden, Germany.

who has her husband left? Were there any Americans left to tell the story of that day? No."

"How did they come on to the attack?"

"I have heard that there are trees which tremble."

"Do you mean the trees with trembling leaves?"

"Yes."

"They call them in some parts of the western country Quaking Asps; in the eastern part of the country they call them Silver Aspens."

"Hah! A great white chief, whom I met once, spoke these words 'Silver Aspens,' trees that shake; these were the Long Hair's soldiers."

"You do not mean that they trembled before your people because they were afraid?"

"They were brave men. They were tired. They were too tired."

"How did they act? How did they behave themselves?"

At this Sitting Bull again arose. I also arose from my seat, as did the other persons in the room, except the stenographer.

As Good Men As Ever Fought

"Your people," said Sitting Bull, extending his right hand, "were killed. I tell no lies about deadmen. These men who came with the Long Hair were as good men as ever fought. When they rode up their horses were tired and they were tired. When they got off from their horses they could not stand firmly on their feet. They swayed to and fro —so my young men have told me—like the limbs of cypresses in a great wind. Some of them staggered under the weight of their guns. But they began to fight at once; but by this time, as I have said, our camps were aroused, and there were plenty of warriors to meet them. They fired with needle guns. We replied with magazine guns

—repeating rifles. It was so (and here Sitting Bull illustrated by patting his palms together with the rapidity of a fusilade). Our young men rained lead across the river and drove the white braves back."

"And then?"

"And then, they rushed across themselves."

"And then?"

"And then they found that they had a good deal to do."

"Was there at that time some doubt about the issue of the battle, whether you would whip the Long Hair or not?"

"There was so much doubt about it that I started down there (here again pointing to the map) to tell the squaws to pack up the lodges and get ready to move away."

"You were on that expedition, then, after the big fight had fairly begun?"

"Yes."

"You did not personally witness the rest of the big fight? You were not engaged in it?"

"No. I have heard of it from the warriors."

How Custer Was Surrounded

"When the great crowds of your young men crossed the river in front of the Long Hair what did they do? Did they attempt to assault him directly in his front?"

"At first they did, but afterward they found it better to try and get around him. They formed themselves on all sides of him except just at his back."

"How long did it take them to put themselves around his flanks?"

"As long as it takes the sun to travel from here to here" (indicating some marks upon his arm with which apparently he is used to gauge the progress of the shadow of his lodge across his arm, and probably meaning half an hour. An Indian has no more definite way than this to express the lapse of time).

"The trouble was with the soldiers," he continued; "they were so exhausted and their horses bothered them so much that they could not take good aim. Some of their horses broke away from them and left them to stand and drop and die. When the Long Hair, the General, found that he was so outnumbered and threatened on his flanks, he took the best course he could have taken. The bugle blew. It was an order to fall back. All the men fell back fighting and dropping. They could not fire fast enough, though. But from our side it was so," said Sitting Bull, and here he clapped his hands rapidly twice a second to express with

what quickness and continuance the balls flew from the Henry and Winchester rifles wielded by the Indians. "They could not stand up under such a fire," he added.

"Were any military tactics shown? Did the Long Haired Chief make any disposition of his soldiers, or did it seem as though they retreated all together, helter skelter, fighting for their lives?"

No Cowards on Either Side

"They kept in pretty good order. Some great chief must have commanded them all the while. They would fall back across a *coulee* and make a fresh stand beyond on higher ground. The map is pretty nearly right. It shows where the white men stopped and fought before they were all killed. I think that is right—down there to the left, just above the Little Big Horn. There was one part driven out there, away from the rest, and there a great many men were killed. The places marked on the map are pretty nearly the places where all were killed."

"Did the whole command keep on fighting until the last?"

"Every man, so far as my people could see. There were no cowards on either side."

* * * * *

Duration of the Fight

I inquired of Sitting Bull:—"How long did this big fight continue?"

"The sun was there," he answered, pointing to within two hours from the western horizon.

"You cannot certainly depend," here observed Major Walsh, "upon Sitting Bull's or any other Indian's statement in regard to time or numbers. But his answer, indeed all his answers, exactly correspond with the replies to similar questions of my own. If you will proceed you will obtain from him in a few moments some important testimony."

I went on to interrogate Sitting Bull:—

"This big fight, then, extended through three hours?"

"Through most of the going forward of the sun."

"Where was the Long Hair the most of the time?"

"I have talked with my people; I cannot find one who saw the Long Hair until just before he died. He did not wear his long hair as he used to wear it. His hair was like yours," said Sitting Bull, playfully touching my forehead with his taper fingers. "It was short, but it was of the color of the grass when the frost comes."

"Did you hear from your people how he died? Did he die on horseback?"

"No. None of them died on horseback."

"All were dismounted?"

"Yes."

"And Custer, the Long Hair?"

The Last to Die

"Well, I have understood that there were a great many brave men in that fight, and that from time to time, while it was going on, they were shot down like pigs. They could not help themselves. One by one the officers fell. I believe the Long Hair rode across once from this place down here (meaning the place where Tom Custer's and Smith's companies were killed) to this place up here (indicating the spot on the map where Custer fell), but I am not sure about this. Any way it was said that up there where the last fight took place, where the last stand was made, the Long Hair stood like a sheaf of corn with all the ears fallen around him."

"Not wounded?"

"No."

"How many stood by him?"

"A few."

"When did he fall?"

"He killed a man when he fell. He laughed."

"You mean he cried out."

"No, he laughed; he had fired his last shot."

"From a carbine?"

"No, a pistol."

"Did he stand up after he first fell?"

"He rose up on his hands and tried another shot, but his pistol would not go off."

"Was any one else standing up when he fell down?"

"One man was kneeling; that was all. But he died before the Long Hair. All this was far up on the bluffs, far away from the Sioux encampments. I did not see it. It is told to me. But it is true."

Not Scalped

"The Long Hair was not scalped?"

"No. My people did not want his scalp."

"Why?"

"I have said; he was a great chief."

"Did you at any time," I persisted, "during the progress of the fight believe that your people would get the worst of it?"

"At one time, as I have told you, I started down to tell the squaws to strike the lodges. I was then on my way up to the right end of the camp, where the first attack was made on us. But before I reached that end of the camp where the Minneconjou and Uncpapa squaws and children were and where some of the other squaws—Cheyennes and Ogalallas—had gone, I was overtaken by one

of the young warriors, who had just come down from the fight. He called out to me. He said:—

" 'No use to leave camp; every white man is killed.' So I stopped and went no further. I turned back, and by and by I met the warriors returning."

"But in the meantime," I asked, "Were there no warriors occupied up here at the right end of the camp? Was nobody left, except the squaws and the children and the old men, to take care of that end of the camp? Was nobody ready to defend it against the soldiers in those intrenchments up there?"

"Oh," replied Sitting Bull again, "there was no need to waste warriors in that direction. There were only a few soldiers there in those intrenchments, and we knew they wouldn't dare to come out."

* * * * *

A Hero's Death

"While the big fight was going on," I asked Sitting Bull, "could the sound of the firing have been heard as far as those intrenchments on the right?"

"The squaws who were gathered down in the valley of the river heard them. The guns could have been heard three miles and more."

* * * * *

Adieu King Bull

As Sitting Bull rose to go I asked him whether he had the stomach for any more battles with the Americans. He answered:—

"I do not want any fight."

"You mean not now?"

He laughed quite heartily.

"No; not this winter."

"Are your young braves willing to fight?"

"You will see."

"When?"

"I cannot say."

"I have not seen your people. Would I be welcome at your camp?"

After gazing at the ceiling for a few moments Sitting Bull responded:—

"I will not be pleased. The young men would not be pleased. You came with this party (alluding to the United States Commissioners) and you can go back with them. I have said enough."

With this Sitting Bull wrapped his blanket around him and, after gracefully shaking hands, strode to the door. Then he placed his fox-skin cap upon his head and I bade him adieu.

The Ogalalla Chief Low Dog. Photo by D. F.
Barry. Denver Public Library Western Collection.

THE STORIES OF LOW DOG, CROW KING, HUMP, IRON THUNDER

(From the *Leavenworth Weekly Times*—
Thursday, August 18, 1881.)

Fort Yates, Dakota, July 30.—Fort Yates is
located on a plateau on the west side of the
Missouri river, 2,000 miles above its mouth, and
ninety miles by river—sixty by road—below Bismarck. It is on the Indian reservation. Cannon-
Ball river, twenty-three miles above here, is the
northern boundary of the reservation, which extends down the river to the northern line of
Nebraska, and west more than one hundred miles.
This is the Sioux reservation. On it are located
the Blackfeet, Uncpapas, Ogalallas, Yanktonnais,
Cheyennes, Sans-Arcs, Brules, Minnecongoes, and
perhaps others. I am not certain that I have named
all. All these are tribes of the Sioux nation, and
they number altogether more than thirty thousand.
Within two miles of this fort on another plateau,
are encamped the hostile Sioux, who came in and
surrendered, with Rain-in-the-Face, Black Moon,
Crow King, Gall, Low Dog, and other chiefs,

who are all here. Sitting Bull and the Indians who
surrendered with him, some three hundred, are on
their way here from Buford, and are expected
within a day or two.

We came from Bismarck, via Fort Lincoln, by
the overland route, Col. Tilford, in command at
Fort Lincoln, five miles below Bismarck, having
kindly furnished us an ambulance and baggage
wagon, each drawn by four mules. On the evening
of our arrival the hostiles, who had been in charge
of the military, were turned over to the interior
department, represented here by U. S. Indian
Agent J. A. Stephan, familiarly known as Father
Stephan. We were invited by Capt. Howe and
Lieut. Ogle, of the Seventeenth infantry, who were
on duty in charge of the hostiles, to be present at
a conference with the chiefs before transferring
them to the care of the agent. At Capt. Howe's
tent we found Rain-in-the-Face, Don't-Go-Out,
Crow King, Low Dog, Bob Tail Hawk, Hump,
Fool Heart, Big Road, Twin Bear, Little Hawk,
Scared Eagle, Circle Bear, Bull Dog, Crawler,
Crazy Thunder and Bull's Ghost—all chiefs,
squatted in a circle on the ground, smoking a pipe
which was passed from one to another. They shook
hands and greeted us with the Indian salutation
"How!" and "cola" (friend). Presently Chief Gall
came riding up, and jumping off his pony walked
to the circle with a stride like Salvini's, and took
his place with the rest. He greeted the chiefs with
a "How," but paid no attention to the whites.
He is a man of fine presence, dignified, slightly
sullen and reticent. His walk is superb, and he
more than any other one of the hostiles, represents
the typical Indian in appearance.

Captain Howe called the chiefs and the interpreter into the inclosed space in front of his tent,
and telling them that he was no longer their father
and that they must look to the agent, said he had
some presents for them as tokens of his good will.
They received this announcement with a "How"
of approval, and Lieutenant Ogle after making
them a neat little speech, distributed the presents.
There were a suit of clothes for each, a flannel
shirt with a flaming red shield in front (which
several of them immediately proceeded to put on
over their own clothes,) papers of tobacco and last
but not least, a quantity of paint. As soon as Rain-
in-the-Face received his proportion of this, he took
some in his hand and, spitting on it, rubbed it
over the upper part of his face and in his hair,
until both were of the color of gold; then Chief
Gall, who was spokesman for the Indians, said
they wanted guns that they might hunt. Captain
Howe told him that he had no authority to give
them, and that he must apply to the agent. The

officers told us that if those Indians had guns and ponies we would need a military escort back to Fort Lincoln. The chiefs then rose, and shaking hands with all of us, went back to their camp.

There has been a great desire to hear the Indian account of the Custer fight. All these hostiles were in it. Captain Howe, who is highly regarded by the Indians, told me that Low Dog, chief of the Ogalallas, and recognized by the Indians as a great warrior, had promised to give him an account of the fight, and invited me to hear it. I took pencil and paper and with Low Dog's consent noted it down. I have it almost word for word as translated by the interpreter, but I regret exceedingly that the interpreter did not give me a literal translation. All the Indians use a great many gestures and signs, and the interpreters tell me that it is very difficult to do more than give the substance of what they say.

LOW DOG'S ACCOUNT OF THE CUSTER FIGHT

"We were in camp near Little Big Horn river. We had lost some horses, and an Indian went back on the trail to look for them. We did not know that the white warriors were coming after us. Some scouts or men in advance of the warriors saw the Indian looking for the horses and ran after him and tried to kill him to keep him from bringing us word, but he ran faster than they and came into camp and told us that the white warriors were coming. I was asleep in my lodge at the time. The sun was about noon (pointing with his finger.) I heard the alarm, but I did not believe it. I thought it was a false alarm. I did not think it possible that any white men would attack us, so strong as we were. We had in camp the Cheyennes, Arapahoes, and seven different tribes of the Teton Sioux—a countless number. Although I did not believe it was a true alarm, I lost no time getting ready. When I got my gun and came out of my lodge the attack had begun at the end of the camp where Sitting Bull and the Uncpapas were. The Indians held their ground to give the women and children time to get out of the way. By this time the herders were driving in the horses and as I was nearly at the further end of the camp, I ordered my men to catch their horses and get out of the way, and my men were hurrying to go and help those that were fighting. When the fighters saw that the women and children were safe they fell back. By this time my people went to help them, and the less able warriors and the women caught horses and got them ready, and we drove the first attacking party back, and that

party retreated to a high hill. Then I told my people not to venture too far in pursuit for fear of falling into an ambush. By this time all the warriors in our camp were mounted and ready for fight, and then we were attacked on the other side by another party. They came on us like a thunderbolt. I never before nor since saw men so brave and fearless as those white warriors. We retreated until our men got all together, and then we charged upon them. I called to my men, "This is a good day to die: follow me." We massed our men, and that no man should fall back, every man whipped another man's horse and we rushed right upon them. As we rushed upon them the white warriors dismounted to fire, but they did very poor shooting. They held their horses reins on one arm while they were shooting, but their horses were so frightened that they pulled the men all around, and a great many of their shots went up in the air and did us no harm. The white warriors stood their ground bravely, and none of them made any attempt to get away. After all but two of them were killed, I captured two of their horses. Then the wise men and chiefs of our nation gave out to our people not to mutilate the dead white chief, for he was a brave warrior and died a brave man, and his remains should be respected.

Then I turned around and went to help fight the other white warriors, who had retreated to a high hill on the east side of the river. (This was Reno's command.) I don't know whether any white men of Custer's force were taken prisoners. When I got back to our camp they were all dead. Everything was in confusion all the time of the fight. I did not see Gen. Custer. I do not know who killed him. We did not know till the fight was over that he was the white chief. We had no idea that the white warriors were coming until the runner came in and told us. I do not say that Reno was a coward. He fought well, but our men were fighting to save their women and children, and drive them back. If Reno and his warriors had fought as Custer and his warriors fought, the battle might have been against us. No white man or Indian ever fought as bravely as Custer and his men. The next day we fought Reno and his forces again, and killed many of them. Then the chiefs said these men had been punished enough, and that we ought to be merciful, and let them go. Then we heard that another force was coming up the river to fight us (General Terry's command,) and we started to fight them, but the chiefs and wise men counseled that we had fought enough and that we should not fight unless attacked, and we went back and took our women and children and went away.

This ended Low Dog's narration, given in the hearing of half a dozen officers, some of the Seventeenth Infantry and some of the Seventh Cavalry—Custer's regiment. It was in the evening; the sun had set and the twilight was deepening. Officers were there who were at the Big Horn with Benteen, senior captain of the Seventh, who usually exercised command as a field officer, and who, with his battalion, joined Reno on the first day of the fight, after his retreat, and was in the second day's fight. It was a strange and intensely interesting scene. When Low Dog began his narrative only Capt. Howe, the interpreter, and myself were present, but as he progressed the officers gathered round, listening to every word, and all were impressed that the Indian chief was giving a true account, according to his knowledge. Some one asked how many Indians were killed in the fight, Low Dog answered, "Thirty-eight, who died then, and a great many—I can't tell the number—who were wounded and died afterwards. I never saw a fight in which so many in proportion to the killed were wounded, and so many horses were wounded." Another asked who were the dead Indians that were found in two tepees—five in one and six in the other—all richly dressed, and with their ponies, slain about the tepees. He said eight were chiefs killed in the battle. One was his own brother, born of the same mother and the same father, and he did not know who the other two were.

The question was asked, "What part did Sitting Bull take in the fight?" Low Dog is not friendly to Sitting Bull. He answered with a sneer: "If some one would lend him a heart he would fight." Then Low Dog said he would like to go home, and with the interpreter he went back to the Indian camp. He is a tall, straight Indian, thirty-four years old, not a bad face, regular features and small hands and feet. He said that when he had his weapons and was on the war-path he considered no man his superior; but when he surrendered he laid that feeling all aside, and now if any man should try to chastise him in his humble condition and helplessness all he could do would be to tell him that he was no man and a coward; which, while he was on the war-path he would allow no man to say and live.

He said that when he was fourteen years old, he had his first experience on the war-path: "I went against the will of my parents and those having authority over me. It was on a stream above the mouth of the Yellowstone. We went to war against a band of Assiniboins that were hunting buffalo, and I killed one of their men. After we killed all of that band another band came out against us, and I killed one of them. When we came back to our tribe I was made a chief, as no Sioux had ever been known to kill two enemies in one fight at my age, and I was invited into the councils of the chiefs and wise men. At that time we had no thought that we would ever fight the whites. Then I heard some people talking that the chief of the white men wanted the Indians to live where he ordered and do as he said, and he would feed and clothe them. I was called into council with the chiefs and wise men, and we had a talk about that. My judgment was why should I allow any man to support me against my will anywhere, so long as I have hands and as long as I am an able man, not a boy. Little I thought then that I would have to fight the white man, or do as he should tell me. When it began to be plain that we would have to yield or fight, we had a great many councils. I said, why should I be kept as an humble man, when I am a brave warrior and on my own lands? The game is mine, and the hills, and the valleys, and the white man has no right to say where I shall go or what I shall do. If any white man tries to destroy my property, or take my lands, I will take my gun, get on my horse, and go punish him. I never thought that I would have to change that view. But at last I saw that if I wished to do good to my nation, I would have to do it by wise thinking and not so much fighting. Now, I want to learn the white man's way, for I see that he is stronger than we are, and that his government is better than ours."

Having heard Low Dog's story of the fight, I concluded I would try to get an account from other chiefs, and going with an interpreter to the Indian camp approached Chief Gall first. He said if he knew anything he would tell it, but he denied that he was in the fight. He said he was helping the women catch the horses and took no other part. If he thought I believed that, he mistook his man, and I shall try him again. Rain-in-the Face refused to talk. I then called on Crow King, a chief of the Uncpapas, Sitting Bull's tribe, and a noted warrior. He has a good face and wields great influence over the Indians. He is one of the few chiefs who speak well of Sitting Bull. After some little talk he came up to the fort and gave me his story.

CROW KING'S STORY OF THE FIGHT

We were in camp and not thinking there was any danger of a battle, although we had heard that the long-haired chief had been sent after us. Some of our runners went back on our trail, for what purpose I do not know. One came back and reported that an army of white soldiers was coming, and he had no more than reported when another runner came in with the same story, and also told us that the command had divided, and that one party was going round to attack us on the opposite side.

The first attack was at the camp of the Uncpapas tribe. The shots neither raised nor fell. (Here he indicated that the whites commenced firing at about four hundred yards distance.) The Indians retreated—at first slowly, to give the women and children time to go to a place of safety. Other Indians got our horses. By that time we had warriors enough to turn upon the whites and we drove them to the hill, and started back to camp.

Then the second band of white warriors came. We did not know who was their chief, but we supposed it was Custer's command. The party commenced firing at long range. (Indicating nearly a mile.) We had then all our warriors and horses. There were eighty warriors in my band. All the Sioux were there from everywhere. We had warriors plenty as the leaves on the trees. Our camp was as long as from the fort to the lower end of our camp here. (More than two and a half miles.) Sitting Bull and Crazy Horse were the great chiefs of the fight. Sitting Bull did not fight himself, but he gave orders. We turned against this second party. The greater portion of our warriors came together in their front and we rushed our horses on them. At the same time warriors rode out on each side of them and circled around them until they were surrounded. When they saw that they were surrounded they dismounted. They tried to hold on to their horses, but as we pressed closer they let go their horses. We crowded them toward our main camp and killed them all. They kept in order and fought like brave warriors as long as they had a man left. Our camp was on Greasy Grass river, (Little Big Horn.) When we charged every chief gave the cry, "Hi-yi-yi." (Here Crow Chief gave us the cry in a high, prolonged tone.)

When this cry is given it is a command to all the warriors to watch the chief, and follow his actions. Then every chief rushed his horse on the white soldiers, and all our warriors did the same, every one whipping another's horse. There was great hurry and confusion in the fight. No one chief was above another in that fight. It was not more than half an hour after the long-haired chief attacked us before he and all his men were dead.

Then we went back for the first party. We fired at them until the sun went down. We surrounded them and watched them all night, and at daylight we fought them again. We killed many of

The Hunkpapa Chief Crow King. Photo by D. F. Barry.

them. Then a chief from the Uncpapas called our men off. He told them those men had been punished enough, that they were fighting under orders, that we had killed the great leader and his men in the fight the day before, and we should let the rest go home. Sitting Bull gave this order. He said: "This is not my doings, nor these men's. They are fighting because they were commanded to fight. We have killed their leader. Let them go. I call on the Great Spirit to witness what I say. We did not want to fight. Long Hair sent us word that he was coming to fight us, and we had to defend ourselves and our wives and children." If this command had not been given we could have cut Reno's command to pieces, as we did Custer's. No warrior knew Custer in the fight. We did not know him, dead or alive. When the fight was over the chiefs gave orders to look for the long-haired chief among the dead, but no chief with long hair could be found. (Custer had his hair cut short before starting on this march.)

Crow King said that if Reno had held out until Custer came and then fought as Custer did, that they would have whipped the Indians. The Indians would then have been compelled to divide

Gall's Warriors Gathering for the Final Rush. From an original painting by
Linde Berg in the Karl May Indian Museum, Dresden, Germany.

to protect their women and children, and the whites would have had the advantage. He expressed great admiration for the bravery of Custer and his men, and said that that fight impressed the Indians that the whites were their superiors and it would be their destruction to keep on fighting them. Both he and Low Dog said that they did not feel that they would be blamed for the Custer fight or its results. It was war; they were attacked; Custer tried to kill them; they killed him.

Crow King said he had two brothers killed in the fight; that from thirty to fifty Indians were killed, and a much larger number, who were wounded, died afterward.

I also had a talk with Hump, chief of the Minnecongoes,* and said to have a larger following than any other chief in the camp.

HUMP'S STORY OF THE CUSTER FIGHT

The sun was about at meridian when the fight began. (This he indicated by pointing; the Indians have no division of time corresponding to our hours.) That was the first we knew that the white warriors were coming. They attacked the Uncpapas first. They were at the upper end of our camp. The Minnecongoes, Sans-Arcs and Cheyennes were near the center of the camp, but nearer the end of the camp furthest from where the attack was made. The charge was from the upper end of the camp. The Indians gave way slowly, retreating until they got their horses and got mounted. Just as soon as they got sufficient force—for our warriors were rushing to help them as fast as they could—they drove the white war-

* A variant of Minneconjous.

riors back, and they retreated. These were Reno's men. I had a horse that I could not manage. He was not mine, and was not well broke; so I went to where the horses were, and the women and the old men and boys were gathering them together, and caught a horse that I could manage better, and when I had caught him and mounted, the other party of white warriors (Custer's forces) charged. The Indians had by that time all got together, and it seemed, the way Custer came, that he started to cut off our retreat, not appearing to know where Reno was, or that he had retreated. When the Indians charged on the long-haired chief and his men, the long-haired chief and his men became confused, and they retreated slowly, but it was no time at all before the Indians had the long-haired chief and his men surrounded. Then our chiefs gave the "Hi-yi-yi" yell, and all the Indians joined, and they whipped each other's horses, and they made such short work of killing them, that no man could give any correct account of it. The first charge the Indians made they never slacked up or stopped. They made a finish of it. The Indians and whites were so mixed up that you could hardly tell anything about it.

The first dash the Indians made my horse was shot from under me and I was wounded—shot above the knee, and the ball came out at the hip (here the interpreter said that he had seen the scar), and I fell and lay right there. The rest of the Indians kept on on horseback, and I did not get in the final fight. It was a clear day. There was no storm nor thunder nor lightning. The report was that it was the long-haired chief that came to fight us, but that was all that we knew.

I know that Sitting Bull was in the fight, but

on account of my wound I did not know anything he did. Every able-bodied Indian there took part in the fight, as far as I could tell. Those that did not join in the fight it was because they could not find room to get in. There were a good many agency Indians in our camp. They all took part in the fight, same as the hostiles. The agency Indians had come out, and all made report to us that Long-Hair was coming to fight us. So the Indians all got together that he might not strike small parties, and not for the purpose of fighting or counciling with Long-Hair what he was coming for, but they were getting ready to be strong to defend themselves.

IRON THUNDER'S STORY

Iron Thunder, brother to Hump, and one year younger—Hump is 34 and Iron Thunder 33 years old—then told his story. He said:

We were encamped on the west side of the Little Big Horn. On the upper side of the camp was a small ash grove, and the camp was strung along from the grove more than two miles down the river. The tepees were close together, one band adjoining another all the way down. I did not know anything about Reno's attack until his men were so close that the bullets went through the camp, and everything was in confusion. The horses were so frightened we could not catch them. I was catching my horse to join the fight. When I caught him and was mounted, our warriors had driven the white men off and were running after them. Then I followed the way they went, and I saw a lot of horsemen—Indians—crossing the river, and went after them. I followed them across the river, and before I overtook them, going up the hill, I found an Indian lying there dead. I knew him. He and I were sworn friends. I stopped to look at him. The whites were still firing back at us. Just as I arrived where our men were, the report came to us that another party was coming to attack us. We could not see them from where we were. The report was that they were coming to head off the women and children from the way they were going, and so we turned around and went towards them. Our men moved around in the direction of a circle, but I cut across to a knoll and looked up the river and saw them coming down. The day before the fight I had come back from a war party against the Crows. I had only one horse, and his feet were worn out (the Indians do not shoe their horses, and they often give out on long marches), and by the time I got half-way back to where Long-Haired Chief and his men were my horse was so lame I could go no further. I

was nearly two miles away when the Indians charged Long-Haired Chief and his warriors. You could not notice the difference in the sun from the time when Custer was charged until he was done away with. Agency Indians, Yanktons and Santees were there. All took part. Every Indian took part in the fight that could, but there was such confusion that no one could tell the particulars of what was done.

———

LIEUTENANT EDGERLY of the Seventh Cavalry who was in Benteen's battalion, was present, and made the following comment: "I have heard the statements made by the chiefs and taken by you, and I believe that they told what they believed to be the truth."

FRANK HUSTON AND HIS COMMENTS

The late Frank H. Huston, whose comments on the 1881 stories of Low Dog, Hump and Crow King appear below, knew more about Indians—and in particular, the Sioux—than anyone with whom I ever came in contact. And he knew more about the battle of the Little Big Horn too, than anyone could know without having been there, or was very closely associated with the Indians who *were* there.

My acquaintance with him was largely through correspondence during the early 20's. He had been a frequent corresponding contributor to the "Camp Fire" section of the Adventure Magazine, which during the reign of Arthur Sullivant Hoffman as Editor, was easily the most valuable and informative debating ground for disputed points of western history to be found in any magazine. Hoffman was convinced, because of some of Huston's observations, that he was in the hostile camp during the battle, though he, of course, understandably enough, would not admit it.

His personal history was a sad one. A native of Richmond, Virginia, during the last years of the Civil War he was a youth doing a man's work in the ranks of Lee's army. When Richmond fell, his Mother, who had remained at the family home, was assaulted and beaten with rifle butts by drunken soldiers of Weitzel's command, who were the first to enter the city. She died as a result of her injuries and her son was never able even to locate her grave.

That this shocking tragedy embittered him is easy to understand; and shortly after the cessation of hostilities, he made his way West without taking the oath of allegiance, and joined the Sioux, determined "to even the score against the blue bellies," as did many others.

In March, 1925, he wrote me: "I differ with you on the point that the 'cognoscenti' of those days owe it to posterity to become garrulous. They were not exactly Sunday School scholars, you know. * * * I will not hint, nor will I talk, but as Hoffman knows, I was one of the bunch that helped Rain (Rain-in-the-Face) escape from the guard house. I saw Tom Custer kick and slap Rain while troopers held him a prisoner, and I got out of the Post Trader's before they came back to get *me*. I was a squaw man, yes; but I was not present at the Little Big Horn. I was 50 miles away headed thereto. But O— how I would have liked to have been there! Yet as a matter of fact, there *were* white men there; *not* with the Sioux, but with other nations present. Put yourself in their place. Would you, *then* or *now,* acknowledge it?

"As to prisoners; from '66 to '81, with some time off, I was mainly in tepees, and in all that time I never saw a *grown* male white taken prisoner, nor heard of one. There might have been, and probably were some, but I relate *my* experience as it was.

"I judge that Reno (as one of his 'skippers' later told me) became rattled, but he did not stampede, and saved his command by pushing up the bluffs. That the battalion *did* stampede I concede, but our people (i.e. the Indians) had 'put the fear of God' into the men. Reno's record in the War between the States refutes any accusation of cowardice; but he was ignorant of Indian methods of fighting and made a convenient 'goat'.

"Among the Sioux, Horse (i.e. Crazy Horse) ranked as senior (like a ranking Major General) of the four principal chiefs of an organization equivalent to the Medicine Lances of the Cheyennes. That is to say, he was of equal rank with the late Roman Nose, Red Cloud, Spotted Tail and others. He wore the long white 'stole' over his shoulders as insignia, and also to tie himself to his planted lance in a fight to the death.

"Bull (i.e. Sitting Bull) I think was a 'Water Pourer': only seven of them at a time amongst all the Lakotah Nation—equivalent to Cardinals of the Church of Rome. Magpi Luta (i.e. Red Cloud) also took that degree and became a sort of Richelieu.

"I find almost no one with a proper understanding of the attitude of Bull et al. As Tatanka (i.e. Sitting Bull) said: 'We ask only to be let alone.' (Kettle (i.e. Black Kettle) said the same). 'All we wish is that you yellow-faces keep out of our country. We don't want to fight you. This is *our* country. The Great Spirit gave it to us. Keep out and we will be friends.'

"While I believe that white men were with the Indians at the Little Big Horn, they were not with the Sioux, because Bull was 'peculiar' and at such times objected forcibly to the presence even of half-breeds—or 'breeds' as we termed them.

"The only purely white man I ever knew that really got under the Indian's skin and *understood* him, his point of view and reasoning, was Philo Clark of the 2d Cavalry. Crook did too; but Crook had Injun blood in him. Frank North understood how to handle them, but even he could not 'stand in their cumpaws' and shed his white preconceptions. Grouard, of course, was part Canuck, part Kanaka and practically an Indian himself. I think he married one of Bull's daughters, but that did not prevent Bull's chasing him out when hostilities prevailed. Bridger did also, and so did the negro Beckworth, but I never met either of them.

"Although somewhat addicted to snobbishness, yet I hate *pretense,* and George Custer has always been anathema to me. His massacre of Kettle's band on the Washita was a fitting supplement to Sand Creek where Kettle's first abuse by whites occurred."

———

The above, and much more, is in the letters of this man who boasted that he was an "Unreconstructed Reb," and who had no good word for any man who wore the blue. Peace to his ashes! But he knew the plains Indians of the 70's, sympathized with them, lived with them: and though he denied that he fought with them, how else did he go about it to "even up the score"? His comments, which follow, are therefore valuable.

HUSTON'S COMMENTS

It is well to remember that the Minnesota affair was yet vivid in the minds of the people, and I doubt if any expected or hoped that the participants in the Custer fight would be treated otherwise than *Little Crow's* people were. That will account for many conflicting stories, denials, and minimizing of important details. Then the desire to placate the conquerors was strong.

Bull had enemies. What strong successful man has not?

Interpreters often rendered "Big Warrior" as "Big Chief."

Even *Rain* was never made a chief, but he *did* have all the *influence* of one, but not the *power*. The word "Chief" is too loosely used by whites.

Leaders or heads of bands were called Chiefs, *by whites* who were ignorant of the fact that these men were *officers* of the military orders and *as such* were chiefs. English rendition of word more comprehensive than Indian.

Friendship was a stronger and closer tie than blood kinship, and it is a human trait to exalt a friend and conceal any possible incriminating acts of his, as also to deprecate an enemy, personal or general. This was done. After a while they got "fed up" on questions and would say what they thought the questioners would be pleased at, or tell any old thing to be rid of the impositive and everlasting queries. This had a greater bearing on the stories than people realize.

Low Dog's casualty list, *I think*, only covers his own band.

As to *Bull's* cowardice: he had as much place in a battle as Gen. Pershing would have had in a trench raid. His job was to make medicine to make the hearts and actions of his people "strong" during a fight as well as before. As a Strong-Heart he had fought well and taken horses and scalps. After he became a Medicine Man, he was to fight *only in great emergencies.*

The Hi-yi-yi—was the Cheyenne war cry. "Hi-yi-yi" like a scared kioodles yipping. Man! but it could stir ones blood.

Crow King's account (mentally edited by him) is good except that they knew the Yank command had divided. This I doubt as I was told Custer's attack was a surprise. *Rain* told me and as he and I were friends I believe it. *Crow's* statement that if Custer had joined Reno the Indians would have been whipped is all "bullcon", told to please the querist. Not an Indian there but was confident that Bull's prophesy would be fulfilled and that they could lick all hell and creation.

Hump's story I like best as to the Custer end; "no man could give any account of it." "They never slacked up—they made a finish of it." They *did*.

You have been in battle. If a melee, then you know how everything is confusion like a disturbed ants nest, or a pig in a girl's boarding school, "only more so." If you go into a fight, highly confident of your ability to whip ten times your weight in wounded wild cats and suddenly find the shoe is on the other foot, then you may get a true idea of "Le Grand Poseur" and his command. I had the esteemed pleasure once of hearing him remark "No enlisted man should ever be made an officer; they bring the barrack room air into the quarters." Had he said "some" I would have concurred. Consider Mike Sheridan, Maj. O'Hara, et al.

Gall, I class as our *Jackson* and your *Grant,* but not steadfast. He was jealous of *Bull*. Put *Horse* as *Hancock,* not quite equal to *Stuart*.

I note that the *Cheyenne* are classed as a Sioux "tribe". Wrong. Newspaper and scientific sharps statements doubtless.

I *think* that some chiefs wanted to remain and fight Terry but that *Bull* said that the signs were inauspicious, so they packed up and got. Scouts and others hastening to join, came in and reported "heap many" coming, with two bang guns. ("They speak twice": artillery using shells). The *Blackfeet Sioux* were a small unimportant band that must not be confounded with the *Blackfoot Nation*. The same holds good regarding the *Gros Ventres* (Grow Vaunts). One bunch were *Arapajo* stock, the other, around Ft. Berthold, were Crows. G. Vt. of Prairie were the Blue Cloud stock.

My theory is that the Arapajo were descendants of Phoenecians, Tirepihu—trader: could write a book on it. I believe the Cheyenne of Norse ancestry, but all pure theory. Europe and Asia uniting with aboriginal America to form the Indian, lots of corroborative indications towards it.

I believe the Maridans Welsh basis, either Ericson or Madoc: prefer former as allied blood of Sanier(?) i.e. Algonquin.

Much to support these theories.

THE NARRATIVE OF MRS. SPOTTED HORN BULL

ONE of the most interesting and graphic eyewitness accounts of the battle is that of Mrs. Spotted Horn Bull, the cousin of Sitting Bull—a woman of the Hunkpapa * Sioux noted for her intelligence and her eloquence. Her story first appeared in the St. Paul *Pioneer Press* of May 19, 1883, at which time she was accompanied by her husband, an active participant in the combat.

The story is important because in 1886, she repeated its substance to General Godfrey, who in the 1908 revision of his 1892 "Century" article, several times refers to this Indian woman as a corroborator of Chief Gall, who took Godfrey over the battlefield during the 1886 reunion, and pointed out to him the ground over which Custer's troops maneuvered; explained to him how and where the Indians met his advance, and demonstrated the manner in which they first repulsed, then surrounded, and quickly exterminated his entire command.

---

* Variant of Uncpapa.

Mrs. Spotted Horn Bull, full cousin of Sitting Bull.

It is important too, because twenty-five years later, when 60 to 65 years of age, she again retold the story to Major James McLaughlin, a former Indian Agent at Standing Rock who knew her well; and who set forth the tale in her own words in his great work "My Friend the Indian," first published in 1910.

Here is the story in its original form, told when her memory was fresh, the events of which she spoke but seven years past, and while her warrior husband, who was killed with Sitting Bull in 1890, was still in his prime, and sitting beside her, aided in the narration.

MR. AND MRS. SPOTTED-HORN-BULL RELATE THE STORY OF RENO'S RE-TREAT AND CUSTER'S CALAMITY

* * *

SUCCINCT AND CREDIBLE ACCOUNT OF THE DAYS PRECEDING THE FATAL TWENTY-FIFTH OF JUNE

* * *

HOW THEY DIED AND WHERE—HE SAVED HIS LAST SHOT—A SQUAW'S DIAGRAM.

The *Pioneer Press* is enabled to give an account of the day from the lips of a pair of Uncpapas, who know as much about it as any living beings. The pair are Tatanka-he-gle-ska and his wife, and it is boldly asserted that a smarter woman does not breathe among the Sioux today than Mrs. Spotted-horn Bull, for such is the translation of the far more euphonious Lakotah.

The Scene and the Story

In the comfortable parlor of Maj. McLaughlin's agency residence, not many nights ago, the hour nearly midnight, and the air outside cold as the glance of a hostile's eye, sat the Major and his wife, Mr. and Mrs. Spotted-horn Bull and the *Pioneer Press* correspondent. Maj. McLaughlin had already heard in part the story which the Indians had to tell; but the recountal, after adroit questioning, was given in full—Mrs. McLaughlin, whose knowledge of Sioux is perfect, interpreting. The woman did nearly all the talking, and her husband—a swarthy Uncpapa, of powerful frame and a reputation for bravery second to none—was evidently proud of his wife's intelligence and ability as a raconteur. The wife, dressed in clean and bright colored calico, with the usual broad leather belt thickly studded with brass nails, encircling what was left her of waist, with bright copper complexion, brighter eyes, twinkling now and then with mirth, but gleaming sometimes with the ferocity which makes the roused Sioux squaw a terror to her own camp, with glistening rows of perfect teeth—rare in an Indian woman over thirty—was a rather pleasing picture. The Major (all Indian agents have the title by courtesy and custom) prefaced the talk by saying that the woman is the full cousin of Sitting Bull and one of the best known individuals in her nation. Only a few days before she had soundly whipped the redoubtable Gall, and prevented him from throwing away one wife, a relative of her own, and taking another. It turned out later that her story of the Little Big Horn had been often told, and Sitting Bull, in whose regard she held, and holds, high place, had nodded many an assent to her related remembrances. It is impossible to describe how animatedly the woman spoke. Her gestures were constant and varied, and such a reader of signs as Philo Clark of Sheridan's staff could almost have translated her story from her fingers. But to the dual tale, thus syllabized:

Sitting Bull Makes Medicine

Eleven days before the Custer fight the Sioux were encamped some distance from the Little Big Horn (known to them as the Greasy Grass) and a solemn sun dance was held, traces of which were afterwards seen by the troops. Though long ago absolved from partaking of its pains and penalties, Sitting Bull, the medicine man and counsellor more than the warrior, was one of those tied to the pole of suffering, and the pierced muscles of his breast still show the scars of that dire observance. One by one the others broke their bonds or succumbed to pain and fasting, but he—not trying especially to tear away—seemed rapt in study. Two days and two nights went by without a morsel of food or a drop of water passing his lips, and on the morning of the third day he fainted. During his trance his faithful squaws and friends—among them the narrator— forced food and drink between his lips, and when he revived, and strength returned, he told, most solemnly, of a dream in which it had been foreshadowed to him that his people were soon to meet Custer and his followers, and would annihilate them. Two mornings after this revelation, and seven before the Custer fight, just as dawn was breaking, a large force of Crows attacked the Sioux, and all day long the battle lasted. The fight could not have been a very hot one, since only seven of the Sioux were slain and the Crows succeeded in carrying away all but one of their dead when, beaten and discomfited, as they were toward evening, they retreated into the heights of the Wolf mountains. The Sioux were not particularly proud of their victory, which they considered as dearly bought, and, though Mrs. Tatanka said the Crows numbered thousands, her husband grunted a stomachic dissent. The next morning the Sioux encampment was broken and moved to the fertile valley of the Little Big Horn, to the spot now historic, about fourteen miles south of the present Fort Custer (located at the junction of the Big Horn and the Little Big Horn rivers) and as nearly as the speaker could recollect, about thirty miles from the scene of the Crow fight.

The Plan of the Hostile Camp

The bodies of the seven Sioux had been brought to the new encampment on travoix and were placed in a tepee on the extreme right, or south, of the town of tepees, which soon spread for nearly five miles along the river, and on its western bank. The correspondent had visited the battlefield in August, 1882, and was familiar with the lay of the land and the salient points of the locality. To test the accuracy of Mrs. Tatanka's memory, she was plied with questions, every one of which she answered readily, and finally, drawing herself up with dignity, said:

"Why shouldn't I know the place? It is a part of my country."

Like most of the Sioux she possesses deftness

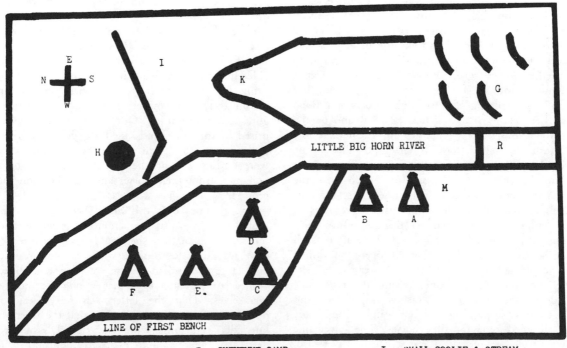

A - BLACKFEET CAMP	E - CHEYENNE CAMP	I - SMALL COOLIE & STREAM
B - UNCAPAPA CAMP	F - MINNECONJOUX CAMP	K - HIGH POINT OF BLUFF
C - OGALLALA & SANS ARC CAMP	G - RENO'S BREASTWORKS	M - WHERE McINTOSH DIED
D - BRULE CAMP	H - CUSTER MONUMENT	R - RENO'S RETREAT CROSSING

Sketch map of the battlefield. Originally drawn on a small card by Mrs. Spotted Horn Bull. First printed in the St. Paul Pioneer Press (1883) in delineating, and taking a visiting card and pencil, and with occasional references to her husband, she drew the appended diagram, saying, as she did so, it would serve to make her story clear, and supplementing it later with a rough sketch of all the streams in the surrounding country, from the Missouri on the north to the Little Missouri on the east.

Explanations of the Ground

Asked as to the number of warriors the seven tribes mentioned mustered at the time, the narrator was unable to give a definite estimate, but her husband after a lengthy and—to a white man—abstruse calculation, said 5,000 would cover the braves and chiefs. This number is probably correct or nearly so, as it agrees with computations of the best posted scouts who saw the encampment before and after the fight. As the diagram shows, the river runs nearly north at the scene of the fight. The ground on the west bank, where the Indians were camped, is level, and the five tribes on the north were on the flat near the river, the other two being on the first bench— a rise of from four to six feet—while above them to the west and south the plain extends. On the east side of the river, where the troops approached, the hills are precipitous and at G, where Reno threw up his shallow earthworks, the height above the river—here an easily fordable stream so far as depth is concerned—an altitude of at least 200 feet is attained. The point K, is the extremity of the highest ground, and to its peak Capts. Benteen and Weir rode before joining Reno, but could see nothing of Custer. The spot where Reno crossed on his retreat is marked as R and on the plain leading thereto, marked M, Lieutenant McIntosh was pulled from his horse and killed, while Hodgson lost his life in the ford. The descent into the river from the side on which were the Indians, is over a bank only a few feet in sheer height, but on the bluff side the shore rises at an angle of more than 45 degrees. Only thoroughly panic-stricken troops could have scaled such an acclivity, and the reason all were not killed is explained by Mrs. Tatanka later, when she tells of the counter panic among the reds. The ride up the hills to the breast works is steep, but not markedly so, and the retreating troops made it in good time for tired horses. The lower line is intended to indicate the first bench. Riverward, below it, is a moderately dense chapparal of willows and cottonwoods. On the plain above, trees are few. Where Custer fell, H, the ground is high and treeless but rolling, and the descent to the river is not as steep as farther south. The

line marked I indicates a coolie in which in June water runs, but later in the year it is perfectly dry.

June Twenty-fifth

The Indian woman continued her account, after drawing the diagram and explaining the positions of the various camps, by saying that very early in the morning of the day of the fight (June 25) seven Cheyennes started southeast to join Spotted Tail. Five of them, it would seem, got through all right, but early in the morning two rode to the brow of the bluffs and signaled with their blankets that white troops in large numbers were advancing rapidly. The troops seen by the scouts were Custer's, for immediately after the signalling, and while the camp was in commotion, Reno's command came up, unseen by most of the Indians, from the south and on the western side of the river, and opened fire. The white men were dismounted and the narrator told how one man was left behind to take care of four horses, as is the custom in dismounted fighting on the frontier. The camp, as said, was in the wildest commotion and women and children shrieked with terror. More than half the men were absent after the pony herd. The story teller waxed excited as she said:

"The man who led those troops must have been drunk or crazy. He had the camp at his mercy, and could have killed us all or driven us away naked on the prairie. I don't believe there was a shot fired when his men commenced to retreat. (Her husband qualified this by saying, "Not much firing by the Indians.") But when they began to run away they ran very fast, and dropped their guns and ammunition. Our braves were not surprised by this time, and killed a good many when they crossed the plain to the river, while they were fording and on the hill beyond. I saw boys pull men from their horses and kill them on the ground."

Several times over this Sioux Scheherazade repeated her disgust at the action of the whites and the only explanation she could give for the retreat was that Reno saw, when he got into it, how large the Indian village was and was seized with a panic greater than that among the Indians themselves. That the latter was very decided, however, was proven by the fact that the warriors hurriedly returning with the quickly rounded herds, met many fugitives from the camp and feared the worst on their own return.

Custer Comes Up

The Reno retreat and its consequent slaughter was scarcely ended before the blare of Custer's trumpets told the Sioux of his approach. But they were prepared for him. The men quickly crossed the river, and by hundreds galloped to his rear, out of range at first, but taking advantage of coolie and mound, soon hemming him in constantly narrowing circles. Mrs. Tatanka mounted her pony and rode to the first bench behind her camp, where she could get a good view of the hills beyond. She saw the troops come up, dismount, each fourth man seize the bridles of three horses beside his own, the rest deploy and advance on the run toward the river. She saw the terrible effect of the withering fire which greeted the approach from the willows on the Indian side of the stream, and laughed as she said:

"Our people, boys and all, had plenty of guns and ammunition to kill the new soldiers. Those who ran away left them behind."

Slowly trotting north, along the outskirts of the encampment, she noted the Indians who had crossed, getting closer to the troops. She watched the latter—those who were left of them—retreat to their horses and mount; she heard the yells of her kindred and the shouts of the whites; but soon, as the former grew plentier and the latter fewer, she could distinguish little, save here and there an animated cluster of men and horses. Slowly her pony jogged down the stream, and she reached the Minneconjou camp on the extreme left—not an hour's ride—she said not one white soldier was visible on the field. Of horses there were plenty. These the Indians spared, of course. Tatanka himself, describing the animals, said they were fat and good looking, but (making a slow motion up and down with both hands) could only canter slowly, while the Indian ponies, "like birds," flitted in and through and about the troopers' broken lines. Less than fifty minutes and more than five lives to the minute!

He Might Have Lived

From the husband was learned one incident of the day. One man, he thought an officer, was the last to live. He was mounted on a splendid horse (the color was forgotten), and seeing all his comrades dead, started up the ravine marked I in the diagram. Two Ogalallas, two Uncpapas and a Brule, all well mounted, started after him. He gained on them all, and one by one dropped off until the Uncpapa, who was unarmed, as it turned out, alone pursued. The latter was about to give up the chase, when the soldier turned, saw his pursuer, noted that his own horse was flagging, drew a revolver from the holster at his hip and blew his own brains out.

"He had a good horse," concluded Tatanka, "and the Sioux (mentioning his Indian name) rode him for years after that."

The Sioux thought the distance ridden by pursuer and pursued was about seven miles from the battlefield, but it might have been more. Lieut. Harrington's body was never found, or at least never recognized, and this sad suicide might have been he.

After the Battle

Custer and his command killed, the Sioux again turned their attention to the troops on the hill and the woman, resuming the story, laughed gleefully as she told what fun the bucks had shooting at the soldiers as they ran that terrible gauntlet, down the hill to the river, for water. The Custer men were soon stripped, of course, and the only way the Indians knew they had killed the Long-Haired Chief was by his buckskin coat trimmed with beaver, which they found on his person. The Sioux lost thirty killed and more than twice as many wounded. Among the killed were boys of twelve and fourteen, who, in the ardor of young warriorhood, rushed across the river on their ponies and into the thickest of the fight. She mentioned two boys who were wounded; one, a young Achilles, in the heel, and another in the right arm, which was shot off. Both recovered and neither of them are yet twenty, though seven years have passed since they counted their first coups. It was with a tone of most noticeable regret that the woman told of the quantities of bank notes found and wasted, being utterly ignorant of the value of the, to them, curiously painted parallelograms of green paper. She naively said:

"We know better about them now, and wouldn't lose them as we did at that time."

Of course, feasting and laudation was the order of the day and night succeeding the slaughter, but the news of Terry's approach with his command compelled a hasty breaking up of the camp. She says they marched day and night for several days, and soon the whole band was safe in the fastnesses of the Big Horn mountains, where they remained some time before a separation took place, and the Uncpapas and portions of other tribes went north. The squaw's story was told straight-forwardly and beyond question she believes it true, every word. Neither she nor her husband had the slightest idea the account was to be published, and the appearance of a pencil and note book would have been the signal for a sudden cessation of the flow of conversation. The correspondent was introduced as a friend by Maj. McLaughlin, and the recountal was given as one which would interest, but was of no special moment to the hearers. To the question whether the bodies of the Custer command were much mutilated, the woman said, almost angrily, "He-ya! he-ya!" (No! No!) but afterward acknowledged that a good many scalps were taken.

The story as recorded by Major McLaughlin during 1908-9, told in the first person, is translated as nearly as may be from "the far more euphonious Lakotah." A long recital, filled with dramatic imagery so characteristic of Indian speech, it differs but slightly in substance, from the *Pioneer Press* report of 1883. Her placement of the various tribal circles is not quite the same, nor does she mention the seven Cheyennes who left the camp in the early morning of June 25, two of whom returned to signal from the heights across the river, the approach of Custer's troops. Her later version says that Custer's column was first discovered when six to eight miles distant, by some women and children who were digging Indian turnips on the east side of the river. As in the *Pioneer Press* story, she makes it clear that Reno's attack was a complete surprise, which, had it been both timely and pressed home, might well have crippled the power of the Sioux; but Reno attacked prematurely, before Custer was within striking distance, thus enabling the Indians to concentrate on Reno first; and having routed him, on Custer, whose command was met with overwhelming force and soon obliterated.

She thus describes Reno's combat in the valley:

"Like * * * fire * * * driven by a great wind * * * the men of the Hunkpapa, the Blackfeet, the Ogalallas and the Minneconjou rushed through the village and into the trees, where the soldiers of the white chief had stopped.

"If the soldiers had not fired until all of them were ready for the attack; if they had brought their horses and rode into the camp of the Sioux, the power of the Dakota nation might have been broken, and our young men killed in the surprise, for they were watching Long Hair only. * * *

* * *

But the Great Spirit was watching over his red children. He allowed the white chief (Reno) to strike too soon, and the braves of the Sioux ran over his soldiers and beat them down as corn before the hail. They fought a few minutes, and the men * * * bore them down and slew many of them—all who did not get across the river we killed, and Long Hair was still three miles away.

* * * Two score of the bluecoats lay dead upon the field, and our people took their guns and many cartridges. * * * The shadow of the sun had not moved the width of a tepee pole's length from the beginning to the end of the first fight."

Her vivid portrayal of the Indian attack that engulfed Custer like the sweep of a tidal wave is dramatic in the extreme; and to receive the full impact of her powerful story, one must read it in its entirety. Even so compact an outline as that which follows leaves the reader tense. Here, in quotation which perforce omits all but the core of the recital, is what she said:

"Down the Greasy Grass river * * * over across from the camps of the Cheyennes and the Sans Arcs, there is an easy crossing * * *. From Long Hair's movements the Sioux warriors knew that he had planned to strike the camp of my people from the lower end as Reno struck it from the upper end. Even the women * * * saw that Reno had struck too early * * *.

"From a hill behind the camp at first, and then from the bank of the river, I watched the men of our people plan to overthrow the soldiers of the Great Father; and before a shot was fired, I knew that no man who rode with Long Hair would go back to tell the tale of the fight that would begin when the soldiers approached the river * * *.

"From across the river I could hear the music of the bugle and could see the column of soldiers turn to the left, to march down to the river to where the attack was to be made. All I could see was the warriors of my people. They rushed like the wind through the village, going down the ravine as the women went out to the grazing ground to round up the ponies. It was done very quickly. * * *

"Our chiefs and the young men rode quickly down to the end of the village, opposite to the hill upon which now stands the great stone put up by the whites where Long Hair fell. Between that hill and the soldiers was a ravine which started from the river opposite the camp of the Sans Arcs, and ran all the way around the butte. To get to the butte Long Hair must cross the ravine; but from where he was marching with his soldiers, he could not see into the ravine nor down to the banks of the river. The warriors of my people * * * had joined * * * on our side of the Greasy Grass and opposite the opening into the ravine. Soon I saw a number of Cheyennes ride into the river, then some men of my band, then others, until there were hundreds of warriors in the river and running up into the ravine. When some hundreds had passed the river and gone into the ravine, the others who were left, still a very great number, moved back from the river and waited for the attack. And I knew that the fighting men of the Sioux, many hundreds in number, were hidden in the ravine behind the hill upon which Long Hair was marching, and he would be attacked from both sides * * *.

"Pizi (Gall) and many of his young men had re-crossed the Greasy Grass River after the white men had been driven off or killed in the earlier engagement * * * where he with some of our warriors had been shooting at the soldiers, who were chased to the hill, * * *. When Pizi (Gall) re-crossed the river, many women followed his party, and we heard him tell his men to frighten the horses of the soldiers, which were held in small bunches. With shoutings that we could hear across the river, the young men stampeded the horses and the women captured them * * *. The Indians fought the soldiers with bullets taken from the first party that attacked the village, and many rode the horses captured from the white men, who had fled to the hill. * * * I remained with many other women along the bank of the Greasy Grass River. I saw Crazy Horse lead the Cheyennes into the water and up the ravine; Crow King and the Hunkpapa went after them; and then Gall, who had led his young men and killed the soldiers he had been fighting further up the river, rode along the bench by the river to where Long Hair had stopped with his men.

"I cannot remember the time. * * * The river was in sight from the battle, and while the whoop still rung in our ears, two Cheyennes tried to cross the river and one of them was shot and killed by Long Hair's men. Then the men of the Sioux nation, led by Crow King, Hump, Crazy Horse, and many chiefs, rose up on all sides of the hill, and the last we could see from our side of the river was a great number of gray horses. The smoke of the shooting and the dust of the horses shut out the hill, and the soldiers fired many shots, but the Sioux shot straight and the soldiers fell dead. The women crossed the river after the men of our village, and when we came to the hill there were no soldiers living and Long Hair lay dead among the rest. There were more than two hundred dead soldiers on the hill, and the boys of the village shot many who were already dead, for the blood of the people was hot and their hearts bad, and they took no prisoners that day."

I asked her if there was any more fighting.

"Not much. The men on the hill (Reno's) were safe to stay there until they wanted water. Gall kept his men along the river. Some of the soldiers were shot as they tried to reach the water. There was some fighting too, but none of our young men were killed.

"That night the Sioux men, women and children, lighted many fires and danced; their hearts were glad, for the Great Spirit had given them a great victory. * * * All night the people danced and sang their songs of victory, and they were strong in their might and would have attacked the soldiers who lay through the night on what you call Reno Hill, but Gall and Crow King and Crazy Horse would waste no lives of the Sioux braves. They said 'We will shoot at them occasionally, but not charge. They will fall into our hands when the thirst burns in their throats and makes them mad for drink.'

"This was the counsel of the chiefs, and the young men saw that it was good; so while many feasted, a few held the hill and the soldiers did not know it, for of those who stole to the river to drink, none went back alive. There was fighting the next day, but the Sioux knew early in the day that many soldiers were coming up from the north, and preparations were made to leave for new hunting grounds. * * * Since the Sioux first fought the men who are our friends now, they had not won so great a battle and at so little cost. Twenty-two dead were counted, and the price was not great, * * *.

"So it was that the Sioux defeated Long Hair and his soldiers in the valley of the Greasy Grass River, which my people remember with regret, but without shame."

THE STORY OF WAR CHIEF GALL OF THE UNCPAPAS

(From a contemporary Chicago newspaper, June 26, 1886)

OBSERVANCE OF THE TENTH ANNIVERSARY OF THE BATTLE OF THE LITTLE BIG HORN

CHIEF GALL, WHO COMMANDED THE HOSTILES, DESCRIBES THE TERRIFIC SLAUGHTER

The Soldiers Killed While Fighting in Line Against a Vastly Superior Force

History Corrected

CUSTER BATTLE-FIELD, Montana, June 25.—[Special.]—The tenth anniversary of the dark and bloody tragedy, which will be a gloomy page in

The War Chief Gall, in winter clothing. Photo by
D. F. Barry. Denver Public Library Western Collection.

American history, was today appropriately celebrated by a few of the survivors of that dreadful June day. Early in the day the great Sioux Chief Gall went over the entire field and described in an intelligent and straightforward manner the exact place in which Custer's command was destroyed. Curley, the Crow scout, who was in reality the only survivor of all who marched into the valley of the Little Big Horn with Custer, was also present, but Gall turned his back on Curley and said: "He ran away too soon in the fight." Gall is a powerful, fine-looking specimen of the red race, 46 years old, and weighs over two hundred pounds. He first appeared reticent, and was

inclined to act sullen, but when he stood on the spot which formed the last sight of Custer on earth his dark eyes lightened with fire, he became earnestly communicative, and he told all he knew without restraint. His dignified countenance spoke truthfulness, and there is little doubt but that the true history of that dreadful day is at last made known.

Gall's Narrative

was as follows: "We saw the soldiers early in the morning crossing the divide. When Reno and Custer separated, we watched them until they came down into the valley. A cry was raised that the white men soldiers were coming, and orders were given for the village to move immediately. Reno swept down so rapidly on the upper end that the Indians were forced to fight. Sitting Bull and I were at the point where Reno attacked. Sitting Bull was big medicine. The women and children were hastily moved down stream where the Cheyennes were camped. The Sioux attacked Reno, and the Cheyennes, Custer, and then all became mixed up. The women and children caught the horses for the bucks to mount them; the bucks mounted and charged back Reno and checked him, and

Drove Him Into the Timber

The soldiers tied their horses to trees and came out and fought on foot. As soon as Reno was beaten and driven back across the river, the whole force turned upon Custer and fought him until they destroyed him. Custer did not reach the river, but was met about half a mile up a ravine, now called Reno creek. They fought the soldiers and beat them back step by step until all were killed."

One of Reno's officers confirms this by saying: "After we were driven back to the hill where the stand was made, there was an interval of over an hour that we had no fighting. This gave us an opportunity to shelter our horses in a ravine and partially intrench ourselves. It was probably during this interval of quiet on Reno's part that the Indians massed on Custer and annihilated him."

The Indians ran out of ammunition and their arrows they fired from behind their horses. The soldiers got shells stuck in their guns and had to throw them away. They then fought with little guns—pistols. The Indians were in coulees behind and in front of Custer as he moved up the ridge to take position, and were just

As Many As the Grass

"The first two companies, Keogh and Calhoun, dismounted, and fought on foot. They never broke, but retired step by step until forced back to the ridge upon which all finally perished. They were shot down in line where they stood. Keogh's company rallied by company and were all killed in a bunch."

This statement seems borne out by the facts, as thirty-eight bodies of Keogh's troops were found piled in a heap. The warriors directed a special fire against the troopers who held the horses, while the others fought. As soon as a holder was killed, by moving blankets and great shouting the horses were stampeded, which made it impossible for the soldiers to escape. Afterward the soldiers fought desperately and hard, and

Never Surrendered

"They fought strong—they fought in line along the ridge. As fast as the men fell the horses were herded and driven toward the squaws and old men, who gathered them up. When Reno attempted to find Custer by throwing out a skirmish line, Custer and all with him were dead." When the skirmishers reached a high point overlooking Custer's field, the Indians were galloping around and over the wounded, dying, and dead, popping bullets and arrows into them. "When Reno made his attack at the upper end he killed my two squaws and three children, which made my heart bad. I then fought with the hatchet"—which means, of course, mutilating. "The soldiers ran out of ammunition early in the day. Their supply of cartridges was in the saddle-pockets of their stampeded horses. The Indians then ran up to the soldiers and butchered them with hatchets. A lot of horses ran away and jumped into the river, but were caught by the squaws. Eleven Indians were killed in Reno creek, and several Indians fell over and died. Only forty-three Indians were killed altogether, but a great many wounded ones came across the river and died in the rushes. Some soldiers got away, and ran down a ravine, crossed the river, came back again, and were killed. We had Ogalallas, Minneconjous, Brules, Teton; Uncpapa Sioux, Cheyennes, Arapahoes, and Gros Ventres. When

The Big Dust

came in the air down the river (meaning Terry and Gibbon), we struck our lodges and went up a creek toward the White Rain mountains. Big Horn ranges covered with snow. We waited there four days and then went over to Wolf mountains."

This ended Gall's narrative. It brings out many new facts and corrects some others. It has been popularly supposed that Custer entered the river, but such was not the case, as the bodies found on the Little Horn were those of a few stampeded soldiers. There were no ceremonies or exercises gone through with, simply an attempt, which was successful, to correct history.

A MORE COMPLETE REPORT

THE STORY OF CHIEF GALL

Fuller Details of the Recent Visit to the Custer Battlefield—The Old Chief Told the Truth

---

Many Erroneous Impressions Corrected—A Lucky Escape for Those Who Failed to Get There

---

(From the *St. Paul Pioneer Press,* 18 July 1886)

FORT CUSTER, Mont., Special Correspondence, July 14.—Much of the history connected with the true fate of Gen. Custer and those who marched with him into the valley of the Little Big Horn on that fateful June morning ten years ago would no doubt forever have remained a mystery had not Gall, the great Sioux chief who commanded on that day, consented to revisit the scene of the terrible disaster, and tell all he knew of it according to the red man's side of the case. Gall was captured at Poplar River in January, 1881, by Col. Guido Ilges, Fifth infantry, since dismissed from the service. He had three hostile villages there (a part of Sitting Bull's great band), and when he became a prisoner the war against the Sioux was virtually over. Gall has been at Standing Rock agency ever since, excepting, of course, the time he has spent junketing around the country as a sort of side show to some of the Wild West combinations, and has—so to speak—become a good Indian, only that he isn't dead yet. Gall is today the acknowledged head of the combined Sioux nation. Sitting Bull seeks to dispute the honor with him, but it is no go; for the Indians know the son of old Jumping Bull better than we do, and so do not take much stock in his fighting abilities. The history of Gall is a very eventful one. He has been at war with the whites off and on for thirty odd years, and the depredations committed by him, not to speak of the lives he has taken, if summed up, would fill many bloody pages in our country's history. This great war chief was once pursued by a detachment of soldiers near Fort Sully, Dak., sent out by Gen. J. N. G. Whistler, commanding that post, for the express purpose of capturing or killing him. He was overtaken on the prairie and killed— so it was supposed. Some half a dozen bullets had been lodged in his body, and he had been bayoneted as many times. While lying apparently dead on the field, a corporal who "knew him well" was about to give him a final prod with his bayonet when an officer came up just in time to stop the corporal in the act. The pointed steel was poised over Gall's heart, and in another minute the Indian would have been pinned to the ground but for the interference of the officer.

"Let me give him one more punch, Lieutenant, just for luck."

"No," replied the officer, "don't mutilate the dead. Leave him alone where he lies."

Strange as it may seem, that pitiful decision made so long ago sealed the fate of Gen. Custer years later, and that of the flower of the Seventh Cavalry. When the two white men had left the spot the wily redskin crawled off into the bushes, where he remained hid during daylight, and as soon as night came on he lost no time in joining his friends down the river.

He Told the Truth

Any one present with Gall at the Custer battle-field on the morning of June 25 last could see at a glance that the chief was telling the truth, the whole truth, and nothing but the truth. When he stood on the spot from which Custer gazed his last on earth, and glanced up and down the valley of the Little Big Horn, once tenanted with thousands of lodges belonging to his people, one could readily see that the old man was visibly affected, by his solemn mien and the suspicion of moisture in his dark, glittering eye. His gaze remained long and fixed on the little grove of timber which marked the point where Reno made his unsuccessful attack on the upper end of the village.

"What is it, Gall?" inquired one of the officers present. "Why do you look so earnestly in that direction?"

"My two squaws and three children were killed there by the pale-faced warriors, and it made my heart bad. After that I killed all my enemies with the hatchet."

Many new facts were brought to light by the visit of the chief who was the leading factor in the destruction of Custer and his troopers; and many popular errors were corrected which were about to go down into history as indisputable truths. The new points brought out were: That Sitting Bull personally had little or nothing to do with the fight. He was a medicine man of the Sioux, and was in his lodge at the time making medicine for the destruction of the whites and the success of the reds. As the battle (or massacre, whichever, you please) turned out favorably for the Indians and to the confusion of their enemies, Sitting Bull at once became the great medicine man of all the tribes, and was from that time forth a leading spirit among them. His prowess as a fighter is simply a creation of the white man's brain and nothing else. When the warriors sallied out to attack the troops, he was really left behind to make medicine and to look after the women and children. If he has any latent fighting qualities, or abilities as a great leader, his kinsmen don't know it, nor does anybody else. Crow King (who died at Standing Rock agency a few years ago) was really the adjutant general of the campaign, and Gall was unquestionably the leader who executed the details and led the young bucks on.

Another Error

Another correction was made of the popular error that Gen. Custer actually reached the Little Big Horn River, entered the same, and was beaten back when in mid stream. The command never did reach the river. In fact, they never came in sight of it again after descending the divide leading into the valley of the Little Big Horn. Gen. Custer was attacked fully three-quarters of a mile back from the river, near the crest of the ridge lining the coulee he was descending, and was forced back step by step, at right angles to his former course, to the summit now crowned by the battle monument where all finally perished. Gall went with the writer and pointed out the exact spot where Gen. Custer stood in person when he was attacked. The brave cavalry leader, some 300 or 400 yards ahead of his command, and alone with his orderly, was slowly descending this coulee toward the river; but when he came in sight of some Indians off to the left and near the high knoll where Benteen came in sight of the Custer field later on, his pace became slower and his actions more cautious, and finally he paused altogether to await the coming up of the command. This was the nearest point any of Custer's party ever got to the river. Gall says that he (Gall) had three Indians with him, and that he sat down on a mound some six hundred yards away, in full sight of the troops, and watched the soldiers file slowly down the ravine. Little did the poor fellows imagine they were marching to their death. Gall is of the opinion that when Custer slowed his pace and finally halted, the latter began to suspect he was in a bad scrape. From that time on Custer acted on the defensive. Poor Custer! He could have saved his well mounted command by flight, but such a thought was no doubt farthest from his mind in that trying moment. The false supposition that the soldiers were not seen until they crossed the divide was also corrected by Gall, who avers that both Reno and Custer had been watched for some hours before they separated to make their respective attacks. Neither Benteen with his three companies nor McDougall with the pack train had been spied else it had gone hard with them. Still another point was made clear in regard to the possible fortune of the day had the soldiers never divided, but made the attack together in one grand sweep down upon the village. The great war chief set all doubts at rest on this point by declaring that "his warriors were just as many as the grass;" and that the consequent result would have been that all would have been killed instead of only a portion. Therefore, whatever may be said of the cowardice of Reno, it is certain he acted wisely in remaining so close behind his trenches. Gall says that only two companies of Custer's command kept any sort of formation at all and from all that could be gathered from the Indian, coupled with what was read from the ground as from an open page, it would appear that Calhoun's men died fighting as skirmishers, while Keogh rallied his company, which was all killed in a bunch. The other companies broke, were shot down individually as they fled in confusion from the field. Considering the point where Custer was first attacked, it would also seem that Calhoun's and Keogh's troops were the first to fall, being nearest the original point of attack; and that Gen. Custer and the others, retreating step by step, were the last to die on the summit where the monument now stands. As a matter of fact, the true condition of affairs was exactly the opposite. The error would never have been cleared up had not Gall contradicted it flatly and positively. He says Calhoun, Keogh and Crittenden (the latter was with Calhoun and fell with him) were the last ones of all to die. When the broken companies fled in dismay to the high point with the intention of escaping over the other side, they were met by hordes of savages who had swarmed up that coulee, ready for the emergency which really did happen. Therefore, Custer personally and those with him were probably the very first ones to fall in the day, and Calhoun and Keogh, taken on both flanks, jammed in between two galling fires and numerous cross fires, and with all possible avenues of escape cut off, had nothing else to do but fight it out in line until the last trooper had fallen in his tracks. It was made clear that the Sioux, particularly the old men, women and young bucks, held Reno in check, while the Cheyennes did all the bloody work at the lower end of the field. Gall asserts with gravity that the Great Spirit was present riding over the field, mounted on a coal black pony and urging the braves on.

Some of Gall's Statements

The following are a few of the questions put to Gall as he rode over the field, with the answers given verbatim by him.

"How long before all the soldiers were killed?"

The chief made the sign of the white man's dinner time which means noon, and then with his finger cut a half, which would signify half an hour consumed in slaughtering everybody.

"Did the red men shoot guns or arrows?"

"Both. We soon shot all our cartridges, and then shot arrows and used our war clubs."

"Did the soldiers have plenty of ammunition?"

"No. They shot away all they had. The horses ran away, carrying in the saddle pockets a heap more. The soldiers threw their guns aside and fought with little guns." (Pistols.)

"Who got the horses?"

"The Cheyenne women. A lot of horses got into the river and I jumped in and caught them."

The chief's mind seemed to dwell particularly upon the number of horses they captured rather than the terrible slaughter which took place.

"Did the Indians fight standing up?"

"No. The soldiers did, but the braves fired from behind their horses. A lot of Indians fell over and died."

"When the soldiers had no more cartridges left what did the Indians do?"

"The braves ran up to the soldiers and killed them with hatchets."

"How many Indians were killed?"

"Eleven down in that creek, (now called Reno Creek) four over there and two in that coulee."

"How many were killed, altogether?"

"Forty-three in all. A great many crossed the river and died in the rushes. They died every day. Nearly as many died each day as were killed in the fight. We buried them in trees and on scaffolds going up Lodge Pole Creek toward the White Rain mountains."

"How many different tribes were in the fight?"

"Uncpapa, Minneconjou, Ogalalla, Brule, Teton, Santee and Yanktonnais Sioux, Blackfeet, Cheyennes, Arapahoes, and a few Gros Ventres."

"Who fought first, Custer or Reno?"

"Reno was whipped first and then all with Custer were killed."

Of course the chief did not understand the names Custer and Reno, but he indicated by pointing and other signs whom he meant.

"How soon after Reno charged did Custer come down the valley?"

"We saw all at one time before they separated. When Reno charged, the women and children were moved down stream: and when the Sioux bucks drove Reno on top of the bluffs, everybody came down and fought Custer. All the Indians were mixed up then."

"How soon after Reno charged was Custer attacked?"

No satisfactory answer could be gotten to this important question; but it would seem that as soon as Reno was lodged safely on the hill the whole village massed on Custer at once and annihilated him.

"Did Custer get near the river?"

"No."

"Then how came the dead bodies of soldiers on the river's bank where we think the white chief crossed or attempted to cross?"

Gall's answer came without a moment's hesitation.

"They were soldiers who fled down another coulee, crossed the river lower down, were chased up stream again toward the village, driven back into the river, and killed on this side."

"Where was Custer first attacked?"

This and other questions have been answered in the narrative above.

"Did the soldiers fight on horseback or on foot?"

"They fought on foot. One man held the horses while the others shot the guns. We tried to kill the holders, and then by waving blankets and shouting we scared the horses down that coulee, where the Cheyenne women caught them."

"Did you kill any soldiers?"

"Yes, I killed a great many. I killed them all with the hatchet; I did not use a gun."

"Who had command of all the red men?"

"I held command of those down stream."

"Who was the first one killed with Reno?"

"I don't know; but some of the Sioux say it was a Crow scout named Bloody Knife."

"Where was Sitting Bull all this time while the white soldiers were being killed?"

"Back in his tepee making medicine."

"Did he fight at all?"

"No; he made medicine for us."

"Did you fight Reno?"

"No; I only fought the white men soldiers down this way."

"Then you know nothing of what happened at the upper end of the village?"

"No, I was down among the Cheyennes looking after horses when the first attack was made on our village."

"Did the old men and boys fight too?"

"Yes, and the squaws fought with stone clubs and hatchet knives. The squaws cut off the boot legs."

"Were there any white men or breeds in your camp?"

"No; we had only Indians."

"Did the soldiers have swords?"

"No, there was only one long knife with them, and he was killed too."

"Who had the long knife?"

"I don't know."

"Did you see Curley on that day?" (Pointing out the Crow scout who is the only survivor of all who marched with Custer into the Little Big Horn valley.)

"No; but my braves say he ran away early and did not fight at all."

"Did you take any prisoners, and if so what did you do with them?"

This question was put to find out if possible the true fate of Lieutenants Harrington, Jack Sturgis, Dr. Lord, and about fourteen others whose bodies were not found on the field, nor has anything been heard of them since the morning when the command was divided.

"No, we took no prisoners. Our hearts were bad, and we cut and shot them all to pieces."

"Do you remember seeing Custer, the big chief, after the fight?"

"I saw the big chief riding with the orderly before we attacked. He had glasses to his face (field glasses). During the fight there were too many soldiers scattered all around for me to see him."

"Did any of the soldiers get away?"

"No, all were killed. About fourteen (indicating the number with his fingers) started toward the Wolf Mountains, but the young braves got on their trail and all were killed."

No doubt Harrington, Sturgis, Lord and the other missing ones were of this party endeavoring to escape toward the Wolf Mountains.

"What did you do after all Custer's soldiers were killed?"

We went back to fight the soldiers on the hill who were digging holes in the ground. We staid there until big dust was seen down the river, when we all moved up Lodge Pole Creek toward the White Rain Mountains. (Big Horn.)

GENERAL GODFREY'S COMMENT ON GALL'S STORY.

(From revised printing of "Custer's Last Battle")
GALL AT REUNION, 1886

IN this narrative of the movements immediately preceding, and resulting in, the annihilation of the men with Custer, I have related facts substantially as observed by myself or as given to me by Chief Gall of the Sioux. His statements have been corroborated by other Indians, notably the wife of Spotted Horn Bull, an intelligent Sioux Squaw, one of the first who had the courage to talk freely to any one who participated in the battle.

In 1886, on the tenth anniversary, an effort was made to have a reunion of the survivors at the battle-field. Colonel Benteen, Captains McDougall and Edgerly, Dr. Porter, Sergeant Hall, Trumpeter Penwell and myself met there on the 25th of June. Through the kind efforts of the officers and of the ladies at Fort Custer our visit was made as pleasant as possible. Through the personal influence of Major McLaughlin, Indian Agent at Standing Rock, Chief Gall was prevailed upon to accompany the party and describe Custer's part in the battle. We were unfortunate in not having an efficient and truthful interpreter on the field at the reunion. The statements I have used were, after our return to the agency, interpreted by Mrs. McLaughlin and Mr. Farribault, of the agency, both of whom are perfectly trustworthy and are familiar with the Sioux language.

At the reunion, 1886, a number of us were sitting near the monument asking questions of Gall. From the volubility of the answers by the interpreter nearly all, including Gall, became satisfied that the interpreter was "padding" and I could see that Gall was quite restive. Finally, Gall, giving me a significant glance and toss of his head and quirt, got up, went to his horse and mounted. Waiting a moment, so as not to attract attention, as I could see he did not want the interpreter with us, my orderly and I mounted and followed Gall over to Calhoun's Knoll. Gall silently surveyed the surroundings for a few moments, then pointed out the direction of Custer's approach, indicating now rapid and now slow march, according to the ground; then the halt, the dismounting of a part and the forward movement of the other troops deploying as skirmishers, opening out his fingers to show this movement, the other troops following. Then these latter made a rapid move to the right front toward Custer Hill. Turning to me, he told me to dismount; then he said: "You soldier; me Sioux," and put me in the several positions of the troops, indicating them; during this he indicated the lines of approach of his own warriors, the stampede of the led horses, the driving back of the soldiers, the final stand. Then the disposition of his warriors; some dismounted near the crest, rising and dropping to draw the fire to cause waste of ammunition; the mounted warriors were lower down on the hill side. Then he imitated the war whoop in a low tone, the quirting of the ponies and then the final charge!

All this was graphically told by the sign language with the occasional interpolation of an English or Sioux word. The old Chief was himself again—it was intensely dramatic! The subsequent relation of the same story through the interpreter after our return to Standing Rock seemed tame indeed.

* * *

Custer's Trail

* * * * * General Custer separated from Reno before the latter crossed the Little Big Horn under

The War Chief Gall, of the Hunkpapas. Photo by D. F. Barry. Denver Public Library Western Collection.

orders to charge the village. Custer's column bore to the right of the river (a sudden change of plan, probably); a ridge of high bluffs and the river separated the two commands and they could not see each other. On this ridge, however, Custer and staff were seen to wave their hats, and heard to cheer as Reno was beginning the attack; but Custer's troops were at that time a mile or more to his right.

It was about this time that the trumpeter was sent back with Custer's last order to Benteen. From this place Custer could survey the valley for several miles above and for a short distance below Reno; yet he could only see a part of the village; he must, then, have felt confident that all the Indians were below him, hence, I presume, his message to Benteen. The view of the main body of the village was cut off by the highest points of the ridge, a short distance from him. Had he gone to this high point he would have understood the magnitude of his undertaking, and it is probable that his plan of battle would have been changed. We have no evidence that he did not go there. He could see, however, that the village was not breaking away toward the Big Horn Mountains. He must, then, have expected to find the squaws and children fleeing to the bluffs on the north, for in no other way do I account for his wide detour to the right. He must have counted upon Reno's success, and fully expected the "scatteration" of the noncombatants with the pony herds. The probable attack upon the families and the capture of the herds were in that event counted upon to strike consternation into the hearts of the warriors, and were elements for success upon which Custer counted in the event of a daylight attack.

* * *

When Reno's advance was checked, and his left began to fall back, Chief Gall started with some of his warriors to cut off Reno's retreat to the bluffs. On his way he was excitedly hailed by Iron Cedar, one of his warriors, who was on the high point, to hurry to him, that more soldiers were coming. This was the first intimation the Indians had of Custer's column; up to the time of this incident they had supposed that all the troops were in at Reno's attack. Custer had then crossed the valley of the dry creek, and was marching along and well up the slope of the bluff forming the second ridge back from the river and nearly parallel to it. The command was marching in column of fours, and there was some confusion in the ranks, due probably to the unmanageableness of excited horses.

The accepted theory for ten years after the battle,

and still persisted in by some writers, was that Custer's column had turned the high bluffs near the river, moved down the dry coulee and attempted to ford the river near the lowest point of these bluffs; that he was there met by an overpowering force and driven back; that he then divided his battalion, moved down the river with the view of attacking the village, but met with such resistance from the enemy posted along the river bank and ravines that he was compelled to fall back, fighting, to the position on the ridge. The numerous bodies found scattered between the river and the ridge were supposed to be the first victims of the fight. I am now satisfied that these were bodies of men who either survived those on the ridge or attempted to escape the massacre.

Custer's route was as indicated on the map*, and his column was never nearer the river or village than his *final position on the ridge*. The wife of Spotted Horn Bull, when giving me her account of the battle, persisted in saying that Custer's column did not attempt to cross at the ford, and appealed to her husband, who supported her statement. On the battle-field, in 1886, Chief Gall indicated Custer's route to me, and it then flashed upon me that I, myself had seen Custer's trail. On June 28th, while we were burying the dead, I asked Major Reno's permission to go on the high ridge east or back of the field to look for tracks of shod horses to ascertain if some of the command might not have escaped. When I reached the ridge I saw this trail, and wondered who could have made it, but dismissed the thought that it had been made by Custer's column, because it did not accord with the theory with which we were then filled, that Custer had attempted to cross at the ford, and this trail was too far back and showed no indication of leading toward the ford. Trumpeter Penwell was my orderly and accompanied me. It was a singular coincidence that in 1886 Penwell was stationed at Fort Custer, and was my orderly when visiting the battle-field. Penwell corroborated my recollection of the trail.

The ford theory arose from the fact that we found there numerous tracks of shod horses, but they evidently had been made after the Indians had possessed themselves of the cavalry horses, for they rode them after capturing them. *No bodies of men or horses were found anywhere near the ford, and these facts are conclusive to my mind that Custer did not go to the ford with any body of men.*

Custer's Battle

As soon as Gall had personally confirmed Iron Cedar's report he sent word to the warriors bat-

---

* See Godfrey's Map, p. 126.

tling against Reno, and to the people of the village. The greatest consternation prevailed among the families, and orders were given for them to leave at once. Before they could do so the great body of warriors had left Reno and hastened to attack Custer. This explains why Reno was not pushed when so much confusion at the river crossing gave the Indians every opportunity of annihilating his command. Not long after the Indians began to show a strong force in Custer's front, Custer turned his column to the left, and advanced in the direction of the village to near a place now marked as a spring, halted at the junction of the ravines just below it, and dismounted two troops, Keogh's and Calhoun's to fight on foot. These two troops advanced at double-time to a knoll, now marked by Crittenden's monument. The other three troops, mounted, followed them a short distance in the rear. The led horses remained where the troops dismounted. When Keogh and Calhoun got to the knoll the other troops marched rapidly to the right; Smith's troops deployed as skirmishers, mounted, and took position on a ridge, which, on Smith's left, ended in Keogh's position (now marked by Crittenden's monument), and on Smith's right, ended at the hill on which Custer took position with Yates and Tom Custer's troops, now known as Custer's Hill, and marked by the monument erected to the command. Smith's skirmishers, holding their gray horses, remained in groups of fours. Twenty-eight bodies, mostly belonging to this troop were found in a big gully near the river, and I firmly believe that these men belonged to Lieutenant Sturgis' Platoon and had been ordered to locate a ford for crossing the river.

The line occupied by Custer's battalion was the first considerable ridge back from the river, the nearest point being about half a mile from it. His front was extended about three-fourths of a mile. The whole village was in full view. A few hundred yards from his line was another but lower ridge, the further slope of which was not commanded by his line. It was here that the Indians under Crazy Horse from the lower part of the village, among whom were the Cheyennes, formed for the charge on Custer's Hill. All Indians had now left Reno. Gall collected his warriors, and moved up a ravine south of Keogh and Calhoun. As they were turning this flank they discovered the led horses without any other guard than the horse-holders. They opened fire on the horse-holders, and used the usual devices to stampede the horses—that is, yelling, waving blankets, etc.; in this they succeeded very soon, and the horses were caught up by the squaws. In this disaster

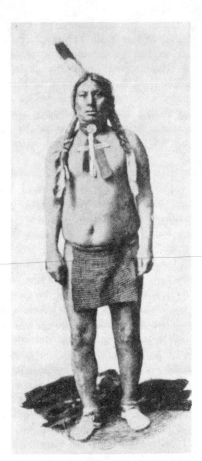

Another photograph of Chief Gall. By D. F. Barry.

Keogh and Calhoun probably lost their reserve ammunition, which was carried in the saddle-bags. Gall's warriors now moved to the foot of the knoll held by Calhoun. A large force dismounted and advanced up the slope far enough to be able to see the soldiers when standing erect, but were protected when squatting or lying down. By jumping up and firing quickly, they exposed themselves only for an instant, but drew the fire of the soldiers, causing a waste of ammunition. In the meantime Gall was massing his mounted warriors under the protection of the slope. When everything was in readiness, at a signal from Gall, the dismounted warriors rose, fired, and every Indian gave voice to the war whoop; the mounted Indians gave whip to their ponies, and the whole mass rushed upon and crushed Calhoun. The maddened mass of Indians was carried forward by its own momentum over Calhoun and Crittenden down into the depression where Keogh was, with over thirty men, and all was over on that part of the field.

In the meantime the same tactics were being pursued and executed around Custer's Hill. The warriors, under the leadership of Crow King, Crazy Horse, White Bull, "Hump," Two Moon, and others, moved up the ravine west of Custer's Hill, and concentrated under the shelter of the ridges on his right flank and back of his position. Gall's bloody work was finished before the annihilation of Custer was accomplished, and his victorious warriors hurried forward to the hot fight then going on, and the frightful massacre was completed.

Smith's men had disappeared from the ridge, but not without leaving enough dead bodies to mark their line. About twenty-eight bodies of men belonging to this troop and other organizations were found in one ravine nearer the river. Many corpses were found scattered over the field between Custer's line of defense, the river, and in the direction of Reno's Hill. These, doubtless, were of men who had attempted to escape; some of them may have been sent as couriers by Custer. One of the first bodies I recognized and one of the nearest to the ford was that of Sergeant Butler of Tom Custer's troop. Sergeant Butler was a soldier of many years' experience and of known courage. The indications were that he had sold his life dearly, for near and under him were found many empty cartridge shells. From knowledge of his personality, and his detached position, I believe he had been selected as courier to communicate with Reno.

All the Indian accounts that I know of agree that there was no organized closequarters fighting, except on the two flanks; that with the annihilation at Custer's Hill the battle was virtually over. It does not appear that the Indians made any advance to the attack from the direction of the river; they did have a defensive force along the river and in the ravines which destroyed those who left Custer's line.

There was a great deal of firing going on over the field after the battle by the young men and boys riding about and shooting into the dead bodies.

DR. EASTMAN'S STORY OF THE BATTLE

(Extract from *The Sioux Narrative* by Dr. Charles Alexander Eastman (O-hi-ye-sa), a full blood Sioux, then an instructor at the Carlisle Indian School. Published in the *Chautauquan Magazine,* 1900.)

* * *

Many were in the midst of their meal when from the south end of the camp came the warning cry: "Woo Woo hay-ay hay-ay. Warriors to your saddles; the white soldiers are now upon us."

* * *

Led by Sitting Bull's nephew Lone Bull they (the young men who had been playing on the flats) would have forced him (Reno) back had it not been for the prompt interference of Gall, Rain-in-the-Face and Spotted Eagle. "Wait-wait," they said—"We are not ready * * * Hold them until there are warriors enough upon their ponies."

In the midst of the confusion Sitting Bull stood by his tepee and addressed his people thus: "Warriors, we have everything to fight for and if we are defeated we shall have nothing to live for; therefore let us fight like brave men."

* * *

Gall, Crow King, Black Moon and Rain-in-the-Face now joined the young men; this encouraged the latter so much that no sooner had Lone Bull given the war whoop for the charge than the soldiers retreated. The first company endeavored to return the way they came, but they were forced toward the east almost at right angles with their trail. Just as the Indians made their general charge the second company of the soldiers turned to flee. They were closely pursued. The Indians, having full knowledge of the ground and the river, were greatly encouraged. The leaders shouted "We can drown them all—charge closer." The first company of soldiers fared tolerably well, but the second lost many men.

* * *

The forces that repulsed Reno numbered not over 500. This was all they could muster up in so short a time. Of this number probably 100 went over to the Custer battle; but they were a little late.

Just as the forces under Gall, Rain-in-the-Face and Crow King made their famous charge, the lower (north) end of the camp discovered General Custer and his men approaching. The two battles were fully two and one-half miles apart.

"Woo Woo—here they come"—shouted the Indians, as Custer with his formidable column appeared on the slope of the ridge. They knew well he could not cross the river at that point. He must go down half a mile. The crossing therefore became at once of first importance.

As Crazy Horse started down to the ford, Custer appeared upon the river bank. Having discovered that it was impossible to cross, he began to fire into the camp, while some of his men dismounted and were apparently examining the banks. Already Crazy Horse and his men had crossed the river, closely followed by Little Horse and White Bull with their Cheyenne Warriors.

Two Moon was still loudly urging the young men to meet the soldiers on the other side, and as he led the remaining Cheyennes in the same direction, the Minneconjous and the Brules were coming down at full speed.

The forces under Crazy Horse and Little Horse followed a long ravine that went east from the crossing until it passed the ridge; it then took a southerly direction parallel with and immediately behind the said ridge. Iron Star and Low Dog, on the other hand, turned southward immediately after crossing the river. The firing from the camp still continued, and as the later forces arrived, they at once opened fire upon the soldiers who were gradually retreating toward the ridge one-half mile back from the river bank.

Up to this time General Custer did not seem to apprehend the danger before him. But when one company of his command reached the summit of the ridge, it was quickly forced behind the brow of the hill by the Indians. The soldiers now took up three separate positions along the ridge, but they were practically already hemmed in.

At first the General kept his men intact; but the deafening war whoops and the rattling sound of the gun shots frightened the horses. The soldiers had no little trouble from this source. Finally they let go of their horses and threw themselves flat upon the ground, sending volley after volley into the whirling masses of the enemy.

The signal was given for a general charge. Crazy Horse with the Ogalallas and Little Horse and White Bull with the Cheyennes now came forward with a tremendous yell. The brave soldiers sent into their ranks a heavy volley that checked them for the moment. At this instant a soldier upon a swift horse started for the river, but was brought down. Again the Indians signalled for a charge. This time the attack was made from all sides. Now they came pell mell among the soldiers. One company was chased along the ridge to the south, out of which a man got away. A mighty yell went up from the Indians as he cleared the attacking forces, as if they were glad that he succeeded. Away he went toward Reno's position. The rest of the company were now falling fast and the ridge was covered with the slain.

* * *

I reiterate that there were not 12,000 to 15,000 Indians at that camp as has been represented; nor were there over 1,000 warriors in the fight. It is not necessary to exaggerate the number of the Indians engaged in this notable battle. The simple truth is that Custer met the combined forces of the hostiles, which were greater than his own, and that he had not so much underestimated their numbers as their ability.

ACCOUNT OF THE CUSTER FIGHT AS GIVEN BY "FEATHER EARRING," A MINNECONJOU SIOUX, TO GEN. H. L. SCOTT, AT POPLAR, MONTANA, SEPT. 9, 1919

RENO'S men came down Reno Creek (no name); they were seen by two (no bow) (Ita-zip-cha) young men who went up Reno Creek to get a horse that had been wounded in the Rosebud fight. "Two Bear" was killed by Reno scouts. "Lone Dog," the other, went back and gave the alarm, riding from side to side. "Feather Earring" (Minneconjou) (mini-con-jou) saw him signaling that soldiers were coming, calling "one of us got killed—they are right close behind me." He had no sooner arrived than Reno's command began firing in the tepees. "Feather Earring" was fighting against Reno. His brother was killed there. Reno was driven across the river into the hills and began to dig in the ground. He was fought by the Cheyennes and Ogalallas. It was thought at first that Reno's was Crook's command. War parties went to watch Crook, but he had gone back. Some war parties had gone down the Rosebud and had seen a steamboat and soldiers, but had not come back. Reno left the bottom for the hills because the Indians were surrounding him in the attempt to cut him off from his train.

It was thought at first that Reno's command was alone. He was fought by the Cheyennes and Ogalallas. Many came from lower down, but about the time Reno reached the hill, word came that the village was being attacked by Custer below. They then left Reno's front for the lower end of the village, but when they got there from Reno's front, it was all over. Custer struck the Hunkpapas. He did not come across the river. He fired on the village. The Indians had crossed the Greasy Grass Creek (Little Big Horn) above where Custer tried to cross, in great numbers, and cut him off from Reno. They got around behind (east) him. They made their main stand on the ridge where the monument now is; they fought very hard. I had put my brother's body in the bushes and came down where Custer was; the fight was over. I drove five horses across the river; gray horses; they were all wounded and trembling. I saw they were mortally wounded and let them go and went back toward monument ridge. About 200 yards from the river I saw two bodies and went to look at them. One was a dead Indian, the other a white man alongside him. I saw the white man's heart beating and called to a Sioux, "Your grandfather has been killed by that man alongside of him; I don't think he is dead; you had better shoot him." He came up and put an arrow through him; he jumped up and was shot and killed by another arrow; he had been playing dead. There were no other marks on him than the two arrow wounds."

Q. What time do you think Custer was killed?

A. The women and children had gone out after berries and had gotten back; it must have been about noon.

Q. Do you think if Custer had kept his men together and attacked at dawn, he would have succeeded?

A. Yes, we would have run away, but we would have come back to attack him. It is a pity Custer did not go into the brush instead of out on that ridge.

Q. Why didn't Custer go back toward Reno, rather than away from him?

A. He couldn't. He was cut off by large numbers of Indians on that side. *If Custer had come up and talked with us, we had all agreed we would have surrendered and gone in with him.*

Q. How many Sioux were killed there?

A. There were sixteen that I can name now. Four of these were near Reno, and three were Cheyennes. There were a terrible number wounded.

Q. Where were they buried?

A. On platforms in the village.

Q. What made you leave Greasy Grass Creek?

A. A man came back and said many soldiers were coming up Little Big Horn, and were digging holes in the ground. We didn't want to fight them when they dug holes.

(Note—Terry's command halted at noon in the bottom near the village till 5 p.m.)

Q. Where did you go?

A. We went toward the Big Horn Mountains, up "Bird Timber" Creek, 20 miles, then 20 miles next day. We got ready to fight Terry's command near the second flat; then we heard they had all gone back.

Q. Who was that man who was buried in the lodge on Reno Creek?

A. His name was Old She Bear who was wounded in the fight on the Rosebud (Crook). He was a brother of Turning Bear, an Ita-zip-cha. The village was right there where that lodge was on Reno Creek when they fought Crook. They went over to the Rosebud to fight and came back. Old She Bear was shot through both hips, and

died in that camp on Reno Creek. The body was put on a scaffold and the lodge pitched over him.

Q. Who got a good reputation at that fight?

A. All: Crazy Horse, Sitting Bull and all that I heard of.

Q. We heard Sitting Bull had run away and was not in the fight.

A. I heard him giving orders. While we were up near the Big Horn Mountains we heard that some soldiers had gone into the Big Horn Mountains, where they dismounted and tied their horses in the timber. The Cheyennes brought back a number of their horses. (This was the noted Sibley Scout.) We did not see the soldiers. After the Terry command went away, we came back down Greasy Grass Creek crossed over where Custer attempted it, up Custer Creek, and then over to the Rosebud.

Q. How many Indians were killed in Crook's fight?

A. Four. Many were wounded.

Q. How many lodges were there?

A. There were very many; three or four young men in a lodge. We gave each man a willow stick in order to count them. I know we counted over 5,000, and they were not all there; many were over on Arrow Creek stealing horses from the Crows.

GEN. SCOTT'S NOTE IN ADDITION

In other conversations later with "Feather Earring" he emphasized the statement that Custer could have led the main body of the Sioux into the agencies by diplomacy, if he had not attacked first. Also that no one knew Custer was present on the Little Big Horn River. His command was thought to be Crook's command that was fought on the Rosebud on the 17th of June, and Custer came from the Rosebud. It was not for more than a month afterward, when someone brought the news out from Standing Rock Agency that it was known that Custer had been killed. *This disposes of all the reasons invented by white men for his not being scalped.* This was confirmed by He Dog, Crazy Horse's head soldier, at Pine Ridge, S. D., in 1920; also that Custer could have led the Sioux into the agencies by diplomacy.

(Signed) H. L. SCOTT.

Note by W.A.G.: Feather Earring's statement that Reno was fought by the Cheyennes and Ogalallas is not in accord with other Indian accounts. Neither is his statement that Custer struck the Hunkpapas. Here is either an error in interpretation or confusion upon the part of the narrator. The overwhelming evidence is precisely the reverse of both these statements.

A MESSAGE FROM THE HOSTILE CHIEFS

Statement of *"The Man that smells his hand,"* an Uncpapa Sioux, to the C. O. Standing Rock Agency, Sept. 6, 1876, including a message from the assembled chiefs of the Ogalalla, Minneconjou, Brules, Sans Arcs and other Sioux Indians encamped on Broken Legged Womans Creek, near the head of Powder River, Aug. 29, 1876.

THREE men spoke, but they all said the same thing. They began by saying: "We are representatives of many bands, and what we have to say is for all these bands. We have heard of your difficulty with the Indians at Standing Rock, that is—you have turned white man. For that reason we should detain you one year; but as we have something to say to the whites we will use you as a courier to them. This land belongs to us. It is a gift to us from the Great Spirit. The Great Spirit gave us the game in this country. It is our privilege to hunt the game in our country. The white man came here to take the country from us by force. He has brought misery and wretchedness into our country. We were here killing game and eating, and all of a sudden we were attacked by white men. You will now depart and return to Standing Rock. Tell the Commanding Officer that we are tired of fighting and that we want the soldiers to stop fighting us. Tell him to repeat these words to the Great Father: The Great Spirit above us gave us this country. It is ours and he is looking down on us today. He sees the bloody deeds going on in this country. Though he gave us the country, he did not give us the right to dispose of it. It is our duty to defend our country. We did not say to the white man "come out and fight us." We did not ask them to come out at all. We did not want to fight them; but now if they wish to withdraw they may. We do not wish to fight them. What we have said is the sentiment of Sitting Bull; he is not here, but if he were he would say the same words to you."

"Sitting Bull says he was out there because there was game, but that he did not want to fight. He had to fight because he was attacked. Perhaps the whites think they can exterminate us, but God, the Great Spirit, will not permit it."

The above is the message. The messenger states that Sitting Bull has all his followers and many Indians from this Agency with him. His camp on the 30th of August was on Tongue River, nearly in sight of the post now being built at the mouth of that river. He is so near that he can see the soldiers any day by riding a short distance. He is on or near the road made by the troops in going out. He was expected however to join the other bands on the head of Powder River, soon, as he had been sent for. A small body of troops had marched near their camp and they could have massacred them all, but they preferred to let them leave the country as they seemed to be doing.

The Indians had any quantity of ammunition and more guns than they needed, most of them "needle guns." They had many mules with galled necks and shoulders, and many of them had died since the Indians got them. They had many American horses, but they had nearly all broken down. The Indians said that if the whites persisted in keeping up the war, they could stand it for three years. They had plenty of game and everything else.

Message sent by Amputated Finger of the Ogalalla Sioux, and other hostile chiefs.

Sgd. by W. P. CARLIN,
Lt. Col., 17th Inf.
Comdg. Post at Standing Rock.

INDIAN GRAPEVINE? A STORY OF CROOK'S SCOUTS

I CANNOT vouch for the authenticity of the following tale by T. R. Porter, which appeared in the Tepee Book for 1916; but as there has long existed a belief (probably superstitious) that the plains Indians had means of inter-communication that were not known to white men, the story is of interest, though I have never seen a confirmation of it by General Crook. However, Major George M. Randall of Crook's staff, who was an intimate of my own Father, related to him during the 80's a somewhat similar incident, though the *time* of the General's talk with his Indian scouts was, as I remember it, the morning of the day *after,* and not the afternoon of the same day, of Custer's defeat. In any event, Crook evidently discredited whatever his Indians told him, just as Terry discredited the Crows the morning of the 26th.

In 1925, Colonel Hugh Reid, a retired officer of Infantry, who was stationed at Ft. Rice, near Bismarck, during the summer of 1876, wrote me that on the evening of 4 July, a party of Sioux arrived at Ft. Rice with news of the battle, bringing with them arrows they claimed to have taken from the bodies of Custer's dead; and that his Commanding Officer at once transmitted the information by telegraph from Bismarck to Army headquarters at St. Paul. On the other hand, General Charles King, then a lieutenant with Merritt's Fifth Cavalry, states that his regiment, awaiting orders at Sage Creek, did not get the news until the morning of 7 July. (See "The Story of the Little Big Horn, p. XXXI). But for whatever it may be worth, here is the Porter story.

(From *The Tepee Book,* 1916)

"On the afternoon of June 25th, 1876, Gen. Crook, the famous Indian fighter, was in camp somewhere in northern Wyoming about a hundred miles south of the Big Horn Country. With him were his command of soldiers and a number of Indian scouts—Sioux.

General Crook had always had the respect and confidence of the Indians, even when he was fighting them hardest. He always kept faith with them, and never broke his word nor a promise made them. Frequently the General stopped in at the tent wherein his Indian scouts lived, and talked with the chief of scouts. In fact, so thoroughly did the Indians trust Crook that they made him a member of the Soldier Lodge.

The Soldier Lodge in Indian life corresponds to the highest degree of Masonry among white men. In war time the members of this lodge took charge of the campaign and waged the conflicts. In time of peace the Soldier Lodge was the most powerful institution among the Red Men. Secrets of the lodge were no more betrayed than are secrets of Masonry.

Few—a very few—white men have ever been initiated into this innermost circle of Indian life. Gen. Crook was one of these. Thomas H. Tibbles of Omaha, for forty years a member of the Omaha Tribe, was another.

On the afternoon of June 25th, 1876, Gen. Crook, in camp a hundred miles south of the Little Big Horn, walked down among the tents of his soldiers. The men were enjoying a rest, after a hard ride, and were sitting around, laughing, talking and joking. Finally the General came to the big tent occupied by his Indian scouts. Every Indian was silent. They were sitting around, "grumpy" and sullen. Gen. Crook spoke to one of them. His only answer was a grunt. He spoke to another and received no answer at all.

The General walked to his quarters. Then he ordered the chief of Indian scouts sent to him.

"What's the matter with you fellows?" inquired the General.

But the Indian wouldn't talk. Gen. Crook could get absolutely nothing out of him. So the Indian was dismissed.

Crook thought the matter over for some time. He knew that something was wrong with the Indians, but he could not figure out just what it was. The Indians were worried. So was Crook.

Finally Gen. Crook sent for the chief scout again. When he came the General had a long talk with him. He finally demanded in the name of the mysteries of the Soldier Lodge, to which the Indian also belonged, to know what was the trouble. Then the Indian gave in.

"Yellow Hair Custer and all his soldiers, every one, were killed on the Little Big Horn this morning," was the startling information the Indian gave Crook. When Crook asked for details, the Indian could not, or would not, give them. He only insisted that a battle had occurred between the white soldiers and the Sioux, and that the soldiers, to the last man, had been killed.

Gen. Crook, having spent many years on the frontier among the Indians, knew that the Red Men had mysterious ways of communicating with each other, and when his scout solemnly assured him, on the word of a Soldier Lodge brother, that the Custer command had been wiped out, he believed the report. In after years he told the incident to Thomas H. Tibbles, another Soldier Lodge White Man, and Tibbles told it to me. However, Gen. Crook told the same story so many times that there is no doubt as to its authenticity.

As to how these Indians, a hundred miles distant from the battle, knew of the affair within a very few hours after the firing ceased, neither Crook, Tibbles, nor any other White Man has ever been able to discover. But that they knew the whole story there can be no doubt."

Well—there it is. Believers in telepathy and the occult will probably accept it: an unbeliever will probably reject it as just another Custer yarn. Having resurrected the story, I suppose it is up to me to state my opinion. Being an unbeliever in anything supernatural, I think Mr. Porter's timing is wrong and that Crook's scouts did not learn on June 25, that a battle was fought that day a hundred miles away. If, however, the timing be shifted to the morning of the day *after,* I see no reason to doubt, as Indian couriers could easily cover a hundred miles in less than twelve hours.

That Crook's scouts named "Yellow Hair Custer" I doubt, for there is no question that Sitting Bull's horde did not learn until long after the battle, who their opponent was. Crook, of course knew that Custer and Gibbon were in the field, and this much his scouts may also have known, but not more.

CHAPTER 6

THE CHEYENNES

GENERAL CUSTER'S LAST FIGHT AS SEEN BY TWO MOON

The Battle Described By A Chief Who Took Part In It.

By HAMLIN GARLAND

(From McClure's Magazine, September, 1898)

A S WE topped the·low, pine-clad ridge and looked into the hot, dry valley, Wolf Voice, my Cheyenne interpreter, pointed at a little log cabin, toward the green line of alders wherein the Rosebud ran, and said:

"His house—Two Moon."

As we drew near we came to a puzzling fork in the road. The left branch skirted a corner of a wire fence, the right turned into a field. We started to the left, but the waving of a blanket in the hands of a man at the cabin door directed us to the right. As we drew nearer we perceived Two Moon spreading blankets in the scant shade of his low cabin. Some young Cheyennes were grinding a sickle. A couple of children were playing about the little log stables. The barn-yard and buildings were like those of a white settler on the new and arid sod. It was all barren and unlovely—the home of poverty.

As we dismounted at the door Two Moon came out to meet us with hand outstretched. "How" he said, with the heartiest, long-drawn note of welcome. He motioned us to be seated on the blankets which he had spread for us upon seeing our approach. Nothing could exceed the dignity and sincerity of his greeting.

As we took seats he brought out tobacco and a pipe. He was a tall old man, of a fine, clear brown complexion, big-chested, erect, and martial of bearing. His smiling face was broadly benignant, and his manners were courteous and manly.

While he cut his tobacco Wolf Voice interpreted my wishes to him. I said, "Two Moon, I have come to hear your story of the Custer battle, for they tell me you were a chief there. After you tell me the story, I want to take some photographs of you. I want you to signal with a blanket as the great chiefs used to do in fight."

Wolf Voice made this known to him, delivering also a message from the agents, and at every pause Two Moon uttered deep-voiced notes of comprehension. "Ai," "A-ah," "Hoh,"—these sounds are commonly called "grunts," but they were low, long-drawn expulsions of breath, very expressive.

Then a long silence intervened. The old man mused. It required time to go from the silence of the hot valley, the shadow of his little cabin, and the wire fence of his pasture, back to the days of his youth. When he began to speak, it was with great deliberation. His face became each moment graver and his eyes more introspective.

"Two Moon does not like to talk about the days of fighting but since you are to make a book, and the agent says you are a friend to Grinnell (George B. Grinnell, whom the Cheyennes, Blackfeet, and Gros Ventres love and honor), I will tell you about it—the truth. It is now a long time ago, and my words do not come quickly.

"That spring [1876] I was camped on Powder River with fifty lodges of my people—Cheyennes. The place is near what is now Fort McKinney. One morning soldiers charged my camp. They were in command of Three Fingers [Colonel McKenzie]. We were surprised and scattered, leaving our ponies. The soldiers ran all our horses off. That night the soldiers slept, leaving the horses one side; so we crept up and stole them back again, and then we went away.

"We traveled far, and one day we met a big camp of Sioux at Charcoal Butte. We camped with the Sioux, and had a good time, plenty grass, plenty game, good water. Crazy Horse was head chief of the camp. Sitting Bull was camped a little ways below, on the Little Missouri River.

"Crazy Horse said to me, 'I'm glad you are come. We are going to fight the white man again.'

The Cheyenne Chief "Two Moon" from a photograph taken during the late 70's. The artist is unknown. This shows Two Moon as he appeared at the time of the battle of the Little Big Horn, though it is probable that in that fight he wore a war bonnet.

"The camp was already full of wounded men, women, and children.

"I said to Crazy Horse, 'All right. I am ready to fight. I have fought already. My people have been killed, my horses stolen; I am satisfied to fight'."

Here the old man paused a moment, and his face took on a lofty and somber expression.

"I believed at that time the Great Spirits had made Sioux, put them there," he drew a circle to the right—"and white men and Cheyennes here,"—indicating two places to the left—"expecting them to fight. The Great Spirits I thought liked to see the fight; it was to them all the same like playing. So I thought then about fighting." As he said this, he made me feel for one moment the power of a sardonic god whose drama was the wars of men.

"About May, when the grass was tall and the horses strong, we broke camp and started across the country to the mouth of the Tongue River. Then Sitting Bull and Crazy Horse and all went up the Rosebud. There we had a big fight with General Crook, and whipped him. Many soldiers were killed—few Indians. It was a great fight, much smoke and dust.

"From there we all went over the divide, and camped in the valley of Little Horn. Everybody thought, 'Now we are out of the white man's country. He can live there, we will live here.' After a few days, one morning when I was in camp north of Sitting Bull, a Sioux messenger rode up and said, 'Let everybody paint up, cook, and get ready for a big dance.'

"Cheyennes then went to work to cook, cut up tobacco, and get ready. We all thought to dance all day. We were very glad to think we were far away from the white man.

"I went to water my horses at the creek, and washed them off with cool water, then took a swim myself. I came back to the camp afoot. When I got near my lodge, I looked up the Little Horn towards Sitting Bull's camp. I saw a great dust rising. It looked like a whirlwind. Soon Sioux horseman came rushing into camp shouting: 'Soldiers come! Plenty white soldiers.'

"I ran into my lodge, and said to my brother-in-law, 'Get your horses; the white man is coming. Everybody run for horses.'

"Outside, far up the valley, I heard a battle cry, Hay-ay, hay-ay! I heard shooting, too, this way [clapping his hands very fast]. I couldn't see any Indians. Everybody was getting horses and saddles. After I had caught my horse, a Sioux warrior came again and said, 'Many soldiers are coming.'

"Then he said to the women, 'Get out of the way, we are going to have hard fight.'

"I said, 'All right, I am ready.'

"I got on my horse, and rode out into my camp. I called out to the people all running about: 'I am Two Moon, your chief. Don't run away. Stay here and fight. You must stay and fight the white soldiers. I shall stay even if I am to be killed.'

"I rode swiftly toward Sitting Bull's camp. There I saw the white soldiers fighting in a line [Reno's men]. Indians covered the flat. They began to drive the soldiers all mixed up—Sioux, then soldiers, then more Sioux, and all shooting. The air was full of smoke and dust. I saw the soldiers fall back and drop into the river-bed like buffalo fleeing. They had no time to look for a crossing. The Sioux chased them up the hill, where they met more soldiers in wagons, and then messengers came saying more soldiers were going to kill the women, and the Sioux turned back. Chief Gall was there fighting. Crazy Horse also.

"I then rode toward my camp, and stopped squaws from carrying off lodges. While I was sitting on my horse I saw flags come up over the hill to the east like that [he raised his finger-tips]. Then the soldiers rose all at once, all on horses, like this [he put his fingers behind each other to indicate that Custer appeared marching in columns of fours]. They formed into three branches [squadrons] with a little ways between. Then a bugle sounded, and they all got off horses, and some soldiers led the horses back over the hill.

"Then the Sioux rode up the ridge on all sides, riding very fast. The Cheyennes went up the left way. Then the shooting was quick, quick. Pop—pop—pop very fast. Some of the soldiers were down on their knees, some standing. Officers all in front. The smoke was like a great cloud, and everywhere the Sioux went the dust rose like smoke. We circled all round them—swirling like water round a stone. We shoot, we ride fast, we shoot again. Soldiers drop, and horses fall on them. Soldiers in line drop, but one man rides up and down the line—all the time shouting. He rode a sorrel horse with white face and white fore-legs. I don't know who he was. He was a brave man.

"Indians keep swirling round and round, and the soldiers killed only a few. Many soldiers fell. At last all horses killed but five. Once in a while some man would break out and run toward the river, but he would fall. At last about a hundred men and five horsemen stood on the hill all bunched together. All along the bugler kept blowing his commands. He was very brave too. Then a chief was killed. I hear it was Long Hair [Custer], I don't know; and then the five horsemen and the bunch of men, may be so forty, started toward the river. The man on the sorrel horse led them, shouting all the time. (This man's identity is in dispute. He was apparently a scout.) He wore buckskin shirt, and had long black hair and mustache. He fought hard with a big knife. His men were all covered with white dust. I couldn't tell whether they were officers or not. One man all alone ran far down toward the river, then round up over the hill. I thought he was going to escape, but a Sioux fired and hit him in the head. He was the last man. He wore braid on his arms [Sergeant Butler?]

"All the soldiers were now killed, and the bodies were stripped. After that no one could tell which were officers. The bodies were left where they fell. We had no dance that night. We were sorrowful.

"Next day four Sioux chiefs and two Cheyennes and I, Two Moon, went upon the battlefield to count the dead. One man carried a little bundle of sticks. When we came to dead men, we took a little stick and gave it to another man, so we counted the dead. There were 388. There were thirty-nine Sioux and seven Cheyennes killed, and about a hundred wounded.

"Some white soldiers were cut with knives, to makes sure they were dead; and the war women had mangled some. Most of them were left just where they fell. We came to the man with big mustache; he lay down the hill towards the river. (Custer fell up higher on the ridge.) The Indians did not take his buckskin shirt. The Sioux said, 'That is a big chief. That is Long Hair.' I don't know. I had never seen him. The man on the white-faced horse was the bravest man.

"That day as the sun was getting low our young men came up the Little Horn riding hard. Many white soldiers were coming in a big boat, and when we looked we could see the smoke rising. I called my people together, and we hurried up the Little Horn, into Rotton Grass Valley. We camped there three days, and then rode swiftly back over our old trail to the east. Sitting Bull went back into the Rosebud and down the Yellowstone, and away to the north. I did not see him again." (This was a wonderful retreat.)

The old man paused and filled his pipe. His story was done. His mind came back to his poor people on the barren land where the rain seldom falls.

"That was a long time ago. I am now old, and my mind has changed. I would rather see my people living in houses and singing and dancing. You have talked with me about fighting, and I have told you of the time long ago. All that is past. I think of these things now: First, that our reservation shall be fenced and the white settlers kept out and our young men kept in. Then there will be no trouble. Second, I want to see my people raising cattle and making butter. Last, I want to see my people going to school to learn the white man's way. That is all."

There was something placid and powerful in the lines of the chief's broad brow, and his gestures were dramatic and noble in sweep. His extended arms, his musing eyes, his deep voice combined to express a meditative solemnity profoundly impressive. There was no anger in his voice, and no reminiscent ferocity. All that was strong and fine and distinctive in the Cheyenne character came out in the old man's talk. He seemed the leader and the thoughtful man he really is—patient under injustice, courteous even to his enemies.

THE STORY OF THE CHEYENNE WARRIOR "WOODEN LEG"

OF ALL the Indian accounts of the battle of the Little Big Horn that through the years have been offered to the public, that of the Cheyenne "Wooden Leg," as recorded by the late Dr. Thomas B. Marquis, is easily the most remarkable. Dr. Marquis, a resident of Montana for many years, became a close and intimate friend of the Northern Cheyennes, to whom the elders of the tribe opened their hearts and talked freely. His best known work "A WARRIOR WHO FOUGHT CUSTER," is a classic in its wealth of circumstantial narration and its descriptions of Indian life and customs during the seventies.

While the book reaches its dramatic climax with the old warrior's story of the manner in which Custer and his men passed into history—he was past seventy when he told it to Dr. Marquis—those fortunate enough to possess a copy of this stirring tale cannot fail to find absorbing interest in every page.

When it first appeared, after correspondence and exchange of views with its distinguished author, I reviewed the book for the Order of Indian Wars. A copy was sent to him before its publication to the Society: and because to quote the old warrior's words would involve reproduction of nearly one hundred of the printed pages, I must content myself with excerpts from that review, reconstructed from the notes from which it was written, and which summarize the salient points of his story of the battle in which as a youth of eighteen, he took a minor, though observing part. The excerpts follow.

After short and meagre description of the Rosebud fight, which occurred June 17, 1876, eight days before the battle of the Little Big Horn, Wooden Leg relates the movements of the Indians following Crook's defeat, which brought them to the valley of the Greasy Grass "one sleep" before Custer and his troops attacked. The Cheyennes led, raising their circle of tepees furthest down the stream, along the western bank of which the camp was pitched. The Sans Arcs and Minneconjous were next in order, their circles being close to the river, with the Ogalallas and Blackfeet Sioux further to the west. The Hunkpapas occupied the lower and southernmost circle. A few Santees, Brulés and Assiniboines were there, but had no independent circles. No white or breeds were present in the camp. He locates the northerly limits of the combined camps slightly north of Medicine Tail coulee, and the southerly limit close to the tip of the river's "Garryowen" loop. He states, however, that after the first day's fighting, there was no jubilant celebration of the victory, but only mourning for the Indian dead, and that all tribal circles were moved to north and west because Death had touched the camp. Sitting Bull of the Hunkpapas was chief of the combined tribes; Crazy Horse chief of the Ogalallas, Lame Deer of

the Minneconjous and Hump of the Sans Arcs. Of the Cheyennes, Lame White Man was warrior chief, and not Two Moon as has been generally supposed.

* * *

On the night before the battle, the Indians held a social dance, and visiting parties of young men went from one circle to another to dance with the girls until daybreak. Then Wooden Leg and his brother, after a late breakfast, went for a dip in the river, after which they lay down in the shade of the cottonwoods that lined its banks, and fell asleep.

About mid-morning, they were abruptly wakened by sounds of shooting that came from the upper end of the camp, where the Hunkpapas were located: they heard shouts that soldiers were upon them, and upon rushing back to the Cheyenne circle, found excitement and confusion among the women and children, some of whom were fleeing to the hills or across the river.

* * *

The young warrior dressed and armed himself while the horse herds were driven in, and having hurriedly painted for battle, mounted his waiting pony and sped south toward the sound of the guns, in the wake of hundreds of warriors who had gone on before. Soldiers, prone upon the valley floor greeted them with rifle fire; the Indians returned few shots, but many arrows.

Soon the soldiers left the valley, and with their horses, hid in the timber, leaving their dead behind. Indians who had come with the soldiers now scattered and fled, and the Sioux, with a few Cheyennes, encircled the timber where the troops were concealed. Suddenly, out they came, mounted, dashing for the river. The Sioux followed, overtook them and killed many before the river was

The Cheyenne Warrior Wooden Leg.

reached; at the crossing they killed many more: and as the soldiers reached the top of a high hill, the Indians were all about them. Wooden Leg joined these Indians and made a few long range shots with a carbine snatched from the back of a soldier during the rush to the river. A few minutes later, an Indian companion pointed out to him, in the hills to the north, another force of soldiers on the eastern side of the stream. The Indians who were shooting at the "first soldiers" now began to leave them and to ride toward those they saw on the northern hills. Some recrossed the river and rode through the camp, to cross the ford at Medicine Tail; others followed down the east side ridges. All the Indians left the "first soldiers" to ride against the others.

* * *

Wooden Leg returned to the Cheyenne camp, which he found almost deserted, the women and children and old men having fled to the western hills. Changing horses, he again crossed the river at the Medicine Tail ford, where, he says, all the Indians crossed to attack the second force of soldiers, and made his way toward the fighting on the northeast hills. Hundreds of warriors rode in that direction—some along the east side ridges, but many more across the ford. The soldiers had formed lines upon a ridge, facing some Indians between them and the river, while others moved up a coulee toward the soldiers' rear. The warriors all dismounted before they began to fight, leaving their ponies in gullies, safe against the firing. Fighting at long range continued for about an hour and a half, during which time the warriors crept steadily closer to the soldiers, who could not see them, though they could see the soldiers all the time. Few warriors had good rifles, and fewer still, repeaters. They used instead, thousands of arrows, shooting them high into the air so that they struck the soldiers and their horses from above, which caused the horses to plunge wildly and knock the soldiers down.

* * *

The ridge along which the troops advanced was about two miles east of the Cheyenne circle. Here a few long range shots were exchanged with Indians. They rode on in a northerly direction, past the camp, and turned in a westerly direction to a lower ridge, where the real fighting occurred, and it was here that most of them were killed. None of the soldiers got any closer to the river than where their bodies were found.

* * *

After long range fighting had proceeded for a long time, a troop of mounted soldiers galloped from the eastern part of the ridge, toward the river. Cheyennes and Ogalallas were massed here, who ran when they saw the soldiers coming; but when they had dismounted, the Warrior Chief (Lame White Man) called the warriors back, shouting out that they now could kill them all. The warriors surrounded these soldiers, and as they closed in, the soldiers began to shoot each other and to shoot themselves. All were dead by the time the Indians reached them, and the warriors secured their arms and ammunition, which they turned against the rest of the soldiers on the ridge above. Wooden Leg mounted his pony and rode to the eastern end of the ridge, but found the soldiers there all dead also. They too had killed each other or themselves as soon as the Indians had attacked and killed a few of them— all except four, who tried to get away, but their mounts were jaded, and three of the four were quickly overtaken and killed. The fourth man, finding that the Sioux were gaining on him, shot himself.

* * *

Wooden Leg rode now to the hill north of the ridge, where the warriors had surrounded another group of soldiers. All these too, shot each other or themselves, all being dead before the Indians reached them.

* * *

There now remained only the soldiers at the west end of the ridge, concealed behind the carcasses of horses. Warriors by thousands surrounded them, creeping ever closer. Neither the soldiers nor the warriors could see each other, but the dead horses that marked the soldiers position were plainly visible. One mounted soldier broke for the east. Where he came from they did not know, but he too was overtaken and killed.

The soldier fire ceased: the warriors rushed forward. All the soldiers were dead but seven, who ran toward the river. But they were surrounded, and as all the others had done, they killed themselves. This ended the fighting on the ridge. The Indians had killed but twenty or thirty soldiers: all the rest had killed each other or had committed suicide.

* * *

As the warriors made their final rush, triumphant shouts proclaimed that all the soldiers had been killed. A crowd of old men and young boys who had watched the battle from a safe distance, now rushed their ponies among the bodies. But not all the soldiers had expired. One wounded officer—a captain—still lived, though in a dazed condition. He raised himself upon an elbow, glaring wildly at the Indians, who shrank from him, believing him returned from the spirit world. A

Sioux warrior wrested the revolver from his nerveless hand and shot him through the head. Thus died the last of Custer's battalion, his identity unknown.

* * *

The rest of the story is anti-climax. Wooden Leg has little to say concerning the fight on Reno Hill, in which apparently, he took no active part, either that day or the next. We know, however, that when Custer's battalion was wiped out, warriors by the hundreds attacked Reno, forcing him to retreat from the advanced position at Weir Point to the hill where his stand was made throughout the 25th and 26th of June. Wooden Leg states that during the night of the 25th parties of young men both came from and went to the hill to shoot at the "first soldiers," who had taken refuge there; that he went himself during the night as a scout to make sure that the soldiers were still there; and that during the next day they were besieged up to the time the Indians moved away. He describes the efforts of the soldiers to get water, and the shooting down of one who reached the stream, and the looting of his body. And he tells, too, of revisiting the Custer field, and of the mutilation of the dead. The details are grewsome and add little but horror to the story.

* * *

Wooden Leg fixed the time of Reno's attack in the valley as about mid-morning, and the end of Custer's fight about noon. He says the Indians were taken by surprise, and that none knew that they were fighting Custer, supposing the soldiers to be the same ones they had defeated on the Rosebud the week before. This statement confirms General H. L. Scott's statement to the same effect.

* * *

Numerous canteens taken by warriors from the bodies of dead soldiers were found to contain whiskey; and it was believed by many of them that strong drink had so crazed the soldiers as to cause them to shoot each other, or to kill themselves, instead of turning their weapons against the Indians. Others believed that the prayers of the medicine men accounted for their strange behavior; but not Wooden Leg—he thought the whiskey did it!

* * *

Until the publication of this work by Dr. Marquis, it was generally believed that Two Moon led the Cheyennes at the Little Big Horn. But Wooden Leg says that Lame White Man was War Chief, and that Two Moon was a minor figure in the battle, owing his later prominence to General Miles, who made him head man of the tribe by appointment. Two Moon was brave enough, he says, but a great liar, who held that it was not wrong to lie to white men. In view of the white man's record of mendacity when dealing with Indians, the old chief had something there!

* * *

It will be remembered that during the morning of June 25, while General Custer was at the Crows Nest, Sergeant Curtis was sent back on the trail to recover a box of hard bread and a bag lost during the night march. He found them; but also found an Indian sitting on the box, examining the contents of the bag! It was this incident that caused Custer to fear that the presence of the troops had been discovered and reported to the Indian camp, and that if he was to strike at all, he must do so without delay, immediately he located them. His scouts had told him at the Crows Nest, that they could see the camp some fifteen miles away, down the Little Big Horn valley, but he did not believe them, being unable himself to see it. But he knew the Indians must be somewhere near, for he had been following their trail for three days. Wooden Leg makes it clear, however, that the finders of the box were members of a small band of Cheyennes led by Little Wolf, who had followed the troops from the upper Rosebud. They had kept to the hills and had made no effort to warn the camp, which they joined only after the first day's fighting was over. The Sioux, indeed, believed them to be allies of the soldiers and were about to kill them when Wooden Leg and other Cheyennes who knew them, assured the indignant warriors that this was not true. This incident probably had far reaching consequences, one of which may well have been the division of the regiment, which contributed heavily to Custer's defeat.

* * *

Wooden Leg told Dr. Marquis that the Cheyenne circle held some 300 lodges—about 1600 people; that the Blackfeet Sioux circle was about equal; the Sans Arcs larger. Both Minneconjou and Ogalalla circles were greater than that of the Sans Arcs; the Hunkpapas twice the size of the Cheyenne's. From these figures Dr. Marquis estimates the population of the hostile camp at about 12,000. Such a figure would easily account for at least 3000 warriors in the combined camps.

Acceptance of the old warrior's estimate that no more than 20 to 30 of Custer's battalion were killed by the Indians, and that all the others killed each other or themselves, leads to the extraordinary statistical conclusion that of Custer's force, which numbered about 225, approximately but 10% were enemy inflicted losses: 90% were self-destroyed!

This charge of wholesale self-destruction upon

the part of Custer's troops, needless to say, is what makes Wooden Leg's story especially remarkable. Dr. Marquis, whose sincerity is beyond doubt, believed and indeed insisted that the tale is true, justifying such belief upon the ground that the Seventh Cavalry of 1876 was composed largely of recruits who, terrorized by fears of savage tortures, destroyed themselves "en masse" rather than to chance it.

While it is true that many enlisted men of the regiment were recruits, the over-all percentage was far below 90%. The commissioned and non-commissioned officers alone of Custer's five troops, of whom none were recruits, aggregated 46 in number—almost double the "twenty to thirty" Wooden Leg estimates as the total number of his soldiers killed by the Indians. Add to these the veteran privates, who constituted a majority of the enlisted personnel, and the recruit theory becomes enshrouded in doubt. But if one discards it because of doubt, there remain only the whiskey—or —the medicine men!

To you, all veteran officers of the Indian wars, I attempt no evaluation of the story. You are better able than I to make one. But I cannot help reflecting that no one has ever charged that any of Reno's men committed suicide, though commanded by an officer who, rightly or wrongly, was accused of cowardice. But Custer's men, commanded by one who above all other qualities was noted for his courage, stand charged with almost universal self-destruction!

Note:

Dr. Marquis wrote and published several booklets having to do with the Battle of the Little Big Horn, which are still in print and available. These booklets carry the following titles, and all are well worth reading and careful study:

(1) Sketch story of the Custer Battle
(2) She Watched Custer's Last Battle
(3) Rain-in-the-Face and Curley, the Crow
(4) Sitting Bull and Gall, the Warrior
(5) Custer Soldiers Not Buried
(6) Which Indian Killed Custer?
(7) Two Days After the Custer Battle

The second booklet of those above listed contains the eye-witness story of Kate Bighead, a woman of the Cheyennes, who saw the combat on the lower ridge and the rout of the Gray Horse troop, as did also Mrs. Spotted Horn Bull, the cousin of Sitting Bull. Kate Bighead's account of the battle is both graphic and grewsome, and in its descriptive features is substantially the same story as that told by Wooden Leg, the young warrior whose exploits are recounted in the book "A Warrior Who Fought Custer."

WHY THE CHEYENNES WERE ALLIES OF THE SIOUX

MUCH more could be added to the Cheyenne stories, and if it were possible to accept the view of some writers that the battle of the Little Big Horn was *primarily* the Cheyenne's fight, rather than that of the Sioux, much more would be added.

But I do not accept that view, which seems to be based in too large a degree upon a theory or belief that because Custer, after the Washita fight, smoked the peace pipe with the Southern Cheyennes, and vowed everlasting peace and friendship thereafter, the Cheyenne Nation took revenge upon him at the Little Big Horn because he had broken his oath.

It has seemed to me that there is little or nothing of substance in this theory, for the reason that it is definitely established that none of the Indians in the hostile camp knew at the time, or indeed, for a considerable time after the battle, that they were fighting Custer. Wooden Leg made this fact clear to Dr. Marquis, and it was made very clear to General Scott by Sioux and Cheyenne alike.

The Cheyennes did take *a* leading part in the battle, but not *the* leading part, which office, as I read the story, was certainly performed by the Sioux themselves.

Sitting Bull was the head and front of the non-reservation Sioux. He was looked upon and looked up to as the leader of the so-called hostile camp, and there can be no doubt that the overwhelming majority of the people in that camp were members of the Sioux Nation.

The Northern Cheyennes were there as allies of the Sioux; and the reason was not because they had gone on the warpath against one man— George Custer; but because the United States Government had sent its soldiers to force unwilling members of the Sioux Nation to live on reservations, where those who had already bowed their necks to the white man's yoke had been cheated, abused and made captives *de facto* whatever may have been their status *de jure*.

And in thus employing force, the United States Government, in its effort to chastise the recalcitrant Sioux, had invaded lands that the Northern Cheyennes claimed as their own; their homeland and their hunting ground. Of course they joined the Sioux. What else could be expected? And why invent a romantic reason when a plain and practical reason is apparent!

CHAPTER 7

THE ARAPAHOES

FIVE STRAY ARAPAHOES

THE ARAPAHOES, as a tribe, had no part in the battle of the Little Big Horn; but a war party, consisting of five young men who were out hunting a chance to lift some Shoshone scalps, ran into a party of Sioux a few days before the battle, and were virtually made prisoners, the Sioux accusing them of being spies for the white soldiers, just as they later accused Little Wolf and his band of Cheyennes. The Arapahoes were cleared of suspicion by the intercession of the Cheyenne Chief Two-Moon, and evidently to show their good faith, went into the fight against Custer's troops.

Two of the group, Waterman and Left Hand, in 1920 the only survivors of the group, were interrogated that year and told their stories to Colonel Tim McCoy, who reduced them to writing. Their statements, which follow, have never heretofore been published.

THE STORY OF WATERMAN

AN ARAPAHOE WARRIOR WHO FOUGHT AGAINST CUSTER

A LONG time ago when I was a young man, it was the custom of the young Indian to go on small war parties looking for Shoshones or other unfriendly tribes. If our medicine was good, we sometimes returned to camp with a scalp or a number of ponies.

Sometimes when an Indian slept he would keep his best horse at the door of his tepee, holding in his hand the rope to which the horse was tied. It was considered a very brave deed for an Indian to slip into an enemy camp at night and cut the rope of a horse outside a tepee, and ride him away.

I had lived twenty-two snows at the time of the great battle on the Little Big Horn River. That was a long time ago, but my mind is clear, and I will tell you all I know about that battle.

There were five of us Arapahoes in that fight. Three have joined the spirits of their fathers, and now only Left Hand and I, Waterman, still live. Soon we too must go to the long sleep, and no one will be alive to tell the story, so I will tell you, whom the Arapahoes call their Soldier-Chief, everything just as I saw it, and nothing that is not the truth.

The Arapahoes were camped at Fort Robinson where they drew their rations from the government, and I, with four other young bucks, slipped out of the agency to go on a scouting party for Shoshones. With me were Yellow Eagle, Yellow Fly, Well-Knowing One and Left Hand. We rode north into the buffalo country, and one day near the Little Big Horn River we met a small party of Sioux. They told us that the Sioux were going to have a sun-dance, and said that we should come along with them to the Sioux village and have a good time. Afterward I learned that these Sioux thought we were scouts for the white soldiers. We rode along with them, and as we came near the village a great many Sioux came out of the camp to meet us. They took all our guns away, and made us prisoners, saying that we were scouts of the white man, and that they were going to kill us. That night we were guarded so we could not escape, and in the morning, Two Moon, Chief of the Cheyenne, learned we were Arapahoes, so he went to the Sioux Chiefs and made them give us back our guns and set us free. The Cheyennes and the Arapahoes have always been brothers. The Sioux gave us our guns, but they kept a close watch on us, so we could not get away. We remained in the Sioux camp and saw the sun rise twice. Then the whole village moved farther down the river and made another camp. It was the biggest camp I ever saw. There were thousands of warriors. I do not know how many. When the sun came up again, that was the day of the fight.

We heard shooting at the upper end of the

village, and we all went that way. The soldiers had crossed the river and were coming toward the camp. At that time the sun was there (position indicating about 9:00 A. M.). There were not many soldiers, and I knew they would be beaten because there were many Sioux and Cheyennes. There was one Indian killed there. The soldiers went back across the river to a ridge where they dug some pits. The Indians kept shooting at them for a long time. After a while we heard shooting at the lower end of the village, and, knowing it must be another body of soldiers, we started down there as fast as we could. These troops were trying to cross the river and attack the camp, but the Indians drove them back. The soldiers could have forded the river at that point, because we crossed over and drove them up the hill. When they got to the top of the hill, they left their horses and the Indians took them. Some of the horses got away and came down to the river where they were caught by some of the Indians. There were grey horses and some sorrels. This left the soldiers on foot completely surrounded by the Indians.

The soldiers were on the high ground, and in one of the first charges we made a Cheyenne Chief named White Man Cripple* was killed. Two Moon then took command of the Cheyennes and led them all during the fight. During the earlier part of the fight, I was with some Indians in a small gulch below the hill where the soldiers were, but later we moved up the hill and closed in on the soldiers. There was a great deal of noise and confusion. The air was heavy with powder smoke, and the Indians were all yelling. Crazy Horse, the Sioux Chief, was the bravest man I ever saw. He rode closest to the soldiers, yelling to his warriors. All the soldiers were shooting at him, but he was never hit. The Indians on horseback had shields and rode on the sides of their horses so the soldiers could not hit them. The soldiers were entirely surrounded, and the whole country was alive with Indians. There were thousands of them. A few soldiers tried to get away and reach the river, but they were all killed. A few did get down to the river, but were killed by some Indians there. The Indians were running all around shooting and yelling, and we were all very excited. I only know of one soldier that I killed. It was just at the last of the fight when we rushed to the top of the hill and finished all that were still alive. I killed him with my gun, but did not scalp him because the Arapahoes do not scalp a man with short hair, only long hair.

* Obviously another English version of the Cheyenne War-Chief's name. Wooden Leg calls him "Lame White man."

When I reached the top of the hill I saw Custer. He was dressed in buckskin, coat and pants, and was on his hands and knees. He had been shot through the side and there was blood coming from his mouth. He seemed to be watching the Indians moving around him. Four soldiers were sitting up around him, but they were all badly wounded. All the other soldiers were down. Then the Indians closed in around him, and I did not see any more. Most of the dead soldiers had been killed by arrows, as they had arrows sticking in them. The next time I saw Custer he was dead, and some Indians were taking his buckskin clothes. The Indians were quarreling, each trying to take the clothes away from the other. I do not know who got them. The fight was all over when the sun was there (position indicating about three o'clock). The squaws then crossed the river and began taking the clothes off the dead soldiers. Sometimes one that was not yet dead would move a little, and the squaws would become frightened and scatter. What the squaws did to the dead soldiers I do not know, because I did not go back to see. I saw many soldiers who were scalped, but do not know whether Custer was scalped or not, because I went back across the river to camp after the fight was over. During the battle I was dressed in beaded leggings, breech-clout, a white shirt and a large war-bonnet. My face was painted yellow and red, and around my neck, tied in a deer-skin medicine bag, was a certain root, which was my medicine. I still have that same medicine. The Sioux kept a close watch on us, because during the fight Left Hand had killed a Sioux warrior, whom he thought was one of Custer's Crow or Arikara scouts, and the Sioux were very angry.

The white people believe that there were a great many Indians killed in this fight. I only know of six Cheyennes and six Sioux who were killed. There were many wounded. That night we stayed in the Sioux camp, but the next night, after it was dark, Yellow Eagle, Yellow Fly, Well-Knowing One, Left Hand and I crawled out under the side of our wickiup, mounted ponies, slipped out of camp and rode on around the foot of the mountains back to Fort Robinson.

That was many moons ago, and since then great changes have come upon us. The buffalo are all gone, and the Indians who once roamed these plains and were happy, are now held on reservations as wards of the government. My people are very poor, and sometimes have not enough to eat. Of the five Arapahoes who were in the battle of the Little Big Horn, only Left Hand and I, Waterman, are now alive. We are old men now, and soon we too must pass over to the great mystery. That is why I have told you this story.

THE STORY OF LEFT HAND

An Arapahoe Warrior Who Fought Against Custer

I WAS BORN in what is now called Powder River country. My father's name was Cherry. I am part Blackfoot and part Cheyenne, but have always lived among the Arapahoes. When I was a small boy, I always used my left hand instead of my right, and as that was strange for an Indian, I was called Left Hand. That has always been my name.

I was in the battle of the Little Big Horn where General Custer was killed. There were four other Arapahoes with me. That was a long time ago, but I remember it as if it were but yesterday.

The Arapahoes were camped at Fort Robinson, and four other young bucks, Yellow Eagle, Yellow Fly, Waterman and a Southern Arapahoe, who was sometimes called Green Grass, and I left the camp to go on a war party for Shoshones. We trailed north toward the country of the Crows, and one day met a small band of Sioux, who told us that their village was on the Little Big Horn, and that the Sioux were going to have a big sundance and that we must go with them. They thought we were scouts for the white soldiers, and watched us very closely. We went along with them to their camp, which was in the valley of the Little Big Horn, and as we approached the village, a number of Sioux came out to meet us. They took our guns away from us, and said they were going to kill us because we were scouts for the white soldiers. The next morning Two Moon, Chief of the Cheyennes, went to the Sioux Chiefs and told them that we were Arapahoes, and that they must give us back our guns and set us free, which they did, but they watched us closely so we could not get away. The second day we were in the Sioux camp they moved farther down the river, and it was the day after this that the battle took place.

The first attack was made at the south end of the village when the sun was there (position indicating about 9:00 A. M.). The soldiers fired a few shots, but when we rushed toward them, they became frightened and started back across the river. Many of them lost their horses and had to swim across. They climbed up on a high ridge and built a barricade. There were many soldiers killed there. The Sioux were all around them.

When the sun was straight up (about noon) we heard shooting at the lower end of the village, and knew it must be more soldiers. I went down through the village and crossed the river with a large party of Sioux and Cheyennes. We Arapahoes had all gotten separated during the first fight.

The soldiers were up on the ridge and the Indians were all around them. There was lots of shooting all around, and the Indians were all yelling. Everyone was excited. I saw an Indian on foot, who was wounded in the leg, and, thinking he was one of the Crow or Arikara scouts with the soldiers, I rode at him, striking at him with a long lance which I carried. The head of the lance was sharpened like an arrow. It struck him in the chest and went clear through him. He fell over a pile of dead soldiers. Afterward I found out he was a Sioux, and the Sioux were going to kill me because I had killed their friend. One Sioux tried to take my horse away from me, but I would not give him up. Everyone was excited. The hills were swarming with Indians, all yelling and shooting. Many of the Indians had bows and arrows. As I came up on the ridge, one soldier, who was on the ground, handed me his gun. I took the gun and did not kill him, but some Sioux who were behind me killed him. I went back and took his belt, which had many cartridges in it.

Once I saw Custer. He was dressed in buckskin. It was almost at the end of the fight. He was standing up and had pistols in his hands shooting into the Indians. I did not see him again until it was all over. I walked around and saw him lying there. He was dead. Most of the soldiers were all dead, but some still moved a little. When the sun was there (pointing to a position indicating about 3 P. M.) all was over, not a white man was alive. The Sioux scalped a great many, then the squaws crossed the river and took all the soldiers' clothes. What they did to the dead soldiers I do not know, because I went back across the river to camp and joined the other Arapahoes. Some of the Indians went back and fought the soldiers who were barricaded on the ridge at the south end of the camp, but I did not go with them.

The next morning the Sioux broke camp and started for the mountains. We heard that some soldiers were coming up the river, and the Indians were scared. That night after they had made camp and it was dark, we four Arapahoes crawled out to the pony herd, and each mounting a pony, slipped away. We travelled as fast as we could back to Fort Robinson where the Arapahoes were.

During that fight I counted thirteen coups. I was dressed in a shirt and breech-clout. My medicine was a piece of buffalo hide made into a cross with two feathers in it, which I wore in my hair.

Custer was a very foolish man to fight the Sioux at that time. He did not have many men, and the Sioux and Cheyenne were as thick as the grass on the hillside. I do not know how many there were, but I have never seen so many Indians together at one time. There were only a few Sioux and Cheyenne killed, and these were buried on the ground on the west bank of the river where the camp was. Not a man of Custer's command escaped, all were killed.

I was a young man then and there were lots of Indians. The white men used to trade us guns for buffalo robes, but now it is all changed. Many moons ago a great medicine man told us that if we would dance a certain dance for a long time, the buffalo would come back, and the Indians would again be free and happy, but that was not true. The Indian is like a prisoner on his reservation. The buffalo are all gone, the antelope are gone, and now we old men can only sit by the fire, sing our war-songs and dream of the past.

At The Crow's Nest (1919). Left to right: Unidentified employee of The Indian Bureau, The Crow Scout White-Man-Runs-Him, General H. L. Scott, Colonel Tim McCoy.

CHAPTER 8

GENERAL HUGH L. SCOTT DISCUSSES
THE SIOUX WAR

CUSTER'S LAST FIGHT:
NOTES BY GEN. SCOTT

* * *

**Facts He Gathered Led Him to Believe
The Tragedy Could Have Been Avoided**

(From an unidentified newspaper)

EARLY in 1876 General G. A. Custer, lieutenant colonel of the Seventh Cavalry, led that regiment gayly out of Fort Abraham Lincoln, Dakota Territory, the band playing "The Girl I Left Behind Me." There were many in that command who never returned alive.

The command marched westward and met General Alfred Terry at the juncture of the Rosebud and the Yellowstone Rivers in Montana. Here General Custer received orders from General Terry on the steamer Far West. [Later the orders, dated June 22, 1876, were reported by General Terry to the War Department.] While attempting to carry out these orders he lost his life in battle with the Sioux, or Dakota, Indians on the Little Big Horn River June 25, 1876.

I was not present at the battle, having graduated from West Point on June 14, only eleven days before. I learned of it while visiting the Centennial Exposition at Philadelphia on July 6, the news having required ten days to reach the nearest telegraph station at Bismarck, Dakota.

I immediately took steps to secure one of the vacancies due to the battle. My commission as second lieutenant, Seventh Cavalry, is dated the day after the fight. The commission and proper orders having been received, I reported for duty to Major Marcus A. Reno, Seventh Cavalry, at Fort Abraham Lincoln, Dakota, and followed the fortunes of that regiment for many years on horseback over a large part of Montana, Dakota, Wyoming, Nebraska, &c., usually on Indian service.

In leisure hours in the tent which I occupied with Lieutenant Luther R. Hare, surviving officers of the Seventh Cavalry would fight the battles of the regiment again until far into the night, especially that of the Little Big Horn. I listened to these discussions with the greatest interest. In addition I have a copy of the testimony of some of these officers under oath before the Reno court of inquiry in Chicago in 1879.*

General Custer with his immediate command separated from Major Reno [on the afternoon of his last battle] near the mouth of [what was afterward called] Reno Creek, went down some distance back from the Little Big Horn River, behind a long, low ridge that masked his approach, to the lower end of the Indian village, and [they] were seen no more by white men until their bodies were discovered by the scouts of General Terry on June 27.

* * *

The Indians were in the Indian country, making meat and robes for the support of their families. There were treaties extant, confirmed by the Senate of the United States, the supreme law of the land, making it a trespass for white men to enter that country. The Indians were as far away as they could get from the white man, 600 miles from the railway.

I have interrogated many agency Indians who were in the fight, asking what they had done and why they were out there. They were perfectly frank with me, saying that they had killed a soldier, for instance, or captured a horse; some said that they were not allowed to be present at the Sun Dance at the agency and had come out to be present at the Sun Dance in what was called the hostile village; others said they were there to make meat and robes for their families.

---

* This was a copy of my Abstract of the testimony, presented to General Scott in 1921. W.A.G.

113

But I never saw one who admitted that he had gone out there to fight. Our ideas about that are altogether wrong. The Indians were attacked at the instance of the Interior Department while they were peaceably attending to their own business, with no desire to fight. To be sure, it was dangerous for white men to be in that country, but white men had no business there, and were trespassers.

Another thing was a surprise to me. I have heard many Indians, at all the Sioux agencies, volunteer the statement (in no way suggested by me) that if Custer had come close and asked for a council instead of attacking he could have led them all into the agency without a fight. I rather doubted that Sitting Bull and Crazy Horse would have come in. The latter had never been to an agency in all his life. But this method of dealing with Indians had not occurred to any one at that time.

It has been charged against General Custer (1) that he disobeyed his orders in going straight to those Indians and attacking before Terry and Gibbon had time to get in position on the other side of them; (2) that he failed to support Reno according to his promise; (3) that he lost the battle by dividing his command. Reno and Benteen were charged with disloyalty in not going to Custer's relief. Reno was charged with cowardice and disobedience for not charging right into the village headlong.

I have never held a brief for either Custer or Reno, and disliked the latter intensely. But I do not like to see either of them censured unjustly. Custer was told in his orders to move toward Tongue River, on the flank of the Indians. It is well known that an Indian has no flanks any more

than a bird. If Custer had demonstrated his attack out in the open, the Indians, if ready to fight, would have overwhelmed him. If not they would have run away toward Terry, whose command was mainly infantry, and the mounted Indians could have passed all around them in plain sight and escaped, as they did when Terry came up.

How it was expected of foot soldiers to catch Indians was always a puzzle to me. Unless they were overwhelmingly strong they would scatter like quail and disappear, and that was just what Custer feared they would do. And if he had allowed them to escape under the orders he had received—putting the whole thing up to his own judgment—he could have expected no mercy.

As it was, Custer had not intended to attack until the 26th, at which time Terry and Gibbon would have reached the mouth of the Little Big Horn River. But his hand was forced by the Cheyenne, Little Wolf, to whose party Custer's attention was called from the "Crow Nest" on the divide between the Rosebud and the Little Big Horn, and who saw Custer and his command. Moreover, an Indian had been seen back on the trail.

Custer had intended to hide on the divide and attack at daylight on the 26th, but he had a right to feel that he had been discovered by those Indians. If he did not attack before they gave the alarm the Indians would escape, for which he would have to answer to a court-martial. He hurried down to prevent the escape.

Why Little Wolf did not hurry down to give the alarm has never been explained. He said himself that he followed along behind, watching the soldiers, and arrived after the fight was over.

CHAPTER 9

PHILO CLARK'S 1877 BATTLEFIELD SURVEY

HIS REPORT AND SHERIDAN'S SUMMARY

IN 1877 a party including Captain Philo Clark, the noted authority on Indian Sign Language and Col. J. W. Pope (then Lieutenant 5th Infantry) went over the battle-field with two Indians who were with the Hostiles in the fight, and an Indian scout who was with Reno's command. "We were * * * led over Custer's trail a distance of ten miles away to the spot where he was killed. This trail was in the valley north of the line of bluffs, on the north bank of the Little Big Horn. These two Indians, one of whom may have been Iron Cedar, stated that after they had followed Reno's command to the hills, they passed on to the north and there saw Custer's command coming down the valley. They hastened and gave the alarm, this being the first intimation they had of Custer's approach. They said that Custer, when he came out in full view of the village, dismounted and formed line; "one troop was formed well forward, making an angle forward with the other troops along the Custer ridge; that this troop made a considerable fight and that nearly all of the Indians killed fell at this fight. (They estimated the loss at thirty or forty.) That this troop was soon driven back to the position where it was overwhelmed with the whole command; that when nearly all the command had been killed, a few men ran down to get shelter in the timber or ravines." (Extracts from letter from Colonel Pope, 1892.)

The foregoing is quoted from General Godfrey's narrative, "Custer's Last Battle," as revised by him in 1908 and reprinted by Mrs. Custer in 1921, under the title, "General George A. Custer and the Battle of the Little Big Horn."

EXTRACT FROM CAPT. CLARK'S REPORT

The following extract from Clark's report probably refers to the survey above described. A battle-field sketch map which accompanies the report has been lost, but is considered unimportant.

"The small number killed is due to the fact that an Indian has a wonderful faculty of protecting himself, and unless he is shot through the brain, heart or back, there is no certainty at all about his dying, for since I have seen many Indians who have been shot in all manner of ways through the body and still enjoying excellent health, I have been convinced that of all animals they are superior in point of tenacity of life, magnificent horsemen and fine shots—doing about as good execution on the backs of their thoroughly-trained speedy and hardy ponies as on the ground, accustomed from their earliest youth to take advantage of every knoll, rock, tree, tuft of grass, and every aid the topography of the country affords to secure game; and their education completed and perfected by constant warfare with other tribes and the whites, each warrior becomes an adept in their way of fighting, needing no orders to promptly seize, push and hold any opportunity for success, or in retreating, protecting themselves from harm. Each tribe is organized by accident or pleasure into several different bands, each band having a chief, but his powers and authority are, in a great measure, limited by the will and wishes of his people.

"Great prominence has been given Crazy Horse and Sitting Bull in this war, the good fighting strategy and subsequent masterly retreats being attributed to them, whereas they are really not entitled to more credit or censure than many others, so far as plans and orders were concerned; but they headed two of the worst bands on the Plains, and were the two fiercest leaders the Sioux nation has produced for years.

* * *

"On June 17th the Indians were camped on a small tributary of the Little Big Horn River about 18 miles above the place where Gen. Custer's troops found them on the 25th. They had at this time about 1200 standing lodges and 400 wickiups, or brush shelters, and numbered about 3500 fighting men.

* * *

"After driving Col. Reno's forces across the river, most of the Indians left his immediate front and went down to join those who were fighting Gen. Custer's column—which came down and made an attempt to cross at the mouth of the little stream (Medicine Tail?) and finding it impossible, turned up the ridge, then turned again as the trails leading down to the ford were reached. The Indians had massed in the ravines and opened such a terrific fire from all sides that the troops gave way; the Indians rushed in and made it a hand to hand conflict. The troops attempted to rally once or twice, but were literally overwhelmed with numbers, and in a few moments not one was left to tell the story.

"The temporary respite gave Reno time to gather his forces on a sort of bluff and partially intrench himself. The Indians, believing they had him anyway, in a measure abandoned the attack for the night, and besides, they had a large number of dead and wounded on their hands to care for. If Reno had attempted to succor Custer's forces he would most surely have met their fate. The next day (27th) the approach of Terry's column was discovered, and as Gen. Custer had fallen upon them so much more quickly than they anticipated, they hurriedly broke camp, leaving much of their camp equipage behind them. The timely arrival of this force saved Reno's party.

"In this fight about 40 Indians were killed and a very large number wounded. They say the white soldiers fought bravely and desperately, and gave instances of personal gallantry which created admiration and respect, even in their savage hearts, but it is impossible to positively identify the individuals from their imperfect descriptions. I am convinced, however, that none were taken prisoners and subjected to torture as has been represented. The Indians say that many of the dead soldiers' carbines were found with shells stuck fast in the chambers, rendering them useless for the time being.

GENERAL SHERIDAN'S COMMENTS

"There is much interesting information in this report, and Lieut. Clark's description of the capabilities of the Indian for offensive warfare is very accurate; but the narratives of the Indians should be read with a considerable degree of allowance and some doubt, as Indians generally make their descriptions to conform to what they think are the wishes of those who interview them.

* * *

"As to the number of Indians in the fight, and the number killed, accounts greatly differ. There certainly were enough Indians there to defeat the 7th Cavalry, divided as it was into three parts, and to totally annihilate any one of these three detachments in the open field, as was proved in the destruction of one of them and its gallant commander. The reasons given why Major Reno should have remained where he was driven, on the top of the bluff, that he afterwards fortified and held, are very good; but there are other reasons no less strong. For instance, he could not abandon his wounded, who would have been slain by the enemy, and furthermore, he had no knowledge of the whereabouts of Custer nor of the straits he was in, and it is natural to presume that he supposed Col. Custer would return to his support when he discovered the superiority in numbers of the Indians, in order that the regiment might be reunited.

"The history of the battle of the Little Big Horn can now be told in a few words. The Indians were actually surprised, and in the confusion arising from the surprise and the attempt of the women and children to get out of the way, Col. Custer was led to believe that the Indians were retreating and would escape him; furthermore, from the point he left Major Reno he could see only a small portion of the Indian encampment, and had no just conception of its size, consequently he did not wait to close up his regiment and attack with its full strength, but, ordering Major Reno to attack the village at its upper end, he started directly down the stream on the further side of the bluffs which concealed the river from his view and hid him from the Indians, with five companies of the 7th Cavalry. Upon reaching a trail that led down to the river, opposite about the middle of the village, he followed it down nearly to the stream, and then, without even attempting to cross (for no bodies of men or horses were found upon either side of the stream near the ford), he went back for a few hundred yards and started directly up the line of the fatal ridge where his body and the bodies of his command were afterwards found, with the evident intention of going to the lower end of the village and crossing and attacking the Indians there. It was upon this ridge that he was completely surrounded and his command annihilated. There are no indications whatever that he attempted to go back and rejoin Major Reno. Had he done this after reaching the ford above named, Capt. Benteen, having in the meantime joined Major Reno, he would have had his whole regiment together, and could have held his own, at least, and possibly have defeated the Indians. If the Indians had really known that he was coming, they would have gone out to meet him, as they did to meet Gen. Crook only eight days before, in order to let the women and children and the village get out of the way. Again, if Col. Custer had waited until his regiment was closed up and crossed it at the point Major Reno did, and had made his attack in the level valley, posting some of his men in the woods, all the Indians there could not have defeated him. I do not attribute Col. Custer's action to either recklessness or want of judgment, but to a misapprehension of the situation and to a superabundance of courage.

"Enclosed herewith a statement of the battle of the Little Big Horn made to the C. O. at Cheyenne Agency by "Red Horse," a Sioux Indian, who evidently took part in the action,* and whose statement of the number killed and wounded of the Indians is greatly in excess of that named by Lieut. Clark's informant.

P. H. SHERIDAN,
Lieut-Gen. Commanding.

---

* See Sioux narratives, supra.

Part II

☆

GODFREY, BENTEEN AND EDGERLY

General Edward S. Godfrey as a Colonel of Cavalry. About 1898.

CHAPTER 1

GENERAL EDWARD S. GODFREY

and

MY RELATIONS WITH HIM

MY FIRST MEETING with General Godfrey occurred during the spring of 1921, at the Army and Navy Club in Washington. I had been engaged for some weeks in the preparation of an abstract of the testimony taken at the Reno Court of Inquiry, a full copy of which I had laboriously made in longhand several months before; and having thus embarked upon a study of Custer's last campaign that (though I did not know it) was to continue for more than thirty years, I wanted some first hand information that books and records did not supply. So I called on General Godfrey, then a guest at the Club.

It was a formal call, such as an officer on post is, by custom of the service, expected, and indeed obligated to make on his Commanding Officer. To be sure, General Godfrey was not my commanding officer, but he did have command (or so I thought) of the information I wanted, which was reason enough for me. I found him a very gracious gentleman, as was usual with officers of the "Old Army," and quite willing and ready to talk about General Custer and his last campaign. He did not have the information I was after, which was the whereabouts of Custer's famous message to Benteen to "Come on and be quick," but he did put me on the track of the man who carried it, a retired Sergeant named John Martin; and the result of my first interview with General Godfrey was my initial attempt at writing history—the personal story of Trumpeter Martin, orderly to General Custer on the 25th of June 1876. It was published by the *Cavalry Journal* in July 1923, together with comments by General Godfrey, under the title "Come On—Be quick —Bring Packs," and is reproduced in this volume.

I found General Godfrey open-minded and charitable in his judgment of other officers of the old Seventh, with one exception. It was plain that he considered Major Reno cowardly and craven. But neither in his conversations with me, nor in his many letters did he ever put his finger on any act of Reno's that he was willing to say was cowardly. He thought Reno "craven" because he did not hold his position in the valley; and having left it as he did, that he was "craven" because he did not immediately advance to the sound of the guns when Custer was fighting for his life in the hills downstream. But he never expressed to me a definite belief that either action on Reno's part would have saved Custer, and he made me feel that the reasons he gave for his attitude toward Reno were but a *part* of his reasons, and that he was holding something back that in his eyes gave weight and color to the reasons he expressed.

Godfrey was partisan. He never denied it, but he maintained always that his partisanship was not built on prejudice. And after knowing him intimately for years, I am free to say that I do not think prejudice, as such, entered at all into his judgment of Reno.

From the time I met him until I left Washington in the late summer of 1924, I had many conferences with General Godfrey. Together we spent hours examining the regimental records of the Seventh Cavalry for 1876; together we went out to the Soldiers Home to interview Sergeant Fremont Kipp and other veterans of the Sioux War, who were in the fight on the Little Big Horn and had signed the enlisted men's petition to the President and Congress, asking that Reno and Benteen be promoted. And when my abstract of the inquiry testimony was completed, I read it, every word, aloud to him. His comments from time to time during the reading, indicated that not until then had he known what other officers of the regiment had testified. And when I finished—(at 3 o'clock in the morning!)—he said—"This has been a revelation to me. I never knew until now the purport of any testimony but my own. Some of it I cannot understand; but it explains the finding of the Court."

I asked him if he had not known that the testimony was published from day to day in contemporary Chicago papers, to which he replied that he had known it, but had refrained from reading it because he did not wish his testimony to be influenced in any degree by that of others.

During all of my acquaintance with General Godfrey, which was continued by correspondence between 1924 and 1927, while I was stationed at Chicago, and by personal contact after I returned to Washington from the Philippines in 1929, almost to the day of his death, I never heard him refer to Reno otherwise than with contempt.

As I could find nothing in the records, or in his own account of the battle (his 1892 "Century" article, revised by him in 1908, an autographed copy of which he had presented to me) that seemed to justify his manner, I did my best to obtain from him a clear and definite statement of his attitude toward Reno, and his real reasons for it, but always he evaded the issue. General Edgerly, on the other hand, usually more reticent than Godfrey, was much more out-spoken, and and said without hesitation that on the hill Reno was cool, though by no means heroic, at the same time contrasting his leadership with that of Benteen.

Three times before my book "The Story of the Little Big Horn" went to press, I sent the manuscript to Godfrey, and each time when I received it back, I revised it because of criticisms or suggestions by him. I sent it also to Edgerly and to Varnum, to General Miles and to Captain R. G. Carter and got much benefit from their generous comments.

In my attempts to draw Godfrey out, I deliberately made over-statements favorable to Reno; but he would not be drawn. The nearest I got was in comments contained in his letters to Capt. Carter, which the latter read or quoted to me. But "the reason behind the reasons" still remained an unknown quantity.

Late in 1924 I took station at Chicago at the Headquarters of the Sixth Corps Area, where I remained until the summer of 1927. During a part of that time General Benjamin A. Poore commanded at Fort Sheridan, and when the Corps Area Commander was temporarily absent, Poore commanded in his stead. Upon one of these occasions he said to me, "Graham, did you ever find out what caused Godfrey to change his attitude toward Custer?" I replied that I had not been aware that Godfrey ever had changed his attitude toward Custer and that I had supposed he had always been one of Custer's most loyal protagonists. General Poore replied—"Oh no! he was not. When I was at West Point, Godfrey was there as an instructor. It was only a few years after the battle, and it was a matter of common knowledge that Godfrey held Custer responsible for the needless sacrifice of some of his most valued friends, and that he would not associate with nor even speak to those who defended Custer."

I expressed surprise, for I was not only surprised but astounded, whereupon Poore said: "Why don't you ask Godfrey what caused the change in his attitude?" I replied, "General, much as I would like to know, I do not feel that I can ask General Godfrey such a question as that. Why don't you ask him? He would probably tell you, but I fear that if I did it, he would think that I impugned his good faith." Poore's answer I do not remember, but it left me with an impression that he would do what he had suggested that I do, and there the matter dropped; and shortly after, I left Chicago to take station at Manila.

I returned to Washington in December 1929, and sometime during the early part of my tour there, I narrated my conversation with General Poore to Dr. Francis Hagner and W. J. Ghent, two Custer partisans (both since deceased), during an evening's discussion at the Doctor's home. Upon my statement that "I couldn't ask General Godfrey a question like that," Ghent exclaimed, "Well, I could; and I will." Whether he did I do not know: at all events, he did not tell me, and I was still in the dark as to "the reason behind the reasons."

But sooner or later, murder will out! In 1930 or 31, I attended the annual dinner of the Order of Indian Wars, of which I was an honorary member. Both Generals Godfrey and Charles King were present, and were called upon for speeches. As I recall the incidents of the evening, the presiding officer, in presenting Godfrey, stated that he had listened that day to a shocking tale, and he asked the General to repeat it. Godfrey then said that though what he had to tell them was hearsay, he believed it to be true, having come to him from the lips of Captain Benteen himself. Benteen had confided to him, he said, sometime during the early 80's, that on the night of the 25th of June, after the Indians had withdrawn, Reno had conferred with him as to what to do; whether, outnumbered as they were, they should stand and fight it out, or whether they should make a run for it under cover of the darkness. Their losses were already heavy, both in men and animals, and they had many wounded men beside. If they stayed and fought, the odds were against them unless Custer came to their relief, and he, apparently, had deserted them, as he had deserted Major Elliott at the Washita. On the other hand, if they could get away during the night, they had a good chance to save themselves, destroying or abandoning to the Indians everything that would not serve in making their escape. Here Benteen interrupted him to interject: "But the wounded; how would you move the wounded?" Reno replied, "those who can ride can be mounted and go; those who cannot ride we would have to leave." Benteen's reply was "No, Reno; *you can't do that."*

Why Godfrey had omitted to tell me of this revelation by Benteen I have never been able to understand. He knew that I was anxious to have the whole truth and nothing but the truth; and he knew also that I had importuned him to tell me the real reason for his attitude toward Reno, *which was obviously more hostile during the early 20's* (when I was working over the material for my story of the battle) *than it was when he testified at Chicago* in 1879, when the farthest he would go in criticism of the Major's conduct was to say that in his opinion "he did not exhibit fear but rather, nervous timidity."

I remarked to Ghent and Hagner, some time after the Indian Wars dinner (at which Ghent was also present), that it seemed strange that Godfrey had said nothing of this incident in his "Century" article. "O yes," they chorused, "Yes indeed he did": and then they quoted the following sentence from that article, which referred to the night of the 25th of June:

"The question of moving was discussed, but the conditions coupled to the proposition caused it to be indignantly rejected."

It may be that had I asked General Godfrey to explain what he meant by this rather cryptic statement, he might have told me the Benteen story; but it never occurred to me (and I doubt that it would occur to any officer of the Army) that a Commanding Officer would be likely to make a "proposition" relative to moving his command, or that subordinates would be in a position to "indignantly reject" any "proposition" made by their Commanding Officer. Commanders do not make "propositions": they issue orders; and the quoted statement, with which I was perfectly familiar,

had meant to me only that some subordinate, during the night of the 25th, had suggested that the command move, and that the suggestion entailed some condition that caused the Commanding Officer to "indignantly reject" it. And that, incidentally, was what it meant to Captain R. G. Carter also who, as spokesman for the anti-Reno clique in Washington, was much more severe in his criticisms of Reno than Godfrey ever was.

After my retirement in 1939, Engene Hart, then a public librarian in Los Angeles, furnished me with a memorandum prepared by Mr. Ghent, which indicated that Godfrey was by no means the only one to whom Benteen had told the story of the Reno "proposition." This Ghent memorandum is printed elsewhere in this volume. *Inter alia,* it includes excerpts from a letter General Godfrey wrote during March 1926 to J. A. Shoemaker of Billings, Montana. In this letter, Godfrey tells Shoemaker that on 28 June 1876, he rode with Benteen to the Custer battlefield, and that on the way he remarked to Benteen that Reno's conduct had been "pretty damned bad," to which Benteen replied, " 'God,' I could tell things that would make your hair stand on end." At that point someone interrupted and Benteen shut up like a clam, but promised Godfrey that at some future time he would tell him what he meant. The promise was not redeemed until the early 80's, when at Godfrey's insistence, Benteen told him that during the night of 25 June, while discussing the situation of the command, Reno "proposed" that the position be abandoned, all property destroyed, and such of the wounded as were unable to ride, left on the field. Benteen replied: *"I won't do it."*

While in general substance the story of the 1926 letter to Shoemaker is similar to what I heard General Godfrey relate at the Indian Wars dinner, his statement of Benteen's reply to Reno's "proposition" differs materially. Instead of the defiant *"I won't do it"* of the Shoemaker letter, it became: "No, Reno: *You can't do that,"* which gives a very different aspect to the entire incident.

But it is easy to understand that General Godfrey, having Benteen's assurance as he did, that Reno had considered and even proposed to flee by night, leaving his helpless wounded to be butchered by the Sioux, if he believed it—and there can be no question that he did—would thenceforth and ever after hold the author of such a plan beneath contempt, for if there was any one thing that any officer worth his salt held unthinkable in Indian warfare, it was a deliberate abandonment of his wounded. It was bad enough to leave the dead to be scalped and mutilated, but to leave the helpless living to undergo the horrors of savage torture until kinder death relieved them, was too shocking an act to contemplate. Such a plan could emanate only from one so crazed by fear as to have lost all sense of self respect and of soldierly honor. Undoubtedly this, or something closely akin, was Godfrey's reaction to Benteen's revelation. And this, in my opinion, though he never told me so, for I never saw him again after that Indian Wars dinner—was "the reason behind the reasons."

I knew General Godfrey well and am proud that I was able to call him friend. During my service on the active list I met and dealt with many officers of low and high degree, but I never knew one more meticulously honest, or who had higher regard for Duty, Honor and Country than did he.

CHAPTER 2

GENERAL GODFREY'S NARRATIVE

For many years after its first appearance in the Century Magazine for January 1892, General Godfrey's article titled *"Custer's Last Battle,"* was generally accepted as the one authoritative account available to the public.

The article has been severely criticized by many later writers, but no symposium of source material could be considered adequate without the inclusion of generous excerpts from Godfrey's first hand narrative.

Such excerpts as hereinafter follow are reproduced from his own 1908 revision, which was republished with some additions in 1921 by Mrs. Custer, under the title *"General George A. Custer and the battle of the Little Big Horn."*

THE INTRODUCTION

ON THE 16th of April, 1876, at McComb City, Missouri, I received orders to report my troop ("K" 7th Cavalry) to the Commanding General of the Department of Dakota, at St. Paul, Minnesota. At the latter place about twenty-five recruits fresh from civil life joined the troop, and we were ordered to proceed to Fort Abraham Lincoln, Dakota, where the Yellowstone Expedition was being organized. This expedition consisted of the 7th United States Cavalry, commanded by General George A. Custer, 28 officers and about 700 men; two companies of the 17th United States Infantry, and one company of the 6th United States Infantry, 8 officers and 135 men; one platoon of Gatling Guns, 2 officers and 32 men (of the 20th United States Infantry); and 40 "Ree" Indian scouts. The expeditionary forces were commanded by Brigadier-General Alfred H. Terry, the Department Commander, who, with his staff arrived several days prior to our departure.

On the 17th of May, at 5 a. m., the "general" (the signal to take down tents and break camp) was sounded, the wagons were packed and sent to the Quartermaster, and by six o'clock the wagon-train was on the road escorted by the Infantry. By seven o'clock the 7th Cavalry was marching in column of platoons around the parade-ground of Fort Lincoln, headed by the band playing "Garry Owen," the Seventh's battle tune, first used when the regiment charged at the battle of Washita. The column was halted and dismounted just outside the garrison. The officers and married men were permitted to leave the ranks to say "good-bye" to their families. General Terry, knowing the anxiety of the ladies, had assented to, or ordered, this demonstration in order to allay their fears and satisfy them, by the formidable appearance we made, that we were able to cope with any enemy that we might expect to meet. Not many came out to witness the pageant, but many tear-filled eyes looked from the latticed windows.

During this halt the wagon-train was assembled on the plateau west of the post and formed in column of fours. When it started off the "assembly" was sounded and absentees joined their commands. The signals "mount" and "forward" were sounded, and the regiment marched away, the band playing "The Girl I Left Behind Me."

The 7th Cavalry was divided into two columns, designated right and left wings, commanded by Major Marcus A. Reno and Captain F. W. Benteen. Each wing was subdivided into two battalions of three troops each. After the first day the following was the habitual order of march: one battalion was advance guard, one was rear guard, and one marched on each flank of the train. General Custer with one troop of the advance guard, went ahead and selected the route for the train and the camping places at the end of the day's march. The other two troops of the advance guard reported at headquarters for pioneer or fatigue duty, to build bridges and creek crossings. The rear-guard kept behind everything; when it came up to a wagon stalled in the mire, it helped to put the wagon forward. The battalions on the flanks were kept within five hundred yards of the trail and not

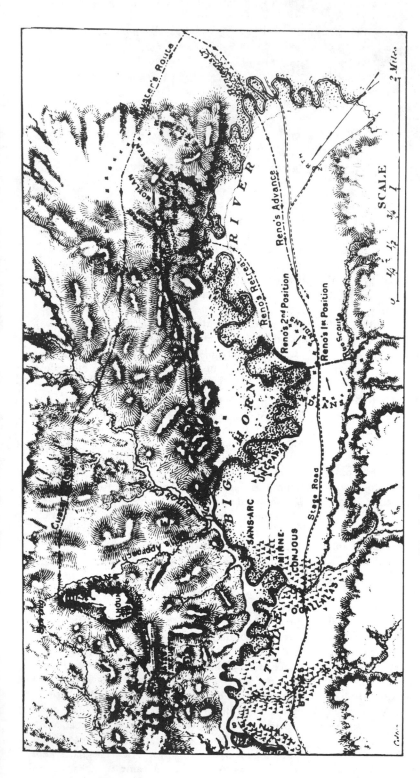

MAP OF CUSTER'S LAST BATTLE

A—Hill where Custer was seen by some of Reno's men during the fight in the valley; Also the point reached by Reno's advance after the retreat from the valley, from which he fell back to the position in which he was besieged. B—Here Keogh's and Calhoun's troops dismounted and advanced along the ridge to where the bodies of their commands were found. C—A few bodies, mostly from the commands of Yates and T. W. Custer, who for the greater part died with General Custer on the hill above, now known as Custer's Hill. D—Ravine where were found bodies of many of Smith's troops who had formed in line on the ridge between Custer's and Keogh's position; Lieutenant Smith's body was found on Custer Hill. E—Hill where Sergeant Butler's body was found; empty cartridge-shells lay about him. He belonged to Captain Custer's troop, and may have been carrying a message to Reno.

The Godfrey Map of the Battlefield. This first appeared in The Century Magazine for January, 1892, as an illustration for the then Captain Godfrey's narrative "Custer's Last Battle."

to get more than half a mile in advance or rear of the train, and to avoid dismounting any oftener than necessary. The march was conducted as follows: one troop marched until about half a mile in advance of the train, when it was dismounted, the horses unbitted and allowed to graze until the train had passed and was about half a mile in advance of it, when it took up the march again; each of the other two troops would conduct their march in the same manner, so that two troops on each flank would be marching alongside the train all the time. If the country was much broken, a half dozen flankers were thrown out to guard against surprise. The flankers regulated their march so as to keep abreast of their troops. The pack animals and beef herd were driven alongside the train by the packers and herders.

One wagon was assigned to each troop, and transported five days' rations and forage and the mess kit of the troop; also the mess kit, tents, and baggage of the troop officers and ten days' supplies for the officers' mess. The men were armed with the carbine and revolver; no one, not even the officer of the day, carried the sabre. Each troop horse carried, in addition to the rider, between eighty and ninety pounds. This additional weight included all equipments and about one hundred rounds of ammunition, fifty in the belt and fifty in saddlebags.

The wagon-train consisted in all of about one hundred and fifty wheeled vehicles. In it were carried thirty days' supplies of forage and rations (excepting beef), and two hundred rounds of ammunition per man. The two-horse wagons, hired by contract, carried from fifteen hundred to two thousand pounds. The six-mule government wagons carried from three to five thousand pounds, depending on the size and condition of the mules. The Gatling guns were each hauled by four condemned cavalry horses and marched in advance of the train. Two light wagons loaded with axes, shovels, pick-axes and some pine boards and scantling, sufficient for a short bridge, accompanied the "pioneer" troops. The "crossings" as they are termed, were often very tedious and would frequently delay the train several hours. During this time the cavalry horses were unbitted and grazed, the men holding the reins. Those men not on duty at the crossing slept, or collected in groups to spin yarns and take a whiff at their "dingy dudeens." The officers usually collected near the crossing to watch progress, and passed the time in conversation and playing practical jokes. About noon the "strikers" who carried the haversacks, were called, and the different messes had their luncheon, sometimes separately, sometimes clubbing together.

When the haversacks were opened the horses usually stopped grazing and put their noses near their riders' faces and asked very plainly to share their hardtack. If their polite request did not receive attention they would paw the ground, or even strike their riders. The old soldier was generally willing to share with his beast.

The length of the day's march, varying from ten to forty miles, was determined in a great measure by the difficulties or obstacles encountered, by wood, water and grass, and by the distance in advance where such advantages were likely to be found. If, about two or three o'clock in the afternoon, a column of smoke was seen in the direction of the trail and a mile or two in advance, it was a pretty sure indication that a camp had been selected. The cavalry, excepting the rear guard, would then cut loose from the train and go directly to camp. The rear guard would send details to collect fuel and unpack their wagons. The adjutant showed the wing commanders the general direction their lines or tents were to run, and the latter then directed the battalion or troop commanders to their camping places. Generally one flank of each line would rest near the creek. The general form of the command was that of a parallelogram. The wings camped on the long sides facing each other, and the headquarters and guard were located at one end nearest the creek. The wagon train was packed to close the other end and was guarded by the infantry battalion. The troops, as they arrived at their places were formed in line, facing inward, dismounted, unsaddled, and, if the weather was hot and the sun shining, the men rubbed the horses' backs until dry. After this the horses were sent to water and put out to graze, with side-lines and lariats, under charge of the stable guard, consisting of one non-commissioned officer and three or six privates. The men of the troop then collected fuel, sometimes wood, often a mile or more distant from the camp; sometimes "buffalo chips." The main guard, or camp guard, consisting usually of four or five non-commissioned officers and twelve or fifteen privates, reported mounted at headquarters, and were directed to take posts on prominent points overlooking the camp and surrounding country, to guard against surprise. Each post consisted of one non-commissioned officer and three privates. The officer of the day, in addition to his ordinary duties in camp, had charge of the safety of the cavalry herds.

Sometimes this latter duty was performed by an officer designated as "Officer of the Herd." To preserve the grazing in the immediate vicinity of the camp for evening and night grazing, all horses were required to be outside of the camp limits until retreat. When the train arrived, the headquarters and troop wagons went directly to the camping-place of their respective commands. The officers' baggage and tents were unloaded first; then the wagons went near the place where the troop kitchen was to be located, always on that flank of the troop farthest from headquarters. The teamsters unharnessed their mules and put them out to graze. The old stable guard reported to the troop commander for fatigue duty to put up the officers' tents and collect fuel for their mess. The troop officers' tents were usually placed twenty-five yards in rear of the line of men's tents and facing toward them. Their cook or mess tent was placed about ten or fifteen yards further to the rear. The "striker" made down the beds and arranged the "furniture," so to speak, which generally consisted of a camp-stool, tin wash-basins, and a looking glass. The men put up their tents soon after caring for their horses. The fronts of their tents were placed on a line established by stretching a picket rope. The first sergeant's was on that flank of the line nearest to the headquarters. The horse equipments were placed on a line three yards in front of the tents. The men were not prohibited from using their saddles as pillows. A trench was dug for the mess fire, and the grass was burned around it for several yards to prevent prairie fires. After this the cooks busied themselves preparing supper. Beef was issued soon after the wagon train came in, and the necessary number of beeves were butchered for the next day's issue; this was hauled in the wagons. Stable call was sounded about an hour before sunset. The men of each troop were formed on the parade and marched to the horse herds by the first sergeant. Each man went to his own horse, took off the sidelines and fastened them around the horse's neck, then pulled the picket pin, coiled the lariat, noosed the end fastened to the head halter around the horse's muzzle, mounted, and assembled in line at a place indicated by the first sergeant. The troop was then marched to the watering place, which was usually selected with great care because of the boggy banks and miry beds of the prairie streams. After watering, the horses were lariated outside the vicinity of the camp. The ground directly in the rear of the troop belonged to it, and was jealously guarded by those concerned against encroachment by others. After lariating their horses, the men got their curry-combs, brushes, and nose-bags and went to the troop wagon where the quartermaster sergeant and farrier measured, with tin cups, the forage to each man, each watching jealously that he got as much for his horse

as those before him. He then went at once to feed and groom his horse. The officer whose duty it was to attend stables and the first sergeant superintended the grooming, examining each horse's back and feet carefully to see if they were all right. When a horse's back got sore, through the carelessness of the rider, the man would generally be compelled to lead his horse until the sore was well. Immediately after stables, the cooks announced in a loud tone "Supper!" The men with haversack and tincup went to the mess fire and got their hardtack, meat, and coffee. If game had been killed the men did a little extra cooking themselves.

The troop officers' mess kits consisted of a sheet-iron cooking stove, an iron kettle, stewing, frying, baking, and dish pans; a small Dutch oven, a camp kettle, a mess-chest holding tableware for four persons, and a small folding table. The table in fair weather was spread in the open air. The early part of the meal was a matter of business, but after the substantials were stowed away, the delicacies were eaten more leisurely and time found for conversation. After supper the pipes were lighted, and the officers, if the weather was cold, went to the windward * side of the camp fire. Each man, as he took his place, was sure to poke or kick the fire, turn his back, hitch up his coat tail, and fold his hands behind him.

Retreat was sounded a little after sunset and the roll was called, as much to insure the men having their equipments in place as to secure their presence, for it was not often we were near enough to any attraction to call the men away. (In 1876 there was not a ranch west of Bismarck, Dakota, nor east of Bozeman, Montana.) The stable guards began their tours of duty at this time. The noncommissioned officers reported to the troop commander for instructions for the night; these usually designated whether the horses were to be tied to the picket line or kept out to graze, and included special instructions for the care of sick or weak horses. At dusk all horses were brought within the limits of the camp. The picket-line was stretched over three wagons in front of the men's tents, or three posts were used when remaining in camp over a day.

During the evening, the men grouped about the fires and sang songs and spun yarns until "taps." The cooks prepared breakfast, which usually consisted of hard bread, bacon and coffee. If beans or fresh meat were to be cooked, the food was put into the Dutch ovens or camp-kettles, which were

_____
* General Godfrey was obviously not a sailor. He means "leeward" here. W.A.G.

placed in the fire trench, covered over with hot ashes and coals, and a fire was built over them. If the wind blew hard all fires were extinguished, to prevent prairie fires. The cooks were called an hour or an hour and a half before reveille. At the first call for reveille, usually 4:20 a. m., the stable guard awakened the occupants of each tent and the officer whose duty it was to attend the roll-call. Stable call followed reveille and was superintended by an officer. This occupied about three-quarters of an hour. Two hours after reveille, the command would be on the march. Of course, there were incidents that occasionally relieved the monotony.

Antelope were plentiful, and the men were encouraged by troop commanders to hunt. General Custer had a number of stag-hounds, which amused themselves and the command in their futile attempts to catch them. One morning they started up a large buck near where the column was marching; Lieutenant Hare immediately followed the hounds, passed them, drew his revolver, and shot the buck. Nothing of special interest occurred until the 27th of May, when we came to the Bad Lands of the Little Missouri River. On the 30th, General Custer was sent with four troops to make a scout up the Little Missouri, for about twenty miles. He returned the same day, without having discovered any recent "Indian signs." On the 31st we crossed the Little Missouri without difficulty. On the 1st and 2nd of June we were obliged to remain in camp on account of a snow-storm.

We remained in camp on the Powder River for three days. General Terry went to the Yellowstone to communicate with the supply steamer FAR WEST, which was at the mouth of the Powder River. He also went up the Yellowstone to communicate with General Gibbon's command, known as the "Montana Column," composed of four troops of the 2nd Cavalry and several companies of the 7th Infantry. Before General Terry left it was given out that the 7th Cavalry would be sent to scout up the Powder River, while the wagon-train, escorted by the infantry, would be sent to establish a supply camp at the mouth of the Powder.

* * *

General Terry having returned, orders were issued on the tenth for the right wing, six troops under Major Reno, to make a scout up the Powder, provided with twelve days' rations.

The left wing was ordered to turn over all forage and rations; also the pack-mules, except four to each troop. Major Reno left at 3 p. m., and the next day the rest of the command marched to the mouth of the Powder. My troop was rear-guard, and at times we were over three miles in rear of the wagon-train waiting on the packers, for we had taken this opportunity to give them practical instruction.

Up to this time we had not seen an Indian, nor any recent signs of them, except one small trail of perhaps a half dozen tepees, evidently of a party of agency Indians on their way to join the hostile camp. The buffalo had all gone west; other game was scarce and wild. The indications were that the Indians were west of the Powder, and information from General Gibbon placed them south of the Yellowstone. Some of the officers of the right wing before they left expressed their belief that we would not find any Indians, and were sanguine that we would all get home by the middle of August.

Major Reno was ordered to scout to the forks of the Powder, then across to Mizpah Creek, follow it down to near its confluence with the Powder; then cross over to Pumpkin Creek, follow it down to the Tongue River, scout up that stream and then rejoin the regiment at the mouth of the Tongue by the time his supplies were exhausted; unless, in the meantime, he should make some discovery that made it necessary to return sooner to make preparations for a pursuit. A supply depot was established at the mouth of the Powder, guarded by the infantry, at which the wagon-train was left.

General Terry, with his staff and some supplies, took passage on the supply steamer FAR WEST, and went up to the mouth of the Tongue. General Custer with the left wing, marched to the mouth of the Tongue, where we remained until the 19th waiting tidings from Reno's scout. The grounds where we camped had been occupied by the Indians the previous winter. (Miles City, Montana, was first built on the site of this camp.) The rude shelters for their ponies, built of driftwood, were still standing and furnished fuel for our camp fires. A number of their dead, placed upon scaffolds, or tied to the branches of trees, were disturbed and robbed of their trinkets. Several persons rode about exhibiting their trinkets with as much gusto as if they were trophies of their valor, and showed no more concern for their desecration than if they had won them at a raffle. Ten days later I saw the bodies of these same persons dead, naked, and mutilated.

On the 19th of June tidings came from Reno that he had found a large trail that led up the Rosebud River. The particulars were not generally known. The camp was full of rumors; credulity was raised to the highest pitch, and we were filled with anxiety and curiosity until we reached Reno's command, and learned the details of their discoveries. They had found a large trail on the Tongue River, and had followed it up the Rosebud about forty miles. The number of lodges in the deserted villages was estimated by the number of camp-fires remaining to be about three hundred and fifty. The indications were that the trail was about three weeks old. No Indians had been seen nor any recent signs. It is not probable that Reno's movements were known to the Indians, for on the very day Reno reached his farthest point up the Rosebud, the battle of the Rosebud, between General Crook's forces and the Indians, was fought. The two commands were then not more than forty miles apart, but neither knew nor even suspected the proximity of the other. We reached the mouth of the Rosebud about noon of the 21st and began preparations for the march, and for the expected battle or pursuit.

PREPARATIONS

On our arrival at the mouth of the Rosebud, Generals Terry, Gibbon and Custer had a conference on board the steamer "FAR WEST." It was decided that the 7th Cavalry, under General Custer, should follow the trail discovered by Reno. "Officers' call" was sounded in the 7th Cavalry camp as soon as the conference had concluded. Upon assembling, General Custer gave us our orders. We were to transport, on our pack-mules, fifteen days' rations of hard bread, coffee and sugar; twelve days' rations of bacon, and fifty rounds of carbine ammunition per man. Each man was to be supplied with 100 rounds of carbine and 24 rounds of pistol ammunition, to be carried on his person and in his saddle bags. Each man was to carry on his horse twelve pounds of oats.

The pack-mules sent out with Reno's command were badly used up, and promised seriously to embarrass the expedition. General Custer recommended that some extra forage be carried on the pack-mules. In endeavoring to carry out this recommendation some troop commanders (Captain Moylan and myself) foresaw the difficulties, and told the General that some of the mules would certainly break down, especially if the extra forage was packed. He replied in an unusually emphatic manner. "Well, gentlemen, you may carry what supplies you please; you will be held responsible for your companies. The extra forage was only a suggestion, but this fact bear in mind, we will follow the trail for fifteen days unless we catch them before that time expires, no matter how far it may take us from our base of supplies; we may

not see the supply steamer again"; and, turning as he was about to enter his tent, he added: "You had better carry along an extra supply of salt; we may have to live on horse meat before we get through." He was taken at his word, and an extra supply of salt was carried. "Battalion" and "wing" organizations were broken up, and troop commanders were responsible only to General Custer. Of course, as soon as it was determined that we were to go out, nearly every one took time to write letters home, but I doubt very much if there were many of a cheerful nature. Some officers made their wills; others gave verbal instructions as to the disposition of personal property and distribution of mementos; they seemed to have a presentiment of their fate.

THE HOSTILES

There were a number of Sioux Indians who never went to an agency except to visit friends and relatives and to barter. They camped in and roamed about the buffalo country. Their camp was the rendezvous for the agency Indians when they went out for their annual hunts for meats and robes. They were known as the "Hostiles," and comprised representatives from all the different tribes of the Sioux nation. Many of them were renegade outlaws from the agencies. In their visits to the agencies they were usually arrogant and fomenters of discord. Depredations had been made upon the commerce to the Black Hills, and a number of lives taken by them or by others, for which they were blamed. The authorities at Washington had determined to compel these Indians to reside at the agencies—hence the Sioux War.

Major James McLaughlin, United States Indian Agent, stationed at the Devil's Lake Agency, Dakota, from 1870 to 1881, and at Standing Rock Agency, Dakota, from 1881 to 1895, and to the present time * Inspector in the Bureau of Indian Affairs, has made it a point to get estimates of the number of Indians at the hostile camp at the time of the battle. In his opinion, and all who know him will accept it with confidence, about one-third of the whole Sioux nation, including the northern Cheyennes and Arapahoes, were present at the battle; he estimates the number present as between twelve and fifteen thousand; that one out of four is a low estimate in determining the number of warriors present; every male over fourteen years of age may be considered a warrior in a general fight, such as was the battle of the Little Big Horn; also, considering the extra hazards of

* 1908.

the hunt and expected battle, fewer squaws would accompany the recruits from the agencies. The minimum strength of their fighting men may then be put down as between twenty-five hundred and three thousand. Information was dispatched from General Sheridan that from the agencies about 1800 lodges had set out to join the hostile camp; but that information did not reach General Terry until several days after the battle. The principal warrior chiefs of the hostile Indians were Gall, Crow King and Black Moon, Huncpapa Sioux; Low Dog, Crazy Horse and Big Road, Ogallala Sioux; Spotted Eagle, Sans-Arc Sioux; Hump of the Minneconjous; and White Bull and Little Horse of the Cheyennes. To these belong the chief honors of conducting the battle; however, Gall, Crow King and Crazy Horse were the ruling spirits.

Sitting Bull

Sitting Bull, a Huncpapa Sioux Indian, was the chief of the hostile camp; he had about sixty lodges of followers on whom he could at all times depend. He was the host of the Hostiles, and as such received and entertained their visitors. These visitors gave him many presents, and he was thus enabled to make many presents, in return. All visitors paid tribute to him, so he gave liberally to the most influential, the chiefs, i. e. he "put it where it would do the most good." In this way he became known as the chief of the hostile camp, and the camp was generally known as "Sitting Bull's camp" or "outfit." Sitting Bull was a heavy set, muscular man, about five feet eight inches in stature, and at the time of the battle of the Little Big Horn was forty-two years of age. He was the autocrat of the camp—chiefly because he was the host. In council his views had great weight, because he was known as a great medicine man. He was a chief, but not a warrior chief. In the war councils he had a voice and vote the same as any other chief. A short time previous to the battle he had "made medicine," had predicted that the soldiers would attack them and that the soldiers would all be killed. He took no active part in the battle, but, as was his custom in time of danger, remained in the village "making medicine." Personally, he was regarded by the Agency Indians as a great coward and a very great liar, "a man with a big head and a little heart."

The War Chief Gall

Chief Gall was born about 1840, of Huncpapa parents. Until Sitting Bull's surrender, 1881, Gall never lived at the agencies, but was sometimes a guest. When 25 years old he was noted for his

bravery and daring. He was so subtle, crafty and daring, that in 1886 (1866?), the military authorities offered a reward for his body, dead or alive; an outrage had been committed, which for daring and craftiness, it was thought no other Indian was gifted. However, he was innocent. Gall knew of the price laid on his carcass and kept away from the military. At Fort Berthold, while visiting friends at the Agency, his visit was made known to the commanding officer at Fort Stevenson, a few miles away. A detachment was sent to the tepee where he was visiting, to arrest him. On their entrance Gall dropped on his belly and pushed himself backward under the tepee. A soldier on the outside bayonetted him through the body and held him till he fainted. The soldiers supposed him to be dead, and so reported to their commander. They were sent back with transportation to get the body. Great was their astonishment to find that Gall had recovered consciousness and crawled away. The men searched faithfully the woods in which Gall had concealed himself, but he was not discovered. Gall then got back to his people and vowed vengeance. He had it in many a foray and numbers of battles. He lurked about the military posts and pounced on luckless promenaders, even at the very gates of the stockade that enclosed the barracks and quarters. He raided settlements and attacked Black Hill stages and freighters. He it was who followed the "Bozeman Expedition" about 1874, for days, when they were searching for gold, compelling them at all times to be in readiness for battle. One of their entrenchments may yet be seen on the divide between the Rosebud and Little Big Horn at the head of Thompson Creek.

In 1872 he led his braves in a raiding attack on the 2nd Cavalry at "Baker's Battlefield" on the Yellowstone, which by reason of its surprise, came near proving a disaster, as Indians rarely made night attacks. August 4th, 1873, General Custer had gone into bivouac on the north bank of the Yellowstone, just above Fort Keogh, waiting for the main command under General Stanley. The two troops had unsaddled and were resting in the supposed security afforded by the absence of fresh "Indian signs," while Gall made his dispositions for attack. His warriors crawled through woods, down ravines and under the river bank to within 300 yards when an alarm called to arms and a lively battle was kept up until the arrival of troops from the main command which had heard and seen the firing from the mesa several miles away. A week later Gall made an attack on the 7th Cavalry at the head of "Pease Bottom," a few miles below the mouth of the Big Horn. In this fight Gall, dressed in brilliant scarlet and war bonnet, rode back and forth in front of the firing line, the target of hundreds of shots, but escaped unharmed. He was the Great War Chief of all the Sioux at "Custer's Last Battle." In 1877 he went with Sitting Bull to Canada, and in 1881 surrendered at Poplar Creek, Montana. The band was taken into Standing Rock Agency, 1882, by steamboat. The boat was met by a great throng of people; the military, settlers and employees and Indians of that Agency were at the landing. When the boat tied up, Gall, in full war paint and regalia ostentatiously walked down the gang plank, halted and surveyed the surroundings. His old mother ran to him and tried to gain his notice; she got on her knees, clasped him about his legs took hold of and kissed his hand; she moaned and cried. Ignoring her caresses, he stalked dramatically aboard the boat. Later Gall became reconciled to agency life and was a good Indian; wise and conservative, he supported the Agent, Major James McLaughlin, in all his efforts for the good of the people. In the grand councils of all the

Chiefs of the Sioux nation, he was the most influential and stood up for what he considered the just rights of his people. He died at Oak Creek, near Standing Rock Agency, in 1895. His features were massive, and in facial appearance was compared to the great expounder, Webster; to Henry Ward Beecher and to Bishop Newman. He was a man of great natural ability, force of character and possessed great common sense.

INSTRUCTIONS

General Custer's written instructions were as follows:

> Camp at Mouth of Rosebud River,
> Montana Territory, June 22nd, 1876.

Lieut.-Col. Custer, 7th Cavalry.

Colonel:

The Brigadier-General Commanding directs that, as soon as your regiment can be made ready for the march, you will proceed up the Rosebud in pursuit of the Indians whose trail was discovered by Major Reno a few days since. It is, of

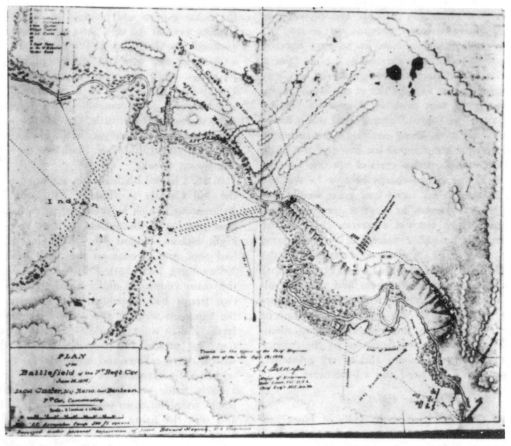

Lt. Maquire's first map of the Custer battlefield. Made for Hq. Military Division of the Missouri, September, 1876.

course, impossible to give you any definite instructions in regard to this movement, and were it not impossible to do so, the Department Commander places too much confidence in your zeal, energy, and ability to wish to impose upon you precise orders which might hamper your action when nearly in contact with the enemy. He will, however, indicate to you his own views of what your action should be, and he desires that you should conform to them unless you shall see sufficient reason for departing from them. He thinks that you should proceed up the Rosebud until you ascertain definitely the direction in which the trail above spoken of leads. Should it be found (as it appears almost certain that it will be found) to turn towards the Little Horn, he thinks that you should still proceed southward, perhaps as far as the headwaters of the Tongue, and then turn towards the Little Horn, feeling constantly, however, to your left, so as to preclude the possibility of the escape of the Indians to the south or southeast by passing around your left flank. The

column of Colonel Gibbon is now in motion for the mouth of the Big Horn. As soon at is reaches that point it will cross the Yellowstone and move up at least as far as the forks of the Big and Little Horns. Of course its future movements must be controlled by circumstances as they arise, but it is hoped that the Indians, if upon the Little Horn, may be so nearly inclosed by the two columns that their escape will be impossible.

The Department Commander desires that on your way up the Rosebud you should thoroughly examine the upper part of Tullock's Creek,* and

---

* Note: On the morning of the 24th, some of the command were quite excited over what they thought were "Smoke puffs" as made by Indians when signaling. At our first halt, I called General Custer's attention to this. He replied that our scouts were well out on the divide, and was sure if any such signals were made our scouts would have reported them, but on the contrary, they reported nothing had been seen. Subsequent observations convinced me that these supposed "smoke puffs" were cloudlets of mist formed during the night in the valleys and wafted over the hill tops by the morning breeze.—E.S.G.

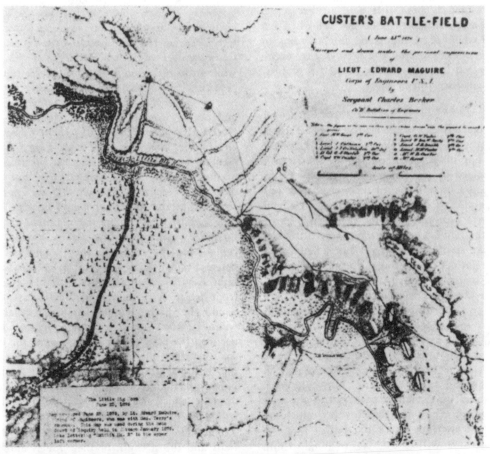

Lt. Maguire's Final Battlefield map made to accompany a report to the Chief of Engineers. This is the copy used at the Reno Court of Inquiry and shows pencil marks made by various witnesses.

that you should endeavor to send a scout through to Colonel Gibbon's column, with information of the result of your examination. The lower part of the creek will be examined by a detachment from Colonel Gibbon's command. The supply steamer will be pushed up the Big Horn as far as the forks if the river is found to be navigable for that distance, and the Department Commander, who will accompany the column of Colonel Gibbon, desires you to report to him there not later than the expiration of the time for which your troops are rationed, unless in the meantime you receive further orders.

> Very respectfully,
> Your obedient servant,
> E. W. Smith, Captain, 18th Infantry,
> Acting Assistant Adjutant-General.

These instructions are explicit, and fixed the location of the Indians very accurately. It has been assumed by some writers that General Terry's command would be at the mouth of the Little Big Horn on June 26th, and that General Custer knew of that—also by some that the two commands were to come together about that date at that place. General Terry's instructions do not say when his command would reach that point, and according to the instructions, General Custer was not necessarily expected there before the 5th or 6th of July, being rationed for fifteen days.

THE MARCH UP THE ROSEBUD

At twelve o'clock, noon, on the 22nd of June, the "Forward" was sounded, and the regiment marched out of camp in column of fours, each troop followed by its pack-mules. Generals Terry, Gibbon and Custer stationed themselves near our line of march and reviewed the regiment. General Terry had a pleasant word for each officer as he returned the salute. Our pack-trains proved troublesome at the start, as the cargoes began falling off before we got out of camp, and during all that day the mules straggled badly. After that day, however, they were placed under the charge of Lieutenant Mathey, who was directed to report at the end of each day's march the order of merit of the efficiency of the troop packers. Doubtless, General Custer had some ulterior design in this. It is quite probable that if he had had occasion to detach troops requiring rapid marching, he would have selected those troops whose packers had the best records. At all events the efficiency was much increased, and after we struck the Indian trail the pack-trains kept well closed. We went into camp about 4 p. m., having marched twelve miles. About sunset "officers' call" was sounded, and we assem-

bled at General Custer's bivouac and squatted in groups about the General's bed. It was not a cheerful assemblage; everybody seemed to be in a serious mood, and the little conversation carried on, before all had arrived, was in undertones. When all had assembled, the General said that until further orders, trumpet calls would not be sounded except in an emergency; the marches would begin at 5 a. m. sharp; the troop commanders were all experienced officers, and knew well enough what to do, and when to do what was necessary for their troops; there were two things that would be regulated from his headquarters, i.e. when to move out of and when to go into camp. All other details, such as reveille, stables, watering, halting, grazing, etc., on the march would be left to the judgment and discretion of the troop commanders; they were to keep within supporting distance of each other, not to get ahead of the scouts, or very far to the rear of the column. He took particular pains to impress upon the officers his reliance upon their judgment, discretion, and loyalty. He thought, judging from the number of lodge-fires reported by Reno, that we might meet at least a thousand warriors; there might be enough young men from the agencies, visiting their hostile friends, to make a total of fifteen hundred. He had consulted the reports of the Commissioner of Indian Affairs and the officials while in Washington as to the probable number of "Hostiles" (those who had persistently refused to live or enroll themselves at the Indian agencies), and he was confident, if any reliance was to be placed upon these reports, that there would not be an opposing force of more than fifteen hundred. General Terry had offered him the additional force of the battalion of the 2nd Cavalry, but he had declined it because he felt sure that the 7th Cavalry could whip any force that would be able to combine against him, that if the regiment could not, no other regiment in the service could; if they could whip the regiment, they would be able to defeat a much larger force, or, in other words, the reinforcement of this battalion could not save us from defeat. With the regiment acting alone, there would be harmony, but another organization would be sure to cause jealousy or friction. He had declined the offer of the Gatling guns for the reason that they might hamper our movements or march at a critical moment, because of the inferior horses and of the difficult nature of the country through which we would march. The marches would be from twenty-five to thirty miles a day. Troop officers were cautioned to husband their rations and the strength of their mules and horses, as we might be out for a great deal longer time than that for which we were rationed, as he intended to follow the trail until we could get the Indians, even if it took us to the Indian agencies on the Missouri River or in Nebraska. All officers were requested to make to him any suggestions they thought fit.

This "talk" of his, as we called it, was considered at the time as something extraordinary for General Custer, for it was not his habit to unbosom himself to his officers. In it he showed concessions and a reliance on others; there was an indefinable something that was *not* Custer. His manner and tone, usually brusque and aggressive, or somewhat curt, was on this occasion conciliating and subdued. There was something akin to an appeal, as if depressed, that made a deep impression on all present. We compared watches to get the official time, and separated to attend to our various duties. Lieutenants McIntosh, Wallace (killed at the Battle of Wounded Knee, December 29, 1890), and myself walked to our bivouac, for some distance in silence, when Wallace remarked: "Godfrey, I believe General Custer is going to be killed." "Why? Wallace," I replied, "what makes you think so?" "Because," said he, "I have never heard Custer talk in that way before."

I went to my troop and gave orders what time the "silent" reveille should be and as to other details for the morning preparations; also the following directions in case of a night attack: the stable guard, packers, and cooks were to go out at once to the horses and mules to quiet and guard them; the other men were to go at once to a designated rendezvous and await orders; no man should fire a shot until he received orders from an officer to do so. When they retired for the night they should put their arms and equipments where they could get them without leaving their beds. I then went through the herd to satisfy myself as to the security of the animals. During the performance of this duty I came to the bivouac of the Indian scouts. "Mitch" Bouyer,* the half-breed interpreter, "Bloody Knife," the chief of the Ree scouts; "Half-Yellow-Face," the chief of the Crow scouts, and others were having a "talk." I observed them for a few minutes, when Bouyer turned toward me, apparently at the suggestion of "Half-Yellow-Face" and said; "Have you ever fought against these Sioux?" "Yes," I replied. Then he asked, "Well, how many do you expect to find?" I answered, "It is said we may find between one thousand and fifteen hundred." "Well, do you think we can whip that many?" "Oh, yes, I guess so." After he had interpreted our conversation, he said to me with a good deal of emphasis, "Well, I can tell you we

are going to have a damned big fight." At five o'clock sharp, on the morning of the 23rd, General Custer mounted and started up the Rosebud, followed by two sergeants, one carrying the regimental standard, and the other his personal or headquarters flag, the same kind of flag he used while commanding his cavalry division during the Civil War. This was the signal for the command to mount and take up the march. Eight miles out we came to the first of the Indian camping-places. It certainly indicated a large village and numerous population. There were a great many "wickiups" (bushes stuck in the ground with the tops drawn together, over which they placed canvas or blankets). These we supposed at the time were for the dogs, but subsequent events developed the fact that they were temporary shelters of the transients from the agencies. During the day we passed through three of these camping-places and made halts at each one. Everybody was busy studying the age of the pony droppings and tracks and lodge trails, and endeavoring to determine the number of lodges. These points were all-absorbing topics of conversation. We went into camp about five o'clock, having marched about thirty-three miles.

June 24th we passed a great many camping places, all appearing to be of nearly the same strength. One would naturally suppose these were the successive camping-places of the same village, when, in fact, they were the continuous camps of the several bands. The fact that they appeared to be of nearly the same age, that is, having been made at the same time, did not impress us then. We passed through one much larger than any of the others. The grass for a considerable distance around it had been cropped close, indicating that large herds had been grazed there. The frame of a large "Sun-Dance" lodge was standing, and in it we found the scalp of a white man. It was whilst here that the Indians from the agencies had joined the Hostiles' camp. The command halted here and the "officers' call" was sounded. Upon assembling we were informed that our Crow scouts, who had been very active and efficient, had discovered fresh signs, the tracks of three or four ponies and one Indian on foot. At this point a stiff southerly breeze was blowing; as we were about to separate, the General's headquarters' flag was blown down, falling toward our rear. Being near the flag I picked it up and stuck the staff in the ground, but it again fell to the rear. I then bored the staff into the ground where it would have the support of a sagebrush. This circumstance made no impression on me at the time, but after the battle, an officer, Lieutenant Wallace, asked me if I remembered the incident. He had observed, and

* Variant of Boyer.

regarded the fact of its falling to the rear as a bad omen, and felt sure we would suffer a defeat.

The march during the day was tedious. We made many long halts, so as not to get ahead of the scouts, who seemed to be doing their work thoroughly, giving special attention to the right, toward Tulloch's Creek, the valley of which was in general view from the divide. Once or twice signal smokes were reported in that direction, but investigation did not confirm the reports. The weather was dry and had been for some time, consequently the trail was very dusty. The troops were required to march on separate trails, so that the dust clouds would not rise so high. The valley was heavily marked with lodge-pole trails and pony tracks, showing that immense herds of ponies had been driven over it. About sundown we went into camp under the cover of a bluff, so as to hide the command as much as possible. We had marched about twenty-eight miles. The fires were ordered to be put out as soon as supper was over, and we were to be in readiness to march again at 11:30 p. m.

Lieutenant Hare and myself lay down about 9:30 to take a nap. When comfortably fixed, we heard some one say, "He's over there by that tree." As that described my location pretty well, I called out to know what was wanted, and the reply came: "The General's compliments, and he wants to see all the officers at headquarters immediately." So we gave up our much-needed rest and groped our way through horse herds, over sleeping men, and through thickets of bushes trying to find headquarters. No one could tell us, and as all fires and lights were out we could not keep our bearings. We finally espied a solitary candle-light, toward which we traveled and found most of the officers assembled at the General's bivouac. The General said that the trail led over the divide to the Little Big Horn; the march would be taken up at once, as he was anxious to get as near the divide as possible before daylight, where the command would be concealed during the day, and give ample time for the country to be studied, to locate the village, and to make plans for the attack on the 26th. We then returned to our troops, except Lieutenant Hare, who was put on duty with the scouts. Because of the dust, it was impossible to see any distance and the rattle of equipments and clattering of the horses' feet made it difficult to hear distinctly beyond our immediate surroundings. We could not see the trail and we could only follow it by keeping in the dust cloud. The night was very calm, but occasionally a slight breeze would waft the cloud and disconcert our bearings; then we were obliged to halt to catch a sound from those in advance, sometimes whistling or hallooing, and getting a response we could start forward again. Finally, troopers were put ahead, away from the noise of our column, and where they could hear the noise of those in front. A little after 2 a.m., June 25th, the command was halted to await further tidings from the scouts; we had marched about ten miles. Part of the command unsaddled to rest the horses. After daylight some coffee was made, but it was impossible to drink it; the water was so alkaline that the horses refused to drink.

Some time before eight o'clock, General Custer rode bareback to the several troops and gave orders to be ready to march at eight o'clock, and gave information that scouts had discovered the locality of the Indian villages or camps in the valley of the Little Big Horn, about twelve or fifteen miles beyond the divide. Just before setting out on the march, I went to where General Custer's bivouac was. The General, "Bloody Knife," and several Ree scouts and a half-breed interpreter were squatted in a circle, having a "talk" after the Indian fashion. The general wore a serious expression and was apparently abstracted. The scouts were doing the talking, and seemed nervous and disturbed. Finally "Bloody Knife" made a remark that recalled the General from his reverie, and he asked in his usual quick, brusque manner, "What's that he says?" The interpreter replied: "He says we'll find enough Sioux to keep up fighting two or three days." The General smiled and remarked, "I guess we'll get through with them in one day."

We started promptly at eight o'clock and marched uninterruptedly until 10:30 a.m. when we halted in a ravine and were ordered to preserve quiet, keep concealed, and not do anything that would be likely to reveal our presence to the enemy. We had marched about ten miles.

It is a rare occurrence in Indian warfare that gives a commander the opportunity to reconnoiter the enemy's position in daylight. This is particularly true if the Indians have a knowledge of the presence of troops in the country. When following an Indian trail the "signs" indicate the length of time elapsed since the presence of the Indians. When the "signs" indicate a "hot trail" i.e. near approach, the commander judges his distance and by a forced march, usually in the night time, tries to reach the Indian village at night and make his disposition for a surprise attack at daylight. At all events his attack must be made with celerity, and generally without other knowledge of the numbers of the opposing force than that discovered or conjectured while following the trail. The dispositions for the attack may be said to be "made in the dark," and successful surprise to depend upon luck. If the advance to the attack be made in daylight it is next to impossible that a near approach can be made without discovery. In all our previous experiences, when the immediate presence of the troops was once known to them, the warriors swarmed to the attack, and resorted to all kinds of ruses to mislead the troops, to delay the advance toward their camp or village while the squaws and children secured what personal effects they could, drove off the pony herd, and by flight put themselves beyond danger, and then scattering, made successful pursuit next to impossible. In civilized warfare the hostile forces may confront each other for hours, days or weeks, and the battle may be conducted with a tolerable knowledge of the numbers, positions, etc. of each other. A full knowledge of the immediate presence of the enemy does not imply immediate attack. In Indian warfare the rule is "touch and go." In fact, the firebrand nature of Indian warfare is not generally understood. In meditating upon the preliminaries of an Indian battle, old soldiers who have participated only in the battles of "civilized" war are apt to draw upon their own experiences for comparison, when there is no comparison.

Troops Discovered

It was well known to the Indians that the troops were in the field, and a battle was fully expected by them; but the close proximity of our column was not known to them until the morning of the day of the battle. Several young men had left the hostile camp on that morning to go to one of the agencies in Nebraska. They saw the dust made by the column of troops; some of their number returned to the village and gave warning that the troops were coming, so the attack was not a surprise. For two or three days their camp had been pitched on the site where they were attacked. The place was not selected with the view to making that the battle-field of the campaign, but, whoever was in the van on their march thought it a good place to camp, put up his tepee, and the others as they arrived followed his example. (This was Gall's explanation.) It is customary among the Indians to camp by bands. The bands usually camp some distance apart, and Indians of the number then together would occupy a territory of several miles along the river valley, and not necessarily within supporting distance of each other. But in view of the possible fulfillment of Sitting Bull's prophecy the village had massed.

The Little Big Horn River, or the "Greasy Grass" as it is known to the Indians, is a rapid, tortuous mountain stream from twenty to forty yards wide, with pebbled bottom, but abrupt, soft banks. The water at the ordinary stage is from two or five feet in depth, depending upon the width of the channel. The general direction of its course is northeasterly down to the Little Big Horn battle-fields, where it trends northwesterly to its confluence with the Big Horn River. The other topographical features of the country which concern us in this narrative may be briefly described as follows: Between the Little Big Horn and Big Horn Rivers is a plateau of undulating prairie; between the Little Big Horn and the Rosebud are the Little Chetish or Wolf Mountains. By this it must not be misunderstood as a rocky upheaval chain or spur of mountains, but it is a rough, broken country of considerable elevation, of high precipitous hills and deep, narrow gulches. The command had followed the trail up a branch of the Rosebud to within, say, a mile of the summit of these mountains, which form the "divide." Not many miles to our right was the divide between the Little Big Horn and Tulloch's Fork. The creek that drained the watershed to our right and front is now variously called "Sun-Dance," Benteen's, or Reno's Creek. The trail, very tortuous, and sometimes dangerous, followed down the bed and valley of the south branch of this creek, which at that time was dry for the greater part of its length. It was from the divide between the Little Big Horn and the Rosebud that the scouts had discovered the smoke rising above the village, and the pony herds grazing in the valley of the Little Big Horn, somewhere about twelve or fifteen miles away. It was to their point of view that General Custer had gone while the column was halted in the ravine. It was impossible for him to discover more of the enemy than had already been reported by the scouts. In consequence of the high bluffs which screened the village, it was not possible in following the trail to discover more. Nor was there a point of observation near the trail from which further discoveries could be made until the battle was at hand.

Our officers had generally collected in groups and discussed the situation. Some sought solitude and sleep, or meditation. The Ree scouts, who had not been very active for the past day or two, were together and their "medicine man" was anointing them and invoking the Great Spirit to protect them from the Sioux. They seemed to have become satisfied that we were going to find more Sioux than we could well take care of. Captain Yates' troop had lost one of its packs of hard bread during the night march from our last halting place on the 24th. He had sent a detail back on the trail to recover it. Captain Keogh came to where a group of officers were and said this detail had returned and Sergeant Curtis, in charge, reported that when near the pack they discovered an Indian opening one of the boxes of hard bread with his tomahawk, and that as soon as the Indian saw the soldiers he galloped away to the hills, out of range and then moved along leisurely. This information was taken to the General at once by his brother, Captain Tom Custer. The General came back and had "officers' call" sounded. He recounted Captain Keogh's report, and also said that the scouts had seen several Indians moving along the ridge overlooking the valley through which we had marched, as if observing our movements; he thought the Indians must have seen the dust made by the command. At all events, our presence had been discovered and further concealment was unnecessary; that we would move at once to attack the village; that he had not intended to make the attack until the next morning, the 26th, but our discovery made it imperative to act at once, as delay would allow the village to scatter and escape. Troop commanders were ordered to make a detail of one non-commissioned officer and six men to accompany the pack; to inspect their troops and report as soon as they were ready to march; that the troops would take their places in the column of march in the order in which reports of readiness were received; the last one to report would escort the pack-train.

The Division of Troops

The inspections were quickly made and the column was soon en route. We crossed the dividing ridge between the Rosebud and Little Big Horn valleys a little before noon. Shortly afterward the regiment was divided into battalions. The advance battalion, under Major Reno, consisted of troop "M," Captain French; troop "A," Captain Moylan and Lieutenant De Rudio; troop "G," Lieutenants McIntosh and Wallace; the Indian scouts under Lieutenants Varnum and Hare, and the interpreter Girard; Lieutenant Hodgson was Acting Adjutant, and Doctors DeWolf and Porter were the medical officers. The battalion under General Custer was composed of troop "I," Captain Keogh and Lieutenant Porter; troop "F," Captain Yates and Lieutenant Reily; troop "C," Captain Custer and Lieutenant Harrington; troop "E," Lieutenants Smith and Sturgis; troop "L," Lieutenants Calhoun and Crittenden; Lieutenant Cook was the Adjutant, and Captain G. E. Lord was medical officer. (It is thought by some that Custer's troops were divided into two battalions, one under Captain Keogh and one under Captain Yates.) The battalion under Captain Benteen consisted of troop "H," Captain Benteen and Lieutenant Gibson; troop "D," Captain Weir and Lieutenant Edgerly, and troop "K," Lieutenant Godfrey. The pack-train, Lieutenant Mathey in charge, was under escort of troop "B," Captain McDougall.

Major Reno's battalion marched down a valley that developed into the south branch of the small tributary to the Little Big Horn, now called "Sun-Dance" Benteen's, or Reno Creek. The Indian trail followed the meanderings of this valley. Custer's column followed Reno's closely, bearing to the right and rear. The pack-train followed their trail.

BENTEEN'S ROUTE

Benteen's battalion was ordered to the left and front, to a line of high bluffs about three or four miles distant. Benteen was ordered if he saw anything, to send word to Custer, but to pitch into anything he came across; if, when he arrived at the high bluffs, he could not see any enemy, he should continue his march to the next line of bluffs and so on until he could see the Little Big Horn Valley.

There is no doubt that Custer was possessed with the idea that the Indians would not "stand" for a daylight attack, that some of them would try to escape up the valley of the Little Big Horn with families, ponies and other impedimenta, and if so, he wanted them intercepted and driven back toward the village. This idea and another that the village might be strung out along the valley for several miles were probably the ones that influenced him to send Benteen's battalion to the left. Benteen marched over a succession of rough steep hills and deep valleys. The view from the point where the regiment was organized into battalions did not discover the difficult nature of the country, but as we advanced farther, it became more and more difficult. To save the strain on the battalion, Lieutenant Gibson was sent some distance in advance, but saw no enemy, and so signaled the result of his reconnaissance to Benteen. The obstacles threw the battalion by degrees to the right until we came in sight of and not more than a mile from the trail. Many of our horses were greatly jaded by the climbing and descending, some getting far into the rear of the column. Benteen very wisely determined to follow the trail of the rest of the command, and we got into it just in advance of the pack-train. During this march on the left, we could see occasionally the battalion under Custer, distinguished by the troop mounted on gray horses, marching at a rapid gait. Two or three times we heard loud cheering and also some few shots, but the occasion of these demonstrations is not known. Some time after getting on the trail we came to a waterhole, or morass, at which a stream of running water had its source, Benteen halted the battalion. While watering, we heard some firing in advance, and Weir became impatient at the delay of watering and started off with his troop, taking the advance, whereas his place in column was second. The rest of the battalion moved out very soon afterward and soon caught up with him. We were now several miles from the Reno battle-field or the Little Big Horn. Just as we were leaving the water-hole, the pack-train was arriving, and the poor thirsty mules plunged into the morass in spite of the efforts of the packers to prevent them, for they had not had water since the previous evening. We passed a burning tepee, fired presumably by our scouts, in which was the body of a warrior who had been killed in the battle with Crook's troops on the Rosebud on the 17th of June.

RENO'S ROUTE

The battalions under Reno and Custer did not meet any Indians until Reno arrived at the burning tepee; here a few were seen. These Indians did not act as if surprised by the appearance of troops; they made no effort to delay the column, but simply kept far enough in advance to invite pursuit. Reno's command and the scouts followed them closely until he received orders to "move forward at as rapid a gait as he thought prudent, and charge the village afterward, and the whole outfit would support him." According to Reno's official report this order was given him near this burning tepee. He says: "Lieutenant Cook, adjutant, came to me and said the village was only two miles above, and running away," and gave the above order.

The Little Big Horn bottom, down which the trail led, is generally flat, and from one to two miles wide; along the stream, especially in the bends at the time of the fight, it was heavily timbered, principally large cotton woods, and obstructed a view of the main villages until Reno got to where he made his farthest advance down the valley; here the village loomed up large among the cotton woods below. Reno following the Indian trail, crossed at a ford; about three and a half miles below it, in a direct line, is a second ford; between these fords, skirting the right bank and paralleling the river is a ridge from one hundred to three hundred feet above the valley, which rises abruptly from river and valley. In following the summit of this ridge the travel distance is considerably increased. The northeast slope declines

rather gently at the upper end, but more abruptly at the lower end, and drains into a usually dry stream bed which joins the river at the second ford. About two miles below this ford is another. These lower fords were used by the Hostiles in swarming to the attack on Custer's troops.

RENO'S FIGHT IN THE VALLEY

Reno's battalion moved at a trot to the river, where he delayed about ten or fifteen minutes watering the horses and reforming the column on the left bank of the stream; both Captain Keogh and Lieutenant Cook were at this crossing for a short time. Reno now sent word to Custer that he had everything in front of him, and that the enemy was strong. Custer had moved off to the right, being separated from Reno by a line of high bluffs and the river. Reno moved forward in column of fours about half a mile, then formed the battalion in line of battle across the valley with the scouts on the left; after advancing about a mile further he deployed the battalion as skirmishers. In the meantime, the Hostiles, continually reinforced, fell back, firing occasionally, but made no decided effort to check Reno's advance. The horses of two men became unmanageable and carried them into the Indian camp. The Indians now developed great force, opened a brisk fire, mounted, and made a dash toward the foothills on the left flank where the Ree scouts were. The scouts ignominiously fled, most of them abandoning the field altogether. Reno says in his report: "I however, soon saw that I was being drawn into some trap, as they would certainly fight harder and especially as we were nearing their village which was still standing; besides, I could not see Custer or any other support, and at the same time the very earth seemed to grow Indians. They were running toward me in swarms and from all directions. I saw I must defend myself and give up the attack mounted. This I did."

During this advance the troops began to cheer in answer to the "whoops" of the Hostiles, and Reno yelled "Stop that noise." Reno, not seeing the "whole outfit" within supporting distance, did not obey his orders to charge the village, but dismounted his command to fight on foot. The movements of the Indians around the left flank and the flight of the scouts caused the left to fall back until the command was on the defensive in the timber and covered by the bank of the old river bed. Reno's loss thus far was one wounded. The position was a strong one, well protected in front by the bank and fringe of timber, somewhat open in the rear, but sheltered by timber in the bottom. Those present differ in their estimates of the length of time the command remained in the bottom after they were attacked in force. Some say "a few minutes"; others "about an hour." While Reno remained there his casualties were few. The Hostiles had him nearly surrounded, and there was some firing from the rear of the position by Indians on the opposite bank of the river. One man was killed close to where Reno was, and directly afterward Reno gave orders to those near him to "mount and get to the bluffs." This order was not generally heard or communicated; while those who did hear it were preparing to execute it, he countermanded the order, but soon afterward repeated the same order "to mount and get to the bluffs," and again it was not generally understood. Individuals, observing the preparations of those on the left, near Reno, informed their troop commanders who then gave orders to mount. Owing to the noise of the firing and to the absorbed attention they were giving to the enemy many did not know of the order until too late to accompany the command. Some remained concealed until the Indians left and then came out. Four others remained until night and then escaped. Reno's command left the bottom by troop organizations in column, but in a straggling formation. Reno was the foremost in this retreat, or "charge," as he termed it in his report, and after he had exhausted the shots of his revolvers he threw them away. The Hostile strength pushed Reno's retreat to the left, so he could not get to the ford where he had entered the valley, but they were fortunate in striking the river at a fordable place; a pony-trail led up a funnel-shaped ravine into the bluffs. Here the command got jammed and lost all semblance of organization. The Indians fired into them, but not very effectively. There does not appear to have been any resistance, certainly no organized resistance during this retreat. On the right and left of the ravine into which the pony-path led were rough precipitous clay bluffs. It was surprising to see what steep inclines men and horses clambered up under the excitement of danger.

Lieutenant Donald McIntosh was killed soon after leaving the timber. Dr. De Wolf was killed while climbing one of the bluffs a short distance from the command. Lieutenant B. H. Hodgson's horse leaped from the bank into the river and fell dead; the lieutenant was wounded in the leg, probably by the same bullet that killed the horse. Hodgson called out, "For God's sake, don't abandon me"; he was assured that he would not be left behind. Hodgson then took hold of a comrade's stirrup-strap and was taken across the stream, but soon after was shot and killed. Hodgson, some days before the battle, had said, that if he

were dismounted in battle or wounded, he intended to take hold of somebody's stirrup to assist himself from the field. During the retreat Private Dalvern, troop "F," had a hand-to-hand conflict with an Indian; his horse was killed; he then shot the Indian, caught the Indian's pony, and rode to the command. Reno's casualties thus far were three officers, including Dr. J. M. De Wolf, and twenty-nine enlisted men and scouts killed; seven enlisted men wounded; and one officer, one interpreter and fourteen soldiers and scouts missing. Nearly all the casualties occurred during the retreat and after leaving the timber. Scout Charlie Reynolds (white), and Isaiah Dorman (Negro), interpreter from Fort Rice, were killed in the timber on the right of Reno's second position. "Bloody Knife" (Ree) was killed by Reno's side. The Ree scouts continued their flight until they reached the supply camp at the mouth of the Powder, on the 27th. The Crow scouts remained with the command. Mr. F. F. Girard, interpreter, informs me that it is his recollection that only one Crow scout "Curley," and "Mitch" Bouyer, Crow interpreter, accompanied Custer's immediate command and that all the other Crow scouts were with Reno. "Curley" probably did not go into the fight at all, but left Custer just before the fighting commenced and went to the high ridge back of the Custer ridge, watched the battle long enough to see that Custer would be defeated and then worked his way to the Big Horn River and waited for the coming of the steamboat "FAR WEST" the smoke of which could undoubtedly be seen for a long distance.

BENTEEN JOINS RENO

Not long after leaving the water hole Sergeant Kanipe, troop "C", met him with an order from Custer to the commanding officer of the pack-train to hurry it up. The sergeant was sent back to the train with the message; as he passed the column he said to the men, "We've got 'em boys." From this and other remarks we inferred that Custer had attacked and captured the village.

Shortly afterward we were met by a trumpeter, Martin, troop "H," bearing this message signed by Colonel Cook, Adjutant: "Benteen, Come on. Big village Be quick. Bring packs," with the postscript "bring packs."

A riderless horse was the only living thing to be seen in our front. Benteen asked the trumpeter what had been done and Martin informed him that "Indians had 'skedaddled,' abandoning the village." The column had been marching at a trot and walk, according as the ground was smooth or broken. We now heard firing, first straggling shots, and as we advanced, the engagements became more and more pronounced and appeared to be coming toward us. The column took the gallop with pistols drawn, expecting to meet the enemy which we thought Custer was driving before him in his effort to communicate with the pack train, never suspecting that our forces had been defeated. We were forming in line to meet our supposed enemy, when we came in full view of the valley of the Little Big Horn. The valley was full of horsemen riding to and fro in clouds of dust and smoke, for the grass had been fired by the Indians to drive the troops out and cover their own movements. On the bluffs to our right we saw a body of troops and that they were engaged. But an engagement appeared to be going on in the valley too. Owing to the distance, smoke and dust, it was impossible to distinguish if those in the valley were friends or foes. There was a short time of uncertainty as to the direction in which we should go, but some Crow scouts came by, driving a small herd of ponies, one of whom said "Soldiers" and motioned for the command to go to the right. Following his directions, we soon joined Reno's battalion, which was still firing. Reno had lost his hat and had a handkerchief tied about his head, and appeared to be very much excited. Benteen's battalion was ordered to dismount and deploy as skirmishers on the edge of the bluffs overlooking the valley. Very soon after this the Indians withdrew from the attack. Lieutenant Hare came to where I was standing and, grasping my hand heartily, said with a good deal of emphasis: "We've had a big fight in the bottom, got whipped, and I am ――― glad to see you." I was satisfied that he meant what he said, for I had already suspected that something was wrong, but was not quite prepared for such startling information. Benteen's battalion was ordered to divide its ammunition with Reno's men, who had apparently expended nearly all in their personal possession. It has often been a matter of doubt whether this was a fact or the effect of imagination. It seems most improbable in view of their active movements and the short time the command was firing, that the "most of the men" should have expended one hundred and fifty rounds of ammunition per man. Lieutenant Hare was ordered to go back and bring up the ammunition pack-mules. Luckily for us the Indians had not gone back on our trail and discovered and waylaid the pack-train. While waiting for the ammunition pack-mules, Major Reno concluded to make an effort to recover and bury the body of Lieutenant Hodgson. Reno asked for a carbine, saying that he had lost his pistols in the charge. At the same time we loaded up a few men with canteens to get water for the command; they were to accompany the rescuing party. The effort was futile; the party was ordered back after being fired upon by some Indians, who doubtless were scalping the dead near the foot of the bluffs.

A number of officers collected on the edge of the bluff overlooking the valley and were discussing the situation.* At this time there were a large number of horsemen, Indians, in the valley. Suddenly they all started down the valley, and in a few minutes scarcely a horseman was to be seen. Heavy firing was heard down the river. During this time the questions were being asked: "What's the matter with Custer, that he don't send word what we shall do?" "Wonder what we are staying here for?" etc., thus showing some uneasiness, but still no one seemed to show great anxiety, nor do I know that any one felt any serious apprehension but that Custer could and would take care of himself. Some of Reno's men had seen Custer's headquarters party, including Custer himself, on the bluffs about the time the Indians began to develop in Reno's front. This party was heard to cheer, and seen to wave their hats as if to give encouragement, and then they disappeared behind the hills or escaped further attention from those below. Major Moylan thinks that the last he saw of Custer's party was about the position of Reno Hill. Major DeRudio thinks he saw Custer on the ridge about opposite where Dr. De Wolf was killed. He says Custer and Tom were dismounted, apparently looking at them through field glasses. Reno was then developing into line of skirmishers. He saw them mount and disappear. Custer's battalion was not seen by Reno's troops after the separation.

It was about the time Custer was last seen that Trumpeter Martin (for the Indians were "ske-

---

* In General Godfrey's narrative as originally published in the Century Magazine for January 1892, this passage reads as follows: "A number of officers collected on the edge of the bluff overlooking the valley and were discussing the situation: *among our number was Captain Moylan, a veteran soldier and a good one too, watching the scene below. Moylan remarked quite emphatically, "Gentlemen, in my opinion General Custer has made the biggest mistake in his life, by not taking the whole regiment in at once in the first attack."*

In his 1908 revision as reprinted by Mrs. Custer in 1921, the language above italicized was deleted. Whether this was done at Mrs. Custer's request or because Godfrey had become increasingly averse to anything that expressed criticism of Custer, is unknown. Perhaps it was both. W.A.G.

daddling"), left Cook with Custer's last orders to Benteen, viz: "Benteen, Come on. Big Village. Be quick. Bring packs. Cook, Adjutant. P.S. Bring packs." The repetition in the order would seem to indicate that Cook was excited, flurried, or that he wanted to emphasize the necessity for escorting the packs. It is possible that from a high point Custer had seen nearly the whole camp and force of the Indians and realized that the chances were desperate; but too late to reunite his forces for the attack. Reno was already in the fight and his (Custer's) own battalion was separated from the attack by a distance of two and a half to three miles. He had no reason to think that Reno would not push his attack vigorously. A commander seldom goes into battle counting on the failure of his lieutenant; if he did, he would provide that such a failure should not turn into disaster.

During a long time after the junction of Reno and Benteen we heard firing down the river in the direction of Custer's command. We were satisfied that Custer was fighting the Indians somewhere, and the conviction was expressed that "our command ought to be doing something or Custer would be after Reno with a sharp stick." We heard two distinct volleys which excited some surprise, and, if I mistake not, brought out the remark from some one that "Custer was giving it to them for all he is worth." I have but little doubt now that these volleys were fired by Custer's orders as *signals of distress* and to indicate where he was.

Captain Weir and Lieutenant Edgerly, after driving the Indians away from Reno's command, on their side, heard the firing, became impatient at the delay, and thought they would move down that way, if they should be permitted. Weir started to get this permission, but changed his mind and concluded to take a survey from the high bluffs first. Edgerly, seeing Weir going in the direction of the firing, supposed it was all right and started down the ravine with the troop. Weir, from the high point saw the Indians in large numbers start for Edgerly, and signaled for him to change his direction, and Edgerly went over to the high point where they remained, not seriously molested, until the remainder of the troops marched down there. The Indians were seen by them to ride about what afterward proved to be Custer's battle-field, shooting into the bodies of the dead men or killing wounded men.

McDougal came up with the pack-train and reported the firing when he reported his arrival to Reno. I remember distinctly looking at my watch at twenty minutes past four, and made a note of it in my memorandum book, and although I have never satisfactorily been able to recall what par-

ticular incident happened at that time, it was some important event before we started down the river. It is my impression, however, that it was the arrival of the pack-train.* It was at about this time that thirteen men and a scout named Herendeen rejoined the command. They had been missing since Reno's flight from the bottom. Several of them were wounded. These men had lost their horses in the stampede from the bottom and had remained in the timber. When leaving the timber to rejoin, they were fired upon by five Indians, but they drove them away.

RENO ATTEMPTS TO FIND CUSTER

My recollection is that it was about half-past two when we joined Reno.** About five o'clock the command moved down toward Custer's supposed whereabouts, intending to join him. The advance went as far as the high bluffs where the command was halted. Persons who have been on the plains and have seen stationary objects dancing before them, now in view and now obscured, or a weed on the top of a hill, projected against the sky, magnified to appear as a tree, will readily understand why our views would be unsatisfactory. The air was full of dust. We could see stationary groups of horsemen, and individual horsemen moving about. From their grouping and the manner in which they sat their horses we knew they were Indians. On the left of the valley a strange sight attracted our attention. Some one remarked that there had been a fire that scorched the leaves of the bushes, which caused the reddish-brown appearance but this appearance was changeable. Watching this intently for a short time with field-glasses, it was discovered that this strange sight was the immense Indian pony-herds.

Looking toward Custer's field, on a hill two miles away we saw a large assemblage. At first our command did not appear to attract their attention, although there was some commotion observable among those near to our position. We heard occasional shots, most of which seemed to be a great distance off, beyond the large groups on the hill. While watching this group, the conclusion was arrived at that Custer had been repulsed, and the firing we heard was the parting shots of the rear guard. The firing ceased, the groups dispersed, clouds of dust arose from all parts of the field, and the horsemen converged toward our position. The command was now dismounted to fight on foot.

*General Godfrey became convinced, after studying my analysis of the time periods, that his entry "4.20" referred to Benteen's junction with Reno on the hill.
** See preceding footnote.

RENO FALLS BACK

Weir's and French's troops were posted on the high bluffs and to the front of them; my own troop along the crest of the bluffs next to the river; the rest of the command moved to the rear, as I supposed to occupy other points in the vicinity, to make this our defensive position. Busying myself with posting my men, giving direction about the use of ammunition, etc., I was a little startled by the remark that the command was out of sight. At this time Weir's and French's troops were being attacked. Orders were soon brought to me by Lieutenant Hare, Acting Adjutant, to join the main command. I had gone some distance in the execution of this order when, looking back, I saw French's troop come tearing over the bluffs, and soon after Weir's troop followed in hot haste. Edgerly was near the top of the bluff, trying to mount his frantic horse, and it did seem that he would not succeed, but he vaulted into his saddle and then joined the troop. The Indians almost immediately followed to the top of the bluff, and commenced firing into the retreating troops, killing one man, wounding others and several horses. They then started down the hillside in pursuit. I at once made up my mind that such a retreat and close pursuit would throw the whole command into confusion, and, perhaps, prove disastrous. I dismounted my men to fight on foot, deploying as rapidly as possible without waiting for the formation laid down in tactics. Lieutenant Hare expressed his intention of staying with me "Adjutant or no Adjutant." The led horses were sent to the main command. Our fire in a short time compelled the Indians to halt and take cover, but before this was accomplished a second order came for me to fall back as quickly as possible to the main command. Having checked the pursuit we began our retreat, slowly at first, but kept up our firing. After proceeding some distance the men began to group together, and to move a little faster and faster, and our fire slackened. This was pretty good evidence that they were getting demoralized. The Indians were being heavily reinforced, and began to come from their cover, but kept up a heavy fire. I halted the line, made the men take their intervals, and again drove the Indians to cover; then once more began the retreat. The firing of the Indians was not heavy. The bullets struck the ground all about us; but the "ping-ping" of the bullets overhead seemed to have a more terrifying influence than the "swish-thud" of the bullets that struck the ground immediately about us. When we got to the ridge in front of Reno's position I observed some Indians making all haste to get possession of a hill to the right.

I could not see the rest of the command, and I knew that that hill would command Reno's position. Supposing that my troop was to occupy the line we were then on, I ordered Hare to take ten men and hold the hill, but, just as he was moving off, an order came from Reno to get back as quickly as possible; so I recalled Hare, again drove the Indians to cover, and ordered the men to run to the lines. This movement was executed, strange to say, without a single casualty.

ON RENO HILL

The Indians now took possession of all the surrounding high points, and opened a heavy fire. They had in the meantime sent a large force up the valley, and soon our position was surrounded. It was now about seven o'clock.

Our position next to the river was protected by the rough, rugged steep bluffs which were cut up by irregular deep ravines. From the crest of these bluffs the ground gently declined away from the river. On the north there was a short ridge, the ground sloping gently to the front and rear. This ridge, during the first day, was occupied by five troops. Directly in the rear of the ridge was a small hill; in the ravine on the south of this hill our hospital was established, and the horses and pack-mules were secured. Across this ravine one troop, Moylan's, was posted, the packs and dead animals being utilized for breastworks. The high hill on the south was occupied by Benteen's troop. Everybody now lay down and spread himself out as thin as possible. After lying there a few minutes I was horrified to find myself wondering if a small sagebrush, about as thick as my finger, would turn a bullet, so I got up and walked alongside the line, cautioned the men not to waste their ammunition; ordered certain men who were good shots to do the firing, and others to keep them supplied with loaded guns.

The firing continued till nearly dark (between nine and ten o'clock), although after dusk but little attention was paid to the firing, as everybody moved about freely.

Of course, everybody was wondering about Custer—why he did not communicate by courier or signal. But the general opinion seemed to prevail that he had been defeated and driven down the river, where he would probably join General Terry, and with whom he would return to our relief. Quite frequently, too, the question, "What's the matter with Custer?" would evoke an impatient reply.

Indians are proverbial economists of fuel, but they did not stint themselves that night. The long twilight was prolonged by numerous bonfires, located throughout their village. The long shadows of the hills and the refracted light gave a supernatural aspect to the surrounding country, which may account for the illusions of those who imagined they could see columns of troops, etc. Although our dusky foes did not molest us with obtrusive attentions during the night, yet it must not be inferred that we were allowed to pass the night in perfect rest; or that they were endeavoring to soothe us into forgetfulness of their proximity, or trying to conceal their situation. They were a good deal happier than we were; nor did they strive to conceal their joy. Their camp was a veritable pandemonium. All night long they continued their frantic revels: beating tom-toms, dancing, whooping, yelling with demoniacal screams, and discharging firearms. We knew they were having a scalp dance. In this connection the question has often been asked, "If they did not have prisoners at the torture?" The Indians deny that they took any prisoners. We did not discover any evidence of torture in their camps. It is true that we did find human heads severed from their bodies, but these had probably been paraded in their orgies during that terrible night.

Our casualties had been comparatively few since taking position on the hill. The question of moving was discussed, but the conditions coupled with the proposition caused it to be indignantly rejected. Some of the scouts were sent out soon after dark to look for signs of Custer's command, but they returned after a short absence, saying that the country was full of Sioux. Lieutenant Varnum volunteered to go out, but was either discouraged from the venture or forbidden to go.

After dark the troops were arranged a little differently. The horses were unsaddled, and the mules were relieved of their packs; all animals were secured to lariats stretched and picketed to the ground.

Soon after all firing had ceased the wildest confusion prevailed. Men imagined they could see a column of troops over on the hills or ridges, that they could hear the tramp of the horses, the command of officers, or even the trumpet-calls. Stable-call was sounded by one of our trumpeters; shots were fired by some of our men, and familiar trumpet-calls were sounded by our trumpeter immediately after, to let the supposed marching column know that we were friends. Every favorable expression or opinion was received with credulity, and then ratified with a cheer. Somebody suggested that General Crook might be coming, so some one, a civilian packer, I think, mounted a horse, and galloping along the line yelled "Don't be discouraged, boys, Crook is coming." But they gradually realized that the much-wished for reinforcements were but the phantasma of their imaginations, and settled down to their work of digging rifle pits. They worked in pairs, in threes and fours. The ground was hard and dry. There were only three or four spades and shovels in the whole command; axes, hatchets, knives, table-forks, tincups, and halves of canteens were brought into use. However, everybody worked hard, and some were still digging when the enemy opened fire at early dawn, between half-past two and three o'clock, so that all had some sort of shelter, except Benteen's men. The enemy's first salutations were rather feeble, and our side made scarcely any response; but as dawn advanced to daylight their lines were heavily reinforced, and both sides kept up a continuous fusillade. Of course it was their policy to draw our fire as much as possible to exhaust our ammunition. As they exposed their persons very little we forbade our men, except well-known good shots, to fire without orders. The Indians amused themselves by standing erect, in full view for an instant, then dropping down again before a bullet could reach them, but of that they soon seemed to grow tired or found it too dangerous. Then they resorted to the old ruse of raising a hat and blouse, or a blanket, on a stick to draw our fire; we soon understood their tactics. Occasionally they fired volleys at command. Their fire, however, was not very effective. Benteen's troops suffered greater losses than any other, because their rear was exposed to the long-range firing from the hills on the north. The horses and mules suffered greatly, as they were fully exposed to the long range fire from the east.

Benteen came over to where Reno was lying, and asked for reinforcements to be sent to his line. Before he left his line, however, he ordered Gibson not to fall back under any circumstances, as this was the key of the position. Gibson's men had expended nearly all their ammunition, some men being reduced to as few as four or five cartridges. He was embarrassed, too, with quite a number of wounded men. Indeed, the situation here was most critical, for if the Indians had made a rush a retreat was inevitable. Private McDermott volunteered to carry a message from Gibson to Benteen urging him to hasten the reinforcements. After considerable urging by Benteen, Reno finally ordered French to take "M" troop over to the south side. On his way over Benteen picked up some men then with the horses. Just previous to his arrival an Indian had shot one of Gibson's men, then rushed up and touched the body with his "coup-stick," and started back to cover, but he was killed. He was in such close proximity to the lines and so exposed to the fire that the other Indians could not carry his body away. This, I believe, was the only dead Indian left in our possession, that is, at Reno Hill.

This boldness determined Benteen to make a charge, and the Indians were driven nearly to the river. On their retreat they dragged several dead and wounded warriors away with them.

The firing almost ceased for a while, and then it recommenced with greater fury. From this fact, and their more active movements, it became evident that they contemplated something more serious than a mere fusillade. Benteen came back to where Reno was, and said if something was not done pretty soon the Indians would run into our lines. Waiting a short time, and no action being taken on his suggestion, he said rather impatiently: "You've got to do something here on the north side pretty quick; this won't do, you must drive them back." Reno then directed us to get ready for a charge, and told Benteen to give the word. Benteen called out, "All ready now, men. Now's the time. Give them hell. Hip, hip, here we go!" And away we went with a hurrah, every man of the troops "B," "D," "G," and "K" but one, who lay in his pit crying like a child. The Indians fired more rapidly than before from their whole line. Our men left the pits with their carbines loaded, and they began firing without orders soon after we started. A large body of Indians had assembled at the foot of one of the hills on the north intending probably to make a charge, as Benteen had divined, but they broke as soon as our line started. When we had advanced 70 to 100 yards, Reno called out "Get back, men, back," and back the whole line came. A most singular fact of this sortie was that not a man who had advanced with the lines was hit; but directly after everyone had gotten into the pits again, the one man who did not go out was shot in the head and killed instantly. The poor fellow had a premonition that he would be killed, and had so told one of his comrades.

Up to this time the command had been without water. The excitement and heat made our thirst almost maddening. The men were forbidden to use tobacco. They put pebbles in their mouths to excite the glands; some ate grass roots, but did not find relief. Some tried to eat hard bread, but after chewing it awhile would blow it out of their mouths like so much flour. A few potatoes were given out and afforded some relief. About 11 a. m. the firing was slack, and parties of volunteers were formed to get water under the protection of Benteen's lines. The parties worked their way down the ravines to within a few yards of the river. The men would get ready, make a rush for the river, fill the camp kettles, and return to fill the canteens. Some Indians stationed in a copse of the woods, a short distance away, opened fire whenever a man exposed himself, which made this a particularly hazardous service. Several men were wounded, and the additional danger was then incurred of rescuing their wounded comrades. I think all these were rewarded with medals of honor. By about one o'clock the Indians had nearly all left us, but they still guarded the river. By that time, however, we had about all the water we needed for immediate use. About two o'clock the Indians came back, opened fire, and drove us to the trenches again, but by three o'clock the firing had ceased altogether.

THE HOSTILES MARCH AWAY

Late in the afternoon we saw a few horsemen in the bottom apparently to observe us, and then fire was set to the grass in the valley. About 7 p.m. we saw emerge from behind this screen of smoke an immense moving mass crossing the plateau, going toward the Big Horn Mountains. This moving mass was distant about five or six miles, but looked much nearer, and almost directly between us and the setting sun, now darkened by the smoke and dust ladened atmosphere; the travois with families and belongings and the pony herds was massed, the long column with wide front was skirted by the warriors on guard; thus silhouetted against the redlined western sky-line, their departure was to us a gladsome sight. A fervent "Thank God" that they had at last given up the contest was soon followed by grave doubts as to their motive for moving. Perhaps Custer had met Terry, and was coming to our relief. "Perhaps they were short of ammunition and were moving their village to a safe distance before making a final desperate effort to overwhelm us. Perhaps it was only a ruse to get us on the move and then clean us out," were the conjectures.

The stench from the dead men and horses was now exceedingly offensive, and it was decided to take up a new position nearer the river. The companies were assigned to positions, and the men were put to work digging pits with the expectation of a renewal of the attack. Our loss on the hill had been eighteen killed and fifty-two wounded.

During the night of June 26th, Lieutenant De Rudio, Private O'Neal, Mr. Girard, the interpreter, and Jackson, a half-breed scout, came to our line.

They had been left in the bottom when Reno made his retreat. In attempting to rejoin on the night of the 25th found the approaches guarded by Indians, so they concealed themselves in the brush some distance up the valley.

AFTER THE BATTLE

Tuesday morning, June 27th, we had reveille without the "morning guns," enjoyed the pleasure of a square meal, and had our stock properly cared for. Our commanding officer seemed to think the Indians had some "trap" set for us, and required our men to hold themselves in readiness to occupy the pits at a moment's notice. Nothing seemed determined except to stay where we were. Not an Indian was in sight, but a few ponies were seen grazing down in the valley.

At 9:30 a. m. a cloud of dust was observed several miles down the river. The assembly was sounded, the horses were placed in a protected situation, and camp kettles and canteens were filled with water. An hour of suspense followed; but from the slow advance we concluded that they were our own troops. "But whose command is it?" We looked in vain for a gray-horse troop. It could not be Custer; it must then be Crook, for if it were Terry, Custer would be with him. Cheer after cheer was given for Crook. A white scout, Muggins Taylor, came up with a note from General Terry, addressed to General Custer, dated June 26th, stating that two of our Crow scouts had given information that our column had been whipped and nearly all had been killed; that he did not believe their story, but was coming with medical assistance. The scout said that he could not get to our lines the night before, as the Indians were on the alert. Very soon after this Lieutenant Bradley, 7th Infantry, came into our lines, and asked where I was. Greeting most cordially my old friend, I immediately asked: "Where is Custer?" He replied: "I don't know, but I suppose he was killed, as we counted 197 dead bodies. I don't suppose any escaped." We were simply dumbfounded. This was the first intimation we had of his fate. It was hard to realize; it did seem impossible. Then I took him to Major Reno and there introduced him to the officers.

TERRY'S ARRIVAL

General Terry and staff, and officers of General Gibbon's column, soon after approached and their coming was greeted with prolonged hearty cheers. The grave countenance of the General awed the men to silence. The officers assembled to meet their guests. There was scarcely a dry eye; hardly a word was spoken, but quivering lips and hearty grasping of hands gave token of thankfulness for the relief and grief for the dead.

During the rest of the day we were busy collecting our effects and destroying surplus property. The wounded were cared for and taken to the camp of our new friends of the Montana column. Among the wounded was Saddler "Mike" Madden of my troop, whom I promoted to be sergeant, on the field, for gallantry. Madden was very fond of his grog. His long abstinence gave him a famous thirst. It was necessary to amputate his leg, which was done without administering any anesthetic; but after the amputation the surgeon gave him a good, stiff drink of brandy. Madden eagerly gulped it down, and his eyes fairly danced as he smacked his lips and said: "M-eh, doctor, cut off my other leg."

WAS THERE A SURVIVOR?

The question has often been asked if any soldier escaped. In August we camped at the mouth of the Rosebud where we found the carcass of a horse *shot in the head;* near the horse was a carbine; on the saddle was a small grain sack made of canvas and used by the 7th Cavalry only to carry oats during the march, when detached from the wagons. At the time of the discovery we conjectured that some man had escaped, and on reaching the river had killed his horse for meat and used the saddle straps to tie together a raft. An Indian would not have left the carbine but the man may have abandoned it, either because he was out of ammunition or could not risk the extra weight on his raft.

WHY CUSTER WAS DEFEATED

The question has often been asked: "What were the causes of Custer's defeat?"

I should say:

First. The overpowering numbers of the enemy and their unexpected cohesion.

Second. Reno's panic rout from the valley.

Third. The defective extraction of the empty cartridge-shells from the carbines.

On the first, I will say that we had nothing conclusive on which to base calculations of the numbers, and to this day it seems almost incredible that such great numbers of Indians should have left the agencies, to combine against the troops, without information relating thereto having been communicated to the commanders of troops in the field, further than heretofore mentioned. The second has been mentioned incidentally. The Indians say if Reno's position in the valley had been held, they would have been compelled to divide their strength for the different attacks, which would have caused confusion and apprehension, and prevented the concentration of every able-bodied warrior upon the battalion under Custer; that, at the time of the discovery of Custer's advance to attack, the chiefs gave orders for the village to move, to break up; that at the time of Reno's retreat, this order was being carried out, but as soon as Reno's retreat was assured, the order was countermanded, and the squaws were compelled to return with the pony herds; that the order would not have been countermanded had Reno's forces remained fighting in the bottom. Custer's attack did not begin until after Reno had reached the bluffs.

Of the third we can only judge by our own experience. When cartridges were dirty and corroded, the ejectors did not always extract the empty shells from the chambers, and the men were compelled to use knives to get them out. When the shells were clean no great difficulty was experienced. To what extent this was a factor in causing the disaster we have no means of knowing.

A possible fourth cause was the division of the command. With all the regiment under Custer's personal direction, the results might have been different; but, on the other hand, the whole command might have been wiped out.

The division of the command was not in itself faulty. The same tactics were pursued at the battle of Washita and were successful. That was a surprise attack and there was *full co-operation* of the separate commands, each commander carried out his instructions. My studies of the battle of the Little Big Horn leaves me in little doubt that had Reno made his charge as ordered, or made a bold front even, the Hostiles would have been so engaged in the bottom that Custer's approach from the Northeast would have been such a surprise as to cause the stampede of the village and would have broken the morale of the warriors.

On the other hand, with the entire command concentrated under Custer's leadership the charge would have been carried *home,* and, I believe, successfully.

General Custer has been accused of selfish motives in refusing to take the additional forces said to have been offered him while at the mouth of the Rosebud. It is a very delicate matter to analyze motives. In going over letters and diary written during the campaign I find references that may help. General Terry, in his official report

makes no mention of the offer, but says: "It was believed to be impracticable to join Colonel Gibbon's troops to Lieutenant-Colonel Custer's force; for more than one-half of Colonel Gibbon's troops were infantry who would be unable to keep up with cavalry in a rapid movement; while to detach Gibbon's mounted men and add them to the 7th Cavalry would leave his force too small to act as an independent body." Thus, it is seen that General Terry had his own reasons for not sending them.

In a letter dated June 10, 1876, I find: "The 2nd Cavalry officers are greatly disgusted; one company has to be mounted all the time; the C. O. selects very poor camps for cavalry and *their horses are in very poor condition.*

The Gatling guns were each hauled by four *condemned* cavalry horses. They were unfitted for long rapid marches and would have been unable to keep up if there had been such a demand upon them. The poor condition of the horses in the 2nd Cavalry and in the Gatling gun battery may have decided against both of them.

Colonel Gibbon in his report says: "The first intimation we had of the force and strategy opposed to us was the check given to Custer's column . . ."

Major Brisbin, 2nd Cavalry, in a letter to me, January, 1892, says he was present at the conference on the steamboat "Far West"; that at General Terry's request he traced the routings of the troops on the map and placed pins to show their probable places en route; that Custer turned to the right and left the Rosebud just twenty miles short of his furthermost point on the Rosebud routing.

General Terry says in his report that at the conference he communicated his plan of operations. "It was that Colonel Gibbon's column should cross the Yellowstone near the mouth of the Big Horn, and, thence up that stream with the expectation that it would arrive at the mouth of the Little Big Horn by the 26th. That Lieutenant-Colonel Custer with the whole 7th Cavalry should proceed up the Rosebud until he should ascertain the direction in which the trail discovered by Major Reno led; that if it led to the Little Big Horn it should not be followed,* but that Lieutenant-Colonel Custer should keep still farther to the south before turning toward that river, in order to intercept the Indians should they attempt to pass around his left, and in order, by a longer

---

* Compare with written instructions, wherein Custer is given discretion when so nearly in contact with the enemy, etc.

march, to give time for Gibbon's column to come up. This plan was founded on the belief that the two columns might be brought into co-operating distance of each other, so either of them which should be first to engage might, by a 'waiting fight' give time for the other to come up."

The length of the marches has been a subject of comment, it being asserted that the command was subjected to long and exhausting marches. They were: June 22nd, 12 miles; June 23rd, 33 to 35 miles; June 24th, 28 miles; then June 24th, at 11:30 p. m., about 8 miles; then from the divide between the Rosebud and the Little Big Horn to the battle, about 20 miles; in all about 113 miles.

A battle was unavoidable. Every man in Terry's and Custer's commands expected a battle; it was for that purpose, to punish the Indians, that the command was sent out, and with that determination Custer made his preparations. Had Custer continued his march southward—that is, left the Indian trail—the Indians would have known of our movement on the 25th, and a battle would have been fought very near the same field on which Crook had been attacked and forced back only a week before; the Indians never would have remained in camp and allowed a concentration of the several columns to attack them. If they had escaped without punishment of battle Custer would undoubtedly have been blamed.

The 29th and 30th of June were occupied in destroying property left in the Indian village, preparing litters to carry the wounded and transporting them at night to the Big Horn, where they were placed aboard the "Far West."

Captain Grant Marsh, master of the "Far West," was the pioneer navigator of the Big Horn and had courageously held his boat there in the face of receding waters, taking chances of stranding his boat on the rocks and shoals of the treacherous river. But Grant Marsh was always ready to take any chances when the services of his government demanded them. He was a man of tremendous energy and resources to fight and overcome all obstacles. July 1st and 2nd the command marched to, and crossed, the Yellowstone and camped on "Pease Bottom," the scene of our fight with the Hostiles in 1873.

At noon July 3rd, the "Far West" loaded with the wounded, Captain Baker's company as escort, and Captain Smith, General Terry's aid-de-camp, and Assistant-Adjutant General of the expedition, with dispatches, etc., cast off, swung into mid-stream, and with "full steam ahead" crashing through willows and carroming against mud banks, made her memorable voyage down the Yellowstone and Missouri rivers, reaching Bismarck 11:30 p. m. July 5th, and then giving to the thirty-nine widows at Fort Lincoln, and to the world, the astounding news of Custer's Last Battle.

CHARGES OF DISOBEDIENCE, RASHNESS & DRUNKENNESS

Recent publications of comments on the movements of the troops and the conduct and characteristics of officers prompts me to add to the foregoing account.

Disobedience of Orders

A careful perusal of the orders issued to General Custer will show that the General was given practically a *free hand*. If any supplemental instructions were given, they were never revealed to the public. General Terry had had no practical experience in Indian warfare. General Custer had that practical experience; he was a student of Indian characteristics; had intimate observations, both in peace and war. He knew that in our centuries of Indian warfare there were more escapes than punishments inflicted for outrages and depredations; that most of these escapes resulted from failure to give vigorous pursuits in following the Hostiles; that the way to find the Hostiles was to follow the trail, stay with it; that success usually depended on surprise attacks; that the most successful surprises came with night approaches and day-break attacks; that forewarned approaches resulted in scatteration into groups or by families and thus escape punishment, and pursuit apt to be disorganized.

It was an absurdity to think that two commands, of 700 and 400, separated by from fifty to one hundred miles, could co-ordinate their movements in that open country and hold the Hostiles for a co-operative attack. In such a case, and the Hostiles had escaped, who would have shouldered the blame?

In the text I have shown that the country toward Tullock's Fork was under surveillance, and it is reasonable to suppose that had circumstances not caused a change of plans for a daybreak attack on the 26th, that Scout Herendeen would have been sent to Gen. Terry's headquarters with information as to plans, etc.

There could not have been any understanding, as contended by some, that the two commands of Custer and Gibbon were to meet at or near the mouth of the Little Big Horn on June 26th.

Rashness

The number of probable Hostiles, one thousand to fifteen hundred, did not cause any dismay in the command. We knew, of course, that there would be many casualties, which would be the misfortune of individuals, but that there would be a disaster was not considered probable. General Custer had no reason to think that there would be a general exodus from the Indian agencies in the Missouri River and from Nebraska to join the Hostile camps without warning being given in ample time by the Agents, the Bureau of Indian Affairs or Interior Department to the military authorities. Such a warning from General Sheridan, via Fort Lincoln, by courier was received about a week after the battle, too late to avert disaster.

Drunkenness

I have seen articles imputing wholesale drunkenness to both officers and enlisted men, including General Custer who was absolutely abstemious. I do not believe that any officer, except Major Reno, had any liquor in his possession. Major Reno had half a gallon keg that he took with him in the field, but I don't believe any other officer sampled its contents. I saw all the officers early in the morning and again at our halt at the divide and when officers' call was sounded to announce the determination to attack, and I saw no sign of intoxication; all had that serious, thoughtful mien, indicating that they sensed the responsibilities before them.

RENO'S LEADERSHIP

Among the questions propounded has been this one: "If" Reno had advanced "to the sound of the guns" when we heard the firing on Custer's field, would he have rescued Custer's command?

Frankly, I do not believe Custer's command would have been rescued under Reno's leadership. At no time during the battle was his conduct such as to inspire confidence. His faltering advances down the valley, his halting, his falling back to the defensive position in the woods in the old river bed before his command had suffered a single casualty in the ranks; his disorganized, panic retreat to the bluffs with practically no resistance, his conduct up to and during the siege, and until the arrival of General Terry was not such as to inspire confidence or even respect, except for his authority; and there was a time during the night of the 25th, when his authority, under certain conditions, was to be ignored. We thought he ought to go, his attention was called to the firing on the Custer field; it was suggested that he go; he was waiting for the ammunition packs to replenish the ammunition; then he waited for the delayed pack train. We started and marched as far as the first ridge when we beheld the dismounted men crossing the valley, men that had been left when he made his retreat. We halted and waited for them to join, to be mounted and have their ammunition replenished; then we advanced to the high point where we could overlook the Custer battlefield. We saw the commotion on that field when the Hostiles started in our direction. Three troops, D, K and M were then ordered to take positions and hold their ground; with the other four and the pack train Reno returned to our first position on the bluffs, nearly two miles away. Then he ordered the troops in position to fall back at once.

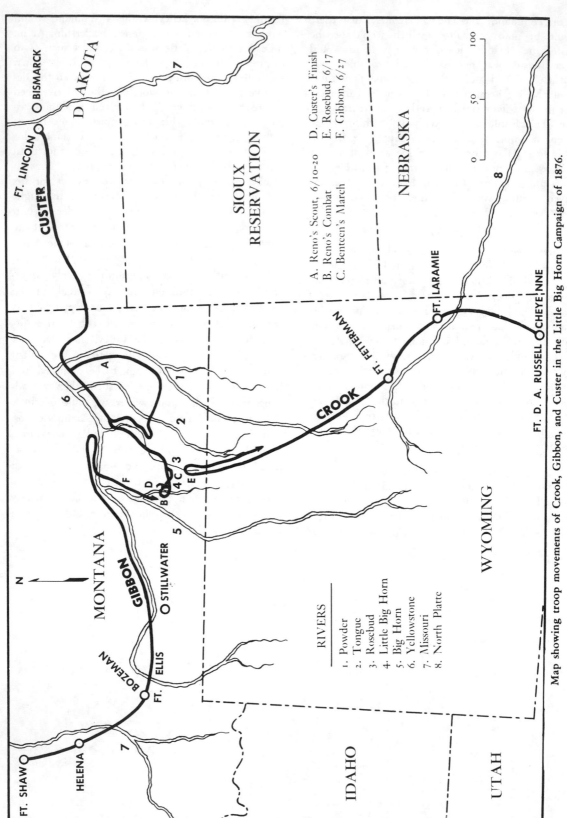

Map showing troop movements of Crook, Gibbon, and Custer in the Little Big Horn Campaign of 1876.

Drawn by Col. W. A. Graham.

RIVERS

1. Powder
2. Tongue
3. Rosebud
4. Little Big Horn
5. Big Horn
6. Yellowstone
7. Missouri
8. North Platte

A. Reno's Scout, 6/10-20
B. Reno's Combat
C. Benteen's March
D. Custer's Finish
E. Rosebud, 6/17
F. Gibbon, 6/27

CHAPTER 3

COMMENTS BY GENERAL J. B. FRY ON GODFREY'S NARRATIVE

(Century Magazine, January, 1892)

CAPTAIN GODFREY'S article is a valuable contribution to the authentic history of the campaign which culminated in "Custer's Last Battle," June 25, 1876.

The Sioux war of 1876 originated in a request by the Indian Bureau that certain wild and recalcitrant bands of Indians should be compelled to settle down upon their reservations under control of the Indian agent. Sitting Bull, on the Little Missouri in Dakota, and Crazy Horse, on Powder River, Wyoming, were practically the leaders of the hostile Indians who roamed over what General Sheridan called "an almost totally unknown region, comprising an area of almost 90,000 square miles." The hostile camps contained eight or ten separate bands, each having a chief of its own.

Authority was exercised by a council of chiefs. No chief was endowed with supreme authority, but Sitting Bull was accepted as the leader of all his bands. From 500 to 800 warriors was the most the military authorities thought the hostiles could muster. Sitting Bull's camp, as Custer found it, contained some 8000 or 10,000 men, women, and children, and about 2500 warriors, including boys, who were armed with bows and arrows. The men had good firearms, many of them Winchester rifles, with a large supply of ammunition.

War upon this savage force was authorized by the War Department, and was conducted under the direction of Lieutenant-General Sheridan in Chicago.

The campaign opened in the winter, General Sheridan thinking that was the season in which the Indians could be "caught." He directed General Terry to send a mounted column under Custer against Sitting Bull, and General Crook to move against Crazy Horse. Bad weather prevented

Custer's movement, but Crook advanced March 1. On March 17 he struck Crazy Horse's band, was partially defeated, and the weather being very severe, returned to his base. The repulse of Crook's column, and the inability of Custer to move, gave the Indians confidence, and warriors by the hundreds slipped away from the agencies and joined the Hostiles.

In the spring Sheridan's forces resumed the offensive in three isolated columns. The first column under Crook, consisting of 15 companies of cavalry and 5 companies of infantry (total 1049), marched northward from Fort Fetterman May 29. The second column under General Terry, consisting of the entire 7th Cavalry, 12 companies (about 600 men), 6 companies of infantry, 3 of them on the supply steamboat (400 men), a battery of Gatling guns manned by infantrymen, and 40 Indian scouts, moved westward from Fort A. Lincoln, on the Missouri, May 17.

It happened that while the expedition was being fitted out, Custer unwittingly incurred the displeasure of President Grant, who directed that Custer should not accompany the column. Through his appeal to the President and the intercession of Terry and Sheridan, Custer was permitted to go in command of his regiment, but Terry was required to accompany and command the column. Terry was one of the best of men and ablest of soldiers, but had no experience in Indian warfare.

A third column under General Gibbon (Colonel of Infantry), consisting of 4 companies of cavalry and 6 companies of infantry (450 men all told), marched eastward in April, and united with Terry on the Yellowstone, June 21. When these columns started they were all some 200 or 300 miles from the central position occupied by the enemy. Gibbon was under Terry's control, but Crook and Terry were independent of each other.

The authorities believed that either one of the three columns could defeat the enemy if it "caught" him; otherwise isolated forces would not have been sent to "operate blindly," without means of mutual support, against an enemy in the interior of an almost totally unknown region. Indeed General Sherman said in his official report of 1876, "Up to the moment of Custer's defeat there was nothing, official or private, to justify an officer to expect that any detachment would encounter more than 500 or 800 warriors." The appearance of 2500 to 3000 in the Custer fight, General Sherman adds, "amounted to a demonstration that the troops were dealing, not only with the hostiles estimated at from 500 to 800, but with the available part of the Agency Indians, who had gone out to help their friends in a fight."

The utter failure of our campaign was due to under-estimating the numbers and prowess of the enemy. The strength he was found to possess proved, as General Sherman said in his report, "that the campaign had been planned on wrong premises." Upon this point Gibbon said, "When these various bands succeeded in finding a leader who possessed tact, courage, and ability to concentrate and keep together so large a force, it was only a question of time when one or the other of the exterior columns would meet with a check from the overwhelming numbers of the interior body."

The first result was that Crook's column encountered the enemy, June 17, and was so badly defeated that it was practically out of the campaign.

In his official report Sheridan claims for Crook a "barren victory," but adds, "Next day he returned to his supply camp on Goose Creek and awaited reinforcements and supplies, considering himself too weak to make any movement until additional troops reached him."

On the 21st of June, Terry, with the column from the east, about one thousand men, was on the south bank of the Yellowstone, at the mouth of the Rosebud. Gibbon was with Terry, and his column from the west, four hundred and fifty men, was some fifteen miles up the Yellowstone on its north bank, nearly opposite the mouth of the Big Horn. The Rosebud and Big Horn flow from south to north about fifteen miles apart, with a high, broken "divide" or ridge between them.

A scouting party had found indications that the Indians were on the Big Horn or its tributaries,

and they were found on the 25th about ninety miles away in the valley of the Little Big Horn, with some 2500 warriors. At that time Terry did not imagine them to be so strong, nor did he know that Crook had been defeated on the 17th. He heard nothing of Crook until July 4.

On the night of June 21, Terry held a conference with Gibbon and Custer, at which he says in his annual report in 1876, he decided upon a plan of operations, by which Gibbon was to move south up the Big Horn valley, Custer was to proceed up the Rosebud and ascertain the direction of the Indian trail, and

"if it led to the Little Big Horn it should not be followed, but that Custer should keep still further to the south before turning to the river, in order to intercept the Indians should they attempt to pass around his left, and in order, by a longer march, to give time for Gibbon's column to come up . . . This plan was founded on the belief that the two columns might be brought into cooperating distance of each other, so either of them which should be first engaged might, by a 'waiting fight,' give time for the other to come up."

Custer's disaster has been directly or by implication attributed to a departure from the "plan." No record of the conference appears to have been made at the time, but Terry's statement concerning it is supported by Gibbon, and no one would dispute it if it stood alone. But it is highly probable that the plan when Custer moved had neither the force nor importance which it subsequently acquired in Terry's mind. Terry made to Sheridan a full and explicit report, June 27, when the subject was fresh, in which he spoke of the conference, but did not say or intimate that a plan of operations had been decided upon in it. He did say, however, "I informed General Custer I would take the supply steamer up the Yellowstone to ferry General Gibbon's column over the river, that I should personally accompany that column, and that it would in all probability reach the mouth of the Big Horn on the 26th instant." If at that time Terry thought the plan of operations mandatory, he probably would have mentioned it in this report of June 27. It was, however, not until July 2 that he reported the existence of a plan. Then he said in his report to Sheridan made in his own defense, *"I think I owe it to myself* to put you more fully in possession of the facts of the late operations," and followed with the account of the plan, above quoted from his annual report, but did not say that he had issued any orders which Custer had disobeyed.

The plan decided upon in conference on the night of June 21 fixes no blame on Custer. His written instructions from Terry were made June 22, the day after the conference, and they were binding upon him. They made no reference to a plan, but said:

"The Brigadier-General Commanding directs that, as soon as your regiment can be made ready for the march, you will proceed up the Rosebud in pursuit of the Indians whose trail was discovered by Major Reno a few days since. *It is, of course, impossible to give you any definite instructions in regard to this movement,* and were it not impossible to do so the department commander places too much confidence in your zeal, energy and ability to wish to impose upon you precise orders which might hamper your action when nearly in contact with the enemy. He will, however, indicate to you his own views of what your action should be, and he desires that you should conform to them unless you shall see sufficient reason for departing from them."

The order Custer received was to proceed up the Rosebud in pursuit of the Indians. Surely he did not disobey that. Everything else was left to his discretion. As Terry did not wish to hamper Custer's action when nearly in contact with the enemy, and found it impossible to give him precise orders, plainly Custer did not, could not, disobey orders in any blamable sense, and plainly, also, he was expected to come "in contact with the enemy."

Captain Godfrey says that the scouts were sent out on the right flank during the 23d and 24th, moving along the divide between Rosebud and Tulloch's Fork, from which the valley of the Fork was in view. It is true Custer does not appear to have examined the upper part of Tulloch's Creek, but there were no Indians there, and the omission if it occurred is colorless. He was directed to endeavor to send a scout through to General Gibbon's column with the result of his examination of Tulloch's Creek, and was informed that Gibbon would examine the lower part of the creek. Whether he endeavored to send a messenger cannot be ascertained (Captain Godfrey says that a scout named Herendeen had been selected for this service, and he is of the opinion that General Custer would have sent him during the day if the fight had been delayed until early next morning as he at first intended); but nothing concerning Tulloch's Creek was material in the campaign.

Even conformity to Terry's "views" was expressly left to Custer's discretion.

In his sermon at General Terry's funeral, December 29, 1890, the Rev. Dr. T. T. Munger said:

"Custer's fatal movement was in direct violation of both verbal and written orders. When his rashness and disobedience ended in the total destruction of his command, General Terry withheld the fact of the disobeyed orders and suffered an imputation hurtful to his military reputation to rest upon himself, rather than subject a brave but indiscreet subordinate to a charge of disobedience."

When called to account for the accusation which he made against one dead soldier at the Christian burial of another, Dr. Munger gave Colonel R. P. Hughes of the army, a brother-in-law of General Terry and for a long time his aide de camp, as authority for his defamatory assertion.

Colonel Hughes denies having authorized Dr. Munger to make the statement, though he admits he was the source of Dr. Munger's information. Called upon more than once, he fails to produce or specify any orders disobeyed by Custer. Indeed there can be no such orders. It is not credible that Terry issued orders which have never been produced by him or any one else, and that these phantom orders if obeyed would have prevented the Custer massacre. Terry was a strict and careful soldier. It was his duty to file with higher authority all the orders he issued in the case, and his orders have passed in due course to their places in the public records, and have been discussed above. Custer disobeyed none of them.*

Returning to the conference plan of operations, it must be noted that, like the general plan of campaign, it was based upon a misconception of the enemy's strength. It required that a well-armed, wary, and vigilant enemy of unknown strength, some ninety miles away in a country well known to him but unknown to us, should be approached by two columns, the enemy, as it turned out, exceeding in numbers the two columns combined. Even if Custer had gone quite to the south and had not attacked, the plan put it in the power of the enemy to defeat at least one of the columns as he had defeated Crook. Custer no doubt thought if he was strong enough to go to the south and wait to be attacked, he was strong enough to make the attack, and Terry's instructions left the matter to his judgment.

*Colonel Hughes, after endeavoring to answer General Fry through the columns of the "Century," which declined his article, published it in the Journal of the Military Service Institution for January 1896. His reply, which covers the question of disobedience thoroughly, will be found reproduced as an Appendix to "The Story of the Little Big Horn," following page 178.

Terry stated in his report that he believed his plan might have resulted in a "waiting fight" through which the column first engaging the enemy might hold him until the other came up, the implication being that advantage from a "waiting fight" was lost through Custer's action. The truth is that a "waiting fight" is exactly what was secured, but there was no advantage in it. Custer's command, south of the enemy, kept him engaged from the 25th until the evening of the 26th, when the column from the north approached. Then the Indians quietly slipped away without the northern column being able to detain or injure them.

Godfrey gives the details of Custer's three days' march and of the fight on the 25th and 26th. When the command was nearly in contact with the enemy Custer directed one company to guard the pack-train, sent three companies under Benteen to the south, no doubt in deference to Terry's advice to see that the Indians did not pass that way, ordered Reno with three companies to charge northward down the valley upon the enemy's flank, and with the rest of his force, 250 men, galloped down the river about three miles to attack in front. The result is known. It is not bad tactics to throw a part of the attacking force upon the exposed flank of the enemy, and support it by a front attack with the other part, and that is what Custer did. To "support" the flanking force is not necessarily to follow it. Custer's "pursuit" to the field where he "caught" the Indians was rapid, but his defeat is not to be attributed to fatigue of horses or men. The offensive is often more fatiguing than the defensive, but the loss of a battle is seldom, if ever, due to the fatigue of the attacking force.

During the Indian outbreak at Pine Ridge Agency, 1890, a battalion of the 9th Cavalry, under Colonel Henry, accompanied by a section of Light Battery E, 1st Artillery, marched as follows: December 24, between 2.30 P. M. and 3.30 next morning fifty miles and six miles further after daylight; scouted actively on the 25th, 26th, and 27th, made forty-four miles on the 28th, and starting at 9.30 A. M. on the 29th made ninety-six miles before 4 P. M. on the 30th; was all the time ready for battle, had a skirmish, and marched six miles after the skirmish, making 102 miles in thirty hours.*

The part taken by the companies under Reno proved that Custer's force was not too tired to go into the fight and maintain it until the evening of the 26th. The command was probably no more fatigued than cavalry usually is when it attacks in a vigorous pursuit.

Having marched leisurely from Fort Lincoln on the Missouri to the Rosebud on the Yellowstone, the men and horses were well seasoned but not worn, and Reno has stated that when the regiment moved out on the 22d of June "the men and officers were cheerful," the *"horses were in best condition."* After Custer "caught" the Indians, their "escape," against which he was warned in Terry's written instructions, could be prevented only by attack. The trouble was their strength was underestimated. Terry reported July 2: "He [Custer] expressed the utmost confidence he had all the force he could need, *and I shared his confidence."* Believing, as he and Sheridan and Terry did, that he was strong enough for victory, if Custer had not attacked, and the Indians had moved away, as they did when Gibbon's column approached on the 26th, Custer would have been condemned, perhaps disgraced. With his six hundred troopers he could not *herd* the Indians, nor, in that vast, wild, and difficult region, with which they were familiar and of which we were ignorant, could he by going further to his left, "south," drive them against Gibbon's column, His fight was forced by the situation. Believing, as Custer and his superiors did, that his 600 troopers were opposed by only 500, or at most 800 warriors, his attack shows neither desperation nor rashness. General Sherman said that when Custer found himself in presence of the Indians he could do nothing but attack.**

In relation to Reno's part, it is proper to state that General Sherman, in his official report, 1876, commends "the brave and prudent conduct of Major Reno," and in 1879 a Court of Inquiry was convened at Reno's request to examine into his conduct in the battle. The court was created by the President and he approved its findings. It reported the facts as it found them, and said "the conduct of the officers throughout was excellent, and while subordinates in some instances did more

---

*Lieutenant A. W. Perry, in the Journal of U. S. Cavalry Association.

**New York City, May 11, 1891. Dear Fry: In reply to your note I cannot recall the whole conversation between General Sherman and myself. I remember distinctly that I was much distressed and greatly excited. The conversation took place not long after Custer's defeat. I condemned everything and everybody, and doubt not I spoke only words of passion without judgment. I think I said that Custer's command was in no condition to fight when he made the attack. To this, or something like it, Sherman said when Custer found himself in the presence of the Indians, he could do nothing but attack.

Very truly, etc. T. L. CRITTENDEN

The only son of the gallant Union general who wrote the above note fell upon the field with Custer.

for the safety of the command by brilliant displays of courage than did Major Reno, there was nothing in his conduct which requires animadversion from this court." Conceding to Reno the right to the benefit of these indorsements, there are some facts which should be noted.

"About the same time that Reno's command was crossing the river in retreat" after it had been engaged only "half an hour or forty-five minutes in all," says the Reno Court of Inquiry, Benteen approached.

His three companies doubled Reno's force, giving him six companies, whereas Custer had only five. Another company with the pack-train arrived a little later. Custer's need of men and ammunition was shown by his last order which Benteen received before joining Reno. "Come on. Big village. Be quick. Bring pack." Under the circumstances Reno might well have treated this order as applying to him as well as to Benteen. As soon as the Indians had driven him back they concentrated upon Custer.

"During a long time" after Benteen joined Reno, says Godfrey, Custer's firing was heard, showing that his five companies were hotly engaged with the opposing force, which Reno had found too strong. If Reno had marched then with his six companies to the sound of Custer's carbines, it would have been conduct to commend, and might have enabled Custer to extricate the command. When he did move out it was too late; Custer's men had been killed, and the enemy was able to oppose Reno with his whole force and drive him back and invest him in his place of refuge.

Crook's and Terry's columns having been defeated, they were heavily reinforced; and on the 30th of July a staff officer from Chicago arrived at Terry's camp with orders for Terry and Crook to unite. After their junction—August 10—there was much marching, but no fighting. The enemy could not be "caught."

James B. Fry.

In re: BRISBIN vs. TERRY AND GODFREY

ON 1 January 1892, General James S. Brisbin, then retired, wrote General Edward S. Godfrey a long letter in which he commented critically and extensively upon Godfrey's article entitled "Custer's Last Battle," which had appeared in the then current number of the Century Magazine. The letter reached Godfrey (at that time a Captain of the Seventh Cavalry) only a few days prior to Brisbin's death, and in consequence, no reply was ever written.

This letter was, however, both referred to and quoted by General Godfrey in a memorandum sent by him to the Rev. Cyrus Townsend Brady in 1904, in which the question of Custer's disobedience of Terry's instructions was discussed. (Indian Fights and Fighters; Brady, pp. 277-8).

Brisbin, in 1876, was a Major in command of the battalion of the Second Cavalry that formed part of Gibbon's column. His 1892 letter to Godfrey, which, with some deletions, is printed as Chapter 16 of E. A. Brininstool's recent work "Troopers with Custer," sets out a material paragraph of the Terry instructions in language that differs sharply from that found in Godfrey's narrative (see p. 132 this volume), and similarly differs from the language of the instructions as found in Terry's official report of 27 June 1876.

In 1923, or thereabout, General Godfrey sent me the original Brisbin letter, with permission to copy it, and to make such use of it as I might see fit; and I accordingly had several verbatim copies made, one of which I sent to Mr. Brininstool. The original letter, I was informed, was later turned over to W. J. Ghent of Washington.

General Brisbin's comments concerning Terry's instructions are set out below, the following being a verbatim copy thereof which reproduces only such italics or emphases as appear in the original letter:

"I read the order you print as being the one given to Custer for his march. If that is the order Custer got it is not the one copied in Terry's books at Department Headquarters. You will remember that after Custer fell, Terry appointed me his Chief of Cavalry. I looked over all the papers affecting the march and battle of Little Big Horn and took a copy of the order sending you up Rosebud. That order now lies before me and it says—

"'You should proceed up Rosebud until you ascertain definitely the direction in which the trail above spoken of leads.' (Terry had already referred to the trail Reno followed). 'Should it be found, as it appears to be almost certain that it will be found, to turn toward the Little Big Horn he thinks' (that is, the Department Commander thinks) 'that you should still proceed southward, perhaps as *far* as the headwaters of the Tongue River, and *then*' ('then' underscored in order) 'turn *toward Little Big Horn,* feeling constantly, however, to your left, so as to preclude the possibility of the escape of the Indians to the South or Southeast by passing around your left flank. It is desired that you conform as nearly as possible to these instructions and that you do not depart from them unless you shall see *absolute necessity for doing so.'* (The absolute necessity mentioned here meant following the Indians alone or attacking them alone with your meager force)."

I asked General Godfrey whether he had checked the Brisbin version of the instructions above quoted against General Terry's Department Headquarters records. He replied that he had never made any effort to do so, being satisfied that Brisbin was mistaken. I considered such a check important, for if the last sentence as quoted by Brisbin was correct, it came close to establishing Custer's disobedience as a fact, whereas the official version raised merely an implication.

For that reason a search began for Terry's Headquarters records for 1876. It took some time and considerable effort to find them, but they were at length located at Ft. Snelling, Minnesota, in storage. The Quartermaster custodian was pre-vailed upon to dig out the desired information, and I received from him a certified copy of General Terry's letter of instructions to Custer as it appeared in those records. The document proved General Godfrey to be correct. General Brisbin was in error.

In justice to General Custer, it must therefore be stated categorically that Terry's Department Headquarters records showed his letter of instructions to Custer to have been *exactly* and *precisely identical* with the instructions as set out in Terry's official report of 27 June 1876, and in Godfrey's narrative of January 1892. The last sentence as quoted by Brisbin, viz: "It is desired that you conform as nearly as possible to these instructions and that you do not depart from them unless you shall see *absolute necessity for doing so,"* did *not* appear either in whole or in part.

CHAPTER 4

FREDERICK WILLIAM BENTEEN
BREVET BRIGADIER GENERAL, U. S. ARMY

IN 1924, WHILE on duty in Washington, I was ordered to visit New Orleans on official business. A friend, then resident in Atlanta, formerly an officer of the Judge Advocate General's Department (my own branch), who knew of my interest in the Sioux War of 1876, had written me that he had lately made the acquaintance of a retired Major, an only son of that famed veteran of the 7th Cavalry, but for whose timely arrival upon the heights of the Little Big Horn, Reno's routed command might well have suffered a fate similar to that of Custer's. The Major, an "Army brat" of tender years when the battle occurred, could, if he would, tell me much of his father's career in the Army, and had in his possession, important letters and documents relating to the campaign against the Sioux, which my friend very much desired me to see.

Acting upon his suggestion that I visit Atlanta, I asked and received permission to stop off there on my return from New Orleans, and through the friendly intercession of my former colleague, I met Major Benteen. He was a reticent man; but he did tell me much about his famous father; and that which follows here is based in part upon what I learned from him, in part upon official records, and in part upon the documents and letters that he showed me.

Frederick William Benteen was a native son of "the Old Dominion," born at Petersburg, Virginia in August 1834. During his early boyhood, the Benteen family, following the star of empire, removed to the state of Missouri, and it was here, during the stirring and stormy times that immediately preceded the War between the States—the Civil War of 1861-65, that he came to young manhood. It was a time when men were called upon to stand up and be counted: one was either for the Union or against it.

Benteen's father was a Virginian of the Virginians: a slave holder who believed in the divine authority of the South's "peculiar institution"; his sympathies and convictions were all with and for the South—for Slavery, and for Secession.

It was a time, too, when brother was arrayed against brother, when all too often, son was arrayed against father; and father against son. And so it was in the Benteen family; for Frederick William Benteen was for the Union and against Secession. And when he, alone of all his family, announced his intention to don the blue of the Union Army, and to take a commission in a loyal regiment of Missouri Cavalry, there was an explosion in the Benteen household.

Benteen as Senior Captain of the Seventh Cavalry. Photo by D. F. Barry.

His father disowned him and dismissed him with a curse. He would pray each day, he angrily declared, that his son, who had disavowed his family's faith and betrayed his family's principles; who had gone forth clad in an alien uniform to fight against his people and his state, should be killed by an avenging bullet; a bullet fired, perhaps, by one of his own kin. But shocking as it sounds, and shocking as it indeed was, his father's curse did not deter the son, whose convictions as to what was right and what was wrong were no less fixed than those of his irate sire, and whose determination to follow those convictions to the end, come what might, was never shaken. And follow them he did, ably, brilliantly, consistently and with marked success. Before the bitter war ended, Frederick William Benteen was to command a troop—a squadron—a regiment, and finally a brigade of cavalry, and because of the merit of his achievements as a combat leader, he was advanced in rank through every grade to that of Colonel, and was recommended by his superiors for the brevet rank of Brigadier General, an honor finally attained; though not until he had retired from active service.

Benteen was commissioned a First Lieutenant in the Tenth Missouri Volunteer cavalry on the first day of September, 1861. One month later he became a captain. On December 19, 1862, he attained a majority which he held until made Lieutenant Colonel and Commander of the regiment, February 27, 1864. After muster out in 1865, he was commissioned Colonel of the 138th colored regiment, which rank he surrendered in July, 1866 to become a captain in the Seventh regiment of cavalry, in the Regular Army.

Frederick William Benteen, however, after he joined the Union Army in 1861, did not forget his father's curse; nor did he fail to remember the oldster's savage wish that he, his son, might be laid low by the avenging bullet of one of his own kin; and with the grimmest of grim humor—for he knew that his sire had entered the Confederate service and was engaged in blockade running on the great inland rivers—he so maneuvered his command that the 10th Missouri intercepted and captured his father's vessel, laden with a contraband cargo, and made a prisoner of war of its owner. And this coup he planned so cleverly that his father never knew, until long years after, that his captor was his own son; that it was he who had caused the confiscation of his vessel and its valuable cargo; he who had been the means of sending him, the defiant old Virginian, to a federal prison, there to remain until paroled in 1865.

From his son, indeed, the old gentleman was never to learn the facts; but—there was a grandson—the same who became the Major Benteen I met in Atlanta in 1924. He was "Freddie" to his grandfather, and the apple of the old man's eye. And "Freddie" it was who "spilled the beans," when, at the tender age of ten, he confided to his doting grandsire the whole story, as he had heard it—or overheard it—from his parents! "Some little boys talk too damn much" was Colonel Benteen's disturbed comment in a letter to his infant son, when he learned from his devoted wife that the family "cat" so carefully concealed since 1862, was now "out of the bag," and rampant. But the Colonel was then very busy with the Nez Perces, and "Freddie" escaped with reprimand only!

Benteen's numerous brevets were awarded him because of outstanding *combat leadership;* during the Civil War "for gallant and meritorious service in the battle of the Osage" and "in the charge on Columbus, Georgia," when he led Winslow's brigade in smashing victories against his southern brethren in rebellion. In 1868, and again in 1890, he was brevetted Colonel and Brigadier General for heroic conduct in engagements with hostile Indians—at the Saline River, Kansas in 1868, at the Little Big Horn in 1876, and at Canyon Creek in 1877.

It was characteristic of this man's leadership that he *led in person;* he was in the forefront of the battle, always. His expeditionary commander, Colonel Florence M. Cornyn of the 10th Missouri, had this to say of him officially with relation to a reconnaissance in force under his command, at Iuka, Mississippi, in July 1863:

"Major F. W. Benteen, Commanding the Tenth Missouri Cavalry, *was where a leader should be, —in the front;*—and by his coolness and great tact and skill, did much toward gaining the day."

Benteen served in the Army of the Tennessee under Generals Grierson, Crocker and McPherson, as lieutenant-colonel in command of the Tenth Missouri; and under Generals Pleasanton and Rosecrans in the Department of the Missouri, when, in the campaign to drive the Confederate leader Sterling Price and his invading forces from the state of Missouri, he distinguished himself for gallantry and daring in sharp cavalry engagements with Fagan's and Marmaduke's divisions of Price's army, at Big Blue River and Little Osage Crossing.

Colonel Winslow of the 4th Iowa, normally commanding the Fourth Brigade of Pleasanton's Cavalry Division, of which the Tenth Missouri was a part, had turned over his command to Benteen because of wounds received in action. At Big Blue River, Benteen, having dismounted his brigade, drove the enemy from a strong position, and pursued him to the vicinity of the Little Osage Crossing, "moving as rapidly as possible after the retreating enemy," to quote from his report to Pleasanton.

At the crossing he found Price's divisions under Marmaduke and Fagan drawn up in line of battle; and again quoting his report:

"Major Hunt of General Curtis' staff came up and told me the enemy's exact position, stating that there was a brigade already in position in his front, but too weak to begin the attack. I at once determined to form on the left of this brigade, especially as a few more paces brought us in view of the line of rebels; seeing the position in which he had his artillery, I immediately surmised that the rebel commander had committed a fatal blunder, and resolved to capture it. I sent an officer to the commanding officer of the brigade on my right with the information that I was going to charge, and a request for him to charge with me, for God's sake, and at the same time formed my command in column of regiments in the same manner I had formed them for marching, and immediately sounded the charge."

The historian of the 4th Iowa Cavalry, one of the regiments brigaded with the 10th Missouri, thus describes the combat, and in so doing draws an unforgettable picture of Benteen in action:

"Colonel Benteen's order to charge was instantly obeyed. The Tenth Missouri started forward with their 'yell' and their bugles sounding, but when they had covered half the distance, the enemy showing no sign of breaking, they hesitated and stopped. Their colonel urged them with great spirit, and they made spasmodic efforts to brace up, but failed. * * * Again and again Benteen ordered the charge, and many of his regiment made brave efforts to overcome the singular balk. Some got forward a little farther, but the line could not be moved. He persisted most heroically in trying to break the unfortunate situation. He rode directly in front of his men, within pistol shot of his enemy, hatless, white with passion, waving his sword and shouting the order to charge. His trumpeters repeated it, and all the trumpets in the column answered with the same piercing notes. Then for a few moments, the two opposing lines of men simply stood, glaring at each other."

At this critical juncture the 4th Iowa swept past the halting Missourians, hurling itself like a thunderbolt upon the enemy's right; and it was followed instantly by the 3d Iowa, which struck hard

at his center. The onset of the Iowa regiments carried the Tenth Missouri with them; and the Militia brigade on Benteen's right, whose commander he had urged "for God's sake" to join him in the charge, seeing that the enemy now was breaking, added its weight to the impact of Benteen's attack, and the break quickly became a rout all along the line. In the pursuit of the fleeing rebels, Generals Marmaduke and Cabell, the rebel leaders, together with five colonels and many lesser officers, were made prisoners of war, the enemy's artillery was captured, two stands of colors taken, and Price's invasion of Missouri was at checkmate.

But Price was not yet done; and Benteen was ordered to report with his brigade to General S. R. Curtis at Cassville. Three days after the fight at Osage Crossing, he notified General Curtis that "though his horses were worn and jaded," and his command "nearly dismounted," he will nonetheless "push on to you with all the speed possible," for Curtis has informed him that "as long as horses can stand on their feet they must be considered fit for duty," and that it is his inexorable purpose "to drive Price beyond the Arkansas."

Price finally disposed of, Winslow's Brigade, still under Benteen's command, was ordered to St. Louis to refit, then to report to Nashville for service in General Emory Upton's cavalry division, a part of the famous "Cavalry" Wilson's corps, which chased the redoubtable Nathan Bedford Forrest through Alabama and Georgia, stormed and captured Selma, and in a grand assault, in which Benteen again distinguished himself, took Columbus, Georgia, *vi et armis,* destroying arsenals, foundries, workshops and vast quantities of munitions.

On June 7, 1865, General Wilson, from the Headquarters of the Cavalry Corps of the Military Division of the Missisippi at Macon, Georgia, forwarding with approval Upton's recommendations for promotions and medals of honor for some twenty-one officers and men of his division, added the following:

"I would also request that Lieut. Col. F. W. Benteen, Tenth Missouri Cavalry, be brevetted brigadier-general for gallant and meritorious service, not only during the recent campaign in Georgia and Alabama, but for distinguished and conspicuous bravery in the pursuit of Price out of Missouri."

Though appointed Colonel of a colored regiment after the Tenth Missouri had been mustered out, Benteen found this service personally distasteful, and in 1866, when the newly organized Seventh Cavalry was added to the Regular Army, he accepted a commission as the Senior Captain of this regiment of which another great cavalry leader of the Civil War was second in command— George Armstrong Custer, whose spectacular rise from "shavetail" in 1861 to Major General in 1865, had brought to him renown second only to that of the great Sheridan himself.

As a captain of the Seventh, Benteen had his first experience of Indian fighting in August 1868, when a large mixed band of Cheyennes, Arapahoes and Sioux raided the advanced settlements along the Saline River in Kansas some distance to the north of Fort Harker, leaving little but death and devastation along their trail. Benteen, leading his troops as usual, made a swift forced march from Fort Zarah to relieve the settlers, and after a sharp encounter, drove the marauding Indians for upwards of ten miles. He was never to be free of Indians during the next decade.

The part he played in the battle of the Little Big Horn and in the Sioux War of 1876, need not be recorded here in detail. Suffice it to say that in the combat in which Custer and nearly half the regiment were wiped out by the followers of Sitting Bull, Benteen, who had been sent with three companies on a fruitless reconnaissance, far to the left and rear, came up in the nick of time to reinforce the reeling troops of Reno, though not in time, unfortunately, to rescue Custer's command, if indeed, to rescue it was within the bounds of possibility. How Benteen supported Reno throughout the 25th and 26th of June at the Little Big Horn has many times been told; how he and Reno held the Indian horde at bay; how he led the charge that cleared the way, and made it possible to obtain water for the wounded; how he formed and organized the charge that Reno led, to scatter the warriors in his front; how by his courage and daring and his very presence, he inspired the confidence that made the surviving troops stand fast to the end; all this has been written many times over. I shall not repeat it here.

Again in 1877, Benteen distinguished himself in the fight at Canyon Creek, during the war with the Nez Perces; and for his heoric conduct there and at the Little Big Horn, he received the long delayed and brilliantly earned brevet of Brigadier General.

The foregoing sketch, for it is a sketch only, is offered to show in broad outline what manner of man Frederick William Benteen was, and thus, in some sort, to shed light upon the papers that follow after.

Benteen retired from active service in July 1888, taking up his residence in Atlanta, Georgia, where he owned a considerable estate. He died there in June, 1898, just as the war with Spain was getting under way. During the years of his retirement, he was a lonely and embittered man: but to the end, his pride endured—he never bowed his head.

Among the papers Major Benteen found among his father's effects in 1898, were two manuscript narratives, both dealing with the Little Big Horn, and a packet of letters written to his wife during the summer of 1876, which Mrs. Benteen had carefully preserved. The two manuscript narratives were loaned by Major Benteen to General Godfrey, and as related elsewhere in this volume, were not returned during the latter's lifetime. The earlier manuscript, apparently written shortly after the battle of Wounded Knee, in 1890, Mrs. Godfrey returned after her husband's death. The final pages were missing and have never yet been found. The later manuscript, however, disappeared and its whereabouts, if it still exists, is unknown.

The earlier narrative is hereinafter produced in Benteen's own hand, together with a "translation," his writing being at times difficult to read. It is considered the more important of the two papers, notwithstanding it is now incomplete. The substance, and most of the content of the *other and later* narrative is mosaiced into Chapter 3 of Brininstool's "Troopers with Custer," and constitutes about half of "Captain Benteen's Own Story." Its original text is interspersed with interpolations and additions taken from an abstract of his testimony before the Reno Court of Inquiry; and while the effect of these interpolations and additions is to modify somewhat the narrative as Benteen wrote it, the modifications are not such as to make necessary a reproduction here of the later narrative in its original form.

Following the reproduction of the earlier of the two narrative manuscripts, there is also reproduced in his own hand, a letter to his wife, dated July 4, 1876, probably the most significant of all the papers found by his son. A "translation" of this long and highly descriptive letter is incorporated in the article "The Lost is found," which originally appeared in *The Cavalry Journal* in 1942, and is reprinted in this volume.

Another letter to his wife, written by Benteen in several installments beginning July 2, 1876 and ending July 30, 1876, is also reproduced, though not in his handwriting. The originals of both these letters, which I was permitted to read, copy and photostat in 1924, have also disappeared, and are probably lost.

1.

On June 22d, 1876, the 7th United States Cavalry, then, on the Yellowstone River, Montana Territory, passed in review, guidons fluttering, horses prancing, before Brevet Major General A. H. Terry, commanding then the Department of Dakota, Headquarters in the Field; the 7th was en route, where? none knew of the Regt. but General G. A. Custer, however, I have since been informed by Brevet Major General John Gibbon, who

2.

was of the reviewing party. That his last salutation to General Custer, was, "Now, dont be greedy Custer, as there are indians enough for all of us"!

On that day we moved up the "Rosebud", marching twelve (12) miles, and bivouacked: in the evening the orderly trumpeter was sent to notify the officers of the regiment that Genl. Custer wished to see them at his headquarters, and after arrival of the last officer, General Custer

3.

commenced his talk; which was to the effect, that it had come to his knowledge that his official actions had been criticised by some of the officers of the regiment at headquarters of the Department, and, that while he was willing to accept recommendations from the junior Second Lieutenant of the regiment, he wished the same to come in a proper manner, calling our attention to the paragraph of Army

4.

Regulations referring to the criticism of action of Commanding officers; and said he would take the necessary steps to punish, should there be a recurrence of the offence.

I said to General Custer, it seems to me you are lashing the shoulders of all, to get at some; now, as we are all present, would it not do to specify the officers whom you accuse? he said, Colonel Benteen, I am not here to be catechised by you.

5.
but for your own information, will state that none of my remarks have been directed towards you: Then, after giving a few excellent general orders as to what should be done by each troop of the regiment in case of an attack on our Bivouac at any time, the meeting of the officers was over, and each adjourned to his palatial "pup tent." On the next day, owing to the report

6. of the lieutenant having control of the marching of the pack-train, the mules or packers of my troop having been reported with two other troops as being the most unmanageable in the regiment, I was directed to assume command of those three troops, and to march the battalion in rear of the last mule of the train: I saluted the General, and awaited the opportunity of crossing the Rosebud in

8.
rear of the regiment: It took exactly one hour and thirty minutes to get that pack-train across the creek, and get it started on other side: — The country through which we were marching was very broken, and over ravines that would have concealed thousands of indians So, after marching, say, seven or eight miles, and the train being scattered for perhaps two miles,

8. it occurred to me that perhaps the Casabianca business might be over construed, and that the pack train had better be "Rounded up", or I might have a knotty explanation to grind out should it be lost; which was one of the easiest of things to have happen; as I was marching, So, a trumpeter quickly galloped ahead with orders to halt the train, and on arrival of the battalion at the train, one troop of battalion

9.) was put in advance of it; one troop on the right-flank of centre of train, nearest the hills; and the remaining troop in the rear of train... The march that day was 35 miles: — Some little while before reaching bivouac of regiment, I missed Dr. Lord from my side, he having accompanied me on the march for the two days. —

10. — However, on arrival at bivouac, the Adjutant of Regt. 2nd Lieut. W. W. Cooke, came out to indicate place of bivouac for each troop, to have it in its proper order for marching on next day: after learning which, I said, See here, "Cookey," "G. A. C." ordered me to march the 3 troops of the battalion composing guard for" packs, in rear of the last mule of train; now as the C. O. of Regt. ? told us last night that he was open for recommendations, &c., I tell you as adjutant of regiment, that the first thing we know, some Casabianca

11. — will be getting such orders about the train, and if the roughness of the country holds out, and the indian signs continue to thicken, why, the train will go up, then, the circus adjourns: — I am willing to admit this was getting close upon infracting the paragraph of Army Regulations to which our attention had been invited on the evening previous; but I was telling it to the adjutant that it might be sandwiched in as were in conversation with the commanding officer of the regiment, and I knew if he did,

12. — that I would not be put in the light of a fault-finder, but that in more elegant language the spirit of my talk would be given, and perhaps might call the attention of the General to a matter that might mar the success of the campaign: however, the Adjt. refused, point-blank, to say anything about it to Custer; saying, I might tell him myself if I chose; So, the next-morning as General Custer was passing, I chose to do so; telling him, that I could not, without endangering the safety of the packs, carry out the orders he

13. had given me concern
ing the marching of the
battalion composing the
"Pack's" guard: I then
told the arrangement I
had made of the battalion;
and this from the fact—
that from the time he
left me at the bivouac
of the night before, not
one sight of his command
had been gotten: the
General said, I am
much obliged to you
Colonel, and I will turn
over the same order of

14. march
for the rear guard
to the officer who relieves
you. Well, after the
2d days march, and
I had seen to the bivouacking of my troop, I
got out my seine for
purpose of seeing the
Kinds of fish the Rosebud
could set up for supper;
the attempt however resulted mostly in "water
hauls", and being ravenously hungry, "S.O.B. and
trimmings" had to serve for
bill of fare; Dr. Lord
not putting in an appearance,

15. at the meal, however,
after I had crawled
under a bullberry bush
for sweet repose, the
Dr. came into camp,
telling me that he had
halted alone some miles
back, being completely
tired out, broken down,
so much so that he had
given up all hopes of
getting to camp; he
declined tea, and wanted
nothing to eat or drink;
— I state this to show what
must have been the physical
condition of the Doctor

16. on June 25th on going
into the fight, after an
almost continuous march
of 84 miles. ——
The repose I found
under the bullberry bush
alluded to, can be
classed with the goose
egg of the cricketer, for
there were myriads of
musquitoes under that
bush where I got there,
and I don't think that any
of them got away.
— 1st night's loss of sleep.—

3d day we marched
to, strange to say, a creek
called "Muddy Creek,"
where, on coming into camp

I heard the voice of my old friend Col. Myles W. Keogh hailing me; saying, come here "old man, I've kept the nicest spot in the whole camp next to me, for your troop, & I've had to bluff the balance to hold it, but here it is, skip off," so I "skipped," putting my my troop in the velo the gallant Irishman had held for me.

It wasn't far from twilight then, so, after getting supper

that we are not going to stay in this camp to night, but we are going to march all night, So, good night..." I had scarcely gotten the words from my lips before the orderly trumpeter notified us that we would meet at the commanding officer's headquarters at once: my preparations for sleep consisted in putting off my cavalry

Keogh came over to my bullberry bush,(he was more luxurious than I was, having a tent-fly for shelter) and the crowd was listening to one of the Italian patriot, De Rudio's recitals, of his hair breadth scapes with Mazzini, or some other man, in some other country, all of which I rudely interrupted by saying, See here, fellows, you want to be collecting all the sleep you can, and be doing it soon, for I have a "Pre."

boots, So little time was consumed in robing: however, that was sufficient, the other officers rapidly their summons, it being quite dark there, and the "Pro." telling us 'twas. a move; I called up my 1st Sergeant, and had him see that the aparejos were O.K. ropes, bridles, &c., all right, and have everything ready about the troop for a speedy move:

21.   I then commenced a search for the Head Quarters; however, before getting far, I met an officer returning from the "Call," saying, tis no use going. You were right — we move at 11 O'clock, P.M. Sharp, to-night: all right, then, there's no sleep for Your humble again to-night.

2d night's loss of sleep. If it took a minute to cross that pack train over the "Muddy," it took two hours;

22d page.) other side, Colonel Keogh hunted me up, he being the officer in charge of rear guard; — he was making the very air Sulphurous with blue oaths, telling me of the situation; however, from having been there very many times myself, I knew it better than he did: So, I consoled him with, "never mind old man", do the best you can, and it will all come out right. — I dont begin to believe that Job ever had much to do with shaved tailed pack-mules. —

23.   Well, my advice seemed to brace Col. Keogh a bit, and I kept the ding-donging of the tin cup, frying pan — or something, that was my guide as to direction, the pounding of that on the saddle of the horse on the left of the troop preceding mine, being all I had to go by, the night being pitch dark, and the gait was a trot, so I hadnt much time to swap words

24. with Col. Keogh, or, my guide would be gone.

This trot was kept up for — perhaps eight or ten miles; then, came a halt, no orders for same being received, and no orders for anything received by me; So, the Packs remained on mules; saddles, & bridles on horses: I crouched down by a Sage bush until daylight, and there spied Colonel Reno and little Benny Hodgson going for Coffee, hard-tack &

25. [Trimmings:] I invited myself
to assist in disposing
of that repast; and
met — with a "1st
class" welcome at sug-
gesting it.
In a few moments,
it seemed, the columns
moved forward; no orders
however for same were gotten
but my troop & I foll-
owed the procession:
there came almost as
sudden a halt:—no
orders for that, i.e. the
rear of column I knew
of none: however, a

27.
to be seen; now,
strange perhaps to say,
I did believe it:—
another "Pre". I knew it,
because, why, I'd sooner
trust the sharp eye of
an indian than to trust
a pretty good binocular
that I always carried;
and I'd gotten that from
experience; however, twant
my "chip in", so I said
nothing. At this halt
General Custer notified
us that the first

26. few moments brought
us a summons thro'
an orderly to "Officers'
Call" at Head Quarters:
where there, General Custer
notified us that he had
been on the mountain
to left, where our Scouts
(Crows.) were all the night,
that they had told him
thro' the interpreter, that
they could see dust,
indians and ponies, &
all that:—he could
see nothing through the
old telescopic glass
they had and didn't
believe there was anything

28.—
Troop commanders who
notified him that the
requirements of an order
issued a few days
before, were being
carried out strictly
in the troop; that
officer and troop should
have the post of honor,
the advance: I notified
him at once that in
my troop the requirements
were being strictly adhered
to:. I feel quite sure
it wasn't expected from
us; but he stammered
out:—well Col. Benteen
—Your troop has the advance:

29.

When all had reported, I was ordered to move in advance with my Troop; which I ~~presented to be~~ did, but had gone but a short distance where General Custer rode up, saying, I was setting the pace too fast; he then rode in advance; and — after going a few miles the Command was halted ~~between~~

30.) hills, on every side, and Genl. Custer and his adjutant stepped aside, and were figuring on paper for quite awhile; at what, we knew not; however, when thro, I was called up, and notified that — my command was 3 Troops, and that I would move to the left to a line of bluffs about 2 miles away. Sending out an officer and a few men as advance guard;

31. —

"to pitch in" to anything I came across, and to notify him at once; I started on my mission immediately; — this was just about 15 miles from where I found the dead body of Genl. Custer. 3 days afterwards.

I omitted stating, that — while en route obeying Custer's last order, I received two other orders from him;

32.) and these through the Chief Trumpeter — and the Sergeant Major of the regiment; the first, to the effect, that, should I not find anything at the first line of bluffs, then, to go on to the second line of bluffs; to pitch in, and notify him at once, being included; the order through Sergt. Major received 15 or 20 minutes later, was, if nothing could be seen from

33.–

Second line of bluffs, then, to go on until I came to a Valley, to "pitch in", and to notify him at once, being also included: now, all of this time the balance of the Regiment was on the march; and the last glimpse I had of them was the Gray horse troop in rapid motion: I thought of course they had struck Something:

34.

however, I had that Valley to find; and ~~So~~ we went away for it; myself and orderly being ~~xxx~~ in advance of the ~~advance~~ guard: the 2d line of bluffs showed no Valley;—only bluffs & bluffs:— So, another of my Preem. came; and said, old man: that Crowd ahead is going to Strike a Snag. indians have too much Sense to travel

35.–

over such country as you have been going unless they are terribly pushed; So, you'd better get back to that trail, and you will find work; ~~xxxxx~~. ~~then~~ "Right Oblique" was the word, until we got out of the hills to the trail; my Command getting to it just ahead of the train of Packs: the horses not having been watered since evening before,

36.–

and this being along about one o'clock P.M of a hot June day, they were needing it badly: So, ~~on~~ the trail I halted at a morass for a few moments for the purpose of giving the men and animals a chance at it: I attended to the watering of ~~the~~ horse I was riding for the brute was tricky and unless you took the precaution to lariat him to Something; ~~xxxx~~ the bit was taken from his

37. mouth, [and he thro' drinking,] you could not hold him by the strap of halter: no one could:— and away he would go; and when he got good and ready, he would rejoin the troop: Well, at this watering, I lariated old Dick to a stump of iron wood before removing the bit; and after drinking he pulled up taut on the stump, and looked as if to say, "Well, I didn't

38. much care to go off this time anyway: but that was the time of times, old fellow, for you would have been saved two wounds, and two days where water was worth its weight in greenbacks, though beautiful and blue, within a stone's throw from our stand.

After leaving the watering place: a few miles brought us to a beautifully decorated tepee of buffalo hide; just on trail;

39. I dismounted, after riding around the lodge, peeped in, and saw the body of an indian on a scaffold or cot of rude poles:— by this time the battalion was up — and away we went again: a mile or two brought orders through a Sergeant to the officer in charge of pack-train: I told him where I had last seen it:— another couple of miles brought

40. an order for me thro' the orderly trumpeter of day, from the adjutant of regiment: to the effect:— "Benteen, Big Village, Be quick; Bring Packs:
P. S. Bring Packs.
W. W. Cooke,
Adjt.

Well, the Packs was safe behind; I knew that better than anybody; I couldn't waste time in going back, nor in halting where I was for them: So, we went = V.V.V.

41. resume
I ~~crossed~~, with the
last order received from
the Adjutant of the 7th
Cavalry; the last lines
penciled by him: Viz:
"Benteen, Come on, Big
Village, Be Quick.
Bring Packs. P.S. Bring
Packs. John Martini,
the Trumpeter, bringing
this dispatch was a
thick headed, dull
witted Italian, just—

42. about as much cut
out for a Cavalryman as
he was for a King:
he informed me that the
indians were "Skedaddling";
hence, less the necessity for
~~retracing~~ retracing our steps
to get the Packs, and
the Same would be gained
by awaiting the arrival
of those where ~~were~~
~~there were:~~
we did, neither, but
took the "3rd"! and,
from the ford where
Reno first crossed the
beautifully blue Little Big Horn

43. We
saw going on
what evidently was not
"Skedaddling" on the part
of the indians, as there
were 12 or 14 dismounted
men on the river bottom,
and they were being ridden
down and shot by 300
or 900 indian warriors:
We concluded
that the lay of the land
had better be investigated
a bit, as so much of
the Italian Trumpeter's story
had "Panned out": So—
Off to left I went, Seeing

44.) a group of 3 or
4 Absaraka or Crow
indians; from them I
learned this; Otoe Sioux,
Otoe Sioux, the "Otoe"
meaning, innumerable, or
Heaps of them: —and
we soon found that
there were enough of them.
From the point
I saw the Crows I
got the first sight of
the men of Reno's bat-
talion who had retreated
from the river bottom,
recrossed the river a couple
of miles below, and were

45. Showing us on the bluffs on the side of the river that my battalion had kept ~~on~~ and was then on: the battalion being in line, Reno, knowing of course we were soldiers; came riding to meet me as I moved towards him: my first query of Reno was,— "Where is Custer?"— Showing him the last order received from the Adjutant of Regt.; Reno replied that he did not know,

46. that Custer had ~~sent~~ ^{ordered} him across the river to charge ~~the indians~~, informing him that he would support him with the whole "Outfit", but he had ^{neither} seen nor heard ~~from~~ from him since:— Well, our battalion got just in the nick of time to save Reno's.— After a few words with Col. Reno I inquired as to the where,— abouts of "D" Troop, of my Battn.— and was informed that Capt. Weir had,

47. without orders, gone down the river; this being the case, I sallied after Weir, and about 3/4 of a mile lower down, from the top of the highest point in vicinity, saw ~~the~~ ^{Weir's} troop returning; hordes of indians hurrying there somewhat: Reno came to same point after I had thrown Captain French's troop in line at right angle with river, to hold that point, dismounted, till Weir's troop got thro. and

48. to then retreat slowly, and I would have ~~that~~ part of command looked after: this didn't ~~go~~ ^{finish} as well as I had hoped and expected it would; however, from fact of the indians not making the most of the opportunity, and Lieut. Ed. S. Godfrey carrying out his instructions more faithfully, and in a more soldierly manner, we had time sufficient to get some kind of a line formed; the first ~~men~~ officer I saw

49. When establishing a line, was Lieutenant Geo. D. Wallace, (recently killed by some of the same Sioux, at the "Wounded Knee" fight in Dak.) I said, Wallace, put the right of your troop here; his answer was, "I have no troop, only three men;" Well, said I, stay here with your three men, and dont let them get away; I will have you looked out for; — and Wallace and the three men stayed, and they

50. were looked out for. Col. Reno was on the left — forming the same line, — which was not a line, but an arc of a circle, rather irregularly described too. — and when we met about centre, my own troop remained to be disposed of; so I put it much ground, almost as much as the other six companies occupied, protecting left flank, and well to the rear; just on the edge of line of bluffs, near river.

51. The formation as described, was dismounted; the horses of command being placed in a saucer prairie, like depression, the lower rim of the saucer, of a rim was, instead of a gentle slope: the hospital was established at the upper rim; and was about as safe a place as there was around, the vicinity; the blue canopy of heaven being the covering: the sage brush, sand, being the operating board:

52. but the stout heart and nervy skilful hand of Dr. Porter, (the only surgeon of the three of command that hadnt been killed,) was equal to the occasion. I state but the facts when I say that we had a fairly warm time with those red men as long as sufficient light was left for them to draw a bead on us, and the same time i.e. free to maintain, in the language of Dante.

53.   I dont know how many of the miscreants there were; — probably we shall never know. — but there were enough.

Now, be it remembered, this wasnt a fight instituted by the Army for glory going purposes, or anything of that kind; but rather, was a little gentle disciplining which the Department of the Interior, (the Department of U.S. Govत. having charge of the Indian Bureau. —

54.   had promised ~~would be given~~ the Indians if they, the nomads of the tribe, declined to come in to agencies in the Spring; be good, and draw their pay; runners having been sent out to the self supporters; ~~to such~~ i.e. those, who gave the Agencies the grand go by, as it were, to the effect, that if they didnt report, ~~troops~~ soldiers would be sent out to bring them in: about the only answer that they returned, as far as I wot, was: "we will be here when

55.   you come for us"! and sure enough, they were there! but little thought anyone that they would be in such hordes.

I judged of the condition of the men of my troop somewhat by my own condition; ~~for that~~ though that is one of almost physical never tire; but not having had sleep the two nights previous to this one, was getting just a trifle weary myself; So, up and down the line of "H" troop 1st Lieut. Gibson and myself

56.   tramped, the night of June 25th & 26th, doing our very best to keep the sentinels awake, but we just could not do it — Kicking them; well, they ~~just~~ didnt care anything about that; however, we two kept awake on our end of line, and at early daybreak ascertained that few, if any of our red friends had given up hope of doing us up: the clatter they made stirred our little bivouac out pretty effectually; then, all being on the qui,

57. Vive; the [thinking] situation was O.K. That I'd "try and Round Up" a few lines of sleep, to make up somewhat for the three nights' sleep that I was short ~~that I was short of~~. So, down I dropped on the hill-side, determined to gather what I could, in; but some grateful red-skin had pretty nearly my exact range, plumping one in the heel of extended boot; another bullet scattered the dry

58. dust under my arm-pit; however, I hadn't the remotest idea of letting little things like that disturb me, and thought that I, at least, had gotten forty winks, when a sergeant of my troop informed me that Lieut. Osborne, of my troop was having a regular monkey & parrot time of it: To say that I felt like saying something naughty to that sergeant, was putting it mildly; but down I ran, led him up, thro' the park.

59. tram, getting together some 15 or 16 soldiers & packers, making them carry up sacks of bacon, boxes of hard bread, pack-saddles, and materials of that kind;— quite a sufficiency to build a respectable little breast work. which, after propping up as well as we could, I turned over with the Falstaff-ian crowd, to "Gib." my 1st lieutenant, telling him to hold

60. the fort, not-withstanding what might become of us: there I walked along the front of my troop and told them that I was getting mad, & I wanted them to charge down the ravine with me when I gave the yell; then, each to yell as if provided with a thousand throats; if the Chinese wail was sufficient, good enough for me, & it would work; but I hadn't so much real.

61. trust in its effic-
iency; however, when
the throttles of the
"Motors" were given
full play, and we
dashed into the
unsuspecting savages
who were amusing
themselves by throwing
clods of dirt, arrows
by hand, and otherwise
for simply pure cussed-
ness among us, to
say that 'twas a
surprise to them, is
but mild form: for
they somersaulted and
vaulted as so many
trained acrobats, heading

62. no order in
getting down those
ravines, but quickly
getting; de'il takes
the hindmost!
There, there, I
had the key to the
beautiful blue water
that had been
flowing so ripplingly
at our very feet
for two days — and
which wounded and
well longed so much
for, — there it was,
ours, for the getting:
well, 'twasn't the
simplest of matters to
get a camp-kettle of
it, even there, but as

13. we were on the brink
of it, to none did it
occur to picture or think
of how it had to be
gotten; we pro-
ceeded to get it, but
at the expense of many
wounded; and this
for the sake of the
already wounded as
well as the dry and thirsty
living; (Speaking for
myself, I am quite
sure that I would
gladly have ever fully given the
very prettiest and newest
twenty dollar silver certificate that I might have

64. persuaded my first
lieutenant to have lent me,
for just one oz. of
Spiritus Frumenti to
have dashed into just
about same quantity of
that pure Little Big Horn
water, if for no other
purpose than to just
brace me a bit; for
to a certainty
I was plumb tired out
and sleepy too; however,
the business for the day
had only fairly opened;
and I got no chance
to steal off and sleep,
or bless me if I would
not have done it.

To say that—I ever had more Serene Satisfaction at Killing a ~~Black~~ Black tailed buck deer, on the bound with a carbine, than I had in putting one of Uncle Sam's .45's ~~thro'~~ as noble a specimen of the ~~[crossed out]~~ Dakotas as ever fluttered an eagle feather in his scalp lock; was every word true at that time; though I'm rather fond of Indians than otherwise, but to plump him thro' his spinal, as he was curvorting

thro. the ravines, there being so many of these around, that one wouldn't be missed, and being so confoundedly mad and sleepy, must say that—I looked on that—dead red with exquisite Satisfaction; (and not because he was maiden hair ~~[crossed out]~~ either; for the present.—but I was so tired, and they wouldn't let me sleep; now, Strong-arm, I, a bit out of luck in losing the ~~[crossed out]~~ night's sleep in the Category of three; still, how tired must—my good friend Dr. Lord have been, when he galloped in with Custer before getting his quietus! as, ~~neither~~ of weak physique,

A TRANSCRIPT OF BENTEEN'S NARRATIVE

ON June 22d, 1876, the 7th United States Cavalry, then on the Yellowstone River, Montana Territory, passed in review, guidons fluttering, horses prancing, before Brevet Major General A. H. Terry, commanding then the Department of Dakota, Headquarters in the Field; the 7th was en route, where? none knew of the Regt. but General G. A. Custer. However, I have since been informed by Brevet Major General John Gibbon, who was of the reviewing party, that his last salutation to General Custer was "Now, don't be greedy Custer, as there are Indians enough for all of us"!

On that day we moved up the "Rosebud," marching twelve (12) miles, and bivouacked: in the evening the orderly trumpeter was sent to notify the officers of the regiment that Genl. Custer wished to see them at his headquarters, and after arrival of the last officer, General Custer commenced his talk, which was to the effect, that it had come to his knowledge that his official actions had been criticised by some of the officers of the regiment at headquarters of the Department, and, that while he was willing to accept recommendations from the junior second lieutenant of the regiment, he wished the same to come in a proper manner, calling our attention to the paragraph of Army Regulations referring to the criticism of actions of commanding officers; and said he would take the necessary steps to punish, should there be reoccurence of the offence.

I said to General Custer, it seems to me you are lashing the shoulders of *all,* to get at some; now, as we are all present, would it not do to specify the officers whom you accuse? He said, Colonel Benteen, I am not here to be catechised by you, but for your own information, will state that none of my remarks have been directed towards you. Then, after giving a few excellent general orders as to what should be done by each troop of the regiment in case of an attack on our bivouac at any time, the meeting of the officers was over, and each adjourned to his palatial "Pup tent." On the next day, owing to the report of the lieutenant having control of the marching of the pack-train, the mules or packers of my troop having been reported with two other troops as being the most unmanageable in the regiment, I was directed to assume command of those three troops, and to march the battalion in rear of the last mule of the train. I saluted the General, and awaited the opportunity of crossing the Rosebud in rear of the regiment: it took exactly one hour and thirty minutes to get that pack-train across the creek, and get it started on other side:—The country through which we were marching was very broken, and over ravines that would have concealed thousands of Indians, so, after marching, say seven or eight miles, and the train being scattered for perhaps two miles, it occurred to me that perhaps the Casabianca business might be over construed, and that the pack train had better be "Rounded up," or I might have a knotty explanation to grind out should it be lost, which was one of the easiest of things to have happen, as I was marching. So, a trumpeter quickly galloped ahead with orders to halt the train, and on arrival of the battalion at the train, one troop of battalion was put in advance of it, one troop on the right flank of centre of train, nearest the hills, and the remaining troop in the rear of train. The march that day was 35 miles. Some little while before reaching bivouac of regiment, I missed Dr. Lord from my side, he having accompanied me on the march for the two days. However, on arrival at bivouac, the Adjutant of Regt. 1st Lieut. W. W. Cooke, came out to indicate place of bivouac for each troop, to have it in its proper order for marching on next day: after learning which, I said, See here, "Cookey," "G. A. C." ordered me to march the 3 troops of the battalion composing guard for "packs," in rear of the last mule of train; now as the C. O. of Regt. told us last night that he was open for recommendations, &c., I tell you as adjutant of regiment, that the first thing we know, some Casabianca will be getting such orders about the train, and if the roughness of the country holds out, and the Indian signs continue to thicken, why, the train will go up, then, the circus adjourns.

I am willing to admit this was getting close upon infracting the paragraph of Army Regulations to which our attention had been invited on the evening previous; but I was telling it to the adjutant that it might be sandwiched in as it were in conversation with the commanding officer of the regiment, and I knew if he did that I would not be put in the light of a fault-finder, but that in more elegant language the spirit of my talk would be given, and perhaps might call the attention of the General to a matter that might mar the success of the campaign. However, the Adjt. refused,

point blank, to say anything about it to Custer, saying, I might tell him myself if I chose. So, the next morning as General Custer was passing, I chose to do so; telling him, that I could not, without endangering the safety of the packs, carry out the orders he had given me concerning the marching of the battalion composing the "Packs" guard. I then told the arrangement I had made of the battalion; and this from the fact that from the time he left me at the bivouac of the night before, not one sight of his command had been gotten. The General said, I am much obliged to you Colonel, and I will turn over the same order of march for the rear guard to the officer who relieves you.

Well, after the 2d day's march, and I had seen to the bivouacking of my troop, I got out my seine for purpose of seeing the kinds of fish the Rosebud could set up for supper. The attempt however resulted mostly in "water-hauls," and being ravenously hungry, "S.O.B. and trimmings," had to serve for bill of fare. Dr. Lord not putting in an appearance at the meal, however, after I had crawled under a bullberry bush for sweet repose, the Dr. came into camp, telling me that he had halted alone some miles back, being completely tired out, broken down, so much so that he had given up all hopes of getting to camp. He declined tea, and wanted nothing to eat or drink. I state this to show what must have been the physical condition of the Doctor on June 25th, on going into the fight, after an almost continuous march of 84 miles.

The repose I found under the bullberry bush alluded to, can be classed with the goose egg of the cricketer, for there were myriads of mosquitoes under that bush when I got there, and I don't think that any of them got away.

1st night's loss of sleep.

3rd day we marched to, strange to say, a creek called "Muddy Creek," where, on coming into camp I heard the voice of my old friend Col. Myles W. Keogh hailing me, saying, come here "old man," I've kept the nicest spot in the whole camp next to me, for your troop, & I've had to bluff the balance to hold it, but here it is, skip off," so I "skipped," putting my troop in the vale the gallant Irishman had held for me.

It wasn't far from twilight then, so, after getting supper Keogh came over to my bullberry bush, (he was more luxurious than I was, having a tent fly for shelter) and the crowd was listening to one of the Italian patriot, De Rudio's recitals, of his hair breadth scapes with Mazzini, or some other man, in some other country, all of which I rudely interrupted by saying, See here, fellows, you want to be collecting all the sleep you can, and be doing it soon, for I have a "Pre." that we are not going to stay in this camp tonight, but we are going to march all night, so, good-night. I had scarcely gotten the words from my lips before the orderly trumpeter notified us that we would meet at the commanding officer's headquarters at once: my preparations for sleep consisted in putting off my cavalry boots, so little time was consumed in robing: However, that was sufficient, the other officers rapidly went to their summons, it being quite dark there, and the "Pre." telling me 'twas a move. I called up my 1st Sergeant, and had him see that the aparejos were "O.K." ropes, bridles, &c., all right, and have everything ready about the troop for a speedy move.

I then commenced a search for the Head Quarters; however, before getting far, I met an officer returning from the "Call," saying, 'tis no use going, *You* were right— we move at 11 o'clock, P.M. Sharp, tonight: all right, then, there's no sleep for your humble again tonight.

2d night's loss of sleep.

If it took a minute to cross that pack train over the "Muddy," it took two hours; other side of creek Colonel Keogh hunted me up, he being the officer in charge of rear guard;—he was making the very air sulphuruous with blue oaths, telling me of the situation; however, from having been there very many times myself, I knew it better than he did: so I consoled him with, "Never mind old man, do the best you can, and it will all come out right."

I don't begin to believe that Job ever had much to do with shaved tailed pack mules.

Well, my advice seemed to brace Col. Keogh a bit, and I kept the ding-donging of the tin cup, frying pan—or something, that was my guide as to direction, the pounding of that on the saddle of the horse on the left of the troop preceding mine, being all I had to go by, the night being pitch dark, and the gait was a trot, so I hadn't much time to swap words with Col. Keogh, or, my guide would be gone.

This trot was kept up for perhaps eight or ten miles; then, came a halt, no orders for same being received, and no orders for anything received by me. So, the Packs remained on mules; saddles & bridles on horses. I crouched down by a sage bush until daylight, and there spied Colonel Reno and little Benny Hodgson going for coffee, hardtack & Trimmings. I invited myself to assist in disposing of that repast; and met with a "1st Class" welcome at suggesting it.

In a few moments, it seemed, the column moved forward, no orders however, for same were gotten, but my troop & I followed the procession: then came almost as sudden a halt: no orders for that. The rear of column knew of none, however, a few moments brought us a summons thro' an orderly, to "Officers' Call," at Head Quarters: when there, General Custer notified us that he had been on the mountain to the left, where our Scouts (Crows) were all the night; that they had told him thro. the interpreter, that they could see dust, indians and ponies, & all that. He could see nothing through the old telescopic glass they had and didn't believe there was anything to be seen; now, strange perhaps to say, I did believe it:— another "Pre." I knew it, because, why, I'd sooner trust the sharp eye of an indian than to trust a pretty good binocular that I always carried; and I'd gotten that from experience. However, 'twasn't my "chip in," so I said nothing. At this halt General Custer notified us that the first troop commander who notified him that the requirements of an order issued a few days before were being carried out strictly in the troop, that officer and troop should have the post of honor, the advance. I notified him at once that in my troop the requirements were being strictly adhered to. I feel quite sure it wasn't expected from me; but he stammered out, Well, Col. Benteen, Your troop has the advance.

When all had reported, I was ordered to move in advance with my troop, which I did, but had gone but a short distance when General Custer rode up, saying, I was setting the pace too fast. He then rode in advance; and after going a few miles the command was halted between hills on every side, and Genl. Custer and his adjutant stepped aside, and were figuring on paper for quite awhile, at what, we knew not. However, when thro, I was called up and notified that my command was 3 Troops, and that I would move to the left to a line of bluffs about 2 miles away. Sending out an officer and a few men as advance guard, to "pitch in" to anything I came across, and to notify him at once; I started on my mission immediately:—this was just about 15 miles from where I found the dead body of Genl. Custer 3 days afterwards.

I omitted stating, that while en route obeying Custer's last order, I received two other orders from him, and these through the Chief Trumpeter and the Sergeant Major of the regiment; the first to the effect, that, should I not find anything at the first line of bluffs, then, to go on to the second line of bluffs, to pitch in, and notify him at once, being included: the order through Sergt. Major received 15 or 20 minutes later, was, if nothing could be seen from second line of bluffs,

Captain Frederick W. Benteen in 1861.

horse I was riding, for the brute was tricky, and unless you took the precaution to lariat him to something, after the bit was taken from his mouth, and he thro' drinking, you could not hold him by the strap of halter: no one could: and away he would go; and when he got good and ready, he would rejoin the troop. Well, at this watering, I lariated old Dick to a stump of iron wood before removing the bit; and after drinking he pulled up taut on the stump, and looked as if to say, "Well, I didn't much care to go off this time anyway": but that was the time of times, old fellow, for you would have been saved two wounds, and two days where water was worth its weight in green backs, though beautiful and blue, within a stone's throw from our stand.

After leaving the watering place, a few miles brought us to a beautifully decorated tepee of buffalo hide, just on trail.

I dismounted, after riding around the lodge, peeped in, and saw the body of an indian on a scaffold or cot of rude poles. By this time the battalion was up—and away we went again. A mile or two brought orders through a Sergeant to the officer in charge of pack-train. I told him where I had last seen it—another couple of miles brought an order for me thro' the orderly trumpeter of day, from the adjutant of regiment, to the effect: Benteen, Big Village, Be quick; Bring Packs.

P.S. Bring Packs,
W. W. Cooke,
Adjt.

Well, the Packs were safe behind. I knew *that* —*better than anybody*. I couldn't waste time in going back, nor in halting where I was for them. So, we went—V.V.V.

I resume with the last order received from the Adjutant of the 7th Cavalry; the last lines penciled by him, viz: "Benteen, Come on, Big Village, Be Quick, Bring Packs. P. S. Bring Packs. John Martini, the trumpeter, bringing this dispatch was a thick headed, dull witted Italian, just about as much cut out for a cavalryman as he was for a King: he informed me that the indians were "skidaddling"; hence, less the necessity for re-tracing our steps to get the Packs, and the same would be gained by awaiting the arrival of them where we then were. We did neither; but took the Trot! and, from the ford where Reno first crossed the beautifully blue Little Big Horn we saw going on what evidently was not "skedaddling" on the part of the indians, as there were 12 or 14 dismounted men on the river bottom, and they were being ridden down and shot by 800 or 900 indian warriors.

then, to go on until I came to a valley, to "pitch in," and to notify him at once, being also included: now, all of this time the balance of the regiment was on the march, and the last glimpse I had of them was the grayhorse troop in rapid motion. I thought of course they had struck something. However, I had that valley to find, and away we went for it, myself and orderly being in advance of the advance guard. The 2d line of bluffs showed no valley,—only bluffs & bluffs:— so, another of my "Prees." came; and said, old man, that crowd ahead is going to strike a snag: indians have too much sense to travel over such country as you have been going unless they are terribly pushed; so, you'd better get back to that trail, and you will find work; then "Right Oblique" was the word until we got out of the hills to the trail; my command getting to it just ahead of the train of Packs, the horses not having been watered since evening before, and this being along about one o'clock P. M. of a hot June day, they were needing it badly. So, on the trail I halted at a morass for a few moments for the purpose of giving the men and animals a chance at it. I attended to the watering of the

We concluded that the lay of the land had better be investigated a bit, as so much of the Italian trumpeter's story hadn't "Panned out." So—off to left I went, seeing a group of 3 or 4 Absaraka or Crow indians; from them I learned this; Otoe Sioux, Otoe Sioux, the "Otoe" meaning, innumerable, or—Heaps of them;—and we soon found that there were enough of them.

From the point I saw the Crows. I got the first sight of the men of Reno's battalion who had retreated from the river bottom, recrossed the river a couple of miles below, and were showing up on the bluffs on the side of the river that my battalion had kept and was then on: the battalion being in line, Reno, knowing of course we were soldiers, came riding to meet me as I moved towards him. My first query of Reno was—where is Custer? Showing him the last order received from the Adjutant of Regt., Reno replied that he did not know, that Custer had ordered him across the river to charge the indians, informing him that he would support him with the whole "Outfit," but he had neither seen nor heard from him since:— Well, our battalion got just in the nick of time to save Reno's.

After a few words with Col. Reno I inquired as to the whereabouts of "D" Troop of my Battn. —and was informed that Capt. Weir had, without orders, gone down the river. This being the case, I sallied after Weir, and about ¾ths of a mile lower down, from the top of the highest point in vicinity, saw Weir's troop returning; hordes of indians hurrying them somewhat. Reno came to same point after I had thrown Captain French's troop in line at right angle with river, to hold that point, dismounted, till Weir's troop got thro, and to then retreat slowly, and I would have that part of command looked after. This didn't finish as well as I had hoped and expected it would. However, from fact of the indians not making the most of the opportunity, and Lieut. Ed. S. Godfrey carrying out his instructions more faithfully and in a more soldierly manner, we had time sufficient to get some kind of a line formed: the first officer I saw when establishing a line, was Lieutenant Geo. D. Wallace, recently killed by some of the same Sioux, at the "Wounded Knee" fight in Dak. I said, Wallace, put the right of your troop here. His answer was, "I have no troop, only three men." Well, said I, stay here with your three men, and don't let them get away, I will have you looked out for:—and Wallace and the three men stayed, and they were looked out for. Col. Reno was on the left—forming the same line—which wasn't a line but an arc of a circle, rather irregularly described too. And when we met

Benteen at his retirement from active service. Photo by D. F. Barry.

about centre, my own Troop remained to be disposed of, so I put it over much ground, almost as much as the other six companies occupied, protecting left flank, and well to the rear, just on the edge of line of bluffs, near river.

The formation as described, was dismounted; the horses of command, being placed in a saucer like depression of prairie, the lower rim of the saucer, instead of a rim was a gentle slope. The hospital was established at the upper rim, and was about as safe a place as there was around the vicinity, the blue canopy of heaven being the covering: the sage brushes, sand being the operating board: but the stout heart and nervy skilful hand of Dr. Porter (the only surgeon of the three of command that hadn't been killed), was equal to the occasion.

I state but the facts when I say that we had a fairly warm time with those red men as long as sufficient light was left for them to draw a bead on us, and the same I'm free to maintain, in the language of Harte.

I don't know how many of the miscreants there were;—probably we shall never know,—but there were enough.

Now, be it remembered, this wasn't a fight instituted by the army for glory going purposes, or anything of that kind; but rather, was a little gentle disciplining which the Department of the Interior (the Department of U. S. Government having charge of the Indian Bureau), had promised would be given the indians if they, the nomads of the tribe, declined to come in to agencies in the Spring; be good, and draw their pay; runners having been sent out to the self supporters; i.e. those, who gave the Agencies the grand go by, as it were, to the effect, that if they didn't report, Soldiers would be sent out to bring them in. About the only answer that they returned as far as I wot, was "We will be here when you come for us"! and sure enough, they were there! but little thought anyone that they would be in such hordes.

I judged of the condition of the men of my troop somewhat by my own condition; though that is one of almost physical never tire; but not having had sleep for the two nights previous to this one, was getting just a trifle weary myself; so, up and down the line of "H" Troop 1st Lieut. Gibson and myself tramped, the night of June 25th & 26th, doing our very best to keep the sentinels awake, but we just could not do it. Kicking them; well, they didn't care anything about that. However, we two kept awake on our end of line, and at early daybreak ascertained that few, if any of our red friends had given up hope of doing us up. The clatter they made stirred our little bivouac out pretty effectually, then *all* being on the qui vive; thinking the situation was O.K. that I'd try and "Round Up" a few lines of sleep, to make up somewhat for the three night's sleep that I was short of. So, down I dropped on the hill-side, determined to gather what I could, in; but some wakeful red skin had pretty nearly my exact range, plumping me in the heel of extended boot; another bullet scattered the dry dust under my arm pit; however, I hadn't the remotest idea of letting little things like that disturb me, and think that I at least had gotten forty winks, when a Sergeant of my troop informed me that Lieut. Gibson of my troop was having a regular monkey & parrot time of it: to say that I felt like saying something naughty to that Sergeant, was putting it mildly, but down I ran and thro and thro' the pack train, getting together some 15 or 16 soldiers & packers, making them carry up sacks of bacon, boxes of hard bread, pack-saddles, and materials of that kind;— quite a sufficiency to build a respectable little breast work—which, after propping up as well as we could, I turned over with the Falstaffian crowd, to "Gib." my 1st lieutenant, telling him to hold the fort, notwithstanding what might become of us. Then I walked along the front of my troop and told them that I was getting mad, and I wanted them to charge down the ravines with me when I gave the yell: then, each to yell as if

provided with a thousand throats. The Chinese act was sufficiently good enough for me if it would work; but I hadn't so much real trust in its efficacy. However, when the throttles of the "H sters" were given full play, and we dashed into the unsuspecting savages who were amusing themselves by throwing clods of dirt, arrows by hand, and otherwise, for simply pure cussedness among us, to say that 'twas a surprise to them, is mild form, for they somersaulted and vaulted as so many trained acrobats, having no order in getting down those ravines, but quickly getting; de'il take the hindmost!

Then, then, I had the key to the beautiful blue water that had been flowing so ripplingly at our very feet for two days—and which wounded and well longed so much for,—there it was, ours, for the getting. Well, 'twasn't the simplest of matters to get a camp-kettle of it, even then, but as we were on the brink of it, to none did it occur to picture or think of how it had to be gotten; we proceeded to get it, but at the expense of many wounded, and this for the sake of the already wounded as well as the dry as dust living. Speaking for myself, I am quite sure that I would gladly and cheerfully have given the very prettiest and newest twenty dollar silver certificate that I might have persuaded my first lieutenant to have lent me, for just one Oz. of Spiritus Frumenti to have dashed into just about same quantity of that pure Little Big Horn water, if for no other purpose than to just brace me a bit, for to a certainty I was "Plumb" tired out and sleepy too. However, the business for the day had only fairly opened: and I got no chance to steal off and sleep, or bless me if I would not have done it.

To say that I ever had more serene satisfaction at killing a Black tailed buck deer, on the bound, with a carbine, than I had in putting one of Uncle Sam's 45s thro' as noble a specimen of the Dakotas as ever fluttered an eagle feather in his scalp lock, was every word true at that time; though I'm rather fond of indians than otherwise, but to plump him thro' his spinal, as he was cavorting thro the ravines, there being so many of them around, that one wouldn't be missed, and being so confoundedly mad and sleepy, must say that I looked on that dead red with exquisite satisfaction and not because he was maiden hair either, for he wasn't—but I was so tired, and they wouldn't let me sleep. Now, Strong man, I, a bit out of luck in losing the 1st night's sleep in the category of three, still, how tired must my good friend Dr. Lord have been, when he galloped in with Custer before getting his quietus, and *he*, A.H.L., was of weak physique.

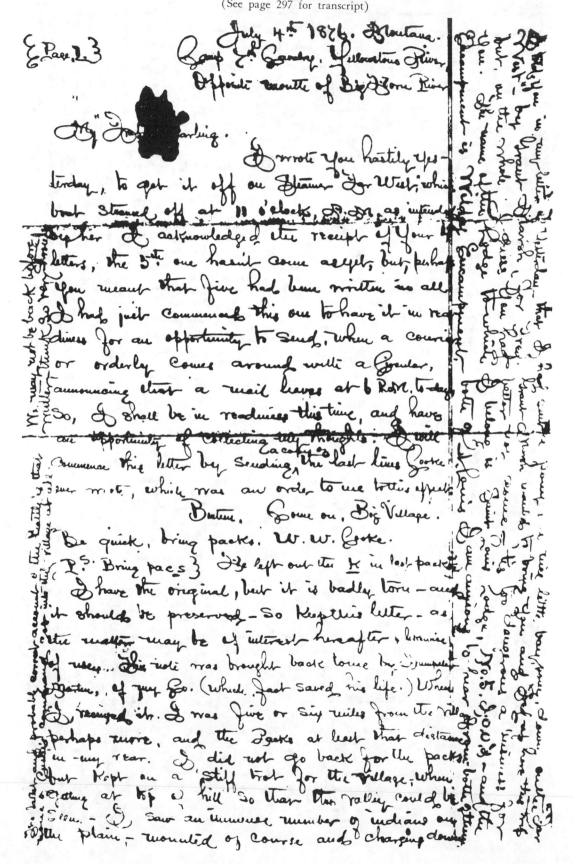

out. Some dismounted men of Reno's command; the balance of R's command were mounted, and flying for dear life to the bluffs on the same side of river that I was. I then marched my 3 Cos. to them — and a more delighted lot of folks you never saw. To commence — On the 22nd of June — Custer, with the 7th Cavalry left the Steamer Far West (and Terry & Genl. Gibbon's command, which latter was then on the side of river and in same camp in which we now are) and moved up the Rosebud, marching 12 miles. the next day — we marched 35 miles up the same stream. the next day we marched 35 more miles up same stream, and went into bivouac, remaining until 12 o'clock P.M. We then marched until about day light, making about 10 miles, about half past five we started again — and after going 6 or 8 miles we halted and officers' call was sounded. We were asked how many were with the companies — and the Co. Packs & methods that only they could remain with them. In the discourse brought up with — that we should ascertain the men — were supplied with the quantity of ammunition as had been specified in orders, and that the Advance that reported itself in readiness to be the Advance. I knew that mine was in the desired condition, and, it being near the point of assembly, I went to it and reported myself, and came then announced to Genl. Custer that Co. was ready, he replied, the Advance is Yours, Capt. Benteen. We then moved four or five miles and halted, between two slopes of two hills — and the Regt. was divided into 4 battalions. After getting "A. B. G. D. & K." I getting "D. H. K." From that point I was ordered over the immense hill to the left, in search of the valley, which was supposed to be very near by, and to pitch into anything I came across — and to perform Custer at once if I found anything worthy of same. Well, I suppose I went up and down those hills for 14 miles — and still no valley anywhere in sight. the horses were fast giving out from climbing — and as my orders had been fulfilled, I struck diagonally for the trail the command had moved on, coming to it just before the Pack train got there or on the trail just ahead of it. I then marched rapidly — and after about 6 or 8 miles came upon a burning depot — in which was the body of an Indian on a scaffold, arrayed gorgeously — none of the command was in sight at this time. The ground from this to the valley was descending — but very rough. I kept up my trot, and when I reached a point very near the ford, which was crossed by Reno's Battn. I got my first sight of the valley and river — and Reno's command in full flight for the bluffs — to the side I was then on — of course I joined them at once. The ground where Reno charged on was a plain 1/2 or 1 miles or 10 miles long, and about one half or more wide; Custer sent him in there — and prevailed of Support.

him – after Reno started in, Custer with his five Cos.
instead of crossing the ford went to the right – around
some high bluffs – with the intentions – as is supposed
of striking the rear of the village; from the bluffs
on which he got he had his first glimpse of the
whole of it – and I can tell you 'twas an immense
one. From that point, Custer sent the note I have to
Martin, which I have quoted on 1st page. Suppose
after the five Cos. had closed up somewhat & he
started down for the village, all throats bursting themselves
with cheering; (So said Martin.) he had 3
or 4 miles to go before he got to a ford – as the
Village ran out the plain, on opposite side to Custer's
Column. So, when he got over those 4 miles of
rough country and reached the ford, the indians
had availed themselves of the timely information
given by the cheering – as to the whereabouts and
intentions of that column, and had arrangements
completed to receive it – Whether the indians allowed
Custer's Column to cross at all, is a mooted question
but I am of the opinion that nearly – if not all –
of the five companies got into the village but was
driven out immediately – flying in great disorder
and crossing by two, instead of the one ford,
by which they entered. E & C going by the left & F,
"I & L" by the same one they crossed – What became
of "C Co." no one knows – they must have charged through
below the village, gotten away – or have been killed
in the bluffs on the village side of stream – as very
few of "C Co." horses are found. Jack Sturgis' &
Porter's clothes were found in the village. After the
indians had driven them across, it was a regular
buffalo hunt for them – and not a man escaped.
We buried 208 of their bodies of Custer's Command
the 2d day after fight. The bodies were as recognizable
as if they were in life. With Custer – was Keogh, Yates,
& Tom Custer (3 Captains), Lieut's. Cooke, D. E. Smith, Porter,
Calhoun, 4 2d Lieut's. Sturgis, Reily & Crittenden
(F. S. of 20th Inf.) Asst. Surgeon Lord was along – but his
body was not recognized; & neither was Porter's nor
Sturgis' nor Harrington's. Lt. Hodgson were killed at
Reno's end of line – in attempting to help back
to bluffs. De Rudio was supposed to have been
lost – but the same night the indians left
their village – he came sauntering in dismounted
accompanied by McIntosh's cook. They had
laid hidden away in the woods. He has a thrilling
romantic story – made out already – embellished
You bet! The stories of O'Neill (the man who was with
him,) & De R's of course couldn't be wanted to agree.

but — far more of truth, I am inclined to think, will be found in the narrating of Ruth's, at any rate it is not at all colored & as he is a cool level headed fellow — and tells it plainly the same way all the time — which is a big thing towards convincing one of the truth of a story.

I must now tell you what I did. When I joined Reno's command we halted for the Packs to come up — & then moved along the line of bluffs towards the direction Custer was supposed to have gone in. Weir's Co. was sent out to communicate with Custer — but it was driven back — we then showed our full force of the hills with Guidons flying, that he might see us — but we could see nothing & could not hear much firing, but could see an immense body of indians coming to attack us, from both sides of the river — we withdrew to a Saucer like hill, putting our horses & Packs in the bottom of Saucer and threw all of our force dismounted — around this Corral; the animals could be riddled from only one point — but we had not men enough to extend our line to there — so we could not do it — therefore the indians amused themselves by shooting at our Stock, dito, men — but they could cover themselves. Both grey horses, (U.S. horses) were wounded. Well they pounded at us all of what was left of the 1st & the whole of the 2d day — withdrawing their line with the withdrawal of their village — which was at dusk the 2d day. Corporal Hall, Meador & Jones were killed; Sergt. Hall — both of the Bishops, Phillips, Rudolph, Black, Ewers, (Copper, &c (21 altogether wounded) I got a slight scratch on my right thumb — which as you see doesn't prevent me from writing you this long scrawl. Better as I am Via West Pellis, it will be a long time in reading you. Genl. Terry with Genl. Gibbon's command came up the morning of the 3d day, about 10 o'clock. Indians had all gone the night before. Had Custer carried out the orders he got from Genl. Terry — the commands would have formed a junction exactly at the village — and have captured the whole outfit of Tepees &c and probably any quantity of Squaws, Papooses &c &c — but Custer disobeyed orders from the fact of not wanting any other command — or body to have a finger in the pie — and thereby lost his life. 3000 warriors were

BENTEEN'S "INSTALLMENT" LETTER

Str. "Far West"
Mouth of Big Horn & Yellowstone
July 2, 1876

My darling Wife—

We have just arrived at this point, marching from the indian village. On the 25th of June, last Sunday, week, Genl. Custer divided the 7th Cav. into 3 Battn's.—about 15 miles from an indian village, the whereabouts of which he did not know exactly. I was ordered with 3 Co's., D, H & K, to go to the left for the purpose of hunting for the valley of the river—indian camp—or anything I could find. I found nothing, and after marching 10 miles or so in pursuit of the same, determined to return to Custer's trail. Reno had 3 Co's. (A, G, M.)

When Custer arrived in sight of indians, he ordered Reno to charge—and promised to support him. R. did so—but Custer went a long way off to the right, behind the bluffs—intending to attack the village at the opposite end to R. the result of which was—that

[Page 2]

Custer, Keogh, Yates, Tom Custer, Cook, Porter, Calhoun, Sturgis, Harrington, Riley, J. J. Crittenden, & A. E. Smith & Dr. Lord were killed —& with them every man of the 5 Co's. who were along. Reno with his 3 Co's. was driven to the bluffs, & I with mine arrived just in time to save them & mine. Tom McDougall, who was back with his Co., in charge of the pack train, got up with us, all right. We endeavored to go where Custer had gone, not seeing or hearing from him however, but we could not do it—and had to fall back to a ravine—or series of depressions in ground—where we corralled our packs, and kept them off nicely—the next day they came at us more fiercely—but could do nothing with us— save shoot the animals—and kill a few men— the 3d day Genls. Terry & Gibbon came up—but the indians struck their village & left the night before. There was 5000 of them—So Genl. Sheridan telegraphs Genl. Terry

[Page 3]

Str. "Far West" July 23d 1876
Mouth of Yellowstone & Rosebud

My Darling Wife:

The Steamer is now taking on wood, at the camp, where one month ago, yesterday, Genl. Custer cut loose from Genl. Terry—and started up the Rosebud. We started out in "Grand Galore," Genls. Terry, Gibbon & Brisbin (Maj. 2nd Cav.) and their staffs, witnessing the Review, which passed them in column of fours, guidons flying, trumpets sounding the March &c. Custer remained until the column passed. Little did he think, that in 3 more days five full companies of that gallant command—along with himself— would be totally annihilated—not one of them left to tell the story! But! 'twas so ordained. It was at this point he issued the order breaking up Wings & Battalions. We are now bound up the river to the command—which is below the mouth of the Big Horn, Gibbon, Comdg. Our trip up has been thus far pleasant and uneventful. I have fully recovered—and feel first rate—tho' I think should feel much better were this Str. heading for Rice.

[Page 4]

July 24, 76

We cached (i.e. hid) 65 tons of freight on the bank today—on account of fearing that there wasn't water enough in the river, but I think they are of the opinion, now, that the proceeding wasn't at all necessary. Met two companies of 2d Cav. with 2 Gatling guns under Lieut. Low, the Dtchmt under command of Capt. Wheelan, of 2d (crossed sabers) who thought they were about 50 miles from command: they were simply scouting around. Wheelan informed us that Capt. Thompson, of his Regt. had blown his brains out in camp,— cause, sickness, whisky etc. Wheelan, by the by, told me some time ago soon after our fight—that he met my father in St. Louis at the Cav. Barracks, was introduced to him by Genl. Sturgis; Queer, isn't it? In one month more—today—I shall be XLII ("Five & Forty cts")! "The Bulk"! I hope you have thought to have the newspapers of the post which contained references to our Expedition preserved for me—as we will not see many of those articles. I have Winsburg & the mare & "Cuff" aboard the Str. Thought it best to bring them up so: "Cuff" would liked to have gone down—but I thought probably 'twould be better to keep the horses up here.

[Page 5]

Lieut. Walker of 17th showed me a portion of a letter from his wife—in which she stated that they had a rumor down there that Moylan, Gibson & DeRudio showed the white feather in fight of 25th: the same rumor prevailed thro' the camp on Powder River: Moylan heard of it and threatened vengeance dire on the perpetrator of the rumor. I think had DeR, made as good use of his eyes as 15 or 20 of the men did—he would have gotten out as they did—and neither M. nor G. exhibited any great degree of activity—according to my light, probably others—the men, may have so seen it—and such things fly fast. Long ere this you will have gotten my long letter, by "Josephine," and I suppose you have answered as lengthily by the boats coming up with 5th and 22d Infty. Tell Fred I shall expect to have him read me some nice little stories by the time I get back: he must learn to ride his pony, but that must be kept for amusement after his studying is done. I have told you how the pay accts. left with you could be used—one being made out for July—the other can be used for any number of months on one. I will quit this now—as I have nothing I can think of to say—So—until then, will leave other page.

[Page 6]
July 25—1876. Str. "Far West"
12:30 P.M.

My Trabbie Darling,

Just one month ago—today—at just about this time of day, Genl. Custer and his command commenced the attack on the indian village—one short half hour finished—I think—that five Co's. One would think that but a short space of time to dispatch so large a number of men, but when the immense number of indians attacked is taken into consideration, and the fact that the cavalry was probably thrown into a panic at the 1st check received—and gotten in just the condition that indians would get a herd of buffalo, suiting their peculiar mode exactly, it is not so very surprising.

I had a queer dream of Col. Keogh the night before last, 'twas, that he would insist upon undressing in the room in which you were. I had to give him a "dressing" to cure him of the fancy. I rarely ever thought of the man—and 'tis queer I should have dreamt of him. We are steaming along very slowly—and 'twill probably take us until tomorrow about this time, to reach camp at Big Horn. I don't think 'tis at all settled that the site of the depot will be at that point—as it cannot—perhaps—be supplied by boats.

[Page 7]
Steamer "Far West" Sunday
July 30, 1876
Yellowstone, opposite Rosebud

My Darling Wife,

We arrived at this point today—marching from the Big Horn. The weather has been hot enough to cook eggs without other fire than the sun furnished. I can tell you it has been terrific.

Grànt Marsh has just told me that the boat was going down to Powder River for the grain that was left there by us—and he wants me to go down with him. I should like very much to do

so, but there are so many things to do around the company that I can illy afford to be absent at this time.

My last letter was sent via Fort Ellis—it will take sometime to get around by that route—if it gets at all—which is exceedingly doubtful. It is a matter of speculation whether we shall (find)

[Page 8]
the indians on other side of Yellowstone. I believe Genl. Crook is impressed with the belief that they are being reinforced from the Agencies— and other officers think we shall find them. I am of the opinion that as soon as we cross to the South side—they will come to the N. side, for on this side is all the game,— i.e. buffalo. I cannot think that such an immense body of indians can have been kept together for so long a period—and can be held in a country where small game, such as Elk, deer & Antelope—is about all they can find.

Sergt. McLaughlin's time is out tomorrow. I don't suppose he will care to re-enlist. Were I in his place I should not. He will have to remain until a boat goes down. There isn't the slightest thing new going on—I am well. I haven't had an opportunity of answering Dr. Taylor's letter as yet, but shall do so. Remember me kindly to everybody. Oceans of kisses & love to you & Fred.

Devotedly—Your husband
Fred Benteen

GENERAL BENTEEN AND MR. GOLDIN

In 1891, one Theodore W. Goldin, a private of "G" Troop, Seventh Cavalry, during the years 1876 and 1877, and then a practising lawyer in Janesville, Wisconsin, contacted Benteen by letter, and a correspondence between them began that extended through the succeeding five years. Goldin's contributions to this correspondence have been lost, but the letters of Benteen were, for the most part, preserved. These are the famous Benteen-Goldin letters, darkly hinted at, indirectly quoted or sparingly referred to by nearly every writer of Custeriana since 1928, but for many reasons, chief of which was the objection of the Benteen family, never heretofore published.

The reproduction of the Benteen-Goldin letters which follows, includes all of their content that is considered of historical value. Camp and garrison scandal and gossip have been eliminated so far as possible, as have also some of the old soldier's more severe strictures against other officers. For these deletions, indicated by stars, I accept full responsibility, believing as I do, that the deleted matter detracts from the value of the letters as historical documents.

It will be noted, of course, that there occurs a long hiatus in the Benteen-Goldin correspondence; an hiatus of more than two years—from 3 April 1892 to 6 July 1894. It was during this period that Goldin, who evidently aspired to be *the* "Enlisted Man Historian" of the Little Big Horn, was preparing manuscripts that were published by the long since defunct "Army Magazine," which was printed at Chicago. His first article appeared in the June 1894 issue, and several others followed. None of these articles have been found, despite a search extending over several years.

As it is obvious from Benteen's letters that Goldin was acquiring much, if not most of his information from the retired veteran officer, it seems highly improbable that during this critical period he failed to remain in touch with his "source of supply," and to keep him advised of the progress of what appears to have been in some sort a joint enterprise.

Notwithstanding Goldin's assertion that the letters hereinafter set out constituted the entire series, it is nevertheless believed that the correspondence was continued throughout the period of the apparent hiatus, and that letters received from Benteen during that period were not preserved.

Long before I saw or even heard of the Goldin letters, I had written of Benteen that he "was Custer's bitter and outspoken enemy. Not even death served to change his attitude: to the day of his own passing he never abated his hatred. But his known character and the habit of his entire life refutes the imputation that at any time or in any circumstances he failed in his duty as an officer and a soldier. He fought as he had lived, fearless, uncompromising, and grimly stern. Benteen was one of the best soldiers the United States Army has ever possessed." (The Story of the Little Big Horn, p. 105-6) The Goldin letters go far to demonstrate the accuracy of that characterization; but they establish even more, for they prove that Benteen not only disliked Custer but despised him. There was a clash of personalities from the very start of their relationship; a clash which, from antipathy, in time developed into contempt, and even hatred.

In reading the Benteen-Goldin letters, however, it should not be forgotten that Benteen wrote them during the sunset of his life, for he died shortly after the last of the series was penned. He, together with Major Reno, had been attacked and charged by Custer's partisans with responsibility for the disaster of June 25, 1876. He had resented and brooded over the injustice of that charge for many years. From his viewpoint, the man who rashly led five companies of his regiment to destruction, and unnecessarily imperiled the rest, because he met death in a heroic setting, had been glorified by propaganda; while he, the man to whom more than to any other, belonged the credit of saving what was left of the regiment, had been slandered and reviled because he had not rescued that man and those who perished with him. He was bitter: and these letters plainly reveal his feeling. Moreover, Benteen was the product of an era of bitterness and strife; of a time when passions ran high; when enmities built upon stern judgments were carried to the grave and even beyond it. All this must be taken into consideration when reading these letters; and the mantle of charitable understanding cast about this stalwart soldier of a bygone day.

THE BENTEEN-GOLDIN LETTERS

The letters from Benteen to Theo W. Goldin, below reproduced in condensed form, were without exception dated at Atlanta, Georgia, and all but the first, which addressed Goldin as "Mr.," are superscribed to "Dear Col. Goldin," and are signed, for the most part, "Very truly yr. friend, F. W. Benteen." Nine letters, dated 12 October and 28 December of 1895, and 15 January, 19 February, 20 February, 23 March, 14 April, 25 April and 26 May, all of the year 1896, have been omitted *in toto* for the reason that they contain nothing of historical value or interest.

October 20, 1891

It is very gratifying to know that my efforts while belonging to the 7th Cavalry were appreciated by the rank and file—i.e., the enlisted men —and your letter of today tells me that they were.

I was with the regiment from its organization to December, 1882, and of course can look far behind the date you came to me, and the backward glance is as full of memories—many of them glorious, and all pleasant, as from the point where you first drew saber. Capt. Owen Hale was the last of our old "mess" of seven to bite the dust, and I alone remain to think of them; I mean the mess association, and cherish their memories in that regard.

In 1866 I could have gone into the 10th U. S. Cavalry as a Major but I preferred a Captaincy in the Seventh. Fate, however, after being a Captain 17 years, threw me into a negro organization of cavalry anyhow; and being well off in this world's goods, and feeling that it was not proper to remain with a race of troops that I could take no interest in— * * * and having served my 30 years—there seemed nothing to do but to commence looking after my property interests.

It cost me $10,000 more than my pay came to, to follow the trumpet calls of the United States, and this amount was not thrown away, or wasted, either. Now, as a retired Major, I am getting along comfortably, and am looking after my flocks and herds—city blocks in prospective—and the interests of Fred, my only child. I lost four children in following that brazen trumpet around.

I am pleased, my dear sir, at having heard from you, and I wish you an uninterrupted run of everything that is good.

November 10, 1891

It pleases me to know that you knew and liked Lieut. Aspinwall of the 7th Cavalry—for he was a good fellow.

I was commanding the post of Fort Rice, D.T., and appointed Aspinwall Assistant Commissary of Subsistence, which office, having funds, ready cash, monthly, completed what was begun in (by?) Custer's coterie in 1869, and ended the army career of poor John. * * *

Capt. E. S. Godfrey wrote to me when I was at Fort McKinney, Wyoming, in 1886, about an article he was engaged at for a magazine concerning the 1876 campaign; my answer to him was to the effect, "That the greatest of these was charity," and asked him if he didn't think Reno had been sufficiently damned?

Pretty nearly ever since the stepping down and out of the more prominent actors in that fight of ours, June 25-26, 1876, Godfrey has been trying to make much capital for himself; and perhaps 'twas well that he didn't undertake to do it sooner * * * Of course I knew a great many things about the fight that 'tisn't essential that the world should know; "qui bono?" but I shouldn't like to see Godfrey attempt to parade himself as an at all prominent actor in it * * * I don't suppose there was ever an officer of the army got such a "cussing out" as I gave Mathey at the L. Big Horn on the eve of June 25th, and before crowds of enlisted men, officers and "packs". Personally, I brought three of the mules of the train back—the mules being loaded with ammunition, and had gotten quite a long way down toward the water, for which they were heading, before I could "round them up. * * * Everybody —I mean most of the captains and all of the subalterns in the 7th, seemed to be positively afraid of Custer. However, without parade, when he did anything that was irregular to me, or infringed on "regulations," where I was concerned, I always went to him in "propria persona" and had the matter adjusted at once. Custer liked me for it, and I always surmised what I afterwards learned, de facto, that he wanted me badly as a friend; but I could not be, tho' I never fought him covertly. * * *

Reno and Weir were never friendly, but the cause of this I never inquired or knew. What was the conversation between Reno and Weir on the little knoll on the bluffs? Weir belonged to my battalion, and, as I always thought, to "show his smartness" sallied out without orders on the march down the river; however, he was glad enough to have us pull his troop (out of?) there and back, and he played a very humble part in the fight till 'twas well closed.

Should you see anything, or hear more of an article from Godfrey, be kind enough to let me know. * * *

(Note: This letter deals almost entirely with the fight at Canyon Creek, during the Nez Perces Campaign of 1877) W.A.G.

November 17, 1891.

I can give you another chapter of the unwritten history of the 7th Cavalry.

I brought the Fort Rice battalion of 7th up river from that post, and while in camp below Lincoln, General and Mrs. Sturgis drove down to my tent —an "A" without cot or any useless paraphernalia —the tent being so small I could not ask Mrs. Sturgis and her daughter in; so they remained in the carriage, being entertained by the usual throng of attendant "youngsters". The general came in, and there he told me that, though he was begged by Mrs. Sturgis to give me the command of a battalion, that he did not see how he could do it. Lt. Col. Otis and Major Merrill going on campaign, Otis must have six troops, and it would not appear well to divide the remaining troops into two battalions; but that he wanted me to "command the reserve."

I said, "General, do not bother yourself about any command for me, as I know it will come when the opportunity for doing something presents itself, and I really am more interested in my own troop than in the whole balance of the regiment."

You know with what a fan-farenade of trumpets we went up the Missouri to the Yellowstone. Otis' and Merrill's battalions seemed to strive as to which could make the most clamor. In camp opposite Keogh we lost Otis, and I shall always be of the opinion that General Sturgis persuaded the doctor to give him a certificate of disability. Gen. Miles then took away the other troops, leaving six for Sturgis; well, soon thereafter we started for the Crow Agency region; and when there I did little else but fish.

At Clark's Fork Canyon, I was up the canyon so engaged, feeling the while that I had no business to be out of the camp, and with such feeling on we returned to camp just as "boots and saddles" were being sounded. I soon learned of the reports that were brought in by the detachments that had gone out under Lieuts. Hare and Fuller, and from the direction (course) taken by the column, pretty soon arrived at the conclusion that if we kept it up, the Nez Perces would not be "in it."

I "pumped" Hare, Fuller and the guides (?) and was the more convinced; so I went to the General on the march (it being then nearly dark) and told him that he was deliberately going away from the Indians. He said, "No, there is only one pass through which they can get; we will go up the Stinking Water and cut them off." My remark was, "General, when you know where Indians are, that is the very best place to find them, otherwise you may not find them at all."

Now this was pretty "brash" talk for a captain to give a colonel, and I soon saw I could not impress my convictions on him, but I at least persuaded him that no fires should be lighted in our bivouac that night, which caused the Indians to "feel around" for us—which they did, running into pickets of "L" Troop.

We went up the Stinking Water and crossed the mountain next day, but found no pass; Sturgis and Major Merrill both telling me during the early forenoon that we were going to have a hell of a fight pretty soon. "No," said I, "you'll find an abandoned camp, and the Indians gone through the gap left by us."

You know how, step by step, we followed their trail through that d——d gorge through which both the Indians and General Howard's command had gone, though we did not find the latter part out till just before we struck Howard's camp.

As soon as I had put my battalion in camp, and before any tents were put up, fishing I went, to get a mess for supper. I soon came back with a beautiful lot, and my Lieut. told me that Gen. Howard had been over, and that Gen. Sturgis had sent for me often, as they were having a council of war; mine was Cambronne's word repeated, though in Saxon phrase. However, as soon as I had gotten outside of as many fried trout as I could carry, over to see the general (Sturgis) I went. He told me they had agreed to "reveille" at 3:30,

"forward" 4:30. I said "General, you will lose time by so doing; it is drizzling rain now; by morning the ropes of the packs will be stiff, and at 3:30 it will be so dark that it will be utterly impossible to pack the mules properly." So he sent around, changing "reveille" to 4:30, "forward," 5:30, and then we marched through Howard's camp before their reveille had been sounded.

After we had followed the trail of the Nez Perces through that gorge, and had gotten into the scantily pine-timbered hills, the officers got into a general group with their respective luncheons, and while eating them, I asked, "Why in the name of all that's good, when we knew where the Indians were, did we not go to them?" General Sturgis's face got as red as a turkey cock's wattle, and he replied, "Colonel Benteen, that is not a fit question for you to ask; there will be too many people asking that same." Merrill (or someone) said, "Well, they are gone now, and we can't catch them." Said I, "O, yes we can." Sturgis then wanted to know how I would do it. My reply was, "40 miles today, 50 miles tomorrow if necessary." Soon after this talk, Major Merrill took me aside, saying, Sturgis wanted to send him with his battalion to check the Nez Perces, but that he did not believe in separating the battalions. I said, "Merrill, get Sturgis to send mine; I'll guarantee that it will check them, and hold them, too, and we will not suffer any unnecessary loss." I asked Hare and Garlington to try and persuade the General to let me go, but I heard no more from it.

You know on reaching the Yellowstone on 2d morning how much time we "monkeyed" away, and how we were actually going into camp, when Howard's scouts alarmed the C.O. by stating that the Nez Perces were coming to attack us; so, off toward Canyon Creek we went, Merrill's battalion in advance. I then learned what the General meant by his Lincoln conversation of wanting me to command the reserve, as order after order came for me to move slower. However, "Old Buckskin" had his war pace on, and I wasn't in a mood for letting Merrill's battalion get all of the glory; then, finding the pace wasn't lessened any, Sturgis came up to the head of my battalion—but I tell you "Old Buck" made his horse jog all the same.

Of course you know how we found Merrill's battalion, dismounted, fighting(?) on foot. The herd of the Nez Perces were on the other side of the canyon. "General, do you want those?" "Can you get them?" "Yes," "Well, do it." I had already sent Lieut. Graham over near the foothills with a platoon of "M" troop. "B" Troop was guard for the packs; so we, "C" Troop, and one platoon of "M"—but we got the horses, didn't we?

In making the movement, one of Howard's scouts coming up from the canyon showed me where the lock of his Winchester had been struck with a bullet and rendered useless, asking me to give him a carbine. Reply: "Can't take a gun from a soldier to give a scout." He told me the canyon was alive with Indians, and to go there we would all be slaughtered—but we were not, were we?

Well, Merrill's boys couldn't "foot it" fast enough to render us any service—other than through moral effect.

My feint through the gap threw the "reds" off, and consequently in the canyon I had time to strip my fine silk fishing line from the pole; yes, and I did not throw the "gut leader" away, either. My fishing pole of birch was my spear on that ride.

From the fact of having struck the reds at Canyon Creek, * * * Sturgis's reputation was saved; but he wanted me to make a "hullabaloo" of a report; but I couldn't. The whole facts of the case came, or should have come under his immediate observation; so, other than complimenting Wallace, Graham and Nicholson in battalion orders, I said naught.

Sturgis got Gen'l. Howard to order him to Lincoln to prepare for coming in of the regiment, and he also wanted Howard to give Merrill a "grave" to keep him from nagging the regiment. This latter, however, Howard would not do, as he thought he had already exceeded his right— but Miles did for Merrill what Howard declined, viz: sending him in charge of wounded to Lincoln. Sturgis was never very warm with me after the Canyon Creek affair.

* * *

So, after all the music, clamor of trumpets, made in coming up the Yellowstone, we went as quietly down as the conditions of our limping horses would permit; and froze and froze, awaiting the coming of the Cheyennes at Buford. I started out with one troop, but got the whole twelve troops back to Buford, and that must have been the "reserve."

Those were pretty rollicking gay days, old comrade; but I tell you in the matter of "dollars and cents" I suffered for my devotion to the clamor of the trumpet. I lost all of $100,000 by neglect of my property interests here during those years; but I've enough, and I don't regret a day I spent in the saddle.

Mathey knew, and I knew that Custer did, that I never fought Custer in any but the most open-handed manner; always going face to face for it.

* * *

I have been solicited time and again to write up reminiscences of the war, and of Indian campaigning; but I've written more to you tonight than I ever wrote before, and I think, too, more than I shall ever write again; for if there is anything I detest it is writing. * * *

January 6, 1892

Yours of the 31st informs me that Captain Godfrey has fired the train at last. Now I haven't seen the article, but shall do so tonight, but I know the facts to a demonstration, and when I read the article I can comment on the same with a thorough knowledge of what is correct or incorrect in the same, and so can you.

Current camp rumor or talk at the time was that Moylan, Godfrey and Gibson did far from well. I know what Gibson did—which was all I told him to do, which wasn't much; but having nothing to do with Moylan or Godfrey, I gave them no orders. At the same time, however, I did not fail to notice that they were pretty well protected from grave danger. How men of a command "tumble" to facts so speedily, you have been in a position to know far more of, and better, than I; but they do get them.

* * *

When I have read Godfrey's narrative—which for 15 years he has been longing to "spring" on N. America—I can tell you—well, not much more than you know—but what I think about his "cheek", if any of the same exhibits itself.

* * *

I expect Godfrey to say in his article that Reno recommended the abandonment of the wounded on the night of 25th, and of "skipping off" with those who could ride; well, so he did, to me, but I killed that proposition in the bud. The Court of Inquiry on Reno knew there was something kept back by me, but they didn't know how to dig it out by questioning, as I gave them no chance to do so; and Reno's attorney was "Posted" thereon.

January 16, 1892

A conundrum suggests itself to me, viz: If Lieut. Godfrey of 7th Cavalry could—and did— so much by himself in 1876, why was it that when sent from Cedar Creek, M. T. in spring of 1877, after hostile Indians that had robbed the U. S. mail—taken it in toto—that he did not pursue them at all, tho' they were in sight, almost?

* * *

Now as for facts as to the holding of the hill in 1876: I had posted French's troop on the ridge at right angles from the river, and told him to send his horses to the rear, but hold the point at all hazards until I could find a place to check the onset of the Indians. I designated the point also for Godfrey to hold. Well, French's command, by some means or other, "flunked" after my leaving there, seeing which I sent word to Godfrey to hold his vantage point, and everything would soon be "O. K." * * *

The searching for a good, very good place, was vain, and I had no such idea, but simply a place to form, where the river would, in a measure afford some protection for that flank, and to be as near it as possible for water, as I was impressed from my sight of the village that we had at least bitten off as much as we could readily chew, and that the chewing was bound to consume some considerable time. Godfrey was not far away, almost in hailing distance.

When I saw French "give way," and knowing that there had been no occasion for his so doing, I grabbed Lieut. Wallace, the first officer I saw, and said, "Wallace, put your troop here!" Wallace replied, "I have no troop—only two men." "Well, then, put yourself and your two men here (I designating the spot) and don't let any of them get away. I will look out for you." And so I went, gathering them in as they came, and had formed the line to the river bluffs nearly where I met Reno. Godfrey, somehow or other, if my remembrance is good, got down to his part of the line about as soon as anybody else. Godfrey, Moylan Mathey and Gibson all know (I am inclined to think) what was said of them then, and Godfrey, now that pretty nearly all of the old fellows have dropped out, intends to sound his horn a bit for the benefit of the bunch.

From the fact that Reno specified me so in his report of the battle, and leaving the balance with, "though they all did well," etc., it has stuck in the craw of everyone of them from that time till now.

Now, personally, Reno, I know, respected me, but I believe had no great regard for me, from the fact that I once slapped his face in the club room of a post trader's establishment before quite a crowd of officers, telling him * * * if I hadn't given him sufficient, that I would be pleased to do so; so therefore 'tisn't to be supposed he was at all dying with love for me that he made me a special mark in his report of the fight; and he certainly didn't consult me about the matter of report.

When midway of the line, or still closer even to bluffs of river than the center of line, I came across Major Reno, who seemed to have been forming a line to meet the one I was forming, though there had been no understanding of the kind between us relative to the matter. And that is how the line was formed.

Answer to query 3d: Reno's line did change position somewhat during the night, Capt. Moylan's troop being changed to left and rear of pack-mules, and facing up the river, and the other troops were "drawn in" somewhat to better positions; all of which I knew nothing of, having had nothing to do with such changes, and having quite sufficient to absorb my undivided attention in the trying position in which I had placed my own troop, which, my dear boy, had by far too much of Montana Territory to look out for; and per consequence, I insisted on Lieut. Gibson keeping me company in assisting to keep the men who were on post from falling asleep, and all the night through (and though I hadn't slept a wink for two nights before) did I, with Gibson, do this act, having to fairly kick the worn-out sleeping sentinels to their feet.

Mathey paid no attention to his pack-train on the hill until I gave him a square heel-and-toe "cussing out" in broad Saxon, which was when I returned to him two mules loaded with ammunition (4 boxes), which mules I had personally caught while they were hell-bent on getting to the blue water which was so plainly in sight. Answer to 3d query is this.

To 4th query, my answer is, yes, I am quite sure that the theory of Godfrey is absolutely correct as to the route Custer pursued and to the very point where the Indians consummated their "surround."

* * *

February 22, 1892

Sickness in the family and multitudinous rounds of duties combined, have thrown me out of all touch with my correspondents, but I trust that "Richard will soon be himself again," then I'll gladly make the comments on the screed sent to me by you. There are few if any changes however to be made in it, and as sent by you is near enough the whole true story.

I would prefer not being known in the matter at all, and this from the fact that the opportunity to make any speeches, were, first, when I made my official report of the part borne by my battalion up to time the battalion joined Reno's; and secondly, before the Court of Inquiry called for by Reno.

Had I not been quite ill when I made the first report alluded to above, I should have had more to say than I said in it; but as to queries before the Court of Inquiry, these I would answer now as I did then, and shield Reno quite as much as I then did; and this simply from the fact that there were a lot of harpies after him—* * *

———

February 24, 1892

I've been on a slight "jag," so am not in good trim for writing, but having a little leisure time now will give you a few comments on the "screed" sent by you to me some time ago.

From where the battalions were formed—the point from which I struck out at about a left oblique with my battalion of three troops, to the spot where Custer's body was found, is estimated by me to be fifteen (15) miles. Now if I had carried out to the letter the last order brought to me from General Custer by the Sergeant-Major of the regiment—which was, to the effect, that if from the furthest line of bluffs which we then saw, I could not see the valley—no particular valley specified—to keep on until I came to a valley (or perhaps *the* valley) to pitch into anything I might come across and notify them at once. Now I don't know how much farther I should have had to go in the direction I was headed to have found the valley of the Little Big Horn river, but think perhaps that six or seven miles more would have brought me to it. What I want you to deduce from this is: supposing I had found up that valley what Reno and Custer found lower down the river—how in the name of common sense was Gen'l Custer to get back to where I was in time to keep the troops from being chewed up as it were by the combined reds?

Now, isn't that the whole and sole reason that we were so badly beaten? i.e. the regiment being broken up into four columns, and none of the four within supporting distance of either of the others, (without any orders even to be such a support to any) true? In right obliquing back to the trail Custer and Reno had gone on, I overtook the pack train and Capt. McDougall's troop, but I didn't stop, and, as I am sure you will allow, got to Reno's assistance in the very nick of time. Tell me, please, was there any generalship displayed in so scattering the regiment that only the merest of chance, intervention of Providence—or what you will—saved the whole 12 troops from being "wiped out."

That is all that I blame Custer for—the scattering, as it were, (two portions of his command, anyway) to the—well, four winds, before he knew

anything about the exact or approximate position of the Indian village or the Indians. Now, don't forget the fact that when Custer descended from the mountain where Varnum and the scouts had passed the night of June 24th, he told the assembled officers that the scouts had told him that they could see the location of the village, ponies, some tepees etc., but that he didn't believe it, and that he looked through the field glass—a telescopic one I believe—belonging to the Indians (Custer had none), and he couldn't see anything, and didn't believe that the Indians could.

Well, right then and there, I, for one, did believe that the Indians had seen and could see all that they had told Custer of; however, I said nothing to anyone, but was convinced that we would see plenty of them before the night came, without the remotest idea though that there would be quite so many of them.

I see nothing in your screed to change, but if you want any special information, why, ask for it, and I'll give it, to the best of my knowledge and belief.

* * *

March 1, 1892

Yours of the 26th ult. I'll proceed to answer as if under oath.

To 1st inquiry: Yes, Nick Boyer*, the halfbreed interpreter and guide, certainly informed Gen'l Custer that he would find more Indians at the point where they had located them, than he, Custer, would care to "handle" with the force he then had; and 'tis just as true that Custer said, "he didn't believe there were any Indians at the point our scouts indicated."

As to the number of able-bodied Indians at the Little Big Horn fight, my belief is that there were eight or nine thousand—8,000 or 9,000—of them.

2d query: Ans. to—viz: "as to what was done when we advanced to pull Weir out of his hole."

I followed, with the remaining two troops of my battalion, the trail that Weir had "sallied on," he having no orders to proceed—some ten minutes later perhaps; anyway, just as soon as I learned of his insubordinate and unauthorized movements. While enroute to the highest point on the river bluffs in that vicinity, Major Reno kept his trumpeter pretty busily engaged in sounding the "Halt" for the purpose of bringing my command to a stand. However, I paid no heed whatever to the signal, but went to the highest point of bluffs, the battalion being in columns

———

*The half breed's name was "Mitch" Bouyer.

of fours. On arriving at elevation I then had my first glimpse of the Indian village from the height. Still I saw enough to cause me to think that perhaps this time we had bitten off quite as much as we would be able to well chew. Then I got the guidon of my own troop and jammed it down in a pile of stones which were on the high point, thinking perhaps the fluttering of same might attract attention from Custer's commands if any were in close proximity. Reno had then gotten up to the point where I was. However, I ordered French to put his troop in line on a bluff near, which was at right angles with the course of the river, and then for the purpose of showing where our command was, if there were any other bodies of our troops in sight.

Weir's troop then "showed up" midway in canyon, coming in hot haste toward us, and, as it seemed, myriads of howling red devils behind him. Of course I knew that Reno's retreat from the bottom had been a rout—a panic—and I made up my mind then and there that there was no necessity of having a repetition of same. So I ordered French to dismount his troop, keep his dismounted men on the bluff, send his led horses to rear, let Weir's troop through, then slowly fall back with his dismounted men, and I'd tell him more when I found it out myself. Well, French "weakened" (no doubt of it!) though he let Weir through; but ye gods! how he came, too! 'Twas then I ordered Godfrey to take position on the point he writes of.

I was intent, of course, on getting the best position we could possibly attain, though I felt the urgent pushing, prodding necessity that was causing the hasty backward movement; but arriving at the conclusion that forming a line couldn't be longer postponed, I grabbed Wallace, then 2d Lieut., saying, "Wallace, put your troop—the right of it—here, facing there." Wallace said, "I have no troop, only two men." "Then," said I, "put yourself and your two there, and don't let any of them get away. I'll look out for you."

That was the nucleus of the line—Wallace on the right, with his brave set of two men (hurrah for G!) I then gathered the procession in as it came, stringing it around an arc of a circle, as it were. Had Reno consulted me about his report, I should have requested him as a favor to eliminate the special reference to me in it; and this from the fact that I had little regard for his opinion in any manner, shape or form, and I had a sufficiency of commendation, proof already established, of what I had done with cavalry commanded by me on many fields during stirring war, to which the episode of 1876 was a mere

incident. However, as I've said, he didn't consult me, and the appearance of his report brought out the remark from Capt. Weir: "But he didn't mention me!" Others were in same category. Now, really, when a man quietly and serenely composed and all that, thinks of it, what could Reno have said of Weir, confining himself strictly to the truth, that would have been at all complimentary to him? If I had been forced to mention him, there would have been nothing special, other than he exhibited a very insubordinate spirit, which came very nearly bringing disaster on himself and troop.

In your reference to what Godfrey says about the charge made by Reno's line on the 26th— I went over to the line and persuaded him to consent to it—the charge. This was after I had driven the Indians from the ravine in my front; but I don't remember the "get back" part of it.

I am writing this in great haste from the fact that I haven't time now to scarcely think of it, but I really should like to hear the story told again from the standpoint of an enlisted man of "Ours." And I know of no one so capable of doing it as yourself, so give it to us. Spare no one! Not even the dead, as they, through their living friends, have assailed everyone who could not think with them, from President U. S. Grant down.

———

March 19, 1892

* * *

Well, I am rejoiced to learn that an account of the battle of the Little Big Horn, from the standpoint of an enlisted man, who was in the field, has been injected into the varied accounts of the same to the great American people; but, my boy, I think "the packs" will be after you. However, then, if you want my corroboration of your account, 'tis at your service. I am quite confident that your version of the affair will be the most correct that has ever yet been unfolded to the G.A.P. McDougall, (French, Weir dead) Mathey, Moylan, Godfrey, Gibson, Varnum, Edgerly, Hare —in fact, everyone, save Wallace, were—well rabidly incensed at Reno at not mentioning them by name in his official report of the battle, and they, in some measure, seemed to hold me responsible for such action on his part, when however, the fact is known that I was scarcely on good terms with Reno, and knew no more of what he intended reporting than you did, and cared as little, too! It can readily be seen that I was in complete ignorance of what he intended reporting to the Asst. Adj. Genl. Dept. Dakota; at any rate, too, I was really ill with a malarious dysentery. However, I was well enough, too, to tell Col. Weir before a dozen or so officers that he was a d——d liar, and this was occasioned by some remarks he made about Custer and Reno, and the fight at Little Big Horn, and occurred while we were in camp opposite mouth of the Big Horn river in August, '76, about the 4th or 6th. Col. Weir said that meant "blood." "Well," said I, "there are two pistols in my holsters on saddle (near him); take your choice of them; they are both loaded, and we will spill the blood right here!" The crowd went off, Weir with them, and the next time I met him he shoved out his hand to me to shake! Aha! I scarcely knew what to make of it, but at same time had his accurate measure. At the organization of 7th Cavalry, Weir had been my first lieutenant.

These old reminiscences are of no manner of interest to anyone, but I doubt if you ever heard of the one I have just given, ere this.

* * *

In conclusion, I shall be pleased to see your account in print. However it is the replies to same from which I expect the greatest source of amusement.

* * *

April 3, 1892

* * *

I have known General Miles since he transferred from the web-footed brunettes to the 5th Infantry, and to date; and I am of the opinion that you are not but a little way off in your diagnosis of the "build" of the man. * * *

Miles' idea was to make a winter campaign against the Sioux and settle a grudge he had against the Milk River half-breeds, expecting me to cooperate therein with him in true cavalry spirit; but you see, I knew the man, and knew his antecedents, too (only too well!) and we couldn't pull together worth a nick. So, when Gen. Terry floated down the muddy Missouri in a mackinac (finding us above the Musselshell) I deliberately knocked Miles' combination into pi, because I informed General Terry of what machinations he was "up to," and so we went Bufordwards instead of camping on the north side of the Missouri, perhaps near Fort Peck, for that winter. I feel that Miles bears me the grudge for that yet. However, I will compromise with him by not voting for him for President—no, not even for president of a football club! * * *

I will be pleased to see your (our) side of the "Narrative of the Big Horn Battle," and as soon as you can get copies of same, please be kind enough to send me at least two of them. I do not think there will be a necessity for "doubling teams" to "stand off" anything the disgruntled folks of the 7th may have to say about your history, but should it come to that, then count me with you. As to taking any kind of notice of what bereaved widows have to say, then I'm "not in it." The game isn't worth the candle.

* * *

July 6, 1894

I underscore to show you that after 19 years of waiting, the U. S. has showered upon me, drenched me with the Bvt. of Brig. Gen'l. for Little Big Horn and Canyon Creek. Same to Col. Merrill.

I thank you very much for having sent me the "Army Magazine" containing first installment of your Big Horn narrative. It is to be regretted that you have had to put it through such a simmering process as it has evidently undergone, for justice cannot be done to the subject in a few columns.

Should not "Sunset Peak," as it appears in June number, be Sentinel Buttes? as that is where we were in the '76 June snowstorm. That, however, is a trifle.

A Mr. Squiers, formerly of 1st U. S. Inf. and who was transferred from that regiment to the 7th Cavalry with Barry of '77 I think, has agreed to put up the l'argent to pay for the getting up of a superfine, double gilt-edge history of the 7th U. S. Cavalry, and per consequence I have been solicited to send a photo for the projected volume and a reminiscence of some of my years of service in the regiment.

I gave Bell, of '78, adjutant of the regiment— sec'y of com., a chit of some 11 pages of "cap," and this bore solely on the "Affair at the Washita," Nov. '68. Ten thousand to one, they don't dare to publish it! Custer was to be the frontispiece. I vote for putting Forsythe "Tony" there. * * *

BENTEEN, Bvt. Brig. Gen. U.S. Army.

_____

August 23, 1894

What's the matter with the Army Magazine's 2d chapter of the Little Big Horn?

I send you the prospectus of the forthcoming history of the 7th Horse, in which you "roughed it" for 6 years (see next page).

How should you like to write a "skit" of the fight at Canyon Creek, M.T. Sept. 13, 1877, and from our leaving Clark's Ford Canyon to the beginning and end of the fight?

I will insure its finding a place in the book under your name, but should like to revise it, as I kept a diary from 1861 to 1888. I don't think the story of that fight will be truly told by any officer who was in it, excepting one only. He is Capt. John C. Gresham, and 'twas his first fight, and he didn't know much then anyway. You will note on front that 7th heading is put in by me.

* * *

Send your photo in Col's "togs" if you write it.

___

HEADQUARTERS SEVENTH CAVALRY
Fort Riley, Kansas ——— 1894.

My dear Sir:

Mr. Herbert G. Squiers of N. Y. City, formerly an officer in this regiment, has made a proposition to its officers to publish at his own expense a handsome history to contain:

1. A history of the regiment from its organization to present time.
2. A sketch of the battle of the Washita.
3. Of the battle of the Little Big Horn.
4. Battle of Bear Paw Mountain.
5. Of Wounded Knee.
6. Short sketches of every officer who has ever belonged to and served with the Regiment, setting forth service with it as shown by the records. Each sketch to be accompanied by a portrait of its subject.
7. What General Merrill saw at Canyon Creek.*

The history will not be a mere recital of the official facts connected with the Regiment's yearly existence, but will be gotten up in a descriptive narrative style, with a view to its being readable by the general public.

The frontispiece of the book will be a portrait of Gen. Custer.** Remington will contribute a few sketches for the work, and Dr. Holmes will be requested to write the dedication.

Mr. Squiers purposes to present to each person whose sketch appears in the book with a copy. The remainder of the edition of about 250 copies to be presented to libraries or disposed of as he may see fit. At the request of Mr. Squiers a committee has been organized which is authorized to add members to itself and to solicit aid from all interested.

It is assumed that every person who has ever been an officer of the Seventh Cavalry will be as much interested in this history as Mr. Squiers or the committee, and the co-operation of all is therefore earnestly solicited in forwarding it to a completion. Mr. Squiers is particularly desirous that everyone should feel as free to offer suggestions and contribute aid as if financially interested in the undertaking. He desires it to be a monument to the regiment and purposes, if duly assisted, to produce a work in every respect worthy of its subject.

No difficulty is anticipated in gathering the necessary material except possibly as to producing pictures and facts pertinent to the history and antecedents of some of the members of the regiment in its early days; co-operation is especially asked in this regard.

Will you kindly forward to the secretary of the committee a photograph of yourself (preferably one taken in uniform while a member of the regiment), such a one as you would like used in the preparation of a portrait to accompany sketch of yourself. Should you already have sent a picture to the secretary of the Seventh Cavalry Mess. for the regimental album, will you be kind enough to state whether you desire to have it used for the portrait.

The Committee earnestly urges the freest correspondence and cooperation, not only in order to forward the work to a completion, but in order to manifest due appreciation of this very munificent generosity of a former comrade.

Very respectfully, THE COMMITTEE
Per. J. F. Bell, 1st Lieut. & Adj. 7th Cavalry
Secretary.

___

August 23, 1894

Yours of the 25th inst. rec'd, and I am somewhat inclined to think the committee in charge of preparation of sketches for "Squiers" 7th Cav. book is somewhat on the close corporation biz., but the hot-shot I threw in protesting against Custer's ugly phiz being shown in front of book, is having its effect, and I think the volume will come out without any frontispiece in shape of a portrait.

* * *

I can give you no idea as to the amount of space nor do I think I could get at what space would be given to the Canyon Creek fiasco. Never mind, though. If you can spare the time, fire away at it, simmering as much as you can, and send same to me, and I'll revise and return to you. I'll get her in or know the reason why, thru Tony Forsyth, but I want "Togs" complete, too, let up on modesty. I want to see the rank and file represented.

___

October 11, 1894

* * *

Rather wondered why you hadn't received copies of the Army Magazine. It is one of the magazines that cannot be purchased here, and the only way I know of seeing a copy would be by going to Fort McPherson, and then most likely only thru one of the army and navy unions, and I haven't had the time to prosecute that.

I haven't had the gall to send "ours" anything as yet on the Canyon Creek—what shall I call it—fiasco? Waiting, rather, the report of Supervising Board on my first "chick of the Washita," then, if they are seeking history sure enough why, 'tisn't a bit of trouble for me to sling it at them; but I'm going to squeal if there's any garbling done. At the Washita we lost Major Elliott, Sergt. Maj. Kennedy—a fine young soldier, and 16 enlisted men, and damme if any search was made for them till a fortnight after. Now, as ever, I want to get at who was to blame for not finding it out

___

* No. 7 apparently added by Benteen, W. A. G.
** Benteen added here: "This is in doubt."

then? 'Tisn't really worth while to know now, but I am not ready to subscribe to any effort of the public's opinion to convince me that Custer was a great man or great warrior; au contraire, he was quite ordinary.

* * *

When I see your second article I will know exactly whether you said too much or too little. Without having seen it, I will wager 'twas too little.

October 19, 1894

I have just rec'd, and have twice gone over your continuation of Little Big Horn story in double number of Army Magazine, and I cannot for the life of me, see how anyone can take exception to your recollections of that affair.

I think Godfrey has endeavored to make more out of it for himself than impartial history from onlookers could grant him, though had I anything to say in the matter, I should have recommended for brevets, first, Hare, then Varnum, and lastly, Godfrey; yes, Wallace, too, before Hare, then I think I should have stopped. Reno brought the wrath of the regiment on me—commissioned officer part, on account of special mention. Well, Lord knows I couldn't help that, and up to the time my battalion joined Reno of course nothing had been done for which to mention anybody. Thus I couldn't do it, and from fact of not being on best of terms with Reno, I rarely ever went near him unless sent for, and then at no time was my opinion called for on any subject. I do not see one thing to be altered in your statement, and I am of the opinion that perhaps that is the last that will be heard from the Little Big Horn.

Charlie King may have talked with some of those would-be B. H. heroes, but by the gods of war, we were there, and know just what we saw.

Had Godfrey wanted to show the mettle of which he was made, he had from (one?) Sunday on Cedar Creek in 1877 a fine opportunity so to do it; but he hadn't lost any Indians then, and didn't look for them when sent to do it! Later on, same year he got plugged by Nez Perces, but that was an illy-managed affair. I haven't heard a word from anyone concerning your article, although I correspond pretty regularly with Lieut. Bell, Adjt. 7th Cav., and it cannot be that at Riley your comments haven't figured among them. Other than to get notes into shape I have done nothing on the Canyon Creek affair, than which I can recall no more thoroughly disgusting campaign, though on few other trips have I ever had such a wonderful lot of amusement in fishing, hunting and the like.

For instance, when we changed camp at mouth of Musselshell River on the Missouri, who will ever see again the same number of antelope together at any one time again that we saw and killed during that change of camp?

* * *

A man with one eye—if he is at all a thoughtful fellow—can see a good many things in the army in even five years, can't he? It seems to me that all of them "soldier for revenue" simply now.

September 14, 1895
* * *

I don't think Hare would have had any ill feelings about anything you might have said about Godfrey, for Hare was essentially a cavalryman, and G.—well, he was anything but!

Hare should have been breveted for L. B. Horn, and would have been had I any say about it. Bell was breveted Lieut. Col. for Canyon Creek. Sam D. Sturgis should have been tried by G.C.M. for the Clark's Ford Canyon idiocy. I labored the best part of the night we moved from there to get him to go where we knew Fuller had seen the Indian camp, but I couldn't phase him. Merrill was "working" him then, and from Aug. 10, '61, I knew neither of them would fight. They had never lost a Reb or an Indian!

* * *

(This letter deals with Nez Perces and Civil War memories. W. A. G.)

January 11, 1896

Well, there's no denying that it warms the cockles of one's old heart to know and have told to him by one of the formulaters of history who was on the spot, that my actions were such as Uncle Sam expects from all of his employees.

As I didn't know you, of course I didn't know that you knew anything about my fishing rod, but she was a daisy, and I wanted to put it to use that night in the Yellowstone, but I didn't, as I need not remark. Of course you didn't know how cussedly mad I was when I saluted those Nez Perces.

You see, we had quite a lot of daylight left, and had two of Howard's mountain howitzers with us that had gone thru the gap, and were not quite up. Well, I wanted to put 20 or 30 shells thru the woods where those N.P.'s. shot at us, but the most peremptory orders came from Sturgis to hustle back to him with all the haste possible—which order was followed up with another to same effect. Therefore I had to leave our red friends with due form.

I wanted to get some more practice with those little bull pups, because in 1862 I was an expert with them and at Pea Ridge, Ark., March 7th, when the Rebs had broken E. A. Carr's brigade, I withstood three separate charges of McIntosh's Indian brigade on my four-gun battery of mountain howitzers, gave Carr time to form in rear; pulled my "little pups" out by hand, and saved the evening at "Elk Horn" and lost no gun. With double-shotted canister I staggered them.

Now, my dear Colonel G. if you think I'm giving you anything of the fairy-tale order, just look, when you get a chance, at the Vol. XII, Series 1, Part 1, Reports Price's Missouri Expedition etc. "Rebellion Records," July 1st to Dec. 31, 1864, Serial No. 83.

At the close of that expedition, Major Gen. Blunt was commanding the 1st Division of Cavalry, and Lieut. Col. F.W.B. the 2d Division of Cavalry which comprised all of Gen. Sam. B. Curtis' Army, Army of the Frontier, which was cavalry wholly.

Doubtless you can find the same (Vol.) without much trouble in your city. Any retired officer or active officer above grade of Captain will have it.

Those were the days, Colonel! You'll see that I didn't have to form the acquaintance of Custer to know something about fighting cavalry—and as to Indians—I fought against them in 1863 and 1864 long before he ever had a whack at them. I know that Custer had respect for me, for at the Washita in 1868, I taught him to have it.

I had received the Jan. copy of Military Service Inst. the day before I received your letter. Colonel Hughes evidently had more in reserve than he paraded at that review. "Tony" Forsythe was the officer on Sheridan's staff who met Custer at R. R. Station in Chicago, and Tony told me that "he put him in arrest" (a fact which Hughes knew but didn't tell.) * * *

In the 1864 Price raid in Mo. Col. Lewis Merrill might have been commanding the 2d division of Curtis' cavalry (not Custer's), but, Colonel Goldin, he preferred the flesh pots of St. Louis, and I don't know but he was correct. I got the glory, he the stewed terrapin. Don't know but in the long run, terrapin and Madeira is the first choice, and you can see from this that Sturgis and Merrill were old compadres of mine, and I knew their full value in 1861.

* * *

January 19, 1896

* * *

Varnum, of 7th, after poor Aspinwall's downfall, came to me one day when I was on a visit to Lincoln to have me sign an application to have Fred Calhoun appointed Lieut. in 7th in "Jack's" place. "No, no," I said to Varnum, "this is premature. Aspinwall, by the statutes is allowed 3 months to "show up," and in any event, Varnum, don't you think that we have quite a genteel sufficiency of that clique at present in the Regiment?"

Of course this decision of mine was soon known at Custer and Calhoun houses, and such decision kept others from signing. At all events, Calhoun didn't get appointed in 7th, but did in 14th Infty., where he got his first lieutenancy, and soon afterwards was retired (A something I look on as a kind of swindling of the Govnt). How does it strike you?

On our trip of '73, with Stanley, Custer got Rosser to give Fred Calhoun a job which necessitated Calhoun's being mounted. "H" Troop was short of horses. Custer had a clay-bank horse for which I was responsible and which I had assiduously endeavored to have returned to troop, but without avail.

Lieutenant Ray, commissary of expedition, from lack of horse, had to content himself with riding a poor mule from his train, so Ray said to me one day, "Benteen, can you not do better for me than this?" "Yes, I think I can," I said, "now I have fourteen dismounted men in troop, but you see that claybank? Well, I'm responsible to U. S. for him, and cannot get him. Custer gives him to that young man to ride, and now he is employed by Gen. Rosser for the N. P. Get the horse if you can."

The correspondence about that horse got Custer in arrest. Stanley got drunk, so the game was thrown into Custer's hand, and thus he "got away with Stanley." Of course the Calhouns never had any use for me; I was not pliable enough.

* * *

Lord, Colonel! We have known for lo, these many years that Custer disobeyed orders, and had not Col. Hughes been the bro.-in-law of Gen. Terry, it is one hundred to one odds that history would never have gotten at the bed-rock facts.

* * *

I owe you many thanks for your complimentary thoughts of me. See the Reb. records I referred you to, and I hope you'll find that my cavalry breast was exposed to the storm for 4 years, 4 mos. and 22 days to help bring my deluded Southern brothers back into the fold.

January 24, 1896

* * *

I plainly told X to divest himself of the idea that there was one or any concealed points concerning the Little Big Horn. If there was one, I didn't know it, and had there been one I should certainly have known it.

As to Custer having been a Michigander, why, that's pure rot. He went to West Point from Ohio, and from the M. A. to the war.

He commanded a Michigan brigade, and had it afterwards in his division, and his father had removed to Michigan. That's all; other than Gen. Custer married Miss Bacon of Monroe.

* * *

January 31, 1896

* * *

I didn't know the men of the regiment had such an aversion to Mylie Moylan, but my! how correct they were in so having!

On 25th June, 1876, when my battalion got to crest of hill where Reno took refuge from his "charge" from bottom, the first thing which attracted my attention was the gallantly-mustached captain of Troop "A" blubbering like a whipped urchin, tears coursing down his cheeks.

Now, I knew he hadn't much of what we call in the South "raising," but I had accredited him in my mind with having some nerve, though I had never seen him in a position before to display it; but as sure as you are born, the bottom tumbled out—and all the nerve with it, before he reached the crest of the hill.

* * *

February 5, 1896

* * *

When I accepted a captaincy in the 7th Cavalry I had no idea whatever of remaining permanently, but was taken to it from the fact that the Indians seemed to have things pretty nearly their own way, and I knew that cavalry, well handled, should more than "stand them off," which wasn't then being done.

Well, I have never heard of anyone accounting for the fact how the profession of arms grows on one, but it certainly does, so I stuck; but it was at pecuniary loss to me at the time. (not complete)

* * *

February 10, 1896

Your announcement of the death of Gen. Gibbon came at time of receipt of A. & N. Register, but I learned it first from your letter.

I knew Gen. Gibbon well, and I suppose he was attached to me somewhat from the fact that my cousin, Gen. Ed. S. Bragg, succeeded to the command of the famed "Iron Brigade" of Wisconsin.

Gen. Gibbon was not only a brave and faithful soldier, but he was far, far better than that. He was an honest and conscientious man, which often brought him in conflict with the staff of the army who notoriously attempted when opportunities offered, the government of the whole; and this Gibbon wouldn't stand in silence—a fact which affected his promotion very seriously, all of which he knew.

Peace to his ashes! The U. S. has need for millions of such men.

* * *

If those defenders of Custer's fame only knew what I know of that man (and not only I know, but can prove), they would be willing to let him rest with the grand aura around him which the public now recognizes, and I know not of anyone who cares to attempt to dispel the ignis fatuus.

Col. Hughes let him down very easily. I would, I think have been scarcely so considerate.

Having been sent off from the command some 15 or more miles from Custer's field, and leaving the whole command dismounted (?), no other disposition of any part of it having been determined upon by Custer, how could McDougall's rear guard become part of my battalion? After getting with Reno, not that I didn't feel free to act in opposition to Reno's wishes, and did so act, but then, what more could be done than we did do?

Like ostriches, we might have stuck our necks in the sand, only that Custer had galloped away from his reinforcements, and so lost himself.

* * *

February 12, 1896

At the risk of tiring, and perhaps disgusting you, I have come to the conclusion of giving you a dissertation on the Seventh Cavalry from the time I joined it in winter of '66 and '67, to death of Gen. Custer.

I think someone in the Great West should have a just opinion of that man, and therefore I give my unbiased views of his character, which you can take as if they were sworn to on a stack of Bibles.

I had never seen Custer before joining at Fort Riley in '66.

At my first formal call at his private quarters, he paraded his orders and books of the old Cav. Div. in the Cav. Corps, as if endeavoring to impress me with the magnitude and eminent success of his operations in it.

I remember his orders shown me said, "No gun has ever been pointed at that Division but what they captured it," etc., etc.

Well, the impression made on me at that interview was not a favorable one. I had been on intimate personal relations with many great generals, and had heard of no such bragging as was stuffed into me on that night.

Col. A. J. Smith, a general who had done far greater work than Custer ever thought of, was the Col. of Regt. and stationed at Riley at the time, commanding the 7th Cavalry and the District of the Upper Arkansas, including Ter. of New Mexico; Custer comdg. post of Fort Riley, Kans.

Gen. Smith, with whom I had served, knew a good deal of my record, and Capt. Noyes, now Lieut. Col. of Cav. was Smith's A.A.A.G., and having been an A.D.C. to Cavalry Wilson in our raid through Ala. and Ga. in '63, so I wasn't at the Post quite an orphan and unknown, but with people who knew what I had done with a cavalry regiment and a division of Cavalry regiments, when war was red hot.

My 2d appearance at Gen. Custer's house was by invitation, given after tattoo roll-call, "to come and play dime ante poker." The result of that "call" and game was that I won every cent of money at the board, and Weir, who was my first lieut. at the time, insisted on giving me his "I.O.U." for $150. * * *

From 10¢ ante the game was, at Custer's request, in which Weir acquiesced, swelled to $2.50 ante, which, with "no limits" is apt to make a pretty steep game, and it was, many having to go up, no "cuff" went. The "swell" of ante sent two of the players out of the game, they not having any money.

At dime ante one can play the game and have some friendship for another player, but at $2.50 ante—well, all "friendship" has got to cease, or one is apt to find himself pretty well begrimed, and a long way from water quite early in the game; so I went for those Heathen Chinee! Being officer of the day, I had to quit at Reveille, and that broke it up. * * *

I started in with my troop to make friends and soldiers of them. I would treat them like men, and everybody else had to; so they got to love me. The four troops at Riley left that post under Custer on the 27th March, 1867, the same day

and year my son Fred was born on my farm in Georgia.

Gen. W. S. Hancock, Comdg. Dept. of Mo. went in command of the expedition in the field. From him, Custer performed his first "cutting loose" act. Hancock didn't relish it, and "rounded him up" at old Fort Hays, Ks. At this point, Custer began his first exploitation with * * * the post sutler.

We had captured the empty village of Roman Nose on the Pawnee Fork of the Arkansas, Hancock present, and in command some days before. Our pursuit of Indians took us via old Fort Hays. The "hard-tack" left over from the war—and bacon too, perhaps—wasn't of the best, and men were tired and hungry. Gen. Custer camped within a base-ball throw of the flagstaff of the post.

What, if any, inducements were held out at this camp to the post sutler, I don't know. This, I know: a cordon of sentries were put around the camp of battln. of 7th Cav. and orders were issued "that no enlisted men would be allowed to visit the post without a written order," which appl. must be sent in with Morning Report Book, and was to be signed by the Adjt. of Battln.

Just at this time I was summoned to return to Fort Riley to take with me five enlisted men of my troop to report as witnesses in the case of a deserter from my troop to the Judge Advo. of the G.C.M.

On return to old Fort Hays with my party of five, Custer had gone toward the Union Pacific R.R., my troop going under command of First Lieut. "Tom" Custer. I was held back with party until news from Custer was gotten, then I was to take a four-gun battery of Gatling guns to the regiment, which I did, joining at Fort Wallace, Kans.

From this point, Custer having received an anonymous letter via the U.P.R.R. that he'd better hustle back * * * did so, I meeting him one day's march before getting to Wallace. Custer had 50 picked men (and picked horses also) as escort. Capt. Hamilton, 1st Lieut. Tom Custer and Lieut. Cooke being along.

On arrival at Fort Wallace next day I received a great awakening. At Old Fort Hays, two of the men of my troop, one of them troop farrier, other just off guard, either or both of which could perhaps have obtained passes by asking, but who had "Frenched it" in preference, were, with many others, arrested at the post for being without passes.

The gang of prisoners were marched thro' company streets, preceded by trumpets sounding the "Rogue's March;" their heads were then shaved, and the poor devils were "spread-eagled" on the plain until they cried "Peccavi." Now my immediate interests were in only two of those men, so I took down their affidavits, the affidavits of responsible witnesses, on which I based my report to Dept. Hdqtrs.

I will say here that on leaving the post of old Fort Hays, Major W. C. being some days from post, and out of whiskey, shot himself—suicide—because the d——d fool Dr. * * * acting under orders from Custer, wouldn't give him even a drink of whiskey to "straighten out" on. C. was 2d Major of Regt. and a most gallant soldier during the war, Col. of a Ky. Cav. Regt. This occurred when I was on G.C.M. duty.

The other awakenings I got on arrival at Wallace were, that on arrival at Fort McPherson, the same orders issued at Hays were carried out. Men of the command arrested were soused in the Platte River, a lariat having been tied to their legs, and this repeated till they were nearly drowned.

Next, and worst of all, the dismounted deserters that were soon on the march from McPherson, and who were shot down while begging for their lives, by Major Joel H. Elliott (2d Major of Regt. vice Cooper), Bvt. Lieut. Col. Tom Custer and Bvt. Lieut. Col. W. W. Cooke (executioner-in-chief). One of the deserters was brought in badly wounded, and in extreme agony from riding in wagon (over the Plains without a road), screamed in his anguish. Gen. Custer in passing by, rode up to the wagon, and, pistol in hand, told the soldier "that if he didn't cease making so much fuss he would shoot him to death!" How's that for high? Now these things are gospel truth! On the arrival of Custer and his 50 picked men and horses at Fort Harker, Kansas, Custer was, by order of Major-Gen. W. S. Hancock, placed in arrest, and the party were ordered back to regiment.

Custer, after leaving me one day's march from Wallace, kept on toward Hays, but at Ellis Springs, a stage station, it was reported to him that a man belonging to him had escaped, so a party of 10 men and non-com. were sent to catch him. They did so, but were jumped by Indians, some being killed, and one man of my troop badly wounded, but who saved his life by tumbling from his horse in a huge buffalo wallow. The Indians seeing the horse going off to command with others, didn't notice that it had no rider on it.

So, Capt. Carpenter of 17th Inf. Comdg. Co. at stage station, was requested by Gen. Custer to send out and scoop in his wounded debris, bury dead, etc., as he, Custer, hadn't the time to stop. Carpenter made a report to Dept. Hdqtrs. by telegraph, which report preceded mine by mail, and

Custer was arrested, tried and dismissed, which sentence was commuted to suspension from rank and pay for 12 months by Gen. Grant, or Pres. Johnson I believe it then was. *(See note at end of letter).

At all events, we were free of Custer till autumn of 1868, then by verbal recommendation made by J. Schuyler Crosby, A.A.A.G. for Sheridan, who came to me from that General, offering (offered?) me the command of the 7th Cavalry in the field. Major Elliott and Capt. Wm. Thompson, who were my seniors, were to be given leaves of absence.

I politely but firmly declined the compliment of being so selected, recommending to Col. Crosby that Sheridan secure the remission of unexpired portion of Custer's sentence, and let him join command, saying that perhaps he would have, and exhibit, more sense and judgment than he had during his former short tour in command. So Custer came!

At the battle of the Washita my Fort Harker squadron broke up the village before a trooper of any of the other companies of 7th got in, and we protected the fifty-five squaws and children we captured. 1st Sergt. Duane of M. Troop, 2 privates, "California Joe" and myself surrounded and drove in the ponies that were killed on that field by Custer—some 800. Custer, in his "Life on the Plains" gives Calif. Joe the credit; but as surely as there's a sun, I conceived, and we carried it out, and Custer knew it. I turned the herd over to Col. West, who had his squadron intact, and was en-route to find something. Godfrey was 2d Lieut. of K, West's troop, at that time.

Elliott, like myself, was "piratting" on his own hook; allowed himself to be surrounded and died like a man. Elliott was a captain in a brigade I commanded during the war. Elliott and West, the latter being a Div. Comdr. under Butler and Kautz (pro tem) and was a distinguished man, but given at times to hellish periodical sprees. These two had, in underhand ways been "peppering" Custer, thinking he was not aware of it, but he was. Elliott being out of the way, and upon arrival at the present site of Fort Sill, Okla., West, feeling that Custer would catch and salt him away surely, at same time succeeded in getting promise from Sheridan—who was with us—of the sutlership of the new post of Sill. He got it. Officers of Regt. Hall, whom it promoted Captain, and all the juniors, chipped in a "pot" for West and everybody signed an application that West be allowed to go around with regiment in the field as Trader. When such application was presented to Custer, he declined signing, saying, though, that he would do so soon.

However, West learned differently, but went on East to purchase goods, did so purchase and brought them to camp of 7th Cav. before his experience was available. The difference there was that he had written to old "Pop" Price sutler at Fort Leavenworth, who was at camp, and informed him that Custer had tendered the appointment to him, and that he was there to buy him out—which he did. On arrival at Camp Supply from site of Sill, via El Llano Estacado, in spring of 1869, we (the regt.) met Major Smith, paymaster U.S.A. waiting for us at Supply, having been ordered to do so by Dept. Comdr. At Fort Meade, Dakota, in winter of '81 and '82, I met the bookkeeper of the firm who were sutlers at Supply in the spring of '69. He was then cashier of First Nat'l Bank of Deadwood, but suffering with sciatica; was the guest of Lieut. Garlington at Meade, and I frequently went to see him to cheer him up.

He said one time to me: "Benteen, do you remember when the regiment was at Camp Supply in spring of 1869 that Major Smith, P.M. had been sent there to pay off regiment, and had been ordered to await the arrival of it there." "Yes," said I "of course." "Well, then, you remember that the regiment was not paid, and that it was taken off at daylight the day after arrival?" "Yes, of course." "Well, do you have any idea of the cause of this?" "Not the slightest," said I.

"Then I'll tell you," said Thumb. "Custer issued his regular pronunciamento on arrival of regt. at Supply, this time the lines being more rigidly drawn, to the effect that neither commissioned officers, non-coms. or privates could visit the post without written orders from Custer. Why was this? A stone's throw from the post?" "Give it up," said I.

"Well, an officer of the 7th Cav. presented himself to Tappan (the trader) saying he came from Gen. Custer, and that if the firm would give Custer $3,500 for which Custer would give them a bill of sale for an (U.S.) ambulance, 4 mules and horses, he would then keep the regiment there for payment, otherwise he'd march the regiment off at daylight, take the paymaster with him and pay off at Fort Hays. Tappan and Weichelbaum wouldn't agree to it, so the 7th marched."

"Now," said Thumb to me, "can you guess the name of the officer bringing the proposal?" "Well, if it wasn't Tom Custer, Cooke or 'Fresh' Smith, I'll have to give it up." "No, to save you trouble, 'twas First Lieut. Wallingford," (who, by the by, had been dismissed from the regiment and had died in the Kansas State Penitentiary, serving sentence for horse-stealing.)

Now, Col. Goldin, this was the first inkling I had as to the cause of the issuing of those orders on arrival at the different posts. 'Tis quite apparent now that we know!

We will skip over now that we are skipping so much, to the time when "Salt" Smith, his Regt. Qr. Mr. lost so many U. S. Gov. Qr. Mr. checks to the "Custer gang" in playing draw poker, in which game Lieut. Aspinwall, just making his advent in the regiment, autumn of 1869, thought perhaps as it seemed so very easy, to see what he could do at pulling in $300 or $400 at a whack with a pair of deuces. "Salt" Smith deserted at once.

The end was, the "Custer Gang" skinned him, and I'm told Jack's poor old father squared up some $1600 in debts to those damned cormorants! Oh, if I only could have known of it and seen him before he did it—but I wasn't there, but was in Colorado.

From this time on, I had never seen Aspinwall play cards, and was the unwitting instrument of putting temptation in his way, and this from fact of being in command of post of Fort Rice, and having the highest opinion of his honor and integrity, made him by appointment Asst. Commy. of Subsistence of the post.

Being "snow'd up" a greater portion of the winter left large amounts of money in his safe. On all of the inspections this money was there, all correct. When Major Tilford relieved me of command I'm inclined to think he might have been neglectful of his duties in that respect, and so the sutler store employes got all the money wasted by poor Jack.

* * *

I'll skip now to 1873: At Memphis, Tenn., Baliran was the proprietor of a restaurant and gaming establishment, doing a good business, and a gambler by profession. Having some money, Custer induced him to come with 7th Cav. as Sutler telling him the officers of the regiment were high players, and he could make a big thing, "catch them going and coming." Baliran told all this to DeRudio on '73 trip, and DeRudio told me Custer had put in 0, but had drawn out to that time $1,100. A few weeks thereafter Baliran and old Vet. Honsinger were killed. What became of the effects of the firm I never heard.

I know that third day out from Rice, that Col. Fred Grant informed Custer that on next day a search of the whole train was to be made; train halted enroute, for whiskey. Baliran's whiskies and wines were put in 7th Cav. troop wagons, and Baliran's wagons carried grain belonging to same troops. Ketchum & Ray, A.C. & C.S. for Stanley, evidently did not inform Fred Grant of the fact that they were going to swoop down on the store in camp of 7th, or they might have been again spirited away; but with the earliest dawn, the two members of Stanley's staff came, axes in hand, and spilt the good red liquor on the dry alkaline soil of Montana at the "Stockade" camp.

Grant, Gibson, Weston and myself had procured a quart about one-half hour before destruction. We were owling! * * * In 1874 Custer was in partnership with John Smith through the Black Hills picnic. As I have this from the original J. S. he ought to know. In 1873 Custer didn't leave Lincoln; in 1876 he did, but he didn't have any opportunity to speak of to organize the sutler dept. of his campaign.

* * *

Note:
Benteen is in error as to Custer's court-martial sentence. He was not dismissed, but suspended from rank, pay and command for one year. The sentence was not commuted, but a portion was remitted at the request of Gen. Sheridan, who needed Custer's service against hostile Indians. Benteen's revelations concerning Custer's sutler "partnerships" seem incredible if not impossible.

W.A.G.

St. Valentine Day, 1896
I omitted saying, in the long scrawl sent you lately, that it was my purpose to exhibit to you what course led to the very, very frequent desertions from 7th Cav. from '67 to '69, at which time Col. Sturgis relieved Custer from command of the regiment.

Those men of my troop who were punished for going to old Fort Hays '67 (a baseball's throw from camp) were wholly sober, having purchased nothing but fresh bread from post bakery, and some canned fruits from sutler, having these in their hands at the time of arrest. This evidently was their offense, only ascertained too late, to make mention of at the proper time.

When Sturgis arrived at camp of 7th below New Fort Hays, in summer of '69, Gen. Custer had a hole deeply dug in ground about 30x30 square feet, about 15 feet deep, entrance by ladder, hole boarded over. This was the guard-house, and a man even absent from a "call" was let down. I don't know how the prisoners laid down. It had been discontinued before I joined at that camp by Gen. Sturgis.

* * *

A fact which you may not be aware of is: there were many officers in the 7th who wouldn't have believed Gen. Custer on oath! Of course,

being in a regiment like that, I had far too much pride to permit Custer's outfit driving me from it, the more particularly as I had taken the initiative to have Gen. Custer disciplined accordingly with Army Regulations, which was done. The suspension of arrest, however, and return to duty, was a mistake, as it made him worse instead of better.

* * *

Gen. Sturgis served in Texas as Lieut.-Col. 6th Cav. under Custer commdg. Cav. Division—after war. When Custer was mustered out of Vols. as Major General, Sturgis remained in Texas. He found the contracts let by Custer for grain, hay, &c., &c., stupendous frauds. Sturgis notified the authorities; the contracts were annulled, and when Sturgis joined the 7th Cavalry he brought all the papers connected with that affair with him, and two weeks after I joined the Regt. under Sturgis at Fort Hays, Sturgis showed me all of the documents, as Custer had commenced war on him through his minions (not showing his own hand then, however). Sturgis knew all about it.

* * *

February 17, 1896
I am pleased to know that I haven't disgusted you in the relation of what I know of Custer's character. Moylan is the only living party that can know of what concerns Custer that I've been giving you in details, and it is presumable that he'd never tell. Neither Mrs. Custer or Mrs. Calhoun or Fred C. know anything about those things, and others who might have known are all dead.

I intend giving you a few more details * * * and not in one word that I extenuate, nor aught set down in malice, because I had and have none, and showed him through all the history of the Seventh Cavalry that I was amply capable of taking care of myself, and never did I attack him in any but a soldierly manner and through military channels.

* * *

In October, 1868, immediately after his suspension was remitted, and he had joined the regiment, which was then in Bluff Creek, Ind. Ter., Custer cast around for some officer to send to Fort Harker, Kans. after 300 horses and 200 recruits there for the 7th Cav. I was selected, and with one orderly I was to go (overland, of course) 180 miles, through a country fairly alive with hostile Indians.

This didn't daunt me a particle, for I knew every mile of the district, and I knew my orderly, who, by the way, was a brother Virginian, had the fullest confidence in my plains skill. Funny, wasn't it? This private of my troop was a major of artillery in the Confederate Army, and born and raised a few miles from my native town, Petersburg, Va. Of course he was under an assumed name in the U. S. Army.

Before starting, which I did at night, Custer sent for me and solicited when I arrived at Harker, to be kind enough to send to his wife (Mrs. E. B. Custer) one hundred dollars (100) at Fort Leavenworth, Kans. I then began to see why I had been selected! It was known that I always had plenty of money in the regiment. I got to Harker O. K. First duty performed was to send to Mrs. Custer my check on First Nat'l Bank of Leavenworth for $100.

2d Lieut. Volkmar, 5th Cav., now Lieut.-Col. and Deputy Adjt. Gen. U. S. Army, was the youth, (Kid) "Johnny" came later, who had the recruits in charge. I gathered them in, took Volkmar and one of his classmates along, his classmate's bride of few weeks, too, which portion of outfit went to 3d U. S. Inf. Fort Dodge.

We arrived at Fort Larned. A Mexican train loaded with arms and ammunition was to be ordered to report to me, but by some means did not do so, and I knew nothing about it. The train pulled out some hour or so ahead of my outfit from Larned, and some mile or so from Big Coon Creek, I came in sight of the train watering the animals at pond of water (surface water) a short piece from roadside. I knew this was done on account of the terrible alkalinity of Coon Creek water; so on arrival of my dtchment. I watered all stock at ponds.

Just as we had straightened out for the march I saw that the train ahead was attacked, surrounded by Indians, pouring the bullets into it, circling around the while. I took the leading platoon, telling Volkmar to bring up the 2d and 3d platoons which were on right and left flanks of my train, and off I pitched into the Indians with my one platoon, scattering them, and saving the life of the wagonmaster who had gone out some little distance to procure a good camp ground for the night. When Volkmar got up, I had the red scamps run off. They broke for the Arkansas River, crossed, and 'twas worse than useless to pursue. However, "the mills of the gods ground exceeding fine," for them, for 'twas this very party that by its trail through the snow, led us to the village of Black Kettle on the Washita.

I reached camp of the 7th, then Camp Sandy Forsyth, and on the Arkansas River, 10 miles below Fort Dodge, in fine fettle, my recruits having been in their first baptism of fire. When I reached camp I learned that my fine mount of horses that Gen. Sheridan told me in August same year, "was the finest mount he ever saw a troop of cavalry have," had been distributed around promiscuously to other troops. In fact, the troops of the regiment had been "colored" in the field at the beginning of the severest campaign that ever cavalry underwent. Fine bays and brown horses taken—other bays given in place. And all this going on with my first Lieut. W. W. Cooke, looking on, permitting—or at least acquiescing—in it. My $100 and horses went about the same time.

Well, this was in October, 1868. In November, 1869, Custer was to march the battalion that went to Fort Leavenworth to winter at that point. I drove my wife and son out to see the regiment start from camp, standing at the head of horses to keep them from scaring at the band in its passing. Custer rode up, shook hands with, and told Mrs. B. goodby, but to me said never a word about refunding (or even spoke of) the borrowed $100 * * *.

In the winter of '69 and '70, I learned from an army officer just up from Leavenworth, that Custer had made a haul at Jenison's faro bank. I wrote him that if he had the money convenient it was high time the debt was paid, telling him it was $91—nine dollars having been absorbed in "calling him" for small amts. when I knew he had the winning hand, and save putting up cash to his pile to ascertain facts. He replied immediately to my dun, sending his check for $92, which he said was his account of it. Now, as one dollar would scarcely be living interest on a hundred doll. for fourteen months and over, and as I was not a Shylock, lending money at interest anyway, I coolly returned on same day a one dollar bill, thanking him for his promptitude in discharging the debt!

* * *

1871—at Louisville, he, Tom Custer and Cooke, Adjt. came to train to endeavor to persuade me to choose going to South Carolina instead of taking Nashville as a station, Custer saying, "J. B. Fry, then A. Genl. for Halleck comdg. Dept. had informed him that the troop going to Nashville would only be there a short time. * * * I told him I'd go up and see Gen. Sturgis, Comdg. Regt. about the matter. Custer remarked to Mrs. Benteen, "that anything he recommended to me

I was pretty sure to choose the exact opposite."
His "guff" imposed on Mrs. B. and she thought
and said I was dead wrong, but she wasn't the
poker player I was * * *. I saw Gen. Sturgis.
His remark was: * * *. "There isn't a word
of truth in it. Custer is trying to keep French's
troop, in which his brother Tom is 1st Lieut.,
from going to South Carolina." But Tom had
to take S. C. in his!

On return of the regiment from Washita—
El Llano Estacado—campaign of 1868—69, and
on arrival at our sub-depot of supplies on the
Washita River, Custer found in the Missouri
Democrat a letter criticising his management of
the battle of the Washita.

Custer had gone ahead with band—one troop
of Regt. taking the "Sharp-shooters" under Lieut.
Cooke, Moylan, Tom Custer, &c. I was to bring
in the remnant of the starved command.

I was about frozen when I dismounted, so
not caring to hunt up Moylan, the adjutant, thinking it his business to put the battln. in camp, I
rushed into the first tent I came to to warm
myself. In a moment or so, Tom Custer and
Lieut. Cooke came in, Tom with a newspaper
in his hand, showing it to me, saying, "Isn't
that awful!" I looked at it, reading down a line
or so, and said, "Why, Tom, I wrote that myself,"
and so I had.

The Civil War turned out no three brighter
enthusiasts and able soldiers than the brothers
Frank, Wm. J. and Jacob De Gresse. Frank
was captain of H. Battery Chicago Artillery—20
lb. Parrots—and his battery threw the first shells
into Atlanta with Sherman in 1864. Wm. J. was
a captain in my regiment, the 10th Missouri
Cavalry. Jacob was a captain in the 6th Mo. Cav.
and A. A. Gen. on same staff. The letter in
Mo. Democrat written by me to Wm. J. DeGresse
from Fort Cobb, I. T., was about the first report
received there after the Washita affair.

* * *

I suppose DeGresse came across a lively newspaper report (reporter?) and the letter then got
to the public, i.e., only the portion affecting the
Washita fight—I wasn't ashamed of it; didn't
care a d—n for Custer, if he did owe me $100
debt of honor, and owned straight up that I was
the miscreant who had given it to the world,
though I hadn't the remotest idea it would be
published—the glimmer of some truth about
Indian fighting.

Well, Custer had given me a fair chance of
getting scalped in sending me 180 miles alone,
almost, for recruits and horses; had endeavored

to the best of his ability to get Col. Myers and
myself killed at the Washita, all of which close
to death embraces I was thoroughly aware of,
and I must say wholly careless of; but the intent was perceptibly plain "allee samee."

Custer paid me off for the letter in almost spot
cash. Col. Wm. Thompson's troop was and had
been stationed at Dodge since the birth of regiment, and Thompson liked Dodge as a station,
and he and his troop both desired to remain
there. I did not want it; this, Custer knew. He
also knew that I had had a child born and
died at Harker since I left there, and that my
wife was very ill, and came very close to death,
and I'm inclined to think he hadn't forgotten
that he still owed me $100 I had sent Mrs. Cus-
ter * * *

Nevertheless, when we arrived at Arkansas
River crossing, opposite site of Dodge, I can
still remember the fiendish gleam of delight that
seemed to sparkle in the eyes of Adjt. Myles
Moylan, as he appeared on south bank of the
Arkansas River, and handed me the written order
to await on that bank of river until all our train
had crossed, though I wasn't in charge of the
train, then to report to the C. O. of the post
of Fort Dodge for duty at that post. Major
Harry Douglas, 3d Inf. was C. O., but had been
"put on" unassigned list. Philip Reade was 2d
Lieut. and Post Adjutant.

I reported to Douglas. His reply was, "Glad to
see you, Benteen. I've been waiting arrival of
somebody to receipt to me for the Ord. and
Ord. Stores. I'll turn over command of post and
stores to you, and be off tomorrow." In those
days Ord. and Ord stores were all invoiced to
the C. O. of posts, and he was the responsible
officer.

I receipted to him for them, and Douglas
skipped. Of course being then Comdg. Post, I
took a seven days' leave and started for Harker,
packed my "lares and penates" and sent my
wife and boy to St. Louis.

* * *

A week or so after getting back to Dodge,
Col. Mitchell, A.D.C. & Insp. Gen. for Gen. W.
S. Hancock, Comdg. Dept. came to Dodge to
inspect and report on some trouble Capt. Geo.
Armes and Capts. Graham & Cox of 10th U. S.
Cav. were having at camp of Battln. near Dodge.
Col. Mitchell was surprised at finding me there
in command, and asked me if I wanted the job.
"Not by a d——d sight!" I remarked, "but Custer
banished me for punishment." I showed him the
copy of letter in newspaper that caused it. "Well,"

he said, "I'll fix this up for you the first thing I do on my return to Fort Leavenworth. You can be making preparations to join regiment at Hays."

As soon as I got my orders I put out for Hays, meeting enroute Tom Custer and Lieut. Cooke, escorting the Inspector Gen. of the Army, with one troop of cavalry to Fort Supply. Custer, of course, didn't know business the Gen. was on, but he had fine spies as an escort to ascertain same.

I had just driven a fat buffalo cow up to the road; had killed her there, and was engaged in cutting her throat, when Cooke rode up with his advance guard, some distance ahead of Gen. Inspec's. ambulance. Cooke said, "At your old business I see," "Yes," said I, "I can't keep out of blood." Cooke was my first Lieut. when I was left on S. side of Ark. at Fort Dodge. He was made aware of my troop's fate, but never intimated it to me, but his troops(?) were put in another wagon, and Cooke given seven days' leave, Custer taking off with him, and Cooke never said good-by even, * * *.

Cooke informed me that Gen. Sturgis had arrived, and was in command of 7th at Hays. I gave 3 hearty cheers! and just then my troop wagons were up ready and men were putting aboard carcass of buffalo cow, while the Inspec. Gen's. ambulance and escort were passing. I didn't speak to him! Had I then known what was told me by "Tom Thumb" at Fort Meade in 1882 about the $3,500 trade Custer offered Sutler at Supply, in 1869, I might have prevented his being killed at the Little Big Horn. Tom Custer and Cooke were sent along to see that that proposal didn't crop out! (?)

You will remember that in 1873, Custer was placed in arrest by Stanley just on arrival at edge of Bad Lands, and I was ordered with G. H. and K Troops to escort R. R. engineers through the Bad Lands. I think 'twas G. and K. I had. Anyway, we so thoroughly satisfied the chief, Rosser, that to please him and punish me for the grand time I had at Stockade in '73 while Custer was Mussell-Shelling, I was sent thru the Bad Lands again with them on return march to Lincoln. He hadn't sense enough to know that nothing was too hard for me to do that took me away from his immediate proximity.

If you were along with Troop G, you will remember that we took five wagons through (the Bad) Lands, and broke only one tongue on way, and that just as we got in sight of camp on the Little Missouri River.

* * *

I cannot tell you any more than you know of affair at the Little Big Horn, as you know that we made the attempt to get through to where we thought Custer was, at the earliest possible moment, and you also know that the attempt was vain; in fact, impossible.

At my own request, Gen. Terry permitted me to mount what was left of my troop and go to Custer's field, soon after he joined us on the 27th. When I returned, I said to Lieut. Maguire of Engineers, "By the Lord Harry, old man, 'twas a ghastly sight; but what a big winner the U. S. Govt. would have been if only Custer and his gang could have been taken!" * * * You know enough of me to know I'd have gone through to him had it been possible to do so. At same time, I'm only too proud to say that I despised him * * *.

All this scribbling is only as a drop in the bucket to what I can tell you of my connection with Custer and 7th Cavalry, but, like Mercutio's wound, "Tis enough," and what's more, all I've said is true as Holy Writ!

February 22, 1896

* * *

Until latter part of August, '68, I was in command of the post at Fort Harker, and had H and M Troops, my squadron, out constantly, commanded by myself, scouting for Indians. After August, till about October, '68, I escorted with squadron Gen. Phil Sheridan from post to post, till Custer joined, as recommended by me, and then we made the Washita—El Llano Estacado campaign '68, '69.

Twenty men of my squadron and the 2d Lieut. of my troop, Eddy Emerson, was a guard for the same P. H. Sheridan, then a Capt. of 13th Inf. and who was the A.A. Qrmr and A.C.S. of the army of the Southwest, in 1862, just before the battle of Pea Ridge, March 6, 7, 8th.

Sheridan declined to obey some of the orders of Gen. S. R. Curtis, Comdg. Army of the S. W., so he was ordered to report to Gen. Halleck at St. Louis, in arrest, charges and spec's. as long as the moral law sent in against him, all of which Halleck paid no attention to, but put Sheridan to buying horses, taking him to Corinth, Miss. with him as Hdqtrs. Qtrmaster. There he got command of a Mich. or Wis. Cav. Regt. and went thereafter like a comet!

Sheridan always had an affection for me from the fact of giving him 20 such good men and such an efficient Lieut. to command his escort in '62.

They were employed in seizing mills, grinding

corn, wheat &c by which means only was our army supplied, and as the mills and sources of supply were widely separated, Sheridan and escort were kept very busy. The Bushwhackers in Mo. and Ark. rendered it necessary to go with escort always.

There are many excellent ways of finding out the disposition and nature of a man. I know of no better way than having to live on shipboard with one for a series of years.

Next, in default of salt-water facilities in the great N.W., campaign with a man in the cavalry, for say 10 or 20 years, playing "draw" with him meanwhile, and if the investigator isn't a dolt straightout, he should garner some valuable statistics as to the matter in question. Thus I became acquainted with Gen. Custer.

Ditto, in case of Gen. J. B. Fry, barring the campaigning; but in the game of "draw" Fry thought that no one from the Vols. had any right to down a Bvt. Maj. Gen. at the game: one who has studied philosophy and "math" at the great National School; but at the same time I used to down him regularly, and he'd try to explain by philosophy why I should not have "called him" on such-or-such a bet. "Oh, yes," said I, "You play poker like the old fellow played the fiddle at the cross-roads in Arkansas, and it wasn't until the Traveler came along that he knew there was a change in the tune."

It is the change (turn) in the tune that I'm giving you now. I hadn't a bit of respect for him if he was Adjt. Gen. Dept. of the South, at last playing with him, A. G. Dept. of the East. He had been Provo Gen. U. S. Army, and by some hook or crook had piled up a stack of coin of the realm. How?

Hon. Roscoe Conklin snubbed and in the U. S. Senate denounced him, refusing always to speak to him, saying he wasn't clean and honest. Fry was a finical, cynical no end of all 'round d——n fool, with an unlimited amount of brass, and little else, though he thought he was an author, genius and all 'round grand man. He and Rodenborough were active in starting the Military Service Institution at Gov. Island, and soliciting me to join. I said, I'd like to, but do not believe in subscribing to lunches for you fellows in N. Y. while I'm out in cactus and sagebrush. I joined, however, though there were a lot of them there I couldn't well tie to—a different gang from the present. "Billy" Mitchell of Hancock's staff, however, induced me to join. Col. Mitchell was A.D.C. to Major Gen. Hancock, and was the officer who rendered nugatory Custer's attempt to banish me to Fort Dodge in spring of '69. From some cause or other,

Gen. Hancock always seemed fond of me, and was always kind, which was by no means the rule to everybody, being at times quite over-bearing I've been told. I never had an axe to grind.

Mine was the only troop of cavalry left in New Orleans in '74 and '75, and when Sheridan came down to assume command, he rather surprised Gen. Emory, 5th Cav. (then in command Dept. of the South), and E's staff, by the way he threw his arms around and hugged me, telling me he was glad I was there, and I know he was, as I had made record in 1862, and he knew some of it.

* * *

Custer, at the time was foaming at the mouth at Lincoln. He was shut out of showing himself up in the newspapers; however he had the relaxation of giving to the "Galaxy" his "Lie on the Plains."*

At Fort Cobb, Ind. Ter. in winter of '68-'69, officers call was sounded one night from Regt. Hdqtrs. I sauntered up, the other officers being mostly there when I arrived. The officers were squatted around the inside of Custer's Sibley tent, (minus a wall), and Custer was walking around the center of tent with a rawhide riding whip in his hand. When all were assembled, he went on with a rambling story, stammering the while, that it had been reported to him that some one—or parties—had been belittling the fight at the Washita, &c., &c., and that if he heard any more of it, or it came to his ears who had done so, he would cowhide them, switching his rawhide the while.

Being right at the door of tent, I stepped out, drew my revolver, turned the cylinder to see that 'twas in good working order, returned it lightly to holster, and went within. At pause in the talk I said, "Gen. Custer, while I cannot father all of the blame you have asserted, still, I guess I am the man you are after, and I am ready for the whipping promised." He stammered and said, "Col. Benteen, I'll see you again, sir!"

Doubtless you can imagine what would have happened had the rawhide whirred! The "call" broke up, sine die, in silence, but no tears from whipping! I then went to Randolph Keim, reporter from N. Y. Tribune (the only man I had spoken to about the matter at all) and told him I wanted him to go with me at once to Custer's tent, taking his notes with him of all I had told him, as a whipping was due somebody, and I didn't want a word I'd said omitted.

Keim went with me, and though I'd told him enough, Custer wilted like a whipped cur.

*A sarcastic reference by Benteen to Custer's "Life on the Plains."

He evidently knew whom to whip! Now all of this kind of business was apt to result disastrously to me when Custer could so work it, but I was determined to "stay right with" him; then the other fellows got a little more of men than formerly, and the Custer power can be said to have commenced to decline. Keim told Gen. Sheridan about the occurrence, and Sheridan gave Custer a piece of his mind about the matter. (Sheridan knew that it was principally through me that Custer was then along, and he was rapidly beginning to learn to know more of the characteristics of the man, and I really think he cared but little for him thereafter.)

In 1876, when Custer came to Fort Lincoln with Terry, he found that Major Reno had divided the regiment into four (4) battalions, captains commanding them. Custer at once changed that order, dividing regiment into two wings, Reno comdg. R. W. and I the left.

Custer sent for me one day after this division of regt., and when at his tent (Mrs. Custer being there), he informed me that my cousin, Lawrence Cobright, had called on him in Washington, in spring of 1876, and wanted to know how I was getting along, seeming, Custer said, to be wonderfully interested in me. "Yes," said I, "we've been very dear friends always."

Now Lawrence Cobright, during the whole war (and from the beginning of the Associated Press) had been at its head, its chief, and no dispatches were given to the public by him affecting the Union cause, until he had presented the same to President Lincoln and the Secretary of War, Stanton. Cobright, though a Southerner, was a Union man to the core, a democrat, too, but as true as steel, and had the whole confidence of the President and Secretary through the whole of it.

I then began to scent out the cause of wing distribution by Custer. However, he had no idea of the pride of my race, for at no time did I seek any preferment through Cobright's influence, and no one knew better than he that I would apply for none. However, he being the "head-monk" of such a power, Custer perhaps feared that I might possibly bring influence to bear at some time. He was fully aware that I'd hold my own like a man and thought that perhaps he might need some such influence probably.

Well, after the disaster, when curs of every grade were hounding Grant, Reno and myself, never did I write one word to Cobright. Had I, the matter would have gone to the world straight.

You see, Colonel, there are wheels within wheels!

March 10, 1896

* * *

I have just come in from reviewing a battalion of the 5th Inf. out from McPherson for a practice march. The C. O. of battalion, knowing he would pass my house, sent me word by his Adjt. that he wanted the battalion to give me a marching salute, so down the terraces I bounded to get there in time. It does rather brace one up to see again a lot of jaunty, well-set-up lot of soldiers, and I doffed my hat with pleasing alacrity to the young aspirants for fame at $13 per mo. They both looked and marched well, and the students of Hispania had better ponder deeply and well o'er it, before starting to ruffle the tail feathers of the eagle-birds; for in my opinion they are a bad lot of birds to monkey with.

* * *

Of course I could do nothing towards a "medal" for Gammon, J. E. Perhaps Nick Wallace forgot to put in the app, for medal for him. All of my app's for such were honored.

But in your case will state that Hon. Asst. Sec'y of War wrote me about the matter, and I thought that I had said sufficient to have insured the granting of it, not knowing till now that it had not been. I could not remember the names or faces even of those I saw spilling themselves over the brink for a camp-kettle of the liquid blue stuff—that was simply an impossibility; and then, my time was fully occupied in endeavoring to make it somewhat feasible to procure a drop of the dear stuff; and so I lamentingly told the Sec'y.

I trust a way may be found that I can render some assistance to you in the matter. You, I suppose, have a personal acquaintance with Gen. Doe, and I am only too willing to do all toward it that lies in my power.

As far as granting them to officers is concerned, and men also, I must say that in my opinion, in the cases of some officers and men to whom they have been given—and I knowing full particulars in such cases—that I'd scarcely give a tinker's dam for one to hand down to my son. That's where, perhaps, the "V.C." is better guarded.

———

Learn if I can do anything to help you in it (if you wish it) and only show me the way. I went through a lot of "cap" to demonstrate to Gen. Doe the general mixed state of affairs existing at the time in question, and I thought that though I didn't, and hadn't known you personally, enough has been said to convince the Hon. Sec'y that I believed you were undoubtedly there, and recommended the "bauble" be granted, "or words to that effect." This, as you know, is all that I could say.

* * *

———

March 14, 1896

* * *

I always thought of the distance lost by my battln. in left-obliquing from the trail, and getting back to same on the morning of the 25th, as something between 10 and 12 miles—perhaps more, as we went in hot haste both ways. From where my battln. obliqued to left, to the spot where I found the body of Custer, I put down as 15 miles. It is rather over than under this estimate.

I think the "probs" very fair, that we shall hear from both Godfrey and Whittaker* on Hughes' dynamite bomb. G. can have easy access to Mil. Service Inst. Journal. W. would have to rely I think on some of the magazines; but as he is a literary cuss, doubtless he'll find little trouble in getting his work in one of the big ones, and perhaps in the "Century."

* * *

The distance and time of day, and a great many minor details, have to remain simply guesswork; which is just as well, as the great fiasco was and is an accomplished fact, "done up" in great shape by the noble aborigines to whom the disobedient Custer had left all lanes open.

* * *

———

March 19, 1896

* * *

Godfrey, in my mind, is rather an obtuse fellow, and like the traditional Englishman, it takes him a good while to see the nub of a joke. That he'll rush up on that intrenched artillery you suggested, why, you can put it down as done. I have known him since he joined the 7th in '67, and am of the opinion that I've pretty well diagnosed his character and capacity.

I've known Major Bell, too, since '66. Bell was H.Q.M. at the Washita fight. 2d Lieut. Mathey took Capt. Hamilton's (Hamilton was killed)

place as Officer of the Day, and Bell left him (Mathey) in charge of the train, and I heard Bell got up with some wagon or so of ammunition from train to scene of fight, but I didn't see him. The little racket at Canyon Creek in '77 was the only one fight I ever knew or heard of his being in with the regiment. His time was put in in looking out for advancement to Qr. Mr., Commy., Adjt. Gen. or any other berth that was in sound or sight, and his services were mostly on "leaves" of some kind of work in the 7th. He got none of the vacancies, and the disaster at L. B. Horn made him a Captain, and the War Dept. hustled Bell and Jackson to their newly-found troops; both of them (of same ilk, had to do some duty then.) (?)

* * *

———

April 3, 1896

Yours of 31st ult., enclosing excerpts from press concerning Miles' chance for stars, (3) just received. Ditto, presentation speech of Gen. Doe in turning over to you medal for most distinguished conduct at the Little Big Horn, June 25, '76. The presentation was well conceived, and I rejoice in it that you rejoice in it, and I congratulate you most heartily thereon.

Now as Capt. L. R. Hare has assisted you in that matter, I shall take immediate occasion to interest myself in endeavoring to secure one for Hare, and I take this occasion to remark that had I then been in command, Hare would have been in possession of one long ago, if my recommendations could have furthered such. The Army & Navy forever! Hurrah for the Red, White and Blue!

Mind, now, should McKinley become president, then Miles will secure the 3 stars triumphantly. But then, you see, McKinley isn't going to wield the baton of Grand Marshal over this grand Republic just yet, my boy; i.e., in my opinion. Let us—as we'll have to—wait and see.

Gen. Miles would have been a grand, strong friend of mine if I'd have let him be; this I know absolutely from intimates of the Gen. But you see this d———d old stubborn Democratic head of mine wasn't built to accept peace offerings from newspaper people, and I never even met him a small part of the way. It is easily to be gleaned from this that I've never been at all politic, and would have made the poorest of poor politicians. "Every one to his liking," or, to way he's built.

* * *

What you say as to any reciprocation toward

---

*This reference is to Frederick Whittaker, Custer's first biographer.

myself, my dear Colonel, I thank you for, but let me assure you that if my scrawl to Gen. Doe had any good effect in your case, then I am fully repaid, the debt canceled—and here's your receipt.

* * *

You are correct, Goldin, about poor "Nick"—Capt. George D. Wallace, and I must say that it gave me the serenest pleasure to "head off" my first lieut. when he was aspiring and conspiring to obtain the command of Troop G, 7th, at Cedar Creek in '77 when Garlington relieved Wallace as adjutant, and it was not that I valued his services, for I really thought there was little of the true man about him; but I liked "Nick" better. But for me, you'd have had Gibson for Troop commander, and for that, I think you should burn an extra roman candle to my memory on the 4th of July next. Look to it that 'tis done!

* * *

———

HEADQUARTERS DEPARTMENT OF DAKOTA

Office of the Chief Signal Officer.

St. Paul, Minn. Aug. 8, 1896.

Mr. Theodore W. Goldin,
Attorney-at-Law
Janesville, Wis.

Sir:

I have just heard that Reno's men while in the bottom, saw Custer's fighting on the bluff, or perhaps it was while his line was extended across the plain before he took to the timber, at any rate, the point is that sometime during Reno's stay in the valley, and before he made the wretched scramble for the bluffs, some of his men are said to have seen Custer fighting across the river, perhaps two miles or so away. I am told you were with Reno, if so, you may perhaps recall me, but in any event I should like to hear whether this story is true or not, so far as your observations went, and would you have been likely to have seen any action going on so far off while yourself engaged? I hear you have written something in a Chicago magazine about the fight. I should like a copy of the paper, or a reference that will enable me to get it. It seems hardly possible that such a material fact as Reno's knowledge that Custer was himself fighting but a short distance away, and his charging (which was of course expected, as it had been ordered) would have relieved him, should have gone all these years unmentioned, yet that is just what the Indians say took place—that Custer's first fighting was done in full presence of Reno's command, and notwithstanding not only was no charge made, but Reno did not try to hold his own in the timber—that is, the bottom—after you came in off the plain. Any light you may be able to throw on any of these matters will be very acceptably received.

Yours very truly,
R. E. THOMPSON
Capt. Signal Corps

August 12, 1896

* * *

Your last inquiry on Custer Big Horn fiasco is from "Dick" Thompson, who was commissary on Terry's staff in the field in '76, Hdqtrs. on "Far West." Thompson was at that time a 2d Lieut. of 5th Inf. Grad. from M.A. of '68. I suppose Dick means at some time to give us a few lines concerning the whys and wherefores of the disaster.

Now 'twasn't physically possible for any of Reno's men to see Custer's men fighting on the bluffs, for no fighting was done by them till they were gotten into the corral into which they wandered in such hot haste, and "Gall" says 30 minutes settled the whole biz for them there.

True, Reno "didn't try to hold his own in the timber," but Custer deceived Reno in assuring him that he would support him "with the whole outfit," R. necessarily supposing that the support would come from the direction from which he had come; in short, his rear, which was natural enough with no other explanation.

I am reckless as to whose feelings I hurt, but it is my firm belief, and always has been, that Custer's command didn't do any "1st-class" fighting there, and if possible were worse handled even than Reno's batt'n. 300 men well fought should have made a better showing.

* * *

From the fact of Thompson having been in the '76 campaign in capacity of A.C.S. on Terry's staff, he may have some information about same, but 'tis by no means possible that he can have as great an amt. of same as had Hughes, who was General Terry's right hand confidential man. Hughes refers to "Dick" in his last article in M. S. I.

———

THE "WASHITA" LETTER THAT ENRAGED CUSTER

FOLLOWING is the text of the letter setting forth some unwritten history concerning the battle of the Washita, that so enraged General Custer. It was written by Captain F. W. Benteen of the Seventh to his friend William J. De Gresse of St. Louis, who furnished it to the *St. Louis Democrat*, in which paper it was immediately published, and was copied by the *New York Times*, 14 February 1869. Benteen refers to it in his letter of 17 February 1896 to Theo. W. Goldin, one of the Benteen-Goldin series of letters included in this volume. General Godfrey told me, as did also Major F. W. Benteen, Jr., that this letter and its publication was the moving cause of Custer's threat to horsewhip his critic, a lively incident which Benteen describes in his letter of 22 February 1896 to Goldin.

THE BATTLE OF THE WASHITA

Death and Barbarous Treatment of Maj. Elliott and His Band—Destruction of the Indian Camp and Property.

(*New York Times*, February 14, 1869)

The St. Louis Democrat publishes the following letter from a participant in the battle of Washita, Idaho (sic) [Indian Territory], which gives some of the secret history of that fight, and accounts for the fact of Maj. Elliott and his men being reported missing:

Fort Cobb, I. T., Dec. 22, 1868.

My Dear Friend: I wrote to you from Camp Supply, which place was left on the 7th, arriving at this post on the evening of the 18th. On the 11th we camped within a few miles of our "battle of the Washita," and Gens. Sheridan and Custer, with a detail of one hundred men, mounted, as escort, went out with the view of searching for the bodies of our nineteen missing comrades, including Maj. Elliott.

The bodies were found in a small circle, stripped as naked as when born, and frozen stiff. Their heads had been battered in, and some of them had been entirely chopped off; some of them had had the Adam's apple cut out of their throats; some had their hands and feet cut off, and nearly all had been horribly mangled in a way delicacy forbids me to mention. They lay scarcely two miles from the scene of the fight, and all we know of the manner they were killed we have learned from Indian sources. It seems that Maj. Elliott's party were pursuing a well-mounted party of Cheyennes in the direction of the Grand Village, where nearly all the tribes were encamped, and were surrounded by the reinforcements coming to the rescue of the pursued, before the Major was aware of their position. They were out of sight and hearing of the Seventh Cavalry, which had remained at and around the captured village, about two miles away. As soon as Maj. Elliott found that he was surrounded he caused his men to dismount, and did some execution among the Indians, which added to the mortification they must have felt at the loss of the village and herds of their friends and allies, and enraged them so that they determined upon the destruction of the entire little band.

Who can describe the feeling of that brave band, as with anxious beating hearts, they strained their yearning eyes in the direction whence help should come? What must have been the despair that, when all hopes of succor died out, nerved their stout arms to do and die? Round and round rush the red fiends, smaller and smaller shrinks the circle, but the aim of that devoted, gallant knot of heroes is steadier than ever, and the death howl of the murderous redskin is more frequent. But on they come in masses grim, with glittering lance and one long, loud, exulting whoop, as if the gates of hell had opened and loosed the whole infernal host. A well-directed volley from their trusty carbines makes some of the miscreants reel and fall, but their death-rattles are drowned in the greater din. Soon every voice in that little band is still as death; but the hellish work of the savages is scarce begun, and their ingenuities are taxed to invent barbarities to practice on the bodies of the fallen brave, the relation of which is scarcely necessary to the completion of this tale.

And now, to learn why the anxiously-looked-for succor did not come, let us view the scene in the captured village, scarce two short miles away. Light skirmishing is going on all around. Savages on flying steeds, with shields and feathers gay, are circling everywhere, riding like devils incarnate. The troops are on all sides of the village, looking on and seizing every opportunity of picking off some of those daring riders with their carbines. But does no one think of the welfare of Maj. Elliott and party? It seems not. But yes! a squadron of cavalry is in motion. They trot; they gallop. Now they charge! The cowardly redskins flee the coming shock and scatter here and there among the hills scurry away. But it is the true line—will the cavalry keep it? No! no! They turn! Ah, 'tis only to intercept the wily foe. See! a gray troop goes on in the direction again. One more short mile and they will be saved. Oh, for a mother's prayers! Will not some good angel prompt them? They charge the mound—a few scattering shots, and the murderous pirates of the Plains go unhurt away. There is no hope for that brave little band, the death doom is theirs, for the cavalry halt and rest their panting steeds.

And now return with me to the village. Officers and soldiers are watching, resting, eating and sleeping. In an hour or so they will be refreshed, and then scour the hills and plains for their missing comrades. The commander occupies himself in taking an inventory of the captured property which he had promised the officers shall be distributed among the enlisted men of the command if they falter or halt not in the charge.

The day is drawing to a close and but little has been done save the work of the first hour. A great deal remains to be done. That which cannot be taken away must be destroyed. Eight hundred ponies are to be put to death. Our Chief exhibits his close sharp-shooting and terrifies the crowd of frighted, captured squaws and papooses by dropping the straggling ponies in death near them. Ah! he is a clever marksman. Not even do the poor dogs of the Indians escape his eye and aim as they drop dead or limp howling away. But are not those our men on guard on the other side of the creek? Will he not hit them? "My troop is on guard, General, just over there," says an officer. "Well, bullets will not go through or around hills, and you see there is a hill between us," was the reply, and the exhibition goes on. No one will come that way intentionally—certainly not. Now commences the slaughter of the ponies. Volley on volley is poured into them by too hasty men, and they, limping, get away only to meet death from a surer hand. The work progresses! The plunder having been culled over, is hastily piled; the wigwams are pulled down and thrown on it, and soon the whole is one blazing mass. Occasionally a startling report is heard and a steamlike volume of smoke ascends as the fire reaches a powder bag, and thus the glorious deeds of valor done in the morning are celebrated by the flaming bonfire of the afternoon. The last pony is killed. The huge fire dies out; our wounded and dead comrades—heroes of a bloody day—are carefully laid on ready ambulances, and as the brave band of the Seventh Cavalry strikes up the air, "Ain't I glad to get out of the Wilderness," we slowly pick our way across the creek over which we charged so gallantly in the early morn. Take care! do not trample on the dead bodies of that woman and child lying there! In a short time we shall be far from the scene of our daring dash, and night will have thrown her dark mantle over the scene. But surely some search will be made for our missing comrades. No, they are forgotten. Over them and the poor ponies the wolves will hold high carnival, and their howlings will be their only requiem. Slowly trudging, we return to our train, some twenty miles away, and with bold, exulting hearts, learn from one another how many dead Indians have been seen.

Two weeks elapse—a larger force returns that way. A search is made and the bodies are found strewn round that little circle, frozen stiff and hard. Who shall write their eulogy?

This, my dear friend, is the story of the "battle of the Washita," poorly told.

A DEFENSE OF COLONEL BENTEEN
(Philadelphia *Times*, March 15, 1879)

To the Editor of THE TIMES:

In your paper of this date there appears a communication, signed "T. G. C.," reflecting on Colonel F. W. Benteen; it contains some truth but much falsehood. Colonel Benteen did write a letter criticising Custer's plan of attack at the battle of the Washita, and well he might, for it was precisely the same which caused the massacre at the Little Big Horn, only in the former case a Major, Elliott, and his command were the victims. Somebody sent this letter to Custer, and being so different from the usual newspaper notices of his achievements, made him furiously angry. "Officers' Call" was sounded, and they assembled to find him walking up and down, switching his legs with a riding whip. He referred to the letter, saying he knew it could only have been written by some officer of that regiment, and directed the author to step to the front. Colonel Benteen did so at once, acknowledging the communication to be his, Custer looked at him, and his eyes were on Custer's all the time. The General then dismissed the other officers, and, when they had broken ranks and dispersed, said to Benteen: "Colonel, I'll see you again on this matter," and walked at once to his tent. The "matter" was never referred to again between them. Custer knew, and I know, and "T. G. C." ought to know, if he doesn't, had that whip touched Benteen he would have most effectually resented the insult before it could have been repeated.

These are the facts of the case, and, as the friend of Colonel Benteen, who is twenty-five hundred miles distant, serving with his regiment, I have the honor to request their publication in reply to an apparently malicious prevarication.

ROBERT NEWTON PRICE,
505 Minor Street,
Philadelphia, March 14, 1879.

BENTEEN DISCUSSES THE CAUSES OF INDIAN OUTBREAKS
(*The Chicago Times*, Saturday, January 25, 1879)

A TIMES reporter had a conversation with Capt. Benteen, one of the dashing cavalry officers which the Reno trial has brought to the city, on yesterday afternoon, in regard to the Indian problem. The captain's experience among the redskins dates back to 1866. Since that time he has paid considerable attention to their habits and propensities, and frequently fought against them. Capt. Benteen entertains some radical notions on the Indian question, and he has the happy faculty of expressing them in a brief form.

"What," asked the reporter, "in your opinion, is the cause of the Indian outbreaks which give your military men so much to do?"

"For the past twelve or fifteen years," replied the captain, "I think the Indian bureau has been entirely responsible, and the cause has been the enormous pilfering and stealing from the Indians."

"Who has done the most of that stealing?"

"The Indian Agents,

undoubtedly. Their acts have created dissatisfaction among the savages which they have been unable to suppress. No agent can save $13,000 or $15,000 annually legitimately out of a salary of $1,500, and yet numbers of them do it."

"What remedy would you suggest for the present state of things?"

"I think if the management of the Indians was turned over to the army there would be none of those disastrous wars with which we are afflicted under the present system. The redskins would be honestly dealt with, and in a couple of years they would be as easily managed as the same number of white men. If they were treated more considerately and received what government allows them, I think there is no doubt they would be perfectly peaceful and tractable. It is

This Constant Robbery

which goads them to outbreaks. Treat them well, and they will be all right and make good citizens. I think a body of Indians preferable at any time to a body of communists; they are better men, with better principles."

"Would this change of system be costly?"

"Certainly not. It would rather be in the direction of economy. In the army we have a large retired list. Three-fourths of the men on that list would make good Indian agents, and that army officers are honest as a class admits of no argument. The government has to pay them three-quarters pay now, and it would be easy to make it full and turn over this agency business to them. All the stealing of the agents at $1,500 a year would be dispensed with; the Indians would get their allowances, and would become satisfied and take more kindly to the arts of peace."

"How does the change of their reservations affect their peace of mind?"

"You have to act with a little consideration for the feelings of an Indian just as with other people. I am a southerner, and I have noticed that you may take a negro far away from home, but he will always have an inclination to return. The same feeling actuates the salmon—it must go up stream to the point where it begun life to deposit its spawn. Well, an Indian is in the same category. No matter at how uninteresting a spot on the plains he was reared, he

Regards it as His Home

and has the same desire to visit it now and then as white people have to visit their native places. Some consideration should be paid to this sentiment. We should treat the Indian as if he possessed some natural feeling. If that were done and the other reforms carried out, the Indian would soon cease troubling us, and more cheerfully give himself up to the processes of civilization."

CHAPTER 5

GENERAL WINFIELD SCOTT EDGERLY
AND
MY RELATIONS WITH HIM

THE neophyte who attempts to solve any one of the numerous puzzles with which the battle of the Little Big Horn fairly teems, frequently finds himself in a state of mental fog. One of the most troublesome of these problems is the time element, not only important to any clear appreciation of what happened, but even more so to an understanding of *why* it happened. All one need do is to read Reno's report, the early semi-official accounts and the statements of scouts and interpreters, and then check these against the time periods of the official itinerary, the testimony taken at the Court of Inquiry, and the "Century" article of General Godfrey to discover confusion worse confused. As for myself, after wrestling with the problem for many months and getting nowhere, I turned to General Edgerly, Weir's lieutenant in 1876 (whom I had never met), in the hope that he might offer a solution.

Edgerly was not the frequent visitor to Washington that Godfrey was, and I had tried in vain to contact him. He had a home somewhere in New Hampshire and another in New York, and it was not until late in 1923 that I was able to reach him. This I finally succeeded in doing by letter, in the course of which I said:

I have been waiting my opportunity to find you sometime in Washington, that I might talk with you in person, but the chance has not come, and so I am writing to ask if you are willing to help me as General Godfrey and Colonel Varnum have done, by giving me your views and recollections as to some phases of the fight that puzzle and mystify me.

It puzzles me greatly that nearly all the early accounts of the fight put its occurrence several hours earlier than do the later ones. According to the first interviews and accounts, Custer went to the Crow's Nest at daylight; the command crossed the divide and was separated into battalions about ten o'clock; Reno's fight commenced about noon; Custer's about 12:30, and Benteen joined Reno about 2:30. But Wallace's itinerary and most of the later accounts, and in particular General Godfrey's story, show that Custer did not go to the Crow's Nest until *after* 10 A. M.; that he stayed there *over an hour* and that the command did not cross the divide until noon; that it was 2 P. M. when the lone tepee was sighted; about 2:15 when Reno got his order to cross the river and charge; from 2:45 to 3:00 before he was engaged in the valley; and about 4:00 P. M. when he reached the hills in retreat. Benteen's column having joined him a few minutes thereafter, their junction occurred about 4:15.

I cannot account for these discrepancies in time. I have asked General Godfrey many times; but he is unable to account for them except upon the theory that everybody was too busy to take account of the hours.

The time element has to me, however, a most important bearing, for if the fight in the valley did in fact commence at noon, and Custer's column was engaged within a half hour thereafter, it is hard to account for Reno and Benteen during the several hours that intervened before their attempt to advance down the river, which occurred, by common consent, about 5 o'clock. On the other hand, if Benteen only reached Reno after 4 P. M., and they were forced to wait for the arrival of the mules and the distribution of ammunition, it is easy to see that this must have consumed an hour or more, and so account for the lateness of the advance. As you were second in command of the troop that led it, perhaps you can clear up these questions of time; and as Captain Weir's

General Winfield Scott Edgerly shortly before his retirement.

lieutenant, it may be that you overheard any conversation he may have had with Reno before the advance was made, and can tell me the substance of what was said.

Was there, in your opinion, any chance to have saved Custer's command or any considerable part of it from destruction, had Reno advanced at once upon Benteen's junction with him, without waiting for the ammunition; or would such a move have resulted only in practical annihilation of the regiment? And, so far as you know, did Captain Weir ever write anything which expressed his views concerning the fight; and if he did, is it by any chance available for reference or information?

I shall not ask you whether you think Custer disobeyed his orders, though there seems to be no doubt as to what General Terry thought. I assume that you are familiar with his "confidential"

report of July 2, but perhaps you do not know that this report was never repeated to Washington as received in Chicago. For some unexplained reason, the last three paragraphs were omitted. The last paragraph, as shown by the Chicago records was:

"I send in another dispatch a copy of my written orders to Custer, but these were supplemented by the distinct understanding that Gibbon could not get to the Little Big Horn before the evening of the 26th."

I have noted, in one of General Brisbin's articles, reference to a paper read by you to the officers at Ft. Clark, and have searched in vain for any copy or resumé of it. If you still have it, I would appreciate an opportunity to see it, and with your permission, to copy it.

* * *

As I read back this letter to General Edgerly after thirty years, I wonder that he answered it at all. It showed unadulterated nerve for a junior officer to put a general officer "on the spot" on such a touchy subject; but answer it he did, and though his letter did not help at all in the time problem (it never has been satisfactorily solved), it was both direct and informative on other questions; and its cordiality led to a valued friendship. I append his answer in full.

Cooperstown, N. Y.,
Dec. 5, 1923

My dear Colonel Graham:

In 1898 I delivered a lecture on the battle of the Little Big Horn, in several cities.

A copy of this address is now stored in my home in N. H. and I haven't a note in regard to it here. I hope to go there next summer and, if I do, will send you a copy of the manuscript. General Miles read it and disagreed with me as to the length of the Custer part of the fight. I think he agreed with nearly or quite all the rest of my acct. I presume that the time of separation into battalions is mentioned in it. My recollection is that it was about 10 A. M. It was estimated that the village was about fifteen miles from the Crow's Nest; this would take about four hours to cover at a walk, the 7th Cav'y being a very fast walking reg't. When Benteen's battalion came in sight of the river the last of Reno's men were climbing the bluff.

The manner of Weir's advance will seem queer to you but the facts are as follows:

Soon after we joined Reno we saw a few Indians in front of us on the bluff; we drove them over the bluff, then stood to horse and then or very soon after heard firing in Custer's direction. We expected immediate orders to advance and I remarked to the 1st Sgt. that we ought to go to the sound of the firing.* About this time Captain Weir came to me and asked if I would be willing to go to Custer's relief if none of the other troops went. I answered in the affirmative and he said he would ask permission of Reno. He told me later that he concluded he had better take a look ahead before asking Reno so he mounted and started to the front with only an orderly.

Presuming that he had permission from Reno and that he was taking it for granted that I would follow him, I mounted the troop and went after him without orders from anybody. Weir told me afterward that he was delighted to see me coming and tho't it a sign of personal devotion to him.

In my opinion there was no 'chance to have saved Custer's command or any considerable part of it from destruction if Reno had advanced at once upon Benteen's junction with him and without waiting for the ammunition', and I believe that 'such a move would have resulted only in practical annihilation of the reg't.'

Capt. Weir never wrote an account of the fight, as far as I know.

Your letter gives me my first knowledge of the last paragraph of Terry's report. On the 24th of June we were on the hot trail of from 600 to 800 bucks and as I did not know of the fixed date for the junction with Gibbon, I always tho't Custer was justified by his orders for advancing as he did. The fact is that a great disaster having occurred, some people believed that either Terry or Custer had to be the scape-goat.

This was unfortunate for it could have been proven that Terry's instructions were excellent and if Custer made a mistake he paid the full penalty. I have answered your questions as fully as I can without my notes and it will give me great pleasure to meet and talk to you.

Yours sincerely,
/s/ W. S. EDGERLY

*OF COURSE WE SHOULD HAVE GONE

The next time General Edgerly visited Washington, he let me know in advance, and from that time forward, I had the benefit of his knowledge and advice. He was wholly unbiased in his appraisals of Custer, Reno and Benteen, though it was easy to see that he considered the latter the outstanding figure of the campaign, whose personality, courage and leadership held high the morale of what was left of the regiment after Custer's debacle.

Sometime before I met Edgerly in person, W. Morgan Shuster of the "Century" Company had sent me a manuscript that had been brought to the magazine by Mrs. Custer, who wished it published. It was, in substance, a severe criticism of General Terry's plan for cooperative action between Custer's column and Gibbon's, as outlined in his confidential message of July 2 to Sheridan. Mrs. Custer, so Mr. Shuster wrote me, had named General Edgerly as the author of this paper, but as it was not signed, the "Century" editors had taken the precaution to submit it to him before publishing it. He had returned it with the message—"I did not write this article, and do not agree with all its statements and conclusions." Mr. Shuster having asked me to ferret out the author if possible, I discussed it with General Edgerly, and we were agreed that certain statements resembled very closely the known and published views of General Miles; and I was deputed "to beard the lion (i.e. Miles) in his den," and attempt to secure from him an acknowledgment of authorship. This I did sometime later with indifferent success. But that is another story.

I had many letters from General Edgerly, and found him always frank in his opinions and clear in his expressions of them. If he talked at all, he talked plainly and without evasion or reserve; and though he was a more reticent man than was General Godfrey, he was much more informative, and far more open-minded. I doubt, however, that he ever heard of the alleged "proposition" by Reno to abandon his wounded on the night of the 25th, and believe his reaction to it, if he credited it, would have been instant and severe.

When the time arrived in 1926 for my study, "The Story of the Little Big Horn" to go to press, General Edgerly, who had been one of its most helpful godfathers, graciously volunteered to fill the breach caused by the refusal of General Godfrey at the last moment to write a "foreword" for the book unless I was willing to modify or delete some passages he considered derogatory to Custer, which I could not do.

General Edgerly passed on in 1927. He was a knightly gentleman of the old school; a man of immaculate character, a loyal and courageous soldier, and an able officer. The Army has not had too many like him.

The Seventh Cavalry's Regimental Standard of 1876. This flag was carried by the regiment on its march from the Yellowstone to the Little Big Horn. It is now exhibited at the Custer Battlefield Museum.

EDGERLY'S STATEMENT, MADE 18 AUGUST 1881, AT FT. YATES.

(From *The Leavenworth Times*)

LIEUTENANT EDGERLY of the Seventh Cavalry who was in Benteen's battalion, which joined Reno's force fifteen or twenty minutes after Reno's retreat, gave me the following account:

At about 10 o'clock in the morning of the 25th of June, 1876, we were, say, fifteen miles from the hostile camp. Our force was then all together. We halted while Custer went on a hill with the Crow and Ree scouts to take a look at the Indian camp, which was in sight. When General Custer came down from the hill officers' call was sounded. The officers all went to where he was, and he told us that our presence was discovered; that his scouts had chased a small number of Indians that they had seen, and they had gotten away and gone in the direction of the Indian camp, and as there was no use in trying to surprise them, as his intention had been, the next morning, we would press on as quickly as we could and attack them in the village if possible. The idea was that the Indians would not stand against a whole regiment of cavalry, and that as soon as they learned of our advance they would try to get away from us. He then ordered troop commanders to mount their troops and report when they were in readiness to move on. In about a minute every troop commander had reported. General Custer and his Adjutant, Colonel Cook, then organized the regiment into four battalions of three troops each, giving to each of the four senior officers the command of a battalion. These officers were Reno, Benteen, Keogh and Yates. He ordered Major Reno to move straight down the valley to the Indian village and attack, and he would be supported. He ordered Colonel Benteen to move off toward the left, at an angle of about forty-five degrees from Reno's course and attack any Indians he could find. The idea was that the Indians would run either to the right or left. He detailed Captain McDougall, with his troop, as rear guard, to take charge of the pack train. The orders he gave to Colonel Keogh and Captain Yates I don't know, but he went off with them—five companies and about 250 to 300 men—in a direction parallel to Reno's. The last that I saw of General Custer alive he was going off in the direction mentioned. Colonel Benteen moved off as ordered, and almost immediately struck a series of high hills. He sent an officer—Lieutenant Gibson—to the tops of several of these hills, to see if any Indians were visible in the direction of his route. Lieutenant Gibson reported several times that there were no signs of Indians, and then Colonel Benteen swung around to the right, and about five or six miles from the starting point we came upon Reno's trail and followed it rapidly. After following it several miles, an orderly trumpeter from General Custer came in and handed Colonel Benteen a note to this effect:

"We have struck a big village. Hurry up. Bring up the packs. Signed.

W. W. COOK, Adjutant."

We then passed on, and when within about three miles of the Indian village we could see that there was fighting going on in the valley, and very shortly we saw a body of men—upwards of a hundred—make a break for the bluffs on the east side of Little Big Horn river, on the west side of which the Indian village was situated, cross the stream and disappear in the bluffs. We were then on the right bank, to the east of the stream, and some distance from it. As the orderly who brought the message from Custer had told us that the Indian village was surprised, and that, when he came away, Reno was driving everything before him and killing them right and left, I supposed that the men we saw running were Indians driven by our men. We hurried forward in the direction of the ford where Reno had crossed, with intent to hurry to his support; but as we approached the ford a Crow scout, Half Yellow Face, came out upon our right and beckoned us to come up on the hill. We immediately turned to the right and went up the hill. When we reached the summit we found Colonel Reno and his battalion there, with several wounded men crying anxiously for water, and then learned to our surprise that they had been driven from their ground. There were a few Indians around, behind rocks and the points of the hills, who were shooting into us at that time. A skirmish line was formed and these Indians driven away in a few minutes. Then I heard heavy firing over in the direction in which we afterwards found the remains of Custer's portion of the command, and could see clouds of dust, and horsemen rushing back and forth on the opposite side of the river and about four miles away. While this firing was going on, Colonel Weir, my captain, came to me and asked me what I thought we ought to do. I told him I thought we ought by all means to go down to Custer's assistance. He thought so too, and I heard the first sergeant express himself to that effect. He then asked me if I would be willing to go down with only D troop, if he could get permission to go. I told him I would. He then walked towards Colonel Reno and Benteen, and very shortly came back, mounted his horse, took an orderly with him and went out in the direction from which we had heard the firing and which had then almost wholly ceased. I supposed that he had received permission to go out with the troop (though he afterwards told me he had not, and had not even asked for it), so I mounted the troop and followed him. After going a few hundred yards I swung off to the right with the troop and went into a little valley which must have been the one followed by Custer and his men, or nearly parallel to it, and moved right towards the great body of the Indians, whom we had already seen from the highest point. After we had gone a short distance down the valley, Col. Weir, who had remained to our left, on the bluff, saw a large number of Indians coming toward us, and motioned with his hand for me to swing around with the troop to where he was, which I did. When I got up on the bluff I saw Col. Benteen, Captain French and Lieutenant Godfrey coming toward us with their troops. We moved along on that bluff for a short distance, when the Indians commenced to fire on us. The troops were all dismounted, formed on the top of the ridge and returned the fire. This firing was kept up about half an hour, when the troops were drawn back to their original position by order of Gen. Reno. Our troops had one man killed in coming back and one horse only, although two or three Indians ran up on the hill immediately after we left and emptied their Winchesters on us. As soon as we got back to where Reno was we found the other troops disposed around on the crest of this elevation, and Weir's troop and Godfrey's fell in side by side so as to prolong their regular line already formed by our troops. Almost as soon as we took this position the Indians came up in our front and opened fire. The firing was heavy, but only a few men were killed, as most of the shots went over our heads. It continued for more than an hour, and until half an hour after dusk. That ended the first day's fight.

The next morning, before daylight, heavy firing commenced again from the hills, five to seven or eight hundred yards from us, and continued until about 10 o'clock. After that there was very little firing, although the Indians in small numbers could be seen on the ridges around us. During the afternoon the Indians on the other side of the river had taken down their lodges, or tepees, and about 4 o'clock they all started off.

From the time we took our position the after-

noon before, we lost but few men. We remained right there, or in a new position adjoining, that night, and the next morning Lieut. Bradley, of Gen. Terry's column, who had command of the scouts came up and told us that Custer and all his men were killed. Shortly after Gen. Terry came along with his column. He then sent our regiment along to bury the dead.

The first dead soldiers we came to were Lieuts. Calhoun, Crittenden, and enlisted men of L troop. The bodies of these officers were lying a short distance in rear of their men, in the very place where they belonged, and the bodies of their men forming a very regular skirmish line. Crittenden's body was shot full of arrows.

The next lot we came to consisted of Colonel Keogh and his troop. They had evidently been falling back toward the knoll where we found Colonel Custer's body—fighting as they retreated. The other men that I saw showed no sign of regular formation; their bodies were scattered over the ground with a general tendency toward the knoll where Custer was.

On the knoll which I spoke of we found the bodies of General Custer, Colonel Cook—his adjutant—Colonel Tom Custer, several enlisted men and several horses, while lower down, just at the base of the knoll were Lieutenant Riley, Captain Yates, and a great many enlisted men and horses. General Custer's brother, Boston, and his Nephew, Reed, were about a hundred yards from the general's body.

The only bodies of officers that I saw mutilated were Colonel Tom Custer and Colonel Cook. All the bodies were stripped of their uniforms. The great majority of the men were stark naked, but in a good many cases they left the undershirt, socks and drawers on the bodies. The bodies were on the east side of the river, below the main village, and about four miles from where Reno had taken position.

When I went out with the troop, on the afternoon of the 25th, I could see quite a number of Indians galloping back and forth on the battlefield, where we afterwards found the bodies, and firing at objects on the ground, but we could not see what the objects were.

When I first reached the top of the hill where Reno was, on the 25th, I heard the heavy firing, and it continued about fifteen or twenty minutes. Then the heavy firing was all over. After we buried Custer and his men on the east side of the river, we crossed to the west side and buried the dead of Reno's command—about forty in number—and then we found two Indian lodges, or tepees, with six bodies of Indians in one and five in the other, beautifully dressed, and fastened to a pole in the center of the tepee. Chief Low Dog has told me since he came here that that is an honorable way of disposing of men who have died fighting bravely, and that their bodies are left to the enemy, to whom they belong. I never knew another such case. My opinion is that they were left because the Indians left in a hurry, being frightened by the approach of Terry's column. Around the tepees where we found the dead Indians were as many dead ponies as there were Indians. The ponies were arranged in a circle around the tepee, with their heads towards the tepee.

From what I saw, I think there were as many as 7,000 warriors. I judged from seeing Terry's command—about 500 men—the size of which I knew, ride down where I saw the Indians the day before. Terry's command looked like a handful compared to the Indians.

Custer's trail showed—and this is what the Indians say—that he passed down the river—which is only about fifteen or twenty yards wide there—on the east side; that is, on the right bank. Reno had crossed and attacked from the west. The river bank was so high and steep that it was impracticable to get down to it from the bluff until he got to a place a little over three miles from where Reno took his position after his retreat across the river. There he found a ford, and the general belief was that he attempted to cross and was attacked and driven back to where he was found dead. Dead bodies were found all the way from the ford to where Custer's body was found.

Custer's hair—which he had been accustomed to wear long—was cut short before he started on the march. His body was naked, but not mutilated.

PART III

✩

MISCELLANEOUS
COVERING A WIDE FIELD

Custer in 1864. Major General of Volunteers.

CHAPTER 1

ROSSER vs. RENO

GEN. ROSSER'S TRIBUTE TO CUSTER

(From St. Paul and Minneapolis *Pioneer-Press and Tribune,* July 8, 1876, reprinted in the *New York Herald,* July 11, 1876.)

Editor: The Evening Tribune,

"The evil which men do, lives after them,
The good is often interred with their bones."

I am surprised and deeply mortified to see that our neighbor the Pioneer-Press and Tribune, in its morning issue, has seen fit to adjudge the true, brave and heroic Custer so harshly as to attribute his late terrible disaster with the Sioux Indians to reckless indiscretion. From what I can gather from Gen. Terry's instructions to Gen. Custer it is quite evident that it was expected, if not expressed, that Custer should attack the savages wherever found, and as to the manner of attack, of course, that was left to the discretion and judgment of Gen. Custer, and viewing the circumstances of this fatal attack, from my standpoint, I fail to see anything very rash in the planning of it, or reckless in its attempted execution. On the contrary, I feel that Custer would have succeeded had Reno, with all the reserve of seven companies, passed through and joined Custer after the first repulse. It is not safe at this distance, and in the absence of full details, to criticise too closely the conduct of any officer of his command, but I think it quite certain that Gen. Custer had agreed with Reno upon a place of junction in case of the repulse of either or both of the detachments, and instead of an effort being made by Reno for such a junction, as soon as he encountered heavy resistance he took refuge in the hills, and abandoned Custer and his gallant comrades to their fate.

It is useless to say that Custer should have amused those Indians as soon as he reached them, or diverted their attention until Gen. Terry could come up with reinforcements, for although it is stated that Gen. Terry was only 20 or 30 miles off, and he moved by forced marches, he did not reach the scene of the disaster until three days after its occurrence. The Indians were running, and it is evident to my mind that Gen. Custer was doubtless ordered to pursue them, cut off their retreat to the south, and to drive them back upon Terry and Gibbon, and thus hemmed in between these commands they were to be crushed.

To do this it was necessary for Custer to strike them wherever he found them, and by vigorous blows and hot pursuit he was to drive them into the trap which Terry had set for them.

Infantry on expeditions against Indians can only be used as guards for supply trains, and in the pursuit of Indians upon a mission such as Custer's they are useless as fox hounds in pursuit of wild geese.

It was expected when the expedition was sent out that Custer and the Seventh Cavalry were to do all the fighting, and superbly did a portion of them do it. As a soldier I would sooner today lie in the grave of Gen. Custer and his gallant comrades alone in that distant wilderness, that when the "last trumpet" sounds I could rise to judgment from my post of duty, than to live in the place of the survivors of the siege on the hills.

I knew Gen. Custer well; have known him intimately from boyhood; and being on opposite sides during the late war we often met and measured strength on the fields of Virginia, and I can truly say now that I never met a more enterprising, gallant or dangerous enemy during those four years of terrible war, or a more genial, wholesouled, chivalrous gentleman and friend in peace than Major General George A. Custer.

Respectfully,
T. L. ROSSER
(Late Major General, C.S.A.)

RENO'S REPLY TO ROSSER

(From *New York Herald,* August 8, 1876)

Headquarters, Seventh Regiment of Cavalry
Camp on the Yellowstone, July 30, 1876.

Mr. T. L. Rosser:—

Sir:—

When I read the first part of your letter, published in the *Pioneer-Press* of the 8th inst., as copied from the Minneapolis *Evening Tribune,* my thought was that your motive had only the object of a defense of a personal friend—a gallant soldier against whom you fought; but after reading all of it I could no longer look upon it as the tribute of a generous enemy, since, through me, you have attacked as brave officers as ever served the government, and with the same recklessness and ignorance of circumstances as Custer is charged with in his attack upon the hostile Indians. Both charges—the one made against him and the one made by you against us—are equally untrue. You say:—"I feel Custer would have succeeded had Reno, with all the reserve of seven companies, passed through and joined Custer after the first repulse"; and after confessing that you are firing at long range say further:—"I think it quite certain that Custer had agreed with Reno upon a place of junction in case of a repulse of either or both detachments, and instead of an effort being made by Reno for such a junction, as soon as he encountered heavy resistance he took refuge in the hills, and abandoned Custer and his gallant comrades to their fate."

As I shall show, both the premises are false, and consequently all the conclusions of your letter fall to the ground, including your talk about the last trumpet. Custer's organization of the regiment into distinct commands was not made until half past ten a. m. of the day he was killed, and was as follows:—Companies M, A, and G to be one battalion, commanded by me; companies H, D, and K another, commanded by the Senior Captain, Benteen; company B, Captain McDougall to be rear guard and take charge of the pack train; companies C, E, F, I, and L to be his own immediate command, with Captains Keogh and Yates as subordinate battalion commanders. He made his own selection of companies. Benteen, with a battalion, was sent far to my left by Custer's orders. When I went into the fight he was out of sight. My battalion was to the left and rear when we approached the village, but brought to the front by Custer. The only official orders I had from him were about five miles from the village, when Col-

onel Cooke, the regimental adjutant, gave me his orders in these words:—"Custer says to move at as rapid a gait as you think prudent, and to charge afterward, and you will be supported by the whole outfit."

No mention of any plan, no thought of junction, only the usual orders to the advance guard to attack at a charge. When the enemy was reached I moved to the front at a fast trot, and at the river halted ten minutes or less to gather the battalion. I sent word to Custer that I had the enemy in front very strong, and then charged, driving the reds before me about three miles or less, to within a short distance of their village, supposing my command, consisting of 120 officers and men and about twenty-five scouts and guards, followed by the column under Custer. The village, about three and a half miles long, was situated upon the Little Big Horn, and the topography of the vicinity may be briefly told. The stream was very crooked, like a letter S in its wanderings, and on the side on which the village was, it opened out into a broad bottom, perhaps half or three quarters of a mile wide. The stream was fringed, as usual, with the trees of the plains—a growth of large cottonwoods, and on the opposite side was a range of high bluffs which had been cut into very deep ravines by the surface water and by the action of the stream. Just at their base the earth had fallen in and left perpendicular banks, making what is known as cutbanks. As I neared the village the Indians came out in great numbers, and I was soon convinced I had at least ten to one against me and was forced on the defensive. This I accomplished by taking possession of a point of woods where I found shelter for my horses. I fought there, dismounted, and made my way to within 200 yards of the village, and firmly believe that if, at that moment, the seven companies had been together the Indians could have been driven from their village. As we approached near their village they came out in overwhelming numbers, and soon the small command would have been surrounded on all sides, to prevent which I mounted and charged through them to a position I could hold with the few men I had.

You see by this I was the advance and the first to be engaged and draw fire, and was consequently the command to be supported, and not the one from which support could be expected. All I know of Custer from the time he ordered me to attack till I saw him buried is that he did not follow my trail, but kept on his side of the river and along the crest of the bluff on the opposite side from the village and from my command;

that he heard and saw my action I believe, although I could not see him, and it is just here that the Indians deceived us. At this time I was driving them with ease, and his trail shows that he moved rapidly down the river for 3 miles to the ford, at which he attempted to cross into their village, and with the conviction that he would strike a retreating enemy. Trumpeter Martin, of Company H, and who the last time of any living person heard and saw General Custer, and who brought the last order his adjutant, Colonel Cooke, ever penciled, says he left the General at the summit of the highest bluff on that side, and which overlooked the village of my first battlefield, and as he turned General Custer raised his hat and gave a yell, saying they were asleep in their tepees and surprised, and to charge. Cooke's order, sent to Benteen, and which I afterwards saw and read, said, "Big village; big thing; bring up the packs." Custer's disaster was not the defeat of the Seventh Cavalry, who held their ground for thirty-six hours after with a force outnumbered ten to one. The Indians made him overconfident by appearing to be stampeded, and, undoubtedly, when he arrived at the ford, expecting to go with ease through their village, he rode into an ambuscade of at least 2,000 reds. My getting the command of the seven companies was not the result of any order or prearranged plan. Benteen and McDougall arrived separately, saw the command on the bluffs, and came to it. They did not go into the bottom at all after the junction. They attempted to go down the trail of General Custer but the advanced companies soon sent back word that they were being surrounded. Crowds of reds were seen on all sides of us, and Custer's fate had evidently been determined. I knew the position I had first taken on the bluff was near and a strong one. I at once moved there, dismounted and herded the pack train, and had but just time to do so when they came upon me by thousands. Had we been twenty minutes later effecting the junction not a man of that regiment would be living today to tell the tale.

As you have the reputation of a soldier, and, if it is not undeserved, there is in you a spirit that will give you no rest until you have righted, as in you lies, the wrong that was perpetrated upon gallant men by your defense of Custer, and I request you will publish this letter with such comments as that spirit will dictate.

Respectfully,

Marcus Reno
Major, Seventh cavalry.

Before General Rosser had an opportunity to reply to the above letter, which he did under date of 22 August 1876, both Reno and Benteen had been interviewed by the New York Herald. These interviews follow, and General Rosser's reply of 22 August indicates that he has seen and read them both.

* * *

STATEMENTS OF CAPTAIN F. W. BENTEEN AND MAJOR M. A. RENO

(To *New York Herald,* August 8, 1876)

BENTEEN

I suppose we had better begin with the formation of the battalion from the point where the battalions were formed. I was sent with my battalion to the left to a line of bluffs about five miles off, with instructions to look for Indians and see what was to be seen, and if I saw nothing there to go on, and when I had satisfied myself it was useless to go further in that direction to join the main trail. After proceeding through a rough and difficult country, very tiring on the horses, and seeing nothing, and wishing to save the horses unnecessary fatigue, I decided to return to the main trail. Before I had proceeded a mile in the direction of the bluffs I was overtaken by the Chief Trumpeter and the Sergeant Major with instructions from General Custer to use my own discretion, and in case I should find any trace of Indians at once to notify General Custer. Having marched rapidly and passed the line of bluffs on the left bank of a branch of the Little Big Horn River, which made into the main stream about two miles and a half above the ford passed by Colonel Reno's command, as ordered, I continued my march in the same direction. The whole time occupied in this march was about an hour and a half. As I was anxious to regain the main command, as there was no sign of Indians, I then decided to rejoin the main trail, as the country before me was mostly of the same character as that I had already passed over, without valley and without water, and offering no inducement for the Indians. No valleys were visible, not even the valley where the fight took place, until my command struck the river. About three miles from the point where Reno crossed the ford I met a sergeant bringing orders to the commanding officer of the rear guard, Captain McDougall, Company B, to hurry up the pack trains. A mile further I was met by my trumpeter, bringing a written order from Lieutenant Cook, the adjutant of the regiment, to this effect:—"Benteen, come on; big village; be quick; bring packs." and a postscript saying, "Bring packs." A mile or a mile and a half further on I first came in sight of the valley of the Little Big Horn. About twelve or fifteen dismounted men were fighting on the plain with Indians charging and recharging them. The body numbered about 900 at this time. Colonel Reno's mounted party were retiring across the river to the bluffs. I did not recognize till later what part of the command this was, but it was clear that they had been beaten. I then marched my command in line to their succor. On reaching the bluff I reported to Colonel Reno and first learned that the command had been separated and that Custer was not in that part of the field, and no one of Reno's command was able to inform me of the whereabouts of General Custer. While the command was awaiting the arrival of the pack mules a company was sent forward in the direction supposed to have been taken by Custer. After proceeding about a mile they were attacked and driven back. During this time I heard no heavy firing, and there was nothing to indicate that a heavy fight was going on, and I believe that at this time Custer's command had been annihilated.

The rest of the story you must get from Colonel Reno, as he took command and knows more than anyone else.

RENO

On the return of the company and the closing up of the pack mules, which occurred about the same time, the whole command moved forward, proceeding about a mile and a half. During this time chopping shots were heard. So numerous were the masses of Indians encountered that the command was obliged to dismount and fight on foot, retiring to the point which had first been selected. It was a crest of hills which formed a depression, in which the pack mules and horses were herded, and men were put in these crests, sheltering themselves as best they could behind a growth of sage brush. This was about half past five P.M. and we had just taken up position when the Indians came on us in thousands. The fight was maintained in this position until night. About nine P.M. the Indians withdrew, and immediately the command was put to work making such rifle pits as the scanty implements at our command enabled us to do—mostly hunting knives, plates and canteens, a few axes, and three spades. We were left undisturbed until half past two in the morning of the 26th, when two sharp rifle cracks opened one of the heaviest fires I have ever witnessed, and which continued until half past nine A.M., when the fury of the attack subsided. In the meantime they fired into the herd through the opening of the valley from a hill which was beyond range of my carbines. About eight A.M. the Indians made a charge on the front defended by Colonel Benteen, one of the Indians reaching near enough to his line to touch a dead soldier with his coup stick. He will never touch another The question of obtaining water was then becoming vital for the wounded, and the water being on the front of Company H, about 600 yards distant, a skirmish line was formed under command of Colonel Benteen to protect the volunteers who went for water. Of these one was killed and six wounded. Water was obtained, and though the Indians remained annoyingly about us during the rest of the day, evidently they had been disturbed, for I saw them making a big fire in the valley, raising great clouds of dust and smoke. The fire was evidently encouraged by the Indians, and about six o'clock we saw their column come out from behind these clouds of smoke and dust on to the bluffs, moving in regular military order in the direction of the Big Horn Mountains, which were about thirty miles distant. I first thought it was the return of Custer which had started the Indians. We could not conceive the awful fate which had befallen him and his command. The question was settled next morning by General Terry riding into camp, who brought the first news of Custer's disaster. Colonel Benteen, with his company, was at once dispatched to the battlefield, and brought us the fact of Custer's annihilation and that he had recognized the bodies of the officers whose names have been published and who fell with Custer. When the battalions were organized I was given the command of Companies M, A and G, and was ordered to proceed at as rapid a gait as I thought prudent and afterward to charge, and that I would be supported by the whole outfit. This order was brought to me by Colonel Cooke, adjutant of the regiment. I never saw Custer again living, and the instructions embodied in these words were received from him. After Colonel Cooke gave me these instructions he rode with me for some time, as also Captain Keogh, and said, in his laughing, smiling, way, "We are all going with the advance and Miles Keogh is coming too." My attention was then taken up with the ford which I was to cross with the companies, and I never saw either alive again. After crossing the ford I sent word to Custer that the Indians were in front and very strong, but charged on down, supposing that I was being followed by him. As

I neared the village I saw Indians passing from the hill behind my left flank. I knew no support could be coming, so I dismounted and took possession of a point of woods about a half mile upstream from the village, sheltered my horses and advanced to the attack, reaching within 200 yards of the village. The Indians then came out in overwhelming numbers, and it was plain to me that the salvation of my command depended on reaching a defensive position, which was accomplished by charging through the Indians to the bluffs, where I was joined by the other companies commanded by Colonel Benteen and Captain McDougall. The ford we crossed in getting to the bluff was not the same we had passed in going to attack the village. It was in front of the bluff, and it was partially by accident that we found it. When I went into action I had only 112 men and officers of the Seventh with me and some twenty-five scouts. If I had not made the charge for the bluffs my command would undoubtedly have been annihilated as Custer's was. The great mistake in the beginning was that we underestimated the Indian strength. The lowest computation puts the Indian strength at about 2,500, and some think there were 5,000 warriors present. The Indians are the best light cavalry in the world. I have seen pretty nearly all of them, and I do not except even the Cossacks. Among the gallant deeds in the Custer fight the splendid conduct of Lieutenant Cooke deserves special mention. He was the last officer to fall, and he remained mounted to the last after Custer's death. The command of the survivors fell on him, and with his small band he repeatedly charged the Indians. The Crow scout, who was the only known survivor, says that the Sioux warriors scattered time and time again before the desperate onslaught of Cooke and his handful of men, who fell at last, overwhelmed by innumerable enemies.

ROSSER'S REPLY TO RENO

(From *New York Herald,* August 22, 1876.)

THE CUSTER MASSACRE.

A Criticism by General Rosser of General Reno's Tactics.

A Sharp Reply to Reno
Rosser's Theory of Custer's Plan of Engagement.

General Rosser has forwarded for publication an answer to the letter of General Reno, in which the former criticized the conduct of the latter in not making an attempt to relieve General Custer. General Rosser says, in the following letter, that he has now read the official report of General Terry, and that he now writes with a fuller information of the details of General Reno's position.

* * *

Minneapolis, Minn., August 16, 1876.

Marcus A. Reno,
  Major Seventh Cavalry
  United States Army:—

Major—

A letter appeared in the New York Herald of the 8th inst., addressed to me and signed by yourself, complaining of injustice having been done you in a letter of mine written to the *Minneapolis Evening Tribune* upon the receipt here of Custer's tragic death. My letter to which you refer, and of which you complain, was written in advance of the receipt of the details of this engagement with the Indians, and before I had seen the official report of General Terry. It was written as a rebuke to the St. Paul Pioneer Press and Tribune, which had arraigned General Custer under charges of unsoldierly conduct, which I believed to have been uncharitable and unjust, and with no view to your disparagement whatever. Having once been a soldier myself I fully appreciate your sensitiveness to criticisms which involved the vital elements of a soldier's honor and reputation. Your patriotism and courage I have never questioned; but as long as you are a public servant you will be fortunate if you escape with simply a criticism of your plan and only your judgment censured. As for the surviving officers and men of the Seventh Cavalry, I am proud to say I know many of them, and I believe that "a more valiant band was never marshaled by gallant knight" than they. They who have followed the immortal Custer in all of his exploits on the plains should be proud of their fame as well as his. The living members of that noble regiment I know are as ready to follow you and Benteen to the other shore as were the few who fell with Custer.

But now, Major, as to the manner in which you, as detachment commander, performed your duty on that unhappy day, I will not assume the office of judge, and, after submitting a few questions to you, I will leave the matter to the department commander, General A. H. Terry, who is eminently qualified to judge of all such questions, and, he being in a position where all the facts can be ascertained, I am willing to rest the case with him, not doubting that he will do you full justice. The errors which I believe you committed in that engagement were attributed to what I believed to have been a lack of judgment and a want of experience in Indian warfare, as I understand you have seen but little service with your regiment on the plains; and, in looking over your plan of attack, I could see no good reason for your gently pushing a line of skirmishers down toward a mounted force of Indians when it was expected that you would attack vigorously with your entire command. The fact of your dismounting and taking to the point of timber to which you refer was an acknowledgment of weakness, if not defeat, and this, too, when your loss was little or nothing. This was an act which I condemn. You had an open field for cavalry operations, and I believe that if you had remained in the saddle and charged boldly into the village the shock upon the Indians would have been so great that they would have been compelled to withdraw their attacking force from Custer, who, when relieved, could have pushed his command through to open ground, where he could have maneuvered his command, and thus greatly have increased his chances of success.

But, if you had charged into the village, and been repulsed, could you not have fallen back upon Benteen in good order, and thus have saved the disaster which befell you in the confusion and haste with which you were forced to cross the river?

You must remember that your situation was very different from the one in which Custer was placed. You had an open field, in which you could handle your command, while Custer was buried in a deep ravine or canyon, and, as he supposed, stealthily advancing upon an unsuspecting foe, but was, by the nature of the ground, helpless when assailed on all sides by the Indians in the hills above him.

Colonel Benteen says:—"When I first came in sight of the valley of the Little Big Horn twelve or fifteen dismounted men were fighting on the plain with Indians, charging and recharging them. Colonel Reno's mounted party was retiring across the river to the bluffs. I then marched my command in line to their succor." Now, in reading this account at this distance, would one be blamed for supposing that those dismounted men had been cruelly abandoned to their fate and were only saved from their fate by the timely arrival of the gallant Benteen? From your letter I infer that your entire command was not called into action in your attack upon the village, and that your loss was but trifling until you began your retreat. You do not state, but I have the impression from some of the accounts sent in from the field, that you began your skirmish with the Indians about half past twelve to one o'clock, and that you recrossed the river and occupied the bluff about two o'clock. Now, to the reporter of the New York Herald you state that you made a reconnaissance in the direction of Custer's trail about five o'clock. The Indians appear to have withdrawn from your front as soon as you recrossed the river. Why, then, could you not have gone in pursuit of Custer earlier? When you did go you say that you heard "chopping shots." Do you not think that, even then, by a bold dash at the Indians, you might have saved a portion, at least, of Custer's perishing command? I have no desire whatever of casting a shadow over you or any one else that the name of Custer may shine the brighter; and, if my criticisms of your conduct in this engagement are unmerited, I deeply regret it, for from the beginning I have never had a thought of doing you or any member of your worthy command any injury, and, on the other hand, perhaps I can never benefit my noble friend who on this field fell a victim to a few combinations of unlucky mishaps. Yet I am proud to know that he sleeps today sublimely in an honored grave, and all patriots and lovers of heroic deeds, performed in devotion to duty, will join in his requiem.

I enclose you a map which I have copied mostly from memory from one which I saw at Department Headquarters in St. Paul a short while ago, on which you will recognize the positions of the various detachments; and as you know no more of the movements of Custer after you separated from him, apart from what you could gather from the position of the dead and the appearance of the ground, than perhaps I do, you will pardon me for submitting to you my theory of the plan of engagement and the result. From your statement, it appears that you, as well as Custer, were deceived as to the strength of the Indians; you, as well as he, believed that they were fleeing; and, without reconnoitering their positions, the command, though broken into detachments, hastened to their capture. The topography of this map leads me to believe that Custer estimated the Indians to be but few, and embraced within the hills which compass the first bottom, or the one in which you deployed your line of attack; and, with this conviction, he passed around behind the hills, hoping to cross the river at the lower end of their village and thus cut off their retreat. He evidently ran in at the first point where his trail approaches the river, thinking that he had gone far enough to accomplish his object; but, finding that the village was still beyond, he hurried on to this point, perhaps before you had crossed the river. He fell upon an overwhelming number at the point where he struck the river, and here, where he expected to find the lower end of the village, he found himself in the midst of a city which extended far (and which to him was before undiscovered) beyond, and while he was warily approaching this point by tortuous canyons, believing that the savages had not discovered him, they had poured out of this to him unseen camp, and, hiding behind the hills, took up a favorable position, which was to him inaccessable, and from which their destructive fire could not be withstood.

I speak of ravines and canyons, and the topography seems to bear me out on this, for all accounts speak of the country about Custer's route as being very broken. While Custer's command was making its way through these gorges to the enemy, he himself, climbing the hillsides wherever he could, and peeping over the broken crests, was observing the condition of the village, and, believing his approach undiscovered, he is heard to exclaim (I suppose to a messenger to you), "Charge! They are asleep in their tepees." Was that last order obeyed? Were the nature of the river banks such, at either of the points where he approached the river, that he could have crossed without great difficulty? Did he approach at the point where these "cut banks," of which you speak, are met? With a river in front which could not be crossed, his command wedged in a narrow ravine, and the hills above covered with sharpshooters, it is not a surprising fact that the command was destroyed.

I know something of those cutbanks of which you speak. I have seen them along the Yellowstone, the Powder and the Little Missouri Rivers; they are usually from forty feet to 100 feet high, and are perpendicular; and a horseman can pass over but few of them, even if there is no other impediment, without great risk of life, both to horse and man; and to accomplish such a thing in the face of a powerful enemy is impossible.

At the verge of this high bank, the deep stream below, a vast city of Indians before him, your command retreating and the Indians rapidly accumulating on his front and flanks, Custer was forced to countermarch and begin his retreat, which he attempted in column of companies. The companies of Tom Custer and Captain Smith, being the first in advance and last in the retreat, fell first in the slaughter which followed this retrograde movement, and were found as I have marked the line on the above map.* Yates' company, with its gallant captain, took up the position on the hill, where all perished, including Custer, the Murat of the American Army, and Cook, Yates, Tom Custer and Riley, as I have indicated on the map; while, a little further along, are found the remains of Keogh's and Calhoun's companies, which perished while fighting their way back to you—a few even reaching the point where Custer first struck the high banks of the river.

I have heard that someone has advanced the theory that Custer was met, at this point where he first struck the river, by overwhelming numbers, and so beaten that his line from that point on was one of retreat. This is simply ridiculous. Had Custer been repulsed at this point his column would have been driven back upon the line on which he had approached and the proposition is too silly to be discussed. I claim that the part which Custer acted in this engagement was that of a bold, earnest man, who believed he had before him a rare opportunity to strike the Indians a blow which, if successful, would end the campaign, and it was worth the bold effort; and, although he was unsuccessful, he was not, in my opinion, rash and risked no more than he had often hazarded before and won. He did that which in ninety-nine cases out of a hundred will succeed, but this by chance was the fatal exception, yet the result does not impair the value of the rule.

You know that even in civilized warfare the bolder movements are generally successful, and the general who plans for the enemy and is counselled by his fears is sure to fail.

Respectfully,

T. L. ROSSER

---

* Gen. Rosser's map was never published, so far as is known. W.A.G.

CHAPTER 2

DEAD MEN DO TELL TALES!

MARK KELLOGG'S LETTERS

(From *New York Herald,* July 11, 1876)

The following private letter and hurried correspondence for publication from the pen of our slaughtered correspondent, Mark Kellogg, will be read with painful interest. We give them both just as written, in order to enable our readers to see the last written messages from our gallant correspondent in all their simplicity and force:—

THE PRIVATE LETTER

In Camp on Yellowstone
June 21, 1876

To the Editor of the *Herald:*—

Enclosed please find manuscript, which I have been forced to write very hurriedly, owing to the want of time given me for the purpose. My last was badly demoralized from wetting, as then briefly explained, and I feared it would not prove acceptable on that account. The officers of the expedition have written generally to their friends to watch for the *Herald,* as they know I am to record their deeds. I will endeavor to give you interesting letters as we go along. I have the liberty of the entire column, headquarters and all, and will get down to bottom facts in all matters connected with the expedition. Very truly yours,

M. H. Kellogg.

THE LETTER FOR PUBLICATION

The following letter for publication was written by Mr. Kellogg four days before the daring charge of Custer, in which the latter and all his followers, including our correspondent, lost their lives:—

At Mouth of Rosebud, on
Yellowstone River, June 21, 1876.

From June 12, the date of my last communication, until June 19, the only occurrences of General Terry's command were the establishment of a supply depot at the mouth of the Powder River and making the steamer Far West a moving base

of supplies, having on board thirty days' rations and forage; the movement of the steamer to the mouth of the Tongue River with the headquarters command on board, and the march of General Custer from the mouth of the Powder River to the mouth of the Tongue River, an estimated distance of forty miles, moving up the valley of the Yellowstone River. During the trip no incident occurred except the display of sharp rifle shooting on the part of General Custer who brought down an antelope at 400 yards and nearly shot off the heads of several sage hens. The country north of the Powder River, for a distance of twelve to fifteen miles, is very poor, low and causing hard marching, with a soil producing no grasses, only sage brush and cactus. *En route,* on the 15th, the column passed through an abandoned Indian camp, apparently less than a year old. It had been a large camp, being two miles or more in length, and must have contained 1,200 or 1,500 lodges. Game was very scarce, and no buffalo at all were seen.

The Yellowstone is looming high, and its current is so swift, eddying and whirling as to create a seething sound like that of a soft wind rustling in the tall grass. Its color resembles yellowish clay at this point. It is cool and pleasant to the taste, and is a larger body of water than that of the Missouri River above its mouth, but very much superior for purposes of steamboat navigation. The waters of the Tongue River are of a deepish red color, running swiftly, and not very palatable to the taste.

On the 19th of June General Custer, with six companies of cavalry, crossed the Tongue River, about three miles from its mouth, by fording, and marching to a point about nine miles from where Major Reno with six companies of the Seventh Cavalry were encamped, having returned from the scout he was ordered upon; but, for some cause unknown to your correspondent, Major Reno was unfortunate enough not only to exceed but to disobey the instructions of General Terry, a copy of which is subjoined, viz:—

Headquarters Department of Dakota
    In the Field, Camp on Powder River,
        Montana Territory, June 10, 1876
Field Special Order No. 2
2. Major M. A. Reno, Seventh Cavalry, with six companies (right wing) of his regiment and one gun from the Gatling battery, will proceed at the earliest practicable moment to make a reconnaissance of the Powder River from the present camp to the mouth of the Little Powder. From the last named point he will cross to the headwaters of Mizpah Creek, and descend that creek to its junction with the Powder River. Thence he will cross the Pumpkin Creek and Tongue River, and descend the Tongue to its junction with the Yellowstone, where he may expect to meet the remaining companies of the Seventh Cavalry and supplies of subsistence and forage.

Major Reno's command will be supplied with subsistence for twelve days, and with forage for the same period at the rate of two pounds of grain the day for each animal.

The guide Mitch Bouyer and eight Indian scouts, to be detailed by Lieutenant Colonel Custer, will report to Major Reno, for duty with this column.

Acting Assistant Surgeon H. R. Porter is detailed for duty with Major Reno. By command of Brigadier General Terry.
            Edw. Smith
            Captain, Eighteenth Infantry
            Acting Assistant Adjutant General

Major Reno made an error in that he crossed, going a due south course, from the forks of the Powder to the Rosebud River, where he found a fresh hostile trail. General Terry had planned to have Major Reno return to the column, marching down the valley of the Tongue River; and after he had formed the junction General Custer was to organize his regiment for a scout up the Tongue, thence across to the Rosebud, striking it near its head; thence down that valley towards General Terry, who in the meantime would move by steamer to the mouth of the Rosebud, join General Gibbon's command, march up that valley until he met and joined General Custer. The plan was an excellent one, and but for the unfortunate movement of Major Reno the main force of the Indians, numbering 1,500, would have been bagged. As it is, a new campaign is organized, and to-morrow, June 22, General Custer with twelve cavalry companies, will scout from its mouth up the valley of the Rosebud until he reaches the fresh trail discovered by Major Reno, and move on that trail with all rapidity possible in order to overhaul the Indians, whom it has been ascertained are hunting buffalo and making daily and leisurely short marches. In the meantime, General Terry will move on the steamer to the mouth of the Big Horn River, scouting Pumpkin Creek en route, with General Gibbon's cavalry as well as infantry, which are marching toward the Big Horn on the north side of the Yellowstone. This part of the command marched up the Big Horn valley in order to intercept the Indians if they should attempt to escape from General Custer down that avenue. The hope is now strong and I believe, well founded, that this band of ugly customers, known as Sitting Bull's band, will be "gobbled" and dealt with as they deserve. General Custer's command made a rapid march from the Tongue River to the Rosebud, over some portion of which the route covered was the mauvaises terres in the ugliest forms; up and down the ascents and descents so abrupt as to appear impassible for locomotion, circuiting and twisting hither and thither —now along a narrow defile, then through a deep, abrupt, canyon, in which the sun's rays created a warm, still atmosphere that caused panting breaths and reeking perspiration. However, the sharp, quick march of the cavalry kept pace with the steamer which was running up the Yellowstone. Frequently by us in the rear, the light colored buckskin on the person of General Custer would be seen, followed closely by the head of the column, as he and they climbed the heights from out the winding, yawning, abysses below.

As we proceeded further up the valley of the Yellowstone River its attractions became more marked, more defined, and more beautiful. Vegetation increases in size, in the grasses as well as in the timber. Beautiful little islands are frequently seen, covered to their very edges with a thick growth of trees whose vivid green foliage hides the branches that reach far outward over the yellowish waters flowing swiftly beneath. The banks of the river are abrupt, the channel unchanging, the bed of which is composed of gravel and its depth sufficient at its usual low stage to allow light draught steamers to navigate its length from its emptying into the Missouri River to the mouth of the Big Horn, a distance of nearly 500 miles. I write of this stream as I see it, for the purpose of informing the thousands of readers of the *Herald* of the magnitude and facilities it affords for commercial purposes in the near future, when its beautiful valley shall become populated, of a stream that has the appearance on the maps of being only a mere creek. A valley of your own "away down East" is merely the area of a race track compared with the valleys of the far west. Here they range from 30 to 500 miles in length, ranging in width from one to fifteen. The upper portion of the Yellowstone valley, that is to say, the upper half of the valley, is superior to the balance in all respects —for grass and timber, not only in quantity but in quality; for richness of soil; for health and climate; for its abundance of game, its quantity of fish and other things besides.

Brigadier General Alfred H. Terry, in command of this expedition, I find to be my ideal of a commanding general—large brained, sagacious, far reaching, cool under all circumstances and with rare executive abilities. He is besides genial, courteous, frank and manly. So far as he is concerned, I contend that his planning has been of the finest character, and unless his subordinates frustrate them by overt acts of their own, must be successful. He has won the hearts of all who have come to know him and is highly, regarded by the whole command. Of his staff, while it may seem invidious of me to mention singly, still it is my privilege to say that I find them all kind, courteous, high toned gentlemen, all of whom fill creditably and well the requisites of their various positions. And now a word for the most peculiar genius in the army, a man of strong impulses, of great hearted friendships and bitter enmities, of quick, nervous temperament, undaunted courage, will and determination; a man possessing electrical mental capacity and of iron frame and constitution; a brave, faithful, gallant soldier, who has warm friends and bitter enemies; the hardest rider, the greatest pusher, with the most untiring vigilance, overcoming seeming impossibilities, and with an ambition to succeed in all things he undertakes; a man to do right, as he construes the right, in every case; one respected and beloved by his followers, who would freely follow him into the "jaws of hell." Of Lieutenant Colonel G. A. Custer I am now writing. Do not think I am overdrawing the picture. The pen picture is true to life, and is drawn not only from actual observation, but from an experience that cannot mislead me.

The officers of the several companies of the Seventh Cavalry, so far as my acquaintance extends, are as brave and gallant a lot of men as ever drew a sword in their country's cause. I can say as much for the infantry. Brave and true hearted, every one of them. In my opinion, based on an experience and familiarity with the army and its men for years, I believe I am safe in saying that the present expedition under the command of General Terry is made up from among the best in the American service, the Seventh and the Second cavalry and the Sixth, Seventeenth, Twentieth and Seventh infantry. My acquaintance with General Gibbon and General Brisbin is limited, but I hear them spoken highly of on all hands. Their record in days gone by bear me out in stating that they occupy positions for which they are eminently fitted, and the commands are made up of the same fearless fellows as compose the Seventh Cavalry.

General Gibbon and command departed from Fort Ellis, Montana Territory, on April 1, pursuant to orders, and marched to a point designated on the Yellowstone, where they have been held in check and prevented from crossing by the extreme high water and rapid current of that stream. While lying in camp not far from the mouth of the Rosebud, during the past four weeks they have been frequently annoyed by bravado demonstrations by hostile Indians on the heights opposite them, who would dash up on their ponies, laugh in derision, shout, whoop and cavort around, like so many gymnasts, and then ride off at a gallop with a war whoop. All this had to be submitted to, for it was simply impossible to cross the boiling, seething, roaring stream that intervened without hazarding valuable lives.

* * *

A VOICE FROM THE TOMB

NOTE: The following "anonymous" letter was believed to have been written by General Custer himself just before the regiment left on its march up the Rosebud June 22, 1876.—W.A.G.

(From the *New York Herald,* July 23, 1876)

* * *

Extraordinary Letter from a Prominent Officer Killed in Custer's Last Charge

* * *

Reno's Contempt of Orders

* * *

Something for Sherman and Sheridan To Investigate

* * *

Big Horn Expedition, on Yellowstone River
At the mouth of the Rosebud, June 22, 1876

My last letter was sent from the mouth of Powder River and described our march from the Little Missouri. I fear it may not have reached its

Custer as he probably appeared at the time of the battle.

destination, or if it did it was in such a condition as to be illegible owing to a sad accident which befell our mail party. The latter consisted of a sergeant of the Sixth Infantry, Hazen's regiment, and two men of the same command. This party was to take the mail of this expedition on a small boat from the mouth of the Powder to Fort Buford at the mouth of the former. Just as the sergeant [Fox] with the mail bag on his arm stepped aboard the small boat and was about to push off the boat overturned, throwing all hands into the water. The sergeant at once disappeared below the surface and was never afterward seen. The other members of the party, being experienced swimmers, were, with the assistance of bystanders, rescued from a watery grave. When the sergeant disappeared in the water the mail sack went with him, but fortunately floated between the steamer and the shore, before sinking below the surface. By means of boat hooks the bag and its contents were recovered, but not until they had been under water several minutes. When opened on shore many of the letters were found opened by the influence of the water, and all the stamps displaced. Captain Grant Marsh, of the steamer Far West, the most popular steamboat captain on the Upper Missouri, took the mail in charge, and, with the aid of his assistants, devoted almost an entire night to dry-

ing and sealing the contents of the mail bag, a task they completed in time to start the mail on its journey at four o'clock the following morning. The sergeant who lost his life had been twenty-two years in the army, and had but recently returned from Washington, where he had been to file his application for appointment as ordinance sergeant, that appointment being considered the crowning ambition of the most faithful old soldiers.

Major Reno, whose departure with six companies of the Seventh Cavalry to scout up the Powder River was mentioned in my last letter, moved under written orders, which in substance directed him to scout up the Powder River as far as the mouth of the Little Powder, then across to the headwaters of Mizpah Creek, down that creek to near its mouth, then across to Pumpkin Creek, down that stream to its junction with Tongue River, then down Tongue River to its mouth on the Yellowstone, where he was informed the main part of the expedition would be by the time of his arrival at that point.

In the opinion of the most experienced officers it was not believed that any considerable, if any, force of Indians would be found on the Powder River; still there were a few, including Major Reno, who were convinced that the main body of Sitting Bull's warriors would be encountered on Powder River. The general impression, however, is and has been, that on the headwaters of the Rosebud and Little Bighorn rivers the "hostiles" would be found.

It was under this impression that General Terry, in framing the orders which were to govern Major Reno's movements, explicitly and positively directed that officer to confine himself to his orders and instructions, and particularly not to move in the direction of Rosebud River, as it was feared that such a movement, if prematurely made, might "flush the covey," it being the intention to employ the entire cavalry force of the expedition, when the time arrived, to operate in the valleys of the Rosebud and Big Horn Rivers. Custer and most of his officers looked with little favor on the movement up the Powder River, as, among other objections, it required the entire remaining portion of the expedition to lie in idleness within two marches of the locality where it was generally believed the hostile villages would be discovered on the Rosebud, the danger being that the Indians, ever on the alert, would discover the presence of the troops as yet undiscovered—and take advantage of the opportunity to make their escape.

Reno, after an absence of ten days, returned, when it was found, to the disgust and disappointment of every member of the expedition, from the commanding general down to the lowest private, that Reno, instead of simply failing to accomplish any good results, had so misconducted his force as to embarrass, if not seriously and permanently mar, all hopes of future success of the expedition. He had not only deliberately, and without a shadow of an excuse failed to obey his written instructions issued by General Terry's personal directions, but he had acted in positive disobedience to the strict injunctions of the department commander. Instead of conforming his line of march to the valleys and water courses laid down in his written orders he moved his command to the mouth of the Little Powder River, then across to Tongue River, and instead of following the latter stream down to its mouth. there to unite with the main command, he, for some unaccountable and thus far unexplained reason, switched off from his prescribed course and marched across the country to the Rosebud, the stream he had been particularly cautioned not to approach.

He struck the Rosebud about twenty-five miles above its mouth, and there—as Custer had predicted from the first—signs indicating the recent presence of a large force of Indians were discovered, an abandoned camp ground of the Indians was found, on which 380 lodges had been pitched. The trail led up the valley of the Rosebud. Reno took up the trail and followed it about twenty miles, but faint heart never won fair lady, neither did it ever pursue and overtake an Indian village. Had Reno, after first violating his orders, pursued and overtaken the Indians, his original disobedience of orders would have been overlooked, but his determination forsook him at this point, and instead of continuing the pursuit and at least bringing the Indians to bay, he gave the order to countermarch and faced his command to the rear, from which point he made his way back to the mouth of Tongue River and reported the details of his gross and inexcusable blunder to General Terry, his commanding officer, who informed Reno in unmistakable language that the latter's conduct amounted to positive disobedience of orders, the sad consequences of which could not yet be fully determined. The details of this affair will not bear investigation.

A court-martial is strongly hinted at, and if one is not ordered it will not be because it is not richly deserved. The guides who were with Reno report that the trail where the latter was abandoned indicates that the Indian village of 380 lodges was moving in such deliberate manner and left so recently that Reno's command could have overtaken it in a march of one day and a half. Few officers have ever had such a fine opportunity to make a successful and telling strike and few ever failed so completely to improve their opportunities.

Of course there was but one thing to do and that was to remedy as soon as possible the effects of Reno's blunder. Custer's entire command, consisting of twelve companies of the Seventh Cavalry and a detachment of Indian scouts arrived at this point yesterday evening, where the steamer Far West, with General Terry and staff on board had already preceded them, General Terry having transferred his headquarters to the Far West before her departure from the mouth of Powder River. Gibbon's command was encamped on the left bank of the Yellowstone, opposite the mouth of the Rosebud.

Yesterday, Terry, Gibbon and Custer got together, and, with unanimity of opinion, decided that Custer should start with his command up the Rosebud valley to the point where Reno abandoned the trail, take up the latter and follow the Indians as long and as far as horse flesh and human endurance could carry his command. Custer takes no wagons or tents with his command, but proposes to live and travel like Indians; in this manner the command will be able to go wherever the Indians can. Gibbon's command has started for the mouth of the Big Horn. Terry in the Far West starts for the same point today, when with Gibbon's force, and the Far West loaded with thirty days' supplies, he will push up the Big Horn as far as the navigation of that stream will permit, probably as far as old Fort C. F. Smith, at which point Custer will reform [rejoin?] the expedition after completing his present scout. Custer's command takes with it, on pack animals, rations for fifteen days. Custer advised his subordinate officers, however, in regard to rations, that it would be well to carry an extra supply of salt, because, if at the end of fifteen days the command should be pursuing a trail, he did not propose to turn back for lack of rations, but would subsist his men on fresh meat—game, if the country provided it; pack mules if nothing better offered. The *Herald* correspondent will accompany Custer's column and in the event of a "fight or a foot race," will be on the ground to make due record thereof for the benefit of the *Herald* readers. Upon the march from Powder to Tongue River, Custer, who was riding at the head of the column as it marched through a deserted Indian village of last winter, came upon the skull and bones of a white man. Near these was found the uniform of a cavalry soldier, as shown by the letter "C" on the button of the overcoat and the yellow cord binding on the dress coat. Near by were the dead embers of a large fire, showing, with attendant circumstances, that the cavalryman had undoubtedly been a prisoner in the hands of the savages, and had been put to the torture usually inflicted by Indians upon all white men falling into their hands as captives. Who the unfortunate man was and the sad details of his tragic death will never be known.

CHAPTER 3

THREE VERSIONS OF THE CUSTER BATTLE

THE NARRATIVE OF JOHN M. RYAN
1ST SGT., "M" CO., 7TH CAVALRY

(From *Hardin, Montana Tribune*, June 22, 1923)

In 1876 another expedition was organized at Fort A. Lincoln, to go against the Indians, under command of Gen. Alfred Terry, who commanded the department of Dakota. My company started with two other companies from Fort Rice, Dakota territory, and went to Fort A. Lincoln, under command of Capt. F. W. Benteen, and went into camp. Other troops assembled from the different forts, and troop K came direct from the southern states.

Start On Way

General Custer was called away from the camp to Washington on some business pertaining to the army, and was detained at Washington for some time against his wishes. He finally returned in time to take command of his own regiment, the Seventh cavalry, under General Terry. This expedition consisted of 12 companies of the Seventh United States Cavalry, numbering about 30 commissioned officers and 700 men: a battalion of infantry composed of the Sixth and Seventeenth United States infantry, commanded by Brevet-Major Sanger, and a company of the Twentieth United States infantry, numbering about 200 men; a battery of four guns, one brass 24-pound Napoleon, one three-inch Rodman, and two Gatling guns. The drivers were cavalrymen, and the cannoneers were a detachment of the Twentieth United States infantry, commanded by Lieutenant Chance, a very brave and efficient infantry officer. We also had about 50 scouts, made up of Reeves (Rees) Sioux, Crows and Santees. We also had about 150 teams loaded with forage, ammunition and rations for the command.

The morning of the 17th of May we prepared to make a move. Custer sent his own wagons ahead with the infantry. The cavalry passed in review through Fort A. Lincoln, where a great many officers and enlisted men took a last look at their wives and sweethearts.

In marching through the fort first came the scouts under command of Lieutenant Varnum, with Chief Bloody Knife and Charlie Reynolds and Fred Girard, two white scouts, and Izar* Dorman, the negro interpreter from Fort Rice.

Off for Yellowstone

Then came General Custer and his staff; next came the Seventh cavalry band, all mounted on their magnificent gray horses, playing one of Custer's favorite battle tunes, "Garryowen." Next came the Seventh cavalry, marching in column of platoons, with their guidons flying and their horses prancing. All the companies wore broadrimmed slouch hats, some black and others gray. The regiment never looked better, as all the men were in good spirits.

Our march was in the direction of the Yellowstone river. After leaving the fort we made a halt for a short time and the officers and some of the men were allowed to go back to the fort and say good-bye to their wives and sweethearts. "Mount" and "forward" was sounded, and we swung into our saddles, and the band played "The Girl I left Behind Me."

Soon after leaving the fort we encountered heavy rains, which made our progress with the heavy wagon trains very slow. When we reached the Big Heart river we camped for two days. There the paymaster joined us under an escort of infantry, and enlivened the boys' hearts with about four months' pay. If he had paid at the fort some of the troopers would undoubtedly have deserted.

Leaving the Big Heart river, we reached the Little Missouri, where we camped for five days. While at this camp General Custer, with four companies of the Seventh regiment, Company M, Captain French; Company A, Captain Moylan; Company B, Captain McDougall, and Company

---

* The man's name was Isaiah.

K, Lieutenant Godfrey, west on a five days' scouting expedition up the Little Missouri.

See Indian Signs

We saw a few signs of Indians, but nothing to indicate anything of importance on the part of the Indians. A few buffalo were killed, but the scout on the whole proved uneventful. Resuming our march, we struck into the bad lands. This is a broken and desolate country abounding in lava beds and other traces of volcanic action.

This strip known as the bad lands runs northwest from the Black Hills, and is a strip of territory about 90 miles long and about 35 miles in width. I passed through this section on five different occasions. At a distance, and when approaching this district, the barren earth, with its high ridges and ascents and descents, resembles the roofs of a large city. We marched through this section with great difficulty, for the greater portion of the way we were obliged to proceed in single file through a narrow pass, lowering our teams by means of ropes down the precipitous descents, and hauling them up again on the opposite sides.

We found the Little Missouri river swollen by the spring freshets, and had to swim our animals, getting our provisions and equipage thoroughly soaked, adding very much to our discomfort. In this vicinity we struck quite a severe snowstorm, which detained us a couple of days. We struck Powder River, and went into camp at a temporary steamboat landing. Here we remained three days. We left our wagon train, the artillery and infantry. Major Reno, with six companies of the Seventh Cavalry, companies I, L, C, F, E, and G, carrying six days' rations for the men, and one-third forage for the horses, with horses and packmules started on a reconnaissance up the Powder river to its headwaters.

Light Marching Ordered

Twelve pack mules were assigned to each of the remaining companies, the remainder of the men carrying five days' rations and forage. The men were in light marching order with no superfluous clothing.

We crossed the Powder river, losing a few of our packs, as the river was deep and the current very rapid. General Terry with one company of infantry went up the river on a steamboat. The remainder of the expedition at the steamboat landing, with one additional company of the Sixth Infantry, and an additional piece of artillery, making five guns in all, followed up the south bank of the Yellowstone, under command of Lieutenant Colonel Moore of the Sixth Infantry.

This detachment traveled up the river four or five days, and struck Tongue river, going into camp. At the mouth of Tongue river Major Reno joined the command with his six companies. During Reno's scout he ran across the Indian trail, so reported to General Terry upon his return. General Custer formed a junction with the expedition under General Gibbon, consisting of a battalion of four companies of the Second United States Cavalry, commanded by Major Brisbin, with six companies of the Seventh United States Infantry, Gibbon's own regiment, some Crow, Snake and Blackfoot Indian scouts, and the famous Diamond R wagon train, from Bozeman, Mont. After being joined by Reno's battalion there were 15 days' rations issued to the men, and one-half forage drawn for the horses.

Hold Grand Review

Each company was issued about 12 or 15 pack mules, laden with rations, forage and ammunition, carrying several thousand rounds of pistol and carbine ammunition. Each company was provided with one Arapahora.

The forenoon of June 22 we had orders to get ready for a grand review, which we expected would soon take place. We got everything in readiness as far as possible, and at noon the Seventh cavalry, numbering a little over 600 men, passed out of camp and passed in review before General Terry, General Gibbon and General Custer. This was the last review for about 322 of those men.

We made a short march of about 15 miles up the Rosebud river and went into camp early. We had orders that no trumpets should be sounded, and to build very small fires, which were to be extinguished immediately after leaving camp. This was done by throwing earth over the fires. This was done also to prevent prairie fires.

On the morning of June 23 we were up early and made a long day's march. We were on a large Indian trail and we passed several of their old camps on that day's march.

We were up early on the morning of June 24 and made another long day's march, passing several of their old camps, and marching until after dark. We were rapidly closing up on the Indians. We went into camp supposing that we were to have a good night's rest. About the middle of the night the officers went around from man to man and woke them up. We had orders to saddle up again, and we marched until just before daylight on the 25th.

Lose Some of Packs

As we marched very rapidly, some of the packs became loosened so we cut the ropes and let them go. One pack belonging to my company was among them and the Indians probably got them afterwards. We rode down into a ravine and went temporarily into camp without unsaddling the horses. We simply dropped down, threw the bridle rein over our arm and went to sleep, which was not an uncommon thing for a cavalryman to do on campaign.

It appears that General Custer and some of the scouts had gone ahead and got some information of the presence of the Indian camp. After Custer came back the officers were called and he gave directions about the battalion formations. We ate a hearty breakfast first and for our bill of fare had raw bacon, hardtack and cold water, which we relished very much.

Here General Custer split the regiment up into three battalions. The battalion that he took immediately under his command consisted of Troop C, commanded by Capt. Thomas W. Custer, the general's brother; Troop I, commanded by Capt. Myles W. Keogh; Troop F, commanded by Capt. George W. Yates; Troop L, commanded by First Lieut. James Calhoun, General Custer's brother-in-law; Troop E, commanded by First Lieut. Algernon E. Smith. He gave another battalion of three troops in command of Maj. Marcus A. Reno, consisting of Troop M, commanded by Capt. Thos. H. French; Troop G, commanded by First Lieut. Donald McIntosh; Troop A, commanded by Capt. Myles Moylan. The third battalion was commanded by Capt. Frederick W. Benteen, consisting of his own Troop H; Troop K, commanded by First Lieut. Edward S. Godfrey, and Troop D, commanded by Captain Thomas B. Weir.

About 150 pack mules constituted the pack train under an escort of Capt. Thomas M. McDougall with his own Troop B; also a detachment from each of the other 11 companies under the command of First Lieut. Edward G. Mathey of Troop M.

This pack train followed Custer's trail, and later joined Reno's battalion on the bluffs, which was very fortunate, as we almost ran out of ammunition.

Find Indian Lodges

We then rode over the divide. Lieutenant Hodgson, who was assigned as adjutant to Reno's battalion, rode from front to rear of the battalion, giving orders to ride a little off from the preceding company, so that we would not raise a large dust cloud, which would warn the Indians of our approach.

After crossing the divide, we moved down through a small valley, and around the foot of the bluff. We saw a few abandoned lodges, with the fronts of them tied up, and it appeared that General Crook's command had an engagement on the seventeenth with some of those Indians, and as some of their chiefs were killed, their bodies were put in these lodges, which accounted for the fronts of them being tied up, although we did not know what they contained at the time, and I think Custer had preparations made to charge that camp, thinking it was an Indian camp. When we got as far as that, we could look down this little valley, and see objects ahead of us. We could not tell whether they were Indians or buffaloes.

At this point I understand that Custer gave the command to Reno to overtake those Indians, and he would support him, although I did not hear that order given myself. This was the last we saw of Custer's battalion until we found their bodies on the morning of the twenty-seventh. Custer took his battalion and branched off to the right.

Reno's battalion followed the valley right down from this point to the Little Big Horn river, and Benteen branched off to the left.

Furlough for Scalp

Reno's battalion started down the valley, first on a trot, and then at a gallop, marching in columns of twos. Lieutenant Varnum, a very brave young officer in command of the scouts, rode ahead of Reno's battalion. He swung his hat around in the air, and sung out to the men, "Thirty days' furlough to the man who gets the first scalp." We were very anxious for the furlough, but not so particular about the scalp.

We arrived at the bank of the Little Big Horn river and waded to the other side, and here there was a very strong current, and there was quicksand about three feet deep. On the other side of the river we made a short halt, dismounted, tightened our saddle girths, and then swung into our saddles. After mounting we came up, "Left front into line," Captain French's Company M, on the right and Lieutenant McIntosh's company on the left, and Captain Moylan's in the rear.

We were then in the valley of the Little Big Horn, and facing down stream. We started down on a trot and then on a slow gallop. Between the right of my company and the river bank there was quite a lot of underbrush, and bullberry bushes. Captain French gave me orders to take 10 men off to the right of my company and form a skirmish line, so as to cover the brush from the right of our line to the river bank, as the Indians might be lurking there. We advanced in that formation from one and a half to two miles, until we came to a heavy piece of timber.

Hears First Shot

Before we arrived at the timber, there was one shot fired away ahead of us. I did not know whether it was fired by Lieutenant Varnum's scouts or one of the hostile Indians. That was the first shot that I heard in the opening of the battle of the Little Big Horn on June 25, 1876, and I had pretty good ears about that time.

Private James Turley of my troop when we arrived at the timber and had orders to halt, could not control his horse which carried him towards the Indian camp. That was the last I saw of him. He was a very nice young man. A little incident happened a day or two before we left Fort Rice to go on the expedition. Turley asked me if I would allow him to put some of his property in my clothes chest. I told him that I would with the understanding that if he was killed the contents of the chest would belong to me and if I was killed it would belong to him. After coming back from the expedition the property belonging to those men that were killed was sold at public auction and the proceeds turned over to the paymaster.

When we got to the timber we rode down an embankment and dismounted. This was where the channel of the river changed and was probably several feet lower than the level of the prairie. We dismounted in haste, number four of each set of four holding the horses.

We came up onto higher ground forming a skirmish line from the timber towards the bluffs on the other side of the valley and facing down stream in the direction of the Indian camp. This was our first view of the Indian camp from the skirmish line. Some of the men laid down while others knelt down.

At this particular place there was a prairiedog town and we used the mounds for temporary breast works. We got the skirmish line formed and here the Indians made their first charge. There were probably 500 of them coming from the direction of their village. They were well mounted and well armed. They tried to cut through our skirmish line. We fired volleys into them repulsing their charge and emptying a number of their saddles.

Lieutenant Hodgson walked up and down the line encouraging the men to keep cool and fire low.

First Man Killed

Finally when they could not cut through us, they strung out in single file, lying on the opposite side of their ponies from us, and then they commenced to circle. They overlapped our skirmish line on the left and were closing in on the rear to complete the circle. We had orders to fall back to our horses. This was where the first man was killed, Sergt. Miles F. O'Hara of my troop M. He was a corporal going out on the expedition and promoted to a sergeant a few days before his death to replace Sergt. John Dolan, who was discharged, as his term of service had expired, and was back with the wagon trains at Powder river. Sergeant O'Hara was considered a very fine soldier in M troop and we missed him very much.

In the Indian camp after the battle, when we were destroying it, we found the heads of three of our men tied together with wires and suspended from a lodge pole with their hair all burned off. We did not see their bodies there. The Indians probably threw them into the river. We got back to our horses and the orders were given to mount and this time some of the men became confused and some of them could not find their horses.

Major Reno had lost his hat and had a red handkerchief tied around his head. As we mounted I looked to the rear in the direction of the river and saw the Indians completing the circle, riding through the brush and lying flat on their ponies. I mentioned the fact to Captain French, saying: "Captain, the Indians are in our rear." He answered: "Oh, no; those are General Custer's men." Just at that moment one of those Indians fired and Private George Lorentz of my company, who was number one of the first set of fours, was shot, the bullet striking him in the back of his neck and coming out of his mouth. He fell forward on his saddle and dropped to the ground. Just at that moment the Indians fired into us from all sides, and I said to Captain French of my company: "The best thing that we can do is to cut right through them." By this time they had us surrounded. They were on higher ground than we were. Major Reno rode up and said: "Any of you men who wish to make your escape, follow me."

Reno Leads Charge

The order was then given to charge, and away we went up the steep embankment, cutting through the Indians in a solid body, Major Reno being in advance. As we cut through them the fighting was hand to hand, and it was death to any man who fell from his horse, or was wounded and was not able to keep up with the command.

After cutting through we went back over the same ground, and then took a circle to the left to gain the bluffs at the nearest point. Here there was some pretty sharp fighting. The Indians were in great numbers on all sides of us. In this charge there were 30 men killed, my company losing 10, but we reached the river.

Bloody Knife, chief of Indian scouts; Charlie Reynolds, a white scout, and Izar Dorman, the negro interpreter, were killed here. Lieutenant Hodgson was wounded, and had his horse shot, and Lieut. Donald McIntosh was killed. McIntosh was a brave and faithful officer, commanding Company G.

Lieutenant DeRudio and Fred Girard, a white scout, and some 10 or 12 men became separated from the command and hid themselves in the brush or in the woods, or under the river embankment, and some of those men told me afterwards that they stood in water up to their necks, under the embankment, to keep out of sight of the Indians. Two of those men were sergeants of my company, Charles White and Patrick Carney. They joined the command in the intrenchments on the bluff, after dark.

At this point the river was about 50 yards wide, and the water about two and a half feet deep, with a swift current. Lieutenant Hodgson asked one of the men to carry him across, he being wounded and his horse being shot. It was reported that a trumpeter from my company named Fisher, better known as "Bounce," told him to hold on to his stirrup, and the horse drew the lieutenant as well as the rider across the river. He was shot a second time and killed. Now I know of three men who claim to have aided Hodgson.

Fighting is Desperate

The opposite bank of the river was very steep, and the only way to get up to the bluffs was through a buffalo trail worn on the bank, and only wide enough to let one man pass through at a time. Before we crossed the river the fighting was desperate and at close quarters.

In many instances the soldiers would empty their revolvers right into the breasts of the Indians, and after these were empty some were seen to throw them away, and grab their carbines, not having time to return their revolvers to their holsters. In my opinion, if Reno had remained in the timber a short time longer not a man would have made his escape as the Indians outnumbered us 10 to one.

In scaling the bluff, Dr. DeWolf, a contract surgeon on the expedition, was killed; also Sergeant Clair of Company K, William D. Myer, a farrier of company M, and Henry Gordon of the same company. Their bodies, with a number of others, lay under cover of our guns, so that the Indians did not get a chance to scalp them.

After we gained the bluffs we could look back upon the plains where the Indians were, and could see them stripping and scalping our men, and mutilating their bodies in a horrible manner. The prairie was all afire. The officers did all in their power to rally the men, and while they were doing so many were killed.

After the companies were formed the firing ceased, and we were joined by Benteen's battalion, which was the first we had seen of him since the division of the regiment. Soon after, the pack train arrived, with company B, under Captain McDougall, which was very fortunate, as our ammunition was nearly exhausted, and we could not get supplies from any other source. We had several wounded men and we attended to them as well as circumstances would permit. I understood at that time that Captain Weir with his company D, left the command there, and started in the direction General Custer took for a short distance, and then returned, although I did not see him.

Leaving two companies with the packs and wounded, Major Reno, with five companies, or what was left of them, proceeded in the direction we had supposed General Custer took, and in the direction of the Indian camp.

We went in that direction for probably half a mile until we gained a high point and could overlook the Indian camp and the battlefield. We saw at a distance of from a mile and a half to two miles parties whom we supposed were Indians, riding back and forth, firing scattering shots. We thought that they were disposing of Custer's wounded men, and this afterward proved to be true.

We halted for a few moments, and saw a large herd of ponies at the further end of the village, and could distinguish a large party of Indians coming towards the Indian camp. The prairie around the village and the first battlefield was all afire, having been set by the Indians to hide their movements.

At the top of this bluff we halted, and at foot there was a ford, and this was where Custer had first encountered the Indians, as we found some of the dead bodies there two days afterwards. While we were on the bluffs the Indians again made their appearance, coming in large numbers from the direction in which we heard the firing. We exchanged several shots with them, and we lost a few men, and then had orders to fall back to our packs and wounded.

On our arriving there we dismounted in haste, putting the wounded in a low depression on the bluffs and put packs from the mules around them to shelter them from the fire of the Indians. We then formed a circle of our pack mules and horses, forming a skirmish line all around the hole, and then lay down and waited for the Indians.

Indians Surround Them

We had been in this position but a short time when they advanced in great numbers from the direction in which we came.

They made several charges upon us and we repulsed them every time. Finally they surrounded us. Soon the firing became general all along the line, very rapid and at close range. The company on the right of my company had a number of men killed in a few minutes. There was a high ridge on the right and an opening on the right of our lines, and one Indian in particular I must give credit for being a good shot.

While we were lying in this line he fired a shot and killed the fourth man on my right. Soon afterward he fired again and shot the third man. His third shot wounded the man on my right, who jumped back from the line, and down among the rest of the wounded. I thought my turn was coming next. I jumped up, with Captain French, and some half a dozen members of my company, and, instead of firing straight to the front, as we had been doing up to the time of this incident, we wheeled to our right and put in a deadly volley, and I think we put an end to that Indian, as there were no more men killed at that particular spot.

Captain French was as brave an officer as ever served in the Seventh cavalry, and was known to have killed several Indians on different occasions. He had a Springfield rifle, caliber .50, breech-loader, and it was his custom, whenever he shot an Indian, to cut a notch in the stock of that gun.

I remember on one occasion he fired at a curlew, two or three shots, and he did not hit it. He felt so discouraged that he took the gun and threw it away. A little later I picked it up and rolled it up in a blanket, put it in one of the government wagons, and brought it into Fort Rice, Dakota, after the expedition broke up, unknown to him, and when he learned that I had it he reclaimed it. He retired from the service some years afterwards, and I have been informed, I am sorry to say, he met with a fatal accident.

When dark set in, it closed the engagement on the twenty-fifth. We went to work with what tools we had, consisting of two spades, our knives and tin cups, and, in fact, we used pieces of hard tack boxes for spades, and commenced throwing up temporary works. We also formed breastworks from boxes of hard bread, sacks of bacon, sacks of corn and oats, blankets, and in fact everything that we could get hold of.

During the night ammunition and the rations reached us where we were entrenched in the lines, but we suffered severely from lack of water. Although the river was only three or four hundred yards away, we were unable to get any water, as the Indians held the approach to it. During the night several men made attempts to get water, but they were killed or driven back.

About the middle of the night we heard a trumpet call, and the men commenced to cheer, thinking it was Custer's men who were coming to our assistance. Major Reno ordered one of our trumpeters to sound a call, but it was not repeated, so we made up our minds that it was a decoy on the part of the Indians to get us out of our works.

Benteen Hard Pressed

The trumpet that they used probably belonged to one of Custer's trumpeters, but we did not know it at that time. We had no thought of leaving our works, as we had a number of our men wounded there, and some of them pretty badly.

At intervals during the night we could hear the Indians riding back and forth across the river. I have an idea that they thought we were going to make a rush and get out of there.

The next morning, being the 26th, two shots were fired just before daylight by the Indians, in rapid succession. All this time we were wondering what had become of Custer and his troops. This began the engagement of another day. In a few moments the battle raged in earnest, the Indians advancing in large numbers and trying to cut through.

Captain Benteen's company particularly was hard pressed, and the men did their utmost to repulse those Indians who were gaining ground on the troops. Captain Benteen called out to Major Reno for re-enforcements, saying: "The Indians are doing their best to cut through my lines, and it will be impossible for me to hold my position much longer." Captain French's Company M was immediately withdrawn from that part of the line which they occupied, and rushed to the assistance of Captain Benteen's company. Both companies made a charge on the Indians and drove them down the hill, but in doing so we lost a number of men. This section of the battlefield was a little higher than the balance of the ground.

Private Tanner Killed

Had the Indians been successful, the day would have been lost, and Reno's command would have shared the fate of Custer's brave men, as Captain Benteen said afterward.

Private James Tanner of Company M, was badly wounded in this charge, and his body lay on the side of the bluffs in an exposed position. There was a call for volunteers to bring him down, and I grabbed a blanket with three other men, rushed to his assistance, rolled him into the blanket, and made quick tracks in getting him from the side of the bluffs to where our wounded lay. Fortunately none of the rescuing party received anything more than a few balls through their clothing. After placing Tanner with the rest of the wounded, he died in a few minutes.

There was a gray horse belonging to my company, that was ridden by Captain French, and he was the best buffalo horse in the command. He was among the other horses near the wounded, and an Indian shot him through the head. He was staggering about among the other horses, and Private Henry C. Voyt, of my company, took hold of him to lead him out of the way of the other horses, and Voyt at the same instant had his brains blown out. We buried Private Tanner, about whom I have made some explanation, and Voyt in the same grave the next morning. Then we made a head board out of a piece of hard tack-box, and marked their names with a lead pencil on the board, and drove it into the ground.

Indian Fire Slackens

Late in the day the fire of the Indians slackened, except on the point of a high bluff in the direction in which it was supposed that Custer had gone. Here the Indians put in a few well-directed shots that laid several of our men low. I do not know what kind of a gun one of those Indians used, but it made a tremendous noise, and, in fact those Indians were out of range of our carbine, which were Springfields, caliber .45.

Captain French of my company asked me if I could do anything with those Indians, as they were out of range of the carbines. I told the captain that I would try, and as I was the owner of a 15-pound Sharp's telescope rifle, caliber .45, which I had had made in Bismarck before the expedition started out, and which cost me $100. I fired a couple of shots until I got range of that group of Indians. Then I put in half a dozen shots in rapid succession, and those Indians scampered away from that point of the bluff, and that ended the firing on the part of the Indians in that

memorable engagement, and the boys set up quite a cheer.

The Indians all scampered from the bluffs across the river and moved back to their encampment. We could see them pulling down their lodges and getting ready for a hasty removal. In a short time they stripped the hides off of their lodges and left the poles standing and moved out from their camp up the valley of the Little Big Horn, and over the field where Major Reno's battalion fought in the beginning of the engagement, and where his dead lay. It was the largest body of Indians that I ever saw move together at one time.

I have seen the Cheyennes, the Arapahoes, the Kiowas, the Apaches and the Comanches move together in the Indian territory, and in Kansas years before, while campaigning there under General Custer. I should say that there were double the number moving out from this camp.

When they moved, the captain of my company, Thomas H. French, and I fired into them while they remained in range of our two guns, and those were the last shots fired in the battle of the Little Big Horn. That was well known by every man in Reno's battalion.

Major Reno, Captain French, Captain Benteen, Captain McDougall, Captain Weir, Lieutenant Godfrey and, in fact all of the officers did all that they could in order to defeat the Indians, and some of the officers must have had a charmed life the way they stood up under this heavy fire.

I think the Indians took some of our men prisoners, and when other reinforcements joined us we found what appeared to be human bones, and parts of blue uniforms, where the men had been tied to stakes and trees. Some of the bodies of our officers were not found, at least not at that time. Among them were Lieutenants Harrington, Porter and Sturgis. I understood that some parts of their clothing, uniform or gauntlet gloves were found on the field, which showed that they were killed. In burying the dead many of the bodies were not identified.

After the Indians moved out of sight we jumped out of our works, built better rifle pits, and un-saddled our horses, which had not been unsaddled since the evening of the twenty-fourth.

45 Men Killed

We also took the packs from the mules. Then we got water from the river in camp kettles, and made a better shelter for the horses and wounded, for we expected that the Indians would attack us again.

Reno's command lost, between the engagement in the bottom and the entrenchments on the bluffs, somewhere about 45 men killed and 60 wounded, which will show how desperate the engagement was. In my company, out of 45 men and horses that went into the engagement, 14 men and the second lieutenant were killed, 10 wounded, and we lost about 15 horses killed or disabled.

That night everything was quiet as far as the Indians were concerned. The next morning at day-light we could look from the bluffs over the timber to where the Indian camp was, and we saw that it was deserted, with the exception of the lodge poles, which remained standing. On the other side, a long way off from the Indian camp, we noticed a large cloud of dust arising, and a body of either Indians or troops coming towards the Indian camp, but at the time we could not distinguish which they were.

Some of the officers turned their field glasses on, and thought they were troops. Reno immediately dispatched a couple of his scouts, and it proved to be the balance of our expedition, and General Gibbon's command under General Alfred Terry. It appears that they came through Custer's battle-field, and they counted the dead bodies of 207 men. They then crossed the river.

Terry Joins Reno

They then crossed the river into the deserted Indian camp, and followed up the valley of the Little Big Horn until they struck that part of the field where Reno's dead lay. They moved a little farther on near the bend where Reno's command retreated across the river, and went into camp. General Terry and his officers rode across the river and joined our officers on the bluffs, and it made our hearts jump to see those men.

As soon as Terry's officers notified Reno and his officers what they had found on the Custer battlefield, Reno's command went to work and buried all the dead that lay on the bluffs. The unexpected news filled the hearts of all the men with sadness.

We took all the extra guns belonging to the dead and wounded, broke the stocks off them, and built a fire and threw them into it. We also destroyed all the extra saddles and bridles, as we had no way of carrying them.

Terry's men removed their clothing and carried our wounded men all down from the bluffs to their camp. After destroying the guns, we ex-amined the horses thoroughly, and any of them that had been wounded and would not live, we killed. Some of the men hated to part with their horses, but there was nothing else to do.

Then five companies of Reno's command moved over the range of bluffs, in the direction of the

Custer battlefield. At the end of this bluff there was a ford, and I think Custer attempted to cross at that point to the Indian's camp, as we found some of the bodies of his men lying there. Those were the first bodies we found belonging to Custer's command.

* * *

Reno Tries to Reach Custer

When Benteen's battalion joined Reno on the bluffs, after Reno arrived from the bottom, five companies started along the ridge in the direction that Custer went, and toward the Custer battle-field, where we could overlook it. Here Reno was attacked by the Indians, and we received orders to fall back to where our packs and wounded were.

* * *

Another Curley Story

It appears that when Custer's engagement opened, Curley, a Crow scout, made his escape in some way. I understand that he mingled in with the Sioux in the engagement, and when he got an opportunity, threw off his Crow blanket and put on a Sioux blanket, and got down into the brush, where he took his pony. He took a wad of grass, jammed it into the pony's mouth, tied his lariat around his horses nose, to prevent his making a noise, and tied him to a tree.

He then jumped on a Sioux pony and made his way down the Little Big Horn in the direction that he knew the re-enforcements were coming. He was pursued by the Indians, but managed to escape. He reported to General Terry and de-scribed the engagement.

An Indian, in describing an engagement will point a gun, then make a noise as if the gun exploded. Then he will drop the gun and throw up his hands. That signifies that the man who fired the gun is dead. He explained that to General Terry. General Terry put down a piece of paper and gave Curley a lead pencil, and he made dots on the paper, showing where the soldiers were on the inside of a circle, the Indians on the out-side. Terry then asked him how many were killed and he picked up a handful of leaves and shook them over the paper, saying: "The white men all dead, and the Indians as thick as leaves."

The story, though not fully understood, seemed incredible and was not accepted, but it proved true in all its details. Curley said he saw that the troops were sure to be massacred, and he managed to reach the river, where he washed off his Crow paint, dropped down his hair, which was peculiar to the Crows, pulled it over his face, put on a

Sioux blanket and pretended to engage in the fight with the Sioux, accompanying them in one of their charges on Custer.

Watching his opportunity, he escaped, and in doing so he picked up a Sioux pony and reported at the mouth of the Little Big Horn, where he knew Terry would arrive on the evening of the twenty-sixth.

Benteen Saves Reno

Too much cannot be said in favor of Captain Benteen. His prompt movements saved Reno from utter annihilation, and his gallantry cleared the ravines of Indians and opened the way for water for the suffering wounded. In Captain Benteen, Reno found one whose advice and assistance was invaluable.

Dr. Porter was in the thickest of the fray in that wild run for life made by Reno and his men in their desperate efforts to reach the ford ahead of the Indians, in their race for scalps. With officers and soldiers passing and being passed by each other, at length running pell mell into the jam of men and horses in the narrow pass at the ford, Porter concedes the highest praise to Lieutenant Mathey, who, as soon as the crest of the hill was reached, with his own hands made a barricade of dead animals and commissary and medical stores from the pack mules, behind which the wounded rapidly increased from 10 to 52. Dr. Porter also spoke in the highest terms of Fred Girard, who aided him during the battle in making a couple of amputations, and gave him invaluable assistance in other respects.

Girard was the only man in the command besides Porter having any medical knowledge. Dr. Lord was killed with General Custer's command, and DeWolf was killed in Reno's command on the side of the hill.

THE STORY OF SERGEANT KANIPE, ONE OF CUSTER'S MESSENGERS

(From the Greensboro, N. C., *Daily Record,* April 27, 1924)

I ENLISTED on August 7, 1872, at Lincolnton. In the spring of 1873 the regiment was moved from the South to Dakota Territory, it was called then. The 7th had been in the south during the Ku Klux ridding and other things. We left Charlotte March 15 and arrived in Yankton, Dakota, April 19. The regiment marched from there to Fort Rice, arriving there on June 9. I was with Company "C." There the expedition of '73 was made up to guard the engineers that were surveying the extension of the Northern Pacific. This road only ran to Bismarck at that time. When the engineers joined us we went on the expedition as planned. This was known as the Yellowstone expedition. We guarded the engineers during the summer while they pushed on up as far as what is now Yellowstone park.

I say we, my troop, "C," and "H" troop didn't go all the way. We stayed at the junction of the Glendive and the Yellowstone rivers at the supply station that had been formed there. This is where the Northern Pacific crosses now.

General Rosser was the chief engineer. He and General Custer, when they were in West Point, before the Civil war, had been roommates. When the war broke out they chose their sides. General Rosser chose the South, Custer the North. I have heard them talk about it several times. You see, I was lucky in those days. Seems like I would be made orderly nearly every guard mount. They said I was the neatest, and if there was anything to that maybe I was. Anyway, I used to catch that most every time, and that is the way I heard what I was telling you. Both of them finally were made Brigadier Generals.

On the last day of September, in that year, the expedition came back to Fort A. Lincoln. Next spring the Black Hills expedition of '74 was made up. We explored the Black Hills that summer under the command of General Custer. There was no expedition in any form in the year 1875. Half the regiment, six companies, were sent to New Orleans. My company, "C," did not go. We stayed at Fort Rice, then later went to Fort Lincoln. In the year '76 the six companies came back, and for the first time, since the regiment was reorganized in 1867, we were all together. We were stationed at Fort Lincoln.

On May 17 we were sent out on what was to prove to be the disastrous expedition. We started to the Yellowstone river. We marched 12 miles to the Big Heart river and made camp. We stayed there a while looking around. About June 10 we went on up to the Powder river. Six companies of the 12 were sent out on a scouting party. Leaving the wagon train at the Powder river and taking 10 days rations on pack mules, we went up the Powder river for two days, then turned across towards the Tongue river and it was on the Rosebud river that we found the Indian trail.

It was about sundown then, so we made a little coffee, then marched up the trail all night. In the morning we made coffee, and hit out up the trail again, marching up it until 12 o'clock. General Reno, who was in command of this detachment, found that his 10-day rations were running low, so we turned back down the Rosebud river and at the junction of it and the Yellowstone we met the other six companies of the regiment, under General Custer.

General Terry, department commander, was there. General Custer was under arrest.* It was said, because of his attitude against the post traders who had been allowed the concessions at the different posts and which were done away with after the airing of scandals concerning post-traderships during President Grant's administration.

Why, those fellows had things so that you couldn't buy anything at the posts without getting it from them. Liquor was 25 cents a glass and the glasses was mostly glass—mighty little whisky. Custer set a maximum price and it caused his arrest. But all the high army officers were with him and he was given a command at the place I spoke of.

On July 22 Custer's outfit drew 15 days' rations off the steamboat Far West that was in the river. There were two Rodman guns, two Gatling guns in a battery with Custer. He thought that he could get along without them, and he turned them over to General Gibbon, who carried them across the river.

There's where he made a mistake, as we see it now, because if he had had one of those Rodman guns and had fired it one time those Indians wouldn't have stopped running yet—no siree, would still be running. And if we'd had one of the Gatling guns there would have been a lot more survivors than me. In fact there would never have been any Custer massacre.

On June 22 we broke camp and started out, marching all day. That evening Custer issued orders that there would be no more bugle calls and only fire enough to make coffee and that commands would be given by signs. On the morning of June 23 we started out. We marched until nearly night, then camped and continued on next morning, June 24. That day we came to a place where the Indians had had a sun dance, and had staged a war dance, too. They had built brush sheds out of the cottonwood trees, and the ground was patted down smooth and hard, where they had been dancing about on it.

Six Crow Indian scouts that were with our regiment had come on ahead and they had found the scalp of a white man. That was from the head of a soldier with Gibbon's command. Well, sir, when those Indians, they hated the Sioux, the ones we were hunting, anyway, found this scalp hanging on a willow twig they sure had a fit.

Just cut up in general and yelled and hollered and danced about.

What did they want? Why, if they had had a Sioux there then it would have been a bad day for him, they were that mad. They brought the scalp back to General Custer, who passed it around to the men, after looking at it. Sergeant Finley, who was the oldest line sergeant in my company, had it in his saddle pockets when he was massacred. We marched all day June 24. Indian scouts that had been sent ahead returned that night about 10 o'clock. It was just good dark. You know that you can see to read at 9 o'clock in the summer time in that country.

We got orders that night to saddle and pack up. We marched all night, coming close to the junction of the Rosebud and the Little Big Horn river. So General Custer took the regiment into a ravine that looked as though we could keep concealed there as long as we wanted to. But, in coming in, as we were riding at a hard trot and a gallop, Quartermaster Sergeant Hearst lost some hard bread from the packs of some of the pack train. Learning this, General Custer ordered the sergeant to go back and get the bread.

But when the sergeant reached the point where the bread had dropped out, there were two Indians helping themselves to it. They ran at the approach of the soldiers. Coming back to camp this incident was reported to General Custer and he ordered us to saddle up.

I reasoned it out that he had planned to surprise the Indians the next morning, but as they already knew that we were there, he was going to do it now. We marched up the divide and halted. General Custer took the chief trumpeter and two scouts and was gone two hours.

When he came back he divided the regiment into three detachments. He gave Major Reno three troops, "A," "M," and "G;" Captain Benteen, three troops, "H," "K" and "D," and gave Captain McDougall charge of the pack train with Troop "B." He then took for himself Troops "C," "E," "I," and "F." *

Leaving that place we went out this way. Major Reno was to the left and abreast with General Custer and Captain Benteen to the left of Major Reno. You could tell that the plan was to strike the Indian camp at three places. Captain McDougall was to bring the pack train on up the main Indian trail. We went at a gallop. Turning down what is now Benteen's creek, we made our way to a crossing and found a vacated Indian camp on the other

---

* See note at end of story.

* See note at end of story. Kanipe forgets Company "L".

side. The fires were not all out. There was a dead Indian in one of the tepees that was still standing. General Custer ordered the tepee fired. Major Reno came in sight and he was signaled to cross Benteen creek and did so. General Custer, with three companies, pushed down the creek.

When we reached within a quarter of a mile of the junction of Benteen's creek with the Little Big Horn I sighted Indians on the top of the range of bluffs over the Little Big Horn river. I said to First Sergeant Bobo, "There are the Indians."

General Custer threw up his head about that time and we—Troops "C," "E," "I," and "F"—headed for the range of bluffs where we had seen the Indians. Tom Custer, brother of the general, was captain of my troop, "C." We rode hard, but when we reached the top the Indians were gone.

However, we could see the tepees for miles. The Crow Indian scouts with our outfit wanted to slip down and get a few ponies. Some of them did slip down, but they got shot for their pains. Chief Scout Mitch Buie (Bouyer), Curley, a Crow, and "Bloody Knife" Reeve (Ree) stayed up on the bluffs with us.*

Well, sir, when the men of those four troops saw the Indian camp down in the valley they began to holler and yell, and we galloped along to the far end of the bluffs, where we could swoop down on the camp * * * (four words illegible).

I was riding close to Sergeant Finkle. We were both close to Capt. Tom Custer. Finkle hollered at me that he couldn't make it, his horse was giving out. I answered back: "Come on Finkle, if you can." He dropped back a bit.

Just then the captain told me to go back and find McDougall and the pack train and deliver to them orders that had just been issued by General Custer.

"Tell McDougall," he said, "to bring the pack train straight across to high ground—if packs get loose don't stop to fix them, cut them off. Come quick. Big Indian camp."

I went back. I thought then that was tough luck, but it proved to be my salvation. If Sergeant Finkle had not dropped back a few minutes before he would have got the orders—and I would not be telling this story.

Away off in the distance, the dust rolling up like a little cloud, I saw the pack train. I went toward that. My company and the others went on down toward the Indian camp. I remember the last words that I heard General Custer say; the men were on the hill, we all gave them three

cheers riding at a full gallop, some of them couldn't hold their horses, galloping past General Custer. He shouted at them, "Boys, hold your horses, there are plenty of them down there for us all." They rode on. I rode back.

Reaching the pack train, I gave Captain McDougall the orders sent him, and went on toward Captain Benteen as I had been told to take them to him, also. McDougall and his outfit rode on to the top of the hill and reinforced Major Reno as he retired from the bottom of the bluffs.

The Indians were following close at their heels, shooting and yelling, and men were dropping here and there. They, the Indians, would hop on them and scalp them before we could rescue them. Dr. DeWolfe was killed just as he reached the top of the hill. If he had gotten a few feet further he would have been saved.

As I went back after Captain Benteen I saw some Indians running along. I thought they were hostile Indians and got ready to give them a few rounds before they got me, but they were scouts that were making their get away from the big battle that was going on. They had come from Major Reno's command and they were that scared that they did not stop until they reached the Powder river.

Delivering the orders to Captain Benteen, I rode back to the top of the ridge with the battalion and there we joined the others under Major Reno and McDougall. The Indians were between this outfit and General Custer, so I could not join my company.

Major Reno started to march out on the range of bluffs there and attack the Indians, but they came at us and we retired, and formed skirmish lines. But, before we could do that we lost several men and they were scalped before we could get to them. They shot at us all day then at night they pow-wowed until daylight on the 26th. Then they started out again shooting and charging. We killed a many a one, just how many I do not know.

We were cut off from water, and there were 68 wounded men in camp. A wounded man wants water bad, and it was pitiful to hear their groans as they called for it and we couldn't get it. Some fellows tried to go for it but got shot and had no such luck as bringing any for the wounded.

I remember the first shot that was fired in that two-day battle. It went right under my horse's belly and lodged in the bank. There were 14 men and two officers, Lieutenant Harrington and Lieutenant Sturgis, that never were found. It was said that the Indians cut off their heads and dragged them around as they pow-wowed during the night.

* See note at end of story.

There were 56 men in our outfit killed on the hill by the Indians.

Well, they kept up the shooting all through the day of the 26th, until late in the evening we could see the camp begin to move. The warriors kept shooting at us and the squaws were getting the camp moved. On the morning of the 27th there was not an Indian in sight.

We got water and made coffee and relieved the suffering of the wounded as best we could. About 10 o'clock General Gibbon and his command arrived. General Terry, department commander, came with him. When General Terry came up lusty cheers (greeted him). He cried like a baby. Then he told us that he had seen 200 men in the valley below and we knew that General Custer and the four companies had been wiped out. We had thought that maybe he had been corralled as we were.

Late on the afternoon of the 27th, Captain Benteen went to the battlefield, and I was allowed to go with him, and look about wherever I wanted to.

I looked over the dead and recognized here and there a buddy and a sergeant that I knew. I recognized Sergeants Finkle and Finley. Sergeant Finley lay at his horse's (Carlo) head. He had 12 arrows through him. They had been lying there for two days in the sun, bloody and the wounded mutilated. You could tell what men had been wounded because the little Indians and the squaws would always, after taking the clothes off the men, shoot them full of arrows or chop them in the faces with tomahawks. They never hurt a dead man, just those that were wounded.

In all this pile of men, not a one had a stitch of clothes on. The Indians had taken it all. They must have gotten about $25,000 in money off of them, too, for we had just been paid at Powder river camp before we left on the campaign and there had been nothing to spend a cent for.

I saw where the last ones fell, they were in a little heap. General Custer lay across a couple of men, the small of his back only, touching the ground. The dead were thick around him. He had been shot through the heart. My captain, Tom Custer, a brother of the general, was near this last bunch, as was his brother-in-law, Lieutenant Calhoun, who was in command of "H" (sic) troop.

In that battle there were fully 4,000 Indians besides the squaws, making a total of between 12,000 and 15,000 Indians in all.

And on the whole field where Custer and those four companies were wiped out not a living being was left to tell the tale. One horse survived—his name was Comanche—when he was found he had seven bullet wounds. He was Captain Keo's (Keogh's) horse.

Well, there were a good many dead Indians. We found three tepees standing with 75 (sic) Indians in them, and there is no telling how many more were carried away when they moved camp. I thought that I would cut one of them out of the blankets and buffalo robes that he was wrapped in. When I did I found that he had a string of scalps as long as your arm and among those were four women's, with hair as long as my arm, two of them having red hair. It was a sight. I dropped them—didn't want them.

They buried the dead and then began to carry the wounded, including the horse Comanche, to the Far West steamboat which had come up the river as far as it could. It then backed down to the Yellowstone river.

Most of the wounded got well. Old Comanche did and there was an order from general headquarters that this (only) survivor, in fact, of Custer's battle was to have a box stall the rest of his life. One man out of the 7th Cavalry Band was assigned to look after him and on dress parade old Comanche would be led at the head of the regiment, draped in black.

What became of the Indians? Why they went on. My regiment did not try to hunt them, we were all shot to pieces.

The many inaccuracies in Sgt. Kanipe's story are characteristic of the accounts of most of the enlisted survivors recounted during the '20s.

* * *

F. F. GIRARD'S STORY OF THE CUSTER FIGHT
(From *The Arikara Narrative*)

ON JUNE 22d, Custer's command left the mouth of the Rosebud looking for Indians. On June 24th, we broke camp and marched all day and in evening went into camp. The men had supper and grazed their horses and then marched all night till 4 A.M., when a halt was called. The horses remained saddled but the soldiers slept on the ground as best they could. Two Arikara scouts arrived from Lieutenant Varnum, who had been sent out to reconnoitre and locate Indian camps. They brought word of a very large camp down in Little Big Horn Valley, but the Indians had discovered us and were on the run. Custer ordered me to go with him and the two Arikara scouts who had come in from Varnum and two of our scouts, to where Lieutenant Varnum was. About daybreak we reached Varnum and could see the large black mass moving in front and down the Little Big Horn and a dense cloud of dust over all and behind. The camp we had found was the smaller camp (the larger camp was downstream farther), and was on the way to the larger camp and this led us all to believe that the Indians were stampeded. Custer and his party with Varnum and his scouts started back to rejoin the command at a sharp gait. Before reaching his troops, about half way back, Tom Custer met us at the head of the troops and Custer addressed him saying: "Tom, who in the devil moved these troops forward? My orders and intentions were to remain in camp all day and make a night attack on the Indians but they have discovered us and are on the run." After joining the troops, Custer with his officers held a consultation and decided it would be better to follow the Indians so he divided his command into three battalions, one under his own command, Benteen in command of the second, and Reno of the third. Benteen he sent to the left of the command to overlook the ridges as we marched down the valley. He then ordered Reno to take his command and try to overtake the Indians and bring them to battle while he himself would support him. Custer said: "Take the scouts with you." Reno started on the double quick down the valley until he came to the Little Big Horn. Up to that time we were all still under the impression that the Indians were running away. Upon reaching the ford of the Little Big Horn, I discovered that the Indians were coming back to give us battle and called Reno's attention to this change in their movements. Reno halted for a few seconds and ordered the men forward. Thinking that Custer should know of this change of front on the part of the Indians, I rode back at once to tell Custer the news. At an abrupt turn I met Cook, (sic) Custer's adjutant, ahead of his command, who said: "Girard, what's up?" On hearing the news he ordered me back to Reno's command and rode to inform Custer of the change in the front on the part of the Indians. I rejoined Reno's command just as he was drawing up his men on the skirmish line. The men were almost six feet apart along the brow of a hill below which was a belt of timber. As the Indians came charging back the men used the timber for cover and the Indians rode by on the left and around to the higher ground at the rear and left. Not more than four rounds had been fired before they saw Custer's command dashing along the hills one mile to their rear. Reno then gave the order: "The Indians are taking us in the rear, mount and charge." This was then about 1:30 P.M. I was surprised at this change of position as we had excellent cover and could hold off the Indians indefinitely, but the orders were to mount and charge. Charley Reynolds was killed as he rode up the slope at the left and Isaiah a little farther out. Reno led his men in Indian file back to the ford above which he had seen Custer's command pass. The Indians picked off the troops at will; it was a rout, not a charge. All the men were shot in the back, some men fell before high ground was reached. As soon as the hill was gained, Benteen and his command came up and the demoralization of Reno's men affected his own men and no attempt was made to go to Custer's aid. They remained where they were though it was about 2 P.M. and no Indians attacked them for more than an hour.

After Reno's command left, I found in the timber Lieutenant de Rudio, Sergeant O'Neill and Wm. Jackson, the half-breed Blackfoot scout, who were also cut off from the command. All the afternoon we could hear the troop volleys, but the scattering fire of the Indians gradually predominated till we were sure that the Indians had won. The fight where Reno's men were began shortly after 4 and kept up till dark. We remained where we were till dark and then struck out west thinking Reno's command had returned. We missed the morning ford and tried the ford Reno used to retreat by but the dead bodies made the horses snort and the water looked too deep so we returned and found a new ford. As we mounted the bank we saw a match lit and called out: "There are the troops, Hello!" and then the match was put out. As we neared the old crossing we saw the Indian lances against the sky and the Indians hearing us turn off suddenly, called out, "Are you afraid, we are not white troops." De Rudio and O'Neill lay down and hid in the brush at this point while Jackson and I rode down and across the stream straight against a cut bank. Both horses threw their riders, our guns were lost, but finally a ford was found and just at dawn we rode out on the prairie. At the left we could hear more Indians coming across the Little Big Horn, coming down to attack Reno. Then we galloped hard to the bunch of willows at the right and reached it before the Indians came out of the water. Here we remained till dark. About 11 A.M. we saw them attack Reno's camp. About one hour before sunset a great talking and confusion arose, the Indians evidently saw Terry coming and began to fall back. Some left for their village to gather their families while others rode away up the Little Big Horn. The retreating warriors passed by hundreds close to where we lay hid in the willows.

This portrait, said to be the last Custer had made, was engraved
on steel and used as the frontispiece of Whittaker's "Life of General
Custer," which was published late in 1876. His hair was even shorter
than shown in this portrait at the time of the battle, as he had it
cropped short with clippers before starting from Fort Lincoln on his
last campaign.

CHAPTER 4

LIEUTENANT CHARLES DeRUDIO'S LETTER

(Alleged to have been written by Major Brisbin though signed by DeRudio)

(From *The New York Herald,* July 30, 1876)

* * *

Camp on N. side Yellowstone,
July 5, '76

I had a narrow escape at the battle of the Little Big Horn on the 25 & 26 of June and I will endeavor to give you my experience of Indian fighting. At about 10 A.M. on the 25th June, Gen. Custer's scouts returned and reported that they had discovered an Indian village about 15 miles distant, on the Little Big Horn, and that from what they had seen, they supposed the Indians to be retreating before our advance. We continued our march two or three miles farther when a halt was ordered and Gen. Custer began preparations for attacking the enemy. He detailed Co's. H, D & K, under the command of Col. F. W. Benteen to take the left of our route, with orders, so I hear, to sweep everything in his way: Co's. M, A, & G were put under the command of Col. Reno; and being temporarily attached to Co. A, I found myself with this division. Gen. Custer took Co's. E, I, F, L & C, and occupied the right of the line of attack. The remaining Company, B, was left to guard the packtrain. After marching two or three miles, our command, the center, was ordered to trot and hold the gait until we reached the river, six or seven miles distant. Having reached the river, we forded, and on reaching the plain beyond the opposite bank, we were ordered into line of battle.

Everything being as was ordered, we started on a gallop and for two miles pursued on the verge of an immense and blinding cloud of dust raised by the madly flying savages ahead of us. The dust cloud was so dense that we could distinguished nothing, so Col. Reno halted the battalion and after dismounting, formed a skirmish line—the right flank resting on the edge of a dry thickly wooded creek. While the horses were being led to shelter in the wood, the Indians opened a galling fire on us which was immediately responded to, the skirmish continuing for about one-half hour. It was now discovered that on the other side of the creek, in a park-like clearing, there were a few lodges, and the whole line crossed the creek to find the lodges deserted, and be received by about two hundred yelping, yelling redskins. The fire from the numerically superior force necessitated a retreat which was almost impossible, as we were now surrounded by warriors. When we entered the engagement we were only 100 strong and the fire of the enemy had made havoc in our little band. When we were half way over the creek, I, being in the rear, noticed a guidon planted on the side we had left and returned to take it. When coming through the wood, the guidon entangled itself in the branches and slipped out of my hand. I dismounted to pick it up and led my horse to the south bank of the creek. As I was about to mount, my horse was struck with a bullet, and becoming frightened, he ran into the Indians, leaving me dismounted in the company of about 300 Sioux not more than 50 yards distant. They poured a whistling volley at me, but I was not wounded, and managed to escape to the thicket near by, where I would have an opportunity of defending myself and selling my life at a good high figure. In the thicket I found Mr. Girard, the interpreter; a half-breed Indian; and private O'Neill, of Co. "G", 7th Cav. The first two of the quartet had their horses, while O'Neill like myself, was dismounted. I told the owners of the horses that the presence of the animals would betray us, suggesting at the same time that they be stampeded. They declined to act on the suggestion and I left them and crawled through the thick underwood into the deep dry bottom of the creek, where I could not easily be discovered, and from whence I hoped to be able under cover of darkness to steal out and rejoin the command. I had not been in this hiding place more than 10 minutes when I heard several pistol shots fired in my immediate vicinity, and shortly thereafter came the silvery, but to me diabolical voices of several squaws. I raised my head with great caution to see what the women were at and to discover their exact location. I found the women at the revolting work of scalping a soldier who was perhaps not yet dead. Two of the ladies were cutting away, while two others performed a sort of war dance around the body and its mutilators. I will not attempt to describe to you my feelings at witnessing the disgusting performance. * * * Finally the squaws went away, probably to hunt for more victims and I employed the time thinking of my perilous position.

While thus engaged, I heard a crackling noise near me, which upon investigation I found proceeded from burning wood, the Indians having ignited a fire. The wood being very dry, the fire made rapid headway, and I was forced from my hiding place. I crawled out of the creek bottom the same way I had approached, and as I was about to ascend the bank, I heard a voice calling "Lieutenant, Lieutenant." I could see no one, but the call was repeated, and advancing a few yards in the direction from which it proceeded, I found all three of the party I had left a short time before, hidden in the bottom of the creek. Mr. Girard told me he had left the horses tied together, where I had seen them, and followed down after me. I found that the party, like myself, was afraid of the progress of the fire; but fortunately for us, the wind subsided, and a little rain fell which, thank God, was sufficient to arrest the flames and revive our hope that we might be able to remain there until night. It was now 3 o'clock P.M.: six more hours to wait, and you may imagine how immensely long we found them. During this time we could hear and often see Indians around us and could hear them talk quite near us. I cannot find words sufficiently expressive to describe my many thoughts during those hours of suspense. * * * Finally the time came when under the protection of night (it was very cloudy) we were able to come out of our hiding places and take the direction of the ford, which was two miles to the south, through an open plain. Mr. Girard and the scout mounted their horses and the soldier and myself took hold, each one, of a horses tail, and followed them. Mr. Girard proposed that, in case he should be ob-

liged to run and leave us, and succeeded in joining the command, he would notify Col. Reno the commander, of my position. During our transit through the open plain we passed many Indians returning to their village and could hear but not see them as the night was very dark. We reached the wood near what we took to be the ford we had passed in the morning, but we were mistaken and had to hunt for the crossing. Once we forded the stream but found it was at a bend and that we would have to ford it again. When we recrossed the river, we ran full into a band of eight savages. The two mounted men ran for their lives, the soldier and myself jumped into the bushes near us. I cocked my revolver and in a kneeling position was ready to fire at the savages if they should approach me. They evidently thought, from the precipitate retreat of the two mounted men, that all of us had decamped; and began to talk among themselves. In a few minutes to my surprise they continued their course, and soon after went out of hearing. I raised up from my position, approached the bank of the river and called to the soldier, who immediately answered. We then saw that all the fords were well guarded by the savages, and it would be very dangerous to attempt to cross any part of the river. * * * The night passed and in the dim dawn of day we heard an immense tramping, as of a large cavalry command, and the splashing of the water convinced us that some troops were crossing the river. I imagined it was our command, as I could distinctly hear the sound of the horses shoes striking the stones. I cautiously stepped to the edge of the bushes to look out (I was then no more than three yards from the bank of the river), and thought I recognized some gray horses mounted by men in military blouses, and some of them in white hats. They were, I thought, going out of the valley, and those that had already crossed the river were going up a very steep bluff, while others were crossing after them. I saw one man with a buckskin jacket, pants, top boots and white hat, and felt quite sure I recognized him as Capt. Tom Custer which convinced me that the cavalrymen were of our command.

With this conviction I stepped boldly out on the bank and called to Capt. Custer, "Tom, don't leave us here." The distance was only a few yards and my call was answered by an infernal yell and a discharge of 300 or 400 shots. I then discovered my mistake and found the savages were clad in clothes and mounted on horses which they had captured from our men. Myself and the soldier jumped into the bushes (the bullets mowing down the branches at every volley), and crawled off to get out of range of the fire. In doing so we moved the top branches of the undergrowth, and the Indians on the top of the bluff fired where they saw the commotion and thus covered us with their rifles. We now decided to cross a clearing of about twenty yards and gain another wood; but before doing this, I took the precaution to look out. The prospect was terribly discouraging for on our immediate right, not more than fifty yards distant, I saw four or five Indians galloping toward us. Near by me there were two cottonwood stumps nearly touching each other, and behind this slender barricade myself and the soldier knelt down, he with his carbine and I with my revolver, ready to do for a few of the savages before they could kill us. * * * They had not seen us and when the foremost man was just abreast of me and about ten yards distant, I fired. They came in Indian file, and at my fire they turned a right-about and were making off when Pvt. O'Neill fired his carbine at the second savage, who at that moment was reining his pony to turn him back. The private's eye was true, and his carbine trusty, for Mr. Indian dropped his rein, threw up his paws and laid down on the grass to sleep his long sleep. The gentleman I greeted rode a short distance and then did likewise. The rest of the party rode on, turned the corner of the wood and disappeared. * * * During all this time the fire from the bluffs continued, but after we had fired our shots, it ceased, and we retired to the thicket, * * *. From our position we could see the Indians on the bluffs, their horses picketed under cover of the hill, and a line of sharpshooters, all lying flat on their stomachs. We could hear the battle going on above us on the hills, the continued rattle of the musketry, the cheering of our command, and the shouting of the savages. Our hopes revived when we heard the familiar cheer of our comrades, but despondency followed fast for we discovered that our wood was on fire * * * and we had to shift our position. We crawled almost to the edge of the wood, when we discovered that the fiends had fired both sides. We moved around until we found a thick cluster of what they call bulberry trees, under which we crept. The grass on the edge of this place was very green, as it had been raining a little while before, and there was no wind. When the fire approached our hiding place it ran very slowly so that I was enabled to smother it with my gauntlet gloves. The fire consumed all the underwood around us and was almost expended by this time.

There we were in a little oasis, surrounded by fire, but comparatively safe from the elements, and with the advantage of seeing almost everything around us without being seen. We could see savages going backward and forward, and one standing on picket not more than 70 or 80 yards from us, evidently put there to watch the progress of the fire. At about 4 o'clock p.m. this picket fired 4 pistol shots in the air at regular intervals from each other and which I interpreted as a signal of some kind. Soon after this fire we heard the powerful voice of a savage crying out, making the same sound four times, and after these two signals, we saw 200 or more savages leave the bluffs and ford the river, evidently leaving the ground. About one hour after, the same double signals were again repeated, and many mounted Indians left at a gallop. Soon the remainder of those left on the bluffs also retired.

Hope now revived, the musketry rattle ceased and only now and then we could hear a far off shot. By 6 o'clock everything around us was apparently quiet and no evidence or signs of any Indians were near us. We supposed the regiment had left the field, and all that remained for us to do was to wait for the night and then pass the river and take the route for the Yellowstone River, and there construct a raft and descend to the mouth of the Powder River, our supply camp. Of course during the 36 hours that we were in suspense, we had neither water nor food. At 8 p.m. we dropped ourselves into the river, the water reaching our waists, crossed it twice and then carefully crawled up the bluffs, took our direction and slowly and cautiously proceeded southward.

After marching two miles, I thought I would go up on a very high hill to look around and see if I could discover any sign of our command; and on looking around I saw a fire on my left and in the direction where we supposed the command was fighting during the day, probably two miles from us. Of course we made two conjectures on this fire: it might be an Indian fire and it might be from our command. The only way to ascertain was to approach it cautiously and trust to chance. Accordingly we descended the hill, and took the direction of the fire. Climbing another and another hill, we listened a while and then proceeded on for a mile or more, when on the top of a hill we again stopped and listened. We could hear voices, but not distinctly enough to tell whether they were savages or our command.

We proceeded a little farther and heard the bray of a mule, and soon after, the distinct voice of a sentry challenging with the familiar words "Halt; Who goes there?" The challenge was not directed to us, as we were too far off to be seen by the picket, and it was too dark; but this gave us courage to continue our course and approach, though carefully, lest we should run into some Indians again. We were about 200 yards from the fire and * * * I cried out: "Picket, don't fire; it is Lt. DeRudio and Pvt. O'Neill," and started to run. We received an answer in a loud cheer from all the members of the picket and Lt. Varnum. This officer, one of our bravest and most efficient, came at once to me and was very happy to see me again, after having counted me among the dead; * * *.

My first question was about the condition of the regiment. I was in hopes that we were the only sufferers, but I was not long allowed to remain in doubt. Lt. Varnum said he knew nothing of the five companies under Custer and that our command had sustained a loss in Lts. McIntosh and Hodgson. * * * It was about 2 A.M. when I got into camp, and I soon after tried to go to sleep; but though I had not slept for two nights, I could not close my eyes. I talked with Lt. Varnum about the battle and narrated to him adventures and narrow escapes I had had. Morning soon came and I went to see the officers, and told them that the Indians had left * * *.

At 8 o'clock we saw cavalry approaching, first a few scouts and then a dense column and soon learned it was Gen. Brisbin's command coming up to our relief. Presently a long line of infantry appeared on the plain and Gen. Gibbon came up. Ah! who that was there will ever forget how our hearts thrilled at sight of those blue coats! And when Gens. Gibbon and Terry rode into our camp, men wept like children.

Yours truly,

CHARLES C. DeRUDIO

P.S.

I should do injustice to my feelings if I should omit to mention the fidelity and bravery of Private O'Neill. He faithfully obeyed me and stood by me like a brother. I shall never cease to remember him and his service to me during our dangerous companionship. This brave soldier is highly thought of by his company commander, and of course ever will be by me and mine.

CHAS. DeRUDIO.

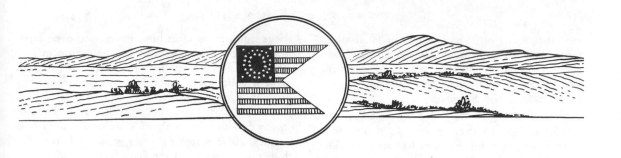

CHAPTER 5

THE STATEMENTS OF SCOUT HERENDEEN

GENERAL TERRY'S confidential report of 2 July 1876, addressed to Sheridan and received in Chicago before the arrival of his first report, dated 27 June, begins as follows:

"I think I owe it to myself to put you more fully in possession of the facts of the late operations. While at the mouth of the Rosebud, I submitted my plan to Genl. Gibbon and to General Custer. They approved it heartily. It was that Custer with his whole regiment should move up the Rosebud till he should meet a trail which Reno had discovered a few days before, but that he should not follow it directly to the Little Big Horn; that he should send scouts over it and keep his main force further to the south so as to prevent the Indians from slipping in between himself and the mountains. He was also to examine the headwaters of Tullock's Creek as he passed it and send me word of what he found there. *A scout was furnished him for the purpose of crossing the country to me.*"

The scout thus furnished General Custer for the stated purpose was George B. Herendeen, who was thoroughly familiar with the country. His name appears in the records in various forms. Sometimes it is Herendon, sometimes Herndon, sometimes Hunbein, and occasionally Haynden. But *he* wrote it *"Herendeen."*

Custer did not examine the headwaters of Tullock's Creek as he had been directed to do by General Terry; nor did he send Herendeen across country to report to Terry, but on the contrary, kept him with the command; and Herendeen went in with Reno's battalion, across the Little Big Horn, and into the valley fight. After the battle he made two interesting statements, the first to a correspondent of the *New York Herald* early in July 1876; and the second by signed letter to the same paper in January 1878. He was called as a witness and testified at length before the Reno Court of Inquiry in 1879; but as his two

prior statements are considered of prime importance they are set out here in full.

The 1876 statement, dated at Bismarck, Dakota Territory, 7 July 1876, was published by the *Herald* the following day:

Bismarck, D. T.
July 7, 1876

George Herendon, a scout sent by General Terry with General Custer's column, relates the following as his experience in the recent battle. He was sent by General Terry from the mouth of the Rosebud with General Custer's command to carry despatches to Terry from Custer:

"We left the Rosebud on the 22d of June at twelve o'clock; marched up the Rosebud about twelve miles and encamped for the night. On the morning of the 23d we broke camp at five o'clock and continued up the Rosebud until nine o'clock, when we struck a large lodge pole trail about ten days old and followed it along the Rosebud until toward evening, when we went into camp on the trail. On the morning of the 24th we pulled out at five o'clock and followed the trail five or six miles, when we met six Crow Indian scouts, who had been sent out the night previous by General Custer to look for the Indian village. They said they had found fresh pony tracks and that ten miles ahead the trail was fresher. General Custer had the officers' call sounded and they assembled around him, but I did not hear what he said to them. The scouts were again sent ahead and moved along at a fast walk. We moved at one o'clock, and, while the officers were eating their lunch, the scouts came back and reported that they had found where the village had been quite recently. They moved again, with flankers well out to watch the trail and see that it did not divide. About four o'clock we came to the place where the village had apparently been only a few days before, and went into camp two miles be-

257

low the forks of the Rosebud. The scouts all again pushed out to look for the village, and at eleven o'clock at night Custer had everything packed up and followed the scouts up the right hand fork of the Rosebud.

"About daylight we went into camp, made coffee, and soon after it was light the scouts brought Custer word that they had seen the village from the top of the divide that separates the Rosebud from Little Horn River. We moved up the creek until near its head, and concealed ourselves in a ravine. It was about three miles from the head of the creek where we then were to the top of the divide where the Indian scouts said the village could be seen, and after hiding his command, General Custer, with a few orderlies, galloped forward to look at the Indian camp. In about an hour Custer returned and said he could not see the Indian village, but the scouts and a half-breed guide, "Nuch Bayer," * said they could distinctly see it some fifteen miles off. While General Custer was looking for the Indian village the scouts came in and reported that he had been discovered, and that news was then on its way to the village that he was coming. Another scout said that two Sioux war parties had stolen up and seen the command; and on looking in a ravine near by, sure enough fresh pony tracks were found. Custer had "officer's call" blown, gave his orders and the command was put in fighting order. The scouts were ordered forward and the regiment moved at a walk. After going about three miles the scouts reported Indians ahead, and the command then took the trail. Our way lay down a little creek, a branch of the Little Horn, and after going about six miles we discovered an Indian lodge ahead, and Custer bore down on it at a stiff trot. In coming to it we found ourselves in a freshly abandoned Indian camp, all the lodges of which were gone except the one we saw, and on entering it we found it contained a dead Indian. From this point we could see into the Little Horn valley, and observed heavy clouds of dust rising about five miles distant. Many thought the Indians were moving away, and I think General Custer believed so, for he sent word to Colonel Reno, who was ahead with three companies of the Seventh regiment, to push on the scouts rapidly and head for the dust. Reno took a steady gallop down the creek bottom three miles to where it emptied into the Little Horn, and found a natural ford across the Little Horn river. He started to cross, when the scouts came back and called out to him to hold on, that the Sioux were coming in

large numbers to meet him. He crossed over, however, formed his companies on the prairie in line of battle, and moved forward at a trot but soon took a gallop. The valley was about three-fourths of a mile wide. On the left (was) a line of low, round hills, and on the right the river bottom, covered with a growth of cottonwood trees and bushes. After scattering shots were fired from the hills and a few from the river bottom and Reno's skirmishers returned the shots, he advanced about a mile from the ford to a line of timber on the right and dismounted the men to fight on foot. The horses were sent into the timber, and the men formed on the prairies and advanced toward the Indians. The Indians, mounted on ponies, came across the prairies and opened a heavy fire on the soldiers. After skirmishing for a few minutes, Reno fell back to his horses in the timber. The Indians moved to his left and rear, evidently with the intention of cutting him off the ford. Reno ordered his men to mount and move through the timber. Just as the men got into the saddle the Sioux, who had advanced in the timber, fired at close range and killed one soldier. Colonel Reno then commanded the men to dismount, and they did so, but he soon ordered them to mount again and moved out on to the open prairie. The command headed for the ford, pressed closely by Indians in large numbers, and at every moment the rate of speed was increased, until it became a dead run for the ford. The Sioux, mounted on their swift ponies, dashed up by the side of the soldiers and fired at them, killing both men and horses. Little resistance was offered, and it was a complete rout to the ford. I did not see the men at the ford, and do not know what took place further than a good many were killed when the command left the timber. Just as I got out my horse stumbled and fell and I was dismounted, the horse running away after Reno's command. I saw several soldiers who were dismounted, their horses having been killed or having run away. There were also some soldiers mounted who had remained behind. I should think in all there were as many as thirteen soldiers, and, seeing no chance to get away, I called on them to come into the timber and we would stand off the Indians. Three of the soldiers were wounded, and two of them so badly they could not use their arms. The soldiers wanted to go out, but I said no, we can't get to the ford, and, besides, we have wounded men and must stand by them. The soldiers still wanted to go, but I told them I was an old frontiersman, understood Indians, and, if they would do as I said, I would get them out of the scrape, which was no worse than scrapes I have been in before. About half

---
* Mitch Bouyer.

of the men were mounted, and they wanted to keep their horses with them, but I told them to let the horses go and fight on foot. We staid in the bush about three hours, and I could hear heavy firing below in the river, apparently about two miles distant. I did not know who it was, but knew the Indians were fighting some of our men, and I learned afterward it was Custer's command. Nearly all the Indians in the upper end of the valley drew off down the river, and the fight with Custer lasted about one hour, when the heavy firing ceased. When the shooting below began to die away I said to the boys, 'Come on, now is the time to get out.' Most of them did not go but waited for night. I told them the Indians would come back and we had better be off at once.

"Eleven of the thirteen said they would go, but two stayed behind. I deployed the men as skirmishers and we moved forward on foot toward the river. When we had got nearly to the river we met five Indians on ponies, and they fired on us. I returned the fire and the Indians broke and we then forded the river, the water being breast deep. We finally got over, wounded men and all, and headed for Reno's command, which I could see drawn up on the bluffs along the river about a mile off. We reached Reno in safety. We had not been with Reno more than fifteen minutes when I saw the Indians coming up the valley from Custer's fight. Reno was then moving his whole command down the ridge toward Custer. The Indians crossed the river below Reno and swarmed up the bluff on all sides. After skirmishing with them Reno went back to his old position which was on one of the highest points along the bluffs. It was now about five o'clock and the fight lasted until it was too dark to see to shoot. As soon as it was dark Reno took the packs and saddles off the mules and horses and made breastworks of them. He also dragged dead horses and mules on the line and sheltered the men behind them. Some of the men dug rifle pits with their butcher knives and all slept on their arms. At the peep of day the Indians opened a heavy fire and a desperate fight ensued, lasting until ten o'clock. The Indians charged our position three or four times, coming up close enough to hit our men with stones, which they threw by hand. Captain Benteen saw a large mass of Indians gathering on his front to charge, and ordered his men to charge on foot and scatter them. Benteen led the charge and was upon the Indians before they knew what they were about, and killed a great many. They were evidently much surprised at this offensive movement, and I think in desperate fighting Benteen is one of the bravest men I ever saw in a fight. All the time

he was going about through the bullets, encouraging the soldiers to stand up to their work, and not let Indians whip them.

"I forgot to state that about ten o'clock in the forenoon, and soon after Benteen made his charge, the men began to clamor for water. Many of them had not tasted water for thirty-six hours, and the fighting and hot sun parched their throats. Some had their tongues swollen and others could hardly speak. The men tried to eat crackers and hardtack, but could not raise enough saliva to moisten them. Several tried grass, but it stuck to their lips, and not one could spit or speak plainly. The wounded were reported dying from want of water, and a good many soldiers volunteered to go to the river to get some or perish in the attempt. We were fighting on the bluffs, about 700 yards from the river, and a ravine led down from the battlefield close to the river's edge. The men had to run over an open space of about 100 yards to get into the head of the ravine, and this open space was commanded by the Indians on the bluffs. The soldiers, about fifty strong, dashed over the open plateau and entered the ravine. They rushed down it to the mouth and found it closely guarded by a party of Indians posted in the timber across the river. The water could be approached to within about thirty feet under cover; but then one had to step out on the river bank and take the Indian's fire. The boys ran the gauntlet bravely. Some would dash down to the river with camp kettles, fill them, and then take shelter in the bend of the ravine, behind the rocks, and there canteens were filled and carried up the hill. Before all the men and wounded men were supplied one man was killed and six or seven wounded in the desperate attempt. One man had the bone of his leg shattered by a ball, and it has since been amputated.

"About two o'clock the Indians began drawing off, but kept skirmishing until late in the afternoon, and near dark all drew off. We now got water for the animals, many of them being almost dead, and they were put to graze on the hillside.

"In the evening Colonel Reno changed his position and fortified the new one, it being higher and stronger than the old one. We expected the Indians would renew the attack next day, but in the morning not an Indian was to be found. Every one felt sure that Crook or Terry was coming to our relief, and Colonel Reno sent out runners. About ten o'clock the glad intelligence was received that General Terry, with a large column of troops, was moving up the valley, six miles distant, and the head of his column soon came in sight."

In reply to questions, Mr. Haynden said:—

"I went in with the scouts on the left of Reno's line. There were about sixty of us, thirty-five being Ree Indians, six friendly Sioux, six Crows and the rest white men. I saw Bloody Knife, a Ree scout, throw up his arm and fall over, and I think he was killed. The two cavalry soldiers I left in the timber when I went out I have no doubt were killed, as they have not been seen since.

"I saw Lieutenant McIntosh soon after he fell. He had his horse shot under him early in the action, and at the time he was killed he was riding a soldier's horse. He was shot on the river bank while riding back to the ford.

"I saw Lieutenant Hodgson also. His horse was shot and he was wounded. His horse fell into the river near the opposite bank of the ford, and to help himself up the steep bank Hodgson caught hold of a horse's tail and had got up the bank when an Indian sharpshooter picked him off. Custer's packs were with the rest, and the Indians did not get any of them. Neither did they get any mules. Most of Custer's horses were shot in the action, and I do not believe the Indians got over 100 animals by the fight.

"I think some of our men were captured alive and tortured. I know the colored scout Isaiah was, for he had small pistol balls in his legs from the knees down, and I believe they were shot into him while alive. Another man had strips of skin cut out of his body. Hordes of squaws and old, gray-haired Indians were roaming over the battlefield howling like mad. The squaws had stone mallets and mashed in the skulls of the dead and wounded. Many were gashed with knives and some had their noses and other members cut off. The heads of four white soldiers were found in the Sioux camp that had been severed from their trunks, but the bodies could not be found on the battlefield or in the village. Our men did not kill any squaws, but the Ree Indian scouts did. The bodies of six squaws were found in the little ravine.

"I think the Indian village must have contained about 6,000 people, fully 3,000 of whom were warriors. The Indians fought Reno first and then went to fight Custer, after which they came back to finish Reno. The same Indians were in all the attacks. I think the Indians were commanded by Sitting Bull in person. There were eight or nine other chiefs in the field.

"I saw five chiefs, and each one carried a flag for their men to rally around. Some of the flags were red, others yellow, white and blue, and one a black flag. All the chiefs handled their warriors splendidly. I think Crazy Horse and his band were in the fight. The Indians must have lost as many men in killed and wounded as the whites did. Custer's men made a good fight, and no doubt killed a great many Indians. I don't think a single man escaped from Custer's part of the field. They were completely surrounded on every side by at least 2,500 warriors."

*A Staff officer has informed me that the haste of General Custer in attacking the Indians was entirely due to himself. General Terry had informed General Custer that he (Terry) would be at the mouth of the Little Horn River on the 26th of June, and Custer might expect to find him there with Gibbon's column. Terry marched as agreed upon, but found the road much more difficult than he had anticipated. The infantry suffered terribly on the 25th for water, the march being over a high and dry divide, under a broiling sun. Terry pushed on from four o'clock in the morning until four in the afternoon, when the infantry, completely exhausted, were left in camp, and Terry continued the march with Brisbin's cavalry all night through a rainstorm and darkness. At daylight on the morning of the 26th Terry was in sight of the mouth of the Little Horn, and had kept his promise to Custer to be there early on the 26th of June.

At eight o'clock Terry heard from Crow scouts of Custer's disaster, and deeply regretted his haste in attacking the Indian camp on the 25th. If Custer had struck the Little Horn one day later, or deferred his attack twenty-four hours later, Terry could have cooperated with him and, in all probability, have prevented the disaster. A Crow Indian scout named "Curley" came in the day after the battle and stated he was in the fight with Custer. He says the fight lasted over one hour, Custer contending against ten times his number. The men fought splendidly until the Big Chief (Custer) fell, and then they became somewhat demoralized. Most of the officers and men had been killed before Custer. "Curley" says the Indians fought Custer on foot, and charged his men again and again. He thinks a great many more Indians were killed in the fight than were in Custer's command.

"Curley" is a truthful Indian, and his statement may be relied on.

* * *

Herendeen's 1878 statement, evidently made because he considered that much misinformation was being fed the public, is contained in the following letter, dated at Bozeman, Montana Territory, 4

*Following the matter in quotation marks, and beginning with the starred paragraph, the language is that of the *Herald* correspondent. (W.A.G.)

January, and was published by the *Herald* 22 January:

CUSTER VINDICATED

A Scout's Story of the Battle of the Little Big Horn

A Brilliant Attack

Reno Precipitately Retreats Before Two Hundred Reds

A ZERO IN THE FIGHT

The Whole Strength of the Village Allowed to Crush the Battalions Engaged

---

Bozeman, M. T., Jan. 4, 1878.

To the Editor of the *Herald*:—

I have read a good deal of late in the *Herald* and other papers about the battle of the Little Big Horn, much of which is incorrect and calculated to mislead the public. I was present with Reno during the whole of his connection with the battle and am personally cognizant of what occurred both before and after the engagement. Of course I did not see all that took place; but I saw a great deal and will relate it just as I witnessed it.

A Council of War

I was with General Gibbon's command at the mouth of the Rosebud when General Terry and General Custer joined Gibbon. General Terry told me I could go with General Custer on his march up the Rosebud. He told me at General Gibbon's tent to go with Custer, and I afterwards saw Terry on the steamer Far West while she lay at the mouth of the Rosebud, and he asked me about the country along the upper part of the Rosebud and Tullock's Fork. I was standing on the forward deck of the boat when I was called into the cabin where I found Generals Terry, Gibbon, Custer and Brisbin around a table apparently holding a council of war. Terry showed me a map and asked me for information about the country on Tullock's Fork and the Little Big Horn. I understood from the conversation had by Terry with Gibbon and Custer that he was trying to find out where the columns of Custer

and Gibbon could best form a junction somewhere in the neighborhood of the mouth of the Little Big Horn, Custer to march up the Rosebud and Gibbon up the Big Horn. I had been over the ground and told the General all I knew about it. Custer seemed pleased with the information I gave Terry and said I was just the man he wanted, and that he would like me to go with him. I went out on the deck again, and soon afterward General Gibbon came out and spoke to me. He said I could consider myself as employed to go with General Custer. I asked him what compensation I would receive and what I would be expected to do, and he replied I would act as a scout, and when Custer's command got to the head of Tullock's Creek, I would come down the Tullock with dispatches to his (Gibbon's) command. There was some conversation about what compensation I would receive, but the above was all that occurred of importance. This was on the 21st of June, and soon after General Gibbon left the boat. General Brisbin came out of the cabin and I asked him where his cavalry would probably be in the next few days, so I could find him and he replied about the mouth of the Little Big Horn.

Starting up the Rosebud

I reported to General Custer at noon on the 21st of June and was sent to Lieutenant Varnum, who had charge of some scouts. I saw with Varnum, Mich Boyer* the half-breed scout and guide. We started out on the 22nd about noon and travelled up to the Rosebud. Boyer and Bloody Knife, a Ree scout, had the lead and Custer traveled with them. Lieutenant Varnum with his scouts followed Custer in advance of the column. We marched about twelve miles and went into camp at five P.M.

An Indian Trail

General Custer ordered reveille to be sounded at four and the command to be ready to march at five o'clock next morning. This was the morning of the 23rd and we marched promptly at five A.M. Our course led up the stream four or five miles, when we struck an Indian trail which Reno had followed a few days before. We followed the trail until five P.M. when we encamped for the night; and in the evening Custer sent the Crow scouts who were with us on in advance to see what they could find out.

On the morning of the 24th we broke camp at five o'clock and continued following the trail up the stream. Soon after starting Custer, who

---

*Also spelled "Mitch Bouyer."

was in advance with Boyer, called me to him and told me to get ready, saying he thought he would send me and Charlie Reynolds to the head of Tullock's Fork to take a look. I told the General it was not time yet, as we were then travelling in the direction of the head of the Tullock, and I could only follow his trail. I called Boyer, who was a little ahead, back and asked him if I was not correct in my statement to the General, and he said "Yes; further up on Rosebud we would come opposite a gap, and then we could cut across and strike the Tullock in about fifteen miles' ride." Custer said, "All right; I could wait."

A Bloody Omen

We had not proceeded far when the Crows came in on the run and reported the trail was getting fresh ahead, and that they had seen some fresh pony tracks. They brought in with them the scalp of a white man which they had picked up on the trail, and which was identified as coming from the head of a man named Stoker, Company H, Second Cavalry, who had been killed a few days before at the mouth of the Rosebud.

Custer on receiving the above intelligence halted his command, dismounted the men and had the officers' call sounded. He held a council with his officers, but I was not near enough to hear what passed.

After halting about half an hour we mounted and moved slowly along the trail, and soon came to the mouth of Muddy Creek, up which about three miles the Second Cavalry had its fight with Lame Deer's band last spring (i.e. 1877. W.A.G.)

A Split Scent

As we passed Muddy Creek I noticed that some lodges had left the main trail on the Rosebud and gone that way. I followed them a short distance and then rode over to Custer and told him some of the lodges had gone up the Muddy. He halted the command at once, and sent Lieutenant Varnum to find out where the trail on the Muddy went. Custer said he did not want to lose any of the lodges, and if any of them left the main trail he wanted to know it.

While Varnum was gone we halted and the men cooked dinner. He was absent about two hours, and when he came back told Custer that the Muddy trail swung over on the Rosebud and joined the main trail again. We then started on the large trail, which freshened every moment. We passed over places where a number of camps had been quite close together, showing that the Indians were travelling very slowly, and only moving for grass.

Aiming to Get the Whole Village

Towards evening the trail became so fresh that Custer ordered flankers to be kept well out and a sharp lookout had for lodges leaving to the right or the left. He said he wanted to get the whole village, and nothing must leave the main trail without his knowing it. About dusk we halted and went into camp on the trail. It was then very fresh and the General sent Varnum, Boyer and some scouts on ahead to examine the trail and adjacent country. The men were given orders to graze their animals, get supper and be ready to start at eleven P.M. Everybody rested until ten P.M., when we packed up again and moved out. The night was very dark and our progress slow. After marching some ten miles, about two A.M. we halted, the horses were unsaddled and the men lay down to rest. The packs were taken off the mules and everything done to rest and recuperate the animals.

Its Great Strength Known

Some time during the night the scouts came in and reported to Custer that the Indian camp was found. We packed up and moved forward at early light. Mitch Boyer and Reynolds, who had been out, said the camp was very large. Boyer said it was the biggest village he had ever seen. Reynolds said there was a heap of them, and Custer replied "he could whip them." Reynolds said it would take six hours hard fighting to whip them.

Custer Reconnoitres in Person

About nine o'clock on the morning of the 25th of June* and the last day of our march Custer halted his troops and concealed them as well as he could. He then took an orderly and rode up on the Divide about four miles to where Lieutenant Varnum and Boyer were. The General was trying to get a look at the village, which was over on the other side of the Divide, on the Little Big Horn. While Custer was gone I rode up the Dry Fork of the Rosebud, along which the trail ran, but had not gone far when I saw two objects going over the hills in the direction of the Little Horn.

Custer was gone perhaps an hour or an hour and a half, and when he came back Boyer, who

* The official itinerary shows this halt to have occurred at 10:07 A. M. to 11:45 A. M. The difference in time is possibly accounted for by the fact that the command moved by Ft. Lincoln time, about 1½ hours later than Montana time.

was with him, asked me if I had seen the Indians. I said, "Yes, I had seen what I thought
were Indians." Boyer replied:—"You were within
150 yards of them and you surprised them and
they have gone to camp as fast as they can go."

The Attack

Custer had "officer's call" sounded, and gave
his orders. I understood him to assign each one
his place, and he divided the column into battalions. As soon as the orders were issued we
started up the Divide at a fast walk and travelled
about three or four miles, when we came to the
top.* The scouts, under Lieutenants Varnum and
Hare, then pushed on ahead at a lope and the
command followed at a trot. I was with the
scouts, and we kept down a creek which led
toward the Little Horn. When we got near the
mouth of the creek we saw a lodge standing on
the bank. We rode up on a hill, so as to flank
and overlook the lodge, and soon saw it was
deserted. From the top of the hill we looked
ahead down the Little Big Horn and saw a heavy
cloud of dust and some stock apparently running.
We could see beyond the stream a few Indians
on the hills riding very fast, and seemingly running away. I said the Indians were running,
and we would have to hurry up, or we would
not catch them. Lieutenant Hare wrote a note
to Custer, but I do not know what he reported.
I presume he thought as the rest of us did, that
the Indians were getting away. Custer was near
at hand, and was riding at a fast trot.

A Dead Man's Lodge

The scouts charged down on the abandoned
lodge, cut it open, and found in it a dead Indian. Custer came up while we were at the
lodge, Colonel Reno having the advance. I heard
Custer say to Reno, "Reno, take the scouts, lead
out, and I will be with you."** Reno started at
a gallop, and as he rode called out, "Keep your
horses well in hand." My horse fell, and for a
few moments I was delayed, but I caught up
with Reno at the ford. As we were crossing I
heard the Crow scouts call out to one another,
"The Sioux are coming up to meet us," and,
understanding the language, I called to Reno,

---

* This does not agree with other accounts, which without
exception place the division into battalions about a mile
after the divide was crossed; and it will be noted that
Herendeen entirely fails to mention the departure of Benteen's battalion, which occurred at this time.

** Herendeen, Girard the interpreter, and Lt. (later Gen.)
Edgerly all have stated that Custer gave Reno this order in
person. All other witnesses state that it was given by the
regimental adjutant, Lt. Cooke.

"The Sioux are coming." Reno waited a few
moments until the command closed up, then
crossed the Little Big Horn, and formed in
line of battle on the prairie, just outside some
timber. The formation was made without halting, and the line kept on moving, first at a trot
and then at a gallop.

The Indians Hold Their Fire

We could see a large body of Indians just ahead
of us and apparently waiting for us. We advanced
probably half a mile, the Indians setting fire to
some timber on our right and in our front. A
few Indians were in the timber and we fired on
them, but no shots were returned.

The Slaughter Begins

Very soon we dismounted, and the soldiers
formed a skirmish line, facing the hills. The
line extended to the left and front, and firing
almost immediately began, the Indians being near
the foot hills of the little valley. In a short time
the firing became quite heavy, the Indians moving
to the left and working to our rear. The horses
were now led into the timber on our right and
rear, and the soldiers fell back to cover among
the bushes and small trees. There was a little
park or meadow just within the timber, and on
this the command formed and mounted. I was
one of the last men to get into the timber and
halted at the edge of the bushes to fire at some
Indians who were coming into the timber on
our left and rear. I got my horse and joined the
command, which I found mounted and sitting
in line of battle in the park or open space among
the bushes. There was little firing for some minutes, and then we received a volley from the
bushes. Bloody Knife was just in my front at
the time, and Reno on my left. The volley killed
Bloody Knife and one soldier. I heard the soldier
call out as he fell, "Oh! my God, I have got it."

Reno's Change of Mind and Precipitation

Reno gave the order to dismount, and almost
immediately gave the order to mount again. The
soldiers were not all on horseback when Reno
started out of the timber toward the prairie, the
men following him. The men scattered, getting
out of the woods as best they could. They ran
quartering toward the Little Big Horn. I had
started out of the timber when the command did,
about half of it being ahead of me and the other
half in my rear. There was such a cloud of dust
no one could see where he was going; just as I
got out on the edge of the prairie my horse fell,
throwing me off and running away. I ran back

to the timber about 150 yards and took cover among the bushes. Just as I turned back I heard some officer call out:—"Halt men! halt! Let us fight them!"

Surrounded

As soon as the troops led by Reno emerged from the timber the Indians closed down upon them, some ahead, some alongside and some in the rear of them.

When I went back to the timber, after my horse threw me, just as I reached the cover I met Lieutenant DeRudio and stopped to talk to him. As we spoke together about a dozen soldiers, some on foot and some on horseback, came along and I called to them to come into the timber and we could stand the Indians off. The soldiers joined us at once and we concealed ourselves, tying the horses to the trees.

The Noise of Custer's Fight

Just as we got settled down firing below us opened up and we knew Custer was engaged. The Indians had been leaving Reno and going down the valley in considerable numbers at full speed. The firing down the valley was very heavy. There were about nine volleys at intervals and the intermediate firing was quite rapid. The heavy firing lasted from three-quarters of an hour to an hour and then it died away.

Escaping from Hiding

I said to the men who were with me, "Boys, we had better get out of this." I told them that the fight below had stopped, and it was a guess how it had gone, but I thought likely in favor of the Indians, and we had better get away before they came back up the valley. I started out and the men followed me. We saw only five Indians between ourselves and Major Reno. We could see Reno's troops on a hill about a mile distant, where they had halted. It was five o'clock when I joined Reno.

Second Attack on Reno

When we had got out of the timber we could see the Indians coming up the valley in large numbers. As I came up the hill Reno started down the way Custer went, but did not go more than a third of a mile before the Indians met him and drove him back to his old stand on the hill. The Indians attacked Reno with great fury and fought him until dark.

On the following day, the 26th of June, the fight opened at daylight and lasted until one minute past four o'clock P.M. The men had no water and suffered greatly. As many as seven men were hit while trying to get water.

Benteen to the Rescue

I think Captain Benteen saved the fight on the hill. None of us knew with certainty what had become of General Custer until General Terry came up with Gibbon's command on the morning of the 27th of June.

Will Reno Answer This?

The number of Indians that attacked Reno's command in the flat on the 25th of June could not have exceeded 200 warriors.* I do not think any one had been killed up to the time when he retreated into the timber, and only one man had been killed at the time when he broke for the bluffs.

Neither Men Nor Horses Were Tired

The horses were not tired and the men worn out and sleepy (as has been represented) when we arrived at the battle field. The animals were fresh and Custer led as well fed and cheerful a set of men as ever went to battle. Everybody thought the Indians were running away when we charged down upon the village and the only fear was that they would escape before we could strike them.

The Changing Tide of Battle

I do not think Custer's fight lasted very long. Certainly it was all over in less than two hours; but at one time the firing was so heavy we thought Custer was advancing, and the Indians seemed to have some doubt as to the result of the battle, for they commenced to take down the lodges and pack up the village as if for flight.**

The Marches Before the Fight

The distance from the mouth of the Rosebud, where Custer started out, to the battle field at the mouth of the Little Big Horn was something over one hundred miles. I think the first day we marched twelve miles, the second day thirty-five miles, the third day thirty-three miles, and the fourth and last day twenty-five to twenty-eight miles. We started at noon on the 22d of June, and did not reach the battle field until about noon† on the 25th of June. All stories about Custer running his men and horses until they were

---

* The testimony taken at the Reno Inquiry almost unanimously estimated the Indians opposing Reno in the valley at from 800 to 1000; the firing, however, being done by about 200 at any one time. This is probably what Herendeen means.

** "We have killed them all; put up your lodges where they were"—Kill Eagle's story. N. Y. Herald, Oct. 6, 1876.

† According to the official itinerist, Reno received his attack order about 2:15 P.M.

W.A.G.

worn out by the time they arrived on the battle field are unqualifiedly false. A heavy pack train kept up with us. The movements of Custer throughout the march, so far as I could judge, were deliberate and soldierly in the extreme.

GEORGE B. HERENDEEN

———

Comment by Colonel Graham: Much has been made by critics of Major Reno of Herendeen's "Mount—dismount—mount" story, which is cited frequently as proof of cowardice. That something of the kind related by Herendeen did occur appears to be beyond doubt, just as it appears beyond doubt that during the night of 25 June, in the course of a conference between Reno and Benteen, consideration was given to moving the command, the idea being abandoned when it developed that such movement would entail leaving the helpless wounded to be butchered by the Sioux.

Consider the circumstances of the "mount—dismount—mount" incident. The horses had been brought to the clearing in the timber, the men called from the firing line and ordered to mount, preparatory to moving out for the purpose of breaking through the attacking Indians. No sooner were they settled in the saddle than Indians who had filtered into the timber in unknown numbers, fired a point blank volley, which killed Bloody Knife at Reno's side and mortally wounded a soldier. Reno instantly ordered the men to dismount, and a few moments later, to mount again, at which time he led them to the plain, where a column was hastily formed and the ride to the river began.

In describing this incident in "The Story of the Little Big Horn" I said that Reno was "startled and disconcerted"; and well he might be, for the sudden volley came as a complete surprise, and to be splattered with the blood and brains of his Indian scout leader was certainly disconcerting.

In ordering his men instantly to dismount, however, he did, as it seems to me, precisely what the occasion required, for if the Indians who fired the volley were to be engaged or driven out, there was no practical way to go about it but on foot. A mounted charge into underbrush and timber was obviously not to be thought of, and it was equally clear that to remain in the clearing mounted would be to make of his men mere sitting ducks. The order to dismount was therefore proper in the circumstances, so long as the concealed Indians continued to be a menace.

Evidently however, in characteristic Indian fashion, they "hit and ran," and for the time being, ceased to be a menace. Reno at once ordered his men to remount; and to obviate another such incident, immediately led them out. That he was startled and disconcerted does not necessarily imply that his action was cowardly. If there is any implication of want of courage in his conduct at this juncture, it is rather to be found in his hasty departure, which left a considerable number of his men behind to shift for themselves as best they could.

Theodore W. Goldin, Benteen's correspondent.

CHAPTER 6

MR. GOLDIN DISCREDITED HIMSELF

A FIGURE which bobs up in some connection with almost every important phase of the battle of the Little Big Horn, is that of Theodore W. Goldin, a private of "G" Company. According to his various and varied tales, he was Custer's orderly on the day of the battle; he carried a written order to Reno, after the latter had crossed the river; he was unhorsed during the retreat to the bluffs, hid with Herendeen in the timber, and joined the command on the heights in time to hear the distant firing down river; he witnessed the deaths of both McIntosh and Hodgson; he overheard a heated colloquy between Weir and Reno on the hill; he was one of the heroes who, under Indian fire, risked their lives to bring water to the wounded, for which he received the Congressional Medal of Honor; after the battle he rode over the field with Martin, the trumpeter, who pointed out to him the place where he turned back with Custer's last message to Benteen to "Come on and be quick." In short, he was present at or participated in almost everything that happened at the Little Big Horn except, of course, the unpleasant experience of being killed with Custer.

Many times during the past twenty-five years I have been taken severely to task because of omission to credit, or even to mention Mr. Goldin's stories, and demand made that I disclose my reason, if reason I had, for such omission. Indeed in 1923, Mr. Goldin himself propounded the same question. The answer I have never made publicly 'till now. It is expressed in the title of this chapter.

I did not discredit Mr. Goldin; he performed that gentle office for himself, alone and unaided; and he did it in the manner below set forth.

In 1904, the Rev. Cyrus Townsend Brady, a well known and highly esteemed Episcopal clergyman who had made many informative contributions to the written history of America, published a book titled "Indian Fights and Fighters." It contains a great deal of valuable and authentic data concerning the Indian Wars that followed the War between the States; and in particular it presents in an appendix a most excellent discussion (in which Generals Miles, Godfrey, Hughes, Woodruff, Carrington and others took part) of some controverted phases of the battle of the Litle Big Horn; a discussion which every student of that disastrous event should read and ponder well.

But the book also contains some features of lesser value, among which is a letter signed by Mr. Goldin, then a practising lawyer of Janesville, Wisconsin, and prominent in state-wide political circles as Chairman of the Republican State Central Committee. The Goldin letter, dated in August 1904, states that it was written in response to a request by the Rev. Mr. Brady for some reminiscences of Mr. Goldin's Indian fighting days when a member of the Seventh Cavalry, and appears as Chapter Six of Dr. Brady's book, in which Goldin is described as "the last, or perhaps the next to the last, man to see Custer alive."

Mr. Goldin wrote a very entertaining letter; and as Dr. Brady's book contained one of the most thorough treatments of the Little Big Horn battle that came to my attention while I was engaged in abstracting the testimony taken at the Reno Court of Inquiry, and about the time I was locating and interviewing John Martin, the retired trumpeter who had carried Custer's last message, the story told by Mr. Goldin was of unusual interest, for reasons that will shortly appear.

"I had known General Custer," Mr. Goldin said, "from the time I joined the regiment in 1873 up to the time of his tragic death, and had campaigned with him and with the regiment, with the exception of the year 1875, when the troop to which I was attached was stationed in the South."

On the day of the battle, he wrote Dr. Brady, he was detailed by Lt. McIntosh, his company commander, to report to General Custer as an orderly, and was directed by the General to ride with the Adjutant, and do whatever he was told to do.

Custer, he said, tried several times to find a place where he could cross the river, but without success: and after perhaps the third unsuccessful attempt, the General conferred with his Adjutant, Cooke, who thereupon called for an orderly. Goldin "happened to be the first one to reach him," and was handed a written order addressed to Major Reno which the Adjutant had "dashed off"; and he was directed to "deliver that to Major Reno, remain with him until we effect a junction, then report to me at once."

Goldin, according to his story, after "a ride of five or six miles overtook Reno *just as he was dismounting to fight on foot.*" He delivered the order, which Reno hurriedly read and "stuck it in his pocket." The contents of the order Goldin did not know; but as no junction was ever effected, he remained with Reno's command throughout the remainder of the action. His description of Reno's fight in the valley, his retreat to the hills, the death of "Benny" Hodgson; the angry colloquy between Weir and Reno and the advance down river of "D" Company, followed by the rest of the command; the onset of the Indians and the desperate defense on Reno Hill, are vivid and graphic.

His story of the six-mile ride to Reno, bearing Custer's order which Reno merely glanced at and then pocketed was a puzzler, for Reno and his officers had testified at Chicago in 1879, that the only order Reno ever got was that given him at or near the "lone tepee," some three miles from the river, to "take as rapid a gait as you think prudent, and charge afterward, and the whole outfit will support you." If Goldin's story was correct, it was obvious that Reno and his officers had testified falsely, and the claim that nothing whatever was received from Custer subsequent to the order to "charge afterward" was not true. It raised a question that was crucial, for if Custer had in fact sent Reno an order after learning from Reno's several messages to him that the Indians were not running, but were meeting him in force, it tended to destroy the claims of the suviving officers that Custer had no plan of battle; and more than that, the directive to Goldin to "remain with him (i.e. Reno) until we effect a junction," tended to prove that he *did* have a plan which was presumably communicated to Reno in the order; and at the very least, it established beyond cavil or question that junction of Custer's force with that of Reno was intended.

Strangely enough, very few persons then knew much of anything about the Reno Court of Inquiry or the content of its record of proceedings, which had been hidden away in confidential War Department files for more than forty years; but I did, because I was even then in the very midst of it; and as that record and the Goldin story did

not "gee," a private court of inquiry of my own seemed to be indicated.

Generals Godfrey and Edgerly were consulted. Both had heard of Goldin's medal of honor (of which more later) but as to his assertion that he had carried an order to Reno, both were skeptical. Godfrey thought it possible, but improbable; while Edgerly "preferred to express no opinion." I wrote Colonel Varnum in San Francisco. His reply was positive. Wallace, who took command of "G" Company after McIntosh was killed, had told him that no word of any kind had been received from Custer after the parting of the two columns at the lone tepee. I also sent a letter to Hare in Texas; but from him got no reply. And then I wrote Trumpeter John Martin, in Brooklyn. As he was Custer's orderly trumpeter, and the unquestioned bearer of his last message, he should know about the movements of the other orderlies. Here is his reply, dated 12 April 1922:

"In regards to this man Goldin, I've never heard the least thing about him, and furthermore don't know who he is. I am the only Messenger who was sendt out from Custer command at that time and also the last. The only Message sendt that I've know off was the one I received from Gen. Custer to deliver to Capt. Benteen on that fatal day for Reinforcement.

Yours Respectfully,
John Martin; Retired, U. S. Army."

Martin's letter settled at least the fact that he did not know Goldin and had never heard of him; but as his letter showed that the message he carried was the only one he knew about, and there was no doubt that Sgt. Kanipe of "C" Company had also carried one, addressed to the Commander of the Pack Train, I thought it only fair, before coming to any conclusions, to get in touch with Goldin himself if possible, and ask some questions. I located him at long last at the Snyderhof Hotel in Kansas City, and in reply to my letter, he said, in substance, that he would be happy to answer any questions I might ask.

Thereupon, I followed an old army custom, and sent him a questionnaire containing 41 questions, which he returned with a letter under date of 19 September 1922. The letter and questionnaire are set out below, with his answers:

Kansas City Mo.,
September 19, 1922.

Col. W. A. Graham, J.A.,
#2101 Munitions Bldg.
Washington, D. C.

Dear Sir:—

I am returning herewith your recent questionnaire, answered as fully and concisely as space would permit.

In making my answers I have had to rely entirely on my memory, as all my diaries and memoranda are in storage with other goods since the death of my wife.

Your questions present some new points to me, some I had never before heard mentioned, one being the fact that the Adjutant and Keogh accompanied Reno to the river. That was entirely new matter to me, and a somewhat surprising statement, as I cannot now recall having missed either officer from the Custer column at any time, and distinctly recall the presence of both of them when Custer's column first moved out to seek another point of egress from the valley in which we halted after our night march.

The man "Kanipe" mentioned as a messenger was a new one to me. Never recall hearing the name before.

It was also the first intimation I ever had that 'G' Troop moved out of the valley into the timber in advance of the rest of the squadron. It seemed to me the move was a simultaneous one all along the line, but of course in a time of action as brisk as that was, one sees and knows but little outside of his immediate surroundings.

Trusting my answers will meet the points you desired light on, and with the assurance that I will be glad to afford you any further information in my power, I am

Very truly yours,
/s/ Theo. W. Goldin."

Snyderhof Hotel
Kansas City, Mo.

THE QUESTIONNAIRE

1. At what time, and where, were you detailed to report to General Custer as orderly?

> Was detailed for clerical work at headquarters a short time before the expedition left Ft. Lincoln.

2. To whom did you report?

> Reported to Lieut. Cook, Regimental Adjutant at the post.

3. At what place in the column did you ride after reporting as orderly? How far from the General?

> On the day of the fight rode most of the time after the night march, near the Adjutant, wherever he went.

4. Were you near enough to the General to hear any conversation he may have had with his Adjutant, or with other officers?

> Only at times.

5. Do you remember Trumpeter Martin (or (Martini), of Benteen's troop, who was Custer's orderly trumpeter that day?

> Yes, very well.

6. Had you any personal acquaintance with Martini, and to what extent?

> No close personal acquaintance, his troop was never stationed at regimental headquarters. Knew him as one soldier knows another.

7. Were you near enough to the head of the column to hear the order to Reno, or the talk, if any (upon the part of Custer and others) which immediately preceded it?

> I did not hear the talk, or orders issued, overheard some conversation. As I recall it there was very little talk until the final orders were issued.

8. Did Custer himself give Reno any orders, or was it all done through the Adjutant?

> My present recollection is that Custer personally made the assignments and issued the final orders to Reno and Benteen.

9. Was there anything in the nature of a conference or conversation between Custer and Reno when the order was given?

> I recall no particular evidence of anything of this nature.

10. From the point where Reno started for the river after receiving the attack order, how far did Custer follow Reno toward the river before swinging off to the right?

> From recollection I should say in the neighborhood of three miles or possibly more. Never was over that part of the trail later.

11. Was Custer still following Reno when the Adjutant and Captain Keogh returned to the column after riding to the river with Reno?

> Have no knowledge that the Adjutant and Keogh rode to the river with Reno. Did not miss them at any time from Custer's column.

12. Did you hear the Adjutant make any report to Custer upon his return from the river, to the effect that the Sioux were coming up the valley?

> I heard no report of this character.

13. If not, what if anything, did you hear either the Adjutant or Captain Keogh report to Custer at that time?

> Recall no report made by either of the officers named. This is my first knowledge that they were away from Custer's column at any time.

14. After swinging off to the right, how far down the river did Custer's column go before he halted it to go up on the ridge with Martini?

> As I recall it, no halt was made, the column merely slowed down and Custer galloped

over to the edge of the bluffs.

15. How far from the river was the column at the time it halted?

At the time it slowed down I think in the neighborhood of a mile and a half (purely guess work).

16. How far from the column and toward the river did Custer go to reach the high point from which he surveyed the Indian village?

As I recall it, possibly about the distance above stated.

17. Who, besides Martini, were with him?

The only one I recall was Sergt. Hughes, Regimental Color Sergeant.

18. About how long was the column halted while Custer was gone to the high point?

My best recollection is that no actual halt was made, the column continuing slowly in a northwesterly direction parallel with the river.

19. With reference to Reno's position on the hill during the afternoon and evening of the 25th, how far down the river was this high point? How close to the river was it?

My recollection is that it was just a few hundred yards below the point where Reno's line was finally formed on the afternoon of the 25th. I never visited the point in question.

20. After Custer returned to the column, what, if anything, did you hear him say to the Adjutant or to other officers as to what he had seen?

The only remark I heard Custer make was to Keogh: "Keogh, those Indians are running, if we can keep them at it we can afford to sacrifice some horses."

21. How far down the river from this halting point did the column proceed before any messengers were sent back?

To my best recollection not more than a mile.

22. Which messenger started back first—yourself, Kanipe, or Martini? Which second?

I believe I was the first messenger sent back. Do not now recall "Kanipe," but do remember Martini (or Martin).

23. Who wrote the message you carried?

Lieut. Cook, Regimental Adjutant.

24. What route did you take in going back?

For some distance practically along the trail, but bearing somewhat to the left after sighting the dust of Reno's column.

25. Where, with reference to Reno's first crossing of the river, did you cross it?

My recollection is within 100 yards of it, down stream.

26. How long did it take you to reach Reno?

Have no idea. Never had. Not long. I was in a hurry to get where I felt safer.

27. To whom did you report after delivering the message?

To no one in particular, merely attached myself to "G" Troop, my own Troop.

28. Did you reach Reno's command from the rear, or from the flank?

If anything, slightly from the rear.

29. How long had Reno been in action when you reached him?

He was not yet in action.

30. How long after you reached him did the skirmish line remain out on the plain?

Time under those conditions very hard to estimate. From the time we deployed until we fell back into the timber probably did not exceed 15 or 20 minutes (estimated).

31. Had "G" troop been withdrawn from the line and placed in the woods when you arrived? If not, how soon afterwards was it so withdrawn?

My recollection is that the entire squadron moved into the timber at about the same time. I know "M" Troop was close on our left almost as soon as we struck the timber.

32. Did Lieutenant Wallace know that you had come through with a message from Custer? Did you ever tell him, or talk to him about it?

I presume he did, possibly not at the time, but we often spoke of it later.

33. Have you any idea what the message was?

My only knowledge in this regard was what Custer said to the Adjutant: "Send word to Reno to crowd them in the rear, we'll soon be with him."

34. What was the situation with regard to Indians on the flanks and in the rear of Reno's command at the time you reached him?

A few Indians were showing in our front as we moved into the river bottom. Soon began flanking us and swinging in our rear.

35. Had Custer's column met any Indians after swinging to the right from Reno's trail, up to the time you left it to go back? If so, where, and in what numbers?

Up to the time I left the column we had seen no Indians, save possibly a half dozen here and there, farther down the valley.

36. Had there been any firing either by or against Custer up to the time you left to go back? If so, to what extent and where?

I recall no firing up to the time I left the column.

37. In what direction, as regards the river, was Custer proceeding when you left the column?

In a northwesterly direction, practically parallel with the river, if anything drawing closer to the river.

38. From all the conversation and talk upon the part of Custer with his officers that you heard, if any, was his intention, at the time you left, to go clear down to the north end of the village to attack, or was it to cross the river and attack in flank? Or, did he then not know or realize how immense the village was?

I am sure Custer knew nothing of the village or its location. His purpose seemed to be to find a crossing and attack on the flank of what he apparently believed to be a retreating column.

39. Did you hear anything which gave you any inkling as to what part Benteen was to take in the attack? If so, what?

Benteen was ordered to scout the bluffs and timber to the southward, attacking anything he met and to send for help if he needed it.

40. What was the fighting strength of the Sioux that day, to the best of your knowledge and judgment?

Judging from the size of the village I always estimated the fighting strength of the Sioux to have been between 4000 and 5000. This is purely an estimate on my part, based on what I saw of the village later.

41. At the time you left Custer to carry the message to Reno, was his column farther down river than the point which Weir afterwards reached in his effort to join Custer late in the afternoon? With reference to "Weir's point," locate the point where you left the column as nearly as you can.

My best recollection is that it was within a mile of the point Weir reached later in the afternoon, that I turned back, but still some distance to the eastward.

* * *

Following the receipt of Mr. Goldin's letter of 19 September 1922, with which he had returned the answered questionnaire, the following correspondence was had between us:

Washington, D. C.
September 25, 1922.

Mr. Theodore W. Goldin,
Snyderhof Hotel,
Kansas City, Mo.

My dear Sir:

I have received your letter of September 19th, with your answers to the questions I asked, and I thank you very much.

Your answers to questions #7, 8 and 9 refer, I take it, to the assignments of battalion commands just after crossing the divide at noon and

the orders then given. My questions, however, referred (perhaps not too clearly) to the order given to Reno some two hours later, just after the "dead warrior teepee" was passed, and which directed him to cross the river and attack. There is some dispute as to whether Custer in person gave the order, or whether Cook gave it at Custer's direction, and also as to just what the order was. I hoped that you might be able to clear that up.

There is, I think, no doubt that Cook and Keogh rode to the river with Reno, and then turned back. This was fully established by the testimony at Chicago in 1879. Girard, the interpreter, testified, among other things that when he reached the river, the Crow scouts told him that the Sioux were coming up the valley in force to meet Reno, who had already crossed over; that he (Girard) rode back, overtook Cook, who was then riding back with Keogh to join Custer (who was then still following Reno's trail), and that he reported the fact to Cook, who said he would tell Custer.

Reno, in a letter written during August, 1876, stated that after he received the attack order, Cook and Keogh rode on with him, Cook saying, laughingly, "I am going in with the advance, and Myles Keogh is coming, too."

The testimony given at Chicago is to the effect that after the dismounting and deploying of Reno's battalion in the bottoms, "G" was on the right of the line, and the horses were concealed in the timber; that in a very few minutes report was made to Reno that the right flank was being turned by Indians in the woods, and that to protect the horses, he at once withdrew "G" to the woods, going with them in person, and that Moylan's troop ("A") was extended to cover the gap. "M" and "A" remained on the line perhaps fifteen minutes longer, when they also were withdrawn because of pressure on the left flank and rear. I thought you might fix the time of your arrival as being before or after this movement of "G" troop, but, as you say Reno was not yet in action when you reached him, of course your arrival must have been before "G" went into the woods to protect the horses.

The man Kanipe was a sergeant of "C" troop, and was sent back by Custer with a message to McDougall to hurry up the packs. He met Benteen, who sent him on to McDougall. He preceded Martin by about a mile, so that, if you were the first, Kanipe must have been the second and Martin the last of the messengers sent back by Custer. Of course, it is clear that when Martin started back, Custer then had seen the village,

272 THE CUSTER MYTH

as the messsage (signed by Cook), you will remember, was—"Benteen, come on; *big village; be quick; bring packs. P. S. Bring packs.*"

In answer to #34 you say that "a few Indians were showing in our front *as we moved into the river bottom.*" Do you mean by that that you reached Reno before he began his charge down the bottom? As I understand it, Reno, upon crossing the river, halted for a few minutes in the timber to reform, and then moved out into the bottom, charging in line, first two troops abreast, and later, all three, for fully two miles, before he halted, dismounted and formed his skirmish line. So I am puzzled by your answer. Had Reno halted and dismounted when you joined him, or did you get to him before he started his charge? Please make this clear.

By question #39 I intended to refer, not to Benteen's original orders, received about noon, to scout to the left, etc., but to what Custer may have had in mind when he sent him the "Come on—be quick" order by Martin. I hoped that you might have heard some talk that would indicate where he was intending to put Benteen in—whether in the center, between Reno and himself, or what his idea was.

If you can elucidate these points for me, I shall be under further obligation to you.

Very truly yours,
W. A. GRAHAM

Room 2101, Munitions Bldg.,
Washington, D. C.

Kansas City, Mo.
September 25, 1922

Col. W. A. Graham
2101 Munitions Bldg.,
Washington, D. C.

Dear Sir:—

Your letter of the 23d, is before me, I am not at all sure that I can add much, if anything to the answers in my previous letter.

My understanding has always been, and my recollection bears me out that the last orders Reno received were given just about the time the command moved out after the halt succeeding the night march.

At the time we passed the "dead warrior tepee" Reno's squadron was some distance in our advance, and so far as I can now recall there was no subsequent communication between the two squadrons, save what followed later by messenger.

Reno's original orders, or the last ones I knew anything about, directed him to follow the trail, attacking anything he might encounter.

Whatever, if any orders were given after the

columns started the forward movement were unquestionably given by Custer himself.

I have not reviewed my copy of the testimony of the Chicago Court of Inquiry for years, in fact am not sure I can find it now, as after the death of my wife I spent some eight years on the Mexican Border and in Mexico, and my personal papers were scattered in half a dozen different places. If that testimony disclosed the presence of Cook and Keogh with Reno's squadron it is doubtless correct, but it does not coincide with my own recollections.

I am still unable to place this man Kanipe. Soon after the fight I heard some talk of a message sent to McDougall, but was finally led to the conclusion that it was the message brought by Martin, as at that time McDougall was having a running fight with small parties of Indians and it was always doubtful in my mind whether a messenger could have passed between Benteen and Reno, but not being in that part of the field I am judging only by what I learned later.

As to question #34. I perhaps did not make myself clear. I overtook Reno's column just as they were mounting after a brief halt in the timber where the men had recinched their saddles and the column had massed together.

Your statement as to Reno's advance down the valley tallies with my general recollection. As we moved out from the timber, after the halt, we could see Indians down the valley, between us and the village, and as we charged down the valley they began to show in constantly increasing numbers, much the larger body of them passing around our left flank, coming in in rear of us, the heavy attack being on our left flank.

My recollection has always been that "A" Troop (Moylan's) was on the extreme left after the skirmish line was formed, with "M" Troop (French's) in the center between "A" and "G".

I have no means of knowing what Custer may have had in mind as to any further disposition of Benteen's squadron, as at the time this message was sent I was with Reno's column.

On the afternoon of the 27th, I rode over the trail with Martin, and he pointed out to me the place where he was turned back, and from that point it was possible to see much, but not all of the village.

From a correspondence with Benteen carried on for years, and a number of personal talks with him, I was always led to infer that Custer had for the first time fully realized the force confronting him and was desirous of massing the two squadrons together, in order to make stronger his line of attack, but this was of course purely supposition on the part of both Col. Benteen and myself.

I am well aware that the testimony at the Chicago Court was "hand picked" that is, very little testimony was given save in answer to direct questions. Benteen at one time gave me his version of the reason for this, but he said it stated pretty fully the general details of the action.

Trusting this will clear up some of the obscurities of my previous letter, I am,

Very truly yours,

/s/ THEO. W. GOLDIN

Snyderhof Hotel
Kansas City, Mo.

September 30, 1922.

Mr. Theo. W. Goldin,
Snyderhof Hotel,
Kansas City, Missouri.
Dear Mr. Goldin:

I have your letter of September 25, and again thank you. I take it, from your answer as to question #34, that you overtook Reno during his momentary halt on the left bank of the river, and before he started on his ride down the valley; and not after he had dismounted at the point of timber to fight on foot.

I wish you would tell me, as nearly as you can, how much farther down the river the point was that Martin pointed out to you as the place he turned back, with reference to the point where you turned back.

I suppose no two men remember an event in exactly the same way, and particularly so after a lapse of 46 years. It would be very strange if they did; and therefore, I want to give to you a summary of the testimony of Wallace, Varnum and Reno with relation to the attack order.

It is, in substance that about 12:15 P.M., the regiment halted, having crossed the divide a few minutes before. At this time the division into battalions was made, and Benteen received his order to scout to the left, departing at once. After Benteen had left, Custer and Reno moved on, Reno on the left bank and Custer on the right bank of a little stream tributary to the Little Big Horn. The columns were from 100 to 200 yards apart. After moving several miles, Wallace says 10 or 12, General Custer, upon sighting the "dead warrior teepee," called Reno over to the right bank of the tributary and the two battalions then moved side by side, so close that the men intermingled and visited together, though the head of Reno's column was, when he crossed over, near the rear of Custer's. Reno then received orders to move his command to the front, and as the heads of the two columns drew together, a

tumult was going on among the Indian scouts. Custer had ordered them forward and they had refused to go, whereupon he had ordered them to give up their guns and horses. As Reno reached the head of the column he was immediately ordered to make the attack. Some of the witnesses say that Custer gave the order in person, but the weight of the testimony is that Cook gave it, in about this language—"The Indians are about 2½ miles ahead, on the jump. Custer says for you to take as rapid a gait as you think prudent and charge them afterward, and you will be supported by the whole outfit." Does this account bring back anything to your recollections?

This occurred, as nearly as I can determine, about 3 miles from the river, perhaps more—perhaps less; it is difficult to tell exactly from the testimony how far from the river the "dead warrior teepee" was. Can you tell me? Reno took a rapid trot and went on to the river, and crossed it, halting. on the other side to re-form. It was then, as I suppose, that you overtook him. Custer evidently followed Reno until about a mile from the river and then swung to the right, evidently sending you back very soon afterward, else you could not have overtaken Reno in the timber during his halt on the other side of the ford. By the time he started down the valley, having received the attack order at about 2:15 P.M., allowing him 10 minutes to reach the river and 10 to re-form, it was at least 2:30 P.M. You must have left Custer within 10 minutes of the time Reno started for the river, and at that time Custer could not have been far down the river. It was at least a half hour later, I should judge, that he sent Martin back, for Reno rode two miles down the valley and was in skirmish line for 15 to 20 minutes, and Martin says he saw Reno in action on his return trip, when he passed the high point where he and Custer had seen the village.

I am surprised to learn that you have a copy of the testimony taken at Chicago in 1879. I was not aware it had been published. Where did you obtain it?

Yours very truly,

W. A. GRAHAM

2101 Munitions Bldg.

Col. W. A. Graham
Washington, D. C.
Dear Colonel:—

Replying to your letter of September 30th, I will say that I overtook Reno's command just as they were remounting to move out after what appeared to have been a brief halt at the ford.

Kansas City, Mo.
October 8, 1922.

I was never over the field after the fight, save on the 27th, when I visited the village, and again on the 28th, when we buried Custer's command, so that my recollections of distances must, of necessity, be indistinct after this lapse of years, but, as I recall it, the point designated by Martin, as the point where he turned back, was all of two miles farther down the river than the point where I left the command. Martin turned back at or near the point where Custer's trail swung to the left, which, according to Martin's story told me at the time, was practically the first sight the command had of the village.

I note the statement as recited in the testimony, but cannot harmonize it entirely with my own recollections. As I recall it, at no time after the squadron formation was Reno's squadron in rear of that of Custer, my recollection is just the reverse of that, but as it is purely a matter of recollection, I take it the chances are that the testimony of Wallace and Varnum, given not many years after the affair, may have been the most accurate. My own recollection is that the scouts bolted some little time after the two commands separated, a few of the Crows remained with us. The others rounded up what they could in the way of straggling horses and ponies and beat it for home.

I am very frank to say that the excerpts from the testimony, as you give them, do not coincide entirely with my recollection.

My recollection now is that the "dead warrior tepee" as the trail ran, was fully 3 or 4 miles from the point where Reno later crossed the stream.

Custer's column was easily more than a mile from the river when he diverged sharply to the right, the trail later drew nearer the river, but, at the time I was turned back we must have been in the neighborhood of a mile from the stream.

Knowing as I did something of the feeling on the part of some of the officers of the regiment at the time of the Court of Inquiry I never gave it the full credence the ordinary reader might have given it.

I have (or had) two copies of the testimony taken in Chicago, one was a copy of so much of the proceedings as the *Chicago Tribune* was able to secure, the second was a copy that came into my possession through an officer of the regiment, now dead, and which I was assured was a complete copy of the testimony.

Very truly yours,
/s/ THEO. W. GOLDIN.

Mr. Goldin, as will be noted from the foregoing correspondence, had changed his story! In 1904 he had written Dr. Brady that he overtook Reno "just as he was dismounting to fight on foot"; but in 1922, he wrote me that he "overtook Reno's command just as they were remounting to move out after what appeared to have been a brief halt at the ford"—"the ford" being the place where Reno crossed the river, prior to his two mile advance down the valley to the place where he dismounted to fight on foot, and before any action had commenced. The two stories were irreconcilable.

In July 1923, the *Cavalry Journal* published my maiden attempt at writing the history of the Little Big Horn, an article entitled "Come on, Be quick, Bring packs." It contained no reference to Mr. Goldin's alleged ride to Reno except a note that in effect rejected the story. I heard from Goldin shortly after. He wanted to know why I had not mentioned this important incident. I did not think it necessary to tell him why.

Some months later, for what reason I do not now recall, I asked the Adjutant General of the Army (through my own Chief, the Judge Advocate General) for an official summary of Mr. Goldin's military record. The following is the Adjutant General's reply:

"The official records show that Theodore W. Goldin enlisted April 8, 1876; was assigned to Troop G. 7th U. S. Cavalry, and was discharged November 13, 1877, per S. O. 174, A.G.O., for minority, a private, character good. At the date of his enlistment he gave his age as 21 years. Under date of August 15, 1877, R. W. Goldin and Elizabeth Goldin requested the discharge of Theodore W. Goldin, their adopted son, and stated that he was born on the 25th day of July, 1858, and enlisted without their knowledge or consent. This statement was substantiated by affidavits from other persons and in paragraph 3 of Special Orders No. 174, A.G.O., August 16, 1877, the Secretary of War directed the discharge of Theodore W. Goldin for having enlisted under false pretenses. In this order it is stated that under paragraph 1371, Revised U. S. Army Regulations of 1863, he was entitled to no pay or allowances and final statements were not to be furnished him."

This record is interesting, in view of the many and varied parts alleged by Mr. Goldin to have been played by him at the Little Big Horn, and his claims to intimacy with various officers of the regiment. A simple computation will disclose that on the day of the battle, he was a very raw and green recruit, less than eighteen years of age, and in the Service exactly two months and seventeen days. As he enlisted 8 April *1876,* what then becomes of his statement to Dr. Brady that "I had known General Custer from the time I joined the regiment in *1873* up to the time of his tragic death, and had campaigned with him and with the regiment, with the exception of the year *1875 * * *"*!

Knowing something of the "Old Army," it is inconceivable to me that General Custer or his Adjutant would select this boy-recruit to perform an important mission under the conditions then existing; and still more so that he was on intimate terms with his officers. That was definitely *not* the way of the "Old Army."

In 1931, DeLand's "History of the Sioux War" was published by the Historical Society of South Dakota. It played up the Goldin story, but in a form that differed from the 1904 letter to Brady and the 1922 letter to me. I do not have DeLand's book before me, and cannot from memory alone point out the differences, but to the best of my recollection, the story had now assumed the form in which it appeared in January 1933, in a letter Mr. Goldin wrote to the late Dr. Philip G. Cole of New York, who had acquired the Benteen-Goldin letters. Here it is:

"Just before we left the Rosebud and on June 21, 1876 I was called to headquarters to assist the Sergeant-major in preparing various orders and in compiling our records for the field desk we carried on a pack mule and when we left the Rosebud the following day I was, by order of Lieut. Cook, regimental Adjutant, retained at headquarters as an orderly or messenger and when the command was divided on June 25th, while still some fifteen miles from the village of the enemy and so far as I have ever been able to learn, without any definite knowledge as to the exact location or strength of the village. I remained with the column under Gen. Custer until we reached a point possibly a mile downstream from the point where we knew Reno was already engaged with the upper end of the huge village. In the meantime Gen. Custer had left his column and ridden to a point out of our sight, but which evidently overlooked the scene of Reno's engagement. I state this because we later learned that men in Reno's command saw and recognized him on the bluffs. In the meantime the rest of his command had continued down the stream but hidden from the Indians by a high ridge paralleling the course of the bluffs above the river. When about a mile

below Reno's position we slowed down to a walk and it was at this point that Custer rejoined us and a few moments later I was given a message to deliver to Major Reno. What the message contained I do not know, but my orders were to get it to Reno at once, remain with him until the two columns effected a junction when I was to report to Lieut. Cook. On my trip back I saw no Indians nor could I see the valley or the village because of the ridge until I sought a place to descend to the river and cross it to reach Reno, then I could plainly see the immense village and Reno's little squadron fighting in the bottoms apparently against heavy odds. While making the descent of the bluffs and fording the river a number of bullets whistled entirely too close for comfort about my ears, whether aimed at me, or whether they were shots fired high by the Indians I do not know. I do know I was a mite uncomfortable for a few minutes. I reached Reno just about the time his Indian allies on the extreme left of his slender line broke and ran, some of them it was reported not stopping until they reached the supply camp on the Powder River, others not until they reached their reservation at Fort Berthold. I delivered my message, Reno glanced at it, asked where I left Custer and what he was doing, folded the message, put it in his note book and turned to watch the movement of the left of his line, which seemed to be forced back into the timber. When I reached Reno the only officers near him were Captain Moylan of "A" Troop and Lieut. Hodgson, Squadron adjutant, killed a short time later. * * *"

In his letter to Cole, Goldin had again changed his story! Version #1 had him overtaking Reno "just as he was *dis*mounting to fight on foot"; in Version #2, he "overtook Reno's command just as they were *re*mounting to move out after what appeared to have been a brief halt at the ford"; but now, in Version #3, he reaches Reno *after the action has commenced,* and "just about the time his Indian allies on the extreme left of his slender line broke and ran." Indeed, some time before, from the other side of the river while seeking a place to cross in order to reach Reno, he "could plainly see the immense village, and Reno's little squadron fighting in the bottoms apparently against heavy odds." And as he delivered the message, Reno merely "glanced at it, asked where I left Custer and what he was doing, folded the message, put it in his notebook, and turned to watch the movement of the left of his line, which seemed to be forced back into the timber."

Here then, we have three stories of the ride to Reno, each one differing materially from the other two. Take your choice; all are priced the same. If you can be satisfied with any one of them, you will have done better than I was able to do.

It is unfortunate that Goldin's letters to Benteen, which formed his part of their extended correspondence between 1891 and 1896, were not preserved, for in several of Benteen's letters to him it plainly appears that the old Seventh veteran believed that Goldin had served with the regiment throughout at least a full five year enlistment; and it is equally obvious that Goldin permitted that belief to continue, if indeed he did not inspire it by some deft reference to the regiment's 1873 campaigns against the Sioux in Dakota and Montana, and to the Black Hills expedition of the following year, just as he did in his 1904 letter to Dr. Brady. It would be interesting too, to read his Little Big Horn articles in the "Army Magazine," that were published during 1894. Some day, somewhere, they will turn up; and I venture to doubt that when and if they do turn up, there will be found therein any reference to Goldin's alleged "Paul Revere ride" to Reno on the 25th of June, 1876.

I have no desire to do Mr. Goldin an injustice: on the contrary, I would lean over backward to avoid it, so long as I did not lose my own balance. But three stories, all different, concerned with the same incident, are *two stories too many*. Any one of them *might* be true, but *only* one. And in the order of their possibility I would place first, what he told me; second, what he told Dr. Brady; and third, what he told Dr. Cole. I would place them in that order *but for a circumstance I have not as yet mentioned*—the sworn testimony of Lt. Wallace in 1879, when he appeared as a witness before the Reno Court of Inquiry.

Here, referring to the advance of Reno's command toward the sound of the guns, in the abortive attempt to go to Custer's relief after the junction of Reno and Benteen on the hill, is what he said:

"When the march commenced, Capt. Moylan had to fall to the rear with his wounded, and he tried to carry them along. He didn't get very far though, until he found he was being left behind, and he sent word to see whether he could get assistance from Capt. McDougall—he sent word that he couldn't go any farther.

Q. Up to this time, had there been any communication whatever between Gen. Custer's command and his?

A. None that I have ever heard of.

Q. Had any communication been received by Major Reno or any officer under him as to where Custer was up to that time?

A. Nothing only a trumpeter had been sent back and said that he had gone that way.

Q. To whom was the trumpeter sent?

A. To Capt. Benteen.

Q. That trumpeter's name was Martin, I believe?

A. Yes, Sir."

In view of the above, what becomes of Goldin's anwser to my question #32—i.e. "Did Lieut. Wallace know that you had come through with a message from Custer? Did you ever tell him, or talk to him about it?" His answer was: " I presume he did, possibly not at the time, *but we often spoke of it later."*

Wallace in *1879*, questioned under oath, knew nothing of any message from Custer except that carried by Martin to Benteen—the famous "Come on—Be quick—Bring packs." Goldin was discharged for fraudulent enlistment in *1877*. If they "often spoke of it later," it must have been *very much* later, after Goldin had been several years out of the service, and Wallace had recovered from a strange case of amnesia! It seems to me that Martin's letter (quoted above) and Wallace's testimony are conclusive.

Mr. Goldin was awarded the Medal of Honor for bringing water to the wounded under fire, an heroic act for which some eighteen other enlisted men were similarly decorated in 1878. Goldin was not, however, one of those originally recommended for the award but received his medal during the year 1896, twenty years after the battle and while he was Chairman of the Republican State Central Committee of Wisconsin. The Benteen-Goldin letters indicate that at his request both Benteen and Hare wrote commendary letters in his behalf to the War Department, and that it was the personal interest of the Assistant Secretary of War, Mr. Doe of Wisconsin, that was mainly effective in securing the award. That Goldin was in fact one of the water-party, I do not question, notwithstanding he was not named for decoration when the other enlisted men were named; and having been a volunteer who braved the fire of ambushed Indians to get water for the wounded, his act was one of heroism above and beyond the call of duty that merited the Medal of Honor. Many of the old time Indian fighters I used to meet around Washington, however, seemed to know about this particular award, and were inclined to criticise it because of the circumstances under which it was bestowed. Some of them, indeed, ascribed it to political influence rather than to heroic conduct. But the record stands "as is"; and the fact that the award was made twenty years after the event, at a time when its beneficiary was Chairman of the State Central Committee of a political party, and his fellow statesman (who happened to be the Assistant Secretary of War) was a prominent member of another and different political party then in power, speaks well and not ill for Mr. Goldin.

He was at the Little Big Horn. There is no doubt of that; and concerning it he wrote both volubly and intelligently to many people. But on the record as he himself made it, his claim that he carried a message from Custer to Reno, is in my opinion, incredible.

* * *

MR. GHENT DISCUSSES T. W. GOLDIN AND HIS RIDE TO RENO

THERE seems to be no way of ascertaining the time at which Mr. Theodore W. Goldin first acquired the notion that at the battle of the Little Big Horn he had carried a dispatch from Gen. Custer through a horde of savages to Maj. Reno. It is likely that the first appearance of the episode in print was in Cyrus Townsend Brady's *Indian Fights and Fighters,* published in 1904. In Mr. Goldin's earlier statements, so far as they are generally known, it is missing. "I have among some of my clippings," wrote Gen. Godfrey to me on Sept. 8, 1927, "an account he [Goldin] wrote in 1886, as I recollect different from that in Brady, in which he accused both Reno and Moylan of cowardice." This clipping has not yet been found among the papers left by the General, but I am sure that if it had contained any mention of the alleged ride he would have remembered the assertion and so informed me.

In 1889 the Acme Publishing Company, of Chicago, brought out a large volume entitled *Portrait and Biographical Album of Rock County, Wisconsin.* The book contains a biographical sketch of Mr. Goldin (then a partner in the law firm of Dunwiddie and Goldin), who is said to be "regarded as one of the leading citizens of Janesville," the county-seat of Rock County. It is obvious that the biography is an authorized one, since it contains personal and family data that could have been obtained only from Mr. Goldin. The birthdate of Mr. Goldin is given as July 29, 1855; the date of his enlistment as April, 1875; of

his discharge as Sept. 29, 1879, and the cause of his discharge as disability from wounds. The part which relates to his share in the battle and in the succeeding campaign is as follows:

"At the time of the battle, which resulted so fatally to Gen. Custer and his command, Mr. Goldin was with Major Reno, but a short distance from the field of combat. He was present on the field soon after the massacre and assisted in burying the gallant general and his brave comrades. He took part in the fight with the Indians at Canyon Creek and Bear Paw Mountain, Mont. He was twice wounded in the second day's fight of the Little Big Horn, and those wounds resulted in his discharge for disability on the 28th day of September, 1879."

It will be observed that there is here no hint of the dramatic episode that he related in Brady's book and that he has been retelling in contradictory versions ever since 1904. It is not conceivable that if Mr. Goldin believed in 1889 that he had carried a dispatch to Reno during the fight of June 25, 1876, he would have failed to mention the feat in this biographical sketch.

Mr. Goldin, it is further to be noted, is inaccurate, or deliberately misleading, in all of his dates. In giving his birth-year as 1855, he neglected to state that in 1877 his father had produced evidence satisfactory to the military authorities that the boy had enlisted some months before his eighteenth birthday. He further neglected to give the correct year of his enlistment and the correct year and real cause of his discharge. His actual birthdate was July 29, 1858 (*not* 1855); his enlistment date April 8, 1876 (*not* 1875); his discharge date Nov. 13, 1877 (*not* Sept. 29, 1879), and the cause of his discharge was the discovery that he had made a false statement regarding his age (*not* that he had become disabled from wounds). A summary of his service record from the Adjutant General's Office contains the notation that he was discharged as a private, "on account of fraudulent enlistment. The War Department holds that his discharge was without honor."

The further record relating to his brief military career is as follows: The board which in October, 1878, awarded honors to survivors of the Little Big Horn battle evidently knew nothing of Mr. Goldin's alleged ride or his alleged bravery in carrying water from the river, since it gave him no recognition. It gave the Congressional Medal of Honor to twenty-three enlisted men, but none to Mr. Goldin. Not until 1895, and then through political pressure exerted by Assistant Secretary of War Doe, of Delavan, Wis., did he obtain the medal, and it was awarded him as a water-carrier and not as a courier. Efforts to bring about the alteration or negation of the War Department record were made, and on March 3, 1927, nearly fifty-one years after the battle, a special act was passed and approved, directing that in the administration of the pension laws Mr. Goldin was to be considered as having been honorably discharged. There was included, however, a proviso that no pension, back pay or bounty should be held to have accrued up to the time the act was approved.

The utter absurdity of the pretence that Mr. Goldin carried a dispatch at the time and place stated is shown by a number of circumstances, any one of which is decisive:

1. His failure to produce any confirmation from any source.

2. His failure to mention the alleged episode for at least thirteen years, and probably twenty-eight years, after the battle.

3. His many contradictory versions of the story, in particular his signed statement of Sept. 19, 1922, to Col. W. A. Graham, in which, though still holding to the pretence that he had carried a dispatch, he repudiated his former assertions by stating that it had been delivered at the first crossing of the river.

4. The certainty that Custer, having learned that the Indians had already confronted Reno, knew that no courier could reach him.

5. The equal certainty that Custer, even had he believed it possible to reach Reno by courier, would not have intrusted a message to a youth not then eighteen years old and with less than four months' service. The four couriers sent by Custer to Benteen or McDougall were the chief trumpeter of the regiment (Koss), the sergeant-major of the regiment (Sharrow), a sergeant (Kanipe), and a trumpeter orderly (Martin).

6. The sworn testimony of Reno, supported by that of Wallace, that no message reached him after he crossed the river to attack.

The genesis of Mr. Goldin's myth is not known. Whether it arose as pure delusion, as did the somewhat similar myth developed by Peter Thompson, of Company C, or began as a deliberate effort at self-dramatization for political purposes and only gradually took on the form of an obsession, is an attractive subject for speculation. It is certain, however, that no credence can be given by any fair-minded student to the statements made by Mr. Goldin regarding his brief military service, and particularly the part played by him in the battle of the Little Big Horn.

W. J. GHENT

Washington, D. C., Nov. 16, 1932.

CHAPTER 7

THE MARY ADAMS AFFIDAVIT

WHEN General Alfred H. Terry, on 2 July 1876, heeded the protests of his staff because of omission from his report of 27 June of any mention of his plan of operations which, through failure of a subordinate to abide by his instructions, miscarried with resulting disaster, he loosed a storm whose lightning flashes and peals of thunder have caused reverberations throughout the pages of western history ever since. If the metaphor is mixed it is because its subject is no less so.

What General Terry did that day was to supplement his original report of the battle of the Little Big Horn with a confidential message to General Sheridan which he entrusted to his Acting Adjutant, Captain E. W. Smith, then ready to depart on the Steamer "Far West," en route to Bismarck with the wounded.

Intended for the eye of Sheridan alone, the message disclosed the fact that at the mouth of the Rosebud, Terry had submitted his plan of operations to Generals Gibbon and Custer, who approved it heartily. It called for cooperation between the two columns, Gibbon to proceed south along the Big Horn to the mouth of the Little Big Horn: Custer to ride up the Rosebud, until he reached an Indian trail discovered by a scouting expedition a few days before. He was then to determine the direction of this trail, and if it led to the Little Big Horn valley, he was to continue south some twenty miles and *then* swing north and west, in order that Gibbon's column and his own might reach the valley the same day, and thus be in position to cooperate.

The message further disclosed that while Gibbon had faithfully performed his mission, Custer had disregarded his instructions, and had followed the trail directly to the Indian village, which he had attacked on June 25 with disastrous results. *Inter alia,* General Terry said: "The movements proposed for Gen'l Gibbon's column were carried out to the letter and had the attack been deferred

until it was up I cannot doubt that we should have been successful. * * * I do not tell you this to cast any reflection upon Custer. For whatever errors he may have committed he has paid the penalty and you cannot regret his loss more than I do, but I feel that our plan must have been successful had it been carried out * * *. I send in another dispatch a copy of my written orders to Custer, but these were supplemented by the distinct understanding that Gibbon could not get to the Little Big Horn before the evening of the 26th."

Unfortunately for Terry's effort to communicate these facts *sub rosa,* General Sheridan was not at his headquarters in Chicago when the confidential message arrived there, and his Adjutant, realizing its urgent importance, repeated it to Philadelphia where Sheridan and Sherman (then Commander of the Army), were foregathering at the Centennial Exposition. Sheridan showed it to Sherman, and the latter, desiring that it reach the Secretary of War without delay, entrusted it to a supposed War Department messenger for immediate transmittal to the Secretary. But the "messenger" proved to be an unscrupulous newspaper reporter, who after relaying the message to Washington, not only purloined it, but published it in the Philadelphia "Inquirer" of July 7.

As Terry's language, quoted above, compelled the inference that he had accused the popular Custer of that heinous military sin—the disobedience of orders—his partisans and admirers—and they were legion—immediately started the hue and cry in their search for a scapegoat on the one hand, and for proof that their hero had been maligned, upon the other. Every student of the campaign knows that failing in their efforts to place responsibility for the disaster on Terry, they turned upon Benteen and Reno, and finally upon Reno alone; but comparatively few knew of the efforts to produce proof positive that Terry had given Custer a completely free hand. This is the story of one of those efforts that was kept secret until after most of those who knew the truth had passed on.

The Custers had in their employ in 1876, and for some time prior thereto, a colored maid who kept their house in order and cooked the family meals. Her correct name was Mary Adams, but Mrs. Custer and the General always called her "Maria."

On 16 January 1878, some officer whose identity has never been definitely established, took Mary (or Maria) Adams before George P. Flannery, then a Notary Public at Bismarck, to execute an affidavit which was to play an important part in a long drawn controversy over Custer's alleged disobedience of General Terry's orders. The affidavit was as follows:

Territory of Dakota: ss:
County of Burleigh:

Personally came before me Mary Adams, who being first duly sworn, deposes and says: that she resides in the City of Bismarck, D.T., and has resided in said City for three months just past. That she came to Dakota Territory with General George A. Custer in the Spring of 1873. That she was in the employ of General George A. Custer continuously from 1873 up to the time of his death in June 1876. That while in his employ she accompanied him on his military expeditions in the capacity of cook. That she left Fort A. Lincoln in the Spring of 1876 with Genl. Terry's expedition in the employ of the said General Custer, and was present in the said General Custer's tent on the Rosebud River in Montana Territory when General Terry came into said tent, and the said Terry said to General Custer: "Custer, I don't know what to say for the last." Custer replied, "Say whatever you want to say." Terry then said, "Use your own judgment and do what you think best if you strike the trail. And whatever you do, Custer, hold on to your wounded" and further saith not.

her
Mary x Adams
mark

Subscribed and sworn to
before me this 16th day of
January, 1878.
   (Notarial Seal)

George P. Flannery
Notary Public
Burleigh Co., D.T.

This affidavit came into the possession of General Miles, then a colonel under General Terry's command, and was by him held for many years.

The existence of such an affidavit was first made known by General Miles in 1897, when he published his well known "Recollections," but without disclosing the name or identity of the affiant; and it was referred to by Dr. E. Benjamin Andrews in his work "The United States in our Own Time," published in 1903. Dr. Andrews' reference, however, was based upon the statements of General Miles.

In 1904, Dr. Cyrus Townsend Brady published his well known book "Indian Fights and Fighters," which contains an appendix that discloses that, though pressed by Dr. Brady, General Miles declined to reveal the name of the affidavit maker; and it was not revealed until, during the early 20's, I learned it from General Godfrey, who at the same time told me that Mary Adams did not accompany the expedition from Ft. Lincoln in 1876, but remained with Mrs. Custer, which information was shortly after orally corroborated by General Edgerly, and by Colonel Varnum by letter. I was not satisfied, however, until I had interviewed General Miles himself, who was then living at the Richmond Apartments in Washington. I twice interviewed General Miles during 1922, and upon each occasion brought up the question of the affidavit, but all he would say about it was "I believe Mrs. Custer has it." This information I repeated to General Godfrey, who said that if Mrs. Custer did have it, he could get me a copy of it. This he did, the copy being set out above.

Upon learning the name of the Notary, I located him at St. Paul, Minesota, where he was President of the Northwestern Trust Company. To my inquiry, he replied as follows:

NORTHWESTERN TRUST COMPANY
SAINT PAUL, MINNESOTA

August 12, 1922.

Lieut. Col. W. A. Graham,
Judge Advocate, U. S. Army,
1806 Arlington Avenue,
Des Moines, Iowa.
Dear Sir:
Your favor of the 10th inst. in re an affidavit made by Mary Adams, Custer's servant, in 1878, is received and noted.

I lived in Bismarck from May 1874 to June 1887. I knew Mary Adams by sight, having seen her in General Custer's home, and later in the home of J. W. Raymond in Bismarck, but I have no recollection about the affidavit referred to by you.

I have quite a distinct recollection of a conversation had with Captain Smith, General Terry's

Adjutant, on his return from the field. It so happened that when he reached Bismarck Dr. Henry R. Porter, the surviving surgeon of the battle of the Little Big Horn, and myself gave a little dinner to Captain Smith, General John B. Sanborn of St. Paul, J. W. Raymond and George H. Fairchild of Bismarck. In the course of the dinner Captain Smith said, in substance:

"General Terry knew where the Indians were. He was afraid they would escape to the South toward the Black Hills. To prevent that he decided to send the cavalry to the South to prevent the Indians getting through that way. The cavalry would have to march about seventy-five miles (two days march for cavalry). The army was then about from two to three days march to where they understood the Indians were. General Terry did not say to General Custer "This will require two days and give time for the infantry to get to a point where connection can be made before attacking the Indians," but it was understood that it would take two days and that the infantry would be at a point near where the Indians were by that time. After General Custer started on his march and got away from the command he marched all night and covered the distance, which it was supposed would occupy two days, in less than twenty-four hours, and went into the battle with his troops weary and without any support."

The rest of the conversation at the dinner related to the part which Major Reno and Colonel Benteen took in the battle, Dr. Porter relating the story of the advance on the Indian village and the apparent surprise, and then the disorderly retreat before there were any casualties, and the disaster which followed in crossing the river and getting up to the high land where they rallied on Benteen's command. I remember him stating that he saw Lieutenant McIntosh pulled off from his horse in the river and tomahawked by the Indians.

The warm and active friends of General Custer at Lincoln after the battle of the Little Big Horn were Lieutenant John Carland, either of the Sixth or Seventeenth Infantry (I have forgotten which), and Lieutenant Weare (Weir) of the Seventh Cavalry. The differences, however, were as to whether or not Reno ought to have gone to Custer's support.

I am sorry I am unable to recall anything in connection with the affidavit. She worked for Mrs. J. W. Raymond for some time after the battle of the Little Big Horn. Mrs. Raymond, I believe, is still living, residing in Pasadena, California.

Very truly yours,
Geo. P. Flannery
/s/ Geo. P. Flannery

From Mr. Flannery, however, I had learned that for some time after the battle, Mary Adams was employed by Mrs. J. W. Raymond, who was then (1922) living, in Pasadena. Mrs. Raymond, upon being located, replied to an inquiry as follows:

85 North El Molino Ave.,
Pasadena—August 24/22
Dear Sir:

I have your request for information in regard to Mary Adams, and am sorry I cannot give you a more satisfactory reply.

The facts in the case are—that on a visit to Fort Lincoln immediately upon receiving the news of the tragedy of the Little Big Horn, I felt that something must be done as soon as possible to get those poor bereaved women to their own people—if they had any. I had been planning to go East soon after, so hastened my going that we might be able to turn over our home to the six widows of the Officers, to use as they would to make ready for the journey.

Mary Adams came with them, and cared for them as long as they remained—afterward keeping house for my husband and a friend until just before I returned to Bismarck—when she left Dakota, as I remember. Since then I have heard nothing.

It seems in the matter of an affidavit that would exonerate Gen. Custer from the charge of impetuosity, or insubordination, his friends would have made public any such information in justice to so brave an officer.

Regretting my information on the Mary Adams incident is so meagre, and wishing you better success in other directions.

Very sincerely yours,
/s/ Rachel A. Raymond

It remained for the late W. A. Falconer of Bismarck, a resident of that city for more than sixty years, to clear up finally the story of Mary Adams and her affidavit. This he did in the course of an article printed in the Bismarck *Capital* 25 June 1925, as follows:

General Fry, now deceased, General Miles, Godfrey and several others, claim that Custer did not disobey Terry's orders, and put the blame for the disaster on Reno. General Miles strongly defended Custer in his very interesting book, "Personal Recollections of General Nelson A. Miles." On Pages 204 and 205, Miles says, "But we have positive evidence in the form of an affidavit of the last witness who heard the two officers in conversation together on the night before their commands separated, and it is conclusive on the point at issue. This evidence is that General Terry returned to General Custer's tent after giving him the final order, to say to him that on coming up to the Indians he would have to use his own discretion and do what he thought best.

This conversation occurred at the mouth of the Rosebud, and the exact words of General Terry, as quoted by the witness, are: "Custer, I do not know what to say for the last." Custer replied, "Say what you want to say." Terry then said: "Use your own judgment, and do what you think best if you strike the trail; and whatever you do, Custer, hold on to your wounded."

Affidavit Was Frame-Up

If what General Miles has quoted had really happened, then, as Miles says, it is conclusive on the point at issue, but there was no such conversation between Terry and Custer. This affidavit that Miles refers to was kept under cover until some time after General Terry's death, and in sporting parlance, the affidavit was a frame-up. The person who made that affidavit that Miles refers to was Mary Adams, better known as Maria, General Custer's colored servant, and at the time that Miles refers to, the evening of the 21st of June, Maria was with Mrs. Custer at Fort Abraham Lincoln, hundreds of miles away from the mouth of the Rosebud river. The affidavit was sworn to by Mary Adams on January 16, 1878, before George P. Flannery, a notary public, in Bismarck.

Now, when the steamer "Far West" brought down the wounded from the battlefield, the boat landed at Bismarck at eleven o'clock at night, July 5th, bringing the first news of the disaster. At about one o'clock in the morning of July 6th, the boat dropped down to Fort Lincoln, about six miles south from Bismarck.

Lieut. C. L. Gurley, Sixth Infantry, who was stationed at Fort Lincoln, has told how the news was broken to Mrs. Custer and the other officers' wives. Gurley said, "The news came to me about two a. m. The commanding officers, Captain William S. McCaskey, 20th infantry summoned all the officers to his quarters at once, and there read to them the communication he had just received per steamer "Far West" from Capt. Ed. W. Smith, General Terry's adjutant general. After we had recovered from the shock, Captain McCaskey requested us to assist him in breaking the news to the widows. It fell to my lot to accompany Captain McCaskey and Dr. J. V. D. Middleton, our post surgeon, to the quarters of Mrs. Custer. We started on our sad errand a little before seven o'clock on the 6th of July morning. I went to the rear of the Custer house, woke up Maria, Mrs. Custer's housemaid, and requested her to rap on Mrs. Custer's door, and say to her that she and Mrs. Calhoun and Miss Reed were wanted in the parlor. There we were almost immediately followed by the ladies of the Custer household, and there we told to them their first intimation of the awful result of the battle of the Little Big Horn."

It will be seen from Lieutenant Gurley's narrative, that he woke up Maria, Mrs. Custer's servant, on the morning of the 6th of July, Maria being the same person who signed the affidavit saying that she was in Custer's tent on the evening of June 21st at the mouth of the Rosebud, and heard the conversation between Terry and Custer. The affidavit that General Miles refers to is the affidavit signed by Mary Adams, or Maria, Mrs. Custer's colored servant. The affidavit is fraudulent, and the conversation that Miles refers to between Terry and Custer never took place.

The widows of the officers who were killed in the Custer disaster all left Fort Lincoln shortly after the deaths of their husbands, and Mary Adams, Mrs. Custer's colored servant, came to Bismarck and worked for James W. Raymond, one of the local merchants, for several years, and it was while she was in Bismarck in the employ of Mr. Raymond that she signed the affidavit that General Miles refers to in his book.

During the past year I talked with Mr. Flannery who took Mary Adams oath, and he says that some officer, a friend of Custer, he believed that Captain Carland was the one, who drew up the affidavit for Mary Adams to sign. Mr. Flannery is now a resident of St. Paul, Minnesota.

CHAPTER 8

THE SIGNERS OF THE ENLISTED MEN'S PETITION TO PROMOTE RENO AND BENTEEN

FOR the past quarter of a century I have been importuned to furnish the names of the enlisted survivors of the battle of the Little Big Horn who on 4 July 1876, at the regimental camp near the Big Horn, on the Yellowstone River, signed a petition addressed to the President and the Congress, asking that Major Reno be promoted to fill the vacancy caused by the death in battle of the regiment's lieutenant-colonel, George A Custer; and that Captain F. W. Benteen be then promoted to fill the vacancy caused by the requested promotion of Reno.

I have not heretofore furnished these names for several reasons, the first and most important being that the signatures, having been made in pencil so many years ago, are in many cases almost if not quite illegible. I had the entire petition including signatures photostated in 1923; and again in 1951, in the vain hope that the photostatic process had been more expertly applied. However, during the past year I have turned up a copy made by me during the 20's from an official copy made in 1878, and which is probably correct. Two hundred and thirty-seven names appear on the petition. Two of them, however, are crossed out, thus leaving two hundred and thirty-five, which number represented approximately 80% of the survivors of Reno's and Benteen's combined commands.

SIGNATURES

Name	Rank	Co.
Geo. McDermott	Sergt.	A
Henry Fehler	Sergt.	A
John T. Easly	Sergt.	A
F. A. Culbertson	Sergt.	A
William J. Hardy	Trmptr.	A
David McVeigh	Trmptr.	A
John Bringes	Farrier	A
Andrew Hamilton	Blksmth.	A
Stanislas Ray	Cpl.	A
Louis Baumgartner	Pvt.	A
John W. Franklin	Pvt.	A

SIGNATURES

Name	Rank	Co.
Andrew Conner	Pvt.	A
Emel O. Jonson	Pvt.	A
Thomas Blake	Pvt.	A
William D. Nugent	Pvt.	A
William McClurg	Pvt.	A
Otto Dinnlen	Pvt.	A
George W. Proctor	Pvt.	A
John M. Gilbert	Pvt.	A
W. O. Taylor	Pvt.	A
Thomas Seayers	Pvt.	A
Antony Labeldy	Pvt.	F
Samuel Johnson	Pvt.	A
Charles Aller	Pvt.	A
Neil Bancroft	Pvt.	A
Wilbur F. Blair	Pvt.	A
Stanton Hook	Pvt.	A
John Crump	Blksmth.	B
Michel Crow	Pvt.	B
John O'Neill	Pvt.	B
James E. Moore	Farrier	B
James Pym	Pvt.	B
Ansgarius Boren	Pvt.	B
James Hill	First Sergt.	B
Rufus D. Hutchinson	Sergt.	B
Thomas Murray	Sergt.	B
Benj. C. Criswell	Sergt.	B
James Dougherty	Cpl.	B
Adam Wetzel	Cpl.	B
John A. Bailey	Saddler	B
John McCabe	Pvt.	B
William McMasters	Pvt.	B
Patrick Crowley	Pvt.	B
William Martin	Pvt.	B
Thomas Carmody	Pvt.	B
William Trumble	Pvt.	B
John J. Casey	Pvt.	B
Charles A. Campbell	Pvt.	B
Edward Stout	Pvt.	B
Stephen L. Ryan	Pvt.	B
Harry Creswell	Pvt.	B
Thomas W. Coleman	Pvt.	B
Daniel Shea	Pvt.	B
James Thomas	Pvt.	B
Richard A. Wallace	Pvt.	B
Philipp Spinner	Pvt.	B
William Frank	Pvt.	B
Frank Clark	Pvt.	B

SIGNATURES

Name	Rank	Co.
Hiram W. Sager	Pvt.	B
Augustus L. Devoto	Pvt.	B
Terence McLoughlin	Pvt.	B
Aaron Woods	Pvt.	B
George Randall	Pvt.	B
William H. Davenport	Pvt.	B
Charles Cunningham	Cpl.	B
William A. Curtiss	Sergt.	E
Wm. H. Shields	Pvt.	F
Henry Sango	Pvt.	F
John Sweeny	Pvt.	E
Henry Miller	Pvt.	E
Able B. Spencer	Pvt.	E
Henry Stoppel	Pvt.	C
William Reese	Pvt.	E
Martin Mullin	Pvt.	C
Isaac Fowler	Pvt.	C
John Brennan	Pvt.	C
John Jordan	Pvt.	C
Frank Berwold	Pvt.	E
John McShane	Sergt.	I
Morris Farrar	Pvt.	C
Edwin H. Pickard	Pvt.	F
T. Mahoney	Pvt.	C
Frederick Schutte	Pvt.	F
Francis Johnson	Pvt.	I
Bernard Lyons	Pvt.	F
James M. Roonay	Pvt.	F
William G. Abrams	Pvt.	L
William Etzler	Pvt.	L
Thos. S. Banet	Pvt.	L
Peter Rose	Sergt.	L
Meier Lefler	Pvt.	F
Daniel Knipe	Sergt.	C
Olaus H. Northey	Sergt.	G
John W. Wallace	Pvt.	G
Theo W. Goldin	Pvt.	G
John Meyers*	Saddler	
J. McCurry	First Sergt.	H
Thos. McLaughlin	Sergt.	H
Patrick Conelly	Sergt.	H
Mathew Maroney	Sergt.	H
George Geiger	Sergt.	H
Daniel Neelan	Cpl.	H
Otto Voit	Saddler	H
John Martin	Trmptr.	H
Romell Williams	Trmptr.	H
J. S. Nicholas		H
Edward Diamond	Pvt.	H
Thomas McDermott	Pvt.	H
Thomas Hughes	Pvt.	H
Henry Hauck	Pvt.	H
John Day	Pvt.	H
Henry Bishley	Pvt.	H
Wm. Channell	Pvt.	H
Wm. C. Williams	Pvt.	H
J. Adams	Pvt.	H
George W. Dewy		H
George W. Glease		
Henry W. B. Mechlin		
Timothy Haley		
Edler Neis		
Thos. Lawhorn		

SIGNATURES

Name	Rank	Co.
James Kelly		
Wm. O. Ryan		
John Hunt		
Chas. Windolph		
James McNamara		
Chas. Fisher	Trmptr.	M
Aloyes Walters		
M. J. W. Lacey		F
W. Oman	Pvt.	D
Thomas Russell	Sergt.	D
George W. Wylie	Cpl.	D
Joseph H. Green	Pvt.	D
Fredrick Deitline	Pvt.	D
C. H. Welch	Pvt.	D
Charles Sanders	Pvt.	D
William Harden	Pvt.	D
William Gibbs	Pvt.	K
John Foley	Pvt.	K
W. W. Lasley	Pvt.	K
Wm. Whitlow	Pvt.	K
Geo. B. Penwell	Trmptr.	K
Geo. Blunt	Pvt.	K
Charles Chesterwood	Pvt.	K
Henry W. Raichel	Pvt.	K
John Rafter	Sergt.	K
Josf Brown	Pvt.	K
Thomas A. Gordon	Pvt.	K
Michael Murphy	Pvt.	K
Patrick Coakly*	Pvt.	K
Christian Schlafer	Trmptr.	K
Alonzo Jennys	Pvt.	K
John Schwerer	Pvt.	K
John Donahue	Pvt.	K
Michael Martin	First Sergt.	D
T. W. Harrison	Sergt.	D
Joseph Kretchmer	Pvt.	D
George Hunt	Pvt.	D
Abram B. Brant	Pvt.	D
William E. Smith	Pvt.	D
George Horn	Pvt.	D
Henry Holden	Pvt.	D
Frank Tolan	Pvt.	D
John B. Ascough	Pvt.	D
George Scott	Pvt.	D
John G. Keller	Pvt.	D
W. M. Harris	Pvt.	D
George Dann	Pvt.	D
David Manning	Pvt.	D
John Hager	Pvt.	D
James Hurd	Pvt.	D
James Flanagan	Sergt.	D
James H. Albertz	Pvt.	D
Henry G. Smith	Pvt.	D
Elwyn S. Reid	Pvt.	D
Aloys Bohner	Trmptr.	D
John Meyers	Saddler	D
John Fox	Pvt.	D
William J. Randall	Pvt.	F
C. H. Houghtaling	Pvt.	D
John J. Fay	Pvt.	D
James Harris	Pvt.	D
Thomas W. Stivers	Pvt.	D
Fremont Kipp	Pvt.	D

*Crossed out on list.

*Crossed out on list.

SIGNATURES

SIGNATURES

Name	Rank	Co.	Name	Rank	Co.
James Wynn	Pvt.	D	Frank Stritter	Pvt.	M
Curtis Hall	Pvt.	D	Edward Pigford	Pvt.	M
William A. Marshall	Pvt.	D	Hugh V. Moore	Pvt.	M
John Ryan	First Sergt	M	Walter L. Sterland	Pvt.	M
John McGlone	Sergt.	M	Frank Sniffin	Pvt.	M
William Lalor	Cpl.	M	Wm. Williams	Pvt.	M
Charles Fischer	Trmptr.	M	Lori Marbrey	Pvt.	M
John Donohue	Pvt.	M	Charles Zewengt	Pvt.	C
John Sivertsen	Pvt.	M	Bernard Golden	Pvt.	M
James Seavers	Pvt.	M	Dan'l Mahony	Pvt.	M
Harris Davis	Pvt.	M	Louis Rott	First Sergt.	K
George Weaver	Pvt.	M	Andrew Fredricks	Sergt.	K
William Rye	Pvt.	M	Jeremiah Campbell	Sergt.	K
Frank Neely	Pvt.	M	George Blose	Sergt.	K
John Whiston	Pvt.	M	Edmund H. Burke	Blksmth.	K
Larry Heid	Pvt.	M	Christian Boissen	Saddler	K
Henry C. Marecz	Trmptr.	M	Ernest Wasmus	Pvt.	K
Robert Senn	Pvt.	M	Cornelius Bresnahan	Pvt.	K
D. Gallenne	Pvt.	M	John Shauer	Pvt.	K
W. Slaper	Pvt.	M	Charles Burkhardt	Pvt.	K
Joseph Bates	Pvt.	M	Wilson McConnell	Pvt.	K
James Miles	Pvt.	M	Thomas Murphy	Pvt.	K
John Seamans	Pvt.	M	Martin McCue	Pvt.	K
James Weeks	Pvt.	M	August Seifert	Pvt.	K
Rollins Thorpe	Pvt.	M	John R. Steiniker	Farrier	K
Charles Weidman	Pvt.	M	Jonathan Robers	Pvt.	K
Morris Cain	Pvt.	M			

Lt. W. W. Cooke, Adjutant, Seventh Cavalry.
Killed on the ridge with Custer.

CHAPTER 9

"COME ON! BE QUICK! BRING PACKS!"

CUSTER'S BATTLE PLAN

The Story of His Last Message, as Told by the Man Who Carried It

By LIEUTENANT-COLONEL W. A. GRAHAM, J. A. With Commentary by Brigadier-General Edward S. Godfrey, U. S. Army, Retired*

(From *The Cavalry Journal,* July 1923)

FORTY-SEVEN years have passed since Custer the Yellow Hair, the dashing, impetuous, and fearless, rode to his death at the battle of the Little Big Horn. And because, out of that greatest of Indian fights, not one of his immediate command escaped alive; because the utter annihilation of nearly half a regiment of cavalry by Indians was a thing unheard of, undreamed of; because it was at once spectacular and terrifying; because of the prominence of the man who led his followers to destruction; because he was a man who, not only in the regiment itself, but in the service generally, had both blindly faithful friends and as blindly bitter enemies, there have been, ever since that day, hardly waiting for the body of Custer to grow cold, and but little abating now after half a century, acrimony and dispute over the whole campaign of 1876 against the hostile Sioux.

One never-failing source of discussion, which engages student, critic, and partisan alike, is the tactics of the combat—the plan of battle, if you will. Volumes have been written upon the subject, but when one has read them all he is still left to conjecture and hypothesis.

Did Custer have a plan of battle? And, if he

had, what was it? When did he resolve upon it; and when and how, if at all, did he communicate it to his detached subordinate commanders. Was it carried out? And, if not, why? Or was the whole fight a hit-and-miss affair, which depended upon luck and chance?

Was the battle of the Little Big Horn only a startling example of fatal division of forces in the face of the enemy, with consequent defeat in detail? Was it a blind, impetuous, dashing attack without thought of the consequence, or even of the possibility of defeat? Or was it a well-planned fight, which failed for lack of co-operation and communication? These are some of the problems which inevitably occur to the student of this extraordinary battle.

Partisan dispute will never clear them up. It seldom clears up anything, though I suppose it is heresy for a lawyer to say so. It is only by delving into authentic records and contemporary statements and accounts, by marshaling all the testimony available, and by searching for new evidence that one gets at the facts. And in presenting the story of Sergeant John Martin, who was General Custer's orderly trumpeter on that fatal day in June of 1876, I am confident that, upon some phases at least of the many disputed questions pertaining to the fight, it is the testimony of the only competent witness who survived the battle, the last man to see Custer alive, except those who rode on and died with him upon the ridge.

Martin is the man who carried Custer's famous last message: "Benteen, come on—big village—be quick—bring packs. P. S.—Bring packs." ** He was then a young man of twenty-five, who was already the veteran of one war. Born at Rome in 1851, he had enlisted with Garibaldi, as a drummer boy of fourteen, in the Army of Liberation, and had seen the backs of the Austrians at Villa Franca in '66. After the restoration

---

* This story of the battle of the Little Big Horn has been prepared with care, from the most authentic available sources, and after much study and research. I thank you for letting me see General Godfrey's comments. The General has been more kind than I deserve, and if I have produced anything worth while out of all my digging, it has been largely due to his kindly interest.—THE AUTHOR.

** The message was signed by his adjutant, Lieutenant Cook.—THE AUTHOR.

of Venice to her rightful allegiance, he left his home in sunny Italy in 1873 and almost immediately upon his arrival in America enlisted in the United States Army. His right name, I should tell you, is Giovanni Martini, and he is still hale and hearty, seventy-one years of age, a resident of Brooklyn, N. Y. He served continuously from 1874 to 1904, when he was retired as a sergeant.

He is rather a remarkable old soldier, who never misses an occasion to honor the Stars and Stripes, and who turns out in the old blue, his left arm literally covered to the elbow with service stripes, every time the call of patriotism sounds, whether it be to honor the dead or to greet the living. His form still erect and soldierly, his salute just as snappy as it was when he marched with Garibaldi and rode with Custer, he is well worthy your respectful attention. A fine old soldier, who has deserved well both of his own and of his adopted country; for, besides his long and honor-

able service, Martin has given two stalwart sons to the American Army.

His 7th Cavalry discharge, which he exhibits with pardonable pride, bears the signature of F. W. Benteen, his old troop commander, the man to whom Custer's last message was sent. And Benteen has described Sergeant Martin in that discharge as "the only surviving witness of the Custer massacre."*

SERGEANT MARTIN'S STORY

A little before 8 o'clock, on the morning of June 25, my captain, Benteen, called me to him and ordered me to report to General Custer as orderly trumpeter. The regiment was then several miles from the Divide between the Rosebud

_____

* Since the story was written, Sergeant Martin has passed on. He died at his home in Brooklyn, on Christmas Eve, 1922. I know that the readers of The Cavalry Journal will be sorry to learn that another of the old guard is gone.—AUTHOR.

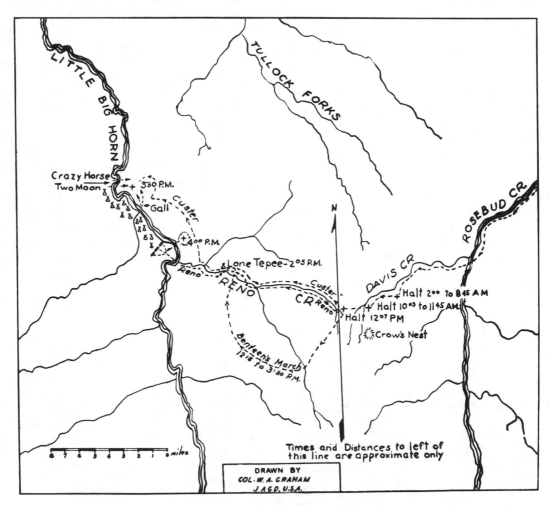

Movements of the several columns of the Seventh Cavalry, June 25, 1876.

and the Little Big Horn. We had halted there to make coffee after a night march.

We knew, of course, that plenty of Indians were somewhere near, because we had been going through deserted villages for two days and following a heavy trail from the Rosebud, and on the 24th we had found carcasses of dead buffalo that had been killed and skinned only a short time before.

I reported to the General personally, and he just looked at me and nodded. He was talking to an Indian scout, called Bloody Knife, when I reported, and Bloody Knife was telling him about a big village in the valley, several hundred tepees and about five thousand Sioux. I sat down a little way off and heard the talk. I couldn't understand what the Indian said, but from what the General said in asking questions and his conversation with the interpreter I understood what it was about.

The General was dressed that morning in a blue-gray flannel shirt, buckskin trousers, and long boots. He wore a regular company hat. His yellow hair was cut short—not very short; but it was not long and curly on his shoulders like it used to be.

Very soon the General jumped on his horse and rode bareback around the camp, talking to the officers in low tones and telling them what he wanted them to do. By 8:30 the command was ready to march and the scouts went on ahead. We followed slowly, about fifteen minutes later. I rode about two yards back of the General. We moved on, at a walk, until about two hours later we came to a deep ravine, where we halted. The General left us there and went away with the scouts. I didn't go with him, but stayed with the Adjutant. This was when he went up to the "Crow's-nest" on the Divide, to look for the Sioux village that Bloody Knife had told him about. He was gone a long time, and when he came back they told him about finding fresh pony tracks close by, and that the Sioux had discovered us in the ravine. At once he ordered me to sound officers' call, and I did so. This showed that he realized now that we could not surprise the Sioux, and so there was no use to keep quiet any longer. For two days before this there had been no trumpet calls, and every precaution had been taken to conceal our march. But now all was changed.

The officers came quickly, and they had an earnest conference with the General. None of the men were allowed to come near them, but soon they separated and went back to their companies.

Then we moved on again, and after a while, about noon, crossed the Divide. Pretty soon the General said something to the Adjutant that I could not hear, and pointed off to the left. In a few minutes Captain Benteen, with three troops, left the column and rode off in the direction that the General had been pointing. I wondered where they were going, because my troop was one of them.

The rest of the regiment rode on, in two columns —Colonel Reno, with three troops, on the left, and the other five troops, under General Custer, on the right. I was riding right behind the General. We followed the course of a little stream that led in the direction of the Little Big Horn River. Reno was on the left bank and we on the right.

All the time, as we rode, scouts were riding in and out, and the General would listen to them and sometimes gallop away a short distance to look around. Sometimes Reno's column was several hundred yards away and sometimes it was close to us, and then the General motioned with his hat and they crossed over to where we were.

Soon we came to an old tepee that had a dead warrior in it. It was burning. The Indian scouts had set it afire. Just a little off from that there was a little hill, from which Girard, one of the scouts, saw some Indians between us and the river. He called to the General and pointed them out. He said they were running away. The General ordered the Indian scouts to follow them, but they refused to go. Then the General motioned to Colonel Reno, and when he rode up* the General told the Adjutant to order him to go down and cross the river and attack the Indian village, and that he would support him with the whole regiment. He said he would go down to the other end and drive them, and that he would have Benteen hurry up and attack them in the center.

Reno, with his three troops, left at once, on a trot, going toward the river, and we followed for a few hundred yards, and then swung to the right, down the river.

We went at a gallop, too. (Just stopped once to water the horses). The General seemed to be in a big hurry. After we had gone about a mile or two we came to a big hill that overlooked the valley, and we rode around the base of it and halted. Then the General took me with him, and we rode to the top of the hill, where he could see the village in the valley on the other side of the river. It was a big village, but we couldn't see it

---

* "While he was riding up" would better express Sergeant Martin's meaning. Evidently Custer did not speak directly to Reno, and the latter never was informed of the General's intention to bring Benteen up to attack in the center.—THE AUTHOR.

all from there, though we didn't know it then; but several hundred tepees were in plain sight.

There were no bucks to be seen; all we could see was some squaws and children playing and a few dogs and ponies. The General seemed both surprised and glad, and said the Indians must be in their tents, asleep.

We did not see anything of Reno's column when we were up on the hill. I am sure the General did not see them at all, because he looked all around with his glasses, and all he said was that we had "got them this time."

He turned in the saddle and took off his hat and waved it so the men of the command, who were halted at the base of the hill, could see him, and he shouted to them, "Hurrah, boys, we've got them! We'll finish them up and then go home to our station."

Then the General and I rode back down to where the troops were, and he talked a minute with the Adjutant, telling him what he had seen. We rode on, pretty fast, until we came to a big ravine that led in the direction of the river, and the General pointed down there and then called me. This was about a mile down the river from where we went up on the hill, and we had been going at a trot and gallop all the way. It must have been about three miles from where we left Reno's trail.

The General said to me, "Orderly, I want you to take a message to Colonel Benteen. Ride as fast as you can and tell him to hurry. Tell him it's a big village and I want him to be quick, and to bring the ammunition packs." He didn't stop at all when he was telling me this, and I just said, "Yes, sir," and checked my horse, when the Adjutant said, "Wait, orderly, I'll give you a message," and he stopped and wrote it in a big hurry, in a little book, and then tore out the leaf and gave it to me.

And then he told me, "Now, orderly, ride as fast as you can to Colonel Benteen. Take the same trail we came down. If you have time, and there is no danger, come back; but otherwise stay with your company."

My horse was pretty tired, but I started back as fast as I could go. The last I saw of the command they were going down into the ravine. The gray horse troop was in the center and they were galloping.

The Adjutant had told me to follow our trail back, and so in a few minutes I was back on the same hill again where the General and I had looked at the village; but before I got there I heard firing back of me, and I looked around and saw Indians, some waving buffalo robes and some shooting. They had been in ambush.

Just before I got to the hill I met Boston Custer.* He was riding at a run, but when he saw me he checked his horse and shouted "Where's the General?" and I answered, pointing back of me, "Right behind that next ridge you'll find him." And he dashed on. That was the last time he was ever seen alive.

When I got up on the hill, I looked down and there I saw Reno's battalion in action. It had been not more than ten or fifteen minutes since the General and I were on the hill, and then we had seen no Indians. But now there were lots of them, riding around and shooting at Reno's men, who were dismounted and in skirmish line. I don't know how many Indians there were—a lot of them. I did not have time to stop and watch the fight; I had to get on to Colonel Benteen; but the last I saw of Reno's men they were fighting in the valley and the line was falling back.

Some Indians saw me, because right away they commenced shooting at me. Several shots were fired at me—four or five, I think—but I was lucky and did not get hit. My horse was struck in the hip, though I did not know it until later.

It was a very warm day and my horse was hot, and I kept on as fast as I could go. I didn't know where Colonel Benteen was, nor where to look for him, but I knew I had to find him.

I followed our trail back to the place we had watered our horses, and looked all around for Colonel Benteen. Pretty soon I saw his command coming. I was riding at a jog trot then. My horse was all in and I was looking everywhere for Colonel Benteen.

As soon as I saw them coming I waved my hat to them and spurred my horse, but he couldn't go any faster. But it was only a few hundred yards before I met Colonel Benteen. He was riding quite a distance in front of the troops, with his orderly trumpeter, at a fast trot. The nearest officer to him was Captain Weir, who was at the head of his troop, about two or three hundred yards back.

I saluted and handed the message to Colonel Benteen, and then I told him what the General said—that it was a big village and to hurry. He said, "Where's the General now?" and I answered that the Indians we saw were running, and I supposed that by this time he had charged through the village. I was going to tell him about Major Reno being in action, too, but he didn't

---

* Boston Custer was a brother of General Custer and went with the column in a civilian capacity, as packmaster.—THE AUTHOR.

give me the chance. He said, "What's the matter with your horse?" and I said, "He's just·tired out, I guess." The Colonel said, "Tired out? Look at his hip," and then I saw the blood from the wound. Colonel Benteen said, "You're lucky it was the horse and not you." By this time Captain Weir had come up to us, and Colonel Benteen handed the message to him to read and told me to join my company.

He didn't give me any order to Captain Mc-Dougall, who was in command of the rear guard, or to Lieutenant Mathey, who had the packs. I told them so at Chicago in 1879, when they had the court of inquiry, but I didn't speak English so good then, and they misunderstood me and made the report of my testimony show that I took an order to Captain McDougall. But this is a mistake.

They gave me another horse and I joined my troop and rode on with them. The pack-train was not very far behind then. It was in sight, maybe a mile away, and the mules were coming along, some of them walking, some trotting, and others running. We moved on faster than the packs could go, and soon they were out of sight, except that we could see their dust.

We followed General Custer's trail until we got near the ridge where the General and I had first seen the village. We could see the fight going on in the valley, and Reno's command was re-treating to the side of the river we were on. As we approached them, Colonel Reno came out to meet us. He was dismounted, his hat was gone, and he had a handkerchief tied around his fore-head. He was out of breath and excited, and raised his hand and called to Colonel Benteen. We all heard him. He said, "For God's sake, Benteen, halt your command and help me. I've lost half my men." Part of his men were still coming up the hill, some mounted and some dismounted, and the Indians were firing at them from the hills and ravines near by. They were pretty much excited and disorganized when we got there.

Colonel Benteen said, "Where's Custer?" and Colonel Reno answered, "I don't know. He went off downstream and I haven't seen or heard any-thing of him since."

We heard a lot of firing down the river; it kept up for a half hour or maybe more. It sounded like a big fight was going on, and the men thought it was General Custer, and that he was whipping the Indians, and we all wanted to hurry on and join him, but they wouldn't let us go. Captain Weir had some words with Colonel Reno, and I could tell by the way he was acting that he was excited and angry. He waved his arms and gestured and pointed down the river. Then we heard some volleys, and Captain Weir jumped on his horse and started down the river all alone. But his troop followed him right away.

The rest of us stayed there until the packs all arrived. The ammunition mules came first, in about fifteen minutes; but it was more than an hour before the last pack-mule was up.

Then we started down the river; but by the time we got as far as where Captain Weir had gone with his company, we had to stop, because the Indians had seen us and were coming up the river toward us by the thousand. The firing down below had all stopped by that time, except for an occasional shot, and we thought that they had stood off the General and that he had gone to join General Terry. We did not suspect then that he and all his men had been killed.

We got down about a mile, or maybe a little more, from the hill where we had found Colonel Reno, and then the Indians came on so thick and fast we had to fall back to the hill again.

By that time they were all around us, and more coming all the time, and we had a hot fight until it was dark.

The next morning it started again before day-light, and they kept it up until the middle of the afternoon. They killed a great many of our horses and mules, and a lot of men were killed and wounded, but we stood them off.

I was in America only two years then, and this was my first Indian fight. I had been in the Black Hills with General Custer in 1875, and we had seen plenty of Indians there, but did not fight them.

I admired General Custer very much; all the men did. He was a fighter and not afraid of any-thing. But he tried to do more than he could that day. They were too many for us, and good fighters, too. They had better weapons than we had and they knew the ground. It is lucky that any of us escaped alive. I don't think we would but for the fact that they heard that General Terry was com-ing.

I am an old man now and have served the United States a long time since I came from Italy in 1873. I enlisted in 1874 and was in the army for thirty years. My memory isn't as good as it used to be, but I can never forget the battle of the Little Big Horn and General Custer.

I have two sons in the army, and one of them is named for the General. I want them both to be as good soldiers as their father was.

It's a long time since I rode with Custer to his last fight—forty-six years—but I still have the old trumpet that I blew officers' call with the morning

Sgt. John Martin (Giovanni Martini) in 1922.

of that fatal day, and still have a lively recollection of, as I have a deep affection for, my old General.

JOHN MARTIN
Sergeant, U. S. Army, Retired.

It is interesting, while reading Sergeant Martin's story, to review what transpired immediately before and after the time he was ordered back with the "Hurry-up" to Benteen and his battalion. Before daylight, the morning of the 25th, the 7th Cavalry, after a night march, had halted to make coffee. They remained where they then were until 8:45, when the march was resumed, until at 10:07 they arrived at a point about three miles from the top of the Divide between the Rosebud and the Little Big Horn, and from which the Indian scouts had reported, just after daylight, the Sioux village was visible.

Here Custer concealed his command in a deep and wooded ravine and went forward himself to the "Crow's-nest" to look at the Indian Camp, then intending to remain in concealment during the day and make his attack the next morning at daybreak, should the report of the scouts be verified. He returned in about an hour and a half, or about 11:30 a.m. George Herendeen, the scout who had been furnished him for the purpose of communicating with Terry, and Benteen and Reno

also, say that when Custer returned to the command he said he "could not see any village, though the scouts and Mitch Bouyer (the half-breed Crow guide) all said they could see it, about fifteen miles off." Benteen and Reno further say that Custer expressed disbelief in the near proximity of any village whatever, at that time.

But during his absence events had transpired which forced him to change his plan to attack at daybreak.

Herendeen states (New York *Herald*, July 8, 1876) that while Custer was gone scouts had come in and reported that the command had been discovered by the hostiles; that two war parties of Sioux had stolen up and seen them and the news was even then on the way to the village. Hasty examination being made in a near-by ravine, fresh pony tracks were discovered. It was necessary to follow the trail at once or the Sioux would be on the move.

Custer thereupon had officers' call blown, as related by Sergeant Martin, and gave his orders.[*] The scouts were ordered forward, the regiment following at a walk, at 11:45. Upon crossing the Divide, Custer, apparently still skeptical about the location of the village, again halted at 12:05 p.m., divided the regiment, and ordered Benteen off to the left to a line of bluffs to scour the country and pitch into anything he might find. He was to go on into the next valley, and if he found nothing, then to the next. Benteen departed at once and was soon out of sight.

The rest of the command, at 12:12 p.m., followed the trail for about six miles, evidently still at a walk, until shortly after 2:00 o'clock an Indian lodge was sighted; whereupon Custer bore down upon it at a trot. It proved to be the remains of a freshly abandoned Indian camp, all the lodges of which had been struck except this one, which contained the body of a warrior who had died from wounds received in Crook's fight on the Rosebud the week before. No Indians in any number had as yet been seen.

_____

[*] It was during this halt that a sergeant of Yates' troop who had been sent back several miles on the trail to recover some articles which had been lost from a pack-mule the night before, returned to the command. He had discovered three Sioux, one sitting on a box of hard bread and examining the contents of a bag. Returning immediately, he reported the incident, which was at once relayed to Custer, then at the "Crows-nest." It was now plain that the Sioux knew of the presence of the troops, and there was no longer any use of secrecy nor hope of surprise.

(The foregoing note was, in 1923, believed correct; but information received in 1931 makes necessary the statement that the three Indians seen by Sgt. Curtis were probably of Little Wolf's band of Cheyennes.)

Near this dead-warrior lodge was a little knoll, from which one could look down the valley of the Little Big Horn, and there heavy clouds of dust were observed, apparently some five miles distant.

Girard, the interpreter, rode up on this knoll, and while looking at the receding clouds of dust in the valley discovered a good-sized party of Indians in flight between the troops and the river. He turned in his saddle and shouted to Custer, "Here are your Indians, running like devils." This was about 2:15 p.m., two hours after Benteen had left the column, and who was then probably some eight or ten miles away, to the left and rear.

Immediately Custer ordered the scouts to pursue. They refused; whereupon the Adjutant, at his direction, gave the order to Reno to "take as fast a gait as you think prudent and charge afterward, and you will be supported by the entire outfit," adding, as Reno moved out, "Take the scouts with you." *

Up to that moment it is fairly clear that Custer had formed no plan of battle. His information of the enemy was insufficient for him to have done so. He gave Reno no other instructions, and no further word was ever received from him by Reno,** who went in apparently expecting Custer to follow and support him from the rear.

It is quite possible, even probable, that this was Custer's intention at that moment, for he did follow Reno for a considerable distance.

The Adjutant, Lieutenant Cook, and Captain Keogh, both of whom were killed with Custer, rode to the river with Reno's command. At the river bank (about 2:30) the scouts saw the Sioux coming up the valley to meet Reno, and Girard,

who had not yet crossed over, rode back, overtook Cook, then on his way back to Custer (who was still following), and reported to him that the Sioux were coming in large numbers to meet Reno. Cook said he would report the fact at once to Custer. This happened about 2:45.

It was at this moment, or very soon after, as it seems to me, that Custer's plan took form. The Indians were coming toward Reno, who would meet them on the plain. By dashing down the river, he would cut in behind them, and hit them from the rear, and he would send for Benteen and put him into action in the center, between Reno and himself.

It is impossible to believe, when he rode to the top of the ridge with Martin, as he did shortly after leaving Reno's trail and starting down the river at a gallop, that Custer thought the Indians were "asleep in their tents," for Cook must already have told him that they were streaming up the valley to meet Reno. He probably said, "We've caught them napping" or "asleep"—an expression which Martin, then a green Italian, unused to American colloquialisms, interpreted literally. But from the ridge evidently he did not see either the Indians or Reno's command. I assume that the timber below hid them from view. But he did see the village, and this, I think, was his first view of it. It was, apparently, deserted by its fighting men. What more natural, then, that he should cheer and shout to his men, "We've got 'em this time!" and dash for a ford, that he might cross and attack in the rear, and on the way send the "hurry-up" message to Benteen. He probably believed that *all* the Sioux were speeding to attack Reno in the valley, and did not know nor had any suspicion of what was in store for his own detachment. The greater part of the Sioux had *not* gone to meet Reno; but, before Martin was out of sight or hearing, attacked him in the ravine which led to the ford; and, as subsequent events show, in such numbers as to force him further down the river than he had intended to go. And there, still driven back by the hordes which cut him off from Reno, he was struck again by the crafty Crazy Horse, who crossed the river below him and attacked his rear. In the meantime Reno, finding the odds too great against him, routed, had fled back across the river. Hundreds of the Sioux under Gall had already left Reno, and dashing down the valley to the point where Custer, already hemmed in, was fighting for his life, they fell upon him like a thunderbolt, and in a short time the fight was over.

Benteen, after receiving the message carried by Martin, and misled, perhaps, by what Martin told

---

* The order was oral and its exact language cannot be reproduced. The witnesses before the Reno Court of Inquiry in 1879 could only repeat its substance. Some said it was to "charge the Indians wherever you find them;" others, "charge the village." I think the first probably the more accurate, as the village was not yet visible. Another version of it was "to make for the dust." All agree, however, that the latter part of the order assured Reno that he "would be supported by the entire outfit." Reno's earlier statements indicate his belief that he was sent in to bring on an advance-guard action.—THE AUTHOR.

** I am aware that it has been claimed that an orderly carried a message from Custer to Reno, who received it while on the skirmish line in the valley. The claim is most improbable, for by the time Reno's skirmish line was formed no messenger could have gotten through. The Sioux were already on Reno's flank and rear, and Jackson, the half-breed scout whom Wallace wanted to send back to Custer to tell him of the situation while the skirmish line was fighting, refused to go, saying, "No man could get through alive." Wallace and Reno both testified at Chicago in 1879 that no word of any sort was received from Custer after the order to attack was given.—THE AUTHOR.

him, had hurried on to join Custer, but instead he found Reno—broken, disorganized, routed. He did not know where Custer was. But Custer had five troops and could, presumably, take care of himself, while Reno was *in extremis*. He heeded the desperate plea for help—and halted.

Not even then, I think, had either detachment of the fated regiment at all realized the strength of the Sioux; and now it was too late. By the time Benteen reached Reno, Custer was hemmed in and doomed to destruction if not already done for.

Reno's ammunition was almost gone. His men had used it wildly, prodigally, and uselessly during the fight in the valley below. Benteen had one hundred rounds to the man—only enough to give his own and Reno's men fifty rounds apiece, when divided between them.

What to do? Did Reno not reason thus?

Custer was five troops strong; he, Reno, now had six, but had lost almost the strength of a troop in killed and wounded; therefore their forces were equal. Custer had all his ammunition, while he had little more than fifty rounds to the man.

If he pushed down the river at once, he must leave the pack-train in the air, at the mercy of the Sioux. And the packs carried all the extra ammunition, 24,000 rounds. He was burdened with wounded; to leave whom was out of the question, and whose presence made fast progress impossible. Surely Custer, with his five troops, could hold his own until the packs were up and the extra ammunition available. It was inconceivable that he was in distress. The thought that Custer could be in danger of destruction never crossed his mind.

So, Hare, on the freshest horse at hand, is sent on the run for the packs; and he, finding them still a mile and a half away, cuts out the ammunition mules and lashes them forward, the rest of the packs coming on as fast as possible, guarded by McDougall's troop.

Reno had attacked about 3:15 p.m. He fought in the valley about a half hour, perhaps forty minutes, and then fled the field, reaching the hills about 4 p.m. About 4:10 Benteen joined him. It must have been at least 5 o'clock, or later before the ammunition mules arrived. What was Custer's situation then?

He had left Reno's trail about 3 o'clock; he started Martin back about 3:15; he had been first attacked, according to Martin, about 3:20. It was now after 5 p.m., more than an hour and a half since the Indians had first fallen upon him.

Gall had left Reno's front about the time Reno withdrew his line into the timber, or 3:30. He had not more than a twenty-minute ride to Custer, which allows more than an hour of his participation in the attack on Custer before Reno had the extra ammunition.

While Hare was gone for the ammunition mules, Weir and his troop moved down the river in an attempt to communicate with or to join Custer. He succeeded in getting about a mile before he was compelled to stop because of the ever-increasing number of Sioux in his front. In the meantime Reno was on the way to join him. Before Reno reached Weir the struggle below was over and the Sioux were coming back. Weir had moved down the river about 4:30 to 4:45 p.m.; Reno followed about 5:30. The Indians checked Weir about the time Reno started, and the retreat up the river to his first position began about 6:00. By 6:30 most of the command was back on the hill; by 7:00 p.m., all of it, and as the covering company (Godfrey's) made its last dash to safety, Reno was surrounded by thousands of yelling Sioux.

At what time was Custer's fight over? Could it have continued long after 5:00 p.m.? I doubt it very much.

Had Reno moved down the river *at once* when Benteen joined him, at 4:10, he might have covered the four intervening miles before Custer was completely wiped out. But whether, encumbered as he was with wounded and possessing insufficient ammunition, such a move would have resulted in anything but greater disaster is a question which will bear thinking about. By the time the extra ammunition was available, was it not too late?

The fighting strength of the Sioux that day was at least six to one; better armed, better prepared, and as well, if not better, led. Was it possible, think you, for Custer to have won?

The tactics of the Indians on that day resulted in their doing to Custer exactly what Custer had planned tactically to do to them. And they were able to do it because they had the leaders, the arms, and the overwhelming forces, none of which facts were known or appreciated by the 7th Cavalry.

Their numbers had been underestimated; their leadership and fighting capacity undervalued; their superiority in arms not even suspected. The 7th. Cavalry paid the penalty for national stupidity.

NOTE:—The time of the various movements is fixed, in so far as is possible, by the official itinerary kept by Lieutenant Wallace, which recorded the halts and marches up to the time of the division into battalions at 12:05. Wallace looked at his watch about the time Custer called Reno across to the right bank of the little tributary they were following. It was then 2:00 p.m. The dead-warrior tepee was sighted immediately after. The others are estimates based upon testimony, map distances, and all available evidence. They are necessarily approximate, but, I believe, very nearly correct.

COMMENTS BY GENERAL E. S. GODFREY

Colonel Graham's contribution to the history of "Custer's last battle" will be greatly appreciated by contemporary and future historians, as well as by writers of stories of that many-sided event, an event that was epochal in the history of the great Northwest, the beginning of the end of the century-old frontier life of the army.

The mystery of the passing of the spirit of the noted and brilliant cavalry leader of the Civil War, of the indefatigable and hitherto-successful Indian campaigner, viewed from all sides and any angle, ends just where it began—in conjecture. There were probably only two men in Custer's entire command who, had they escaped, could have cleared up the mystery of his intentions and his plans—Captain Tom Custer, his brother, and Lieutenant Cooke, his adjutant; but they and their gallant comrades passed on to the Great Beyond with their hitherto-indomitable leader. The commanders of the detached battalions were his irreconcilable, bitter enemies and critics; but he trusted to their regimental *esprit* and soldier honor for loyal and efficient support.

One orderly alluded to by Colonel Graham states that he carried and delivered a written message from Custer to Reno. While this testimony may be of doubtful value, who knows but that this message contained important instructions, hastily glanced at, that were pocketed, ignored, destroyed, and never revealed?

Colonel Graham, when seeking in the dusty archives of the War Department, came across the proceedings of the Reno Court of Inquiry held at Chicago in 1879, became interested, and has sought and brought to light much information from newspapers of that period and elsewhere—from wherever he could get a lead; from original official documents and from survivors of the expeditionary forces. I have reason to believe that his investigations have been made with an impartial, judicial frame of mind, not only deserving praise, but helpful assistance. It is to be hoped that we may have further contributions on this and kindred subjects from him.

Colonel Graham's time periods of events and movements, his deductions or conjectures, for they can only be conjectures, as to the plans and intentions of General Custer, are about the best that have been suggested.

I confess to considerable surprise that Reno and Benteen had testified at the Court of Inquiry "That Custer expressed a disbelief in the near proximity of any village whatever at that time." A number of us were already grouped when Keogh came up and told of the incident of Sergeant Curtis and the lost pack. Tom Custer jumped up and said that he was going to report that to the General. He and the General soon returned and officers' call was sounded. At the conclusion of his talk the General ordered us to return to our troops, inspect them, and report when we were ready for the march; and he said that the troops would take their places in the column of march in the order of reports. As we dispersed, Benteen and I walked toward our troops together. We had proceeded not more than fifty yards when, to my surprise, Benteen faced about and reported his troop ready. Benteen was beside me at the officers' call. I relate this to show that what one could hear the other could hear. I feel perfectly sure that such an expression of disbelief from the General would have made an unforgettable impression on my mind.

The difference in vision from the "Crow's-nest" on the Divide may be accounted for. The scouts saw the smoke at the village and the pony herds moving in the bottom when the vision was at the best, through a clear, calm atmosphere, with the early morning sun at their backs; General Custer's observations at the same place were made at near midday, with a high overhead sun; he had a hazy atmosphere from the heated earth. At all events, the General must have accepted the scouts' point of view, because he made their location of the village his objective.

Our observations in locations of large Indian villages had shown that, for grazing their pony herds and perhaps for sanitary reasons, the village would consist of a series of groups or bands, separated by considerable distances. It is quite probable that General Custer had this in mind when he ordered Benteen's battalion to the left front to scout as far as the valley of the Little Big Horn, to pitch into anything he found, and to report. The fatigue of crossing ridges and valleys heavily distressed our horses, many falling behind. Lieutenant Gibson, with a detail, was sent on to the ridge, where he had a view of the valley of the Little Big Horn. He signaled, "No enemy in sight," and Benteen resumed the march, heading toward the trail of the main command, which we struck just ahead of the pack-train. On our march to the left I had glimpses of General Custer's command moving at a trot.

In recent years some newspapers have given space to self-styled "Last Survivors of the Custer

Massacre" to proclaim their trashy, unbelievable tales of adventures and heroisms. I think there are now about twenty of these frauds, fakers, and imposters on the rolls.

As to many of the so-called Indian versions of the battle of the Little Big Horn, it must be remembered that the Indian in battle is an individualist; he is not anchored to a unit; he rides furiously in a circle or back and forth, as the spirit moves him, hoping for a chance to make a *coup* or get a scalp. Only the commanding personality of the war chief can hold him to a fixed or set purpose. In this battle, Gall, the noted Huncpapa Sioux war chief, when he learned that Custer's troops were approaching the village on the flank, called his warriors from the attack on Reno and assembled them in a deep ravine on the flank held by Keogh and Calhoun. He sent a detachment to attack and stampede the led horses; others he posted under cover, awaiting the opportunity for the rush and charge. Apparently there was no guard left with the led horses and the stampede was soon accomplished; that seemed to be the

opportune moment and Gall gave his war whoop; the charge was made, overwhelming first Calhoun and then Keogh (troop commanders with Custer).

Crazy Horse, another noted war chief, when he learned that Custer was approaching, left Reno's front and rushed down the valley through the approaching warriors and through the village, calling, "All who want to fight, follow me." He assembled his warriors on Custer's flank, under the cover of a ridge. He sent a detachment to Custer's rear, and at the opportune moment he gave the war whoop for the charge that destroyed Custer's command.

———

EDITOR'S NOTE.—General Godfrey wrote a full account of "Custer's last battle," which was published in the CENTURY MAGAZINE in 1892. A reprint of this article was made and published in 1908, and still another reprint was done in 1921. We are informed that this is no longer obtainable, although General Godfrey has kindly given a copy to the U. S. Cavalry Association.

———

THE LOST IS FOUND—CUSTER'S LAST MESSAGE COMES TO LIGHT!

By COLONEL W. A. GRAHAM, *Retired*

(From *The Cavalry Journal*, July-August 1942)

TWENTY YEARS ago this month, after searching for him many months, I found John Martin, the man who carried Custer's last message; the famous message to Benteen that bid him to "come on and be quick" and to "bring the packs."

The dispatch of that message marked the crisis of the battle of the Little Big Horn, where Custer, and nearly half the Seventh Cavalry, found death instead of glory waiting for them at the trail's end.

Having read avidly all War Department records of this dramatic fight, in which the American Indian achieved his greatest triumph over the American soldier, I keenly wished to write the story of that message.

The messenger was found; but the message itself had disappeared. I turned the records inside out in efforts to locate it, until I became a nuisance to The Adjutant General. Then, early in 1923, Major Fred Benteen, son of the gallant officer to whom the message was sent, told me that all his father's papers were destroyed when their home had burned long years before; that

Sgt. Martin at his retirement in 1904.

the famous message with many another relic of the Little Big Horn had then gone up in smoke. And so I ceased my search, and wrote John Martin's story of how he carried Custer's final message to Benteen. The *Cavalry Journal* published it, with comments by General Edward S. Godfrey, a distinguished participant in the battle, in its July, 1923, number.

It now appears that the younger Benteen was mistaken. The message had not gone up in smoke as he supposed, for it has lately become known that after producing it to supplement his testimony before the Court of Inquiry held in 1879 to determine whether Major Reno, Custer's second in command, had been guilty of misconduct at the Little Big Horn, the elder Benteen had presented it to a friend, a certain Captain Price of Philadelphia. Apparently he told no one about it, for Godfrey also believed the paper destroyed by fire. Thus lost since 1879—Custer's last message has now been found, and through the commendable efforts of Colonel Charles Francis Bates, Retired, it now rests safe in the library at West Point.

The story of its recovery is interesting. For the past fifty years it has been in the possession of the family of a New Jersey collector who acquired it from Price, and who, so far as I can learn, valued it only as a curio. How many other historic documents, I wonder, now accounted for as lost, might be restored to public record if only the collections of relic hunters could be made to give up their secrets?

The original message, with other treasures of the collector, was recently advertised for sale at auction. Colonel Bates thus learned of its existence, and arranged with the owner to secure it for West Point. There can be no doubt of its authenticity. Not only is the script of the message itself plainly the hand of Lt. W. W. Cooke, the 7th's regimental adjutant, who died with Custer within an hour of the time he wrote it, but the unmistakable penmanship of Benteen himself, once seen, never forgotten, attests its genuineness in the "translation" made for his friend Price's benefit, and which he inscribed above its penciled words.

It was far from easy to get Martin's story of his ride to Benteen. He was very old and very feeble when I found him deep in the jungle of Brooklyn's Italian quarter. His memory was as feeble as his body, and it was only after I had made three separate visits, each time reading to him (for he was almost blind) his testimony before the Reno Inquiry, that recollection of that

fateful June day of 1876 came back. But when it did come back, it came with a wealth of incident and detail that was surprising. And so I wrote his story, just as he told it to me, and he signed it.

Between visits to Martin I made an official trip to New Orleans in an attempt to adjust a dispute between the Government and the local "Dock Board" over the title to lands upon which the Army's multi-million dollar warehouses had been built during the World War. Having permission to stop over in Atlanta, I there saw Major Benteen, and it was then he told me that the famous message had been burned: but he told me also that he had some letters written by his father during the campaign of 1876 that had escaped the flames only because his mother had them safely stored away in a fireproof vault. He had never read them, he said, nor shown them to anyone, but he would let me see them; and he did. Two of those letters were written less than ten days after the battle—the first July 2d—the other July 4, 1876.

The letter of July 4th is of especial significance. In it Benteen tells not only of the receipt of Custer's last message, but recounts the harrowing experience through which the regiment had passed; and it tells also all that then was known of what had happened to Custer and his immediate command. But little more has been discovered since. Those two letters Major Benteen permitted me to take back to Washington, where photostatic copies were made. The letter of July 4th, I both showed and read to General Godfrey, saying to him as I did so—"this letter is of historical importance." The general replied—"It is far more than that. It was written long before any controversy had arisen over the way the battle was conducted, and under circumstances that give it special credit. It is history itself."

Omitting only such parts as are purely personal, here the letter is:

> July 4th 1876, Montana,
> Camp 7th Cavalry, Yellowstone River,
> Opposite mouth of Big Horn River.

My . . . . Darling,

. . . I will commence this letter by sending a copy of the last lines Cooke ever wrote, which was an order to me to this effect.

Benteen. Come on. Big village. Be quick, bring packs.

W. W. Cooke. (P. S. Bring pac-s)

He left out the k in last packs.

I have the original, but it is badly torn and it should be preserved. So keep this letter, as the matter may be of interest hereafter, likewise of use. This note was brought back to me by Trumpeter Martin of my Co. (which fact saved his life.) When I received it I was five or six miles from the village, perhaps more, and the packs at least that distance in my rear. I did not go back for the packs but kept on a stiff trot for the village. When getting at top of hill so that the valley could be seen—I saw an immense number of Indians on the plain, mounted of course and charging down on some dismounted men of Reno's command; the balance of R's command were mounted, and flying for dear life to the bluffs on the same side of river that I was. I then marched my 3 Co's. to them and a more delighted lot of folks you never saw. To commence—On the 22d of June—Custer, with the 7th Cavalry left the Steamer "Far West," Genl. Terry and Genl. Gibbon's command (which latter was then in on the side of river and in same camp in which we now are) and moved up the Rosebud, marching 12 miles—the next day we marched 35 miles up the same stream. The next day we marched 35 more miles up same stream and went into bivouac, remaining until 12 o'clock P. M. We then marched until about daylight, making about 10 miles; about half past five we started again—and after going 6 or 7 miles we halted and officers' call was sounded. We were asked how many men of the companies were with the Co. Packs and instructed that only six could remain with them—and the discourse wound up with—that we should see that the men were supplied with the quantity of ammunition as had been specified in orders and that the 1st Co. that reported itself in readiness should be the advance Co. I knew that my Co. was in the desired condition and it being near the point of Assembly I went to it, assured myself of same, then announced to Genl. Custer that "H" Co. was ready; he replied the Advance is yours, Col. Benteen. We then moved four or five miles and halted between the slopes of two hills and the Regt. was divided into Battalions—Reno getting Co's. "A. G. and M." I getting "D. H. K." From that point I was ordered with my Battn. to go over the immense hills to the left, in search of the valley, which was supposed to be very near by and to pitch into anything I came across—and to inform Custer at once if I found anything worthy of same. Well, I suppose I went up and down those hills for 10 miles—and still no valley anywhere in sight, the horses were fast giving out from steady climbing—and as my orders had been fulfilled I struck diagonally for the trail the command had marched

on, getting to it just before the Pack train got there—or on the trail just ahead of it. I then marched rapidly and after about 6 or 7 miles came upon a burning tepee—in which was the body of an indian on a scaffold, arrayed gorgeously—None of the command was in sight at this time. The ground from this to the valley was descending but very rough. I kept up my trot and when I reached a point very near the ford which was crossed by Reno's Battn. I got my first sight of the Valley and river—and Reno's command in full flight for the bluffs to the side I was then on—Of course I joined them at once. The ground where Reno charged on was a plain 5 or 6 miles or 10 miles long and about one mile or more wide; Custer sent him in there and promised to support him—after Reno started in, Custer with his five Co's instead of crossing the ford went to the right—around some high bluffs—with the intention—as is supposed—of striking the rear of the village; from the bluff on which he got he had his first glimpse of the whole of it—and I can tell you 'twas an immense one. From that point Cooke sent the note to me by Martin, which I have quoted on 1st page. I suppose after the five Co's had closed up somewhat Custer started down for the village, all throats bursting themselves with cheering (So says Martin). He had 3½ or 4 miles to go before he got to a ford—as the Village was on the plain on opposite side to Custer's column. So, when he got over those 4 miles of rough country and reached the ford, the indians had availed themselves of the timely information given by the cheering—as to the whereabouts and intentions of that column, and had arrangements completed to receive it. Whether the indians allowed Custer's column to cross at all, is a mooted question, but I am of the opinion that nearly—if not all of the five companies got into the village—but were driven out immediately—flying in great disorder and crossing by two instead of the one ford by which they entered. "E" Co. going by the left and "F. I. and L." by the same one they crossed. What became of "C" Co. no one knows—they must have charged there below the village, gotten away—or have been killed in the bluffs on the village side of stream—as very few of "C" Co. horses are found. Jack Sturgis and Porter's clothes were found in the Village. After the indians had driven them across, it was a regular buffalo hunt for them and not a man escaped. We buried 203 of the bodies of Custer's command the 2d day after fight—The bodies were as recognizable as if they were in life. With Custer—was Keogh, Yates and Tom Custer (3 Captains) 1st Lieut's. Cooke, A. E. Smith, Porter, Calhoun (4) 2d Lieuts. Har-

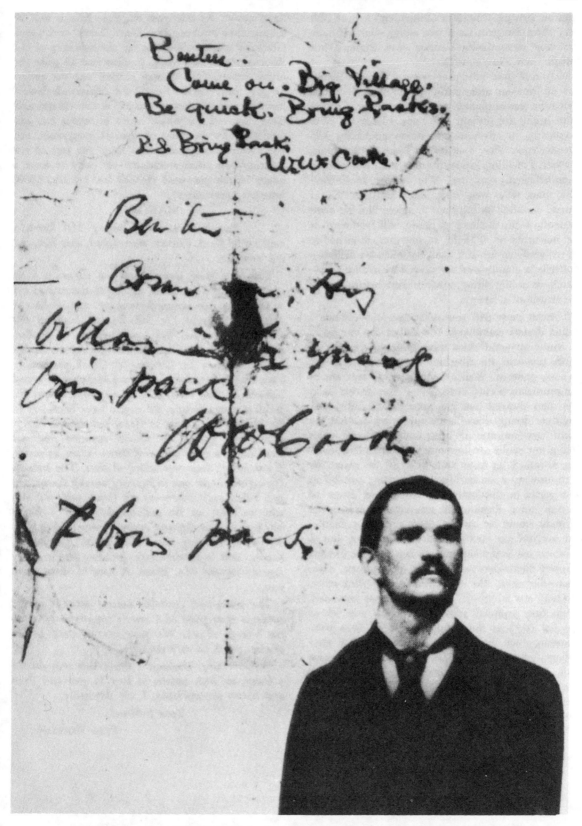

The Famous Last Message and the Man Who Carried It, as he looked in 1879.

rington, Sturgis, Riley and Crittenden (J. J. of 20th Inf.) Asst. Surgeon Lord was along—but his body was not recognized. Neither was Porter's nor Sturgis' nor Harrington's.

McIntosh and Hodgson were killed at Reno's end of line—in attempting to get back to bluffs. DeRudio was supposed to have been lost, but the same night the indians left their village he came sauntering in dismounted, accompanied by Mc-Intosh's cook. They had hidden away in the woods. He had a thrilling romantic story made out already —embellished, you bet! The stories of O'Neill (the man who was with him) and De R's of course, couldn't be expected to agree, but far more of truth, I am inclined to think, will be found in the narrative of O'Neill; at any rate, it is not at all colored—as he is a cool, level-headed fellow— and tells it plainly *and the same way all the time*— which is a big thing towards convincing one of the truth of a story.

I must now tell you what we did—When I found Reno's command. We halted for the packs to come up—and then moved along the line of bluffs towards the direction Custer was supposed to have gone in. Weir's Company was sent out to communicate with Custer, but it was driven back. We then showed our full force on the hills with Guidons flying, that Custer might see us—but we could see nothing of him, couldn't hear much firing, but could see immense body of Indians coming to attack us from both sides of the river. We withdrew to a saucer like hill, putting our horses and packs in the bottom of saucer and threw all of our force dismounted around this corral; the animals could be riddled from only one point— but we had not men enough to extend our line to that—so we could not get it—therefore the indians amused themselves by shooting at our stock, ditto, men—but they, the men, could cover themselves. Both of my horses (U. S. horses) were wounded. Well they pounded at us all of what was left of the 1st day and the whole of the 2d day—with-drawing their line with the withdrawal of their village, which was at dusk the 2d day. Corporal Loll, Meador and Jones were killed; Sergt. Pahl, both of the Bishops, Phillips, Windolph, Black, Severs, Cooper, etc. (21 altogether) wounded. I got a slight scratch on my right thumb, which, as you see, doesn't prevent me from writing you this long scrawl. As this goes via Fort Ellis it will be a long time reaching you. Genl. Terry, with Genl. Gibbon's command—came up the morning of the 3d day, about 10 o'clock. Indians had all gone the night before. Had Custer carried out the orders he got from Genl. Terry, the commands would have formed a junction exactly at the village, and have captured the whole outfit of tepees, etc. and probably any quantity of squaws, pappooses, etc. but Custer disobeyed orders from the fact of not wanting any other command—or body to have a finger in the pie—and thereby lost his life. (3000 warriors were there).

MARGIN:

. . . Boston Custer and young Mr. Reed, a nephew of Genl. Custer, were killed, also Kellogg, the reporter. . . .

This is a long scrawl—but not so much in it after all—and I am about getting to the end of my tether. Reno has assumed command and Wallace is Adjutant. Edgerly, Qr. Mr. By the death of our Captains, Nowlan, Bell and Jackson, 3 "coffee-coolers" are made Captains and Godfrey is Senior 1st Lt., Mathey 2d, Gibson, 3d. Quick promotion. I am inclined to think that had McIntosh divested himself of that slow poking way which was his peculiar characteristic, he might have been left in the land of the living. A Crow indian, one of our scouts who got in the village, reported that our men killed a great many of them—quite as many, if not more, than was killed of ours. The indians during the night got to fighting among themselves and killed each other—so the Crow said—he also said as soon as he got possession of a Sioux blanket, not the slightest attention was paid to him. There was among them Cheyennes, Arrapahoes, Kiowa and representatives probably from every Agency on the Mo. River. A host of them there sure.

The latest and probably correct account of the battle is that none of Custer's command got into the village at all. We may not be back before winter, think so very strongly.

Well—Wifey, Darling, I think this will do for a letter, so with oceans of love to you and Fred and kisses innumerable, I am devotedly,

Your husband

FRED BENTEEN.

CHAPTER 10

MY DEBATE WITH CAPTAIN CARTER

THE late Captain Robert G. Carter, Retired, was a distinguished Indian War veteran, having been an officer of Colonel Ronald Mackenzie's famous regiment, the Fourth Cavalry, whose record of success in Indian fighting was second to none.

Carter has been considered as Spokesman-in-chief for the anti-Reno critics; but as a matter of fact, he was a critic of the Seventh Cavalry, rather than of its individual members, who regarded with derision the usual characterization of the regiment as "The Fighting Seventh." His estimate of the Seventh's record in the Indian Wars was anything but complimentary, and he ascribed responsibility for its defeat at the Little Big Horn more to Custer than he did to Reno. His opinion of both, and of the regiment also, may be deduced without too much difficulty from the letters which follow.

In 1935, E. A. Brininstool of Los Angeles, was in the throes of his long continued effort "to cut Custer down to size" and to make a hero out of Reno. In some way unknown to me he had obtained a copy of one of my letters to Carter dated 18 March 1925; and during my tour of service at the Baltimore headquarters, he requested, through a mutual acquaintance, permission to publish it, together with some comments and remarks of his own. The intercessor was informed that I could not consent to such publication unless it met with Captain Carter's approval, and then only if Brininstool submitted to me his comments and remarks, as I did not wish to be drawn into controversy other than that which might arise from the letter standing alone. In other words, while willing to be bound by the text of my letter to Carter, I was not willing to be bound by the comments of a hero-maker who might easily drag me overboard with him by expressing extreme views.

I called on Carter the next time I was in Washington, and told him of Brininstool's request. He said he would have no objection, *provided* the entire correspondence was published —his memoranda and letters as well as mine. That, however, being at the time out of the question, he at length consented upon condition that at some future time, if found possible, I would publish the entire correspondence between us. The letters that follow may therefore be considered as a belated redemption of my pledge, no opportunity having heretofore presented itself.

As to the letter of 18 March 1925, Brininstool published it during 1935 in booklet form (with a considerable amount of interpolated emphasis of his own) under the title "Major Reno Vindicated," with comments which he submitted to me: and this same letter, but *without* the comments and interpolated emphasis, has now been reprinted as a part of Chapter 6 of his recent "Troopers With Custer," in which is discussed the question of Reno's alleged cowardice. As the letter, as reproduced by Brininstool, is not an exact copy, it is repeated here as I wrote it, as a necessary part of the series.

The first of the series is a Memorandum setting forth Captain Carter's criticisms of the manuscript of "The Story of the Little Big Horn," which I had sent to him for examination and comment, just as I had sent copies to Generals Godfrey and Edgerly. This began the debate, which continued throughout 1925, and until "The Story of the Little Big Horn" was published by the Century Company in 1926. It will be found informative, in that it sets forth the views of the *military,* as distinguished from *civilian* critics of the tactics employed at the Little Big Horn. While General Godfrey took no *active* part in this correspondence, his desire that Carter's views be published, as expressed in his letter of 14 April 1925 (which is included as part of the series) furnishes an interesting sidelight on his own views.

All of Captain Carter's memoranda and letters are herewith reproduced. Some of mine have been misplaced or lost: but they were, I think, of minor importance, except one dated on or about 20 April 1925, which apparently contained a summary of my notes relating to Reno's conduct, and with which I enclosed a copy of General Edgerly's letter of 16 April. Captain Carter's reply ignored the Edgerly letter completely. The series follows:

Washington, D. C.,

March 13, 1925.

MEMORANDA

Comments and notes on Lt. Col. W. A. Graham's article "The Story of the Little Big Horn— Custer's Last Fight."

It is for the most part a fine story for publication; a very fair and reasonable statement of facts, and intended to be perfectly free from bias and prejudice or desire to provoke controversy which for so many years, at least while many of the participants in this great tragedy were living, provoked so many bitter statements and criticisms.

It is my belief, however, that this article is not entirely free from error in some of its conclusions, as noted in a paper with comments and notes which I prepared several years ago, before Colonel Graham began his study of the Custer campaign and battle. This article I have never published. This is but a brief resumé of that paper.

On page 6, of Col. Graham's MS, he refers to Gen. Terry's plan of operations after a conference on the "Far West" with General Gibbon and Gen. Custer, as he (C) was about to start out on his fatal expedition, and on page 7 to Terry's letter of instructions as a "written order." It was signed by E. W. Smith, Captain, 18th Infantry, A.A.A.G., and not by Gen. Terry. It was not "by command" or "by order" of Gen. Terry, as was usual in the field or when a battle was contemplated or impending. It was then simply a *Letter of Instructions,* and a very elastic one at that. Knowing Gen. Hughes (Gen. Terry's brother-in-law) as well as I did, I am quite sure that he (Hughes) wrote it. It is his language. It does not order Custer to do what a battle order would actually compel him to do,—unless he was willing to take the risk of actual disobedience. The first sentence *"directs"* him (Custer) to *"proceed* up the Rosebud in pursuit of the Indians whose trail was discovered by Major Reno a few days ago," etc. etc. That is the only sentence that is

really an *order*. It would be a profitless task to fully analyze this so-called "order," for it soon departs from the language of an *"order"*. "It is, of course,' impossible to give you any definite *instructions"*—showing that Gen. Terry regarded it as a letter of instructions and not an "order," for he adds: "and were it not impossible to do so, the Department Commander places too much confidence in your *zeal, energy* and *ability* to impose upon you *precise orders* which might hamper your actions when *nearly in contact with the enemy."* And here we will stop, for the rest of this letter of instructions gives Custer ample latitude and the use of his own judgment when he shall have found himself so far away from his Commanding Officer that he could only communicate with him by courier over a country then swarming with hostile Indians. After this Gen. Terry uses the words—*"indicate,"*— "He *thinks you should* proceed up the Rosebud until," etc., (still no positive order),—"Should it be found, however, etc. x x x he *thinks* you should still proceed southward," etc. All this is an endeavor to *herd* (*"enclosing* and *capturing"*—Col. Graham) 4000 or 5000 savages, the finest light cavalry this world has ever seen—across the country in the hope of corralling them in the near vicinity of either Gibbon or Terry, or both, and then by Custer closing in on them, capture or destroy the entire Indian outfit—an anomalous condition, an absurdity, and something unheard of in the annals of Indian warfare in this country. Indians could never be herded nor corralled. The pony herds, with good herders could be herded, but the Indians generally got them all back the same night unless, perchance, in the meantime, we had had them all shot. I have two instances in mind in my own experience with Comanche Indians. Again the Department Commander uses the words *"It is hoped"* (is that an order?). Later he *"desires* that on your way up the Rosebud you *should* (not must) thoroughly examine the upper part of Tullocks Creek, etc." —again using the word "desire" in the concluding paragraph of his letter (not *order*) of instructions.

General Hughes, in his able defense of his brother-in-law, published in the Journal of the Military Service Institution for January, 1896, lays too much stress on these words, thus quoted from Terry's letter of instructions. He very lamely claims that Terry's instructions was an "order." Gen. Sickles, at Gettysburg, disobeyed Gen. Meade's *wishes, desires* and *verbal* instructions, as to where he should post his Corps (3d) on the morning of July 2, 1863, because Gen. Meade, arriving on the field late at night, exhausted mentally and physically by such grave responsibilities having been so suddenly thrust upon him, and having no opportunity to make a personal reconnaissance of the field, gave Sickles no *positive order*. He (S) used his own judgment—poor enough at best and jeopardized the safety of the entire army by the faulty disposition of his command. Custer used his own judgment when he felt compelled to, and then by failing to reveal his plans to one or more of his immediate subordinates—so that they could fully cooperate with him when he went into action—he lost his own life and those of his own attacking column. If all of the Civil War generals had issued such *orders*(?) as Terry did, no one can doubt the result. General Hughes says, "All military men know that the *polite words* (italics are mine,) 'he indicates,' 'he desires,' 'he thinks,' 'he wishes,' have all the force that can be conveyed in the words '*he orders.*'" That was the trouble with Terry. In such an important movement then impending, with so much at stake as there was bound to be, he was *too polite* in his phrases with a man of Custer's impulsive temperament, and not explicit enough in giving him (C) *positive verbal,* or better still, *written* orders, as to just what he was to do, with, perhaps, some qualifying clause, as to what he *should* do, not when "nearly" in contact with the enemy (he was *nearly in* contact just so soon as he started in *pursuit*) but when he *was in contact,* ready for battle. All that Terry seemed to have in mind in this letter was that Custer should *carefully herd* this savage horde of warriors and then slip them into a corral whenever Gibbon and he (Terry) should be ready for them. Who knows what these same Indians might not have done to Gibbon and Terry had not Custer attacked them on the 25th instead of the 26th, in the fear that they might escape, and moving towards them (Gibbon and Terry) do that very same thing—overwhelm them by force of numbers. Custer was supposed to do not only this herding, but to be in a position to cooperate with both Gibbon and Terry on the 26th, the date on which Custer's fifteen days rations expired. Both on the 25th and the 26th Gibbon's and Terry's columns were known to have been much scattered out or widely separated, which would have made it impossible for Custer to have so timed his movements, being then so closely in fighting contact with the Indians as to have made any close connection or to have been in a position to have fully cooperated with

the other two columns. All this Col. Graham seems to have lost sight of.

Col. Graham seems to assume that Reno was fully justified before Benteen came up, in leaving his defensive position in the timber to save his command from annihilation, because then he did not know the conditions, and the Indians were filtering into the timber from several directions and endangering his communications to the rear. I do not find any positive proof that at any time the Indians were "filtering" into the timber in any considerable numbers. If this were the fact, more than one (Bloody Knife) would have been killed or wounded during the period in which he (R) remained there.

He (Col. Graham) admits, however,—but not in his story—that "knowing all the *circumstances as they afterwards occurred, and as is now well known,*" that Reno *could* and *should* have remained in the timber until Benteen arrived, not only to save his command from annihilation— which he afterwards exposed them to by his cowardly flight in an utter rout—but in the hope that the two commands could probably have done much by a possible advance, with Benteen as the directing spirit, in the direction of the village, in drawing away a large body of the Indians whom he (G) seems to think were then advancing to head Custer off and block his crossing of the lower fords to get to the rear or on the flanks of the Indian village, even if they were not already attacking him across those fords. The truth is that from the moment Reno suddenly decided to abandon his first line and enter the timber for the better protection of his men, he lost all control of them as an organized force, permitting them to scatter through the timber; gave no orders to anybody as to fire control, and displayed less leadership than might have been credited to or expected of any sergeant or corporal in his command; and when he emerged from that position, after many confusing orders to "mount and dismount," repeated several times, he failed to display any more control of his men than any other leader of a mob would have done under like circumstances. It was a disgraceful run for the river, every man for himself, and the devil (in this case a horde of wild, yelling Indians) take the hindmost.

I could cite many instances, but more notably Gen. Geo. F. ("Sandy") Forsythe's command of but 50 well trained and disciplined scouts in his fight with Roman Nose's Cheyennes at Beecher's Island in 1868, where he "stood off" 700 or more well armed Cheyenne warriors for nearly eight days, and this after his second in command (Lieut. Beecher) and his surgeon had been killed and he himself had been wounded three times. There was *no timber* for cover, nothing but a low sand spit in the middle of the stream, protected only by low banks and a few stunted willow trees. There were many instances when fewer men in a buffalo wallow hole on the open prairie stood off ten times their numbers. I myself in 1871 with but five men held back several hundred Comanche Indians with no cover, for quite a long while, or until the main command could come to my rescue. Of course in all of these instances there were some casualties. That is always expected. *It is a part of the game.* I lost one killed and two wounded of my little bunch of five perfectly disciplined soldiers, armed with Spencer 7 shooting carbines and pistols; the men, by my orders, locking off their magazines and using their guns as single shooters, until the rush was made when the magazines were ordered to be opened and to "pump it into them at close range." This did the trick! The Indians fell back. Indians always hesitated, except in the Custer fight when they clearly saw their overwhelming numbers could be used to smash and crush his tired command, and annihilate them—to "close in" and fight in the face of a well directed fire by which they knew they would lose many of their warriors, killed or wounded. Reno showed the white feather from the start, and his entire conduct was that of a white-livered, yellow-streaked coward. He was terrorized and panic stricken, absolutely in a state of "blue funk." There was no excuse then, and there can be none now, although 50 years have passed, for such conduct on the part of a supposed leader of cavalry in the face of an Indian foe. He should have been tried and cashiered for the part he took in "Custer's Last Fight." If ever there was a pusillanimous poltroon in the army whose name should be handed down to future generations as an arrant coward, Marcus A. Reno is the man.

What shall we say in commenting on the conclusions of Colonel Graham's story of the Little Big Horn?

"While Reno did not show himself to be a great commander (*Ye Gods!!*) who could rise above the demands of trying and desperate conditions, it was due to his *sanity* and *prudence* (italics are mine—R.G.C.) and to Benteen's leadership that any of the 7th Cavalry survived." All this rests upon the meaning of the words— "prudence" and "sanity" and whether they are synonymous with the words—"Cowardice" and "insane" or "ignoble flight."

History records many instances where a commander through cowardice or refusal to fight his command to a finish has saved a part or the whole of it. That is easy to do. Reno, however, by his shameful flight to the rear in a rout led by himself, *invited annihilation;* and only *good luck* or *fate* then saved himself and a part of his men. It was not "sanity" or "prudence." By staying in the timber where he had lost but one man, he might have lost some more—as Forsythe did on Beecher Island, or as I did at the mouth of Canon Blanco in the Panhandle of Texas—but it would seem now—after a lapse of 50 years—as though "prudence" and "sanity" should have dictated his staying where he was under good cover, and to play a waiting game, even had he lost a few more men, than to have exposed his gallant battalion by cowardly flight to the murderous fire of hundreds of yelling savages riding along his flank, subjecting them to almost certain destruction, a situation which—so far as our gallant little army was concerned—has never had a parallel in its long history of splendid deeds.

There is one point in this long complicated problem, which Col. Graham in his carefully prepared and well written story has brought out and as I believe solved, and finally disposed of, at least to my satisfaction, one which I had never thought of before and which could only have been disclosed by a very close study of the Reno Court of Inquiry proceedings—which Col. Graham had access to and has examined many times within the past three years. It is this. When Reno left Custer's column about three-fourths of a mile from the river (Little Big Horn), and where Custer turned off to go to his right and then on up over the ridge, Cook, the Adjutant, and Captain Keogh are known to have accompanied Reno as far as the ford. Girard, the interpreter, was with them. Custer believed that the Indians were trying to get away and would escape, although his scouts had said that that was not the case. Shortly before Reno deployed his column across the valley, Girard saw that the Indians were swarming up from the upper end of the village to boldly attack Reno. He went back to the ford as rapidly as possible and communicated this fact to Cook, who, with Keogh, returned to Custer, rejoining him on the trail. The former doubtless informed Custer of this sudden move on the part of the Indians. Col. Graham believes, and there seems to be no doubt in the absolute correctness of his assumption, that Custer had up to the moment of this information, intended to closely follow Reno in his attack and support him from the rear, thus carrying out his order to Reno to "charge, and I will support you with the whole outfit." It was just at this moment that Custer changed his mind and, without disclosing his reasons for so doing, turned off from the trail and proceeded on his long and exhausting march over the ridge to his fate.

Nobody will ever know positively his reasons for this, or what plan he had in view, except that he was afraid—never doubting that Reno would push through to the village—that the Indians might cross the river and escape over the hills into the Bad Lands, and by this detour he would be able to head them off by crossing himself at one of the lower fords and attacking them there, drive in towards Reno, thus crushing them between the two commands. The inability of Reno to get through on account of his rank cowardice prevented this, and Custer's fate was sealed just as soon as Reno retreated, first to the timber, and then back to the river and bluffs, thus leaving the entire Indian outfit—after leaving enough warriors to hold Reno in check—to go back and head off and surround Custer by an overwhelming force. It is my belief that Custer could not have been reinforced or rescued after he (Reno) and Benteen had joined their commands and had taken up their defensive stand on the bluffs.

It was only by their joining in the timber, reorganizing, and then charging in on the village, thus drawing the bulk of the warriors away from Custer, that gave any hope of success for any plan that could then be hastily determined on.

/s/ R. G. CARTER,
Capt., U.S.A., Ret'd.

————

March 18, 1925.

Dear Captain Carter:—

Thank you for your comments on my Little Big Horn story, which I received yesterday. I had previously received those of Generals Edgerly and Godfrey. I am revising the story in the light of the various comments received, and am preparing a set of notes to go with it which will cover most of the ground taken by the criticisms.

The use of the word "order" in describing Terry's written instructions to Custer was a "lapsus linguae," and I owe you thanks for calling it to my attention. I agree that it should be called a letter of instructions rather than an order, and I will make the change.

I cannot agree with you about Reno. Nor do I believe, if you will take the time to make a careful and comprehensive study of the fight in the valley, that you yourself would hold to the views you have expressed.

I do not know whether you have read the testimony taken by the Reno Court of Inquiry at Chicago; but if you have, you cannot reach the conviction you now hold without discrediting the sworn statements of every military witness, whether called by the prosecution or the defense, who recounted what occurred in the valley. These were Wallace, Hare, Varnum, Moylan and DeRudio of the officers, and Sergeants Culbertson and Davern of the enlisted men.

In all their testimony you cannot find one word in criticism of Reno's action in halting and deploying in skirmish line, instead of charging headlong into the village. On the contrary, you will find only commendation, and unanimous agreement that had he not done as he did, his little force would have been swallowed up and exterminated in five minutes.

And you will find no criticism, but only approval of his action in getting out of the timber; and unanimous opinion that had he remained there, without support (which he might have done a short time longer), his command would have been completely wiped out.

I am not ready to agree that Reno was a "cowardly poltroon" because he did what all these officers say was the only thing he could have done with the knowledge he had of the situation; and which they all agree, saved what was left of the regiment.

I do not doubt that Reno was alarmed; that he was frightened, and lost his head during the retreat. But that fact does not justify any such charge against him. If every officer who gets alarmed and frightened during an action is a "cowardly poltroon," the Army is full of them, always has been and always will be.

The test—if one wishes to be fair and impartial—should be, not—was he scared? nor—might he not have done something else? but, did he do what, under the circumstances which confronted him, he ought to have done? I think he did, up to the time that his column reached the river in retreat. And I believe that you will think so, too, if you will study the situation with care, and with an open mind.

You would not say that Wallace and Hare and Varnum and Moylan and DeRudio were all "cowardly poltroons," I feel sure. Yet, to be consistent, you must say either that, or that they wilfully and deliberately perjured themselves at Chicago in 1879. And you would not say that, either.

The truth is—and I think you will recognize it when you think it over—that most of the criticism and condemnation of Reno comes from men who were not with him in the valley, and whose ideas upon that matter were based on hearsay, not always too accurate; and upon the natural disdain that arose from his passing of the buck to Benteen, as soon as the latter came up.

I hold no brief for Reno, but I believe in giving even the devil his due; *and it is not necessary to attack and condemn Reno in order to account for what happened to Custer.*

Don't forget that Reno's 112 were opposed in the valley by not more than twenty-five percent of the Indians *at any time.* There never were to exceed eight or nine hundred of them. The rest— fully 2500 to 3000, *were attacking Custer before Reno's retreat got under way.* There was no hope for Custer from the moment he abandoned his intention to support Reno from the rear. His command was doomed as soon as it rode down the river. If he, with *five* companies, was unable to even *reach* the river, what chance had Reno, with *three,* to charge through the camp? The idea is absurd. There were enough Indians there to defeat the whole Seventh Cavalry, just as Crook had been defeated the week before at the Rosebud fight.

Was Crook a "cowardly poltroon" because he, realizing that they [the Indians] were too strong for his force—much larger than the Seventh Cavalry and not divided into far-separated detachments—withdrew? And there were fewer Indians against Crook than were then against the Seventh, for several large bands had joined Sitting Bull during that week.

I don't think you can compare Forsyth's Beecher Island fight with the Little Big Horn fight, at all. Forsyth's men were all picked men, while the Seventh was from thirty to forty percent raw recruits, who had never been in the field before. Forsyth, moreover, was entirely alone, cornered, and had to fight to the death, whether or no. Reno *could* get out, and had a chance at least to rejoin the rest of the regiment. The two situations are in no sense comparable.

Now, Captain, put yourself in Reno's place for a minute. Just forget all you know of what happened *afterward,* and confine your estimate to the situation as it had developed up to the time he made his retreat.

What are the facts?

Custer's order was, "Take as rapid a gait as you think prudent and charge afterwards; and the whole outfit will support you." That's the only order he ever got. He starts, reaches the river, and sends word twice to Custer that "the enemy is in force in my front." Nothing comes back from Custer. Reno has every reason to believe that Custer is following him in support. He gets down the valley two miles from his crossing. He finds himself confronted by a force of Indians which outnumbers him ten to one. He can see that the village is an immense one, and that there are hordes of Indians in the distance. His scouts, who form his left flank, run, as soon as the Sioux attack. His left flank is in the air, and the Sioux by hundreds are massing there and to his rear.

I concede that he might have gone on, just as the Light Brigade went on at Balaklava. But the promised support was not coming, as everyone could see. To go on meant that in less than a minute he would be in the midst of a thousand warriors, which you aptly describe as "the finest light cavalry in the world." They were not only ready for him, but inviting him to continue his advance. His little command wouldn't have lasted five minutes if he had gone a thousand yards further. It would have been utter lunacy to have gone on.

When he halted, remember, Custer was on his way down the river, on the other side. He was not attacked for a good half hour after Reno halted and dismounted. If Reno had charged into the village, his command would have been wiped out and gone the better part of a half hour before Custer reached the point where the Sioux met him. His failure to charge, therefore, could not and did not have any bearing whatever on what happened to Custer. Its only result was to prevent the annihilation of his [Reno's] own battalion.

What did he do next?

He formed a skirmish line, dismounted, and that line advanced a hundred yards or more, and until the nearest tepees were within range, for many of his bullets reached them. As soon as he did this, the Indians massed against his left flank, and came into the timber, where he had put his horses, from right flank and rear.

What did he do then?

He took G Troop off the line and put it in the timber to protect the horses, and Moylan (A Troop) extended to the right to fill the gap. And this extension made the line so weak that the left flank was crushed in, and he was forced to change front, and bring the line in to the edge of the timber.

So far, certainly, he has done nothing that indicates cowardice and poltroonery. He has preserved his command from utterly useless and senseless sacrifice, and has it in a position where the support, which Custer had promised, can reach it. I call that good leadership, so far. Can you find any flaw in it? I think not.

How long did he stay out in the open, in skirmish line?

You know how long military movements take. Figure it out. Could it have taken less than fifteen or twenty minutes to do the things he did? He did all these things—not one right after another as if on a schedule, but as the necessity for them developed. You have had long experience in handling troops. I have had a little myself. But we both know that situations do not develop, nor are troop movements made, in an instant.

What next?

He is on the bench now, his men along the edge of the timber, as far as they will reach. So far, only one casualty. He finds that he has not enough men to cover the position and keep the Indians out of the timber. If he puts his men at the long intervals necessary to line the edge of the timber, they will be so far apart as to be beyond supporting distance—and also beyond control of his officers. The Indians are creeping up along the front; they are slipping into the woods on the right, and from the rear. He is being fired on from all sides, *and Custer's promised support still does not come!*

I grant you that Forsyth, with his picked and experienced men, might have held that timber as long as their ammunition lasted, and that they would not have wasted ammunition. But do you think it was possible to exercise any great fire-control—always a difficult thing, even with the best of troops—over a command that was forty per cent raw recruits, every one of whom was probably scared stiff!

All the time—and don't lose sight of this—Reno and his officers and men expected to see Custer come charging through from the rear. They had no reason to believe that he would not do what his order promised. They had no reason to be very sparing of ammunition, so far as they knew; and there would have been no need of it had Custer supported the attack.

How long was Reno in the timber?

It is hard to tell; but at least as long as he was on the plain. And long enough to become convinced (from the fact that in every direction from which support could come, the country was full of Indians), that Custer was not coming!

He made up his mind to get out and go where

he had a chance to save his command, and to connect with other parts of the regiment. For this you condemn him!

Well, let's see: If he had stayed there half an hour longer (if not wiped out by that time), Benteen's command would have come along, following Custer's trail (not Reno's) and might, or might not, have discovered where he was. But don't overlook the fact that Reno didn't know that Benteen was coming; and Benteen, on the other hand, didn't know that Reno was across the river, in the timber.

By the time Benteen could have crossed the river and gotten to where Reno was, if he had stayed there, it would have been at least as late in the afternoon as when Benteen did join him on the hill, or after 4:00. Probably later, as Benteen would have had to fight his way through.

By the time that the remnants of Benteen's battalion had joined him (conceding that he could have cut his way through), he must have used much of his ammunition, lost some horses and had some casualties. Upon joining Reno (after 4:00) the two together might have made a charge into the village, leaving their wounded in the timber.

Suppose they had done so. Custer was already hotly engaged, and had been for some time, and was at least three miles away, on the other side of the river. The combined force of Reno and Benteen might have created sufficient diversion in Custer's favor to have drawn from him a part of the Indian force. Whether it could have been done soon enough to have saved any considerable part of Custer's command, is problematical, and I think rather doubtful. I think most of Custer's command was dead by the time it was possible for Benteen to have joined Reno in the timber (conceding for the sake of speculation that he would have tried to do so).

You say in your comments that you do not think it possible to have done anything for Custer after Benteen and Reno united on the hill. How, then, would it have been possible to do anything more, had Reno remained in the timber and Benteen had joined him there, after fighting his way through? The time element, to say nothing of others, is more unfavorable to the chance in the latter case than in the former.

No, Captain, I don't think it was "in the cards," however played, to have saved Custer's command. From the time he divided the regiment and separated the various detachments so widely, without any plan for co-operation, what happened was bound to happen. The enemy was too strong

—too cohesive—too confident—too well equipped. The Seventh Cavalry could not have beaten them.

Supposing, however, that Benteen had joined Reno in the timber, and the two together had charged into the village. They had at least *two miles of village* to go through before reaching a point anywhere near Custer, *whose whereabouts they did not know and could not have known.*

It is within the bounds of possibility, I grant you, that the Indians *might* have left what remained of Custer's command, if any, to oppose them. And what was then left of Custer's command (if they had any horses, ammunition or spirit left), *might* have crossed the river and tried to fight through to the south. What chance would either force have had to fight through to the other?

And in the meantime, what would have become of the packtrain which had *all* of the reserve ammunition?

But Reno didn't stay in the timber—so all this speculation is beside the point. I have merely called to your attention some grave objections to your assumption that *if* he had remained there, and *if* Benteen had joined him there, and *if* together they had charged the village, it *might* have saved Custer's battalion.

When Reno decided to get out and re-cross the river, both you and General Godfrey seem to be under the belief that he made a break, and that officers and men followed, helter-skelter, each man for himself. But this is very far from the fact, unless again all the military witnesses at Chicago deliberately perjured themselves. Wallace, Hare, Moylan and Varnum all describe what was done—how the word was passed to get to the horses—how the companies were formed in the clearing—how the Indians who had gotten into the timber fired into them point-blank, killing Bloody Knife at Reno's side, and mortally wounding another; how they broke from the timber and formed on the plain in column of fours, and with pistols drawn, cut their way to the river. It's all in that testimony, and perfectly clear, if you read it with an unbiased mind.

And I am free to say, that in my opinion, based upon the most careful and painstaking study, with no reason in the world to be biased one way or the other, Reno, up to the moment that Bloody Knife was shot down by his side, and the Sioux fired a point-blank volley into his troops, had done only what a commander should have done in the circumstances.

At that point, however, he became excited and lost his head. He broke out of the woods, instead of waiting to collect all his men—many of whom, belonging to G Troop, were scattered through the timber; and once out, the companies were hastily formed in columns and the retreat began.

And it was just as I have described it. The head of the column reached the river in very good order; but along the length, what with the Indians firing into it, it became a rout, a panic at the rear.

And what happened to Reno's column on this retreat gives you a very fair picture of what would have happened to Benteen's, had he tried to cut through to Reno in the timber (supposing Reno to have remained there.)

The character of the retreat is the only thing that can rightly be charged against Reno. And even that, the evidence showed, was intended by him, and understood by everybody, to be a charge, to cut through the surrounding enemy and gain contact with the regiment.

The most that can fairly be charged against Reno is that he became excited and lost his head when this charge or retreat began; that he failed to cover his crossing and temporarily lost control of his men. That much is true. But to blame him for the disaster to Custer is not only unfair and unnecessary, but, in the light of the demonstrated and demonstrable facts, most unjust.

Sincerely yours,

(*Signed*) W. A. GRAHAM.

To Capt. R. G. Carter, Ret'd.
Army & Navy Club
Washington, D. C.

———

25 March 1925

My dear Colonel Graham:—

In view of the testimony of the officers of the 7th Cavalry as shown in the abstract which you have furnished me, and which I read several years before, all of which you have had before you for reference for more than 3 years, your argument would seem to be almost unanswerable unless, as you say, I "discredit" their testimony as being willful, premeditated perjury.

That is just the point. While I do not think that these witnesses intended to wilfully perjure themselves, or not to tell what they thought might be the truth before that Court, I do most emphatically discredit their statements, and in view of what I myself have heard and read from equally credible witnesses, I am sure they did not tell the *whole truth;* and I also believe that it was predetermined among themselves after their previous discussions about Reno's conduct in the Post Trader's store at Fort Abraham Lincoln, when it had become known that the regiment was being assailed by the press and people on all sides. Reno was being ostracized to the extent that he felt forced to demand a Court of Inquiry, and the stigma of cowardice was likely to be attached to their regimental colors and guidons, and handed down to future generations as a part of the history of the United States Army. Since that testimony at the Reno Court and the finding was promulgated—notwithstanding much adverse criticism since—and many damaging facts which have since come to light, the regiment has been known as the "Fighting Seventh."

It never has appeared that those officers who testified at that Court were ever cross-examined by anybody as to anything they were trying to hold back. The testimony clearly shows that they were doing this very thing. While they may have felt that they were telling the truth so far as it went, not one of them *volunteered* to tell the *whole truth,* as conditions and facts have since developed—so long as no one asked them to do so. This, of course, was not wilful or premeditated perjury, and I make no such charge, or accuse them of so doing. But, do you now consider that they *did tell the whole truth* in the light of what *you yourself now know,* and as they *might* and probably *would have done,* being under oath, had you yourself as a Judge Advocate been there conducting the case, to bring it out by a drastic course of cross questioning, and as you yourself know and as I know has generally been the policy at any Court of Inquiry or General Court Martial. Even Godfrey expected to be recalled to give additional testimony, but found that the Court had closed and adjourned. Of course in its finding no Court Martial was found necessary or for the best interests of the service, therefore the *whole truth* has long been buried in oblivion. Why does Hare pay no attention to your letters? Why is Edgerly so mealy-mouthed, even to me, his own classmate?

I simply discredit, I repeat, the testimony of these officers—after knowing of their daily conversations in the Post Trader's store at Fort Lincoln, the ostracizing of Reno for nearly 3 years, or until he felt compelled to ask for a Court of Inquiry, and then their going as a body before that Court and testifying just exactly to the reverse of what their talk had been. Even Benteen testifying in Reno's favor.

I feel that if they had been properly cross-examined, his (Benteen's) act in throwing down the Chicago paper in the train when he was travelling with Godfrey to Chicago, and in which paper was a bitter article accusing the entire 7th Cavalry outfit of cowardice, would have been brought out; also, the story that he (Benteen) told Godfrey—his *"most amazing"* story—five years later, of how Reno came to him at night (25th) and proposed to abandon their works, leaving the wounded to their fate, etc., and Benteen's reply to him (Reno); also, the charge made by some of the packers, whose testimony was discredited, and is now discredited by you yourself, that Reno was drunk while they were besieged by the Indians; also, the conversations which took place between Weir and Reno as to his (Reno's) conduct. All of these matters *could* and *should* have been brought out. If one set of witnesses were to be discredited, then all, in view of what occurred, both during and after the fight should have been drawn out. Don't you think so? I was not so persistent in my comments in urging that Reno should have gone on into the village when he was directed to make his charge; but if he found that he could not do so without subjecting his command to annihilation he should have remained in the timber as his only salvation. But he could only have done this by a different disposition of his battalion. You admit that it was scattered instead of holding the edge of same and that he exercised no fire control. You also admit that when he formed column outside of the timber for his "charge" to the rear, he left those scattered units in there. That shows then that he had no knowledge of where they were, or in his haste to get out, that he gave any thought of whether he was or was not abandoning them. It was like abandoning ship—*every one for himself.*

I asked you once if you had ever seen Curtis' story. I think you said "no." (It is "The North American Indian, Vol. 3, pp. 44-49). You can get this at the Newberry Library. His is the most detailed account, as shown by the Indians he had on the ground, of every movement of Custer's after he left Reno. According to him the Indians had not engaged Custer before Reno left the timber—not until Reno took his position on the bluff and Benteen had joined him; and Gall seeing him comfortably disposed of, left his front and swarmed down to the fords and not only cut off Custer, but crossing herded him up on the hill.

General Miles tells me the same thing (March 22) that when he went over the ground after the battle with some of the chiefs who were in the fight and afterwards surrendered to him, they pointed out all the places where both Reno and Custer went, and emphatically stated that had Reno stayed in the timber, or made a sortie from the edge nearest the village, or had Benteen joined him (Reno) there and both made an attack from the timber upon the upper end of the village; or had Benteen followed Custer's trail after Custer's message reached him and attacked the center across one of the fords while Reno made his attack from the timber (all of this, of course, on the supposition that Reno held on to his position in the timber and held his command well in hand) —in any one or all of these eventualities, they (the Indians) told General Miles, they were prepared to get out, abandon their village and make for the Bad Lands. He (General Miles) also stated to me that they told him that they did not attack Custer where and when you state (I don't know where you get this) with from 2000 to 3000 Indians, while at least 1000 were holding Reno in the timber; but not until Reno had gone back in his headlong flight from the timber to the bluffs and Benteen had joined him, making it safe for Gall to leave Reno's front to go down and attack Custer, —(I had always supposed that was originally your own belief)—for Custer had not gone to any point near enough to the river, or to any ford where it was supposed he intended to cross, for his attack.

You will doubtless recall what Colonel (?) Shields stated in his book. "The Blanket Indian," Chapter 3, pp. 33-47, where he claims that he talked with several officers of the 7th who told him that they clearly heard the firing for some time when Custer was being headed off, and after Benteen had joined Reno on the bluff, but that they had agreed that on account of their hatred of him not to go to his rescue. (I am not now attempting to quote Shields' exact language.) Of course I not only discredited Shields' statement, believing it to be a barefaced lie, absolutely incredible, but when I wrote and told him this and asked for the names of those officers to clear up an almost unheard of situation in the annals of our army, he offered the lame excuse that in the lapse of time he could not possibly recall their names. I called him a "traducer" and left him to chew his cud.

Perhaps a rigid cross-examination of all who testified at that Court ought and could and should, at least *might* have brought out the truth or perfidious falsehood of this story. Benteen testified just exactly the reverse of his talk with Godfrey, whom he wanted to read the newspapers, which Godfrey refused to do as he wanted to go before the Court with an open mind, without bias or prejudice. Benteen also, you will recall, wanted Godfrey to go to Reno's room in a hotel in Chicago, where he kept "open house," with plenty of cigars and whisky for all those officers who talked *one way* at Fort Lincoln, and when their tongues had been limbered up by Reno's booze, gave testimony such as you have furnished me in that abstract;

Godfrey refused to accept Reno's open handed hospitality.

No, Colonel Graham, all this was a *"cooked up"* and *"cut and dried" affair*—a predetermined effort to save their own faces and protect the honor of the regiment even if they had to conceal Reno's cowardice by white-washing if necessary. Nothing to the contrary was dragged out of them, as would undoubtedly have been, had they all been subjected to a rigid cross-examination. You must remember that at that period—which is far different from the conditions in our army at the present time—there was a very strong regimental *esprit de corps*, an *intense regimental pride*. The 7th Cavalry had been assailed in the public press, its fighting conduct severely criticized all over the country—after the first shock of such astounding news had somewhat abated and Custer's and Terry's friends had sought out the causes—the former's asserting that he had been abandoned, the latter's that he had been unjustly blamed for such a catastrophe.

It does not appear that when Reno left the timber he was leaving it for "a place which he could defend better." He was *heading for the ford where he had crossed, not for the bluffs to which he was forced by the Indians riding along his right flank*. What point did he have in view "which he could defend better," when he was riding pell-mell for the rear to recross that ford? I think Reno was right, as you and others contend, when his left flank was turned, to get into the timber, and I do not think he should have gone in on a charge upon that end of the village just then when he saw the Indians coming up to meet him in such numbers, but waited for events and better conditions; i.e., until he could know where Benteen was and whether it was or was not possible for him (Benteen) to cut his way in and join him. My contention is that his formation in the timber was not only faulty, but that he had no control over his battalion as an organization from start to finish after his first formation, nor any fire control. In other words, I believe he had entirely lost his head as soon as he saw them (the Indians) swarming up, and had then decided to take up a defensive position in that timber. Instead of trying to hold the outer edges of the timber or that post with the *old river bed as a cover*—which, all three Generals, Miles, Gibbon and Godfrey, declare was a perfect defensive work, as also did the Indians later,— he went too far in, lost control, and then, as soon as one man had been killed, became panic stricken and lost his head. General Miles agrees with me in this. If Reno did not know where

Benteen was or where he might be able to connect with him, when he started on his route to the rear—where was he (Reno) going or what did he expect to do in seeking safety for his men by his cowardly flight, when he headed for the ford where he had crossed, but which the Indians forced him away from to the crossing a mile or more away? What was in the back of his head, so far as saving his men was concerned, when he broke towards the ford? Was he to be any safer anywhere along that route to the rear than he would have been by remaining in the timber waiting for the possibility of either Custer or Benteen coming up and joining him?

General Miles still adheres to his original statement that he not only saw the sworn affidavit of Gen. Custer's cook relating to the last conversation between Gen. Terry and himself (Custer), but had it in his possession. I have been told that Mrs. Custer now has it. He also states emphatically that an officer who was with Benteen when he (Benteen) viewed Custer's body, repeated to him (Gen. Miles) that Benteen remarked "There he is, G-d d-n him, he will never fight any more." General Miles says he walked his horse from Reno's position on the bluff to where Custer's body was found in about 30 minutes, at a slow or hand gallop he could have covered the distance in about 10 or 15 minutes. E. S. Curtis gives about the same time.

Very sincerely yours,

/s/ R. G. CARTER,

Captain, U. S. Army, Ret.

P. S. Are the statements of all these parties to whom I have referred to be discredited simply because they have never been sworn, while the testimony of those officers who were before that Court and on their oath, is to be fully credited in the light of all the knowledge we now possess regarding many of the facts connected with the Custer tragedy?

R. G. C.

———

March 30, 1925.

Captain R. G. Carter,
U. S. Army, Retired,
Army and Navy Club,
Washington, D. C.

Dear Captain Carter:

I have received and read your letter of March 25th. I am sorry that I cannot, with my present lights, agree with your views. Even if I were prepared to admit that the witnesses whom I have quoted to you did not tell the whole truth, it would be impossible to follow your reasoning unless I carried it to its only logical conclusion, which would be that in what they did say, they had deliberately lied. It would be out of the question for what they did say to be true in whole or in part, if what you say you have heard from equally credible witnesses is the fact. In other words, the situation which you insist upon is so utterly and totally inconsistent with what these witnesses all testified to that one *must* take the position that they deliberately perjured themselves in order to maintain your position.

I am not willing to do that. I would like to know who are the equally credible witnesses of whom you speak. And I would like to know what they say. In my studies, which you know have been impartial and thorough, I have not found any other equally credible witnesses. The ones I quoted were *all* of the surviving officers who were in the valley fight, except French. I cannot consider any officer *who was not there* an "equally credible witness." Manifestly he is not, whoever he may be. I have talked with a number of the enlisted men who were there, but very little information of value is obtainable from them.

I think that you are in error when you state that the *regiment* was being assailed by the public and the press. I have read reams of contemporary newspaper articles and editorials and have never found any which assailed the *regiment*. On the contrary, all the bitterness, all the criticism and all the disturbance of the atmosphere arose from the implied criticism of Custer contained in Terry's confidential telegram, which was published by General Sherman's mistake, in the Philadelphia papers, July 7, 1876. It was also published, in somewhat garbled form, in the Army and Navy Journal for July 15, 1876. Have you ever read it? The controversy became a personal one between those who admired Custer and those who did not. And, of course, throughout the years it grew by what it fed on and became more bitter as time passed.

I do not understand why General Godfrey should have expected that he would be recalled as a witness. He was given full opportunity to tell everything he knew concerning Reno's conduct. And he said nothing very damaging. The worst he said was that he was "not particularly impressed by Reno's qualifications either as to courage, coolness or efficiency" but he later qualified that by saying *"I do not think Major Reno exhibited cowardice,* rather nervous timidity."

Now Captain, one cannot split hairs on a question of perjury. When General Godfrey swore that "I do not think that Reno exhibited cow-ardice," knowing General Godfrey as I do and as you do, I do not feel justified in thinking that he was swearing to something which he did not believe, or that he knew was not true. And hav-ing sworn as he did I do not see why he should have expected to be recalled. Certainly, having thus committed himself under oath, he did not propose, if recalled, to swear otherwise and thus discredit himself.

You asked why Colonel Hare has never answered any letters. That question I cannot answer; but I think the reason is not that which your letter implies. A short time ago I had a long talk with Mr. W. M. Camp of Chicago. Among other things he told me that years ago he had a long interview with Hare, who gave him his own story of what happened in the valley. He said that Hare told him that he was unwilling, so long as Mrs. Custer was alive, to talk for pub-lication about the battle of the Little Big Horn; and he did not want Camp to make use of any-thing he said. He told Camp that *in his opinion General Custer was to blame for the entire dis-aster,* but because of the great regard he held for Mrs. Custer, he would not permit himself to be quoted to that effect.

Camp told me this; and I tell you: but I do not want you to make any use of it as Colonel Hare's wishes should be respected until and un-less he himself removes his objection.

There are some things to which you allude in your letter which it appears to me are irrelevant to the subject. One of them is the testimony of the packers that Reno was drunk during the night of the 25th of June. You say that I discredit it. In that you are mistaken. I neither credit nor discredit it for, to my mind, even if Reno was drunk as a Lord during the time they claimed he was drunk, the fact would not have the slight-est significance in scanning his conduct in the valley. Neither do I see what significance Ben-teen's remark (if he made it), over Custer's body can have. Benteen hated Custer, everybody knew it, and I have no doubt that whether he said it or not, he at least thought it. But it is too mon-strous a supposition for any reasonable being to hold that because Benteen hated Custer he was willing to sacrifice the lives of 225 other men whom he did not hate; some of whom were his best friends, in order to "get" Custer. That is to ascribe to him the character of a wholesale murderer.

You mention the affidavit of Mary Adams, Custer's negro cook. I have read it and know something of its history. I enclose you a copy of it. It was taken before a gentleman who is now President of the Northwestern Life Insurance Company at St. Paul and who was, in 1877, a Notary Public at Bismarck. I have corresponded with him. I tell you frankly that I do not attach any importance whatever to this affidavit. In my opinion, it is incredible; and the very fact that it was kept secret and concealed until after Gen-eral Terry's death is enough alone to cast sus-picion upon it if not to discredit it as evidence of anything. I would not send a dog to the pound on that kind of evidence. I could not find out, for Flannery does not remember, who brought Mary Adams to him, but in my opinion, it has all the ear-marks of a deliberately framed tale made for the purpose of excusing Custer's failure to follow the instructions which Terry set out in detail in his confidential telegram to Sheridan. And unless one thinks that Terry was a man who did not know his own mind and could not ad-here to any plan for more than a few minutes it must be conceded that after having given to both Custer and Gibbon explicit instructions as to what he expected them to do in a cooperative movement he would not within a few minutes tell Custer to do whatever he might think best. To me, the proposition is so absurd as to be un-worthy of consideration. Perhaps General Miles can tell you something about the origin of this affidavit. He had it in his possession a long time, but I do not know where he got it, or how, or when. See if he will tell you about it.

You allude to conversations between Weir and Reno. Can you tell me what they were? General Edgerly has talked to me very freely. From him I gathered that Weir's supposed attitude has been greatly misrepresented. He was Weir's own Lieu-tenant and he knew what Weir's ideas were. It was freely asserted about the time of the Court of Inquiry and there were some letters published in the Philadelphia papers at the time which stated in plain terms, that Frederick Whittaker, whose letter to Congress caused Reno to ask for the Court of Inquiry, had endeavored by every means possible to get Weir, while on recruiting duty in New York, to accuse Reno: and that Weir complained bitterly about it and refused. I have tried to run this down but both Weir and Whittaker are dead.

You ask where I get the idea that Custer was attacked before Reno left the timber. I got it from the testimony of Trumpeter Martin, the stories told by the Indians and what seems to me the inevitable logic of the situation. Unless Custer stood still for three quarters of an hour, he must have reached the point where the Sioux met him, before Reno retreated. Martin left him more than two miles down the river from the point at which he left Reno's trail, and he was then proceeding to turn toward the river. His fight commenced about a mile and a half from the point where Martin left him. Martin reached Benteen when the latter was at least two miles from the hill to which Reno retreated. You cannot piece together these circumstances and facts with the times and distances without seeing that unless Custer sat down somewhere and waited for three quarters of an hour or so his fight must have commenced within five or ten minutes of the time that Martin left him. The story of Mrs. Spotted Horn Bull and her husband, which is generally considered to be the most accurate of the Indian accounts, makes the claim that the bulk of the Indian forces were waiting for Custer in the ravines and gulleys on the other side of the river and that he rode directly into an overpowering ambush. She says that the Indians were watching Custer for some time before his column turned toward the river and that they were fully prepared for him. It was Reno's attack at the southern end of the village that they were not looking for but there were enough of them near the southern end to hold him. McLaughlin's account, which he says is derived from hundreds of Indians who were present, corroborates this. He says Crazy Horse and the Cheyennes crossed the river and laid in ambush. DeRudio, who was left in the timber, and therefore had the best chance to observe, testified that those of the Indians who left Reno, did so *after* the heavy firing was heard down river. How long before the retreat the firing commenced, no one can tell; obviously a very few minutes—but Reno's command, being in action, would not be able to hear it.

I talked twice with General Miles and I have read Curtis' account. I do not think that all the Indians support General Miles' views; although as to both General Miles and Curtis I am conscious of the fact that it is difficult to imagine any account which will not find more or less support from some of the stories told by some of the Indians. The fact is that it is difficult, if not impossible, to reconcile the statements that they make. No two of them tell the same story. It is undoubtedly true that that part of the Indians who defeated Reno did not take part in the fight on Custer until after Reno's retreat. But they, as I have said, were only about 25% of the force. Were the other three quarters doing nothing? Those who opposed Reno were largely Hunk-

papas and Blackfeet. Those who began the attack on Custer were the Cheyennes, Minneconjous and Ogalallas. Gall rode with a band of warriors half the length of the camp after Reno attacked and it was his arrival that crushed in Reno's left. And as soon as Reno retreated, Gall went immediately back to where the fight on Custer had already begun. So I read the riddle.

One striking example of the unreliability of Indian accounts is furnished by the fact that when Gall left Reno some of his warriors told the people at the other end of the camp that they had killed all of Reno's men, and to this day many of the Sioux believe that. And you will find in the stories of many of them, the statement that all of the soldiers who attacked the southern end of the village were killed and that not one got back across the river alive. Mrs. Spotted Horn Bull says that, for one; and I have read numerous others to the same effect.

I can see, however, that I have a long job on my hands if I ever convince you, but I am not discouraged on that account. I am only afraid that when I do convince you, as I know I will sooner or later, you will be "a man convinced against his will."

Sincerely yours,
W. A. GRAHAM,

—— — —

7 April, 1925.

My dear Colonel Graham:

I have received your last two letters of March 30 and April 3, the last referring to Varnum's testimony, also Benteen's letter. I am not going now to try and "convince a man against his will," but merely point out to you several apparent inconsistencies in some of your conclusions, and try to place the onus of "splitting hairs" upon you rather than to admit that charge myself.

You state that you do not understand why General Godfrey should have expected that he would be recalled as a witness, etc., as he had already testified that "I do not think Major Reno exhibited cowardice, rather *nervous timidity*,"— and then you add: * * * "When General Godfrey swore to that, 'I do not think that Reno exhibited cowardice,'—knowing General Godfrey as well as I do and as you do, I do not feel justified in thinking that he was swearing to something which he did not believe, or that he knew was not true, and having sworn as he did I do not see why he should have expected to be recalled. Certainly having thus committed himself under oath, he did not propose, if recalled, to swear otherwise and thus *discredit* himself."

Now here is just where the "hair splitting" comes in. He did not intend to *discredit* himself had he come back and emphatically declared his belief that Reno was a coward. He had already used the synonymous words—"nervous timidity," —and it was his intention, as I believe *(he has never declared this to me)* to use the other word —"cowardice."

Now, Colonel, look at your Webster's Unabridged Dictionary for the two definitions of *coward* and *cowardly*. The first is "one who shrinks from *duty* or *danger;* one who *yields to fear;* a *poltroon;* to *make afraid.* Cowardly: *lacking courage* to *face danger; fearful; timid; pusillanimous.* Cowardice: the state of *being a coward;* or of giving way to *fear.*

I have known Godfrey for 60 years and I had rather accept his version of Reno's cowardice, viz: "nervous timidity," and Webster's definitions as I have quoted them to you, than I would the testimony of all those officers whom you quote in justifying his (Reno's) conduct, especially Varnum's—who by firing his pistol into the air and by his other acts shows that he himself was sacred almost stiff and juiceless. Reno had communicated his fear to almost all of them, especially when he emerged from the timber and, as you declare, formed a column for his charge to the rear. Tell me, if you please, just how this column could have been formed if there were 1000 Indians, or 25% of all the Indians all about Reno, filtering into the timber, etc., who finally tore down along the right flank of that mob, firing into them at every jump, and killing them all the way to the crossing. I also rather accept Godfrey's judgment and declaration of Reno's "nervous timidity"—synonymous, according to Webster, to "cowardice"—to your own opinion that he (Reno) by his "prudence and sanity" saved what were left of the 7th Cavalry.

I have no doubt, in view of what he (Godfrey) knew of the talk in the Post Trader's store at Fort Lincoln, of his conversation with Benteen on the train going to Chicago, of Reno's keeping open house there where he freely dispensed whisky and cigars to all of the officers who testified before the Court, and to which he (Godfrey) was urgently invited but which he declined for reasons which I have given, that he felt he was almost if not quite alone in the testimony he might give before the Court, based, of course, not so much on his actual knowledge of what took place in the valley both before and during Reno's gallant (?) charge to the rear, but what he himself had heard talked over and what he saw himself of Reno's conduct that night and the

night of the 26th—so he modified the word *cowardly* or *cowardice* to *"nervous timidity,"* intending, if recalled, to use the former word so that there might be no mistake or misunderstanding as to his exact meaning. Consult Webster's definitions and see if you do not think that any man being afflicted with "nervous timidity" in the face of, or in a run out against an enemy, is not a coward, and if they are not synonymous terms which Godfrey alone of that entire bunch trying to shield the conduct of their regiment— now the "Fighting Seventh"—was trying to convey to that Court and which he probably would have done had he been recalled without in any way violating his oath, prejuring himself, or *"discrediting"* his testimony.

General Miles does not hestitate in his talks with me to call Reno's conduct rank cowardice, and I had much rather take his, General Gibbon's and General Godfrey's judgment as to Reno's ability to stay in that timber till h——l froze over—eating his horses if necessary—as "Sandy" Forsythe did on Beecher's Island in 1868, than Hare's, Varnum's and others, who after Reno's *fear, timidity,* or whatever Webster or any one else may term it, had communicated itself to them, to the extent of stampeding them so that they themselves were not loath to get out of that timber and make the charge to the rear with him. That would not do, however, to tell the Court. The question again comes up, however, where in the h——l were they all expecting to go when they headed for the ford, and when they could not see Custer or know where he had gone; could not see Benteen, and, as you have several times declared, had no reason to expect the latter to be near or that either he or Custer could come to their assistance.

Where do we get this stuff—"The Fighting Seventh?" The 4th Cavalry went into Mexico in May 1873, into an unknown desolate country. It marched 160 miles in 32 hours—this a part of the way with a pack train, wounded men, and women and children prisoners, and captured stock, the horses 49 hours under the saddle, and on the way back—after completely destroying three villages with all of their accumulated stores —being harassed by hundreds of Mescalero Apaches and Mexicans, we were four nights without sleep and more than three-fourths of the men were so exhausted that they were half crazy and suffering from delusions and hallucinations, so that the officers—also exhausted—had to ride the column all night, shaking the men in their saddles so that they would not fall off and be captured. And yet, as soon as Lawton met us at the Rio Grande with plenty of rations (we had been feeding on cracker dust and water) and ammunition, we placed ourselves in a defensive position at the ford and dared the raging horde on the other side—then aggregating several thousand—to cross. We were in a critical position and far from our base either at Fort Duncan or Fort Clark, and everybody at the point of a breakdown. Did we weep and put up any sob stuff when Lawton came to our relief? We did not. And yet the "Fighting Seventh" is pictured as going into a frenzy of nervous cry baby stuff when Terry's command came over the hill so that they could see that they were not the dreaded Sioux who had stampeded Reno, annihilated Custer, and corraled the balance for two days and nights.

Varnum must have been far-sighted to have seen a grey troop at the distance he gives. Ordinarily in that country it was difficult to tell the color of horses a half mile away, especially if there was dust. Again—Martin's statement to you would seem to indicate that it Custer could not or did not look down into the valley and see Reno's column, the officers in that command *could not* and *did not* see Custer; or, if so, only for a brief moment,—and not, as Wallace declared, in a swinging of hats or cheering of Reno's command—for Martin told you that the hat swinging was towards his own command. The element of time in this entire riddle, all of which you seem to have worked out with so much precision, is not so conclusive with me, especially after Custer left Reno and until Benteen came up and joined Reno, for no two officers before the Reno Court seemed to give the time alike as to how long Reno was in line, how long in the timber, how long it took them to reach the crossing and up on the bluff, the periods when Benteen came up, or how long the packs were in closing up. I kept the time or tried to, in our Mexican Raid and have always said we halted to cut off the packs only a few minutes. It must have been *nearly an hour if not more.* Time goes "blewy" when men are exhausted and are marching night and day. I consider Varnum's testimony as of little or no value *knowing him as well as I do.* Here is where my knowledge of some of those officers, and the personal equation makes me discredit their testimony.

In writing all this I have never sought to put the blame for Custer's disaster upon Reno. I do not now, for that would be, as you have previously stated, "not only unfair and unnecessary, but in the light of demonstrated and demonstrable facts, most unjust."

I put that tragical affair just where you yourself and where now you say Hare puts it in his conversations with Mr. Camp—directly upon Custer for not informing any of his officers of his plans, if he had any, so that they could have cooperated with him; and when he told Reno he would support him and then when he suddenly changed his mind, if he was going to follow Reno—as Reno naturally expected—in not telling the battalion commanders his exact reasons for the change. Gen. Miles agrees with me in this.

In quoting Mary Adams' affidavit, and Benteen's remark upon viewing Custer's body, etc., it was done with no idea of changing either your own views or mine upon the salient points as they have been revealed or to insinuate for a moment that Benteen's hatred for Custer would have caused him to halt a rescue of Custer had it been possible for it to have been done. Custer by separating himself by miles from his other units invited the disaster which inevitably befell him. In this we both quite agree as I now understand the riddle.

Mary Adams' affidavit makes no change whatever in so far as concerns Custer's disobeying Terry's letter of instructions. Custer *did not disobey them* as Benteen declares in his letter to his wife. I am not so sure but what Benteen is right in his surmise that Custer did cross some of his advance into the village and was wiped out before he could retreat, or the balance of his command could cross to his support. In this the Indians have never quite agreed. The finding of Porter's coat, Sturgis' underclothes, and several heads in the village would indicate this, besides shod tracks in "double column of fours," as General McClernand tells me, were found at the ford. Of course that alone would not be proof since that trail might have been made by captured animals being driven back by the Indians across that same ford. Whatever is mere conjecture I am willing to eliminate from the problem.

In your last letter (April 3) you use Varnum's testimony to "bear out my theory that Custer was attacked before Reno's retreat began." In your letter of March 30 you do not refer to this as a "theory" but that you "got it from the testimony of Martin, the stories told by the Indians and what seems to be the *logic* of the situation." Again, later on you say you are "conscious of the fact that it is difficult to imagine any account which will not find more or less support from some of the stories told by some of the Indians. The fact is that it is difficult, if *not impossible,* to reconcile the statements that they make—*no two tell the same story."* Then, in other words, any support of your "theory" seems inconclusive, even this last of Varnum's that "General Custer must have been in action before Benteen joined Reno." His guess then was the same as other guesses. He does not state it as a fact. Not all of the officers on the bluff with Reno seemed to have heard the firing where Custer then was. Weir did, for he moved without orders towards that point, believing that the balance would closely follow him. *This was after Benteen joined.* If, as Varnum states, Custer was in action before Benteen joined, why was it that nobody heard the firing or that Weir himself upon hearing it started his troop towards it, before Reno could gather his wits?

I do not agree with you that because Custer committed the fatal error of not disclosing his plan to his battalion commanders and thus securing cooperation between his fighting units, that Indians proved themselves such superior strategists or tacticians, any more than I believe that because General Hooker got drunk at Chancellorsville and jeopardized the safety of his entire army it brought "Stonewall Jackson" to the fore as the greatest military genius in either the Union or Confederate armies. Indians knew little of strategy or tactics but relied upon wily stratagems, ruses, trickery, treachery, ambushes, etc., and having thousands of fresh ponies, could out march a pursuing enemy and could concentrate quicker, but that was all. What a force of good fighting white troops needed more than anything else was a leader with guts, fighting spirit, resourcefulness, and a cabeza on him that was not afflicted with "nervous timidity." Such was "Sandy" Forsythe.

Sincerely yours,
(s) R. G. CARTER
Captain, U. S. A., Ret.

N. B.:

I have just read Benteen's marginal note where he expresses the belief that Custer *never did get into the village.* I had not seen this before.

P. S.

Since writing the foregoing and after quoting the substance of my correspondence with you relating to the Custer tragedy to a Brigadier General of the Army now retired, and my absolute belief that the testimony of those officers you have quoted to me who went before that Court is not only worthless but, in view of what has come to light since the battle of the Little Big Horn, should be utterly discredited, he volunteered to tell me that in conversation with one of those officers he was told by him that *they had all agreed to tell but one story.* This general officer declined to give me the name of that officer, saying, "he is dead," and "it would now serve no good purpose, especially as Mrs. Custer is yet living." This is practically the same reason for your wishing me to hold back the statement which Mr. Camp says he got from Hare, and which Camp gave to you with an injunction. This general is an absolutely reliable man and I can have no reason for discrediting his story. The fact is that I have always believed those officers went to Chicago pledged to give that testimony in order to uphold the good name and honor of their regiment. In this they have thus far succeeded and pinned the proud name "The Fighting Seventh" to their regimental colors and guidons, but I believe a stiff cross-examination might have brought out the *"whole truth."* Your hope in trying to save Reno's name from the stigma of cowardice will, I fear, my dear Colonel Graham, result in a "forlorn hope" and in your well written story of the Custer Fight I would not go so far as you have, based merely upon such evidence.

Colonel Merrill (son of former Col. Lewis Merrill of the 7th Cavalry), is the man who told me that when he was a boy of about sixteen he frequently heard the officers of the 7th in the Post Trader's store discussing the details of the battle. Their principal subject of conversation was the cowardice of Reno. I have never heard Godfrey say that he himself heard them talk that *but he was well informed that such was the fact.*

Why has no officer of the 7th Cavalry ever defended the honor of his regiment by demanding of this so-called Colonel (?) Shields, who wrote "The Blanket Indian of the Northwest," and branding his statement as a lie and himself as a traducer, after he had put in cold type his alleged conversations with several of them that they plainly heard the firing from Reno's position in the direction of Custer's command, but had agreed among them that they *would not go to his relief on account of their hatred of him.* I have given you the chapter and page. There has always been a "nigger in the woodpile" all through that Custer battle riddle, which, as certain facts come to light, seem very obvious, in view of the strange importance which you as a lawyer seem to attach to such testimony as you have quoted, and which you believe cannot be discredited unless willful perjury is charged. Many a woman's honor has been defended and saved by *a part of the truth,* but not the *whole truth* being told. The honor of the "Fighting Seventh" Cavalry was bound to be saved in the same way.

Sooner or later "murder will out." This will, perhaps seem almost unbelievable; really unthinkable, but in my experience of nearly 80 years wrestling with the problems of life nothing now today seems *impossible*.

R. G. C.

(COPY TO CARTER)

Cooperstown, N. Y.,
April 16, 1925.

Dear Colonel Graham:

I have read your story of the Custer fight with a great deal of interest.

It shows great care and is I believe as nearly accurate as it is possible to make it at this late day.

I wish to call your attention to Reno's conduct after we joined him on the hill. He was greatly excited at that time but soon calmed down and from that time showed no undue excitement or fear. I hate to see him carried down in history as a coward for I am not at all sure that he was altho' his conduct was by no means heroic. The greater part of the time the Indians were shooting from a long distance and there was no reason why any officer should do much walking around. All the walking that I saw the gallant Benteen do was from his line to Reno's and that lasted but a few minutes.

Benteen at that time thrilled us with admiration but the men were not demoralized and obeyed every order promptly. Some men slept during the lulls and there wasn't a sign of panic. In fact I was very proud of them and my high estimate of the valor of the American soldier dates from that fight.

I have never spoken of the "Custer massacre" but always of the "Custer disaster" and am glad you handled it the way you did.

I wish you could see your way to state that Custer found the trail of the village told of by Bradley, that it was approximately about the size estimated by him, that we had no means of knowing or reason for suspecting that it had been reinforced by thousands and finally that upon nearing the village he had every reason to believe the Indians were running away.

* * *

With kindest regards believe me,
Sincerely yours,
W. S. EDGERLY.

23 April 1925.

My dear Colonel Graham:

Your notes on Reno's conduct, while you have materially changed them, still seem inconsistent to me or can not be reconciled with other parts of your story. Reno never had any *leadership*, either in the timber, after he began his retreat, or after he got up on the bluff—before or after Benteen joined him. You still stick too closely to the testimony of those officers who since they *agreed* as to what they should state before they went before that Reno Court, and for other reasons which I have given you, I utterly discredit. You state that up to the time of his retreat, in the opinion of his officers Reno exercised "*proper* discretion and *good leadership* and that the disposition and movements ordered by him were correct and requisite to meet the military situation." From that time on, however, it seems clear to you that "he *lost his head and with it all control of his men.*"

At just what time do you fix this most important period of Reno's cowardice, "nervous timidity," or whatever Webster, Godfrey or I choose to term it, and which now you yourself declare you "personally believe he showed the white feather." Just a little further on you seem to fix it by this statement:—"When Bloody Knife was killed at his side he became *startled* and *unnerved*." "His formations were made with *undue* haste," etc. Well then, all this occurred before he left the timber in his retreat or headlong flight and rout to the rear, and yet you have stated that officers testified that Reno coolly formed his column outside of the timber for his gallant(?) charge towards the ford which he had crossed. How in the h——l could he form a column for a charge to the rear in the face of 1,000 yelling, shooting Indians whom you state were all about him and filtering in and firing into the timber if he had already become "startled and unnerved" by Bloody Knife being shot by his side while he was already in and protected as much as any Indian fighter could expect to be by the merciful sheltering timber? You say now that "perhaps the Indians gave way long enough for him to do that when he (Reno) broke out of the woods." Colonel Graham, those Indians seeing that Reno was *unnerved* and fleeing from the timber would never do that. They would do just what they did do—both to Reno and to Custer—*close in* and *shoot* and *club* them to death. If they had stopped long enough to form a column none would have reached the crossing. You overleap and overstraddle yourself here by your persistent efforts to stick so closely to Hare's, Varnum's, Wallace's and other discredited officers' testimony of the "Fighting Seventh."

You have, through the testimony of those officers, carefully fixed the time of Custer's, of Benteen's and John Martin's movements; also of the possible attack on Custer before Reno left the timber. Now you need definitely to fix the time when Reno lost his head, when he first became afflicted with "nervous timidity," when he lost control of his men, and became panic stricken, not only while he stayed in the timber, but after he left it, formed column and made his cowardly, yellowstreaked run and rout to the rear.

Have had a long letter from Godfrey; am sending you his letter, which please return. Varnum's *opinion* as to Custer having been attacked before Reno left the timber, carries no weight with me. You may call all of my statement of facts which have developed since the fight, as *hearsay evidence,* but they are as good as *Varnum's opinion* and much better than all the testimony of those officers who, after they had drank up Reno's whiskey and smoked his cigars went before that Court and testified to what they had previously agreed on.

You will observe that Godfrey says Girard told him that but two or three Indians (bold warriors) ever "filtered" into the timber from either side of the river while Reno was in there. He also tells me a good deal more about what occurred at Reno's room in Chicago when he kept an open house; also says that some of those who signed the petition at the Soldiers Home here in Washington denied that they ever signed it until shown their signatures. Can you send him the photostat letter of Benteen's which I returned to you?

I do not see how Varnum was able to mark on Curtis' map the exact point at which he saw "momentarily" the front and rear of the Gray Horse Troop as it was disappearing over the ridge. Curtis marks on this same map—"Custer's route over this ground unknown," and Godfrey found a trail *still further* to the north which he firmly believed Custer took and which would have made it still further impossible for Varnum to have seen the color of that troop with the naked eye. I am not so sure that it was Wallace who said he saw Custer's column, the waving of the hat or heard the cheers, but it was seen by somebody *with glasses,* at the point and at the time Martin states Custer *waved his hat to his own men.*

I do not believe, from the picture you have drawn in your finely constructed story, and the sworn testimony which you have offered of those officers who went before the Reno Court, that the average reader of today, totally ignorant of Indian warfare, can come to but one conclusion, unless these other facts can be given to them in the shape of notes, as Godfrey and myself have been giving them to you; i.e., that Reno was justified in his judgment in doing as he did, etc., regardless of whether you paint him as a hero or not, certainly not unless they know fully under just what conditions the testimony of those officers was given. By giving these notes, even if you do consider all of it as "hearsay," you *do not give it as your own opinion,* nor do you yourself *impeach* those officers or declare them to be *perjurers.* The public can still draw their own *"inferences."*

The general reading public would, upon the testimony of these officers, necessarily believe that Reno's exoneration by the Court was a perfectly just finding.

All that part of your story, without including *(not your own opinion)* all these facts which have come to light since the Reno Court, is clearly misleading and falls short of the true history of "Custer's Last Fight." It is perpetuating that kind of history (his—story) which, in my judgment, ought to be corrected *now,* for probably no one will ever write it up again for future generations.

The same applies to Waterloo, Gettysburg, and other great battles, much of the history of which—to my own knowledge—has been the purest *bunk.* Sickles should have been tried for advancing and posting his Corps (3d) in a false position in disobedience of General Meade's orders on the field, thereby jeopardizing our left on July 2, 1863, and he probably would have been had he not lost a leg. But John B. Bachelder, a loud-mouthed, blatant photographer, artist at Sickles' headquarters, and *henchman* of Sickles, made the people believe by an avalanche of propaganda that Sickles held back Longstreet, and all *writers began to believe it* and praised Sickles' act. They know better now and that part of the battle of Gettysburg has been corrected.

* * *

Very sincerely yours,
/s/ R. G. CARTER,
Captain, U.S.A., Ret.

———

HEADQUARTERS
ARMY AND NAVY LEGION OF VALOR OF THE
UNITED STATES OF AMERICA.

Cookstown, New Jersey,
April 14, 1925

My dear "Bob":—
Yours of recent date came yesterday and I

hasten to reply, regretting that I have held the "comments" to give you uneasiness. 1st, I've been sick, and not myself; a lack of ambition, or power to sustain effort. I have been in a state of mind to run down to Walter Reed for removal of polypus in nose; but that has apparently been absorbed, nearly. So much for *excuses.* Please pardon. One other reason was that Graham promised to revise and send me copy. I'm glad he sent one to you. He has evidently had a second thought on several of his conclusions. I endorse every word of your comment.

I took Hare, June 28th, after we had buried the dead, and went down to examine Reno's position in the Valley, the old river bed. I said after explanations, etc. by Hare that Reno could and should have held that position. Hare did not agree with me. Years later General Gibbon told me he had examined the position and came to the same conclusion. General Brisbin in his letters or articles to the Omaha *World Herald* in 1886, said the same thing. That *"filtering"* business that Graham rather emphasises, did not amount to a half dozen Indians, and no attempt seemingly was made to meet it. Girard told me that only two or three Indians were in the timber across the river opposite the old river bed. A sustained, orderly retreat *could* have been made to the bluffs. A similar or analogous situation or condition was presented when Reno had withdrawn to his final position in the afternoon, after leaving three troops to cover his *safe* retirement, and then ordering the three troops to retire to his position nearly *two miles* distant. (One might infer from Graham's article that Weir's troop had been in that position of advance from soon after the meeting of Reno and Benteen and had been in contact with hostiles.) Well, to go back to that retirement:—My troop was the nearest to the main command when Hare came with the order to retire. (See page 25, my pamphlet). Only a few shots were being fired by Weir's and French's troops, but when later they came pell-mell over the hill or ridge (the highest point), I dismounted my troop for a rally of the retreating two troops. Did they rally? Not much! But left me to hold the sack! Fortunately I could hold my men to meet the situation. Now, suppose when I saw French & Edgerly coming pell-mell, I had put spurs to Troop K? Would not "that horde" (as Hare calls the attacking Indians,) have followed right up and into the main command? I had not only the attack to meet, but was harassed by Reno's *repeated* orders "to retire at once." But he made no attempt to give me reinforcement. I had 22

men, after my horse holders had been sent to the position. Did he see any merit in my actions? Weir did, so did Hare. But the contrast with his own retreat from the bottom seemed to incense him—render him insensate.

Graham did not send me a photostat copy of his letter to Mrs. B. Please send me yours and I'll return it at once.

I never heard that there was a compact by officers as to testimony. I only know that I was importuned many times by Benteen, and by others, to call on Reno and visit in his room, drink his whisky and smoke his cigars, etc. I did know by circumstances that there was a lot of drinking going on in his room. I refrained from reading the proceedings of the Court, when I overheard some one express surprise at the testimony given by one witness, which was summarized by "he believes in Reno." So, I did not visit Reno nor read the testimony given *during* the trial.

Graham in his revised copy mentions with approval the signing of petition for Reno's and Benteen's promotion. The fact is that we were so stunned, overcome as it were, from the fatigue and strain of the several days before, during and after the battle, and its results, that we did not *sense* its real importance, nor did we fully coordinate the events. The men were grateful that we had escaped the disaster and the petitions were put before them at the psychological time to gain their signatures. We know how such things can be set in motion. There were several men of the 7th Cavalry at Soldiers Home and in Washington in 1921 & 2, who when asked if they had signed the petition denied ever having had such a thought, yet their signatures proved genuine. Not one would admit that he had signed, till shown his signature.

I hope your comment will be published as well as those of Graham's—which is well written and will command great interest.

Cordially and faithfully yours,

E. S. GODFREY

———

April 29, 1925.

Capt. R. G. Carter,
U. S. Army, (Retired)
Army and Navy Club,
Washington, D. C.

Dear Captain Carter:

I yesterday received a letter from the Department of Justice which indicates that I will probably have to return to Washington for a few days in the near future. If I come on, I shall take pleasure in going over our points of difference with you.

I am sorry that we continue to disagree, but I see no help for it. While I realize, of course, that your comments are all entitled to the greatest weight (and I have, I assure you, very carefully considered them all), yet I cannot accept your view of the situation, because I do not think that you give proper credit and weight to the recorded evidence, while, in my opinion, you give undue weight to what at the best, is nothing more, as it seems to me, but hearsay.

You assume, what I do not by any means agree to, that the testimony of all the officers who testified at Chicago, except Godfrey, *has been discredited*. And even though Godfrey himself testified that he *did not* think Reno exhibited cowardice, you still insist that he meant the same thing, when he said that he did exhibit "nervous timidity." I don't agree to your construction, no matter what the dictionaries may say. To my mind, dictionary or no dictionary, when Godfrey made a distinction as between "cowardice" and "nervous timidity," it clearly shows that in his mind there was a distinction, and therefore one must interpret his testimony in that light. And that is why I say that he could not, had he been recalled, have testified that Reno *did* exhibit cowardice, without stultifying himself and completely discrediting his oath. And I do not believe he would have said anything more or anything different, had he been recalled.

All the officers agreed that Reno was excited and throughout their testimony they make it plain that he was rattled and discomfited; but they drew a distinction between that and cowardice. And I think there is a very clear distinction.

To my mind, whatever my personal opinion, (and it is as I have stated it), the testimony of the men who were there is the best evidence; and until I see some better reason for discrediting what they said than I have so far had, I do not intend to accuse these men of wilful and deliberate perjury.

General Godfrey has never done it in any of his many talks with me; and I do not believe he ever will do it, in the face of his own testimony.

I think my note 12 makes it very plain that Reno's loss of control began when he was forming the command in the clearing, before he rode out of the woods to form on the plain: i.e. when Bloody Knife was killed.

Whatever Girard may have told General Godfrey about the number of Indians who "filtered in," the testimony of Herendeen, (who was one of the strongest witnesses against Reno) is conclusive that they had done so in considerable numbers. And Reno's officers claimed that the "filtering" was due to the fact that the force Reno had was not sufficient to line the edge of the timber, or to cover the position well enough to keep the Indians out.

I am not prepared to say that the Indians knew that Reno was unnerved when he rode out of the timber. Perhaps they thought that he intended to do just what he says he intended to do, charge through them. If so, it would not be strange if they gave back from what looked like a threatening move, just as they gave back when he started for the river.

I never said that he "cooly formed his column outside the timber for his gallant charge etc., etc."—nor anything which even approaches that. What I did say was that he broke out of the timber, the men following him, and that they hastily formed into column—so hastily, indeed, that many of them were left behind, not having heard or understood the order. I am quite willing to be bound by what I did say, but not by what I think a misconstruction of what I said.

General Godfrey is in error about those men at the Soldier's Home. They did *not deny* that they signed the Reno petition. On the contrary, they said they did not *remember* it; and even after I showed them the signatures, which they said were their own, they did not recall it. Certainly there is the widest possible difference between *forgetting* an incident and *denying* that it ever occurred. The General's letter to you rather leaves the impression that they denied having had anything to do with it until confronted by their signatures; which is quite an erroneous impression.

I am not nearly so old as these men were when I talked to them about an incident that had occurred nearly fifty years back: yet when I was called as a witness last year to testify whether or not I had written a certain opinion only three years back, I could not, even when shown the papers, remember it at all. And I have not a weak memory, by any means.

I am doing my level best to have this story right, all the way through, before I let it go out: and it may be that I will still further revise some parts of it: but not by putting in my opinions, which I don't think the proper function of a historian. Too much history has been written that way, and particularly is that true about this particular campaign.

I think the public is entitled to the demonstrated and demonstrable facts, from which each can draw his own conclusions. I may be wrong, but that is the way I feel about it.

I was surprised to learn from General Godfrey's letter that he had probably not received my revised copy. I sent it to him by the same mail that took the copy to you. I have written him about it.

He has already seen the Benteen letter. I showed the original to him at Washington. If he wishes to see it again, I'm perfectly willing to send it.

Of course, the important consideration as to that letter is that it was written less than ten days after the battle; before any controversy had started, and anybody knew that there would be any controversy. And being a private letter to his wife, the circumstances under which it was written remove it from any suspicion of being framed for a purpose. This letter, I may tell you, *was never seen by anyone* outside Benteen's own family, until I persuaded Fred Benteen to show it to me. And so, when Benteen, at that time, charged disobedience to Custer, his accusation carries weight. He had some reason beside his hatred of Custer, for saying it. And the reason was, undoubtedly, that he knew that Custer had not carried out Terry's plan for cooperation between his column and that of Gibbon.

I hope to see you in Washington shortly.

Sincerely yours,

W. A. GRAHAM.

———

The "Sherwood,"
Portland, Me., July 27, 1926.

My dear Col. Graham:

Many thanks for your "Story of the Little Big Horn" upon which you have labored so hard. It is certainly well told, and has been a carefully considered one. In its details and graphic descriptions, it is probably the best story of Custer's battle which has ever been written—and is illuminating throughout the text. After reading over the first M. S. you sent me I was glad to see that you had somewhat modified your first views and have now given it out as a finished product.

Of course, as I told you at first, I have never fully agreed with you as to Reno's conduct—or as to the value of the testimony which the officers of the 7th Cav. gave at the Court of Inquiry in his behalf—and in swearing that they would tell *the truth,* the *whole truth* and *nothing but the truth* after talking as they did about him at Fort Abraham Lincoln and ostracising him to the ex-

tent that he felt compelled to ask for that Court, especially Benteen. Their efforts in withholding "the whole truth" were pitiful in the extreme and, I repeat, I attach no value, or little value to their efforts to shield his cowardice.

Furthermore, I do not agree with Gen. Charles King that this story is now practically a *sealed book* after 50 years of most bitter controversy—or in Gen. Edgerly's "Foreword" that your story "contains all the facts of importance that *will ever be known.*" The members of the O.I.W.* are considering the disposition of Mr. Camp's voluminous notes and data gathered over a period of about 18 years—much of it not transcribed. It may—when Mrs. Camp releases it, go to the His. Branch of the Army War College, there to have the notes transcribed and all of the material edited and co-ordinated. Should that be done, it is my belief that many more facts will come to light than have ever been known because, before his death he told me of much that you have not included in your story, and could not, for you never knew of these facts. To publish them now so soon following upon such an apparently complete and exhaustive study as you have printed and given to the public, would be like throwing a monkey wrench into your pages—but, I believe the time will come when an effort will be made to inject into the story these new facts—for the sake of history—which will throw a new light upon what now seems to be a closed incident. You refer to Gen. Godfrey's testimony before the Reno Court and his words "nervous timidity" in lieu of the word "cowardice." I think I called your attention to the definition of this word in Webster's Unabridged Dictionary.

I note that you yourself on p. 363, use the word as applied to Reno when Bloody Knife was killed—"He became *startled and unnerved.*" You therefore reinforce Gen. Godfrey's words. If he exhibited "nervous timidity" in the face of the enemy—or became "unnerved" as you concede, then according to opinion of all soldiers who have ever been in battle either during the Civil War, or in action with Indians since, he (Reno) had a yellow streak and was a white livered coward long before it became necessary, if he was a coward, to show it before his men. From that time he lost his leadership which he never regained as you practically admit when you praise Benteen for his gallantry and whom you declare saved what was left of "The Fighting Seventh"(?)

Did "Sandy" Forsythe and his scouts show "nervous timidity" or become "unnerved" at

———
* Order of Indian Wars.

Beecher Island? Did the men in the "Wallow Hole Fight" display either? Did Capt. Powell and his men of the 18th Inftry display either in the "Wagon Box Fight"?

And yet, Col. Graham, your story is a fine one in the general summing up of which and conclusions I most unreservedly agree.

There is a Gen. Samuel Miller in the A&N Club—formerly of the 5th Inftry who has recently told me several times that a few years after the fight he was camped on the Little Big Horn for several weeks. He talked with the Cheyennes who were in the fight. Their principal Chief took him to the middle ford and showed him where Custer came down the Coulee to the ford and *went into the water* with the head of his column. All of the Cheyennes were there—and massing on Custer's front drove him back and circling up along his right flank were soon joined by Gall returning from Reno's front (After R. had reached the bluff) who with his Sioux circled along Custer's left flank—both herding him up on the hill*—and then joining, cut him off from any escape and then closing in finished him.

Col. C. F. Bates writes me that he went to Billings and joined in the Anniversary stunts. He does not mention meeting either you or Gen. Godfrey—but I presume you went and saw both.

Three nights out and the same back seemed to preclude my undertaking such a journey, much as I wanted to go on account of my long continued chronic insomnia.

Again please accept my grateful thanks for your kind thought in sending me such a well rounded, comprehensive story—and with my best wishes,

I am, most Sincerely Yours,
/s/ R. G. CARTER

*This is shown in Russell White Bear's (a Carlisle graduate) sketch map which I presume you have seen.

EDGERLY & VARNUM REFUTE CHARGE OF FIXED TESTIMONY

The following letter was written under date of July 9, 1925, to Brigadier General Winfield S. Edgerly, Retired, then residing at Cooperstown, N. Y., and to Colonel Charles A. Varnum, Retired, residing at San Francisco, Calif.:

Since last hearing from you I have had a letter from a retired officer of the Army, containing certain statements credited by him to W. M. Camp of Chicago, and which are of such a character that I think they should be submitted to you for comment.

Inasmuch as Mr. Camp is, and has for years been engaged in collecting material for a book on the Indian Wars, and presumably intends to publish, at some time in the future, his views and conclusions as to the conduct of the troops at the battle of the Little Big Horn, I believe that in fairness to everybody concerned, the statements contained in this letter ought to be commented on, as fully as may be, by the officers of the 7th who now survive, and not permitted to go into history only after all those who took part in the fight, have passed on.

I have, for several years, as you know, made a most careful study of the fight on the Little Big Horn, and have been, and still am, a most assiduous seeker after the truth; and the story which I wrote, (and which you have read), is as accurate as I can make it with my present knowledge of the facts.

To quote, however, from the letter just received:

"He (Camp) had an interview of 5 hours with Hare; one of 7 hours with Edgerly; and a long one with Varnum. * * * All of these interviews he has autographic copies of in his safe at Chicago.

1. "He has positive evidence that Reno was drinking before he crossed the ford; before his deployment and skirmish in the valley: was seen to drink in the timber and throw the bottle away: was drunk during the night of the 25th and was also drunk when Terry came up on the morning of the 27th."

2. "He scouts the idea that Custer became engaged before Reno left the timber on his retreat; or that Reno ever climbed out of that timber in any other way than a disorderly, disorganized mob, with no leadership whatever."

3. "He has positive evidence that those officers who testified before the Reno Court, after reading the testimony of the day, which was published in the papers gathered in Reno's room and *rehearsed the programme for the next day*: and Girard and Godfrey were urged to sit in with them, but both refused. This, and very much more, he told me * * *

4. "He says he has positive proof that Custer *did stop* on the trail after Martin left him with the message to Benteen, *at least ¾ of an hour.*"

In justice to yourself, and to those who are no longer able to speak in their own defense, I ask you to comment on the statements thus accredited to Mr. Camp—*and particularly the statement Numbered 3,* since that, in effect, is an imputation, if not an accusation of bad faith upon the part of every officer except Godfrey, who testified at Chicago in 1879.

You are the only ones now living who can refute it; and I hope that your comments will be both so direct and so emphatic that there will be no chance for cavil or question in the future.

Sincerely yours,
W. A. Graham,
Lieut. Col., Judge Advocate.

A similar letter was sent to Colonel Luther Hare, Retired, to which no reply was received.

2691 Union St.,
San Francisco, Calif.
July 15, 1925.

Col. W. A. Graham
Dear Sir:

Replying to yours of the 9th Inst. 1st. I did not see Col. Reno drink liquor, or see any sign of his having drank any liquor on the two days of the fight June 25 & 26th 76, or the 27th either for that matter. I do not believe a word of the charge referred to in your Art. 1.

No. 2. The first part is all surmise. No one knows. The second part is covered as far as I know by my testimony before the Court of Inquiry.

No. 3. As far as I am concerned the statement is absolutely untrue. I was never in Reno's room in Chicago and was never asked by any one to go there and I never discussed, even with my most intimate friend (Lt. Wallace) what my testimony would be. I do not believe a word of it.

No. 4. I know nothing about but do not believe it. Any one who knew Geo. A. Custer would find it hard to believe that he could keep still for five minutes under the circumstances.

Respectfully yours,
Chas. A. Varnum,
Col. U. S. A.

Cooperstown, N. Y.
July 15, 1925.

My dear Colonel Graham:

I was very much surprised by the contents of your letter of the 9th inst. I have never met Mr. Camp and his interview of seven hours must have been taken from my correspondence with him. He wrote me several years ago stating that he intended to write a story of the Custer fight and I replied. I do not think I wrote him more than once but may have. In regard to statement 1. I have to say that Col. Reno had the only whiskey that I had any evidence of during the fight. He (Reno) had a bottle of whiskey which he carried quite openly and from which he took an occasional sip.

I had been with Col. Reno for two summers '73—'74 on the Neschim Boundary survey and knew him very intimately. He was, in those days when almost everybody drank, what was called a moderate drinker and I never saw him drunk.

During the fight I was near him much of the time and saw no sign of intoxication on him or any other officer or soldier.

2. I think you have all the facts in regard to this in your story.

3. I have absolutely no recollection of any meeting in Reno's room for the purpose of rehearsing to shield Reno or for any other purpose, and the feeling of the officers toward Reno was not of the kind that would lead them to conspire for his benefit even if they were dishonorable enough to do so which I indignantly deny.

4. I think you know as much about Custer's movements after he separated from Reno as anybody and altho' I know nothing positively as to whether he halted on his march for more than ¾ of an hour, I do not think it probable.

Yours sincerely,
W. S. Edgerly

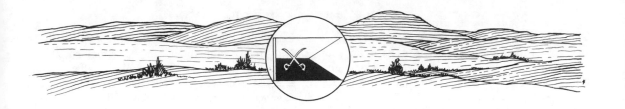

CHAPTER 11

TRIPLE PLAY: WHITTAKER TO BENTEEN TO PRICE AND BACK!

NONE who knew him ever doubted that Frederick W. Benteen, by instinct and by practice, was a soldier who never shrank from a fight; on the contrary he was usually found in the forefront of the battle. But he could, and upon occasion did, inspire others to carry an objective, holding himself in readiness should reserves prove necessary.

When Custer's biographer, Frederick Whittaker, in a letter to the New York "Sun", dated 26 February 1879, expressed profound dissatisfaction with the acts and doings of the Court of Inquiry that exonerated Major Reno from charges Whittaker had made against him, and in voicing his disapproval lambasted Generals Sheridan and Merritt, and condemning Major Reno, together with most of the officers of the Seventh Cavalry, even took pot shots at Benteen himself, it was to be expected that the old war horse would accept the gage of battle. And he did.

In Philadelphia there resided one Robert Newton Price, a former officer of volunteers who had served with Benteen and admired him greatly. He shared Benteen's estimate of Custer and his contempt of Whittaker, and had expressed his views in print with sarcastic vigor. He had, moreover, followed closely the reported sessions of the Court, and heartily approved its findings; and in a letter to Benteen commending his stand during the proceedings, he enclosed some promised photographs of himself and wife and asked, whenever Benteen had no further need of it, that the now famous message to "Come on; Be quick; Bring packs," be given him as a relic of the battle of the Little Big Horn.

Benteen replied to Price 6 March 1879, and thanking him for the photographs, sent him the historic document he had asked for; and then, calling to his attention the Whittaker diatribe,

he asked Price to "rasp up his bolts of sarcasm" and to flay its author therewith. Price at once complied, his answer to Whittaker being printed in the Philadelphia "Times" of 13 March 1879.

The three letters appear below; and as they made the pattern followed ever since by both critics and defenders of the Court of Inquiry, they are well worth reading.

Lincoln March 6th, '79

My dear Price:

Yr. notes of 5th & 25th came along today. Ditto Photos of yourself & Doll. They are exquisite. Thankye for them. They are the shadows of two nice young folks. Clean young people. I also got the copy of Bay Window paper you sent me, (Torey's) and a nice paper 'tis too. The review of the Nigger's book was well, very well thought—and I liked it muchly.

I send you the relic you request, as I have no use for it. I heard not a criticism on the nature of my evidence in Reno case, tho' Gilbert has written me since that it was wholly satisfactory to Army people, which of necessity it must have been, as it was true, and they knew just what I thought long before trial. I was close mouthed as I could be, or my testimony might possibly looked like a too high flying of my own kite to have met with favor among those unacquainted with me. I almost regretted I was not allowed to turn loose on Custer, tho' Qui Bono?

Cadets for ages to come will bow in humility at the Custer shrine at West Point, and—if it makes better soldiers and men of them, why the necessity of knocking the paste eye out of their idol?

Whittaker had a recent letter in the N. Y. Sun, in which Genl. Merritt, Reno, Mike Sheridan,

Genl. S. and myself catch, well, Merry H. Can't you go for that Heathen Chinee? Rasp up your bolt of sarcasm which is so well hurled and give him a shake up for me. If you haven't seen the article, will send it to you.

Kind remembrances from all of us to yr. family and self. Thanks for the photos.

Truly yrs.,

BENTEEN

* * *

(From *The Sun,* Wednesday, February 26, 1879)

GEN. CUSTER AND MAJ. RENO
ONE WHO DIED AT THE LITTLE BIG HORN AND ONE WHO RAN AWAY.

Enemies Wracking their Spite on a Hero's Memory—Reno Finding a Friend in Need in R. B. Hayes—A Whitewashing Court of Inquiry—Damaging Evidence—Benteen and Col. Mike—"It will Hurt the Army Badly."

To the Editor of the Sun—Sir: Ever since the nation was startled in 1876 by the news that Custer and five companies of United States troops had been massacred by the Indians of Sitting Bull, speculations as to the reasons for his fate have been rife. The so-called official reports, emanating from Gen. Terry and from Major Reno, who had been second in command to Custer himself in the Seventh Cavalry, expressed little doubt. Terry openly ascribed the defeat to the rashness and disobedience of Custer. The *cidevant* second in command, now become first by Custer's death, proceeded to criticise the orders he had received from Custer, attributing the death of that officer to unwise measures and an alleged state of exhaustion among the horses of the regiment, produced by overmarching, under Custer's direction. A few months later appeared the biography of Gen. Custer. This book, published just six months after the battle, openly charged that "had Reno fought as Custer fought, the battle of the Little Big Horn might have been Custer's last and greatest Indian victory." It further charged Reno with timidity and demoralization, and with standing an idle spectator of Custer's battle for at least two hours, after a needless retreat and the arrival of reenforcements to Reno's help.

Time passed on, and Reno, in 1877, in the full dignity of a post commander at the West, had a fresh opportunity of exhibiting his qualities as an officer and a gentleman. One of the Captains under his command had a young wife, whom he left behind him in the fort while he went out on scouting duty with the rest of the command. It seems that the regiment had had enough of Reno as a field commander, so he remained at the post. The history of the rest of the affair, as far as Reno was concerned, is told in the records of a general court martial convened a few weeks later. It seems that Reno addressed insulting proposals to the wife of his absent comrade, and when these were repulsed with indignation, he made use of his power as commanding officer to persecute this helpless woman by branding her in public orders as a person of bad character. At all events her husband came back, heard what had passed, and at once sought Reno. He had two courses open to him—to kill Reno or to have him tried by court martial. Fortunately for Reno's skin the Captain was a cool man, of great self control. He satisfied his natural anger by stigmatizing Reno, before witnesses, in terms that a hare would have resented, but Reno would not fight. Then the Captain brought charges against him. On these charges Reno was tried, and the unanimous verdict of the court was that he be "dismissed the service."

The Sentence Hayes Commuted

Now comes the best part of the whole proceeding. Reno's friends went to Washington, where resides a person by the name of Rutherford Burchard Hayes, and this person commuted the sentence of the model Major to a suspension of two years, on the ground of Reno's supposed "gallant conduct" in the war of the rebellion and the battle of the Little Big Horn. It perhaps seems strange, but it is nevertheless true, that Hayes did this, knowing well the public accusations made against Reno. Therefore, the present status of that remarkable officer is that of a suspension from rank, which expires next spring.

In May, 1878—not quite two years after the battle—a solemn official accusation was laid before Congress, referred to the Military Committee of the House, and favorably reported by them. This accusation, contained in a letter to Mr. Corlett of Wyoming, charged Major Reno with showing cowardice in the battle in which Custer was killed, with abandonment of his commander, and with making a false report libellous to Custer's memory.

The report of the Military Committee, owing to the hurry of business at the close of the spring session, was not brought up. After the adjournment of Congress without action, Reno played a smart trick, for which he deserves credit. Waiting until June 22, 1878, just two years from the date when Custer left Terry and Gibbon for his last march, the gallant Major boldly asked the

Adjutant-General—for what? Not for a court martial, but for a court of inquiry into his (Reno's) conduct in the battle of the Little Big Horn. The non-military reader may not comprehend the smartness of this trick, but a glance at the state of the law will explain it. Under the military law a court martial on any person must be ordered within two years of the time of commission of the offense for which he is charged, otherwise he escapes scot free. No officer can be dismissed from the service save by sentence of a court martial or by special act of Congress. Thus, even if Reno's request were granted, he could not be dismissed the army. The court, at the worst, could only censure him; and his previous record shows how much he would care for censure, however severe. As if to show him that his trust in the Military Ring at Washington was not unfounded, The Adjutant-General considerately delayed ordering even the court of inquiry for another six months, and at last it was convened at Chicago, Jan. 13, 1879.

It consisted of Col. King, Ninth Infantry; Col. Merritt, Fifth Cavalry; and Lieut.-Col. Royall, Third Cavalry; and had Lieut. Lee, Adjutant Ninth Infantry, for Recorder. But for Recorder Lee the case would soon have progressed to a complete and scientific whitewash. Thanks to his efforts, the following facts were developed on the trial, which can never be contradicted hereafter.

The Facts Proved

On the morning of the 25th June, 1876, Gen. Custer, in command of the Seventh United States Cavalry, advanced down the valley of the Little Big Horn to attack a camp of Indians of unknown force. He had with him twelve companies, or about 600 men of the regiment, and a pack train of 150 mules. Within twelve miles of the village, he detailed Capt. Benteen to the left with three companies, to scour the country up to a certain point, to strike any Indians he might meet, to report if he found them, and, if he found none, to return to the main trail at a certain point. These orders were very strict and precise, and were delivered by three different persons at intervals—namely, Adjutant Cooke, the chief trumpeter, and the Sergeant-Major, successively. With the main column, Custer kept on until within five miles of the village, when he detailed Major Reno to the left with three companies, ordering him to follow the Indians and to "charge them." These orders were explicit, and made no mention of retreat unless driven back. They were accompanied by the assurance: "We will support you with the whole outfit."

These orders given, Custer and Reno both advanced at a fast trot or gallop, Reno diverging to the left and crossing the Little Big Horn, while Custer kept on the right bank, following the arc of which Reno had the chord. They arrived in sight of the Indian village almost at the same time, the Indians running from before Reno in a cloud of dust, caused by driving in the herds of ponies with which they had been surprised in the valley, and by a panic which had seized them.

Within a thousand yards of the village Reno suddenly halted, dismounted his men, and sent his horses into a patch of timber on the left bank of the stream, where a perfect natural fortification existed. All around was an open prairie, and the timber was sunk below the prairie, bordered by a steep bank. As soon as the Indians saw Reno halt they took heart, and began to come back to defend their women and children. The troops opened from the prairie a wild, aimless fire, in which Major Reno himself joined with a carbine, the officers paying very little attention to regulating the expenditure of ammunition. After about ten minutes, the men of a sudden fell back to the timber. When the line first opened fire Custer heard them on the right bank of the river, left his column along with Adjutant Cooke, galloped to the edge of the bluffs, looked down and waved his hat to cheer them on in the fight, then went back to his column to attack the Indians in rear. He was seen by one officer in the fight, Lieut. de Rudio. From thence the lay of the ground hid each column from the other. Custer had hardly been gone five minutes when Reno suddenly made up his mind to retreat, and accordingly ordered his men to their horses. While this was doing the fire of the troops ceased, and the Indians came near the timber. When all were mounted in column of fours, headed away from the village, a few Indians who had sneaked clear around the column during the lull in the action, suddenly fired, killing Custer's favorite Indian scout, "Bloody Knife," who on that day was attending Reno. The scout's brains were spattered over Reno, who immediately yelled out, "Dismount!" and then "Mount!" At the same moment a soldier shouted: "My God, boys, I've got it." and then Major Reno struck spurs to his horse, and led a wild stampede of all the men into the prairie, running for dear life to the river. He lost his hat, carbine, and one pistol in the wild race; but came in first. The Indians did not attempt to stop the column, but galloped after it, slaughtering twenty-seven men as security as so many buffaloes. Over the river and up the bluffs went Reno and his men, till they ran right into the advancing column of Benteen, who had come back to the main trail some time before.

In the meantime Custer had sent back an urgent order to this same Benteen to "Come on. Be quick. Bring packs," and it was while obeying that order that Benteen met Reno.

"Where is Reno?"

A few minutes after these two joined on the hill, Custer struck the Indians at a ford four miles down the river. He went into action with the full belief that Reno was fighting in the bottom, and Benteen "coming on" to join in the fight. His firing was distinctly heard by every witness who testified on the trial except Reno and Benteen, and it lasted for two hours. It was reported to Reno by Capt. McDougall, who brought up the pack train nearly an hour after his meeting on the hill. Reno made no reply, but went down the bluffs to look at the dead body of one of his officers. All the Indians had left his front and had gone to Custer, and still he remained quiet. At last Capt. Thomas B. Weir, who had been fretting and fuming, started off alone to join Custer, and was followed by his company without orders. When they had gone about a mile Reno let the rest go after. By that time the firing down the river had ceased, and they met the Indians returning. In another hour they were attacked themselves, and Reno practically disappeared from the scene, leaving the actual command to Capt. Benteen. It is true that he gave a few orders and was now and then visible to his acting Adjutant, but many times the question was asked: "Where is Reno?" He turned up after dark with a flask of whiskey and a carbine, struck an unarmed man in the face for no offence but answering his question civilly, and threatened to shoot him at once. The man was a poor citizen packer, and therefore safe game. In fact, Reno seems rather proud of this than otherwise, for he asked on the trial through his counsel, "So Reno slapped your face, did he? He wasn't a coward then, was he?" It is unnecessary to remark that this question produced quite a little sensation in court—it sounded so brave. This little scene terminates all that is of importance in the behavior of Reno on the first day: and the second was a repetition of the same sneaking policy, without the addition of the Dutch courage at night. On the third day the consequences of his conduct became manifest when Terry rescued the remnant of the regiment from the Indians. The dead bodies of Custer and all his men were then found.

Sneering at the Dead Custer

It only remains to describe a few scenes that transpired during the trial in Chicago this year, now closed. While the case was in progress Reno and Benteen were inseparable; and Reno's counsel, a gentleman strongly resembling the lamented Oily Gammon, made up a happy trio. They ate and drank together at all times, and the hotel loungers said they frequently slept three in a bed, though this we cannot vouch for. When Benteen was giving his evidence, Mr. Gammon—we should say Gilbert—could not control his feelings, and kept jumping up and down, prompting the witness to such an extent that the President of the Court, Col. King, openly rebuked him with: "Mr. Gilbert, sit down and don't interfere with the Recorder or make suggestions to the witness." It was clear that Benteen was Reno's great gun. He had been puffed in advance as a hero and a martyr, as a wonderful Indian fighter and lady-killer, and the room was crammed with ladies come to hear the great Indian fighter testify. [N.B.—Most of these ladies came from Sheridan's headquarters.] And yet what was the testimony of this vaunted Benteen? It is enough to say that before he had left the stand he had convinced every one in the room except Reno and Gammon that he could not be trusted. His statements were confined to a series of malignant sneers at his dead commander, Custer; to an expression of opinion that Custer had given "senseless" orders; that he had blundered into a trap; that he had been killed in a "panic"; that his fight had only lasted about ten minutes, and so on, in spite of the firing heard for two long hours on Reno's hill by every one else. And here comes in the true inwardness of the Reno inquiry. Every witness who wanted to slander Custer was allowed to do so, but no word was allowed on the other side, because it was Reno, not Custer, who was to be investigated. Gen. Sheridan sent in his brother, the Colonel, better known in Chicago as "Mike Sheridan," to swear down Custer, and Mike, who never was in action, was permitted to offer his military judgment on the probable fate of Custer, though he only visited the field in 1877. Poor Mike, by the by, was suffering from a recent wound contracted by bumping his head against the top of an ambulance while campaigning after imaginary Indians; so we must not be severe on him. He gave his evidence like a little man.

A Mockery of Justice

Reno himself was allowed to sneer at Custer for his civil war record, an appeal to the old rivalry between Custer and Merritt, now one of

Photo by Illingworth during Custer's 1874 Black Hills Expedition. Two stars-and-stripes guidons shown.

cision, the Recorder having no voice save to present the case on trial. His remark shows the spirit in which he looked at the case. Better to continue Reno in the army and try to hush things up than to cut out this festering sore and save the army by honesty at the eleventh hour. The American people will know how to treat this verdict when it appears, if it be a clean whitewash, and to whose influence to ascribe it.

F.W.

(From the Philadelphia *Times,* March 13, 1879)

CUSTER AND RENO

* * *

Another View of the Much Discussed Indian Massacre

* * *

THE COURT OF INQUIRY REVIEWED

* * *

The Whole Matter Claimed to Have Been an Advertising Dodge.

* * *

To the Editor of The Times:

Since the fall of 1876 the officers of the Seventh Cavalry who survived Custer have silently borne more vicious abuse and malignant defamation than any equal number of the most notorious criminals in the country. These attacks would never have become so general nor so bitter had not the army and its friends been restrained by a unanimous and heartfelt sympathy for Mrs. Custer, and an aversion to resurrecting evil after it has been decently buried and mourned for; but as their generous silence has come to be construed into admissions of guilt, the writer feels constrained to dispense a portion of the information in his possession and warrants it to be reliable. This one-sided controversy was begun and has been pushed on by a person named Whittaker, who professes to have been a warm friend of General Custer, and whose present sole ambition in life is to vindicate the general's memory.

Immediately after the battle of the Little Big Horn, when the whole nation and, in fact, the civilized world stood aghast at the unexpected disaster, he recognized it as being the grand opportunity to distinguish, not Custer—for to him it was then a useless luxury—but Custer's dear friend Whittaker, and imagined it could best be achieved by publishing a book. Knowing that even a nine day's wonder ceases before a readable and profitable literary work can be put on the market, with bold ingenuity he surmounted these dilemmas by taking the General's "Life on the Plains,"

the court, and not without effect. Benteen was allowed to sneer at Custer, but a question as to his relations toward Custer was ruled out. Benteen, too, was not on trial. In short, by the rulings of the court and the terms of the order under which they acted, the whole proceeding became at last the merest mockery of justice, despite of the honesty of Cols. King and Royall, and the energy of Recorder Lee. All that could be done was to accumulate facts; and, thanks to the Recorder, enough facts were established to sink Reno ten times over. It was proven that Custer went into action on that fatal day with two subordinates who hated and distrusted him, affecting to despise his ability as a soldier, and that these men deliberately refused to hear the firing in his direction though their attention was called to it.

The verdict of the court on these facts has gone to Washington, sealed, and is supposed to be secret, but enough has leaked out to show that it will be a partial whitewash, though the court cannot avoid censuring Reno on some of the counts, if not all. The reason of this whitewash and the excuse offered for it is found in an unwary remark of Col. Merritt, made on the last day but one of the trial. "It is a pity," in substance said the gallant Colonel—Custer's old rival—"that this thing was brought on now. It will hurt the army badly. It ought not to have been allowed to come out." Col. Merritt was afterward closeted with the Recorder alone for several hours, and, it is understood, did most of the work of the de-pictures included, and the correspondence published by the New York press relating to the campaign of that year; then by the interjection of a sentence here and the elimination of one there, and changing the persons of the pronouns, he evolved "Whattaker's Life of General Custer." Meanwhile the public was invited to show its appreciation of the dead hero "by subscription, only four dollars and twenty-five cents each." On the publication of this valuable biography sympathy seemed to wane, and the ordinary advertising schemes seemed futile, so recourse must be had to something startling. About this time Colonel Weir, of the Seventh Cavalry, was detailed on recruiting service and stationed in New York. Weir's only weakness was that of many other generous and whole-souled men—too craving an appetite for exhilarating stimulants, and through it Whittaker endeavored to take advantage of him. As it had become pretty generally understood that Custer's mistake had been a fatal one for him in more senses than one, his "biographer" concluded to follow Josh Billings' advice as to the proper method of making a correction—"by cussing sumbody else fur it." Weir died suddenly, and immediately after his demise there began to appear from time to time, throughout the press of the entire country, insinuations against Reno and Benteen. Hints soon became definite charges and Custer was promoted from hero to martyr; even the subscription limitation on the circulation of the book was less rigorously enforced. Whittaker returned to the attack nobly and was again equal to the emergency.

Whittaker's Attack

Counting on the silence of the maligned officers for the reasons above given, he wrote a letter, in which Reno was accused of having violated all the articles of war, and Benteen all but two or three (or words to that effect), and in order that it might not call attention to the literary venture, and yet be deposited in the care of a statesman commanding unquestionable and undisputed influence in Congress, the biographer of the life of General Custer sent it from New York, via the Associated Press, to the Congressional delegate of one of the Western Territories! As an official investigation was being so earnestly sought for, Colonel Reno thought he would assist in bringing one about by applying for a Court of Inquiry. This put Whittaker to his trumps, so, as Weir was very dead by this time, he trotted him out as partner. He announced, or caused to be announced, that he had in his possession an affidavit of his ghostly ally's, setting forth that Custer was

overwhelmed because of the treachery and cowardice of Reno and Benteen. With this assertion and a few quotations from the "Life of Custer" as evidence, he tried these officers in the newspapers. Preponderance of evidence was the verdict, and it has been coming in ever since. The Court of Inquiry convened and Whittaker reported, to coach the Judge Advocate. On invitation to produce the potent paper he declined. Two reasons effectively influenced its suppression; the first and merely nominal one was, that Weir had never made the affidavit alleged; the second and material drawback was the presence of Captain Charles Braden, late of the Seventh, now retired because of wounds received in the Yellowstone fight of 1873. This gentleman was in Chicago to testify that he had been a guest at the same hotel in New York with Weir, some time before, and up to within a few days of the latter's death, and that Weir had frequently complained that Whittaker was constantly pestering him to sign a paper which stated that Reno failed to assist Custer when he could have done it, and was therefore responsible for the massacre. He further expressed not only his intention of not doing it, but expressed his opinion of the self-sacrificing patriot who made the proposal in the strongest language and most emphatic eloquence of a trooper. This unexpected development transmuted the affidavit into a few notes of conversations had with the officer in question, alleged to have been indited from memory. Braden was therefore relieved from attendance on the court and his testimony not taken. After a few day's evidence was in, the self-appointed champion made a public retraction of his charges against Benteen. The investigation being completed and the officers of the court being of unquestioned integrity and fitness, the result was a foregone conclusion. Therefore appeared the following in the Chicago papers of February 12: "As the biographer of the late General Custer, he deemed it his duty to promise the people of the United States that he would see that Congress righted the reputation of General Custer, and that at no late day." So much for Frederick Whittaker, friend and biographer, the inventor and sole proprietor of one of the most novel and stupendous advertising schemes of this or any other age, and with apologies to the reader for occupying so much time with such a subject, let us look at some of the results of the Court of Inquiry.

The Court of Inquiry

"A Court of Inquiry may be considered more a council than a court," says the text-book on military law used at the West Point Academy, and this case is a fair illustration of the definition. Colonel Reno availed himself of the customary redress of an officer assailed with informal charges and requested the official investigation known as a Court of Inquiry; if the allegations were not proven the fact would be reported to the President through the proper channels and this report published to the army in general orders, if there was found to be any truth in the accusations made they would be incorporated into formal charges and a general court-martial recommended; this last court would determine his innocence or guilt. The newspapers are just now full of his "acquittal" of this or the other charge, but, as is frequently the case, their information is still-born.

During the twenty-six days' patient examination every officer swears positively in so many words, or else substantially testifies, that Reno did the very best thing which could have been done under the circumstances; that they saw no indications of cowardice, and that it was impossible to have averted Custer's fate. Of Colonel Benteen's conduct there was admiration only expressed. After the court had been in session some time, and a majority of the officers had returned to their posts, every one interested, except the "biographer of the late General Custer," was astounded to learn the hitherto unrevealed cause of the disaster, divulged by two mule-packers. These discerning patriots testified Reno was under the influence of liquor! They intoxicated him about six hours too late to make his drunkenness of any effect, and then all the witnesses available, officers, privates and employes, swore it was all news to them; but as Weir's affidavit had miscarried, and something had to be done to maintain the status of the "biographer," the mule-packers, for sympathy or some other cause, generously contributed to the extent of their small ability. Yet, notwithstanding these unexpected reinforcements for the prosecution, the court has decided the charges made are groundless and that the official records of the War Department testifying to his "judicious and skilful conduct" must remain unaltered, and that "there was *nothing* in his conduct which requires animadversion from this court." As there is a Congressional investigation threatened, however, and as there is little likelihood of it ever taking place or the demand for the "Life of the late General Custer" increasing, these two officers must be again tried by the press on the old charges, but with additional specifications, to wit: That they had the temerity to openly proclaim their doubts of Custer's ability as a commander and their consequent lack of confidence in his judgment. It will here be pertinent to inquire who

these critics are that they question the military skill of their late commanding officer.

Colonel Marcus A. Reno entered the service in 1857, from the Military Academy, and having been assigned to a cavalry regiment, has remained in that corps ever since, during the war rising to Colonel and Brevet Brigadier General. His courage and skill have been tried over and over again, and never questioned until Whittaker compiled the "Life of the late General Custer." Col. Fred W. Benteen was appointed First Lieutenant in a Missouri cavalry regiment, from civil life, in September, 1861, and fought with most enviable distinction throughout the war, attaining the rank of Colonel, but frequently wielding commands of higher rank in closely contested battles. The fact of his being a Virginian, and his not being a West Pointer, militated against his receiving the promotion he fairly earned. At the close of the war he accepted the senior captaincy of the Seventh Cavalry, and has not been absent from duty with it since, except in the fall of 1876, when, being ordered on recruiting service, he immediately applied to be relieved when he reached his station; the application being granted, he returned at once to his post and company. As for bravery, prowess and experience he need not envy the reputation of any cavalryman in the United States Army. And to him particularly applies that finding of the court which says: "Subordinates in some instances did more for the command by brilliant displays of courage than did Major Reno."

These gentlemen, who can count their triumphs by the dozens, and have each had as much, if not more, experience against Indians than Custer, are perfectly competent critics of warfare, either civilized or savage. They were asked their opinions of General Custer as a commander and gave them. They were not called on to explain their reasons for forming their judgment, and the public, tutored by the "biographer," infers that it arises from their jealousy. There are a few interesting facts in relation to Custer's record, which may throw some light on the heresy of his subordinates.

Without attempting to quote so large a portion of the history of the rebellion as that detailing the services rendered by him, it is only necessary to suggest at this writing that most of the lauded victories, as reported by his staff of newspaper correspondents, were the results of battles in which some larger force than his own was obliged to go to his rescue. His foolhardiness got him and his commands into dire extremities and it took all of "Custer's luck," with the assistance of others' brains and bravery, to retrieve his disasters, and this rule was general. In the subsequent Indian wars, if to suffer the greater loss and to fail to accomplish the object of a campaign was a defeat, he never won a victory. The one serious battle he had before the Little Big Horn affair was the Battle of the Washita in the '68-69 campaign, and with nearly similar results, only in this case it was the Major and his command who were butchered. One expedition, fitted out at enormous expense, and started under the most flattering auspices, with every indication favoring a speedy and successful undertaking, he rendered practically fruitless by riding into the hostile camp unawares, accompanied only by his orderly, when the command was several miles in the rear. The ignoble savage held him as a hostage, and made his safe deliverance depend on theirs. The Yellowstone campaign of 1873, after the return of the Seventh from Ku Klux duty, was a failure in so far as he succeeded in making "good Indians."

Custer's Romance

Common error seems to confound and confuse Custer's literary with his military ability; his narratives were always readable, whether they appeared in a popular magazine, credited to the author, or found their way into a newspaper office, signed by his brother-in-law, Calhoun; and the interest of the reader was rarely allowed to flag, if romance had a stimulating effect upon it. He went into the campaign of 1876 under a cloud, and it was a heavy one. Having been most em-

phatically snubbed at Washington for using the means he took to get East, he was additionally troubled by the relatives of two soldiers who were pistoled under his orders by his brother and brother-in-law, in the campaign of '68-69, after having surrendered as deserters. These people had been posting themselves on military and civil law, and learned entirely too much about them and their relations to each other to appreciate the necessity for such sudden and merciless punishment. His natural recklessness was spurred beyond all precedent, and after wilfully disobeying positive and explicit orders, he forced his "luck" against too great odds, failed to retrieve his former reputation, and wrecked another, his last, campaign. Had he survived he would have most likely been dismissed the service by court-martial, and the censure implied by the decision of the late Court of Inquiry expresses the opinion of the whole army.

If these remarks hint at a lack of overwhelming confidence in General Custer's military superiority, it is because his "biographer" has for the last three years unceasingly decried and derided the unexampled pluck and skill which won the toughest Indian battle in our history, and loaded the survivors with infamous and shameful calumny merely to advertise a book without merit as it is without readers.

ROBERT NEWTON PRICE.

Philadelphia, March 13, 1879.

CHAPTER 12

THE "EVIDENCE" AGAINST RENO

W. J. GHENT'S SUMMATION OF THE "ABANDON THE WOUNDED" EVIDENCE

THE late W. J. Ghent of Washington, D. C., was known as a "Custer historian" and so he was, though a very jaundiced one. He belonged to that class of historians who, because they are unable or unwilling to see but one side of a picture, are also unwilling to admit that by any possibility, there could be another side. The battle of the Little Big Horn has been, and I am afraid still is, cursed with too many such "historians"; and they are by no means massed on one side of the picture. Hence the age old controversy, which bids fair, like "Ole Man River" to keep on rolling along indefinitely.

Ghent was a pro-Custer propagandist who could see no fault in the "Boy General," and who dipped his pen in vitriol whenever and wherever he expressed his views. To him both Benteen and Reno were anathema; and when in 1930, General Godfrey made his speech at the Indian Wars dinner, in which he recounted the "abandonment of the wounded" story, Ghent began at once to busy himself in an effort to prove that Godfrey's recital was supported by overwhelming evidence.

To that end he collected and put together in a "dossier" all the odds and ends he could find that seemed to corroborate the story, and to show that Reno was both cowardly and recreant, not only during the night of 25 June, but throughout the action.

I

MR. GHENT SUMMARIZES THE EVIDENCE ON RENO'S COWARDICE, AND HIS PROPOSAL TO ABANDON RENO HILL

(Excerpts from a letter of Gen. E. S. Godfrey to Mr. J. A. Shoemaker, Billings, Mont., March 2, 1926).

MY judgment of his (Reno's) conduct was made up on the field, during the engagements. And I am, and was, satisfied that Ben-teen had the same feeling toward him or his conduct on the day we buried the dead on Custer field. Also that Weir was of the same opinion, emphatically. On June 28, as we were marching to Custer field to bury the dead, Benteen and I were riding together, apart from the rest of the command, and I said to him, "Benteen, it's pretty damned bad."

Benteen asked, "What do you mean" I replied, "Reno's conduct." Benteen then faced me and said, with great earnestness, "'God' (my nickname among my fellows), I could tell things that would make your hair stand on end." I responded, "What is it? Tell me." Just then some one rode up near us, and Benteen jerked his head in the direction of the intruder and said, "I can't tell you now." I asked, "Will you tell me some time?" and he replied, "Yes." Time after time I besought him to tell me, but always there appeared some excuse for putting off the narration.

In 1881 we were on a fishing trip at Point Pleasant, N. J., and one evening all the other members of the party had gone to the beach for a swim. I recalled his statement to me on June 28, and said, "Benteen, now we are absolutely alone, and no one can hear. You promised to tell me what you had in mind, and I want you to tell me now." He hesitated a moment, and then asked, "Don't you think it is just as well to let bygones be bygones?" I replied, "No, I insist on your promise." A moment of silence followed, when he said:

"Well, on the night of the 25th Reno came to me after all firing had ceased and proposed that we mount every man who could ride, destroy such property as could not be carried, abandon our position and make a forced march back to our supply camp. (The supply camp was on the Yellowstone River, at the mouth of the Powder, distant about 120 miles, map measurement.) I asked him what he proposed to do with the wounded, and he replied, "Oh, we'll have to abandon those that can not ride." I said, "I won't do it."

On the night of the 25th Capt. Weir had come to me and said (alluding to my dismounting and deploying my troop to protect the retreat from the high point to Reno Hill), "I want to thank you, Godfrey, for saving my troop." A few moments later he asked, "If there should be a conflict of judgment between Reno and Benteen as to what we should do, whose orders would you obey?" I replied, "Benteen's." Whether or not Weir went to the other troop commanders with the same question I do not know.

After hearing Benteen's statement at Point Pleasant I put the two incidents together and assumed that Benteen had told Weir of Reno's proposal and probably asked him to sound me on my attitude. We both belonged to Benteen's battalion.

(The foregoing statement, with a few technical emendations, is taken from the Shoemaker letter. On Jan. 25, 1930, at the dinner of the Order of Indian Wars, in Washington, D. C., Gen. Godfrey repeated the statement in substance, and in virtually the same language. At the same dinner Gen. William J. Nicholson, who has since died, arose and said that in 1877, when he was a young lieutenant, Benteen had told him the same story of Reno's proposal, pledging him not to reveal it while he (Benteen) was alive. Gen. Nicholson concluded by saying: "I have never mentioned it until now.")

II

Statement about Reno's proposal related by Benteen to Moylan in 1883, according to latter's letter to Godfrey, Jan. 17, 1892.

Reaffirmed by Benteen to Godfrey, Jan. 3, 1886.

Reaffirmed by Benteen in letter to Theodore Goldin, Jan. 6, 1892.

Admitted by Gen. Jefferson R. Kean to have been told him by Benteen, presumably about 1887. Kean's statement made at Order of Indian Wars banquet, Feb. 20, 1937.

III

GEN. GODFREY TO W. J. G., JAN. 13, 1930.

Dear friend Ghent:

Mr. H. Lyday Sloanaker, 1-11 Everett St., Cambridge, Mass., was the correspondent to whom I gave an account of Benteen's revelations about Reno. The understanding at the time was that it was confidential and we were quite surprised to see it in Print in the Sunday Boston Post—and I cannot now find my copy. Mrs. Godfrey says she thinks the date was the *Sunday* before the Reunion (June 25), I think 22nd 1926. We have not heard from Mr. S. since altho we sent card of greeting and Mrs. G. wrote to him. Only one copy was sent to me . . .

Sincerely yours
E. S. GODFREY
1-13-30

(The reference is to an article by Lyday Sloanaker, published in the Boston *Post* on June 20, 1926, and giving the first printed mention of Reno's proposal to abandon the desperately wounded and attempt to escape from the battlefield of the Little Big Horn.)

IV

EXTRACT FROM A LETTER BY BENTEEN TO GODFREY

(The letter from which the following extract is taken was written by Major F. W. Benteen to Capt. E. S. Godfrey in 1886. Godfrey was then at Fort Yates, and Benteen at Fort McKinney. It is apparent that Godfrey had written Benteen of his intention to recast his West Point lecture of 1879 for general publication. It is further apparent that Benteen feared Godfrey would divulge the information given him in 1881 as to Reno's proposal on the night of June 25, 1876, to abandon his wounded and attempt an escape from the position on the bluffs. When Godfrey's article appeared (*Century Magazine,* January, 1892), it carried no more than a hint of the incident. "The question of moving was discussed," the account reads, "but the conditions coupled to the proposition caused it to be indignantly rejected."

Fort McKinney, Wyo, Ter.
Jan. 3d 1886.

Dear "God."

Your favor just rec'd. To commence, Don't you think that Reno has been sufficiently damned before the country that it can well be afforded to leave out in the article the proposition from him to saddle up and leave the field of the Little Big Horn on the 1st night of fight

Don't think that I would do it, but that he did so propose, there is no manner of doubt. "But the greatest of these is Charity"!

* * *

Happy New Year to you all, love from all the B's to thine,

Yr. friend,
BENTEEN.

V

EXTRACT FROM LETTER OF CAPT. MYLES MOYLAN TO CAPT. E. S. GODFREY, 1892.

(Moylan's letter, which consists of nearly five closely written pages, was written at Fort Riley, Kan., Jan. 17, 1892. The writer refers to Godfrey's *Century* article, though he acknowledges that he has read it but hurriedly. "I can say, however," he continued, "that my opinion of the article is that it covers all the points of the expedition in an able manner. I fully endorse all you say except some of your conclusions as to the causes of the defeat of the 7th Cavalry." He thereupon attributes to Custer the blame for the disaster, because of his division of the regiment, and defends Reno's action in leaving the valley. He continues:

I desire to be understood that my defense of Reno is entirely confined *to his act of taking his three troops out of the bottom* (italics by Moylan). Of his personal conduct in the bottom or subsequently on the hill the least said the better. If what Col. Benteen told me at Meade in 1883 was true, and I know of no reason to doubt it, then Reno ought to have been shot.

* * *

P.S. What I have written as to my conclusions of the responsibility of the Little Horn disaster is *strictly confidential.* (Italics by Moylan).

Yours,
Moylan.

————

VI

MEMORANDUM BY W. J. G., SEPT. 6, 1929

To me the most important letter (of the 48 written by Benteen to Goldin) was one of the earliest, written on Jan. 6, 1892, in reply to one from Goldin of Dec. 31, 1891. Goldin had evidently just read Godfrey's article in *The Century Magazine* for January, 1892, on the Little Big Horn battle. Benteen, at the time of his reply, had not seen it, though he expected to read it that night. He speculates to some extent on what Godfrey will say. He (Godfrey) will probably assert, writes Benteen, that on the night of June 25 Reno proposed "skipping out" with such of the wounded as could be mounted, leaving the remainder to the mercies of the Sioux. "So he did —*to me*," writes Benteen, "but I killed the proposal."

VII

Cookstown, New Jersey,
January 18th, 1929.

C. H. Asbury, Agent,
Crow Agency, Montana.

My dear Major Asbury:

Your letter of January 2nd has been before me as a matter of great interest. Several times when in Washington I have been tempted to see the Interior officials in reference to the appropriation for grounds and marker at the upper battlefield, but thought better to await progress of purchase, etc.

I have always felt that no individual names should be placed on the marker.

1st—Because I have always felt that Major Reno utterly failed in his part in the valley attack in the disposition of his command when he fell back in the old stream bed; that he failed to exercise any fire control; that he *could* and *should* have held that position.

2nd—Having made the decision to retreat, he made no disposition to cover that retreat or to properly inform the command of such decision; that he in person led a panic, straggling retreat, thereby sacrificing many lives and the morale of his command. The shock from the killing of Bloody Knife at his side or near him seems to have bereft him of the sense of official responsibility and to impel him to seek safety in flight.

3rd—After the command had taken the position, when we were besieged he seemed resigned to inactivity except when urged by Captain Benteen. After all firing had ceased the night of June 25th, he planned to abandon the position, destroy property that could not be transported, mount all men who could ride and retreat to the supply camp at the mouth of Powder River. When asked what he proposed to do with the wounded who could not ride, he said they would have to be *abandoned* and Benteen then told him he would not do it. This I had from Captain Benteen himhelf.

I protest the name of Major Reno on the marker and as the titulary commander's name should not be engraved thereon, therefore no individual names of survivors should appear and I suggest the following inscription:

This area was occupied by Companies A, B, D, G, H, K, and M, 7th U. S. Cavalry, and the Pack Train where they were besieged June 25th & 26th, 1876. * * * * *

With best wishes for you and yours,
Cordially,
(Sgd) E. S. Godfrey

VIII

GEN. HUGH L. SCOTT ON HERENDEEN'S TESTIMONY

(In the spring of 1926 Gen. Scott borrowed from Gen. Godfrey the latter's copy of George B. Herendeen's account of the battle of the Little Big Horn, which had been published in the New York *Herald* Jan. 22, 1878. In this account, as most students of the battle are aware, Herendeen defended Custer and condemned Reno. Gen. Scott, in a letter inclosed to Godfrey with the returned copy, bears witness to the close resemblance of Herendeen's statements to those expressed by officers of the 7th Cavalry within a year or two after the battle but before the holding of the Reno Court of Inquiry, Jan. 13-Feb. 11, 1879. The part of the letter relating to the subject is as follows:)

April 3, 1926.

My dear Godfrey:

. . . I inclose the Herendeen paper I borrowed from you to copy—it seems very straightforward and true to me just about as I heard it from all you fellows in 1877-8—drinking hotscotches made on my flat topped stove while engaged in fighting the battles of the Washita and the Little Horn—

Very sincerely yours,
H. L. SCOTT.

———

IX

EDGERLY'S STATEMENT TO HEIN

(From "Memories of Long Ago," by Lieut.-Col. O. L. Hein, (1925), pp. 143-45)

On June 25th (1886), the tenth anniversary of Custer's last fight was celebrated at the Post (Fort Custer), by a reunion of the surviving officers of the Little Big Horn campaign, including my old friend and classmate, Captain W. S. Edgerly, at the conclusion of which a number of the officers and ladies of the garrison made a visit to the battlefields.

Interesting information with reference to Custer's campaign was imparted to me by Edgerly in the following account that he indited for me:

Extract from General Terry's Order to Custer. "The Department Commander desires that on the way up the Rosebud you should thoroughly examine the upper part of Tulloch's Creek."

When we arrived in the neighborhood of Tullock's Creek we ran on a hot trail that led straight to the Indian village. It would have been useless to scout this creek, for we knew the Indians were in front of us.

After Reno crossed the Little Big Horn, he proceeded at a trot towards the village. Custer seeing that Reno met with very slight resistance and seeing that the creek was only knee high to the horses, changed his mind about following Reno in support and swung to the right, thinking he could cross anywhere. Unfortunately he had to go several miles before he came to a practical crossing.

Instead of charging through the village as Custer expected him to do, Reno halted, and later recrossed the creek to the high bluff. This was his fatal error. We of Benteen's squadron saw this recrossing and joined Reno before all his men had recrossed, which shows that we were near enough to come to his support in a few minutes. As soon as this second recrossing was made, nearly all the Indians left Reno and went to meet Custer. From this moment nothing could have saved Custer's command.

If Reno had charged through the village, Custer would have joined him in a very short time and Benteen later, and we might have had an expensive victory.

General Custer was severely criticized by some people for not obeying General Terry's order to scout Tullock's Creek. I show you why it would have been absurd, and do not believe any good officer would have obeyed it under the circumstances.

———

X

OFFICERS' ATTITUDE TOWARD RENO, JUNE 27, 1876

Memorandum by Captain Robert G. Carter, July 6, 1923.

General D. S. Brainard told me this date that he has often heard Capt. (later Gen.) Whelan and Lieut. (later Gen.) C. F. Roe, both of the Second U. S. Cavalry and of Terry's command, say that when they reached Reno's defensive line on the bluff all of Reno's officers talked wildly and excitedly about the fight, and of Reno's cowardice, etc. A little later they shut their mouths like clams and would not talk. It seemed to them (Brainard was later in Whelan's troop) that there suddenly sprang up among the Seventh Cavalry officers an understanding and resolve among themselves that they would say nothing further about that affair which would reflect in any way upon the honor of their regiment or regimental esprit, even if they had to sacrifice their own individual opinions concerning the plan of campaign or the conduct of the battle, either by Reno or Custer. This was later shown by their testimony before the Reno Court of Inquiry, where all but Godfrey refused to charge Reno with cowardice.

It is also shown by my interview with Col. (John) Merrill (son of Major Lewis Merrill, 7th Cavalry) who as a boy heard the battle discussed in the post trader's store at Fort Abraham Lincoln for months and was astounded to learn that three years later (1879) nearly every officer went before the Reno Court and testified to absolutely nothing which, in 1876, they had uttered as a positive conviction.

XI

MEMORANDUM

THE ARMY AND NAVY CLUB
Washington

I have frequently heard Major-General Eben Swift, who for a period was Adjutant of the Fifth U. S. Cavalry when Gen. Wesley Merritt commanded it—declare that Gen. M. who was a member of the Reno Court of Inquiry held in Chicago in 1879 told him that the Court in its findings— *"damned Reno with faint praise"*— because they were compelled to base that finding according to the evidence—and most all of the witnesses seemed reluctant to *"tell the truth, the whole truth and nothing but the truth"* but testified only to such facts as would *sustain the honor* and *uphold the reputation* of the Seventh U. S. Cavalry.

R. G. CARTER
Captain U. S. Army, Ret'd.

(Italics by Capt. Carter.)
Washington, D. C.,
    July 11, 1932.

W.J.G.

COMMENT ON GHENT MEMORANDA BY
COLONEL GRAHAM

I have many times been asked the question:— "What actually occurred during the night of 25 June, that gave rise to the story that Reno 'proposed' to 'skip out' and to abandon such of the wounded as were helpless and unable to ride."

While I would prefer to let the record stand as made, without comment, merely answering the question put to me by saying "I do not know," the situation as developed by Mr. Ghent is such that some comment seems desirable, for whatever it may be worth.

One cannot read intelligently the record of the Reno Court of Inquiry without realizing that though Reno was the ranking officer present, and as such, was technically in command during the whole of the action on Reno Hill, Benteen was the power behind the throne, and that it was he, not Reno, to whom the command looked for advice and leadership. There can be no doubt that Reno himself, an able and experienced officer in all but Indian fighting, sought out Benteen during the night of the 25th and discussed with him the desperate situation of the command, and what, if anything, could be done to extricate it from the threat of what the morrow probably would bring.

It must be kept in mind that during the night of the 25th there existed in Reno's command no slightest hint of what had happened to Custer. On the contrary, memories of what had happened to Major Elliott and his little band at the Washita reasserted themselves, and among officers and enlisted men alike the belief was general that Custer had found the Indians too strong and had gone to meet Terry, leaving *them* to fight it out as best they could.

And it must not be forgotten too, that it was Benteen who had written the Washita letter denouncing Custer's abandonment of Elliott—the letter which, published in the St. Louis "Democrat," had so enraged Custer that he proposed to horsewhip its author. And Benteen was Reno's chief, if not his only consultant during the night of the 25th.

No doubt the two went over the whole situation—they checked the animals, which had suffered badly from Indian long range fire; they counted the dead and discussed the wounded; the lack of water and of medical care. They made a general estimate of the situation, whose background probably was—"Damn Custer—this is another Washita affair."

And during the discussion, there can be no question that the matter of moving was considered, and carefully examined. And after such consideration it was rejected, not alone by Benteen, but by them both, when it became evident that a move would mean that such of the wounded as could not ride would have to be left. I have no doubt that it was Reno's answer to Benteen's question—"How could we move the wounded?" that brought forth his own reply: "No Reno, you *can't* do that!"

I do not for a minute believe, as the Ghent memoranda seem intended to imply, that Reno made a bald "proposal" to abandon his wounded which Benteen at once "indignantly rejected." I do not think he made any "proposal" whatever, in the sense that it was an independent proposition, rather than a conclusion to which their joint estimate of the situation inevitably forced him—

that *if* the command was moved, the *helpless* wounded must be left behind.

And I think it evident that when Benteen said —"No, Reno, you *can't* do that!" Reno assented without argument. He knew, quite as well as Benteen, that he could not do it. And we know that the command was *not* moved, and that the wounded were *not* abandoned.

In my opinion, altogether too much has been made of this "abandonment" story.

* * *

As for the Edgerly statement to Hein, I doubt that Edgerly ever made it in this form, as it clashes with his sentiments expressed on other occasions, and as expressed to me, both orally and by letter. Captain Carter's memoranda are consistent with the views he many times expressed. See "My debate with Carter," in this volume.

THE FIRST AND ORIGINAL CHARGE OF DRUNKENNESS AGAINST RENO

ONE of the "star" witnesses produced in 1879 at the Reno Court of Inquiry, was John Frett, who was employed during the Little Big Horn expedition as a packer. This man was summoned to Chicago to testify against Major Reno, upon the recommendation of Custer's biographer, Frederick Whittaker, whose charges against Reno, contained in a widely publicized letter to Wyoming's delegate to Congress, Mr. Corlett, caused Reno to demand the Court. It was Frett who swore that during the night of 25 June, Reno was drunk; in which testimony he was corroborated by another packer, named Churchill.

Other witnesses interrogated on the subject denied that Reno showed any evidences of intoxication during the time in question, and that they never heard of any such claim until the two packer's testified, from which it has been inferred by some writers that the packers' testimony was "framed" by Whittaker.

The fact is, however, that Frett first made his accusation upon his return to St. Paul in July 1876, and it was published by the Chicago *Tribune* on the 28th of July, as follows:

St. Paul, July 27

John Frett, formerly a policeman in this city, recommended by his acquaintances here as reliable, furnished an account of Major Reno's operations in the battle of the Little Big Horn, differing from all others in the assertion that Reno, from the effects of liquor, was unable to direct his command; that Captains Benteen and Weir saved all who were saved; that soldiers and others were united in accusing Reno of cowardice, and laying the responsibility of the defeat and Custer's death to him. Frett was a train employee who came up with a train after Reno's charge and his assertions concerning Reno are discredited by his own admission that during the day preceding the battle, for some offensive answer by him, Reno gave him a slap in the face.

He assisted to bury the dead, and though he served in the late war, and once saw 1500 dead in a narrow space, never saw a sight so horrid. The bodies had been greatly mutilated and were in all stages of decomposition. A German born soldier named Ackerman had by actual count, 75 well defined wounds in his body. His limbs were cut off.

Lt. McIntosh's scalp was torn and cut off from the forehead clear back to the neck. Many dead Indians were found and the soldiers generally believed the Indian loss was much heavier than the whites.

DID RENO "ACKNOWLEDGE THE CORN"?

On 7 September 1904, the Northwestern Christian Advocate, a well-known religious magazine, published the following in its editorial column.

"WHY GENERAL CUSTER PERISHED"

"General George A. Custer was and will always be regarded as one of the most brilliant officers of the United States Army. His career abounds in romantic interest; and his death, together with that of every officer and soldier fighting with him, was one of the most tragic and memorable incidents in Indian warfare. The story of Custer's last fight with the Indians, which took place on the Little Big Horn River in the summer of 1876, is graphically described by Cyrus Townsend Brady. It is not our purpose to relate the story of the battle, but to call attention to the real cause of Major Reno's conduct, which resulted in Custer's defeat and death."

Following an interpolated quotation from Cyrus Townsend Brady's well-known description of the battle of the Little Big Horn, the editorial then concludes:

"Major Reno was not a coward, as many believe. His career in the army during the Civil War and his promotion for gallant and meritorious services at Kelley's Ford, March 17, 1863, and at the battle of Cedar Creek, October 19, 1864, are evidence of his courage. What, then, was the ex-

A newspaper cut of the Reno Court of Inquiry held at Chicago in 1879. From a photo by Copelin.

Major Reno (seated in front of the middle window); Lt. De Rudio; the Recorder, Lt. Jesse M. Lee; and members of the court, Col. John H. King (center), flanked by Col. Wesley Merritt and Lt. Col. Wm. B. Royall, in order of rank (Royall is the partly bald officer with mustache); at the center table, the official reporter, Mr. Hollister.

planation of his conduct at the Battle of the Little Big Horn? Dr. Brady does not give it. Perhaps he does not know. But Major Reno himself told the late Rev. Dr. Arthur Edwards, then editor of the *Northwestern,* that his strange actions were due to the fact that HE WAS DRUNK. Reno's conduct in that battle lost him many of his military friends. To Arthur Edwards, who knew him well, and continued his faithful friend, Major Reno often unburdened his heart, and on one occasion in deep sorrow said that his strange actions were due to drink, and drink ultimately caused his downfall. His action at the Battle of the Little Big Horn was cited as one instance of the result of his use of intoxicating liquor. Liquor finally caused his expulsion from the army in disgrace. In 1880 he was found guilty, by a general court-martial, of conduct unbecoming an officer and a gentleman. While in an intoxicated condition he engaged in a brawl in a public billiard saloon, in which he assaulted another officer, destroying property and otherwise conducted himself disgracefully. For this offense the court sentenced him to be dismissed from the army.'

CHAPTER 13

A BOAST, A GRAPHIC LETTER AND A GRUMBLE

DID "RED HORSE" MEAN FRENCH?

*Capt. French, "M" Tp., to Mrs. Cooke, wife of
Dr. A. H. Cooke, 234 Dearborn Ave.,
Chicago, June '80*

Excerpt

"I fear that the information which you have received as to the duration of the combat of the five companies has much truth in it.

What those people who first reached that memorable hill heard, I have no means of knowing. I reached there late, and listened, attentively, and heard nothing to denote the progress of a battle. Along in the lower valley I heard a few scattering shots, such as may be heard near an Indian camp at any time. I paid no attention and attached no importance to that.

I talked with noted chiefs; men of that ferocious but truthful band of Northern Cheyennes—such men as "Brave Wolf," "White Bull" and "Two Moon." They agreed in saying that they drove those (meaning us) at the upper end of the Greasy Grass Creek (The LBHorn) and then swarmed on those below (Custer's command) so thickly that scarcely half of them could fight, for fear of killing each other. Everything showed a fierce fight, especially at the point where lay dead the two Custers, Cooke, Yates, Reilly, Smith and about 35 others—Keogh a little way off.

* * * These Indians *all* had Winchester 17 shooting breech loaders, which may be fired as rapidly as a slight turn of the hand can be made. They had, some of them whom I have seen at the agencies, four belts of cartridges—two about the loins, one each way from the shoulder over the chest; they also had from one to two six shooters (pistols). In such a storm of leaden hail I doubt if the slaughtered band could have lived more than half an hour.

* * * "What made Major R run away when he did I cannot positively know, and he did not tell me. What made him halt and dismount when he did is a matter in regard to which I am equally ignorant. It was not the kind of warfare to which I had been accustomed—and that was this—to be watchful, and prudent and never to take less than an even chance, but when once in to do as is said to be the custom at Donnybrook Fair—"if you see a head, hit it." I thought that we were to charge headlong through them all—that was the only chance. To turn ones back on Indians without being better mounted than they is throwing away life. When he started to that hill he had told me, not one minute before, that he was going to fight—this was in reply to a question of mine.

And when all had gone for safety was when I sought death—and tried to fight the battle alone —and did so for nearly a mile. If one man could hold back seven or eight hundred, what might not a hundred and twenty have done at the right instant. Sometimes one minute is of far more value than years afterward, or before—and military life consists simply in waiting for opportunities.

I hate to leave active service, as I would like one more chance at those Sioux. Not that they owe me anything personally—but I want revenge for my friends. No—they owe me nothing. I don't wonder that old Red Horse thought me a spirit from the bad place—for—and there is no mistake in this—I saw them fall—8 of his men who rode up to within a few yards of me—tumbled off as I fired, and their ponies ran loose. How many were dead I don't know and did not stop to see. Just before I had killed one with my rifle, and on crossing the creek two more and on the next day, one—this is in the evidence taken at Ft. Lincoln in January 1879, given by men who saw it. And in 1873 (see Gen. Custer's report) I fought an open duel with one and killed him. It is not nice, I know, to mention these things, but they do not rest on my version. What I mean to get at is this. If I were able to do all this single handed, what might I not have done with the coveted opportunity—but a friendly bullet did not come to assist me—and although the idea flashed through my mind, yet I did not dare to resort to murder —the latter I now believe would have been justifiable.

                              T. H. FRENCH

* * *

FIGHTING THE INDIANS

From Lowell, Mass., *"Weekly Journal,"*
August, 1876.

Letter from Lieutenant Varnum, of this city—A full description of the Late Massacre—Death of General Custer.

* * *

We take the following letter from Lieut. Varnum to his father, who now lives in Tallahassee, Fla., and who formerly lived in Dracut, from a Tallahassee paper:

                    Camp on the Yellowstone,
                         July 4, 1876.

Dear Father and Mother:

Having an opportunity of sending off a letter this evening, I will try and give you an account of our operations since I wrote you last. On the 22d of June General Custer took the entire regiment, numbering about 605 strong, with my squad of about thirty-six scouts and guides, interpreters, etc., and started up the Rosebud river after the Indians, whose trail was discovered by Major Reno. We made about twelve miles the first day and thirty-two or three on the second, and early on the morning of the third day we got on a very heavy trail going up the Rosebud. About ten miles from camp we found a circle surrounded by a brush fence arranged for a sun-dance, a description of which I have given you before, for making warriors. We found a stick with a fresh scalp attached and the trail of two or three Indians, evidently made that morning. We marched twenty miles, and then I was sent back six to examine a creek to see if any Indians had left the trail, and on my return we started again and made eight miles more, and camped in an Indian camp about two days old. The signs indicated an immense force, and we were in a hurry to take them by surprise. Custer came over to see the scouts. Six Crows with us, who knew the country well, said that the trail from here led on towards the Little Horn, a fork of the Big Horn, and they wanted to go ahead about twenty miles to a high bluff from which the valley of the Little Horn

could be seen. Custer wanted some intelligent white man to go ahead with them to send him information. I took the six Crows, five Rees, and a white man, who was an old frontiersman, and we marched all night, making about sixty miles. I had rode without rest or any sleep for thirty-six hours. Custer said he would start at 11 p. m., and come somewhere near us by morning. At 2:30 o'clock we reached the hill, and lay there in scrub bushes until daybreak, when we discovered the smoke of a village, and by 5 a. m., I started the Rees back with a dispatch to General Custer. The Crows said there were about two or three thousand ponies on the plain twelve miles off, but I could not see them, as their eyes were better than mine. Custer had come ahead, and we could see his camp about eight miles off. He got my dispatch at 8 a. m., and started again and came to the hill. In the meantime two Sioux were seen going in the direction of Custer's column. Charley Reynolds, myself, the Crow interpreter and two Crows started out to kill them, and prevent Custer being discovered. We failed to do it, however, and when Custer came up we informed him of the state of affairs, and he concluded, as we were discovered, to hurry up and strike them as soon as possible. At about 2:30 we came up to the neighborhood of the camp, and three companies, A, G and M, under Major Reno, started in. I saw them going, and Lieutenant Hare, who had been ordered to report to me for duty with our scouts, went in with them. They pretended to run away and we charged up the valley, near the village, dismounted, put our horses in the timber near the stream, and fought on foot. My scouts scattered about so I had no command near me, and I reported to Captain Moylan for duty with Company A. In half an hour we were not only surrounded, but the odds against us were so fearful that we were obliged to retreat, and we returned up into the woods and started on a run for the bluff. The Indians did not press us very hard, and we knew from the fearful firing at the other end of the village that some one was getting it hot and heavy up there. On the bluff we reorganized, and found that Lieutenant McIntosh and DeRudio were gone, and Lieutenant Hodgson was killed close by. Only five men and Lieutenant Wallace came out with company G, and more than one-third of our command was gone. Just then Colonel Benteen and three companies came in from a trip they had endeavored to make to the rear of the village, and the pack-train came up with one company more. This gave us four full companies with the remains of three others and the citizen portion, numbering in all about three hundred men. We could hear heavy firing about two miles off, and knew that Custer, with the remaining five companies, was having a hard fight beyond the village. As soon as we could get into any sort of shape we started along the bluff to try and unite with Custer, and after a mile's march we could see no sign of him; while the firing was very distant. As we were encumbered with wounded and had the whole pack-train on our hands, and hundreds of Indians were turning their attention to us, we selected a good place for defence on the bluffs, and prepared to receive them. The place was well selected, while the horses were in a sort of hollow where they could be shot at from only one direction, and here the ball opened.

We fought, God and ourselves only know how hard, until about 9 o'clock, and then the firing ceased until the first streak of daylight, when the ball opened again. We fortified as much as the four spades we had would let us, and all day long they piled lead into us at a fearful rate. The men fell fast, but young boys soon became old men, and men lay in the trench beside corpses with flies and maggots, and struck and fought like old veterans of years' standing. The hospital held about forty wounded, but was protected by the mules and horses which surrounded it, and which must be hit before the bullets could hit the men. I will not attempt to describe the horror of the situation. We had no water, and the men became furious, and detachments were sent under heavy fire to try and get some. Many were killed and wounded in that way. The horses suffered fearfully, as they, of course, got no water, and could not eat what oats we had without. The firing ceased on the afternoon of the 26th, and we could see that the village was leaving. After dark we changed our camp a little, so as to get away from the stench of the dead animals. In the morning the Indians were gone, and the cause was soon explained. General Terry, with five companies of the Seventh Infantry, and four of the Second Cavalry, was coming to our relief. They had seen the Crow scouts, who had escaped, and hurried to our assistance. They reached us about 10 a. m., and then the sickening details were seen in all their horror. General Custer, with his five companies, had been exterminated. About three hundred men had been killed, and their bodies stripped and horribly mangled. Sixteen officers had fallen, viz: General Custer, Captain Keogh, Captain Yates, Captain Custer, Lieutenant Cooke, First Lieutenants Smith, McIntosh, Calhoun and Porter; Second Lieutenants Hodgson, Harring-

ton, Sturgis and Reilly, of the Seventh Cavalry, Lieutenant Crittendon of the Twentieth Infantry; Doctors Lord and DeWolf. Colonel Benteen and myself were slightly wounded. I have received two slight flesh wounds, one in each leg, below the knee, while charging, dismounted, to drive the Indians from a hill where they were killing our men very rapidly. It seems horrible to think it all over now. Mrs. Custer loses her husband and his two brothers—one a citizen travelling with us, and Mrs. Calhoun loses her husband and three brothers (She is the General's sister), and a nephew—a Mr. Reed travelling with us also. Half of the officers with us are killed, and the regiment sadly cut up. I will give you some more of the incidents hereafter. I have been put in command of the remnant of Company I. This makes me a First Lieutenant, and No. 11 on that list. We are encamped on our old battle ground of August 11, 1873, and a boat has gone to Lincoln to open communication with Sheridan, and receive orders. When we got a mail yesterday by a carrier from Fort Ellis, we received a letter from Sheridan, a month old, cautioning Terry not to split his command, as he had information that at least five thousand warriors were assembled, and I don't think there is any doubt but that we fought four thousand of them. Gen. Crook, with sixteen companies of cavalry, was coming up from the south, and this despatch says he has been reinforced by the whole Fifth Cavalry, giving him twenty-eight companies to fight what we struck with twelve. This is a brief account of affairs. Don't worry for me.

> Your affectionate son,
> CHARLES A. VARNUM

EXCERPT FROM A LETTER TO GENERAL GODFREY

(From WM. O. TAYLOR of "A" Troop, 7th Cavalry, 74 East Main St., Orange, Mass.)

February 20, 1910.

I enlisted in Troy, N. Y., Jan. 17, 1872, went to St. Louis and was there assigned with many others to the 7th and soon after joined Capt. French's troop "M" at Unionville, S. C. Was with Troop "M" at Ft. Rice until the latter part of 1875 or early in 1876 when I sought and obtained a transfer to Capt. Moylan's Troop "A" at Ft. Lincoln. * * * and therefore was with Troop "A" and took part in the fight at the Little Big Horn. It so happened that both times the troop counted fours that 25 June 1876 I was a number four man and as such had to care for led horses when the troop was dismounted, hence I did not see much of the firing line in the first part of the valley fight, being in the woods with the led horses. I do not know if I can add anything to the story of that unexpected and demoralized rout that you do not know. It seemed but a very few moments after we had taken the horses into the timber before the men came rushing back for them. I did not see any officers in there except Lieut. Varnum I think, nor did I hear any orders as to what we were to do. After my led horses were taken, I followed in the direction the men had taken, mounting and dismounting several times, but for what purpose I did not know. As I came out of the timber into the open I saw the soldiers heading for the bluffs and firing their revolvers at the Indians, who were rushing in the same direction, but a few yards away, with a tendency to crowd us. My horse played out just after crossing the river and things looked rather dark as I trudged up the steep bluff, a comrade with whom I was talking being shot dead at my side; but the top was soon reached, and most unexpectedly the Indians seemed to draw off and left us alone. Then Benteen came up and you know the rest. * * *

Reno proved incompetent and Benteen showed his indifference—I will not use the uglier words that have often been in my mind. Both failed Custer and he had to fight it out alone. This is but one of my theories—a theory of one who has had no chance of studying the field or talking with survivors of the battle. Among the several things that impressed me greatly, one was the general demoralization that seemed to pervade many of the officers and men, due in great measure, I think, to Major Reno. When an enlisted man sees his commanding officer lose his head entirely and several other officers showing greater regard for their personal safety than anything else, it would be apt to demoralize anyone taught to breathe, almost, at the word of command. * * *

I have seen but one member of the 7th since I was discharged in January 1877: that was Sergt. John Ryan of "M" Troop. He is now a Captain of Police at West Newton, Mass.

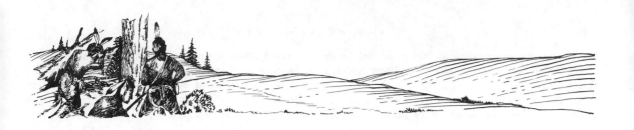

CHAPTER 14

UNIFORMS, EQUIPMENT AND AMMUNITION

GODFREY DESCRIBES MOUNTS, UNIFORMS AND EQUIPMENT

(Montana University Historical Reprints)

UNDER date of January 16, 1896, General (then Major) E. S. Godfrey, answered several questions relating to the mounts, uniforms and equipment of the 7th at the Little Big Horn, and the general conditions obtaining on Custer's field, as follows:

"1st: Gen. Custer rode "Vic" into the fight; Vic was a sorrel, with four white feet and legs and a blaze in the face; he was not found on the field. I have heard that he had been identified in the possession of some Indian in the hostile camp after they went into the British possessions. The dogs were left with the wagon train.

2nd: General Custer carried a Remington Sporting rifle, octagonal barrel; two Bulldog self-cocking, English, white-handled pistols, with a ring in the butt for a lanyard; a hunting knife, in a beaded fringed scabbard; and a canvas cartridge belt. He wore a whitish gray hat, with broad brim and rather low crown, very similar to the Cowboy hat; buck skin suit, with a fringed welt in outer seams of trousers and arms of blouse; the blouse with double-breasted military buttons, lapels generally open; turn-down collar, and fringe on bottom of shirt. (skirt?)

3rd: Captain Tom Custer was dressed about the same as the General. He was found near the top of the hill, north, and a few yards from the General, lying on his face; his features were so pressed out of shape as to be almost beyond recognition; a number of arrows had been shot in his back, several in his head, one I remember, without the shaft, the head bent so that it could hardly be withdrawn; his skull was crushed and nearly all the hair scalped, except a very little on the nape of the neck.

The General was not mutilated at all; he laid on his back, his upper arms on the ground, the hands folded or so placed as to cross the body above the stomach; his position was natural and one that we had seen hundreds of times while taking cat naps during halts on the march. One hit was in the front of the left temple, and one in the left breast at or near the heart.

Boston, the youngest brother was dressed similar to the other brothers, his body was found about two hundred yards from "Custer Hill," between that and the Little Big Horn, at the foot of the ridge that runs up from the river, and as it were, forms the lower boundary of the battlefield. The body was stript except his white cotton socks and they had the name cut off.

4th: Yates, Cooke, Smith and Reilley lay on Custer Hill in the vicinity of the General but nearer the top of the hill, the General's body was slightly down the slope, toward the river. Calhoun was in the vicinity of the hill, but farther removed from the others, as if he had been killed while going toward Custer, from the position of his troop on the left. Crittenden was on the hill on the extreme left of the line (when facing the river). Keogh was in a depression just north or below Crittenden Hill * and on the slope of the ridge that forms the defensive line furthest from the river; the body was stript except the socks, and these had the name cut off; in life he wore a Catholic medal suspended from his neck; it was not removed.

All of the officers wore the dark blue shirt with rather wide falling collar, which when the blouse was worn, was over the blouse collar; most of them had cross-sabers and 7, like the old cap ornament, worked in white or yellow silk on the points of the collar.

Yates, Cooke, Smith, Porter and Calhoun, and sometimes Keogh, wore buckskin blouses, but I don't think any of them wore other than blue trousers; Harrington wore the blue blouse and

_____
* Now known as Calhoun Hill.

white canvas trousers, with fringe on the outer seams. The day was very warm and few had any kind of blouse.

In describing the dress, I give it as generally worn, for when the bodies were found, after the fight, they were stript.

I found Porter's buckskin blouse in the village, while destroying the property, and from the shot holes in it, he must have had it on and must have been shot from the rear, left side, the bullet coming out on the left breast near the heart. Dr. Lord and Lieutenants Sturgis and Reilley wore the blue; Dr. Lord wore eye-glasses.

Sergeant Robert Hughes of Troop K, who carried the General's battle flag, was killed near the General on the hill. Nearly all the men wore the blue, but many, perhaps most of them, had their trousers reenforced with white canvas on the seat and on the legs from the knees half way up. Nearly every one wore the short top boot (that was then uniform) not high like those now worn, although a few of the officers wore the Wellington boot and had white canvas leggings.

5th: The command was armed with the Springfield and the Colt revolver; every officer carried a revolver. NO ONE CARRIED THE SABER. (Nearly every illustration I have seen of that fight or campaign have had the officers and men armed with the saber. Adams' painting of "Custer's Last Fight," last winter presented to the regiment by Mr. Busch, has the men armed with the Winchester and the saber. In a historical painting, I think, if I may be allowed the suggestion, that the equipments, etc. should conform to those used at the time of the fight.) The bridles were different from the present pattern; the carbine socket was a small sack about 20 inches long in which was carried about 12 pounds of oats, strapped on the cantel (sic); there was no hood on the stirrup used by the men.

6th: There were no "good Indians" left on the field after the time we saw it; they were all removed; our dead were alone. There were not so many dead ponies found on the field, nor many dead horses, indeed surprisingly few, and most of them were on or near Custer Hill. It would seem that they were turned loose that the men might better defend themselves, or were wounded and broke away. The scene on the left (N & E of Crittenden Hill or near the point on the map marked "spring")* where the Indians stampeded the "led horses" of Troops I and L, must have been a wild one; and their loss must have made their hearts very heavy and perhaps

* See Godfrey's Map.

caused many a man to give up hope at the very beginning. A representation of that scene in the background would add immensely to the effect from the realistic point of view, whatever it might be from an artistic point!

Troops F, I, and L had bay horses; Troop C had light sorrels, and Troop E had grays; the trumpeters rode grays; Cooke rode an almost white horse; as a rule the officers rode horses the same color as the troops to which they belonged.

As to "accessories" on the battlefield, there were none. The marble white bodies, the somber brown of the dead horses and the dead ponies scattered all over the field, but thickest on and near Custer Hill, and the scattering tufts of reddish brown grass on the almost ashy white soil depicts a scene of loneliness and desolation that "bows down the heart in sorrow." I can never forget the sight: The early morning was bright, as we ascended to the top of the highest point whence the whole field came into view, with the sun to our backs. "What are those?" exclaimed several as they looked at what appeared to be white boulders. Nervously I took the field glasses and glanced at the objects; then almost dropped them, and laconically said, "The Dead!" Col. Weir who was near sitting on his horse, exclaimed, "Oh, how white they look! How white!" No, there were no "accessories"; everything of value was taken away; arms, ammunition, equipment and clothing. Occasionally, there was a body with a bloody undershirt or trousers or socks, but the name was invariably cut out. The naked mutilated bodies, with their bloody fatal wounds, were nearly unrecognizable, and presented a scene of sickening, ghastly horror! There were perhaps, a half dozen spades and shovels, as many axes, a couple of picks, and a few hatchets in the whole command; with these and knives and tin cups we went over the field and gave the bodies, where they lay, a scant covering of mother earth and left them, in that vast wilderness, hundreds of miles from civilization, friends and homes,—to the wolves!"

* * *

SGT. JOHN RYAN TELLS HOW THEY WERE DRESSED

(1st Sgt. John Ryan, M Troop, 7th Cavalry, in the Hardin *Tribune*, June 22, 1923)

Going out into this engagement General Custer wore a broad brimmed slouch hat, buckskin shirt and trousers, and high top cavalry boots. He was armed with a Remington sporting rifle which used a brass shell. He also carried in his belt two pistols, one a .45-caliber Colt, and the other a French Navy, and a hunting knife. He rode a large sorrel horse. His favorite horse, "Dandy," was with the pack train.

His brother, Thomas W., wore a broad brimmed slouch hat, a buckskin shirt and carried a .45-caliber Colt pistol, and I think a Springfield sporting rifle, caliber .45.

* * *

The men all wore high topped boots, going into the engagement, and when we found the bodies of the men we found nearly all of the lower parts of their boots near the bodies, the legs of the boots being cut off and carried away by the Indians. We supposed that this was for making soles for their moccasins.

———

RYAN DESCRIBES THE INDIAN ARMS AND AMMUNITION

(1st Sgt. John Ryan, M Troop, 7th Cavalry, in the Hardin *Tribune,* June 22, 1923)

In regard to the ammunition and the arms that the Indians used on Reno's command, it appears that when Custer's five companies were wiped out of existence the Indians got all their Springfield .45-caliber breech-loading carbines, and in addition to getting what cartridges the men had left in their waist belts, they probably got the 60 extra rounds that each man carried in his saddlebag, and also the 24 rounds of pistol ammunition, caliber .45. All this ammunition, with the carbines, were used against Reno's men by the Indians, as a number of our men were wounded with the same caliber ammunition.

———

COL. VARNUM ON INDIAN ARMS

My dear Col. Graham:

I return your manuscript herewith. I have no comment to make and think you have written a very fair and complete account of the campaign and its results.

Personally I think and always have that the best guns in the hands of the Indians, were the carbines taken from Custer's men and the 70 grain ammunition they got from the same source. We took, at least I think they all took, rifle ammunition instead of carbine 55 gr. On the hill most of the bullets came in with a *zip* sound. When a zing-g-g sound came, that made you take notice. However that is only *my* opionion.

Yours,

CHAS. A. VARNUM

"Custer's Last Stand" by Elk Eber. Original painting in
Karl May Indian Museum at Dresden, Germany.

CHAPTER 15

WHY HELENA INSTEAD OF BOZEMAN
SCOOPED THE NEWS IN 1876

COLONEL LOUNSBERRY of Bismarck, publisher of the *Bismarck Tribune,* claimed for many years that he (which is to say, his paper), first gave to the world the news of the Little Big Horn disaster. Lounsberry's *Tribune,* did, as a matter of fact, in an Extra dated 6 July 1876, publish the first account that included a list of the dead and wounded; but two Montana papers, the *Bozeman Times* and the *Helena Herald,* both preceded the *Tribune* story with stories of their own.

The *Bozeman Times* was first, having put out an "Extra" at 7 P.M., 3 July 1876, and was followed by the *Helena Herald,* which got the news the next day, during Helena's Fourth of July celebration, and by working far into the night, printed a late Extra dated 4 July 1876. Andrew Fisk, editor of the *Herald,* after getting his paper on the street, flashed the news to the *Associated Press* at Salt Lake City, from which point it was relayed to the east, and made late editions of eastern papers 5 July 1876, one day ahead of the *Bismarck Tribune,* thus scooping the most sensational news of the year.

These are the bare facts; but the reason that Bozeman did not make the scoop at least twenty four hours ahead of Helena has never been told. But that Bozeman had the news on 3 July cannot be gainsaid, for the *Times Extra* was as follows:

THE BOZEMAN TIMES
EXTRA

July 3, 1876
7 P. M.

Mr. Taylor, bearer of despatches from the Little Horn to Ft. Ellis, arrived this evening and reports the following.

"The battle was fought on the 25th, 30 or 40 miles below the Little Horn. Custer attacked the Indian village of from 2500 to 4000 warriors on one side and Col. Reno was to attack it on the other. Three companies were placed on a hill as a reserve. General Custer and fifteen officers and EVERY MAN BELONGING TO THE FIVE COMPANIES WAS KILLED. Reno retreated under the protection of the reserve. The whole number killed was 315. General Gibbon joined Reno.

"The Indians left the battleground looking like a slaughter pen, as it really was, being in a narrow ravine. The dead were much mutilated.

"The situation now looks serious. Gen. Terry arrived at Gibbon's camp on a steamboat and crossed the command over and accompanied it to join Custer, who knew it was coming before the fight occurred. Lieut. Crittenden, son of Gen. Crittenden, was among the killed."

The facts appear to be that when on 27 June General Terry wrote his first report of the Battle, he placed it in the hands of the scout known as "Muggins" Taylor, to be delivered to the Commanding Officer at Ft. Ellis, for immediate transmittal by wire from Bozeman, the nearest telegraph office.

Taylor, as will be apparent later, got through to Stillwater the night of 1 July, and the next day, before proceeding to Ft. Ellis, told the story of the battle to one W. H. Norton, a representative of the *Helena Herald.* Taylor then rode on, reaching Ft. Ellis the afternoon of 3 July, and delivered General Terry's report to the Commanding Officer, Captain D. W. Benham of the 7th Infantry, who at once took it in person to the telegraph office in Bozeman for immediate transmittal.

On 5 July, upon being informed at Bozeman that the report had not been transmitted by wire, but had been sent by mail *that morning,* he made the following report:

Fort Ellis, M. T.,
July 5th 1876

To the
  Asst Adjt Genl
    Mil Div of the Mo
      Chicago, Ills.

Sir:

I have the honor to inform you that on the afternoon of July 3d, '76 a scout, Taylor, arrived at this post from Genl. Terry's command with important dispatches for your headquarters.

I immediately in person took the dispatches to the telegraph office in Bozeman and was there informed that the line was in working order to Pleasant Valley.

On the 4th day of July I went to town to see if the telegrams above referred to had been sent and found the telegraph office closed.

This afternoon on visiting Bozeman, I inquired if the telegrams left at the office on the 3d had been sent and was informed that they had been forwarded by mail this morning.

I deem this neglect of duty and criminal negligence on the part of the telegraph operator and report it accordingly.

If telegraph rates are charged on the dispatches above referred to between Bozeman and Helena, the bill should be repudiated and proceedings instituted against the company for neglect of duty because the dispatches were sent by mail from Bozeman to Helena, and if the agent had informed me that the telegrams could not have been sent I could have forwarded them by courier and thereby have gained twenty four hours time.

Copies of telegrams above referred to are sent you by this mail.

I am, Genl
D. W. BENHAM,
Capt. 7th Inf. Comd'g. Post

In the meantime, however, Mr. Norton, the "Special Correspondent" of the *Helena Herald* was letting no grass grow under his feet, and succeeded in sending his story of the fight by courier, presumably the Mr. Countryman who figures in the Fisk story of the scoop,* who arrived in Helena 4 July and immediately sought out Mr. Fisk, the editor of the *Herald.* Fisk's *"Extra"* dated 4 July 1876, reads as follows:

---

* See *Brininstool* "Troopers with Custer," Chapter 12.

HELENA DAILY HERALD
EXTRA

July 4, 1876

A TERRIBLE FIGHT

Gen. Custer and his Nephew

KILLED

The Seventh Cavalry cut to pieces

The Whole Number Killed 315

---

*From our Special Correspondent
Mr. W. H. Norton*

Stillwater, M. T.,
July 2nd, 1876.

Muggins Taylor, scout for Gen. Gibbons, got here last night, direct from Little Horn River with telegraphic despatches. General Custer found the Indian camp of about two thousand lodges on the Little Horn, and immediately attacked the camp. Custer took five companies and charged the thickest portion of the camp.

Nothing is Known of the Operation

of this detachment, only as they trace it by the dead. Major Reno commanded the other seven companies and attacked the lower portion of the camp. The Indians poured in a murderous fire from all directions. Besides the greater portion fought on horseback. Custer, his two brothers, a nephew and a brother-in-law were

All Killed

and not one of his detachment escaped. 207 men were buried in one place and the killed are estimated at 300 with only 31 wounded. The Indians surrounded Reno's command and held them one day in the hills

Cut Off from Water

until Gibbon's command came in sight, when they broke camp in the night and left.

The Seventh Fought Like Tigers

and were overcome by mere brute force. The Indian loss cannot be estimated, as they bore off and cached most of their killed. The remnant of the Seventh Cavalry and Gibbon's command are returning to the mouth of the Little Horn, where the steamboat lies. The Indians got all the arms of the killed soldiers. There were seventeen commissioned officers killed.

The Whole Custer Family

died at the head of their column. The exact loss is not known as both Adjutants and the Sergeant Major were killed. The Indian camp was from three to four miles long and was twenty miles up the Little Horn from its mouth. The Indians actually pulled men off their horses in some instances. I give this as Taylor told me, as he was over the field after the battle.

The above is confirmed by other letters which say Custer met a fearful disaster.

———

The next day, the *Herald* followed its July fourth Extra with a short editorial which read:

HELENA DAILY HERALD

Wednesday, July 5, 1876

EDITORIAL

The news received last evening of the defeat of Custer and the massacre of his entire command, fell upon the festivities of the day with a gloom that could not be shaken off. There is only too much reason to believe that the facts given in the extras of last evening are literally true. The parties from whom the facts were received are too well known to leave a reasonable doubt.

* * *

BOZEMAN and HELENA, however, were not alone in beating the *Bismarck Tribune,* for on 5 July 1876, the Commanding Officer, Ft. Rice, near Bismarck, had news of the battle, and at once wired it to the Adjutant at St. Paul. The following extract from letter of Colonel Hugh F. Reed, Ret'd., dated 14 April 1926, tells the story:

"We officers at Fort Rice and the Post Trader made up a purse, and had a pony race on the Fourth of July. * * * The day after the pony race three Sioux Indians arrived at the post. One of them had a bow and half a dozen arrows. I bought them. * * * The Indian from whom I bought the bow and arrows said that he had pulled the arrows from the dead bodies of soldiers that the Indians had killed with Custer. This was our first news of a fight. The Indians said that a big force of Indians had killed Custer and all his soldiers. I then took the three Indians to Lieut. Humbert the post commander, and they repeated their story of the fight. * * * As Adjutant I wrote a message which Humbert signed and sent it by a courier thirty miles to Bismarck, the nearest telegraph office, to the Adjutant General, Dept. of Dakota, St. Paul. This was the first news sent of the fight. There was an old stockade south of the post buildings, and Humbert put his company in one bastion and I put my company in the other bastion, where we stayed all night on watch for an attack. The next day Capt. Grant Marsh with his steamer The Far West arrived at Bismarck. He had on board some wounded soldiers from Reno's battalion."

———

But why the telegraph operator at Bozeman failed to transmit Terry's report the afternoon of 3 July has never been explained: nor has it ever been explained why the editor of the *Bozeman Times* did not round up the operator and scoop the news himself. Certainly the opportunity was wide open.

It has been stated that the wires were down and that no message could be sent from Bozeman on that day; but Captain Benham's official report gives the lie to that assertion.

Perhaps the Bozeman telegraph operator had already commenced to celebrate the Glorious Fourth when Benham rode in with Terry's report. In the "good old days" many celebrants of Independence Day absorbed their patriotism from a bottle. Perhaps—but it is idle to speculate. Quien sabe!

The Thrill That Comes Once in a Lifetime BY H.

CHAPTER 16

FIVE TALES WITH THE REAL HOLLYWOOD TOUCH

ELSEWHERE in this volume allusion has been made to the product throughout the years, of the Diabolical Twins, and my offering would be incomplete without the inclusion of a few selected samples.

When I was practising law, many years ago, we of the profession were wont to say that liars were divisible into three classes; liars, damned liars and expert witnesses. I think I would amend that classification now, and for expert witnesses, substitute another class—the fabricators of fantastic tales about Custer's Last Fight.

There follow here five such tales that the movies haven't as yet taken over. Two were sent to Mrs. Custer; two were sent to me; one was published in 1876 by the New York Herald.

No. 1: the frenzied message from Custer to Reno deposited with the Heye Foundation by the Ft. Wadsworth teamster is perhaps the quaintest of the lot. The copy I possess was sent me by an excited student of the battle at least twenty-five years ago—a school girl who thought she had discovered the key to the Custer mystery. And I still receive letters, happily less frequently now than formerly, asking whether the "message" is "the real McCoy." The Heye Foundation has cost me a pretty penny in postage, and I venture to express the hope that more efficient use may be made of the Foundation's waste basket than has heretofore been evident.

No. 2, The Benner story, was sent me years ago by some chap in San Francisco. It really is a wondrous tale—a tale that grows and grows each time one reads it. That "Custer horse" which Benner rode 150 miles to find Reno 65 miles away was a better performer than Sheridan's "Rienzi," which carried him from Winchester: better even than the famed mount of Paul Revere, which visited every Middlesex village and farm. The San Franciscan who sent the Benner story to me believed it; or said he did, which was even more wonderful than the story;—and he became quite peeved when told that parts of it seemed to me to approach debatable ground. It never was clear to me whether Benner rode 150 miles or 300, before his return on the third day to assist in burying the dead. His description of Indian hunting in Colorado, too, and Wild Bill's inspired enterprise which ended in shocking disappointment and a no less shocking waste of whiskey and strychnine, (notwithstanding he killed 59 Indians with it), makes one wonder whether his heirs have a valid claim against the government. At $50 per Indian, Wild Bill should have netted $2950 for a few minutes work, which amount, with accrued interest to date, would now be a tidy sum, even in New Deal dollars.

The two letters (Nos. 3 & 4) sent to Mrs. Custer must have amused the dear lady, if it was possible for her to find amusement in the distortion of what to her had been a life long tragedy.

But to have the real low-down from "the only living white man that saw that fight" was an experience, even for her; and it must be conceded that the Carlyle Chemical man's letter had its points.

His graphic description of Custer's last moments is a word picture that should appeal to every Hollywood producer. The brave General stands alone with all his comrades lying dead around him! And does he blanch? Not he! With a sweep of his trusty saber he all but decapitates a warrior, even as his last shot strikes another between the eyes; and two red-skins bite the dust as the hero falls dead, a bullet in his breast. And the Carlyle Chemical fellow, as he stands over the body fifteen minutes later, detects a smile upon his face, as if he were thinking of his home, his wife, and mother!

The Towers' letter from Sawtelle is interesting too, the *duello* between Reno and Hazen, and the interference of other officers, apparently having prevented everyone else from going out to assist Custer in his last fight.

No. 5, The New York Herald story of 1 August 1876 is worthy of especial attention, combining as it does, more fantasy and misinformation than any concoction I have seen, except perhaps, some of the Curley stories.

But here we have a tale of an ambush into which the trusting but impulsive Custer is led by a half breed guide named Billy Cross—a headlong charge into an apparently deserted village, with no resistance until its further side is reached, when the troops receive a terrific volley, and find themselves in the very center of an immense camp, entirely surrounded, and all avenues of retreat cut off. And to prove the cunning of the Indians and the perfidy of Billy Cross, the grass and brush has been tied and knotted together, to trip and otherwise impede the horses of the troopers; while hidden Indians fire upon them from behind a screen of wickerwork, made of willow boughs, which conceals not only the warriors, but hides part of the village also! It is indeed a stirring tale.

Upon the roll of Varnum's Arikara scouts, one there was whose name was *CROSS WILLIAM;* and it may be he that is named in the story as "Billy Cross;" but no Arikara went beyond the lone tepee with Custer, and his only guide was the half-breed Sioux, Mitch Bouyer, who died with him on the ridge. There was no half-breed guide, nor any guide named "Billy Cross" with the Seventh Cavalry that day, or any other day.

Number 1

AN AGONIZING MESSAGE

Reno

For God's sake send help. I am surrounded and can't break through. I have only 40 troopers left and cannot hold out another minute. I can't send Boston to you, he's dead. I haven't enough men to break through. Evacuate your position and join me: for God's sake hurry. Am intrenched in the Big Horn Basin.

CUSTER.

(Manuscript in Museum of the American Indian Heye Foundation, Bway. & 155th St., N. Y. Sent in by a teamster named Floyd, Ft. Wadsworth, who states that his uncle, a Civil War vet. gave it to his grandmother who in turn gave it to him.)

Number 2

BUCK BENNER RIDES AGAIN!

On January 29, 1902

A. G. Lamson brought into my office (Templeton Bldg) and introduced to me Henry L. Benner.

Mr. Benner incidentally mentioned the Custer massacre and spoke of being there.

On making inquiry and asking many questions he made the following statement. He was one of Custer's guides and was present with him the day the fight began.

The Custer party was passing along a valley perhaps a mile wide and noticed many Indians along the side of the hills who as soon as the Custer party passed fell in the rear.

The valley gradually narrowed and the fight commenced there.

Before the attack Custer rode forward to the guides (there were three) and complained that none of his men would go in search of Reno for help, the surrounding country being full of Indians and Reno's whereabouts uncertain.

Custer had no authority to send a guide as a messenger, but Benner offered to make the trip if Custer would give him his best horse, Custer having three fine horses.

Custer consented at once and gave verbal orders and also written orders, the latter to be destroyed in case of capture.

Benner left after changing his saddle to the Custer horse.

A number of Indians followed but their ponies could not run more than half as fast as the Custer horse.

He was shot at many times but was soon out of their reach.

Reno was found 65 miles away, but Benner had to go 150 miles to get around Indians and to cross streams.

He returned the third day and helped care for the dead.

Mr. Benner stated that Black Kettle was in command, and Red Cloud and Sitting Bull were there.

The Indians were good shots, many having Winchesters.

Many of them were mounted police who drew pay and arms from the Government up to the time of the outbreak.

Custer and three others, one a brother-in-law, cut their way out and could easily have escaped with their superior horses, but on reaching high ground looked back and seeing his men surrounded fighting for their lives all four returned to their aid from which none escaped.

Mr. Benner also stated that in Colorado, while a Territory, a bounty of $50. each was paid for Indian scalps. The money was paid by the Governor, but it was not known who supplied it; it was not paid by the Territory unless accounted for in some other way; it is not likely that it was the Governor's private money, and it was supposed to be furnished by the U. S.

This was supposed to be paid for wild Indians and not on those in camp.

One man (Wild Bill) bought whiskey, put strychnine in it and killed one entire camp of 59 persons and collected the bounty. When found out the bounty was withdrawn.

It was quite common to go out with a party of men and make from $300 to $800 each in a day hunting Indians.

The Indians had inferior arms and all the Whites had to do was to keep at a safe distance (200 yards) if not ambushed.

So many men, women and children on their way to California had been killled and mutilated by Indians that the Whites were determined to destroy them.

Number 3

NOT CHEMICALS ALONE ARE SYNTHETIC!

CARLYLE CHEMICAL CO., INC.
BOSTON, MASS.

July 4, 1926.

Mrs. George A. Custer,
71 Park Avenue, New York.

Dear Madam:—

I was very much interested in an article in the Boston Sunday Globe, June 20th, on what is known as "Custer's Last Fight," written by Marguerite Merington.

The reason of my interest was because I am the only living white man that saw that fight, and I can say that it was the best article on that fight that I ever read.

One article that I read stated that the Indians tried to lasso Custer, and in so doing, take him alive, but there was nothing to that, the same as hundreds of other statements.

If Reno and Benteen had carried out Custer's orders, they would have wiped out the whole Indian camp, for the reason that the red-skins did not know that Reno and Benteen were just out of sight of their camp.

When they found out that Reno and Benteen were just over the hill, about a mile away, they lost no time in packing up their goods and chattels, and when it was dark enough so they would not be seen, they beat it for the North.

After they had gone a short distance, they broke up into small companies and went every which way. The company that I was with did not stop for two days.

When the red-skins made their rush down the valley that morning, I did not know what was going on, but I climbed a hill and there in full sight was the terrible battle going on. The Indians road around in a circle and kept picking off the horses first.

After they had shot all the horses, killed or wounded them, then they started to close in on the men, and they done it slow too.

Custer and his men then retreated to a small rise of ground, and there made their last stand.

Those of the red-skins who had lost their horses, closed in on foot and slowly but surely they picked off the white men, one by one, until at last only the brave General Custer was left with his comrades dead around him.

One sweep of his saber and an Indians head was split in two, one flash of his revolver, his last shot, and a red-skin got the bullet between the eyes, then he fell with a bullet in the breast, the last of that brave band.

I saw him within 15 minutes after he was shot, and there was still a smile on his face. Perhaps he was thinking of his home, his beloved wife or Mother. Who can tell.

The battle ground was an awful sight, and I never want to see such a horrible sight again. One red-skin cut out the heart of Col. Tom Custer and carried it around on a pole. The General's body was not even touched by one of their hands.

About six months after, I managed to escape and came back to God's country.

Sometime when I am in New York, I would like to call on you.

Sincerely yours,
WILLARD J. CARLYLE

Number 4

A TERRIBLE SITUATION

SOLDIERS HOME CALIF.
P. O. Bx. 15.
Sept. 24th, 1921

Mrs. G. A. Custer.
New. York. City N. Y.

Dear Friend,

Years ago I was ordered to go, to help your Husband in his last fight, but Gen Hazen &

Gen. Reno had some trouble in regard of Rank & Gen Reno challenged Gen. Hazen to fight a Duel. When we reached FT Bufort N. ORTH DEkota, The officers interfered & they were placed under arrest laid two day when Curley a scout came in & said all were killed I. brought in one of his stag dogs in camp I. also bought from a Indian a gold ring for one dollar said to belong Tom, Custer made out of native gold &. I. sold it to the Post Trader at FT BUFORT N. DAKOTA. After wards he told me you recd it from him O.K. is that true? I. was in the, Sixth U. S. Infintry at that time, I. was your Husband Mounted—Orderly During the civel war, I. saw your AD in the VETERANS-ENTERPRISE, Sawtelle CAL. would like PAMPHLET. REVIEWED. NATL. TRIB.

YOURS VERY TRULY.

W. F. TOWERS

NUMBER 5

CROSS AND DOUBLECROSS

New York Herald, August 1, 1876.

THE CUSTER FIGHT. *A New Story of the Little Big Horn Massacre. Allegations of a Guide's Treachery. The Indians Warned and Enabled to Prepare an Ambush. Interesting Incidents of the Battle. Evidence that White Men Were With the Redskins.*

Bismarck, D. T., July 31, 1876

A letter written by a sergeant in the Sixth Infantry, dated Yellowstone Depot, July 15, has the following interesting points in relation to the Custer massacre. You will note a new theory of Custer's attack and defeat which is at least plausible; but to the letter:—

The impression prevails here, as well as above, that Custer was given away treacherously by a half-breed guide he had with him, by the name of Billy Cross, and every circumstance, so far as ascertained, tends to confirm the impression that the guide had an understanding with the Indians beforehand, and treacherously led Custer's command into a snare, where they were all massacred, with the exception of one Crow scout and two guides, named respectively Girard and Jackson. Cross, with the Indian scouts that came from Lincoln with Custer, deserted the command shortly after the fight began, and nothing was heard of them until they came into this camp, about 100 miles—four days' travel—from the scene of conflict. Had they joined Gibbon or Reno, the latter of whom was in close proximity

and the former no more than twenty-five or thirty miles away, and informed the one or the other of Custer's situation the lives of at least some of the brave men who perished might have been saved.

They came in two distinct parties. Cross and one party about two o'clock in the afternoon of the 28th of June, and another party of about nine or ten more, leading surplus ponies, in about five hours after. When their stories were compared they were found to want in harmony in several very essential details. Most of the Indians' cartridge frills were full and none of them had expended more than two or three rounds. This, in connection with their contradictory stories, created in the minds of many, myself included, doubts as to their courage and honesty toward Custer on this occasion, and I for one find it difficult to eradicate this impression from my mind. Most all of them are mere boys, and one of them gave evidence the other day that he was deficient in courage, and he is doubtless a fair criterion by which to judge the whole. Parties who have arrived from Terry since with dispatches inform us that the men who were fortunate enough to escape this dreadful carnage, the Crow scout especially, charge these Indians with cowardice, and say they ran away at the beginning of the fight.

They also say that the night before the fight this Cross was sent out to scout and reconnoitre and was gone ten or eleven hours; that he returned in the morning and informed General Custer that the village was a small one and he would encounter but very little difficulty in obtaining an easy victory. Custer, who is said by his men to be very impulsive, without first satisfying himself as to the truth or falsity of the report, mounted his command and gave the command forward. The command came in sight of the village within an hour and a half and he gave the order to charge it, which was gallantly done, but no resistance was met with until they arrived at the other side of the village location, when they received a terrific volley, which put an end to many a noble fellow's existence, and the troops then found themselves in the centre of a large camp of many villages and completely surrounded by the red devils.

At this spot the grass and brush were found tied and knotted, so as to impede the progress of the horses, and the Indians and some of the villages were screened from view by a sort of wicker breastwork of willow brush, behind which these red sleuthhounds of hell could quietly pick off any of the soldiers without endangering their own precious hides. All retreat being cut off there was nothing to do but go forward. Custer then designated a knoll for his command to rally at, which they did, breaking through the bronze wall of savages like a streak of barbed lightning and gained the knoll, where they made the last stand, all hands fighting desperately, as men only can fight whose lives are at stake and where the fight became a hand to hand conflict.

The squaws made themselves conspicuous, knocking in the skulls with a heavy club with a stone at the end of it, and mutilating in divers other ways, too sickening to mention, every soldier that fell.

The breastworks referred to, and the knotted grass especially, presented every indication of having been freshly done, and that the Indians were fully informed and aware of Custer's intentions toward them, and had accordingly made every necessary preparation for giving him a warm reception. Everybody was scalped and otherwise mutilated, excepting General Custer and Corporal Tiemann, whose scalp was partly off and who had the sleeve of his blouse with the chevron uplaid over it in a peculiar manner. This enabled a good many men of the Seventh cavalry, who are here dismounted, to detect one of the participants in the fight on the Indians' side in the person of Rain-in-the-Face, who was in the guardhouse last winter and chained to a corporal, also a prisoner at the time. Not even a button was removed from Custer's uniform, while his brother and the rest of the officers were terribly mutilated.

Reno's command was several miles away from the scene of Custer's fight, but was not aware of his having been engaged until after the battle was all over and General Gibbon had arrived with this command to reenforce him. To the timely arrival of Gibbon with his "Dough boys" is due the salvation of Reno and his command, for they were also surrounded and fighting desperately and with very slight hope of ever coming out alive.

To the coolness and bravery and foresight of Colonel Benteen, of the Seventh cavalry, at the beginning of Reno's engagement, is due the salvation of Reno and the greater portion of his command. He now occupies the very enviable position of idol in the esteem of those who were engaged with him and came out with their lives.

One of the wounded of Reno's command, who is in the hospital here, says that at one time during the fight they heard the advance sounded on the trumpet from Indians; they all rose up, thinking it was Custer coming to reinforce them, and cheered lustily; when the Indians let forth a derisive yell at them, fired a terrible volley and made a charge which they repulsed, as they did several others that were made in rapid succession.

The Indian loss was very heavy, and it is said that after the battle was over, when Gibbon's and Reno's commands were burying the killed, they were found piled up like cordwood, so effective was the fire of the soldiers. Many more of the Indians were tied to their ponies and thus their bodies were carried off, and others were carried away by their friends.

The carbines of our cavalrymen, with breeches similar to our infantry guns, are represented to be almost useless after the first and sixth rounds have been fired from them, the spring refusing to throw the shell, thus necessitating the use of the ramrod to eject it.

Great complaint is also made of the cartridges, many of them hardly having enough powder in them to force the ball from the socket of the shell.

There is quite a number of white men with the Indians, English having been spoken in their ranks plentifully during the engagement. One of the Indians that was shot by Reno's men attracted peculiar attention, and upon going up to him he was found masked, and upon removing the mask the features of a white man were disclosed, with a long, gray, patriarchial beard. This individual was seen several times by Gibbon's command, in charge of small parties of Indians, but they never could get close enough to him to make his acquaintance, so they took him to be an Indian sporting false whiskers for a blind. But when he was pointed out on the field, dead, they recognized him as the same individual. A bugler who was dishonorably discharged in 1869, from the Second infantry, is said to be with them, and it is supposed that he is the one who blew the call on the trumpet.

PART IV

☆

Section 1

•

FRED DUSTIN DESCRIBES
THE BURIALS & REBURIALS OF CUSTER'S DEAD.
Also,
ACCOUNTS BY SHERIDAN, GODFREY ET AL.

FRED DUSTIN

CHAPTER 1

PRESENTING A MASTER OF RESEARCH

FRED DUSTIN of Saginaw, Michigan, whose portrait accompanies this sketch, is well known to every earnest student of Custeriana. His great work "The Custer Tragedy," published in a severely limited edition in 1939, and now much sought after by collectors, is a masterpiece of detailed research.

Mr. Dustin is a native of northern New York, where he was born 12 October 1866, the son of James and Jennie E. (Greene) O'Donnell. His mother died during his early infancy, and as a baby, he came to the care of his aunt, Mrs. Ira M. W. Dustin, who, with the aid and cooperation of her husband, both adopted and raised him, legally changing his name to Fred Dustin.

His early education was scant, consisting as it did of five years in the old time country district schools, and three years in a village graded school. There was no opportunity for more, as from the age of fifteen on, he was under the necessity of making his own way, which he did as a common laborer in lumber yards and saw mills, until he reached the age of twenty. In his twenty-first year he came to Michigan, and was employed as a lumber yard foreman until 1890, when he left that employment to enter the business world as a small building contractor. From this he graduated into the role of building custodian, remaining in this type of employment until early in 1929, when the University of Michigan deputized him to conduct an archaeological survey of Isle Royale, as Special Agent of the University. He completed this survey during the summers of 1929 and 1930, making his final report late in the latter year. Isle Royale is now a National Park.

In 1931, Mr. Dustin was commissioned by the Cranbrook Institute of Science at Bloomfield Hills, Michigan, to conduct an archaeological survey of four extensive prehistoric earthworks located in Ogemaw County, Michigan. This work he completed during the autumn of 1931.

Mr. Dustin is an archaeologist of note, and has authored many archaeological and historical papers which have been published by various societies. Among them may be noted the following "Old Indian Trails in the Saginaw District"; "Some Ancient Village Sites in Saginaw County"; "A Summary of the Archaeology of Isle Royale"; and "Report on Indian Earthworks in Ogemaw County." He has at the present time ready for publication an extended work entitled: "A History of Saginaw County, Michigan." Though Archaeology has been Mr. Dustin's vocation for many years, like many other busy men, he has had also an absorbing avocation. His has been a research over forty years for the facts and circumstances that reached their culmination in the destruction at the Little Big Horn of Custer and his men. To that research he has devoted both much time and much energy, as every lucky owner of "The Custer Tragedy" well knows. Another contribution made by Mr. Dustin to the subject is his pamphlet printed in 1936, entitled "The Custer Fight: Some Criticisms of General E. S. Godfrey's 'Custer's Last Battle,' in the Century Magazine for January 1892, and of Mrs. Elizabeth Custer's Pamphlet of 1921."

In this volume appear two lately completed studies by Mr. Dustin, grouped under the title "Some Aftermath of the Little Big Horn." The first of the articles deals with the burial of the dead after the battle; and the second, with the several re-burials since. Though the subjects are rather gruesome, students of the battle will find them both interesting and like all of Mr. Dustin's work, thorough.

His third contribution to this volume is his remarkable bibliography of Custeriana, which will later be separately discussed.

So, Readers: meet Fred Dustin, *Master of Research*.

CHAPTER 2

SOME AFTERMATH OF THE LITTLE BIG HORN FIGHT IN 1876

THE BURIAL OF THE DEAD

By FRED DUSTIN

DURING the fifteen years preceding 1952, new interest has been awakened in the Battle of the Little Big Horn, owing largely to the publication of several books of importance, one of these being "Legend Into History" by Charles Kuhlman, Ph.D. It is a work of extraordinary merit, both in its construction and Dr. Kuhlman's approach, study and conclusions as to Custer's movements after he had crossed Medicine Tail Coulee to his fall on Monument Hill.

In his "Foreword" he makes especial mention of the burial of the dead, and their several reburials. Like some others, his conception of these interments is that there was considerable completeness from first to last. To the writer this conception seems natural to a certain turn of mind; but in a study of over fifty years, it is felt that a closer and more realistic examination of the matter may present a different picture. "Burial," like many other words, is but a relative term, for even as the traditional "six feet down" has been discarded in some public cemeteries (where three feet is considered quite sufficient; and doubtless is), so it appears to us that force of circumstances may reduce the traditional six feet to one foot; to a few shovels of earth, or even to a mere covering of grass, weeds or brush, in short, to a mere gesture, exactly as I have seen in the case of a man killed by an automobile, whose face was covered with newspaper to hide the poor mortality from the gaze of the curious or horror-stricken. Moreover, our feelings of sympathy for relatives and friends cause us to do what we can to assuage grief, and thus to make the ordeal as little painful as possible. After the lapse of three-quarters of a century, however, the whole truth about the burials on Custer's and Reno's fields can now be told without reservation, for those nearest and dearest are gone, time has softened poignant memories, the horror of 1876 has passed, and Death has taken all the actors.

For several years the writer has had it in mind to assemble the fragmentary accounts in a summary or symposium composed of the statements of those who took part in or were eye-witnesses to the burials and reburials of 1876 and later years. No minor event in our history has produced as much myth, pure invention, garbling and complete misinterpretation as the Little Big Horn, to say nothing of speculation, wise or otherwise; but some serious efforts have been made to bring out the truth which have been in part at least successful, and fact has gradually taken the place of fiction. Yet there remain unsolved puzzles, and the public, which in increasing numbers visits the Custer Field each year, usually leaves with strong impressions, some of which will be noted later.

Where differences arise as to the adequacy of the testimony to follow, it must be remembered that *circumstances governed and NOT wishes; we are not offering theories,* but a series of factual relations, largely in the words of the witnesses themselves.

Of the few accounts in print of the first burials, most are very brief, especially the earlier ones. There were reasons for this. The families of over two hundred and sixty men were to be considered. The fact of their deaths was bitter enough without adding to it that the "burials" even of the officers (with the exception of Colonel Custer and his brother Thomas), were no more than gestures, so far as actual interment was concerned. For years after the battle there was a reticence on the part of survivors of the fight, officers and men alike, even those in Gibbon's command, caused by the same feeling. Privately, however, the facts were known to many outside the army. But as time passed, it was realized that suppression could serve no good purpose, for under the circumstances which existed, regular burials would have entailed almost criminal negligence of the wounded, who must be moved to some place where they could in part, at least, be adequately treated. There were about forty sorely wounded soldiers, three of whom died later, and in addition, there were a dozen with lesser wounds.

The first report concerning the burial of the dead on the Reno and Custer fields the writer has found is that of General Terry in his brief official dispatch to General Sheridan, dated from the camp on the Little Big Horn, June 28, 1876, the last sentence of which reads: "The dead were all buried to-day."

The next is the official report of Major Reno to General Terry, dated at the camp on the Yellowstone River, July 5, 1876, in which appears the following passage: "The wounded in my lines were, during the afternoon and evening of the 27th, moved to the camp of General Terry, and at 5 A.M. of the 28th I proceeded with the regiment to the battle-ground of Custer, and buried 204 bodies, including the following named citizens: Mr. Boston Custer, Mr. Reed (a young nephew of General Custer) and Mr. Kellogg (a correspondent for the *New York Herald*.)"

It will be noted that Reno does not include in the list "Mitch" (Minton) Bouyer, but does include Kellogg, whose body was not discovered until after all the burials for which Reno was responsible had been made, and also the soldier found by Gibbon and his party. Neither of these could then have been buried, having been overlooked by the burial parties.

Aside from the two official reports, we have been unable to find any further record from an official source, and from here on, no sequence of time will be followed in recording available accounts of the first burials on Custer's Field, those on the site of Reno's valley fight and its continuance on Reno Hill, for this designation is certainly as proper and as factually correct as that of the field where Custer and his immediate command fell.

In January, 1892, an article on the battle by General Godfrey, then a captain, was published in the *Century Magazine* in which he says: "On the morning of the 28th we left our intrenchments to bury the dead of Custer's command. . . . We buried, according to my memoranda, 212 bodies."

It will be noted that neither Reno nor Godfrey give any details as to how the dead were buried.

After reaching the field, however, Major Reno ordered the several company commanders each to take over a certain strip of the terrain, advance in a sort of skirmish order and bury all bodies found, thus thoroughly covering the field from the easternmost group just below the end of the battle-ridge (southward) to the farthest group northward, where Custer fell.

Lieut. Charles A. Woodruff of Gibbon's infantry, stated in an unsigned article in the *New York Herald* of July 13, 1876, that they found on the Indian camp-site—"new axes, spades" and many other articles, and Colonel Gibbon in his admirable account of the campaign in the *American Catholic Quarterly Review,* 1877, says: "The Seventh Cavalry . . . moved down to the scene of Custer's conflict to perform the mournful duty of burying the remains of their slaughtered comrades. This would have been an impracticable task but for the discovery, in the deserted Indian camp, of a large number of shovels and spades, by the aid of which the work was performed." (We shall revert later to these statements of Gibbon and Woodruff).

We now proceed to report how the sad duty was performed. One or two writers seem to have felt that some stigma attached to the fact that of stern necessity the burial of enlisted men, and to a lesser degree of officers also, was superficial—a gesture, so to speak; so much so that in one instance only do we find a detailed description of what might be termed a *real burial*—that of Custer and his brother Thomas. The author of this analysis has the manuscript and only full account of these burials by First Sergeant John Ryan, of "M" Company, who supervised them. From all we have learned of Ryan, we believe that he was as competent to command a company as was his captain, French: indeed, we may go farther, and express the opinion that his military ability, record and aptitude for command was equal or better than that of several of the regiment's commissioned officers on that June day of 1876.

Many years ago, the writer purchased a copy of Mrs. Custer's "Tenting on the Plains" (New York, 1893). On the inside of the front cover is written: "From *Boston Daily Advertiser,* July, 1876" and below is pasted a clipping giving the first news of the Little Big Horn fight, which came by way of Salt Lake City July 5, and was dated at Stillwater, Montana, July 2, with another account from Bozemen, dated July 3. On the first fly leaf is General Terry's first report (not the stolen confidential one) with a list of the casualties following on three pages, and on the next two pages are written accounts of Rain-in-the-Face and Tom Custer with their pictures. On other blank leaves in the back of the book, appears the account of the capture of Rain-in-the-Face, 2½ pages, with two written pages signed by Ryan, thus describing the burial of Custer and his brother Thomas.* "We dug a shallow grave 15 to 18 inches deep. We laid the General in as tenderly as a soldier could with his brother Captain along side of him, covering the bodies with pieces of blankets and tents and spreading earth on top, spreading it as well as we could, making it look as near a mound as possible. We then took a basket off an Indian 'travois' placing it upside down over the grave and pinning it to the ground with stakes, placing large stones around it to keep the wolves from digging it up, and this simple and sad mode of burial was the best of all those heroes on that terrible field of Little Big Horn, and I helped bury 45 enlisted men and commissioned officers." There are a few lines more, but they are not material to this account, except as showing Ryan's competence both as a soldier and as a recorder of carefully prepared historical data. He states that his company entered the fight with 45 men and 45 horses. Fourteen were killed and ten wounded, and all the horses killed but nine.

In the *Billings (Montana) Gazette,* another account by Ryan in the June 25, 1923 issue is in considerable detail as to the burials he superintended, and the story in part is as follows: "The company commanders went in a body over the field, to find the bodies of the commissioned officers. The first sergeants of each troop had orders to advance with their companies over a certain space of the field, burying what men were found, and keeping an account of the number and who they were. . . . The burials did not amount to much, as we had only a few tools, so we simply dug up a little earth beside the bodies and threw it over them. In a great many instances their arms and legs protruded. . . . Some of the companies burying those men had no shovels. They had a few axes and chopped down some sage brush and put it over the bodies. I also saw where 20 or 28 men belonging to Company 'E,' Lieut. Smith's 'Gray Horse Troop,' . . . had gotten into a ravine. They traveled into the ravine quite a distance, until it got so steep they could not get out, and we saw the marks where they tried to get out of there, and where afterwards they were shot by the Indians and fell back into the ravine."

We now return to General (then Captain) Edward S. Godfrey, another eye-witness, and to Sergeant M. C. Caddle, a member of Company "I" who had been left in charge of the Seventh's property at the Powder River base, and in 1877 was with his company when it went to the battle-field to remove the remains of the officers and "rebury" the enlisted men.

From time to time we have been disconcerted at passages recording various circumstances relating to this subject, and in Caddle's story we find one of those puzzling situations, for the Sergeant declares "that when Colonel Sheridan's (Michael, brother of the General) burial party arrived at the field . . . they found all the skeletons lying on top of the ground," and that the survivors and Gibbon's column had not sufficient tools to bury the dead. The disturbing element lies in what Caddle goes on to say; i.e., that No. 1 grave (Custer's) would seem to have been disturbed or that something unnoted by Sergeant Ryan or any officer had occurred, for the bones were lying on a corporal's blouse: but Caddle says: "I think we got the right body (bones) the *second* time."** At the present, however, we are interested only in the *original* burials, and so General Godfrey has his say as follows in a letter written around 1908 to the author of "Conquest of the Missouri," Major Joseph Mills Hanson:

"What Sergeant Caddle says as to the greater number of the bodies is pretty correct. There were very few tools in the command. Each troop had a certain part of the ground to go over and bury the dead within its limits. But I feel quite sure that in the cases of the officers greater care was exercised. Captain H. J. Nowlan told me that he had marked the grave of each officer with a stake driven below the surface of the ground. The name of the officer was written on a slip of paper and put in an empty cartridge shell, and this driven into the top of the stake. He made a sketch of the ground to show the location of the grave of each officer, and he went with Colonel Mike V. Sheridan when the bodies were removed. In some cases part of the bones were somewhat removed from the places of burial, but Capt. Nowlan told me great care was taken in their collection."

Let us call this witness again: his testimony is dramatic, but it is to the point. On January 16, 1896, Godfrey writes to E. S. Paxson, Butte, Montana, closing his letter as follows: "The marble-white bodies, the somber brown of the dead horses and dead ponies scattered all over the field, but thickest near Custer Hill, and the scattering tufts of reddish brown grass and almost ashy-white

*"The Custer Tragedy," by Fred Dustin, copyrighted and privately printed, 1939.

** From "The Conquest of the Missouri," by Joseph Mills Hanson, copyright 1946 by Rinehart & Company, and reprinted with their permission.

soil depicts a scene of loneliness and desolation, that 'bows down the heart in sorrow.' I can never forget the sight; the early morning was bright, as we ascended to the top of the highest point whence the whole field came into view, with the sun to our backs. 'What are those?' exclaimed several as they looked at what appeared to be white boulders. Nervously I took the field glasses and glanced at the objects; then, almost dropped them, and laconically said: 'The dead!' Colonel Weir who was sitting near on his horse, exclaimed: 'Oh, how white they look! How white!' . . . Occasionally there was a body with a bloody undershirt or trousers or socks, but the name was invariably cut out. The naked, mutilated bodies, with their bloody, fatal wounds, were nearly unrecognizable, and presented a scene of sickening, ghastly horror! There were perhaps a half-dozen spades and shovels, as many axes, a couple of picks and a few hatchets in the whole command; with these and knives and tin cups we went over the field and gave the bodies where they lay, a scant covering of mother earth and left them, in that vast wilderness, hundreds of miles from civilization, friends and home—to the wolves!"

Lieutenant (later General) Edward J. McClernand in his valuable paper in the *Cavalry Journal* (1937) says: "As we had but a few spades, the burial of the dead was more of a pretense than reality. A number were simply covered with sage brush. Yet we did our best. "As McClernand was acting engineer officer for Gibbon's column, his opportunities for observation were excellent, and his laconic description really covers the whole subject.

Corporal John E. Hammon, Company "G," Seventh Cavalry, in a statement to Charles E. DeLand, February 28, 1898, says: "Each troop burying dead to a certain point, covering the whole battleground. . . . Many times in taking hold of a body to lift it into the grave the skin would slip from the wrists, or the shoulders became dislocated, etc."

Private William E. White of Co. "F," Second Cavalry, is quoted by T. B. Marquis in the pamphlet entitled "Two days after the Custer Battle." White told Dr. Marquis, in substance, that the so-called burials of Reno's dead were no more than "respectful gestures" and that none of the bodies were buried in the ordinary sense, but were merely covered over with sage brush and scraped up dirt. He did not witness the burials on Custer's field, but was told by others who did, that Custer's dead were "buried" in the same manner.

With the exception of a few bodies close to Gibbon's camp near the river, the dead in the valley were buried by the Seventh Cavalry.

Private George C. Berry, Seventh Infantry, in "Winners of the West," Vol. XIX No. 7, September 1942, in one of the best stories of Gibbon's part in the Little Big Horn campaign wrote as follows: "A lieutenant named McIntosh was lying on his face directly in our line of march, and he had on a buckskin shirt with his name written or printed on it. A captain, Logan (of Gibbon's Seventh Infantry) said he knew McIntosh in life." Berry says of their arrival: "The first chore we did that morning was to bury the dead and haul off the horses that lay on the ground where we were camped."

Lieut: Luther R. Hare, page 257, Reno Court of Inquiry:

"Probably 300 yards from where the final stand was made (on Monument Hill) there were 28 men of 'E' Company. I assisted in burying the men of 'E' Company and remember more about them."

Page 261: "Lieut. Smith's (Company) was the only one I saw, and 28 of his men were in a coulee." Asked by Major Reno's counsel—"Did the position of those men indicate a prolonged resistance?" Hare answered: "It indicated skirmish order. They were about at skirmish intervals." (Referring evidently to the bodies on the bank.)

Captain Thomas M. McDougall, Page 477, Reno Court of Inquiry:

"Major Reno ordered me to go to the village and get implements to bury the dead. On returning, he ordered me to bury Company 'E,' the one I had formerly commanded for five years, and to identify the men as far as possible. I found most of them in a ravine." (McDougall identified the ravine marked 'H' as the spot, and said: "That is where most of Company 'E' were found to the best of my recollection; about half were in the ravine, and the other half on a line outside. . . . All the men were lying on their faces, and appeared to have been shot mostly in the side."

Page 494:

"On the night of the 26th of June, 1876, I took privates Ryan and Moore of my company, and we went and got Lieut. Hodgson's body and carried it to my breastworks and kept it until the next morning, the 27th. After sewing him up in a blanket and a poncho, I proceeded with those two men to bury him."

Captain Myles Moylan, Page 201, Reno Court of Inquiry:

"In deploying the men to hunt for the bodies, my company was on the left next the river, and there were but few evidences of fighting there, but when Lieut. Calhoun's body was reached, I had permission to go and identify it as he was a brother-in-law of mine. As soon as his body was found, I was sent for, and that is the way I happened to see those bodies."

"After leaving the place I rode up to this point (where Custer's body was found) I think in company with Major Reno. In the ravine marked H on the map we found twenty-odd bodies of E Company. They were undoubtedly fighting and retreating. I could see where they had passed down the edge and attempted to scramble up on the other side, which was almost perpendicular. The marks were plain where they had used their hands to get up, but the marks only extended half way up the bank."

"It was generally understood that the bodies were counted. I know there were some men missing that could not be accounted for. I have always been under the impression that the (missing) officers were buried with the men."

Page 202:

"I understood (later) a number of bodies have been found a considerable distance from the field, which I think make up the number." (missing)

Private Theodore W. Goldin, Company G:

In a letter to the writer, dated May 12, 1934, says: "Reno's dead on the hill were some of them buried soon after they were killed, the others late on the afternoon of June 26th. My recollection is that most of them, if not all, were buried under the picket line, and the horses put back, and the graves trampled down so as to be almost obliterated; there may have been one or two buried close at hand, but I do not now recall any."

We find some difficulties as to the above burials, for Private Peter Thompson, of Company "C" stated definitely (Page 205, "Black Hills Trails"): "The rifle pits came into use as graves." It seems improbable that graves sufficiently deep under the picket lines where horses and mules were tied could be dug, and the Indians gave little opportunity for such work except at night. A little good digging would solve the problem. Reno's report shows that eighteen were killed on the hill on the 26th, but we find nothing said of any burials except that of Hodgson who was buried the morning of the 27th.

In a letter to Mr. Albert Johnson of Marine-on-St. Croix, Minn., Mr. Goldin under date of December 29, 1931, says: "In burying the bodies we spread out from where the first bodies were found . . . (the end of the battle-ridge near the gate opening toward Medicine Tail) in a sort of skirmish line advance, we covered the entire field so that only the men in each sector saw the bodies in their front, so it isn't strange that there were

errors of judgment, and in failure to report all the bodies who were really identified."

On December 30, 1929, he said:

"In going in there (the ravine down which Custer rode) with the burial party, we followed a well-marked trail of shod horses through this draw, as I recollect the first break in the high bluffs."

In a letter of January 15, 1930, he is very specific in his statements, and perhaps it will be best to tell his story in running form, for otherwise there would be repetitions:

"My recollection is that we saw nothing to indicate that the White Horse Troop approached the river much nearer than the point where they entered the valley. We turned in at a little opening, following a well-marked trail of shod horses not very far from the southwest corner of the present fenced enclosure. This brought us to the first group of several soldiers, now marked by headstones, and it was from this point we discovered the faint trail leading along the lower edge of the bluff (battle ridge) to the point where we found the men and horses of Smith's troop in what proved to them to be a *cul de sac,* as men and horses were piled up together, and the odor was such that we did not go down to them but shoveled dirt from the top covering them in one big grave. From the point where we found the first bodies there were evidences of shod horses in broken order, leading back in the direction where we later found Calhoun's troop."

"The trail of the White Horse Troop left the main column and swung to the left."

On October 27, 1928, he said:

"We found the bodies of a number of men and horses of 'E' Troop (White Horse). To all appearances they had angled off along the hillside, finally entering the dead-end ravine where the bodies of men and horses were found, with a high bank in front and on both sides."

Though several witnesses remain, it is not necessary to confirm the foregoing testimony by further evidence; but in closing, we cite two who were on the field later, the first Thomas H. LeForge, whose reminiscences, recorded by Thomas B. Marquis, were published in 1928 under the title, "Memoirs of a White Crow Indian."

LeForge related that during the summer of 1877, he frequently visited the Custer battlefield, as he had previously done after the battle in 1876, and that on these visits he saw many skulls and bones, some partially covered and some entirely uncovered, the evidences being plain that wolves had disturbed the bodies. Because of lack of digging tools, none of the graves were more than a few inches in depth, and varying weather conditions during the year that elapsed before the 1877 reburials had brought about a situation that he characterized as "ghastly."

One further witness is Captain John S. Payne, Fifth Cavalry, who under orders made measurements at the battlefields, and was called to the stand at the Reno Court of Inquiry. At page 233 of the proceedings he stated:

"I made one measurement on the field upon the 22nd day of last August, 1878." Asked by the Recorder—"What were the evidences also that the place you measured from was the place where General Custer fell?" his answer was: "It was unmistakably the spot where the struggle had taken place. The bones of men and horses were there, and it was the extreme northern limit of the battle-field."

The death of Lieut. James H. Bradley in 1877, before he had completed his story of the campaign, was a loss not only to the army but to history. His account ending with the discovery of the dead on the Custer field, carefully written, along with General Gibbon's relation and Lieutenant McClernand's itinerary of the march, form an almost complete history of the whole summer's events in which Gibbon's command took part. The statement of Colonel Gibbon as to the discovery of numerous digging tools at the Indian camp site has already been quoted.

In contrast with Colonel Gibbon's statement, however, we have the statements of officers under oath, and of others credible and of good report, which have been cited in the preceding pages, and there are still others of equal credibility that might be quoted. Such cumulative testimony, however, seems unnecessary: nor is it necessary to charge Colonel Gibbon with misrepresentation. We have no evidence that his statement was the result of personal observation. He was a very busy commander with a heavy responsibility. *Some* shovels, spades, picks, axes and hatchets were undoubtedly found at the site of the Indian camp, as the witnesses have plainly indicated; but it is equally plain that the number was not large; and if we put the almost unanimous testimony as to these implements against Colonel Gibbon's statement, we may safely conclude that he was misinformed —not a serious matter. Indeed, were it not for the minute scrutiny which in the last fifteen years has characterized the study of the whole Custer matter, it would never have been given a second thought, and the brief summary by Dr. Thomas B. Marquis in his little brochure, "The Custer Dead Not Buried," might well have stood as "The Last Word" on this phase of a tragic event.

As to Lieutenant Woodruff's *Herald* article, it informs us only that on the Indian camp site, "new axes, spades" and many other articles were found, but there is no suggestion that *"many"* such implements were found. We may therefore accept the statements of those who actually performed or superintended the work as factual.

Keogh's Grave, 1877.

CHAPTER 3

DUSTIN DESCRIBES THE

RE-BURIALS

O F THE many visitors to the Custer and Reno Battlefields, there is perhaps one out of half a dozen who ever sees Reno's battlefield near the Garryowen store or the scene of the fight across the Little Big Horn on the Heights: the Be-All, Center and End-All is the monument on the Custer field. The tourist may read the names of a few of the officers or civilians on the granite blocks, and possibly learn that there are 266 names altogether, and naturally supposes that all fell on the field dominated by the monument. If he is unusually curious, he may be shown a map of the field made by the United States Geological Survey from surveys made in 1891; and if statistically-minded, he will try to count the dots on it, for each represents the place where an officer or soldier fell. If he succeeds, he will find 202 instead of 261, and wonder at the discrepancy, just as the writer did until he had unlearned some alleged "history." Fifty-three of those names on the monument belonged to officers, soldiers, and Indian scouts; and three more, to a white scout, a negro interpreter and a civilian packer, all of whom fell over four miles away up the Little Big Horn. True, there is now a monument on Reno Hill, but without a single name on it, not even that of the commander; for Prejudice prevented Justice from awarding their just dues to an officer and fifty-six men who

died in the valley or on the heights under his command.

Dr. Charles Kuhlman in his excellent work, "Legend into History," in part explains the reason for the discrepancy between the list on the monument on Custer Hill and the dots on the survey sheet, and tells *how* it happens that there are *now* many more markers on the Custer field *than were killed with Custer:* they are scattered among the 202 earlier ones. Many years ago, the writer had known of this disturbing discrepancy; he had tried to count the dots on the Survey sheet, but found that impossible until he divided the sheet into little squares, and counted the number in each square. Since the erection of the monument, the twelve or fifteen missing soldiers have been accounted for by the discovery of their unburied skeletons in spots hidden or distant from those grouped together on the Battle Ridge or below, with the surplus markers which actually belong on the Reno fields. *There* we find three only, that of Lieut. B. F. Hodgson (which until recently stood on the bluff far from where he fell); that of Lieut. Donald McIntosh, whose marker is far distant from where it should be, and that of Dr. DeWolfe, the surgeon, whose marker stands, pathetically alone, on a little knoll half way up from river to the heights, properly placed where he died, and sadly also, his soldier-orderly who fell with him and who has no marker to his memory.

In 1876 the average enlisted man counted for little: in the army he was only a number on the rolls. By the comfortable civilian he was despised. The Civil War was ten years away, and the few veteran enlisted men formed a mere nucleus. From twenty-five to fifty per cent of each company were fresh recruits. To the general public, the army was in poor standing, and justly so. The swarm of officers who owed appointment largely to President Andrew Johnson and certain congressmen who supported him, were of small credit to the army, to their sponsors or to the President; and the Seventh Cavalry with its variegated assortment of officers, perhaps owed its prominence over other regiments, to the fame of its lieutenant-colonel and some of its nepotistically-appointed officers.

In consequence, the regiment gained an undeserved reputation, for basically, its enlisted men were like others of the time. Especially in the cavalry, many were very young, not a few of whom got into the army through perjury. Boys of eighteen (and sometimes less) were far from uncommon. They had families and friends, of course, but their situations in life were usually humble, and when the time came to rebury their bones (if re-burying it could be called), it is not strange that the first "re-burials" were no more carefully done than the original "burials."

We cannot doubt that there were three actual interments, those of the Custers, colonel and captain; and that of Lieut. Hodgson, who was a general favorite, and whose captain, McDougall, definitely tells us how he was buried (Page 494, Reno Court of Inquiry, Graham). And it is quite possible that McIntosh also was carefully taken care of, for his brother-in-law Lieut. Francis M. Gibson, in a letter to his wife says that on the twenty-seventh he buried McIntosh and that his grave was nicely marked. (Page 271 "With Custer's Cavalry," Fougera).

In June, 1877, the newly-recruited Company "I," Seventh Cavalry, under its new captain, Henry J. Nowlan, with Lt. Hugh L. Scott (later Major-General), was dispatched from the camp at the mouth of the Tongue River for the especial purpose of gathering up the remains of the officers, and incidentally, "reburying" the soldiers. At the camp on the grounds where Fort Custer was to be erected, Scott relates that they picked up Col. M. V. Sheridan, brother of General Sheridan, with "all the Crow scouts that had gone with Custer the year before, and went out fifteen miles to the battle-field and were there on June 25, exactly a year after the fight. The valley was a different sight; whereas the year before it had been thick with dust from drought and the trampling of innumerable hoofs, now the grass grew luxuriantly, higher than the stirrups, and flowers were everywhere."

He says that Nowlan had a chart showing where each officer was buried, so it was easy to find them. It seems that he had nothing to do with collecting

the officers' remains, for Nowlan and Sheridan worked all the morning while Scott kept the camp, "but the work was finished sooner than expected. I went out with a detachment to bury all the others I could find. There was no time to dig deep graves, and I was told to cover the bones made up into little piles where they were lying. This I did, but the soil was like sugar and I have no doubt the first rain liquified it and exposed the bones later. We had neither the time or the force to bury the whole command in deep graves, as we were obliged to join the main command." (Page 48, "Some Memories of a Soldier," Scott)

While casually made, Scott's statement is very definite as to this *first* "reburial." Practically, the entire purpose of the expedition was to collect the bones of the officers, *not* to bury the bones of enlisted men. If stakes were driven at *their* heads with their names in cartridge shells, and the shells driven into the stakes, we have not learned about it. As will be noted later, poles had been, or were at that time, driven into the ground at the location of each body or skeleton, but whether after the fight the previous year or by Scott's party does not appear.

Ten years before, Capt. Fetterman and his eighty-two men had been carefully picked up and carried to Fort Phil Kearny, and buried in one great common grave, and each body was carefully marked for future identification; but the Custer burials were under very different circumstances. The Phil Kearny fight was so close to the Civil War that sentiment was strong for the individual soldier; but in 1876, sentiment centered on a single figure, and Politics could do its part in using the circumstance for its own purposes.

It has seemed to the writer that Scott's account so well summarizes the "reburials," that no other witnesses need be called. However, as it is evident that a *second*—and indeed a *third* "reburial" have been completely overlooked by some writers, an account of these will follow.

Nowlan's party did make one genuine burial, however, that of young Lieut. John J. Crittenden, whose father, Colonel Thomas L. Crittenden, 17th Infantry, had said: "Let my boy lie where he fell." The Sheridan-Nowlan party dug a grave three feet deep, and the frail bones were placed therein. Later, a large marble headstone sent by the father was placed at the grave, and there remained until 1932, when the government in inexcusable vandalism, dug up the remains and moved them to the cemetery to make room for a roadway along the crest of the battle ridge.

We come now to a report of Captain K. Sanderson, Eleventh Infantry, dated April 5, 1879, a copy of which was kindly furnished me by Dr. Charles Kuhlman who says: "I have copied it as it is, mistakes and all," referring in part at least, to obvious errors in wording, as well as several in spelling, but not apparently, to errors of fact. The date, April 1879 we may assume to be an error, or that previous report had not been made; or possibly, that a timely report had been lost or mislaid. The work was unquestionably done very soon after Nowlan had collected the bones of the officers, and made a gesture of reburial. As to the *year* that Captain Sanderson did his work, there is positive proof. Two photographers, S. J. Morrow and L. A. Huffman were on the field with him, and took many photographs both of men and objects, in several instances duplicates from different positions. Examples are those of the "monument" erected by Sanderson and the Crittenden cross. As these pictures were taken in 1877, no doubt as to the year exists. The report follows, a few errors in spelling and one in wording being corrected or noted.

Fort Custer M.T.
April t (probably April 7) 1879.
Post Adjutant:

Sir: I have the honor to report that in obedience to your instructions I went to Custer battlefield, to carry out orders in regard to graves at that point.

I found it impossible to obtain rock within a distance of five miles. I accordingly built a mound as illustrated below, out of cord wood, filled in the center, with all the horse bones I could find on the field in the center of the mound. I dug a grave and interred all the human bones that could be found, parts of four or five officers' bodies, this grave was then built up with the wood for four feet above ground, well covered, and the mound built over and around it. The mound is ten feet square, and about eleven feet high, is built on the highest point, immediately in rear of where Gen'l Custer's body was found.

Instead of disinterring any remains, I carefully removed [obviously *renewed*] all graves that could be found. At each grave a stake was driven where those that had been previously placed had fallen. . . . The ground to the north and east of the field was well searched for six miles in each direction but no trace of any remains were found nor anything to indicate that any persons were killed in that direction.

The whole field now presents a perfectly clean appearance. Each grave being re-mounded.
. . . Lieutenant Crittenden's grave is well marked. I had it remounded, it ought to be understood that if the bodies are to be removed to the

Custer point, that his grave should remain undisturbed it being generally known that it is the desire of his family not to have the remains disturbed. A stone should be sent to replace the wooden cross now over his grave, which though in good condition now cannot long remain so."

If any of the suggestions made are acted upon, it should be done as soon as possible.

> I am Respt.
> Your Obedient
> (Signed) C. K. Sanderson
> Capt. 11 U. S. Infantry.

In April and May, 1877, six companies of the Eleventh Infantry were sent to the future site of Fort Custer at the mouth of the Little Big Horn, to begin its erection, and it was to the post adjutant that Capt. Sanderson made his report.

A tour of inspection by General Philip Sheridan having been planned, his brother, Colonel Michael V. Sheridan of his staff who had been with the Nowlan party, undoubtedly informed the commander at Fort Custer, Lieut.-Colonel George P. Buell, of the conditions on the Custer field; and Captain Sanderson, having been provided with the proper facilities for the work, very soon proceeded to the battlefield and the work was done as noted. Shovels were undoubtedly used this time to cover the bones of the dead, with a neater bit of work on Lieut. Crittenden's grave.

General Sheridan arrived at the Custer Battlefield July 21, 1877, and on April 8, 1878, made his official report in part as follows:

To the Adjutant General of the Army, Washington, D. C.

Sir: In compliance with the request of the General of the Army, I have the honor to state that I visited the Custer Battlefield, July 21, 1877. Shortly after reaching the field, I made a detail of Major Geo. A. Forsyth, of my personal staff, and seventy men, with Sioux guides who had been in the battle, to scout the country around the battlefield and thoroughly examine for any body or bones, and if found, to carefully bury them. I visited the main portion of the battlefield myself, and found all the graves neatly raised as in cemeteries inside civilization, and most, if not all, marked with headboards or stakes. I respectfully refer to Major Forsyth's report herewith enclosed as to what he and his party accomplished. . . . I am half inclined to think, strange as it may appear, that nearly all the desecration of graves at the Custer battlefield has been done by curiosity hunters in the shape of human coyotes. I have myself known of one or two cases where bones were exhibited as relics from the Custer Battlefield.

> Very respectfully,
> Your obedient servant,
> P.H. Sheridan,
> Lieutenant General.

Forsyth's report is as follows:

"Headquarters Military Division of the Missouri, Chicago, April 8, 1878.

Lieut. Gen. P. H. Sheridan,
Commanding Mil. Div. Missouri,
Chicago.

I have the honor to make the following supplementary report, regarding the condition of the graves on the Custer battleground on the Little Horn or Custer River, as they appeared on the 21st of July, 1877. The original report made upon this subject shortly after your return from your tour of inspection has, in some manner been lost or mislaid.

By your direction, a detail of 60 enlisted men and three commissioned officers made from the detachment of troops accompanying your headquarters and with this force, equipped with all the spades, shovels and picks of the command, Maj. V. K. Hart, 5th Cavalry, commanding the escort, and myself made a thorough and careful survey of the battlefield on both sides of the river, with the following results: We found that, as a general rule, the graves were in as good a condition as, under the circumstances and considering the extreme lightness of the soil and the entire absence from it of clay, gravel or stones, could have been expected. The grave of Lieut. Crittenden—the only officer's body that had not been removed for burial, was plainly and distinctly marked by a wooden cross, as were also the graves of several of the citizens who fell in the fight. The soldiers' graves were generally grouped together in four distinct places, and with two exceptions where wolves had dug for prey, were well covered.

On the side of a ravine where a number of bodies had been buried, we found several skeletons that had been exposed by rains washing the side of the ravine, as it was as easily washed out as so much ashes. Upon the west side of the river, we also discovered parts of several skeletons disinterred by wolves.

Our search over the whole field was thorough and exhaustive, and when we returned to camp I do not think there was a human bone unburied on the field. The total skeletons and parts of skeletons reburied were seventeen (17). Our party was divided into three detachments, each commanded by a commissioned officer, and the time spent reburying and searching for graves that had been disturbed was over four hours. I do not think that there will ever be a time in the spring, or after the spring rains, that portions of skeletons will not be exposed, if the remains are left there, for the soil is so light, bakes so hard and disintegrates to such an extent in summer, that washouts from four to ten feet in depth among the bullocks (undoubtedly *hillocks*) are not at all unusual.

> I am, General,
> Very respectfully,
> Your obedient Servant,
> (Signed) Geo. A. Forsyth,
> Maj. & A.A.D.C.

In that portion of Captain Sanderson's report not quoted, he speaks of "sensational newspaper reports" that bodies still laid exposed. The reports *were* sensational, but they were based on facts, and these facts are to be found in the preceding pages. It all made good newspaper "copy," and was of course, exaggerated to give the stories color, and thus to sell papers: it was the vogue, the pattern. The reporter saw some bones, but he neither knew or cared to learn the conditions that had made adequate below-ground burial impossible. Under the conditions, no blame could be laid against the army, but of course the army was sensitive to criticism, so we have the story of *Three* Reburials, the first, like the original "burials," a mere gesture: the second by Captain Sanderson, perhaps a complete covering up of the bones "piled in little piles" by Nowlan; and finally, the third reburial by Forsyth, as to the adequacy of which we shall call two witnesses to corroborate what Forsyth says in the last paragraph of his report.

The first witness will be Dr. William A. Allen, who in his book, "Adventures With Indians and Game, or Twenty Years in the Rocky Mountains" writes (p. 63):

"On the morning of August 18, 1877, we camped on the Little Big Horn River, just opposite Custer's Battlefield. . . . After a careful survey of the valley we decided to cross the river and examine the battlefield. . . . When our party gained the other side, a horrible sight met our eyes. Each soldier . . . yet lay where he had fallen on that ill-fated day . . . each with a small amount of earth thrown over him, with his head protruding from one end of the grave and his feet from the other. A very noticeable feature presented itself to me, the boot tops had been cut from the dead. Their skulls in many instances had been crushed. . . . No bullets or shells of the enemy were found near the last stand, showing conclusively that the battle and last stand were fought to a finish at some distance as Rain-in-the-Face told me afterward."

Dr. Allen further states that the party located the firing lines of the Indians surrounding the soldiers, marked by expended shells of several kinds. [If the party had been thoughtful enough to have made a fairly accurate sketch, they could have portrayed the Indian lines for future use. F.D.]

It would seem to me that Dr. Allen's story is somewhat exaggerated. There is little doubt that skulls and foot-bones were seen in some instances, but not of "each soldier." This is an example of the misleading literature that has loaded the whole Custer story with superlatives and made single incidents appear applicable to many, or even to all.

However, we shall not leave Dr. Allen without corroboration, for Dr. Thomas B. Marquis, an unusually careful writer, in his pamphlet "Custer Soldiers Not Buried" (page 7), relates that an old soldier told him of observations at the battlefield in the late summer of 1877, and that he and some companions had gathered up eleven battered and decayed human skulls which they buried in a pit below the site of the monument.

There yet remains the *final* reburial; and we close this account with a brief story of the monument on Custer Hill which was put in place during the spring and summer of 1881, by a party under the command of Lieut. Charles F. Roe, Second Cavalry. Three granite blocks weighing respectively 14,000, 12,000 and 10,000 pounds; were hauled by teams from the bank of the Big Horn River to which point they had been transported by boat. The foundation was laid and the stones erected, the work being completed July 29, 1881. Lieut. Roe's report is not available, but Dr. Kuhlman informs me that it indicates that

"wherever he found the remains of a man, he planted a stake well into the ground," a further confirmation of surface burial only, as the preceding narrative has shown to be the fact.

General Terry's official report, however, is explicit. It is dated October 9, 1881, and is found in the Report of the Secretary of War, No. 1, Part 2, Vol. 1, at pages 97-98. It is as follows:

July 6, 1881, Lieutenant Roe, Adjutant Second Cavalry, placed in charge of the Custer battle-field monument, left Fort Custer with Troop C, Second Cavalry, Lieutenant Fuller, commanding, to establish a camp near the Little Big Horn battlefield, between the first and second crossings of that river, to erect the monument and inter the remains from the battle-field around the side of the monument.

July 30, 1881, Troop C, Second Cavalry, returned to Fort Custer, having completed under the direction of Lieutenant Roe, Second Cavalry, the erection of the monument, prepared by the Quartermaster-General of the Army, in memory of the officers and men who fell in the battle of the Little Big Horn June 25, 1876. The monument is located on the point of the hill, six feet from where the remains of General Custer were found. Great pains were taken in collecting all the remains from the battle-field and interring them at the base of the monument. The monument has 261 names cut on the four faces of the two upper stones, and bears this inscription on one face of the lower stone: "In memory of officers and soldiers who fell near this place fighting with the Seventh United States Cavalry Against Sioux Indians, on the 25th and 26th of June, A.D. 1876." The remains of Lieutenant Crittenden were buried where he fell, and the stone provided by his father was placed in position.

Sketch of the Battlefield made during Col. Sheridan's 1877 visit.

(From New York Graphic, July 1877.)

CHAPTER 4

COLONEL SHERIDAN'S REPORT

LT. GENERAL PHILIP H. SHERIDAN, commanding the Military Division of the Missouri, with headquarters at Chicago, in common with the country at large, had for months been perturbed and distressed because of the unfortunate, but undeniable fact that following the battle of the Little Big Horn, circumstances had made impossible other than a nominal burial of those who fell in that disastrous combat.

During the Spring of 1877, therefore, he instructed Lt. Colonel Michael V. Sheridan, his brother and Aide-de-camp, to proceed to the battlefield for a two-fold purpose—to return to civilization the remains of the fallen officers, and to re-inter the bodies of the enlisted men. Colonel Sheridan, traveling by boat from Bismarck, arrived at a cantonment located at the mouth of the Tongue River 20 June 1877, and was there met by Captain Henry J. Nowlan of the Seventh Cavalry. From this point he proceeded by boat to the mouth of the Little Big Horn and thence to the battlefield. His report to General Sheridan, dated 20 July 1877, which was given to the public through the Chicago papers a few days after his return, detailed what was done to carry out his mission, as follows:

"My original intention had been to take with me on the boat to the mouth of the Little-horn

Capt. Nowlan and about twenty dismounted men, but I found this would be impracticable on account of the already crowded condition of the steamer, and also that it would be unwise for the reason that that force would be too small to take out to the battle-field from the mouth of the Little-horn, and Col. Buell's command at that point was so small that he could not well spare me any men. I therefore directed Capt. Nowlan to march his whole company to Col. Buell's camp by the road on the north bank of the Yellowstone, taking with him fifteen days' rations and forage, while I proceeded up the Yellowstone on the steamer intending to use it at the mouth of the Big-horn for ferrying Capt. Nowlan's command over the Yellowstone in case he had not in the meantime found means of getting across. I arrived at the mouth of the Big-horn after many delays on the evening of the 27th June, and found that Capt. Nowlan had finished swimming his horses across the river that morning, having employed a mackinaw belonging to some citizens at Big-horn City (a new town established two miles above old Fort Pease) to carry over his men and baggage. As the cavalry had gotten over one day's march ahead of me, I now concluded to abandon the boat, and next morning, accompanied by Lieut. G. C. Doane, 2nd Cavalry, whom I met near the Crow village, and one man, started on horseback for the mouth of the Little-horn, overtaking Capt. Nowlan at that point. The crossing the Big-horn River was begun by swimming the horses, on the morning of June 30th and accomplished by noon of July 1st, and finding it almost impossible to take over our wagons, I left them on the north bank and borrowed four ox-teams from Col. Buell. That afternoon we started for the battle-field, where we arrived on the morning of July 2nd.

"The command was put into camp, and Capt. Nowlan and myself, with a small detachment and some Crow Indians, proceeded to make an examination of the battle-field. Lieut. Doane had kindly sent with me the Crow Indian named Curly who has claimed to be the only person who escaped from Col. Custer's party, and also Half-yellow-face, another Crow Indian who accompanied Maj. Reno in his attack on the village, in the hope that by going over the ground with them some intelligible account of the massacre might be obtained. Curly showed me the route he had taken and where he had hidden during the fight, and also described through a good interpreter the time and place at which he deserted Custer, and I soon became fully convinced that he had run away before the fight really began, and that the greater portion of his tale was untrustworthy. Half-yellow-face was of no more account to me than Curly

and I therefore gave up the idea of obtaining from these Indians any account of the battle.

"After crossing to the east bank of the Little-horn, at the ford where it has been supposed Custer attempted to cross, we followed the route indicated on Maguire's map and at a distance of about a fourth of a mile back from the ford and on the slope of the hill, we began to find the graves of the killed, and all the way from this slope to where Custer fell the route is marked by these graves.

The first officer's grave was that of Lieut. Jas. Calhoun, the next Lieut. John J. Crittenden, the next Capt. Myles W. Keogh, and then no more until we reached the point of the hill, where we found Col. Geo. A. Custer, Capt. Thomas W. Custer, Capt. Geo. W. Yates, Lieut. Wm. W. Cooke, Lieut. Algernon E. Smith and Lieut. Wm. Van W. Reily, surrounded by the remains of about sixty men. From this hill we pursued the route laid down in the map in a south-easterly direction towards the river, still plainly marked by the line of dead, in the hope that something might be discovered to identify the bodies of Lieut. Jas. G. Sturgis, Lieut. Jas. E. Porter, Lieut. Henry M. Harrington and Dr. Geo. E. Lord, but our search was unsuccessful.

"As some rumors had been circulated last year

Sketch map showing locations of the graves of Calhoun, Crittenden, Keogh and Custer, drawn by Captain Nowlan, Seventh Cavalry, in July, 1877, for use by Col. M. V. Sheridan.

stating that a party had escaped from the battle-field and been massacred some three or four miles from it, I directed the scouts and Indians to scour the country in a circuit of about ten miles from Custer's hill with the hope of finding the remains of this party. This search was followed up the next day by a more thorough one, and on the third day by Capt. Nowlan with the greater portion of his company and all the Crow Indians and scouts, and not an indication was met with which would go to show that any portion of the command had made its way through the Indians.

"The remains of Col. Custer, Capt. Keogh, Capt. Custer, Capt. Yates, Lieut. Cooke, Lt. Smith, Lieut. Calhoun, Lieut. Donald McIntosh, Lieut. Reily, Lieut. Benj. H. Hodgson and Dr. DeWolf, were identified by Capt. Nowlan and some of the men of the 7th Cavalry who had assisted in their burial, without difficulty, by a distinct recollection of the ground, and also by a numbered cedar stake that had been driven into the ground at the head of each grave at the time of burial, and which corresponded with a number given in Maguire's map.

"The remains of each of the above named officers were carefully transferred to pine boxes, that had been made for me by Col. Buell at Post No. 2, and taken across the river to my main camp, while those of Lieut. Crittenden were enclosed in a coffin and buried where he fell. In the meantime parties had been sent out in all directions over the field to find and mark the graves of the enlisted men. As soon as these were found, details of burial parties were made, and the work of recovering the bones of those who had been partially exposed by the ravages of coyotes was carried on until it was concluded on July 4th. As I had no lumber with which to make coffins, it was thought best to simply re-cover the graves and mark them with cedar stakes, so that the remains could be collected hereafter and buried in a cemetery, if one be declared there, or else removed to the cemetery at Post No. 2. No identification of the remains can, however, be made, for the bodies were not identified and marked when they were originally interred.

"After the completion of this work, the command thoroughly searched all the country on the east bank of the river, as far as the cedar bluffs, and extending from Reno's crossing, down the river to within about ten miles of its mouth, for any missing bodies, and I believe that all have now been buried, though it is possible that in the breaks and ravines, some may have escaped us.

"Late on the evening of July 4th, the remains of the officers arrived at Post No. 2, and were immediately placed under charge of a guard in the only building at the post, remaining there until July 7th, when they were transferred to the steamer Fletcher, and brought by me down to Fort Lincoln where they have been temporarily interred awaiting the arrival of caskets from Chicago, on receipt of which they will be shipped to their various destinations."

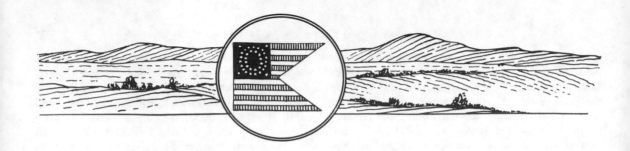

CHAPTER 5

GENERAL GODFREY DESCRIBES THE BURIALS

(From "Custers Last Battle," *The Century*, 1892)

ON THE morning of the 28th, we left our intrenchments to bury the dead of Custer's command. The morning was bright, and from the high bluffs we had a clear view of Custer's battle-field. We saw a large number of objects that looked like white boulders scattered over the field. Glasses were brought into requisition, and it was announced that these objects were the dead bodies. Captain Weir exclaimed: "Oh, how white they look!"

All the bodies, except a few, were stripped of their clothing, according to my recollection nearly all were scalped or mutilated, and there was one notable exception, that of General Custer, whose face and expression were natural; he had been shot in the temple and in the left side. Many faces had a pained, almost terrified expression. It is said that "Rain-in-the-Face," a Sioux warrior, has gloried that he had cut out and eaten the heart and liver of Captain Tom Custer. Other bodies were mutilated in a disgusting manner. Much has been said and many times I have been asked about the mutilations of General and Tom Custer's bodies. When we got to the battle-field to bury the dead, the regiment was deployed by troop so as to cover the whole front embracing the battle-ground, and each troop was apportioned a part of this front with orders to bury the dead on its territory. The ground covered by my troop took me two or three hundred yards below the monument. I had just identified and was supervising the burial of Boston Custer, when Major Reno sent for me to help identify the dead at Custer Hill. When I arrived there General Custer's body had been laid out. He had been shot in the left temple and the left breast. *There were no powder marks or signs of mutilation*. Mr. F. F. Girard, the interpreter, informed me that he preceded the troops there. He found the naked bodies of two soldiers,

one across the other and Custer's naked body in a sitting posture between and leaning against them, his upper right arm along and on the topmost body, his right forearm and hand supporting his head in an inclining posture like one resting or asleep. There was no sign for the justification of the theory, insinuation or assertion that he committed suicide. When I asked Chief Gall if he knew why General Custer was not scalped, he replied that he "didn't know unless it was because he was the Big Chief, that they respected his rank and his bravery."

When I went to Tom Custer's body it had not been disturbed from its original position. It was

Lt. Sturgis' Grave, July, 1877.

lying face downward, all the scalp was removed, leaving only tufts of his fair hair on the nape of his neck. The skull was smashed in and a number of arrows had been shot into the back of the head and in the body. I remarked that I believed it was Tom and he and I had often gone in swimming together and the form seemed familiar. We rolled the body over; the features where they had touched the ground were pressed out of shape and were somewhat decomposed. In turning the body, one arm which had been shot and broken, remained under the body; this was pulled out and on it we saw "T.W.C." and the goddess of liberty and flag. This, of course, completed our identification. His belly had been cut open and his entrails protruded. No examination was made to determine if his vitals had been removed.

There were forty-two bodies and thirty-nine dead horses on Custer's Hill. The bodies of Dr. Lord and Lieutenants Porter, Harrington, and Sturgis were not found, at least not recognized. The clothing of Porter and Sturgis I found in the village, and they showed that they had been killed. We buried, according to my memoranda, 212 bodies. The killed of the entire command was 265, and of wounded we had fifty-two. The killed included sixteen officers, seven civilians, and three Indian scouts.

The loss of the Hostiles has never been determined. Thirty-eight dead were found in the village, some of them were killed in the Rosebud fights, one at Reno Hill and on the reconnaissance up the Little Big Horn valley, numerous bodies were found sepultured in trees and on scaffolds. They had no statistics of their dead and wounded.

A "marker" in the battle-field cemetery, as a rule, shows where a body was buried; some bodies were moved from where they fell; they were not buried in deep graves or trenches as we did not have the tools necessary to dig them in the hard, dry ground.

In 1877 the bones of the men were collected and deposited where the monument now is; stakes were driven to show where the bodies or graves had been. Some years later a marker was put up where the stake indicated a grave, but some of these stakes had been taken away; some places were marked where vegetation grew rank or there was a depression to give a clue to a former grave. It is reasonable to suppose that the elements destroyed evidences of some graves before markers were placed, and consequently that all graves are not marked.

The remains of Lieutenant Crittenden were left on the field where he fell. The remains of General Custer were buried at West Point, New York; those of the other officers were buried in the Post Cemetery at Fort Leavenworth, Kansas. Captain Keogh's remains were subsequently removed to Fort Hill Cemetery, Auburn, New York.

EXCERPT FROM A LETTER TO GENERAL GODFREY FROM
CAPT. MCDOUGALL

May 18, 1909.

* * *

I took my Troop "B" to the Indian village to look for implements to use in burying the dead. Upon crossing the river I found Keogh's horse in the small bushes, and detailed one of the men to look after him until I reported the same to Reno.

Reno * * * ordered me to bury Troop "E" which I had commanded so many years. In the ravine I found most of the troop, who had used the upper sides of the ravine for a kind of breastwork, falling to the bottom as they were shot down. In burying the men the stench was so great that the men (my men) began to vomit, so we had to pile large chunks of earth upon them, broken off from the sides of the ravine. This was not very far from the village. Only a few men were found upon the ground from the extension of the ravine. * * * Only a few of the men could be recognized. I knew Sergeant Hohmyer at once; he had one sock left on his foot with his name on it.

CHAPTER 6

TRUMPETER MULFORD'S DESCRIPTION
OF THE BATTLEFIELD IN 1877

ON SCOUT TO LITTLE BIG HORN

Accompany Officers to Battlefield Where Custer and All His Force Were Killed

Skeletons Strewn Over Scene of Battle

ABOUT fourteen months after "Custer's Last Charge," on the Little Big Horn, while our force was on Tongue River, I was included in a detail ordered on a scout into the Big Horn country, and also to act as escort of a few officers who wished to see the battlefield where Custer and his men met death.

Some say that the distance from Tongue River, near the mountains, to the battlefield, does not exceed twenty-five miles; others place the estimate at thirty and none over thirty-five—but we, after two long and hard days' ride from the head of the Little Horn in the mountains, a point nearer than Tongue River, at present General Miles's headquarters, carefully compute the distance to be at least forty-five miles.

Beginning with the noble table-land upon which we stood, the ground gradually and gently fell towards the river, straightening out as level as a floor, and with both sides clearly defined by the sparsely shaded streams and the bluffs.

Beyond the water appeared the rugged embankment, extending from the south (where Reno held his force while Custer and his command were struggling in "the jaws of death,") to the limit of vision on the north, standing perpendicular, save an occasional gap through which some trickling stream contributed its mite to the general volume of the Little Horn, or through which entrance to the fords are made, and through which we must ride if we would gain the other side.

Still farther back, towards the Rosebud, the silent timberless, sandy Wolf Mountains loomed high, casting a mild and pleasing shadow over the landscape, while at the other extremity of the valley the gradual divides, rich with verdure and bright-hued with full blown flowers, completed as beauti-ful a scene as the eye of an artist ever rested on, or the hand of a master ever transferred to canvas.

At last, after a weary march, and not without the many little incidents which go to liven up, and sometimes to still further depress the drooping spirits of man and beast, we arrived at and entered the site of the old Indian village, hard by which General Custer and his men were trapped and slaughtered.

This camping place was about four miles long, a half-mile wide, and located by the river side, upon a depressed table-land with a thin growth of timber, which at one time extended all over the bottom, but the felling of the trees by the squaws to secure the bark for food for ponies during the winters, had left the central portion of the strip almost barren.

At the southern side, we passed through a dense, bushy grove, covering three or four acres, where the squaws and papooses were concealed when Custer approached, and until the Cavalry were securely trapped.

Beyond this the ground presented a strange spectacle. Teepee and lodge poles were as thick as they could stand, while all about camp equipage and hides were scattered in confusion.

An outstanding feature was the great quantities of leggins lying about, and the only explanation is, that the Indians discarded them for articles of clothing taken from the dead soldiers.

Farther down we saw six burial scaffolds, and on the ground beneath them were the bones of as many Indians, the skull of one of them having been pierced by and still containing a rifle bullet.

It was nearly dark when we reached the lower ford, about half-way through the abandoned Indian village, where we camped for the night, wet, cold, hungry and greatly fatigued. Supper was quickly prepared, and after eating and taking a short smoke, we spread our wet blankets on the ground, and all turned in for the night; but not to sleep, for coyotes and wolves kept up their horrid din, as though angry at being deprived of their accustomed nightly hunt for scraps of muscle and flesh on bones scattered about.

We had been lying down some time, when a yell rent the air, and Jack Healey sprang to his feet shouting "snakes!"

Jack, while nearly asleep, had felt a cold, slimy something crawl over his face, and then followed the warning cry of "snakes!"

We were soon on our feet, quickly replenished the dying fire, and with sabers in hand began to hunt for the unwelcome intruders. No snakes were found, but we found lizards, hundreds of the slimy green things, and the slaughter continued until the last one found was dead. Then we tried our blankets again but dread of another attack by the repusive things did not allow us to fall asleep. Soon another man felt one of the reptiles crawling over him, and then all arose and there was another slaughter of lizards. Sleep was out of the question. So we lay and sat around until morning dawned.

After a hasty breakfast we passed on over the battlefield, where a little over one year ago, General George A. Custer and three hundred brave troopers of the Seventh Cavalry, while in the line of duty, were massacred by between three and four thousand Indian warriors under the immediate command of Sitting Bull. Not one of the hostiles having part in that massacre has ever been called to account for the awful deed. Worse than that, some of these very same savages are now fed and supported by the government they fought against, and are the forced associates and companions of members of the Seventh Cavalry!

The bodies of our dead had never been properly buried. All these months had passed, yet the little band whose brave deeds of heroism will ever remain a matter of history, have not received decent burial. Their bones, divested of clothing by the heartless and brutal savages, and of flesh by wolves and other animals, lie bleaching on the ground where they fell, a sad result of the failure of Major Reno to give expected support.

Two days after the battle a small detachment was sent to bury the bodies, but not one was given proper interment—graves were shallow, and dirt thrown but sparsely over bodies was soon washed away by rains or dug away by scavenger animals and birds.

Crossing the Little Horn, or Custer River as it is now called, to the east side, a well-defined trail leads up the gradual slope a quarter of a mile in length. The ground is covered with sage brush, coarse grass, prickly pears, and is destitute of rocks or timber. We reach the summit, and see a ravine with gentle sloping sides, near a half-mile in length—and free from rocks, timber, or anything that could furnish shelter. Nearby are the uncovered remains of eighteen men, in six piles, with a piece of tepee pole sticking in the ground at each pile. Upon one of these "tombstones" hung a white sombrero, relic of a member of the Seventh Cavalry, with two bullet holes through it, and a long cut as if made with an axe; and near by we found an axe, with a dark stain on the rusty blade, it having undoubtedly been used by the squaws in their frenzied mutilation of the wounded and dead of the Custer command. Near here were the carcasses of two horses; to the north, a few yards away, were heaps of bones so mixed that it was not possible to count the number of persons represented. A little farther on, and another heap containing the bones of three men appear beside the skeleton of a horse, evidently killed to be used as a breastwork.

A heavy trail runs along the crest of the divide, which separates the river from the ravine, and it was thickly strewn with whitened bones, rotting equipments and clothing.

Three hundred yards up the trail, we came upon the knoll where Custer and the remnant of his command made their final stand. We picture him in our mind, as he coolly loads and fires with the rest of the men, frequently glancing over the bluffs to see if Reno, whom he had so urgently requested to hasten to his support, is at hand. Reno's utter failure to respond is generally condemned.

This elevation of the battlefield is but a little above the divide of which it is the terminus, and is, apparently, a commanding position. But the enemy were too powerful for the small body of troops who were there. On top of the hill where Custer was killed, we saw the skeletons of four men and horses, among the latter being the skeleton of the horse that Custer rode.

We returned to Tongue River, with the picture of that field of death vividly impressed on our minds, and wondering if Custer and his men would have perished had Reno tried to fight his way to Custer's rescue. Trumpeter Martin says Reno could have got there; and Trumpeter Martin knows, as he is the man Custer sent back to ask Reno to hurry to his assistance.

(The foregoing constitutes Chapter Thirty-Three of the Booklet "FIGHTING INDIANS!" by A. F. Mulford, a former enlisted man of the Seventh Cavalry. It was published in 1878 by the Paul Lindsley Mulford Printers of Corning, New York.)

SECTION 2

✧

THE DUSTIN BIBLIOGRAPHY

IN THE following pages will be found the most complete and comprehensive bibliography concerned with CUSTERIANA in all its aspects that has ever been compiled. It is the work of that renowned scholar and researcher Fred Dustin, whose monumental work "The Custer Tragedy," was published in a tightly limited edition in 1939.

The Dustin Bibliography, like Caesar's Gaul, is divided into three parts which, for the convenience of its users, are denominated "A," "B" and "C." Part "A" is the original as it appeared in "The Custer Tragedy." Part "B" consists of additions made by Mr. Dustin between 1939 and 1952. Part "C" is an addendum completed by him during 1952. Altogether some 641 items of reference material are listed, which cover the whole field of Custeriana to date. *All three lists should be consulted.*

This Dustin Bibliography should prove of inestimable aid to all students of the subject, and they are fortunate indeed who have access to it.

Mr. Dustin, as is well known, is a stout defender of Major Reno, and his evaluations of many of the listed works, together form an excellent brief in support of that much criticized officer. From such evaluations I am constrained to dissociate myself; not because I do not agree with them (for with some I do agree heartily and with some I definitely do *not*); but because I have ever refrained from carrying the torch for *any* controversial figure of the 1876 campaign, and I prefer to preserve that attitude intact.

But I repeat—this Bibliography is of inestimable value, and a veritable treasure house of informative material.

W. A. GRAHAM

Bibliography Additional to that in "The Custer Tragedy"

By FRED DUSTIN

SINCE "The Custer Tragedy" was published in 1939, the author has collected much additional material—some in newly published books, some in various newspapers and other periodicals, some from personal or loaned letters, and some from documents in the compiler's hands that have been more carefully scrutinized or brought to light.

I am indebted to several persons for typed copies of letters in their possession, or which have been deposited in public institutions, or for calling my attention to important items or sources of information. Some of this material was furnished by persons who for excellent reasons did not wish their identity to become known. For instance, I received from one correspondent a considerable number of typed copies of articles from an unusually authoritive perodical of a semi-official nature of the period of the Custer fight, and of the Reno Court of In-

quiry, which otherwise was not available to me except at a prohibitive cost. From another person whose name could not be used owing to his position, certain writings against Major Reno and others, that were in his possession, which with other information were freely and generously given.

Some of the most valued friends and correspondents of the compiler have deceased, among them Charles E. DeLand, Robert S. Ellison, Theodore W. Goldin, Albert S. Johnson, I. D. O'Donnell of Billings, Mont., William A. Falconer of Bismarck, North Dakota, and Alson B. Ostrander. In their passing they leave a deep sense of personal loss that is soothed by the memory of their worth and worthiness.

There are a few whose contributions can be publicly acknowledged, but as the number is quite large, and acknowledgments have already been made in the "Custer Tragedy," I can only say that those still living have continued to contribute, and to Mr. E. A. Brininstool, and Col. William A. Graham, my thanks are due as well as to several new correspondents, one a young man of only graduate high school age, but of a singularly matured mind, who has furnished me with several invaluable copies of important papers that are in a large public library in the original, but which have never been put in print.

In this compilation there will be found a number of somewhat unrelated titles, but all having a bearing on the subject directly or indirectly, for they were part and parcel of The Great Sioux War, with its tragic Fort Phil Kearney "massacre," its culminating Custer "massacre" with the Wounded Knee aftermath. The Phil Kearny and Little Big Horn fights were not massacres in any sense of the word; Sand Creek and the Washita were, with Wounded Knee as a final culmination and "honor" of being the third—and we hope the last—of what to the Indian were very definitely massacres according to that good old authority, Webster, who defines "Massacre" as "A killing of human beings by indiscriminate slaughter: to kill where resistance cannot be made; to slaughter."

Some of the titles listed are annotated if thought worthy of a more particular attention, which may make them more useful to the student and investigator who is looking for the hidden springs of certain transactions and events, a very definite example of which will be found under the caption of "ARMES, GEO. A", or NYE, ELWOOD L."

There are several publications in which Colonel George A. Custer has appeared in various situations that have not been listed, for this is not intended to be a definitive Custer bibliography in any sense, but is for the student of history. Long "Custer" articles have been written—some of them quite recently—which are so largely the result of imagination on the one hand, and lack of any investigation on the other, that they deserve to be classed as fiction. Some of these are in this bibliography because they contain a few grains of truth which have a bearing on the story. Three works of pure fiction have been admitted, and the annotation will explain why. Some general Indian and historical works also appear, not for their accuracy, but to provide a setting for the tragedy.

A NOTE AS TO FRED DUSTIN'S MANUSCRIPTS

My first Custer Manuscript was in long hand-written in 1908, about 100 pages.

No. 2 was typed copy of the same with carbon copy.

No. 3 was a greatly expanded mansucript of about 250 pages with carbon copy made around 1910-11. Sold to George Heckroth, of Royal Oak, Mich.

4. My Final Typed Manuscript with carbon copy, from which Robert S. Ellison had a typed copy (with carbon copy), made for the printer in 1938.

No. 5, The Robert S. Ellison (as above noted) manuscript from which "The Custer Tragedy" was printed.

ITINERARY TO CUSTER BATTLEFIELD IN 1938 by Fred Dustin.

FIELD BOOK, CUSTER FIELD, etc., Fred Dustin's, 1938 (There are *Two*).

With the exception of No. 3, all of the above are in my possession as of June 18, 1952.

(Signed)

FRED DUSTIN

BIBLIOGRAPHY OF THE
BATTLE OF THE LITTLE BIG HORN

LIST "A"

By Fred Dustin

THIS BIBLIOGRAPHY contains the following material; first, reports and writings of those who participated in the campaign; second, the work of careful students like Graham and De Land; third, books, magazine and newspaper articles having an indirect bearing or containing incidental information. My letter files contain hundreds of pages written by various persons, both participants and others, naturally not noted in the following titles, but which have been of extreme value.

Maps are listed, both separate and in the various works cited, and the campaign should be studied not only in the light of present-day mapping, but from the maps that were available to the Department Commander in 1876. It must be realized that from the Powder River westward, the region was largely unknown. I have seen a map drawn by an ingenious individual, taking Captain (General) Hughes' inadvertent statement that "Reno bolted straight to the Rosebud, which he struck near its mouth," as a literal truth, marking Reno's course from the Powder River camp as two sides of a triangle without any curves or deviations. The ridiculousness of such a "map" is easily seen by a casual reference to Terry's official report.

Notes have been appended to some of the items, most of which are out of print, a few being practically unobtainable, and some of quite recent date already scarce.

Titles marked with an * are in the author's library.

MAPS

*1. Black Hills, Reconnaissance of, With Troops Under Command of Lieut. Col. G. A. Custer, July and August, 1874. By Capt. Wm. Ludlow, Corps of Engineers, Washington, 1875.

*2. Black Hills of Dakota. Topographical and Geological Atlas of. To Accompany the Report of Henry Newton, E.M. 22" x 32". New York, 1879. (U.S. Geological Survey, J. W. Powell, Director.)

*3. Crow Indian Reservation, Montana, Map Of, Compiled and drawn by Frazer C. Hilder, 1921; revised June, 1929 by E. H. Coulson: Department of the Interior, Office of Indian Affairs, Washington, 1929.

A useful map showing roads and trails, irrigated lands, settlements, and other features. Scale, one-half inch equals one mile.

*4. Custer Battle-Field. Prepared under the personal direction of Lieut. Edward Maguire by Sergeant Charles Becker, Corps of Engineers. (In Report of Chief of Engineers, Appendix. Fiscal Year ending June 30, 1876.) Washington, 1877.

This is the most valuable original map of the battlefields, and gives the correct route of Custer's advance. Maguire and his sergeant went over the ground and the sketching was done on the spot.

*5. Custer Battlefield, Montana Territory, 1876. Surveyed in 1891, by U.S. Geological Survey. Scale, 5 5/16" equals two miles. (Edition of 1908.)

This map has an inset on a very much larger scale showing by dots where the individual bodies of Custer and his men were found. Scale, 6 1/8" equals one mile. Should be used in conjunction with the Maguire map which shows elevations by hachures, while all Geological Survey maps show them by contour lines.

*6. Dakota, Department of, Including Minnesota, Dakota, and Montana. By authority of Gen. A. H. Terry, under the Direction of Lieut. John Biddle by E. H. Racowicz, Top. Asst., March, 1886. Published by Chief of Engineers, 1886, Washington.

*7. Dakota Territory, (2 sheets) Originally compiled under direction of Capt. D. P. Heap, Corps of Engineers, by W. H. Wood, 1872. Fourth edition revised and corrected under direction of Lieut. Edward Maguire, by Julius J. Durage, Prvt., Top. Asst., 1881. Published by Chief of Engineers, n.d. (1881)

*8. Fort Custer Quadrangle, Montana Territory. Surveyed in 1891-1892, by U.S. Geological Survey. Scale, 1 1/16" equals two miles. (Edition of 1902)

*9. Big Horn and Yellowstone Expeditions, 1876, showing many battlefields in the Indian Wars. This was based on the Raynolds Map as revised in 1876. Prepared by Gen. Chas. King and Gen. W. C. Brown with notes, and shows locations of Indian fights up to publication, as well as lines of marches. Very useful. Clason Map Company, Denver, Colorado, n.d. (recent)

*10. Montana, State of, (2 sheets) Scale, about 1 1/4" equals ten miles. U.S. Geological Survey, revised edition of 1923: reprinted 1930. Washington.

*11. Montana, Land Office Map of, Washington, 1907.

*12. Montana Territory, (2 sheets) Compiled under the direction of Capt. D. P. Heap, Corps of Engineers, W. H. Wood, Top. Asst. Fourth Edition, 1881, Compiled under direction of Lieut.

Edward Maguire, by Private Julius Durage, Top. Asst.

*13. North Dakota, Land Office Map of, Washington, 1910.

*14. Rosebud Quadrangle, Montana. Scale, 1 1/16" equal two miles. Surveyed in 1891-1892. U.S. Geological Survey, 1901.

Shows upper course of Davis Creek (erroneously called "Rosebud Creek" on the map) along which the Seventh Cavalry marched, and over the divide down Reno's Creek to near its mouth. Very necessary, in tracing the separate battalions' marches.

*15. Wyoming, Land Office, Map of, Washington, 1907.

*16. Yellowstone and Missouri Rivers and their Tributaries Explored by Capt. Raynolds and Lieut. Maynadier in 1859-60. (2 sheets) Revised and enlarged by Maj. G. L. Gillispie, 1876. Published by Chief of Engineers, 1876.

This was the map that Gen. Terry had to rely on in the campaign.

*17. Yellowstone National Park, Big Horn Mountains and Adjacent Territory. Prepared in Office of Chief Engineer, Military Division of the Missouri, 1881. Published by Office of Chief of Engineers, 1881.

*18. Yellowstone National Park, Upper Geyser Basin. Drawn under direction of Capt. Wm. Ludlow, Corps of Engineers. To accompany Report of Capt. Ludlow, n.d. (1876)

BOOKS AND OTHER REFERENCES

1. ALLEN, DR. WILLIAM A. *Adventures With Indians and Game, Or Twenty Years in the Rocky Mountains.* Chicago, 1903.

Contains a few useful facts concerning his visit to the Battlefield in 1877, but this part must be read with caution, as there are many errors.

*2. ANDREWS, E. BENJAMIN. *The United States in Our Own Time,* New York, 1903.

Statements in an earlier edition concerning Terry and Custer brought out much valuable material.

*3. *Army Regulations, Revised, 1863.*

*4. *Army, Reorganization of the.* Report of Sub-Committee, March 21, 1878. House Miscellaneous Document No. 56, 45th Congress, Second Session.

Contains material indirectly bearing on the campaign.

*5. BARRY, D. F. "The Custer Battle." *Tepee Book,* 1916, p. 65.

*6. BARRY, DAVID F., edited by Usher L. Burdick, Indian Notes on "The Custer Battle;" Baltimore, 1937.

Contains a few notes of value, and interesting plates.

*7. BARLOW, MAJ. J. W. and GILLISPIE, MAJ. G. L. *Outline Description of the Posts in the Military Division of the Missouri Commanded by Gen. Philip H. Sheridan.* Accompanied by Tabular Lists of Indian Superintendencies, Agencies and a Summary of Certain Indian Treaties. (Ninety Posts are described, each with a full-page detailed plan.) Chicago, 1878.

*8. BATES, CHARLES FRANCIS. *Custer's Indian Battles.* Bronxville, New York, n.d. (1936) n.p.

Contains several new reproductions of photographs; gives a few new facts and many old fictions. Bitterly criticizes Reno and lauds Custer.

*9. BATES, COL. CHAS. FRANCIS. *Fifty Years After the Little Big Horn Battle.* n.p. n.d. (New York, 1926)

*10. .... *Westchester-Hudson River-West Point.* Bronxville, New York, n.d. (1926)

*11. BEAR, RUSSELL W. Letters and original maps to the author, 1938.

Much valuable information.

*12 BEARDSLEY, J. L. "Could Custer Have Won?" *Outdoor Life,* March, 1933, Mount Morris, Illinois.

Reply to an article by Lieut. Col. W. W. Edwards in February, 1933, issue of *Outdoor Life.* Contains many erroneous statements, but no new facts or theories.

*13. BELKNAP, WILLIAM W. Trial of, in the Senate of the United States, 1876. 44th Congress, 1st Session. Washington, 1876.

A very important document. A strange revelation to one who holds the key to one of the most (at its time) dramatic and tragic mysteries concerning a man prominent in public life. Custer's testimony before the House Committee had much to do with Belknap's impeachment.

*14. BENTEEN, CAPTAIN FREDERICK W. Report made July 4, 1876, to Major Reno. In Executive Document 1, Part 2, House of Representatives, 44th Congress, 2nd Session.

*15. BEYER, W. F. and KEYDAL, O. F. *Deeds of Valor,* 2 volumes, Detroit, 1903.

Gives descriptions of acts for which medals of honor were conferred on soldiers in Reno's command.

*16. *Billings Gazette* June 25, 1925, and June 21, 1931. Billings, Montana.

*17. *Bismarck Tribune* July 26, 1908, and August 23, 1908. Bismarck, North Dakota.

The last number contains a copy of the Custer Battle story as it appeared in the *Tribune* of July 6, 1876. It contains lists of killed and wounded.

*18. BLAINE, JAMES G. *Twenty Years of Congress,* 2 volumes, Norwich, Connecticut, 1886.

Contains much bearing on Custer's relations with President Johnson, and to the "Soldiers' and Sailors' Convention" at Cleveland.

*19. BOURKE, JOHN G. *On the Border With Crook.* New York, 1891.

Considerable incidental material relating to Custer. Very reliable.

*20. BOWEN, COL. W. H. C. "Custer's Last Fight." In Brady's *Northwestern Fights and Fighters;* also in *California Joe,* Milner.

A well written account but no new material.

*21. BRACKETT, WILLIAM S. "Custer's Last Battle," *Montana Historical Society Contributions,* Volume IV, 1903.

*22. BRADEN, LIEUT. CHAS. "Experiences of, on the Yellowstone Expedition of 1873." (From *Journal of U.S. Cavalry Association,* October, 1904) with leaf of addenda. n.p. n.d.

*23. BRADLEY, LIEUT. JAMES H. "Journal of Sioux

Campaign of 1876." *Montana Historical Society Contributions,* Volume II, 1896.

A day-by-day diary, and of great importance. One of the few first-hand records of complete authenticity.

*24. .... Letter to the *Helena Herald,* (Montana) published July 25, 1876. Quoted by Graham in *Story of the Little Big Horn,* 1926. Describes condition of bodies on the field carefully. Authentic.

*25. BRADY, CYRUS TOWNSEND. "Captain Yates' Capture of Rain-in-Face." In *Tepee Book,* 1916, page 16. Some useful information about Yates.

*26. .... *Indian Fights and Fighters.* New York, 1904.
Some original material. Valuable because it brought out a considerable amount of new material as well as creating some controversy.

*27. .... *Northwestern Fights and Fighters.* New York, 1907.
The same may be said of this book as of the preceding one.

*28. BRININSTOOL, E. A. *Captain Benteen's Story of the Battle of the Little Big Horn June 25-26, 1876.* Hollywood, California, 1933. Based upon letters from Captain Benteen and his testimony before the Reno Court of Inquiry.
Several points of interest.

*29. .... "Custer Battle Water Party: The Experience of Theodore W. Goldin, Medal of Honor Cavalryman of Troop G, 7th U.S. Cavalry, in Custer's Last Fight." *Hunter-Trader-Trapper,* August, 1932, Columbus, Ohio.
A clearly told story of heroic action, related without exaggeration.

*30. .... "DeRudio's Thrilling Escape: Sensational Experience of One of Custer's Officers at the Battle of the Little Big Horn." *Hunter-Trader-Trapper,* March, 1933. Columbus, Ohio.

*31. .... "I Was There: Col. Charles A. Varnum's Experience with Custer At The Battle of the Little Big Horn." In *Winners of the West,* March 30, 1936, Vol. XIII, No. 4; St. Joseph, Missouri.

*32. .... "Kidder Massacre, The," *Hunter-Trader-Trapper,* December, 1932.

*33. .... "Major Reno Vindicated"—From A Letter written in 1925 by Col. W. A. Graham, U.S.A., With Comments by E. A. Brininstool, Hollywood, California, 1935.
An unanswerable defense of Major Reno's tactics in the Valley fight, logical, sound, and decisive. Brininstool's pointed comments are enlightening.

*34. .... *My People the Sioux,* by Luther Standing Bear. London, England; n.d. (1928)
Contains a few paragraphs on the Custer fight, and other information of considerable value.

*35. .... "A Trooper With Custer," (Story of W. C. Slaper) *Hunter-Trader-Trapper,* Columbus, Ohio, 1925.
Considerable fresh and authentic material by a private in Reno's battalion. This book also contains the story of Private Thomas O'Neill and his escape with Lieut. DeRudio, the story of Trumpeter Martin and Charles Reynolds, the scout.

*36. BRININSTOOL, E. A. "With Col. Varnum at the Little Big Horn." *Hunter-Trader-Trapper,* Vol. 54, pp. 15-17; Vol. 55, pp. 13-16, June and July, 1927.
Contains considerable new material compiled by Mr. Brininstool. Reprinted in *Winners of the West,* Mch. 30, 1936, under title "I Was There."

*37. BRISBIN, JAMES S. (MAJOR) Valuable first-hand material sent by him to the *New York Herald* in July, 1876, but not published over his name.

*38. ., ... Long letter to Capt. E. S. Godfrey, early in 1892. (Copy) Godfrey quotes considerable of it, (see page 377, Brady, "Indian Fights and Fighters"). This letter, containing much important matter, has never been published in full. Of intense interest to the student of the campaign.

*39. BROWN, JESSE, and WILLARD, A. M. *The Black Hills Trails.* Rapid City, South Dakota, 1924.
Contains Peter Thompson's story of the Battle of the Little Big Horn. There is so much that was, under the known circumstances, impossible in Thompson's account that I feel he was a victim of *someone's* vivid imagination so far as a portion of the relation is concerned.

*40. BRUCE, ROBERT, Editor. *Custer's Last Battle,* New York, 1927.
Contains, "Custer's Last Battle" by Chas. Francis Roe; "Comment on Custer's Last March" by Col. Chas. Francis Bates; "Terry's Last Order to Custer" by Col. Bates; "Comanche Still Lives," by Herbert E. Smith; "The Fight on Custer Hill" by Lieut. (General) E. J. McClernand, and some other articles previously listed or in works cited.

*41. BURDICK, USHER L. *The Last Battle of the Sioux Nation.* Fargo, North Dakota, n.d. (1929)

*42. BURDICK, USHER L., Compiler. *The Army Life of Charles "Chip" Creighton.* Story of a soldier who was in Godfrey's troop in the Custer battle. Very inaccurate: so much so that it is nearly worthless, but contains a few items of possible value. Paris, Md., 1937.

*43. BURT, MARY E. *The Boy General (Custer).* A compilation principally from Mrs. Custer's books; (a "hero" book).

*44. BYRNE, P. E. *The Red Man's Last Stand.* London, 1927.
A useful book containing some new facts.

*45. .... "When War Came to the Indian—A Chapter of Neglected Truth in American History With a Letter From the Commissioner of Indian Affairs." Document 68, 73rd Congress, 1st Session (Senate). (Reprint from *North Dakota Historical Quarterly,* April, 1932, with additions.) Washington, 1933.
A valuable contribution.

*46. *Cadiz Republican,* Cadiz, Ohio. June 2-9-16-23-30, 1932. "Dedication of Custer Monument at New Rumley, Ohio." The June 23 number contains some original pictures and a life of Custer.

*47. CAMP, WALTER MASON. Address Before the Annual Meeting and Dinner of the Order of Indian Wars, of the U.S., Washington, D.C., January 17, 1920. In *Winners of the West,* Vol. X, No. 11, October 30, 1933, St. Joseph, Missouri. Covers the Chief Indian Fights from Sand Creek to Wounded Knee.

*48. CARNAHAN, JOHN M. "Telegraphs 'First' News

of Custer's Fight." *Courier-Herald,* April 4, 1915. Saginaw, Michigan.

*49. CARRINGTON, COL. HENRY B., and MRS. HENRY B. *Absaraka: Land of Massacre.* Philadelphia, 1878.

An authoritative work; contains material bearing on the Custer fight.

*50. .... Col. Henry B. "Indian Operations on the Plains." Senate Executive Document No. 33, 50th Congress, 1st Session, Washington, 1888. (In Volume I, Executive Documents.)

A suppressed report of Fort Phil Kearny and the Fetterman affair. Records an event which was a forerunner of the Little Big Horn. Exposes disreputable newspaper fictions and leaves some individuals in a rather unenviable position.

*51. .... *The Indian Question.* Boston, 1884.

This very scarce volume of only thirty-two pages contains matter not before published and of much value; also, two very fine maps of the Missouri River and Platte River regions.

*52. .... FRANCES C. *My Army Life and the Fort Phil Kearny Massacre.* Philadelphia, 1910.

Mrs. Carrington's first husband was Lieut. Grummond, killed at the Fetterman "massacre." Her book, giving her experiences at that time and at the celebration held in Wyoming in 1908, contains much new material and throughout is of intense interest.

*53 CARROLL, MATTHEW. "The Diary of Matthew Carroll for Gibbon's campaign in 1876." In *Montana Historical Society Contributions,* Volume II, 1896.

Carroll was in charge of the pack train of Gibbon's command on its march to Custer's field. Source material of value.

*54. Cheyenne Indians, Massacre of. (Sand Creek Massacre) See *"Conduct of the War,* Volume 3, 1865. Washington, 1865.

Congressional investigation of a horrible affair.

*55. *Chief Flying Hawk's Tales: The True Story of Custer's Last Fight As Told to M. I. McCreight.* New York, n.d. (1936)

Contains a number of very good illustrations. His account of the Custer fight is told with the usual reservation exhibited by Indian participants, but is straightforward and bears the marks of truth. It adds little or nothing not already known.

*56. CHITTENDEN, HIRAM M. *History of Early Steamboat Navigation on the Missouri River: Life of Jos. De Barthe.* 2 Volumes, New York, 1903.

*57. CLYMER, HEISTER, CHAIRMAN. Report of Committee on, Sale of Post Traderships: August 5, 1876. Published as "House Report," No. 799, 44th Congress, 1st Session.

This "Report" has been fully commented on in the preceding pages. No student of Custer, or the affairs in which he took part subsequent to the Civil War, should fail to read this book carefully; to an open mind it is a revelation.

*58. COCKERILL, JOHN A. (*New York Herald* correspondent) *The Custer Battlefield.* Passenger Department, Burlington Route, 1906.

*59. CODY, WILLIAM F. (Buffalo Bill). *Story of the Wild West and Campfire Chats.* Philadelphia, n.d.

Contains a few facts of interest, but as a whole, very unreliable.

*60. .... *True Tales of the Plains.*

The same comment as noted above applies to this book.

*61. COMMISSIONER OF INDIAN AFFAIRS, REPORT, November 1, 1875. House of Representatives, 44th Congress, 2nd Session. Executive Document 1, Part 5.

*62. .... The same, October 30, 1876. House of Representatives, 44th Congress, 2nd Session, Executive Document 1, Part 5.

*63. The same, November 1, 1877. House of Representatives 45th Congress, 2nd Session, Executive Document 1, Part 5.

*64. .... The same, November 1, 1878. Report of Secretary of the Interior, Volume 1, at beginning of 3rd Session, 45th Congress, 1878.

All these "Reports" of the Indian Commissioner have considerable matter bearing on the war.

65. COUGHLAN, COL. T. M. "The Battle of the Little Big Horn." *Cavalry Journal,* January, 1934.

Col. Coughlan's article is both of interest and value. Should be read carefully.

*66. *Court-Martial, Custer's.* Composition of Court, Letter to author from Maj. Wm. J. Bacon, Department of Military Justice, U.S.A., March 17, 1932, giving names of officers.

Custer claimed that this court was "packed" against him. No ground can be discovered to support the claim, but quite the contrary.

*67. .... Review of the Trial of Gen. George A. Custer, 1867, by Gen. Joseph Holt, J.A.G. (Manuscript Copy)

*68. *Courts-Martial, Statistics of.* March 4, 1857 to March 4, 1861 and for March 4, 1877 to March 4, 1881. *Also:* These Cases in which the findings were disapproved, or the sentences remitted or partly remitted for those periods. House of Representatives, 48th Congress, 1st Session, Executive Document 104.

Not an edifying record, but as to the last period, enlightening as to the character of many officers.

*69 *Court-Martial of Major M. A. Reno resulting in his dismissal from the Service.* Senate Report No. 926, 47th Congress, 2nd Session. 1883. (Manuscript copy)

*70. CRAWFORD, LEWIS F., *Rekindling Campfires— Exploits of Ben Arnold* (Connor) Bismarck, North Dakota, n.d. (1926?)

*71. *Custer Battlefield.* Published by the Passenger Department, Burlington Route, 1906.

*72. *Custer Battlefield Monument.* Report of Secretary of War, 47th Congress, 1st Session, Volume 1. Washington, 1881.

*73. CUSTER FIGHT, THE. *Leavenworth Weekly Times,* August 18, 1881.

Contains accounts by the following Indians: Low Dog, Crow King, Hump, and Iron Thunder. Also an account by Lieut. Winfield S. Edgerly. Of considerable value.

*74. CUSTER, ELIZABETH B. *Boots and Saddles.* New York, 1885.

*75. .... "The Custer Statue." *Michigan Historical Collections,* Volume 39, Lansing, Michigan, 1915.

*76. .... *Following the Guidon.* New York, 1890.

*77. .... *Tenting on the Plains*. New York, 1893.

78. ...., three-page circular tract, dated June 21, 1897, replying to an article by Col. (General) Robert P. Hughes in *Journal of the Military Service Institution*, January, 1896. (Hughes' castigation of Fry.) Privately printed, n.p., 1897.

*79. CUSTER, GEORGE A. Anonymous Papers in the *New York Herald* as follows: "In Camp on the Little Missouri," June 19, 1876; "Camp on Yellowstone, mouth of Powder River, June 27, 1876; "A Voice from the Tomb," July 11, 1876.

*80. .... "Battling With the Sioux on the Yellowstone." *Galaxy Magazine*, July, 1876.

*81. .... *My Life On The Plains: Or, Personal Experiences With Indians*. New York, 1874. (Ends with recapture of two white women.)

*82. .... *Wild Life on the Plains (And Horrors of Indian Warfare)*, St. Louis, Missouri, n.d. Pirated edition of *My Life On The Plains* with much added material.

*83. .... "War Memoirs," *Galaxy Magazine*, Volume XXII, 1876. (Civil War)

*84. *Cyclorama of Custer's Last Fight*, Boston, 1889.
Pamphlet descriptive of Cyclorama. Contains considerable interesting matter, including lists of officers and men killed. A very rare pamphlet.

*85. CULLUM, G. W. *Biographical Register of the Officers and Graduates of the U. S. Military Academy at West Point, New York*. 4 Volumes, New York, 1891 and 1901. (Lieut. Chas. Braden compiled the last two volumes.)

86. DE BARTHE, JOE. *Life and Adventures of Frank Grouard, Chief of Scouts, U.S.A.* St. Joseph, Missouri, 1894.
Interesting reading, but the author drew on his imagination in regard to some of Grouard's doings, relating to the Custer fight.

*87. DE LAND, CHARLES EDMUND. "Aborigines of South Dakota." Part I. (Arikara Indians.) *South Dakota Historical Collections*. Volume III, 1906, Aberdeen, South Dakota.

*88. .... Letters to Fred Dustin. Much valuable material; first-hand studies of battlefield and analyses of events as well as copies of interviews (original) of participants in the campaign.

*89 .... "The Sioux Wars." Volume XV, *South Dakota Historical Collections*, Pierre, South Dakota, 1931.
The most complete, authentic, and accurate history of the Sioux Wars as a whole, up to and including the Custer battle. A history in which a just viewpoint is taken. Complete and fully documented, it corrects many errors and demolishes popular fictions and mendacious fabrications.

*90 .... "The Sioux Wars." Continued from Vol. XV, *South Dakota Historical Collections*: Vol. XVII, 1934, *South Dakota Historical Collections*, Pierre, South Dakota, 1934.
Like all of Mr. DeLand's work, this conclusion of his Sioux War studies is marked by long research and investigation, closed by his death shortly after its completion.

91. DELLENBAUGH, FREDERICK S. *George Armstrong Custer*, New York, 1926.

*92. DISTURNELL, J. *United States Register and Blue Book for 1866*. New York, n.d. (1866)

*93. DIXON, DR. JOSEPH K. *The Vanishing Race— The Last Great Indian Council . . . and The Indians' Story of the Custer Fight*. Garden City and New York, 1914.
Contains some first-hand material from Indian survivors of the fight.

*94. DOBBIN, C. E. "Forsyth Coal Field in Rosebud, Treasure and Big Horn Counties, Montana. *U. S. Geological Survey, Bulletin 812-A*, Washington, 1929. Map shows part of course of Rosebud Creek.

*95. DODGE, COL. RICHARD I. *Hunting Grounds of the Great West*. London, 1877.

*96. .... *Our Wild Indians*. Hartford, Connecticut, 1883.

*97. DORSEY, JAMES OWEN. "Siouan Sociology." *Fifteenth Annual Report, Bureau of Ethnology*, Washington, 1897.

*98 DUNN, J. P. JR. *Massacres of the Mountains*. New York, 1886.

*99. DUSTIN, FRED. "The Custer Fight:" Some Criticisms of Gen. E. S. Godfrey's "Custer's Last Battle," in the *Century Magazine* for January, 1892; and of Mrs. Elizabeth Custer's Pamphlet of 1921; Hollywood, California, 1936, n.p.

*100 EASTMAN, DR. CHARLES A. "Rain-in-theFace, A Story of a Sioux Warrior." *Outlook*, October 27, 1906.

*101. .... "Story of the Little Big Horn, The," *Chautauqua Magazine*, Volume XXXI, No. 4, 1900.
Of some value as checking "white men's stories" of the battle. Written in part at least from information received from Indian participants.

*102. EDWARDS, WILLIAM WALLER, LIEUT. COL., U.S.A. "The Battle of the Little Big Horn. A fair and authentic account with an analysis of the various movements." *Outdoor Life*, February, 1933. Mount Morris, Illinois.

*103. "EL COMANCHO," The Custer Fight. *Outdoor Life*, October-November, 1928.

*104. EWERT, COL. THEODORE. Letters Regarding General Custer. (See Brady, *Northwestern Fights and Fighters*, page 357.)

*105. FINERTY, JOHN F. *War Path and Bivouac*. Chicago, n.d. (1890)
Contains much on the Custer battle; reliable; has lists of killed and wounded.

*106. FISKE, FRANK BENNETT. *Life and Death of Sitting Bull*. Fort Yates, North Dakota, 1933.
Pamphlet. Little or nothing new or of value.

*107. FORREST, EARLE R. "Two men who were with Gallant General Custer at Little Big Horn Battle are still living." (Stories of Edward Pigford and George A. Roberts.) *Morning Observer*, October 3 to October 19, inclusive, Washington, Pennsylvania, 1932.
Some facts in these stories are of value, but parts of the Pigford relation are imaginary; under the known conditions, impossible.

*108. FORSYTH, GEORGE A. Story of the Soldier, New York, 1900.

*109. FORSYTH, JAMES W., and GRANT, FREDERICK D. *Expedition up the Yellowstone River, 1875*. Washington, 1875.

*110. FREEMAN, LEWIS R. *Down the Yellowstone*. London, England, 1923.

*111. FRINK, MAURICE MAHURIN. "— And Battles Long Ago," *Outing Magazine,* Vol. 67, pp. 87-91; Oct., 1915.

*112. FRY, GEN. JAMES B. "Comments on Custer Battle." *Century Magazine,* Vol. XLIII, No. 3, January, 1892.

113. .... Military Miscellanies.

*114. GARLAND, HAMLIN. "General Custer's Last Fight as Seen by Two Moon." *McClure's Magazine,* Vol. XI, No. 5, 1898.

*115. "Geology of Big Horn County and the Crow Reservation, Montana." Thom, W. T. Jr., Hall, C. M., Wegeman, C. H., and Moulton, G. F., Washington, 1935. *(Bulletin 856, U. S. Geological Survey)*
Includes Custer Battlefield. Good map.

*116. GHENT, W. J. "Varnum, Reno and the Little Big Horn." In "Winners of the West," April 30, 1936, Vol. XIII, No. 5; St. Joseph, Missouri.

*117. GIBBON, COL. JOHN. "Last Summer's Expedition Against the Sioux" (continued as "Hunting Sitting Bull") *American Catholic Quarterly Review,* Vol. II, April and October numbers, 1877.
A most important work written very soon after the campaign from Colonel Gibbon's diaries. Unknown to most writers and very scarce. Indispensable to the student.

*118. .... Official Report, (in part) October 17, 1876, to General Terry. In Executive Document 1, Part 2, House of Representatives, 44th Congress, 2nd Session. Washington, 1877.

*119. GODFREY, EDWARD S. "Custer's Last Battle." *Century Magazine,* Vol. XLIII, No. 3, January, 1892.

*120. .... Memoranda for Rev. C. T. Brady. (See *Indian Fights and Fighters.*)

121. ...... "Some Reminiscences of the Battle of the Washita." *Cavalry Journal,* October, 1928.

*122. GODFREY, EDWARD S., and CUSTER, ELIZABETH B. A partial rewriting of Godfrey's article in the *Century,* 1892, with about ten pages of additions, as well as several omissions. The Fry "Comments" are omitted. Issued by Mrs. Custer with a preface and sketch of Custer by her. The Century Company, New York, 1921.

*123. GOLDIN, THEODORE W. "Custer Battle Water Party." (See Brininstool, E. A.)

*124. .... Letters to the author giving some unpublished details of the fight and much other information about the Seventh Cavalry.

*125. GRAHAM, COL. W. A. *Story of the Little Big Horn.* New York, 1926.
An authoritative work, well documented. Like nearly every other writer on the subject, the dominating personality of Captain Benteen has involved him in the usual disparaging tone of Reno's leadership on the bluffs. In this he has failed to do Reno complete justice. The manufactured prejudice against that officer has affected even well balanced and judicial minds, and Col. Graham is no exception, although his unqualified defense of the Major in "Major Reno Vindicated," (which see under Brininstool, E. A.) goes far toward making amends.

*126. GRANT, GENERAL U. S. Dispatch to Secretary of War Stanton, January 18, 1865, recommending General Terry for appointment in the regular army following the capture of Fort Fisher. "The confirmations of Generals Thomas and Sheridan to the rank of Major Generals in the regular army make two vacancies. I hope Gen. Terry will get one of these."
A very interesting sidelight on Grant's confidence in Terry, which, on the latter's endorsement, permitted Custer to march to the Little Big Horn in command of the regiment.

*127. GRANT, JESSE ROOT. *In the Days of My Father, General Grant.* New York, 1925.
Some revealing pictures of Grant the man, the general, and the President; also, the intrigues against him by politicians.

*128. GREENE, JACOB L. Greene's defense of Custer. (See *"Indian Fights and Fighters,"* Brady.)
Greene follows Rosser, Whittaker, and others, "that THE KING could do no wrong."

129. GRINNELL, GEORGE B. *The Cheyenne Indians,* New Haven, Connecticut, 1923.
An authoritative work.

130. .... *The Fighting Cheyennes.* New York, 1915.

*131. HAIRY MOCCASIN, (Crow Scout), Statement of. (See *Tepee Book,* 1916, p. 54).

*132. HALL, COL. HENRY, "Stories of John Sivertsen and James Wilber." (See *Tepee Book,* 1916, p. 33.

*133. HAMMON, CORPORAL JOHN E. The Custer Battle; statement made to C. E. DeLand, February 28, 1898. (Copy) Hammon was in "G" Troop of the Seventh Cavalry.

*134. *Handbook of American Indians.* 2 volumes. Washington, 1907 and 1910.
Indispensable to student of Indians and Indian affairs.

135. HANSON, JOSEPH MILLS. *Conquest of the Missouri.* Largely a biography of Captain Grant Marsh, Chicago, 1909.
Contains considerable first-hand matter on the Custer battle and events preceding and following. A valuable work.

*136. HARRISON, J. B. *Latest Studies on Indian Reservations.* Philadelphia, Indian Rights Association, 1887. (Custer Battle and Monument, page 79.)

*137. HAZEN, COL. WILLIAM B. Report to Gen. Terry, November 2, 1876. In Executive Document 1, Part 2, House of Representatives, 44th Congress, 2nd Session.

*138. .... *Some Corrections of "Life on the Plains."* St. Paul, Minnesota, 1875.
This very rare pamphlet gives some facts about the Battle of the Washita that were rather disturbing to General Sheridan and Colonel Custer. Of great importance if one wishes to see both sides of the Indian question.

*139. HEBARD, GRACE RAYMOND, and BRININSTOOL, EARL A. *The Bozeman Trail.* 2 volumes. Cleveland, Ohio, 1922.
A valuable work, but some important facts omitted.

*140. HEITMAN, F. B. *Historical Register and Dictionary of the United States Army.* 2 volumes. Washington, 1903.

*141. *Herald, The New York,* June 1 to August 31, 1876, inclusive.
Contains much valuable first-hand material; also, an equally large amount of fantastic fiction, unscrupulous assertion, and unwarranted statement.

*142. HOLLEY, FRANCES CHAMBERLAIN. *Once Their Home,* Chicago, 1890.
A useful work written with candor and sincerity of purpose. Contains much on the Dakota Indians and the Custer affair.

*143. HUGHES, ROBERT P. (Colonel, later General) "The Campaign Against The Sioux In 1876." *Journal of the Military Service Institution,* Vol. XVII, No. LXXIX, January, 1896.
Indispensable to the student of the campaign. Very rare.

*144. HUMFREVILLE, CAPT. J. LEE. *Twenty Years Among Our Savage Indians.* New York, 1897.
Much of this work is a compilation, but there is considerable original matter.

*145. HUNT, FRAZIER. *Custer—The Last of the Cavaliers.* New York, 1928.
Written from the standpoint of the hero-worshipper. It contains so many erroneous statements that it might well be classed as a Western dime novel. Some have thought that it was written as an "answer" to Colonel Graham's "Story of the Little Big Horn"; if so, it well represents the attitude of Custer partisans.

*146. HUNT, FRED A. "A Purposeful Picnic." (Gen. Miles' visit to the Custer Battlefield) *Pacific Monthly,* Vol. XIX, Nos. 3 and 4. Portland, Oregon, 1908.

*147. "Imaginative Writing, a Good Sample of, seen in 'The Human Interest of the Custer Battle.'" *Tepee Book,* 1916, p. 47.

*148. Indian Bureau, Transfer of. (See "Reorganization of the Army and Transfer of the Indian Bureau")
Much valuable material; testimony of army officers.

*149. Indian Hostilities 1866-7. Senate Executive Document 13, 40th Congress, 1st Session. Washington, 1868.

*150. *Indian, The; The Northwest, The Red Man, War Man, White Man.* Traffic Department, Chicago and Northwestern Railroad, Chicago, 1901.

*151. Indian scouts. Muster Roll of First Lieutenant Chas. A. Varnum's Detachment of Indian Scouts from April 30 to June 30, 1876.
There are a number of errors in this Roll.

*152. "Indians Taxed and Indians Not Taxed." *Census Report,* 1890. (See under Porter, Robert P., and Wright, Carroll D.)

*153. "Indian Tribes, Difficulties With. (Battle of the Washita and surrounding events) House of Representatives, 41st Congress, 2nd Session, Executive Document 240. (In Volume II, Executive Documents, House, 2nd Session, 41st Congress)
Much valuable data.

*154. JACKSON, HELEN HUNT. *A Century of Dishonor.* Boston, 1886.
Contains a series of facts for which there can be no adequate apology.

*155. JOHNSON, W. FLETCHER. *Life and History of Sitting Bull, and History of the Indian War.* Edgewood Publishing Co., n.p. n.d.
The "War" was the Wounded Knee affray and surrounding events.

*156. KANIPE, SERGEANT DANIEL A. "The Messenger's Story." *Montana Historical Society Contributions,* Volume IV, 1903.
Kanipe was the soldier who carried a message from Custer to the pack train.

*157. KAPPLER, CHARLES J. *Indian Affairs, Laws and Treaties.* 3 volumes, Washington, Volumes 1 and 2, Washington, 1904; Volume 3, 1913.

*158. KEATING, EDWARD. "Pensions for Indian War Veterans." (Contains Historical resume of certain Indian campaigns.) House Report No. 115, 64th Congress, 1st Session. Washington, 1916.

*159. KEIM, DE B. RANDOLPH. *Sheridan's Troopers on the Border.* Philadelphia, 1885. Battle of the Washita; contains list of killed with the nature of their wounds.

*160. KELLY, FANNY. *My Captivity Among the Sioux Indians.* Chicago, 1891.

*161. KEYES, GEN. E. D. *Fifty Years Observation of Men and Events.* New York, 1884.

*162. KIMBALL, MARIA BRACE. *A Soldier-Doctor of our Army, James P. Kimball.* Boston and New York, 1917.
Dr. Kimball was surgeon in Stanley's Yellowstone Expedition; also, a friend of Custer. Book contains some quite pertinent facts.

*163. KING, CAPTAIN CHARLES. *Campaigning With Crook.* New York, 1890.

*164. .... "Custer's Last Battle." *Harper's Magazine,* Volume 81, New York, 1890.

*165. .... "Faster than the Fastest Pony." *Youth's Companion,* February 9, 1911. (See also Wagner, Arthur L.)

*166. KUHLMAN, CHARLES. Many original photographs of the field and its environs, also much valuable information as to the topography and locations, furnished the author. Billings, Montana.
Dr. Kuhlman has made a remarkable study of the movements of Custer's battalion, based on the known facts, the position of dead soldiers, and the topography of the battlefield.

*167. LAFORGE, THOMAS. Statement of. (See *Tepee Book,* 1916, p. 52.)

*168. LANMAN, CHARLES. *Biographical Annals of the Civil Government of the United States.* New York, 1887.

*169. LARSEN, OLE. Statement made to C. E. DeLand, March 8, 1907. (Copy)
Larsen was a member of the crew of the "Far West."

*170. LETTERS from various persons, historians, military officers, and others who have either studied the campaign, written upon it, studied the battlefields and photographed many scenes, persons, and objects. They cannot all be mentioned individually, but among them are C. E. DeLand, E. A. Brininstool, Col. W. A. Graham, A. B. Ostrander, R. S. Ellison, Dr. R. A. Burnside, Theodore W. Golden, C. A. Asbury, F. F. Van de Water, O. G. Libby, Dr. T. W. Marquis, and Charles Kuhlman.

*171. LIBBY, O. G., Editor. "Arikara Narrative of the Campaign Against the Hostile Dakotas, June, 1876." *North Dakota Historical Collections,* Volume 6, Bismarck, North Dakota, 1920.
There has been no volume published on Custer's last fight of more interest than this. While it requires a careful analytical study, it furnishes a surprising number of facts which before its publication were unknown.

*172. LINDERMAN, FRANK B. *Plenty-Coups, Chief of the Crows.* London, England, n.d.

*173. LUDLOW, CAPTAIN WILLIAM. "Reconaissance of

Black Hills of Dakota," in 1874." Washington, 1875.

*174. McBLAIN, JOHN F. With Gibbon on the Sioux Campaign of 1876. *Cavalry Journal,* Vol. 9, pp. 139-148, June, 1896.

McBlain was an enlisted man, probably a sergeant, in one of Brisbin's troops of the Second Cavalry, and his account is one of the best, ranking closely to that of Gibbon. Gives a number of new facts and descriptions that make the article of much value. McBlain was appointed second-lieutenant of the Ninth Cavalry in 1880.

*175. McCLERNAND, LIEUT. EDWARD J. "Journal of March of Gibbon's Forces, 1876." *Report of Chief of Engineers, for Fiscal Year ending June 30, 1877.* Appendix PP.

A very valuable day-by-day record of Gibbon's march. This also has appeared in a quarto pamphlet with some abbreviations, under the title of "Custer's Last Battle," edited and published by Robert Bruce. (See under Roe, Charles Francis, and McClernand, Edward· J.)

176. .... "With the Indians and Buffalo in Montana." *Cavalry Journal,* 1927.

*177. McCORMACK, GEORGE R. "A Man Who Fought with Custer." (Jacob Adams of Vincennes, Indiana, in Benteen's troop.) *National Republic,* March, 1934. Washington, D. C.

*178. McGEE, W. J. "The Siouan Indians." *Fifteenth Annual Report, Bureau of Ethnology,* Washington, 1897.

*179. McLAUGHLIN, JAMES. *My Friend The Indian.* Boston, 1910.

*180. MAGUIRE, LIEUT. EDWARD. "Explorations and Surveys in the Department of Dakota, 1876." *Report of Chief of Engineers for Fiscal Year ending June 30, 1876.* Appendix 00.

Important day-to-day record of Terry's march from Fort Lincoln to Custer's field. Contains much not to be found in any other publication.

*181. .... "Explorations and Surveys in the Department of Dakota, 1876-'77." *Report of Chief of Engineers, for Fiscal Year ending June 30, 1877.* Appendix PP.

Describes battlefield, and has map referred to under "MAPS," which see.

*182. MALLERY, GARRICK. *Picture Writing of the American Indians.* (See under "Red Horse.")

*183. MANYPENNY, GEORGE W. *Our Indian Wards.* Cincinnati, Ohio, 1880.

184. MARTIN, JOHN. "Custer's Last Battle." *Cavalry Journal,* July, 1923.

This was "Trumpeter Martin."

*185. MARQUIS, THOMAS B. *Sketch Story of Custer Battle.* Privately printed, Hardin, Montana, 1933.

186. ....Custer Soldiers Not Buried. Privately printed, Hardin, Montana, 1933.

*187. .... *Memoirs of a White Crow Indian,* (Thomas H. Laforge). New York, n.d. (1928)

A very useful, carefully written, and authentic work.

*188. .... *Rain-in-the-Face and Curly, the Crow.* Privately printed, Hardin, Montana, 1934.

*189. .... *She Watched Custer's Last Battle, Her Story, Interpreted, in 1927.* Privately printed, Hardin, Montana, 1933.

*190. .... *Sitting Bull and Gall, the Warrior.* Privately printed, Hardin, Montana, 1934.

*191. .... *Two Days After the Custer Battle.*

The Scene as Viewed by William H. White, a Soldier with Gibbon in 1876. Privately printed, Hardin, Montana, 1935.

*192. .... *A Warrior Who Fought Custer.* Minneapolis, 1931.

This book takes the highest rank as invaluable source material. The Cheyenne warrior whose biography it really is, speaks without reserve, and has a faithful interpreter in Doctor Marquis. Many heretofore puzzling matters are cleared up. The author's decease in 1935 was a great loss to all who are interested in authentic Western history.

*193. .... *Which Indian Killed Custer?* Privately printed, Hardin, Montana, 1933.

This little pamphlet is most interesting, and sets at rest the fictions concerning Custer's death.

*194. .... Letters to the author. Interesting data.

*195. Marsh, Prof. O. C., Charges of, Against Indian Agents, Etc. (See Red Cloud Agency, Investigation . . .)

*196. MATHEWS, WASHINGTON. *Ethnography and Philology of the Hidatsa Indians.* Washington, 1877.

*197. Medals of Honor, War Department. Official lists of soldiers who have received the same, with services for which awarded. Washington, 1904, with supplements, 1910 and 1915.

*198. Miles, General Nelson A. *Personal Recollections of Gen. N. A. Miles,* Chicago, 1897.

*199. .... Report of, September 14, 1891. Washington, 1891.

*200. .... Serving the Republic, New York, 1911.

*201. Military Posts of the United States Army, With Barracks and Hospitals. Description of, (Circular No. 4, Surgeon-General's Office, December, 1870.) 12 full-page plates of plans of Army Posts with 59 figures, some large. 154 Posts described.

There is no other publication containing the vast amount of information about frontier posts; contains much natural history.

*202. MILES, GEN. ANSON. *My Story.* Privately printed. Washington, 1918.

*203. MILNER, JOE E., and FORREST, EARLE R. *California Joe.* Caldwell, Idaho, 1935.

The appendices have considerable value, containing lists of the killed and wounded in the Little Big Horn fight.

*204. *Minnesota In The Civil And Indian Wars.* Compiled by the Commissioners of Minnesota. St. Paul, Minnesota, 1890.

*205. MOONEY, JAMES. "Ghost-Dance Religion and Sioux Outbreak of 1890." *Fourteenth Annual Report, Bureau of Ethnology.* Washington, 1896.

206. MOORE, COL. HORACE. *The Nineteenth Kansas Cavalry in the Washita Campaign.* Oklahoma City, 1923.

*207. MOORE, MAJ. ORLANDO. Report of, August 4, 1876. In Executive Document 1, Part 2, House of Representatives, 44th Congress, 2nd Session.

*208. MORRIS, WILLIAM E. Letter to Cyrus T. Brady. (See *Indian Fights and Fighters*)

*209. .... Seven-page typed letter to Robert Bruce, New York, with copies to A. B. Ostrander and Earl A. Brininstool, dated New York, May 23, 1928. (Copy)

A valuable account of the fights by a soldier in Reno's command.

*210. MULFORD, AMI FRANK. *Fighting Indians in the Seventh U.S. Cavalry.* Corning (New York) 1878.

This scarce pamphlet has considerable value as giving a good picture of the *quality* of the very young recruits who enlisted in the cavalry in the seventies. Mulford joined after the Custer fight, and saw some plains service.

*211. NEIHARDT, JOHN G. *Black Elk Speaks: Being the Life Story of a Holy Man of the Oglala Sioux.* New York, 1932.

Contains chapters on Crook's and Custer's fights in 1876. One of the better class of books of its kind; well written.

212. NESBITT, PAUL. The Battle of the Washita, *Oklahoma Historical Chronicles,* Volume 3.

*213. NEVINS, ALLAN. *Hamilton Fish: The Inner History of the Grant Administration.* New York, 1936.

On page 821, a paragraph is given to Custer in part as follows: "One of the most effective witnesses before Heister Clymer's Committee . . . had been General George A. Custer. He had testified courageously to waste and abuse in the War Department's management of Indian affairs. . . . For this the resentful President had removed him from his command on the eve of an expedition against the Sioux. . . . Only after loud public outcry and pronounced manifestations of protest from the army did Grant relent sufficiently to permit him to lead one regiment of 600 men with the rank of major. . . ." This work is quoted, not as an authority, but as an example of one kind of present-day "history." Instead of Custer being "one of the most effective witnesses," he was one of the poorest. The War Department did not manage Indian affairs. There was no loud public outcry; no manifestations of protest from the army, nor was Custer demoted "to the rank of major." We are reminded of that other grossly inaccurate and one-sided chronicle of reconstruction days, *The Dreadful Decade,* by Claude Bowers.

*214. OSTRANDER, MAJ. A. B.; ELLISON, R. S.; GODFREY, GEN. E. S., and HAWKINS, M. E. Custer Semi-Centennial Ceremonies, June 25-26, 1926. Casper, Wyoming, 1926.

Contains some valuable original matter.

*215: PARKER, W. THORNTON, M.D. Records of the Association of Acting Assistant Surgeons of the U.S. Army. Salem, Massachusetts, 1891.

216. PERKINS, J. R. *Trails, Rails and War.* (Life of Gen. G. M. Dodge) Indianapolis, Indiana, 1927.

*217. PORTER, DR. H. R. "His Story of the Little Big Horn Fight." St. Louis *Globe-Democrat.*

*218. PORTER, ROBERT P., and WRIGHT, CARROLL, D. Indians Taxed and Not Taxed in the United States (Except Alaska), Census of 1890. House Miscellaneous Document No. 340, Part 15, 52nd Congress, 1st Session. Washington, 1894.

*219. PRICE, MAJOR SIR ROSE LAMBART. *A Summer on the Rockies.* London, 1898.

*220. PRILL, L. M., "Distant Relative of Famous General," Custer's Last Battle. *The Sample Case,* August, 1925.

Some new errors.

*221. QUAIFE, MILO M. *Yellowstone Kelly, Memoirs of Luther S. Kelly.* New Haven, Connecticut, 1926.

*222. RAYNOLDS, W. F., BVT. BRIG. GEN. *Exploration of the Yellowstone River.* Washington, 1868.

223. *Recruits For Seventh Cavalry.* Muster and Descriptive Roll of a Detachment of United States Recruits (General Mounted Service) forwarded by Col. S. D. Sturgis, Supt. Genl. Mounted Service, for the Seventh Cavalry, Sept. 13, 1875.

*224. Red Cloud Agency, Investigation of Affairs at. *Report of Special Commission,* July 1875. Washington, 1875.

*225. "Red Horse, Narrative of, and Pictures, Battle of the Little Big Horn." Bureau of Ethnology, Tenth Annual Report, Washington, 1893.

*226. Register, U.S. Army, 1866 to 1876, inclusive, and 1912. Adjutant General's Office, Washington, n.d.

*227. RENICK, B. COLEMAN. Geology and Ground-Water Resources of Central and Southern Rosebud County, Montana. U.S. Geological Survey, Water Supply Paper, 600, Washington, 1929.

The map shows Rosebud Creek from its mouth to above Lame Deer Creek. The text contains information as to the topography, water, soil, and minerals.

*228. "Reno Court of Inquiry, Chicago." See *Chicago Times* for year 1879.

The complete stenographic report was kept and published in the *Times* from day to day during the hearing. The file of this paper may be found in a few of the large libraries. The basis of my own information has been a photostat copy, from which a careful summary was prepared, directly quoting from the original.

*229. RENO, MAJOR MARCUS A., Report of, July 5, 1876. In Executive Document 1, Part 2, House of Representatives, 44th Congress, 2nd Session.

*230. RENO, MAJOR M. A. "The Custer Massacre." *Americana Magazine,* Vol. 7, pp. 255-266, Mch. 1912, and pp. 357-368, Apr. 1912.

On page 256 is the following: "An account of the circumstances attending the massacre of General George A. Custer and his command, by the Sioux Indians, in the summer of 1876, found among Major Reno's effects after his death."

There are passages that would seem to suggest that it was a compilation by another hand than that of Reno, with running extracts from that officer's official report, also palpable errors, which hardly appears likely that Reno would make. However it contains some original material that might well be credited to Major Reno.

*231. Reno Hill, Marker on, *National Geographic Magazine,* Vol. LIV, No. 1, July, 1928.

*232. Reorganization of the Army and Transfer of the Indian Bureau. House Report No. 354, 44th Congress, 1st Session, March, 1876.

233. ROBINSON, DOANE. *History of the Dakota or Sioux Indians.* Vol. II, South Dakota Historical Collections.

*234. RODENBOUGH, T. F., and HASKINS, W. L. *The Army of the United States.* New York, 1896.

*235. ROE, CHARLES FRANCIS, and McCLERNAND, EDWARD J. *Custer's Last Battle—March of the Montana Column.* Edited by Robert Bruce. New York, 1927.

Contains some original material of value.

*236. ROGERS, G. S., and LEE, W. Geology of the Tullock Creek Coal Field. Bulletin 749, U.S. Geological Survey, Washington, 1923.

Maps show Tullock Creek from its mouth to the Crow Reservation.

*237. RONSHEIM, MILTON. *Life of General Custer.* Cadiz, Ohio, 1929.

Contains some new material about Custer, but as to the battle, is a repetition of Whittaker, Rosser, Hunt, and others who have tried to load the odium of "inefficiency, cowardice and disobedience" on Reno and Benteen.

*238. RYAN, SERGEANT JOHN, TROOP M, 7TH CAVALRY. Manuscript account of Custer's burial and the capture of Rain-in-the-Face, (also newspaper clippings). In Mrs. Custer's book, *Tenting on the Plains* written and pasted on flyleaves. Owned by author.

*239. .... "Reno's Part of the Fight on The Little Big Horn, Told by One of Custer's First Sergeants." Billings, Montana, *Gazette,* June 25, 1923.

At the time this was written by Ryan, he was seventy-seven years old and his story shows a few lapses of memory, but as a whole is a remarkably clear and authentic account giving facts not before published.

*240. "Sand Creek Massacre, November, 1864." Senate Executive Document 26, 39th Congress, 2nd Session. Washington, 1865. (In Senate Documents, Vol. 2, 2nd Session, 39th Congress.)

*241. "Sand Creek, Massacre of Cheyenne Indians At." *Conduct of the War.* Volume 3. Washington, 1865.

*242. SCHMIDT-PAULI, EDGAR VON. *We Indians: The Passing of a Great Race Being the recollections of the last of the Great Indian Chiefs, Big Chief White Horse Eagle.* New York, n.d. (First edition, 1901)

A fantastic concoction. Contains considerable Custer "history" of a very unreliable character. Cited here as an example of literary invention, from a factual standpoint, utterly worthless.

*243. SCHULTZ, JAMES WILLARD. *William Jackson, Indian Scout.* Boston, 1926.

Jackson was one of the "Ree" scouts; was not a Ree, but a Pikuni, Piegan, or Blackfoot, different designations for the same tribe. This book contains some very useful data, as Jackson not only had a thrilling experience but being able to understand and speak English, his story is of interest, especially as relates to certain officers and scouts.

*244. SCOTT, GEN. HUGH L. Accounts of the Custer fight given to Gen. Scott by the two Crow scouts, White-Man-Runs-Him and Curly, August 24, 1919. Manuscript.

These interviews on the field and competently interpreted, are of great value. When read in connection with the Arikara Narrative, we have several heretofore unexplained matters quite adequately elucidated.

*245. .... *Some Memories of A Soldier.* New York, n.d. (1928)

246. Seventh Regiment of Cavalry. Return of Alterations and Casualties, Month of June, 1876.

Gives the names, rank, station, and status of all the officers and men in the Seventh Cavalry: the names of those killed, and wounded: Report on horses serviceable, lost in action and unserviceable: the absentee enlisted and officers:

enlisted strength present and absent, and a brief record of events for June, 1930.

There are some errors to be noted, but they are not material.

*247. SHERIDAN, LIEUT. GEN. P. H. *Record of Engagements With Hostile Indians Military Division of the Missouri, 1868 to 1882.* Washington, 1882.

This very scarce pamphlet gives a chronological list of fights of the dates noted. An invaluable record.

*248. .... *Report of, November 25, 1876.* In Executive Document 1, Part 2, House of Representatives, 44th Congress, 2nd Session.

*249. SHERMAN, GEN. W. T. *Report of November 10, 1876.* In Executive Document 1, Part 2, House of Representatives, 44th Congress, 2nd Session.

*250. SMITH, HERBERT E. "This Was A Man, Such Could Have Been the Epitaph Upon the Tombstone of General Custer." *Recruiting News,* December 1, 1933. Governor's Island, New York, 1933.

251. SPOTTS, DAVID L. *Campaigning With Custer.* Los Angeles, 1928.

252. STANLEY, GEN. DAVID S. *Personal Memoirs.* Cambridge, Massachusetts, 1917.

*253. STONE, MELVILLE E. *Charles De Rudio.* (Carlo di Rudio) *Collier's Weekly,* May 15, 1920.

*254. TAYLOR, JOSEPH HENRY. *Frontier and Indian Life.* Bismarck, North Dakota, 1897.

*255. .... "Kaleidoscopic Lives." Extracts from *A, to Bloody Knife.* Washburn, North Dakota, 1902.

*256. Tepee Book, The, Official Publication — The Fiftieth Anniversary of the Custer Battle. A reprint of *The Tepee Book,* Vol. II, No. VI, published, June, 1916.

Contains considerable useful data.

*257. TERRY, GEN. ALFRED H. *Report November 21, 1876.* (In Executive Document 1, Part 2, House of Representatives, 44th Congress, 2nd Session.)

*258. .... Reports immediately after the arrival of his troops at the battlefield and later have been quoted in full; all but the stolen "confidential" report will be found in the document cited in 247.

*259. THOMPSON, PETER. *Story of the Little Big Horn Battle.* (See Brown, Jesse, and Willard, A. M.) Thompson's story first appeared in the *Belle Fourche Bee,* Belle Fourche, South Dakota.

260. TREMAIN, GENERAL H. E. *Last Hours of Sheridan's Cavalry.* New York, 1940.

*261. VAN DE WATER, FREDERIC F. *Glory-Hunter— A Life of General Custer.* Indianapolis and New York, 1934.

The first adequate biography of Custer the man and not the myth. He is faithfully pictured as he really was, not as his worshipers saw him.

*262. VARNUM, LIEUT. (COLONEL) C. A.; HARE, LIEUT. (COLONEL) LUTHER R.; BARRY, D. F.; RENO, JAMES ROSS. Personal letters from them. Various dates, and letters from some others of the regiment. Some contain confidential matter which cannot be quoted.

263. VESTAL, STANLEY (Pseudonym of WALTER STANLEY CAMPBELL). *Warpath; The True Story of the Fighting Sioux Told in a Biography of Chief White Bull.* Boston, 1934.

264. .... *Sitting Bull.* Boston, 1932.

265. WAGNER, ARTHUR L. *The Service of Security and Information.* Kansas City, Missouri, 1895.

*266. WAGNER, GLENDOLIN D. *Old Neutriment (John Burkman).* Boston, 1934.

Mrs. Wagner's way of spelling Mrs. Custer's designation of Burkman is perhaps an up-to-date method of spelling an old word. The incidents related by Burkman of Custer are interesting.

*267. WALKER, JUDSON ELLIOTT. *Campaigns of Gen. Custer in the Northwest and the Final Surrender of Sitting Bull.* New York, 1881.

This rather scarce pamphlet has a few facts of interest, but its value is greatly impaired by vagueness, erroneous statement, and failure to give names of persons against whom accusations are made. Statements sometimes contradictory.

*268. WALLACE, LIEUT. GEORGE D. *March of the Seventh Cavalry June 22 to June 25, 1876.* Report of Chief of Engineers for Fiscal Year ending June 30, 1877, Appendix PP.

*269. WEBB, LAURA S. *Custer's Immortality.* Poem with some text notes. New York, n.p. n.d.

*270. *West Point Military Academy, Centennial of, 1802-1902.* 2 Volumes. Washington, 1904.

*271. WHEELER, COL. HOMER W. *Buffalo Days.* Indianapolis, Indiana, n.d.

Contains considerable Custer matter.

*272. WHITE-MAN-RUNS-HIM, Crow Scout, Death of, *Saginaw News,* June 4, 1929. Saginaw, Michigan.

*273. ....Statement of, (See *Tepee Book,* 1916, p. 52).

*274. WHITTAKER, FREDERICK A. "General George A. Custer." *Galaxy,* Volume XXII, September, 1876.

Considering his later attitude, this paper is of interest as to Whittaker and his "Biography" of Custer.

*275. .... *Life of Maj. Gen. George A. Custer.* New York, n.d. (1876)

This "Life" has been referred to several times in my text. After a careful study, only one conclusion can be arrived at; namely, that so far as relates to the last battle it is a tissue of violently prejudiced misstatements.

*276. WILSON, JAMES G. "Two Modern Knights Errant." *Cosmopolitan,* May-October volume, 1891.

*277. WILSON, SERGEANT JAMES E. Report of Trip of Steamer "Far West" up the Big Horn River, June 24-29, 1876. Report of Chief of Engineers for the Fiscal Year ending June 30, 1877, Appendix PP.

*278. WISHERD, EDWIN L. "Crows, Friendly, In Festive Panoply." *National Geographic Magazine,* September, 1927, Volume LII, No. 3.

*279. WOODRUFF, GEN. CHARLES A. Letter to C. T. Brady on Custer's Last Battle. (See *Indian Fights and Fighters*)

*280. .... "The Sioux Campaign of 1876, and The Last Battle of General Custer." In *Addresses . . . Calif. Soc. Sons of American Revolution* published June, 1913.

Lieut. (General) Woodruff has contributed some useful material on the campaign from first-hand knowledge.

*281. YOUNG, JOHN RUSSELL. *Men and Memories.* Vol. II, New York and London, n.d., (1901)

Some very pertinent remarks about President Grant, and his relations to politicians, both civil and military. "The politicians understood and feared Grant. They could not use him and therefore sought to slay him. He had seen the calamity of patronage—jailbirds sent to command troops because they had a " 'political pull'—"are fair samples.

LIST "B"

ADDITIONAL BIBLIOGRAPHY
OF THE
BATTLE OF THE LITTLE BIG HORN

By FRED DUSTIN

282. ADAMS, JACOB. *A Man Who Fought With Custer.* See MCCORMACK, GEORGE R.

283. ARMES, GEORGE A. *Ups and Downs of an Army Officer.* Washington, 1900.

A curious story by a curious person in which he informs the reader that he had been under military arrest twenty-five times, had been repeatedly court-martialed and dismissed from the service. Had kept up a constant lobby with certain senators and representatives to get back into the service, and through an intrigue with Custer, Clymer and others, was able to bring about the Clymer Committee of the alleged sale of post traderships. Custer figures quite prominently in the picture. As General Belknap had

to pass on the sentence of both, each developed a hatred for him that resulted tragically for Belknap and Custer. Armes wrote one or two blackmailing letters to Belknap, in which he had company, a cashiered army captain. Armes was the "Washington real estate dealer" of one or two writers as the inciter of the Clymer Committee investigations in 1876, based on the Fort Sill post tradership of four years previous.

The devious methods of Armes, aided by certain congressmen, to finally attain to the rank of "Lieutenant-Colonel, retired" were capped by a final court-martial sentence of suspension, on the expiration of which he often appeared at various formal functions in the full dress uniform of his rank of lieut.-colonel in which he deceased.

After reading this remarkable story, only one conclusion can be reached, and it is that the assurance, conceit and enormous ego of Armes was so over-developed, that along with his naive self-revelation it amounted to insanity. His tie-in with Custer, Clymer and Meeker, of the *New York Herald* was not at all strange, and his whole history is a scathing commentary on the appointment of army officers following the Civil War, and the utterly unworthy, and at times almost if not wholly criminal acts by representatives in Congress to get commissions for men who should never have been permitted to disgrace the service.

*284. BALDWIN, ALICE BLACKWOOD (Mrs. Frank D. Baldwin). *Memoirs of the late Frank D. Baldwin, Major-General, U.S.A.* Privately printed, Los Angeles, Calif., 1929.

See also under, HUNT, FRED A., also letter from Gen. Baldwin's daughter, Mrs. Juanita Baldwin Williams-Foote to Fred Dustin.

*285. BARRY, D. F. "Photographer of Soldiers, Indians, Historic Places and Objects." *Winners,* Vol. X, No. 12, Nov. 30, 1933.

*286. "Beecher Island Fight." As told by Scout John Hurst to E. A. Brininstool; *Winners,* Vol. XVII, No. 7, June 30, 1933.
Beecher Island Rescue. See CARPENTER, BREVET COL. I. H.

*287. BEEDE, A. McGEE. "Custer Died By His Own Hand." *Chicago Herald and Examiner,* April 18, 1923: with marginal notes in script by Beede. Photostat copy.
A fantastic story and a good example of imaginative writing.

*288. .... "The Indian Who Shot Custer." Typed manuscript deposited with the Chicago Historical Society, sealed, "Not to be opened in less than twenty-five years," and opened in 1949. Photostat copy sent to Fred Dustin by the Chicago Historical Society.
The story has no foundation in fact. The author was strong in folk-lore and legend, and wrote a very creditable book, *Toward the Sun,* its value being enhanced by the commentary notes by the late Dr. Melvin R. Gilmore, University of Michigan.

289. .... *Sitting Bull and Custer.* Bismarck, N. D., 1913.

*290. BELKNAP, WILLIAM W. Secretary of War: as to his Knowledge of Marsh's payments to Mrs. Belknap: *Army and Navy Journal,* Vol. 13, No. 3 Mch. 18. 1876.

*291. .... Reception of, at Fort Abraham Lincoln by Custer. Letter of Col. James W. Forsyth to Belknap in regard to: *Army and Navy Journal,* Vol. XIII, No. 37, Apr. 26, 1876.
A sharp refutation of Custer's testimony before the Clymer Committee as to his reception of Belknap.

*292. BENTEEN, CAPTAIN FREDERICK W. Letters to Theodore W. Goldin: in manuscript.
The unexpurgated text of these remarkable letters has been suppressed for very good reasons. The originals were bought from E. A. Brininstool by Dr. Philip Cole of New York, and

after his decease, were sold to the Thomas Gilcrease Foundation, Tulsa, Oklahoma.

*293. .... Letters to Goldin in the hands of E. A. Brininstool, Los Angeles, Calif. *Hobbies,* Vol. 36, No. 12, Dec., 1931.
.... Letter to Edward S. Godfrey as to "abandoning the wounded." See GHENT, W. J.

*294. .... Comments on Whittaker's "Life Of Custer." *Army and Navy Journal* Vol. XIV, No. 24, Jan. 20, 1877.

*295. BERRY, PRIVATE GEORGE C., SEVENTH INFANTRY. "The Little Big Horn Campaign." *Winners,* Vol. XIX, No. 7, Sept. 28, 1942.

*296. BETHUNE, FRANK, Crow Indian, Finds Skeleton on Custer Field. Clipping from newspaper (*Saginaw News?*) Oct. 19, 1928, with letter to C. H. ASBURY, Supt. Crow Agency by Fred Dustin and Asbury's reply.

*297. *Billings Gazette,* Billings, Mont., "Founder's Section," June 30, 1927. First Half-Century of Billings. Much of Custer interest.

298. *BISMARCK TRIBUNE:* Golden Jubilee Edition, August 15, 1939; memorializing North Dakota's 50th anniversary of statehood. This special issue of the Tribune contains much Custer material, including the last notes of the reporter Mark Kellogg; a story of Dr. H. R. Porter and the Arikara "Bloody Knife"; P. E. Byrnes on Custer's alleged disobedience; Fred Dustin on "Curley's" alleged claims; Dr. Kuhlman on "Red Horse and Keogh"; life sketches of General Thomas I. Rosser and W. A. Falconer, and other items of interest.

*299. "Bloody Knife and Goose, Ree Scouts." *North Dakota Historical Colls.,* Vol. 7.
.... See under TAYLOR, JOSEPH HENRY.
.... See under BRININSTOOL, E. A.
.... See under BISMARCK TRIBUNE.

*300. .... See under NORTH, LUTHER H.
Bob-Tailed Bull. See under VAN OSTRAND, FERDINAND A.

*301. BOURKE, JOHN G., "Mackenzie's Last Fight with the Cheyenne Indians." *Winners,* Vol. VII, No. 1, Dec. 30, 1929.

302. BOYD, JAMES R. *Red Men on the Warpath.*

303. BOYD, ROBERT K. *Two Indian Battles, The Little Big Horn, 1876, and Birch Coulee, 1862.* 8vo, wrappers, 18 pages, privately printed, 1928.

*304. BRADLEY, LIEUT. JAMES H. "History of the Sioux. *Contributions to the Montana Historical Society,* Vol. 9, Helena, Mont., 1923.

*305. BRIGHAM, EARL K. Letters from, to Fred Dustin, of much interest, as well as copies of useful documents.

*306. BRILL, CHARLES J. *Conquest of the Southern Plains.* Oklahoma City, 1938.
An excoriating study and relation of the Washita fight and the events preceding and following it. Sheridan and Custer, but more especially the latter, are bitterly attacked. In the light of actual history, Brill seems to be largely justified.

*307. BRININSTOOL, EARL A. "Buffaloing Buffalo Bill." *Hunter,* Vol. 76, April, 1938.

*308. .... *Crazy Horse, Chief, His Career and Death.* Los Angeles, Calif., 1949. A symposium of accounts, edited by Brininstool, as follows: Gen. Jesse M. Lee, Dr. V. T. McGillicuddy, Major H. R. Lemly and others.

*309. ....Crazy Horse, "The Murder of. What Captain Lemly Saw Personally." *Hunter*, Vol. 66, May, 1933.

*310. .... "Captain Benteen's Story." (Reprint of pamphlet) *Winners*, Vol. XII, No. 9, Sept. 28, 1944.

*311. .... "Custer Battle Heroes: How twenty-four Troopers Won the Medal of Honor in the Battle of the Little Big Horn." *Winners*, Vol. IX, No. 10 Sept. 30, 1932.

*312. .... "The Kidder Massacre." *Hunter*, June 1933.

*313. .... "Lame Deer's Surrender and Death." *Hunter*, Vol. 55, July, 1932.

*324. .... McINTOSH, LIEUT. DONALD. Letters to Fred Dustin by Mr. Brininstool as to McIntosh.

*315. .... "RED MEN." (Part of a paper by Col. John Gibbon in *American Catholic Quarterly Review*, 1877.) Reprinted by Mr. Brininstool in *Hunter*, June, 1933.

*316. .... Remarkable Anonymous Letter to Mr. Brininstool: contains much of interest.

*317. .... "Who Killed Chief Yellow Hand?" *Outdoor Life-Outdoor Recreation*, (Date?)

*318. .... "Memories. (Of early life in Western New York)." Autobiographical sketches by Mr. Brininstool. *American Rifleman*, June, 1938.

*319. BRINKERHOFF, HENRY M., Sergeant in Troop "G"-McIntosh. Letter to Albert Johnson criticising General Godfrey for his anti-Reno stories.

320. BUEL, J. W. *Heroes of the Plains, or Lives and Wonderful Adventures of Wild Bill, Buffalo Bill, Kit Carson, . . . Gen. Custer's Last Fight.*
A florid account, well seasoned with western "expansiveness."

*321. BURDICK, USHER L. *"The Last Days of Sitting Bull, and the Wounded Knee Massacre."* Baltimore, Md., 1941.

322. .... *Tales From Buffalo Land, or the Story of FORT BUFORD, Dakota Ter.* Baltimore, Md., 1940.

*323. .... "Tragedy in the Great Sioux Camp: A historical novelette based on fact."
First Sergeant James Butler of Troop "L," the hero of the story, was killed in the Little Big Horn fight. Baltimore, Md., 1936.

*324. .... and HART, EUGENE D. *Jacob Horner and the Indian Campaigns of 1876 and 1887.* Baltimore, Md., 1942.

*325. "Marking Historic Sites." *Tepee Book*, November, 1916.
Shows the necessity of marking the route of Custer's march. Through Camp's efforts, a bronze marker indicates the place where the Seventh Cavalry crossed the divide between Davis Creek and Reno Creek.

*326. .... "The Records of Indian War History." Edited by Gen. William C. Brown. *Winners*, Vol. X, No. 11, Oct. 30, 1933.

*327. "Calamity Jane." *Billings, Gazette*, Sept. 8, 1940, Billings, Mont.

*328. CAMPBELL, EDWARD G. "Saving the Custer Muster Rolls." *Military Affairs*, Vol. X, No. 2, 1946.
Tells how some of the dilapidated muster rolls of the Seventh Cavalry's Little Big Horn campaign were preserved. Valuable.

*329. *Casper, Historic Fort.* Leaflet, n.p. n.d.

*330. Casper, Wyoming. Better Casper Association, Casper, Wyo. n.d. 1939?
CARTER, CAPT. R. G. See under GHENT, W. J.

*331. "Civilians, Unaccredited, Order as to," by Gen. A. H. Terry. Order No. 40, Hdqs. Dept. of Dakota, St. Paul, Minn., June 9, 1875. *Army and Navy Journal*. Vol. XII, July 3, 1875.
Interesting on account of its bearing on the presence of Mark Kellog with Custer's command, and in view of Sherman's order to "take no newspaper men along."

*332. COLLINS, ETHEL A. "Pioneer Experiences of Horatio H. Larned, and Some Account of John Smith (liquor-seller on the *Far West* in 1876.)" Vol. 7, *North Dakota Historical Collections*, Grand Forks, N. D., 1925.

*333. COMANCHE (Keogh's horse). "Charger on a Stricken Field." By Fairfax Downey. *Adventure Magazine*, Sept. 1941.

*334. "........ THE HORSE." *Winners*, Vol. XI, No. 3, Feb., 1934.

*335. .... *Winners*, Vol. XI, No. 2, Jan. 30, 1934.

*336. .... *Winners*, Vol. XI, No. 5, Apr. 30, 1934.

*337. "Crazy Horse. His Version of the Custer Battle." *Chicago Times*, May 25, 1877.

*338. .... Dedication of a Monument to North-west Nebraska News, Sept. 6, 1934.

*339. "...... and Lieutenant Robinson's Monuments." *Winners*, Vol. XI, No. 11, Oct. 30, 1934.

*340. "Crown King, The Custer Fight." *Leavenworth Weekly Times*, Aug. 18, 1881. Leavenworth, Kas.
An Indian's account of the Little Big Horn Fight.

*341. Crow's Nest, Notes on, by Gen. Charles Woodruff.
Woodruff's "Crow's Nest" was not the actual Crow's Nest of the Crow Indians. He was seriously in error.

*342. *CROOK, GENERAL GEORGE, Autobiography.* Edited, annotated and completed by Martin F. Schmitt. Norman, Okla., 1946.
A very valuable book. Gives story of Crook's early army life in California etc., after the Mexican war: drunken and demoralized officers of that period. Mentions Custer and his florid report of his captured guns, flags and prisoners, with a quizzical remark as to *who* made it possible for Custer to get the credit. Crook's sudden death left the work unfinished, and it was finished by Schmitt.

*343. CUSTER, GEORGE A., Expedition to the Black Hills, 1874. *Black Hills Engineer*, Nov., 1929.

*344. "........ In the Black Hills." *Cadiz Republican*, Cadiz, O., June 23, 1939.

*345. "........ Reckless Blunder; Career Revived at Widow's Death." *Detroit Free Press*, Apr. 9, 1933, Detroit, Mich.
.... Camp Homes of. See under DAVIS, THEODORE R.

*346. .... Sketch of, *Winners*, Vol. VIII, No. 7, July 30, 1931.

*347. .... Sale of Autographed Letters, Signed, from Custer to Postmaster-General, J. A. J. Creswell, Louisville, Ky., Mch. 14, 1872, asking the latter's influence in getting Boston Custer, his brother, appointed as a second-lieutenant in the Seventh Cavalry. Sold at auction in December,

1931, Chicago Book and Art Auctions. Listed by Forest H. Sweet, Battle Creek, Mich., May, 1938 at $15.00, and same month and year by Whitlock, New Haven, Conn., at $22.00.

*348. ...."How Did Custer Die?" *Waterbury Republican,* Waterbury, Conn., May 15, 1927.
A fantastic story.

*349. "........ at Gettysburg." (The third day at Gettysburg) *Century,* Vol. XXXIII, Nov. 1886, p. 451.
Two portraits with notes.

*350. .... "Found after the Fatal Massacre." By John E. McPherson. *Winners,* Vol. VI, No. 12, Nov. 30, 1929.

*351. .... At Monroe, Mich., ALSO, Custer Killed 62 years ago to-day: *Monroe Evening News,* June 25, 1938, Monroe, Mich.

*352. .... Mutilation (At L. B. H. fight). *Winners,* Vol. V, No. 9, Aug. 30, 1928.

*353. .... Relics, Statement as to their disposition. *Winners,* Vol. XI, No. 6, May 30, 1934.

*354. .... Report on Reconstruction in his District by Gen. Custer, at the First Session, Thirty-Ninth Congress, Washington, 1866, Part IV, page 72, to the Joint Committee on Reconstruction.
Custer's testimony leaves no doubt that his early lukewarm view as to the Union cause had been dispelled by four years of war, but far more his experience in the deep South after the war. To a correspondent during his command in Texas he wrote that the Simon Legrees in that region were plentiful. His former experience in Maryland and Virginia where the close touch with free States made conditions very different in the treatment of slaves when escape was comparatively easy, a vast contrast to the brutish conditions that existed in Texas and Louisiana.

*355. .... "Finding the Bodies of the Slain after the Massacre." *Winners,* Vol. VI, No. 1, Nov. 30, 1929.

*356. .... "George Armstrong, American Soldier." *Winners,* Vol. VII, No. 3, Feb. 28, 1931.

*357. .... Unveiling the Statute of, At Monroe, Mich. *Saginaw Courier-Herald,* June 4, 1910.

358. .... *and Others, In Memorium.* Brevet Maj. L. M. Hamilton. n.p., 1869.
Hamilton was killed at the Washita fight.

*359. Custer Monument, New Rumley, O. Dedicated June 22, 1932: Program *Cadiz, Ohio Republican,* Dedication Supplement, July 23, 1932.

*360. CUSTER, MRS. ELIZABETH BACON. In "Half-Forgotten Romances of American History," by Elizabeth E. Poe. *Winners,* Vol. X, No. 5, June 30, 1935. (From *Washington D. C. Post*)

*361. .... Custer's letter to, June 9, 1876, from "Boots and Saddles."
.... Expresses her displeasure over the first Custer statue at West Point, but pleased with the second one which displaced the first.

362. .... Unusual picture of General Custer and. *Winners,* Vol. XII, No. 6, May 30, 1935.

*363. ....The Passing of. *Winners,* Vol. X, No. 5, Apr. 30, 1933.

*364. "Thousands Visit the Custer Battlefield." *Winners,* Vol. XII, No. U, June 30, 1935.

*365. *Custer Battlefield National Cemetery* (Park). Guide leaflet, 6 pages, 8vo, 5 ills., and one map. Natl. Park Service, n.d.

*366. Later issue with same map and one additional map, with 4 different Ills. n.d.

*367. ...... 16-page, quarto, with 13 ills. and 2 maps. Wash., 1943.
A very adequate guide.

*368. .... By Edward J. and Evelyn S. Luce: Natl. Park Service, Wash., 1949. 16 pages, with 13 ills. and 2 maps.
Well-written with reasonable restraint and quite adequate.

*369. .... Discoveries on the. Letter from Robert S. Ellison to Fred Dustin.

*370. Custer, FORT, The Building of, *Winners,* Vol. X, No. 5, Apr. 30, 1933.

*371. .... Reminiscences of. By Corporal Maurice J. O'Leary, First Cavalry. *Winners,* Vol. VII, No. 11, Oct. 31, 1930.

372. Custer, Milo. *Custer Genealogies,* Bloomington, Ill., 1944.

*373. *Custer Tragedy, The.* Dustin: Review in *Billings Gazette,* Billings, Mont., June 25, 1939.

374. "Custer in Wall Street." *Army and Navy Journal,* Vol. XX, Jul. 21, 1883.
A questionable transaction in which Custer was the chief figure.

*375. DALY, H. W., Chief Packer, U. S. Army, *Manual of Pack Transportation.* Washington, D. C., 1910.
Refers to Custer, Crook: Very complete.

376. DAVIS, THEODORE R. "With Generals in their Camp Homes." Custer. *Westerners Brand Book,* Chicago, 1947.

*377. .... "A Summer on the Plains." *Harper's New Monthly Magazine,* Vol. 36, Feb., 1868.
Davis was an artist for Harper's, and accompanied the Hancock Expedition in the campaign which resulted in Custer's courtmartial. Davis had a great opportunity, but wasted much time and ink in denouncing the Indians instead of giving a full account of the expedition; still, it has some value.

*378. DE WOLFE, DR. J. M. (Killed with Reno). His last letter to his wife—copy of.

*379. DE LAND, CHARLES E. Basil Clement (Claymore). "The Mountain Trappers-Stanley's Yellowstone Expedition in 1873." *Historical Collections of South Dakota,* Vol. XI, 1922, Pierre, S. D.
Considerable useful matter on Stanley's expedition.

*380. DIXON, CAPTAIN JAMES W. "Across the Plains with General Hancock." *Journal of the Military Service Institution,* Vol. VII, June, 1886.
This was the expedition which brought about Custer's courtmartial and suspension.
DOWNEY, FAIRFAX. "Charger on a Stricken Field." See under COMANCHE.

*381. ...."Indian Fighting Army." New York, 1941.
A well-written work: a compilation of outstanding Indian fights based on authoritative accounts by many writers. Useful for general reader; considerable on Custer's fights.

382. DODGE, COL. RICHARD IRVING. *The Black Hills.* New York, 1876.
An excellent work.

*383. Drannan, Captain, his picture, with E. A. Brininstool's penciled comments. This remarkable individual seemed to have the ability of being in two or more different places several hundred miles apart at the same time. *Hoofs and Horns,* Tucson, Ariz. May, 1941.

*384. DUSTIN, FRED. *The Custer Tragedy.* Ann Arbor, Mich., 1939.

Considerable research and detailed account. Bibliography of 18 maps and 300 printed works.

*385. .... "George Armstrong Custer." *Michigan History Magazine,* Vol. 30, No. 2, Apr.-June, 1946.

Biographical sketch.

*386. .... A Few Corrections of Old Neutriment (John Burkman) by Glendolin D. Wagner.

"Old Neutriment" is an interesting book, but its errors of fact are so numerous that aside from certain relations of which Burkman had actual knowledge, it is extremely misleading from the historical standpoint. As a "human document" it is of value. (In Manuscript)

*387. .... A criticism of Beardsley, J. I., "Could Custer Have Won?" In *Outdoor Life,* Mch. 1933, which see in Addenda: Also, under ED-WARDS, LT. COLONEL WILLIAM W., No. 102. In Manuscript.

*388. EDGERLY, WINFIELD S. "An Account of the Custer Battle." *Leavenworth Weekly Times,* Aug. 18, 1881.

Good source material.

.... See also under GHENT, W. J.

389. ELLISON, ROBERT S. "Portugee Phillips and His Famous Ride." Typed autographed presentation copy to Fred Dustin from Mr. Ellison, dated at Tulsa, Okla., Oct. 11, 1940.

390. ENGLISH, LIEUT. WILLIAM. Manuscript Field Diary, Mch. 17 to Sept. 5, 1876. Deposited in Yale University Library, New Haven, Conn. The contemporary record of a lieutenant in the cavalry company of Gibbon's command that first reached the scene of Reno's first fight.

*As noted in the *Yale University Library Gazette,* Vol. 23, No. 2, October 1948, to which this entry—390—alludes only.

*391. FARLEY, JOSEPH P. *Three Rivers: The James, The Potomac and The Hudson.* New York and Washington, 1910.

While not a "Custer" book in the sense of a historical relation, it is an idealistic picture of the better part of what West Point stands for by a man who graduated from it in 1861 and served in the Union Army.

*392. .... *West Point in the Early Sixties.* Troy, N. Y., 1902.

Considerable on Custer and much of high quality on the Civil War.

*393. FINKEL, "FRANK, Custer Battle Survivor." By Kathryn Wright, *Billings Gazette,* Billings, Mont., June 22, 1947.

A "Frank Finkel" was listed as one of the killed in the Little Big Horn fight, and the Frank Finkel of the story was probably one of the "sergeant and six men" from his troop who were detached to accompany the pack train, and his "survival" was likely due to that fact. The story has several impossibilities, and may be safely added to the seventy-five or more other "survivors" of Custer's five troops who died with him.

394. Finding Bodies of the Slain in Custer Massacre. See No. 355.

*395. FOUGERA, KATHERINE GIBSON. *With Custer's Cavalry.* Caldwell, Ida., 1940.

Mrs. Fougera was the daughter of Lieut. Francis M. Gibson of Benteen's troop, and the book was written from the records and memories of her mother in the first person. Like Mrs. Custer's books, it is quite revealing in many ways: contains a long letter from Lieut. Gibson to his wife, written July 4, 1876, with the story of the fight. Well-written and useful.

*396. FREEMAN, CAPT. HENRY B., Seventh Infantry. Part of the diary of, from June 12, to July 26, 1876, with notes by Fred Dustin. Capt. Freeman commanded Gibbon's infantry battalion in the campaign.

A very important historical document: revealing. Mss.

397. FRY, JAMES B. *Military Miscellanies.* New York, 1890. Chapter XIV "Custer's Defeat By Sitting Bull," is characteristic of those blind idolators whose worship led them into imaginative eulogy.

*398. "GARRY OWEN. Seventh Cavalry Battle Song." History of and use in the Seventh Cavalry. *Cavalry Journal,* July-August, 1942.

*399. GATCHELL, THEODORE J. Fort Phil Kearny and Environs, and History of old Fort McKinney. Gatchell Drug Store 50th Anniversary Souvenir, May 22, 1950.

Autographed copy. Reliable information.

400. GERRISH, THEODORE. *Life in the World's Wonderland.* Biddeford, Me., 1887.

Contains descriptions of Indian battlefields in the west.

*401. GHENT, W. J., Letters from, to William A. Falconer, with comments by Earl A. Brininstool. Also, several from Ghent to Fred Dustin with copies of the latter's replies to Ghent.

*402. .... A collection of anti-Reno attacks etc., secured by Ghent as follows:

Capt. Benteen to Godfrey in 1886 as to "abandoning wounded."

Capt. R. G. Carter as to "Reno's cowardice," and officers at the Reno Court of Inquiry, "practically perjuring themselves and reluctant to testify."

Lieut. Edgerly as to advance to Weir's Peak, and criticising Reno for "not charging through the village."

Ghent on letter from Benteen to Goldin.

Gen. Godfrey as to "Why Reno's name should not appear on the Reno Hill Monument," and Godfrey's letter to Mr. J. A. Shoemaker, Billings, Mont.

Capt. Moylan as to the *Century* article by Godfrey, and as to Reno.

Gen. Hugh Scott's notes on the Herendeen story in the *New York Herald,* Jan. 22, 1878.

(Typed copies of the originals which were collected by Ghent)

*403. "........ Varnum, Reno, and the Little Big Horn." *Winners,* Vol. XIII, No. 5, April 30, 1936.

A venomous attack on Reno with plenty of errors of fact. It was replied to by F. F. Van de Water, author of "Glory Hunter," and E. A. Brininstool, but the publishers of *Winners* refused to print these replies. See also manuscript by Fred Dustin analyzing the Ghent article.

*404. GODFREY, EDWARD S. "Cavalry Fire Discipline." *Journal of the Military Service Institution,* Vol. XIX, Sept., 1896.

In this paper Godfrey gives a much clearer picture of his actions in the Little Big Horn fight than he does in his *Century* paper. Also notes actions in the Washita fight.

.... "Custer's Last Battle." Reprint of the Mrs. Custer-Godfrey pamphlet in Vol. 9, *Montana Historical Collections.*

*405. .... First printed comment by, on the Little Big Horn fight. *Army and Navy Journal,* Vol. XIV, No. 58, Sept. 2, 1876.

*406. .... "Medicine Lodge Treaty, 60 years ago." *Winners,* Vol. VI, No. 4, Mch. 30, 1929. (This is the preliminary chapter to the Battle of the Washita which follows)

*407. .... "Battle of the Washita." *Winners,* Vol. VI, Nos. 5-6-7-8, Apr., May, June, July, 1929.

*408. .... Wounded Knee Creek," "Battle of, *Winners,* Vol. XII, No. 2, Jan. 30, 1935.

.... Why Reno's name should not appear on the Reno Hill Monument. See under GHENT, W. J.

.... Letter to "Mr. J. A. Shoemaker, Billings, Mont." See under GHENT, W. J.

*409. GOES AHEAD, "(Crow scout and Custer)" Reminiscences of. *Tepee Book,* November, 1916.

*410. GOLDIN, THEODORE W. "Finding Bodies of the Slain." See No. 355.

*411. .... "Regimental Band and Others of the Seventh Cavalry left at the Powder River Camp." *Winners,* Vol. XII, No. 5, Apr. 30, 1935.

*412. .... Story of the Little Big Horn, Milwaukee Journal, Wis., Oct. 27, 1929.

*413. .... Extract from Brady's "Indian Fights and Fighters," page 263.

*414. GRAHAM, COL. WILLIAM A. "The Lost is Found! Custer's Last Message Comes to Light." *Cavalry Journal,* Vol. LI, No. 4, 1942.

A very interesting story of the "Be quick" order to Benteen. This order was offered to Fred Dustin by a New York bookseller some time previous to its sale at a high figure.

*415. "Come On, Be Quick, Bring Packs," Custer's Last Message as told by Trumpeter Martin to Col. William A. Graham, with comments by Gen. Edward S. Godfrey. *Cavalry Journal,* July 1923.

HAMILTON, BREVET MAJOR LOUIS M. Memorial of, See under Caster.

*416. HAYCOX, ERNEST. *Bugles in the Afternoon.* Boston, 1944.

A novel based on some of the history of the Seventh Cavalry, culminating at the Little Big Horn. Unusual for its fidelity to history, and as such, is entitled to a high place in the lighter type of historical fiction.

417. HEBARD, GRACE RAYMOND. *Washakie, an Account of Indian Resistance to Invasions of Their Territory.* Arthur H. Clark Co., Cleveland, O. Much on the Little Big Horn Fight as to its prelude.

*418. HIXON, JOHN C. Custer's "Mysterious Mr. Kellogg" and the Diary of Mark Kellogg. Pamphlet reprint from *North Dakota History,* Vol. 17, No. 3, July, 1950, Bismarck, N. D.

Mr. Hixon has regarded the letters written to the *New York Herald* by Custer during the march from Fort Abraham Lincoln as the production of Mark Kellogg. The only authentic letter by Kellogg to the *Herald* was written June 21, 1876, and was printed in the *Herald* July 11.

The Reynolds diary has been in question, but proof or disproof should be easy if any manuscript of Kellogg remains for comparison with the *original* Kellogg diary if such exists.

Much of the value of Mr. Hixon's paper lies in his copious footnotes.

*419. HAMMON, JOHN E. Corporal Troop "G," Seventh Cavalry. Statement made and signed by him, to Charles E. DeLand, Feb. 28, 1898. Has considerable value.

*420. HERENDEEN, GEORGE. Notes on his story in the *New York Herald,* Jan. 22, 1878, by Gen. Hugh L. Scott. See under GHENT, W. J.

*421. .... Notes on, by Albert W. Johnson. See under JOHNSON, ALBERT W.

*422. HETLER, JACOB. "Story of, in Little Big Horn Fight." *Winners,* Vol. XII, No. 12, Nov. 30, 1935.

*423. HETTINGER, AUGUST. Personal Recollections of Messiah Craze Campaign. *Winners,* Vol. XII, Nos. 1, 2, 3, Dec. 30, 1934; and Jan., Feb. 1935.

*424. HORNER, "JACOB, Why He Missed Being in the Custer Fight." *Winners,* Vol. XII, No. 9, Sept. 30, 1935.

*425. .... Extracts From His Story as told to Bruce Nelson, *Sensation Magazine,* Feb., 1943, Denellen, N. J.

.... See also under BURDICK, USHER L., and HART.

426. HUBBARD, ELBERT, *Custer's Last Fight at Little Big Horn.* East Aurora, N. Y., 1917.

*427. "Hump, Indian Chief. His Account of the Custer Fight." *Leavenworth Times,* Aug. 18, 1881, Leavenworth, Kas. Quite important.

*428. HUNT, FRAZIER and ROBERT. *I Fought With Custer; The Story of Sergeant Charles Windolph.* New York, 1947.

The first half of the book is largely the result of interviews with Windolph, and as a whole, has considerable value. The last half is a mixture of speculation and history, and is in part, made up of quotations from official records. It is in such contrast to Frazier Hunt's "Custer, The Last of the Cavaliers," that we wonder at the change of attitude. The very good bibliography seems to have followed the pattern of that in the Custer Tragedy.

429. "Indian Fighters Recall Little Big Horn Defeat." *Winners,* Vol. VIII, No. 8, July 30, 1931.

*430. "Indian Warfare and the Custer Massacre." By Tom Hale, First Cavalry. *Winners,* Vol. V, No. 10, Sept. 30, 1928. (Reprinted from *The Wave,* Rockaway Beach, N. Y., Jan., 1925.)

*431. *INDIAN WAR VETERANS, PENSIONS FOR.* House Report No. 115, 64th Congress, 1st Session, with a twenty-five page resume of Indian campaigns, 1866-1882, by Capt. S. J. Bayard Schindel, July 22, 1914.

*432. "Iron Thunder, His Story of the Custer Fight." *Leavenworth Times* Aug. 18, 1881. Of considerable value.

*433. JACKER, REV. EDWARD. "Who is to Blame for the Little Big Horn Disaster?" *American Catholic Quarterly Review,* Vol. I, 1876, pages 712-741.

From its title and length we would expect an analysis of the Little Big Horn fight, its antecedents, personalities and basic causes, but instead, we have twenty-one lines expressing sympathy for the fallen, etc. Then beginning with these words, "The full significance of the fact, however, especially from a Catholic point of view, seems not quite generally understood nor candidly acknowledged."

In this single sentence the whole matter is summarized, for in the twenty-six pages following, the cause of the disaster is due to a lack of Catholic missionary effort. So far as the Custer fight is concerned, the article is valueless, and its worth lies in an account of the work of certain missionary priests, and a two-page appendix, "A Comparative Vocabulary of the Dakota Language and the Non-Aryan Tongues of India" is of considerable interest.

*434. JOHNSON, ALBERT W. Notes on George Herendeen in letter to Theodore W. Goldin: Also, Extracts from the Diary of Charles Reynolds. Very useful.

*435. .... Kennedy, Francis Johnson, soldier of Seventh Cavalry, Statement of, also note on Herendeen, Of considerable value.

*436. .... Photographs of Noted Indians, and historic views, list of in Johnson's possession. Largely by Barry.

*437. .... "Sioux War in Minnesota, 1862-1863." *Winners,* Vol. XIII, No. 10, Sept., 1936.

A well-written and summarized account of the "Minnesota Massacres."

*438. .... Unknown Soldier. Letter to Johnson from W. B. Plympton, Field Service, Indian Affairs, Crow Agency, Mont., as to the Unknown Soldier.

*439. JOHNSON, ROY P. "Jacob Horner of the Seventh Cavalry." Reprint from *North Dakota History,* Vol. 16, No. 2, Apr. 1949.

*440. .... "Gustave Korn, Blacksmith, Troop "I," Seventh Cavalry, as told to Johnson by Jeremiah Finley." *Fargo Forum,* N. D., Jan. 30, 1949.

The story makes Korn a "survivor" of the Custer battle. That he survived is certain, but *how* is not satisfactorily explained, for the story is third-hand, vague, and of little if any, value historically.

*441. .... Three articles in the *Fargo Forum.* Fargo, N. D., on Terry's march from Fort Abraham Lincoln to the Little Big Horn Field.

The remainder of the series are not in the compiler's possession, but those noted above show considerable research, and are of value.

*442. KANIPE, MRS. MISSOURI. "Her Soldier-Husband." (First Sergeant Bobo, killed with Custer). *Winners,* Vol. IX, No. 6, May, 1932.

*443. KELLOGG, MARK, "His presumed diary." *Bismarck Tribune,* N. D., Aug. 13, 1939.

*444. .... "Notes on the Little Big Horn Expedition under General Custer." *Montana Historical Society Collections,* Vol. 9, Helena. Mont., 1923. This was Mark Kellogg's presumed diary.

*445. KEOGH, FORT, The History of. *Billings Gazette,* Sept. 8, 1940, Billings, Mont.

446. KIDD, A. J. *Recollections of a Cavalryman.* Privately printed, 1908, Ionia, Mich.

*447. Koehler, Mrs. Clark, of Saginaw, Mich. Long letter from her brother from Miles City, Mont., in which he writes of the Little Big Horn fight, and gives some interesting information.

*448. KUHLMAN, CHARLES. "Did Custer Disobey Terry's Orders?" Paper read before the Billings, Mont., Rotary Club, Aug. 26, 1946. A well-prepared paper in which Dr. Kuhlman takes the negative side.

*449. .... *Custer and the Gall Saga.* A remarkable analysis and study of Custer's fight. Speculative, but bringing out certain new facts. May not be accepted as a whole, but very useful.

*450. .... Long Custer Article, informative and of much value, *Bismarck, N. D., Tribune,* Aug. 13, 1939.

*451. KITTREDGE, WALTER. "Tenting on the Old Camp Ground," words and music. A beautiful souvenir edition with fine illustrations.

The Custer interest lies in the frontispiece, a fine steel engraving from an autographed photograph of Custer in his perhaps most modest pose, in striking contrast to nearly all of his pictures. In the uniform of a major-general, half-length. Fine half-tone of the author.

*452. *Leavenworth Weekly Times,* Aug. 18, 1881, Leavenworth, Kas.

Contains accounts of the Custer fight by the following Indians: Crow King, Hump, Low Dog, and Iron Thunder, also, Lieut. Winfield S. Edgerly, all of whom see under their names.

*453. LOUNSBERRY, COL. CLEMENT A. *Early History of North Dakota.* Washington, D. C., 1919.

A useful work, but as to Custer and the campaign of 1876, we find numerous errors. As a newspaper man of long standing, the author followed the dictum of the craft, supplying what pleased him best where real authority was either entirely lacking at the worst, or dubious at the best.

*454. LORENTZ, UPTON 'Expedition to re-establish old Fort Phil Kearny.' *Frontier Times,* Bandera, Texas, July, 1935.

Contains some information about California Joe, Custer's scout.

*455. LOWIE, ROBERT H. *The Crow Indians.* New York, N. Y., 1935.

Informative work on the Crows, past and present.

*456. LUCE, CAPTAIN EDWARD S. *Keogh, Comanche and Custer.*

Comanche had so many "biographers" that Captain Luce could add little about him. Comanche has figured time and again, "as the only living creature to survive the battle" when as a matter of fact, a considerable number of Seventh Cavalry horses were captured by the Indians, and turned up later in their hands. A chapter in the small volume by Dr. Charles Kuhlman adds to the value of the book.

*457. "Low Dog, His Account of the Custer fight." *Leavenworth Weekly Times,* Aug. 18, 1881.

Considerable value.

458. Martin, John, Custer's orderly trumpeter the day of the fight.

See under CAMP, WILLIAM M.

459. MARQUIS, DR. THOMAS B. Two typed extracts from "A Warrior Who fought Custer."
Describes the Indian camp and the rovings of the Indians after the battle.

*460. McCLERNAND, GEN. EDWARD J., *Winners,* Vol. XI, No. 11, Oct. 30, 1934.

*461. .... "With the Indian and Buffalo in Montana." *Cavalry Journal,* 1927.
Typed copy of the part covering the participation of Gibbon's command in the campaign of 1876. Of much interest and of value as source-material.

*462. McCONNELL, H. B., and RONSHEIM, MILTON, Compilers. "A Custer Bibliography." *Cadiz Republican,* Cadiz, O., June 23, 1932.

*463. McGILLICUDDY, JULIA B. *McGillicuddy, Agent.* Stanford University, 1941.
Much on government relations with the Indians. Useful.

*464. McGILLICUDDY, VALENTINE P. Letter to E. A. Brininstool as to Dr. George W. Lord (Killed with Reno).

*465. McINTOSH, LIEUT. DONALD. Letter from E. A. Brininstool to Fred Dustin as to McIntosh.

*466. MERINGTON, MARGUERITE. *The Custer Story—* "Based on the letters left by Mrs. Custer." New York, 1950.
A review of this book indicates that the author has been quite discreet in her selection of letters, and it seems likely that had she realized the connection of some of them with certain passages of Custer's life, they might have been omitted. In some instances she has been free in giving names, but in others only initials, a mistake from the historical view-point. Altogether too much has been concealed, garbled or distorted on this subject, and now that all the actors in the scene have passed from the stage, there is no reason for the suppression of facts. A senseless hero worship invited revelations, and the publication of historical truth has resulted.
As a whole Miss Merington's work is revealing and is well edited, and the running comments and narrative give a sequence of events to the close of Custer's career that adds to the value of the book.

*467. MERRILL, "MAJOR LEWIS, and Custer" *Army and Navy Journal,* Vol. VIII, No. 39, May 6, 1876.
An interesting side-light on Custer's relations with other officers of the Seventh Cavalry.

*468. MILES, GEN. NELSON A. *Personal Recollections and Observations.* Chicago and New York, 1896.
It may be said with truth, that General Miles' observations on the Little Big Horn Fight were based on his opinions as to certain matters which were at variance with the facts, and while his book has a high value as a whole, it is marred by his occasional lapses, that, coming from a supposed authority, cause perversions of history and mislead his readers.

*469. *Montana, Land of the Shining Mountains.* 2 copies, 19— and 1946.

470. Moore, Major Orlando. Report of, to Gen. Terry, Aug. 4, 1876.

*471. MOORE, CHARLES. "The Days of Fife and Drum." *Michigan Historical Collections,* Vol. 28, 1897-1898.
Considerable on Custer.

*472. Moses, W. W., "of the *Great Falls Tribune"* (Montana). "Sitting Bull, Sioux Medicine Man." *Winners,* Vol. X, No. 12, Nov. 30, 1933.

*473. Moylan, Capt. Myles, As to Godfrey's *Century* article and Reno.
See under GHENT, W. J.

*474. MURPHY, WILLIAM. "Fort Phil Kearny and Wagon-Box Fights." *Winners,* Vol. V, Nos. 6, 7 and 8, May, June and July, 1928.

*475. Museum, A Public Historical, In Custer Battlefield National Cemetery. A Bill for the Erection of, 76th Congress, 1st Session Jan. 4, 1939.

*476. MYRICK, HERBERT. *Cache La Poudre, The Romance of a Tenderfoot in the Days of Custer.* New York, 1905.
Much about Custer, but of a fictional character. Part of the illustrations have a historical value, for they are reproductions of historic places and persons, and there is a realism that does not offend, while it stirs the feelings, and is a dream-picture of what might have reasonably occurred.

477. NEWSON, T. M. *Thrilling Scenes Among the Indians, with a Graphic Description of Custer's Last Fight with Sitting Bull.* Chicago, 1884.

*478. NIXON, CAROLYN A. Custer Bibliography of about one hundred titles in manuscript, some of which are included in this list.

*479. NORTH, LUTHER H. Letter to Major A. B. Ostrander as to Bloody Knife, the Unknown Soldier and White Shield's story of the Custer fight.

*480. NUGENT, W. D., late of Troop "A," "Seventh Cavalry." *Winners,* Vol. IX, No. 7, June 30, 1932.

*481. NYE, ELWOOD L. "Marching With Custer." *Army Medical Bulletin,* April, 1941.
This paper by Colonel Nye (U.S.A. Retired), presents in strong colors the fatigue of horses and men on Custer's march from the Rosebud's mouth to the battlefield. Custer partisans from Whittaker to Godfrey have endeavored to prove that Custer's attack was neither premature nor in conflict with Terry's orders. Col. Nye's analysis of the marches very clearly indicates that men and horses were tired out when the command reached the divide, and had been over-marched. From his position in the Army, Col. Nye was especially interested in the horses of the Cavalry and field artillery, and made a study of those of the Seventh Cavalry from its leaving the Yellowstone on June 22 to the fight, and his conclusions are well-weighed and authoritative.

482. O'HARA, C. C. Custer's Black Hills Expedition. See No. 344.

483. "Old Neutriment" (John Burkman.) See under BURKMAN.

484. OTIS, GEORGE A. Transportation of Sick and Wounded. Drawings of Carrying Soldiers from Reno's Hill to Gibbon's Camp. Surgeon-General's Office, Washington, D. C.

485. PARTOLL, ALBERT J. Editor. "After the Custer Battle." *Sources of Northwestern History,* No. 39, Missoula, Mont.

*486. PAYNE, CAPTAIN JAMES S. "Indian Story Land." *United Service Magazine,* June, 1880.
During the late summer of 1878, Captain Payne visited the Custer field with his troop of

the Fifth Cavalry, arriving Aug. 22nd. Gives a few useful facts.

*487. PHILLIPS, JOHN, (Portugee), Monument To. *Winners,* Vol. IX, No. 4, Mch. 30, 1934.

488. PHILLIPS, JOHN, (Portugee) See under ELLISON, R. S.

*489. PORTER, DR. H. R. *Charles Reynolds,* Where He Fell.

*490. PRIDE, CAPTAIN W. F. *The History of Fort Riley.* n.p. (Fort Riley) 1926. Considerable as to the Seventh Cavalry.

491. Recruits for Seventh Cavalry. See under STURGIS, COL. SAMUEL D.

492. REMSBURG, J. E. and G. J. *Charley Reynolds,* Kansas City, Mo., 1931.

493. Reno, Major Marcus A., Report of, to Gen. Terry, July 5, 1876.

*494. .... Death of.

495. .... Court of Inquiry, Proceedings of. See under GRAHAM, WILLIAM A.

*496. .... Testimony at Court of Inquiry, Abstract of about 100 pages with carbon copy.

*497. .... Testimony—208—Supplemental Abstracts in addition to above, by Fred Dustin, 22 pages, with carbon copy.

*498. .... Second Supplement by Fred Dustin, 23 pages with carbon copy.

*499. .... Court-Martial of, May 8, 1877. Suspended from pay and rank for two years.

*500. .... Court-Martial of, Nov. 28, 1879. Dismissal from the service.

*501. "Reno Hill Monument Dedicated." *Winners,* Vol. VI, No. 11, Oct. 30, 1929.

*502. RENO TRIAL, (Court of Inquiry) The Secret of. *Army and Navy Journal,* Vol. XVI, No. 33, Mch. 22, 1879. Whittaker scored for his part in the matter.

*503. Reno, Old Fort, on the Bozeman Trail. See under ELLISON, ROBERT S.; REYNOLDS, CHARLES, See under BRININSTOOL, E. A., REMSBURG, J. E. and G. J.; PORTER, DR. H. R. and JOHNSON, ALBERT W.

.... DIARY OF. See under JOHNSON, ALBERT W.

*504. .... Plan for Ceremony of Dedication of Bronze Plaque at place Where He Fell, Aug. 17, 1938. *Billings Gazette,* Aug. 1938.

*505. .... "Honored With a Marker"—Ceremony of Dedication, Aug. 17, 1938:

Brininstool, Ellison, Kuhlman and others mentioned. *Billings Gazette,* Mont., August 18, 1938.

*506. RICHESON, VOORHEIS. "History of the Seventh Cavalry." *Winners,* Vol. VII, No. 5, Apr. 30, 1930.

*507. ROGERS, G. SHERBURNE, and LEE, WALLACE. *The Geology of the Tullock Creek Coal Field.* U.S. Geological Survey, Bulletin 749, Wash., 1923. Of use as to the topography of the region.

*508. ROOSEVELT, THEODORE. "On Indians and Indian wars," *Winners,* Vol. X, No. 5, Apr. 30, 1933.

Roosevelt's opinion as to the Indian seems to be in line with Judge Taney's decision as to the negro, that he had no rights that the white man was bound to respect, and in his paper we find that bitter hatred of the Indian that was characteristic of his type. For a more just view, see in the same number of *Winners,* page 3, General James Parker's article.

*509. SABIN, EDWIN L. *On the Plains With Custer.* Philadelphia, 1913.

A boy's story, and one to be commended, for the author has to a great extent followed history. The real hero is Custer, although the tale is of a boy's adventures. Naturally, there are some errors of fact, but not pure inventions by the author. This little book is listed as an example of a certain type of literature at its best.

*510. SCHAFF, MORRIS. *The Spirit of Old West Point, 1858-1862.* Boston and New York, 1907.

This finely written work covering a crucial period of our history, mentions Custer several times and the strained relations of the period are well treated: a revealing book.

511. SCHMITT, MARTIN F., and BROWN, DEE. *Fighting Indians in the West.* New York, 1948. (Reviewed in *Military Affairs,* Vol. 13, No. 2, Summer, 1949.)

*512. SCHULZ, EDWARD H. Report on Yellowstone River, Montana; House Document 83, 62nd Congress, 1st Session, July 1, 1911.

Deals with proposed improvement of the navigation of the river, with some descriptive and historical material: good map.

*513. Scott's Bluff National Monument, National Park Service.

*514. SCHREYVOGEL, CHARLES, Picture by. "Custer's Demand," with full-page portrait of the artist and explanation of the picture. *Everybody's Magazine,* Vol. 9, 1903, Page 121.
Shining Mountains, Land of the. See under Montana.

515. SHERIDAN, GEN. PHILLIP H., and SHERMAN, GEN. WILLIAM T., Report of Travel in the Big Horn Mountains and the Yellowstone River in 1877, with Custer Battle Maps. Washington.
Seventh Cavalry, History of, See under RICHESON, VOORHEIS.

*516. "Skeleton Discovered on Custer's Field, Aug. 25, 1884." *Army and Navy Journal,* Vol. XXII, No. 148, Sept. 20, 1884.
(Was it that of Dr. Lord? See under WHEELER, OLIN D., in Wonderland, 1901.)

*517. Spotted Tail's Daughter, Shang-Tag-a-Lisk, The Burial of.
(Typed copy received from Major A. B. Ostrander)

*518. SMITH, JOHN HENRY. *A Soldier's Report of the Custer Massacre and the Battle of the Little Big Horn.* n.d. (about 1946)
This neat 16-page pamphlet has a few points of interest, but the aged soldier's memory caused him to mix unrelated events and persons.

*519. SMITTER, WESSEL. "The Red Warrior Who Licked Custer." *Coronet.*
Some extremely fantastic statements; perhaps useful as an example of what a vivid imagination can do.

*520. Standing Bear's Story, A Criticism of, by O. Kay. *Winners,* Vol. V, No. 10, Sept., 1928.

*521. STRINGHAM, ALONZO. "A Rescue Incident of June, 1877." *Winners,* Vol. XI, No. 7, June 30, 1934.
(See Scott's "Some Memories of a Soldier," page 47)

522. STURGIS, COL. SAMUEL D. Scrap-Books of Contemporary Press Accounts of the Little Big Horn

Fight, etc., in Yale University Library, *Yale University Library Gazette,* Vol. 23, No. 2, Oct., 1948, New Haven, Conn.

*523. Survivors, Two Indian, of the Little Big Horn Battle. *Indians at Work,* Oct. 15, 1937.

*524. Sydenham, Lieut. Alvin H., *The Daily Journal of.* Edited by Deoch Fulton, New York Public Library, New York, 1940.

This young officer's journal covers his service for most of the period while stationed at Fort Keogh in 1889 and 1890, and contains some useful information. Supplementing the Journal are five pages of notes on the artist, Frederick Remington, who was at Fort Keogh for some time while Sydenham was stationed there, and it is presumed that Remington got most of the material for his book, "John Ermine of the Yellowstone" at that time. He was with General Miles and an Indian Commission.

*525. TAFT, ROBERT. "Custer's Last Stand: The Pictorial Record of the Great West." *Kansas Historical Quarterly,* Vol. XIV, No. 4, November, 1946. (Reprint)

Dr. Taft's masterly studies, in the series noted, has no finer subject than this title with its accompanying illustrations and text. The reproductions of pictures are from the most notable, one of which is so realistic, although purely imaginative, that it brings a thrill of horror when its implications are realized.

*526. TAYLOR, JOSEPH HENRY. Frontier and Indian Life, and Kaleidoscopic Lives, Extracts from, as to Bloody Knife.

*527. TAYLOR, THE SERGEANT. Scrap-Books "On the Campaign and massacre" (Little Big Horn) are said to contain "useful data." In Yale University Library, Yale University Library Gazette, Vol. 23, No. 2, Oct., 1948, New Haven, Conn.

528. TERRY, ALFRED H. General Grant's recommendation for his promotion to Brigadier-General in the Regular Army after his capture of Fort Fisher. Quoted from T. F. Madigan's "Sale of Autographed Letters," etc., Catalogue.

*529. .... Message to Gen. Sheridan from camp on the Little Big Horn, June 27, 1876. *Winners,* Vol. XII, No. 4, Mch. 30, 1935.

*530. THOM, W. T., JR.; HALL, G. M.; WEGEMANN, C. H., and MOULTON, G. F. "Geology of Big Horn County and the Crow Reservation, Montana." Bulletin 856, U.S. Geological Survey, Washington, 1935.

Useful as a reference in studying the terrain of the region.

*531. THOMPSON, PETER, Death of. Typed copy with notes.

*532. Thornburg Fight, The. *Winners,* Vol. X, No. 6, May 30, 1936.

Reprint from Chicago *Inter-Ocean,* Oct. 9, 1879.

*533. TRAUB, PETER E. "Sioux Campaign of 1890-91." (Wounded Knee) *Winners,* Vol. VIII, No. 3, Feb. 28, 1931.

*534. TROBRIAND, PHILIPPE REGIS DE. *Army Life in Dakota.* Chicago, 1941.

Colonel de Trobriand was stationed for two years or more in Dakota with his headquarters at Fort Stevenson on the Missouri River. There is much in his journal that reveals the discredit-

able actions of white traders, Indian agents and squaw-men, and perhaps it is for this reason largely, that it seems to be almost unknown to the average student of the period, 1867 to about 1870, but it is a mine of factual wealth. His comments on Custer while not at all flattering, are of interest. With the curiosity of the Frenchman, and the peculiar insight of that race, he saw with a clear vision, detached and isolated as it were, therefore more just by far, than even the judgment of an average high-grade American of the usual English or mixed descent.

*535. TURNER-HIGH, HARRY. *The Practice of Primitive War.* Montana State University, Missoula, Mont., 1942.

Refers to Custer briefly.

Unknown Soldier, The. See under JOHNSON, ALBERT W., and NORTH, LUTHER H.

536. UTLEY, ROBERT M. *Custer's Last Stand with a Narration of Events Preceding and Following.* Dayton, Ind., 1949.

The author states that he received information and assistance from "Captain and Mrs. Luce, Maurice Frink" and several others. Follows Whittaker, but in a milder vein. Well-written, but with many errors.

*537. VAN OSTRAND, FERDINAND A., Diary of. Edited by Russell Reid. *North Dakota Historical Review,* Vol. IX, No. 4, continuing through Vol. X; Bismarck, N. Dak., 1943-1944.

Van Ostrand was clerk for Indian traders at Missouri River posts, and his diary gives much of interest as to the traders, army officers and some frontiersmen, also about Bob-Tailed Bull.

*538. VARNUM, LIEUT. CHARLES A. Muster Roll of Varnum's Detachment of Indian Scouts from April 30 to June 30, 1876.

There are several errors in this roll.

539. VESTAL, STANLEY. (Pseud. for Walter Stanley Campbell). *War Path and Council Fire; The Plains Indians' Struggle for Survival in War and Diplomacy; 1851-1891.* New York, 1948.

540. .... "White Bull's Story of the Custer Battle," *Blue Book,* Aug.-Sep. 1933.

*541. Veterans, Indian War. Pictures of many, including Charles ("Chip") Creighton, Alson B. Ostrander and Theodore W. Goldin: also a picture of Beecher Island Monument. *Winners,* Vol. IX, No. 2, Jan. 30, 1932.

542. VICTOR, FRANCIS E. *Eleven Years in the Rocky Mountains . . . also a History of the Sioux War and a Life of Gen. George A. Custer, With a Full Account of his last battle.* Hartford, Conn., 1877.

Wagon-box Light. See under MURPHY, WILLIAM

*543. WARREN, GOUVERNEUR K. "In South Dakota. *South Dakota Historical Collections,* Vol. XI, 1922.

Much topographical and other information.

*544. WATSON, ELMO SCOTT. "Echoes of the Custer Tragedy." *Winners,* Vol. XII, No. 5, Apr. 30, 1935.

*545. WEBB, GEORGE W. *Chronological List of Engagements, Indian Wars, 1790 to 1898.* St. Joseph, Mo., 1939.

A useful compilation.

*546. WHEELER, OLIN D., "Wonderland, 1901." Northern Pacific Railway, St. Paul, Minn., 1901.

An unusually well-written article with fine

illustrations of the Custer Battlefield and some of the participants in the fight. Largely factual and not imaginative.

*547. White Shield's Story. See under NORTH, LUTHER H.

*548. White, William H., Guide at the Custer Battlefield. Was a soldier in Gibbon's command through the campaign. *Winners*, Vol. XII, No. 2, Jan. 30, 1935.

*549. WHITTAKER, WEIR, and GENERAL MILES. Article in the *New York Herald*, reprinted in *Army and Navy Journal*, Vol. XVI, No. 22, Jan. 4, 1879.

After the death of Weir in the fall of 1876, Whittaker began to talk about an alleged affidavit from Weir as to Reno's "cowardice," etc. Like many other anti-Reno allegations from the Whittaker source, it does not appear in the Court of Inquiry records, and the compiler does not find that it was produced in open court.

Miles' connection was in regard to certain firing experiments at Custer Hill as to their being heard at Reno's position after ascending the bluffs.

*550. WINDOLPH, CHARLES. *The Battle of the Little Big Horn*.

*551. Winners of the West. Index of Historical Data from its start, December, 1923, to November, 1935.

Over forty articles on Custer's career, mostly on the Little Big Horn fight.

*552. WISE, JENNINGS C. *The Red Man in the World Drama*. Washington, D. C., 1941.

An unusual book; historical with a "politico-legal study," in which the author presents many unpalatable truths of our dealings with the Indians.

*553. WISHERD, EDWIN L. "Friendly Crows in Festive Panoply." 18 fine colored plates. *National Geographic Magazine*, Vol. LII, No. 3, Sept., 1927.

*Wonderland. See under WHEELER, OLIN D.

*554. WOODRUFF, GEN. CHARLES A. "Montana Has Seen Bloody Fighting." *Winners*, Vol. VIII, No. 1, Nov. 30, 1931.

*555. Wounded Knee Creek, Battle of. See under GODFREY, EDWARD S.

*556. .... "The Last Major Fight." *Northwest Nebraska News*, Jan. 7, 1937. Crawford, Neb.

*557. .... "Report on Pension Bill for the victims and heirs of victims." (Indian) *Indians at Work*, July 15 and Aug. 1, 1937.

*558. Wyoming, Highway Map of, 1937.

*559. .... *WONDERFUL*. Cheyenne, Wyo., 1936.

Exceptionally fine pictures, including one of Devil's Tower.

*560. Yellow Hand Fight, Chief. Dedication of Monuments Marking the Sites. *Northwest Nebraska* News, Sept. 6, 1934; Crawford, Neb.

*561. .... "Monument," by Chris Madsen, *Winners*, Vol. XII, No. 1, Dec. 30, 1934.

*562. .... "Versus Buffalo Bill." *Winners*, Vol. VI, No. 11, Oct. 30, 1929.

LIST "C"

ADDENDA TO THE BIBLIOGRAPHY

OF THE

BATTLE OF THE LITTLE BIG HORN

BY FRED DUSTIN

563. Barry, D. F. See under GILMAN, SAMUEL C.

564. Battle Flags, Custer's. See under GRAHAM, W. A.

565. BEARDSLEE, J. L. "Could Custer Have Won?" Reprint in Hardin, Mont., *Tribune-Herald*, June 16, 1933.

*566. BENTEEN, CAPT. F. W. Letter to his wife, describing the Little Big Horn fight. See under GRAHAM, W. A., in "The Lost is Found," *Cavalry Journal*, Vol. LI, No. 4, 1942.

*567. BLAKE, HERBERT CODY. *Blake's Western Stories, California Joe, Yellow Hand and others*. Brooklyn, N. Y., 1929.

568. BRININSTOOL, EARL A. Charley Reynolds (By Remsburg). First Printed at Potter, Kansas, in 1914 and 1915. Typed Copy by Brininstool with additional information supplied by Charles A. Reynolds, a nephew of the scout. In manuscript.

*569. BRININSTOOL, E. A. *Troopers With Custer*. The Stackpole Company, Harrisburg, Pa., 1952. On the verso of the title-page, the author says: "Revised and expanded edition, with many new illustrations, of a small book titled *A Trooper*

With Custer, by the same author, published in 1925 by the Hunter-Trader-Trapper Co., Columbus, Ohio."

In the first thirty pages, Mr. Brininstool summarizes the fight, and follows with the accounts of various participants, such as Benteen, Varnum, Goldin and others, and in Chapter 16, puts in print with some deletions, the famous letter of Major Brisbin to Godfrey on the latter's *Century* story. With a single exception, we can see no reason for the deletions, for there was nothing either scandalous or scurrilous in the letter. The remainder of the letter brings together much valuable matter outside the Custer fight, most of it having been long out of print but still in strong demand. The format is excellent, and the new illustrations add much to the value of the book.

*570. Brisbin, Maj. James S., Statement of, on the Little Big Horn Campaign in *Omaha Daily Herald*, May 30, 1886, with another article in the same paper of June 10, 1886, with notes by Col. Charles F. Bates and comments by Fred

Dustin. Typed copy of originals, with the additional notes.

.... See also under GHENT, W. J.

571. BURDICK, USHER L., *Editor*. See under McLAUGHLIN, JAMES.

*572. BURKMAN, JOHN, (Old Neutriment), Shoots Himself." *Waterbury, Conn., Republican*, May 15, 1927.

*573. BURNETT, F. G. "History of the Western Division of the Powder River Expedition." *Annals of Wyoming*, Vol. 8, No. 3, January, 1932.

574. "Comanche Still Lives." See under SMITH, H. E.

575. COBURN, WALLACE DAVID. *The Battle of the Little Big Horn*.

I have never seen this pamphlet: it was called to my attention by Hon. Clare F. Hoffman, Rep. Fourth District, Michigan, Allegan, Mich., whose quotations from it remind me of Whittaker, Allan Nevins and other writers of that type.

*576. COPELAND, FRED. "Sitting Bull's Last Trail." *Youth's Companion*, July 15, 1920.

577. COX, JOHN E. *Five Years in the United States Army*. Reminiscences and Records of an Ex-Regular. The author, Rev. John E. Cox, was a sergeant in Company "K," First U. S. Infantry. A very rare book, 171 pages, printed at Owensville, Indiana, 1892.

Not first-hand as to the Little Big Horn fight.

*578. Curley, A Crow Scout. "Narrative of, to Charles F. Roe, Adjutant Second Cavalry." *Army and Navy Journal*, Vol. XIX, No. 34, Mch. 25, 1882. (SEE also under ROE)

*579. .... Statement of as to Battle, in *Tepee Book*, Anniversary Number, 1926.

*580. CURTIS, EDWARD S. *The Teton Sioux*, Vol. III. Typed extracts from.

Curtis was deeply interested in the Indian, and his story of, the Little Big Horn fight is of considerable value. His means and opportunity made it possible for him to collect much source-material. While sincerely honest, he was at times careless of facts, and accepted interpretations of locations or movements that were plausible but erroneous. An example is his location of the Crow's Nest.

581. Custer Battle Flags. See under GRAHAM, COL. W. A.

*582. Custer Battlefield Burials. See under DUSTIN, FRED.

*583. Custer Battlefield Re-burials. See under DUSTIN, FRED.

*584. Custer Battlefield Museum, Dedication of, June 25, 1952. *Billings Gazette* (Montana) June 22 and June 26, 1952.

*585. Custer Battlefield National Cemetery. Guide Leaflet, 6 pages, Hd. Ninth Corps Area, Presidio of San Francisco, Sept. 1, 1937.

*586. DUSTIN, FRED. "Analysis of W. J. Ghent's 'Varnum, Reno and the Little Big Horn.' " Mss. (See also F. F. Van de Water).

*587. .... "Some Aftermath of the Little Big Horn Fight in 1876: the Burial of the Dead." Mss., fifteen pages.

*588. DUSTIN, FRED. *Echoes From the Little Big Horn Fight*. Reno's Positions in the Valley. Privately printed, 1953, by the author.

In his circular, Mr. Dustin says: "I have never been satisfied with my version of Major Reno's positions in the Valley, for there was something lacking." In the 22 pages and five sketch-maps, he has corrected what he frankly concedes to be his mistakes, and we think, produces a clear picture of what has been a seeming confusion of accounts, but have now been clarified by the use of Col. Graham's complete publication of the Proceedings of the Reno Court of Inquiry, supplemented by other new material from authentic sources.

*589. Re-burials, The Custer; Mss., fifteen pages.

*590. The Little Big Horn Fight. Reno's Positions in the Valley, June 25, 1876, with map and notes on the same, 26 pages.

*591. EDGERLY, WINFIELD S. Letter to Capt. Edward S. Godfrey as to Reno's advance to Weir's Peak, June 25, 1876. Informative.

Carbon copy.

*592. ELLIS, HORACE. "A Survivor's Story of the Custer Massacre on American Frontier." Testimony of Jacob Adams. *Journal of American History*, Vol. III, No. II, 1909, page 227.

A brief laudatory introduction by Dr. Ellis who was President of Vincennes University, is followed by the story by Adams in the first person, but whether it was written by Adams or told by him to Dr. Ellis does not appear. There are something over five pages of text from which it seems that he was a member of Company "H", Captain Benteen, but was detailed with the pack train on the day of the fight.

It must be said that the article abounds with errors of fact, as well as by implication, and as a historical paper has little value. Much is evidently not related from Adam's own observation or experiences.

On page 200 is an "Original photograph of Custer with Maj. Gen. Alfred Pleasanton" on the battlefield at Brandy Station, Va.

*593. ELLISON, ROBERT S. "Old Fort Reno and the Bozeman Trail." *Midwest Review*, April, 1924.

Fort Reno was named after Jesse I. Reno, a graduate of West Point. He was breveted for "gallant and meritorious conduct" in the war with Mexico. Captain in the Regular Service at the outbreak of the Civil War, and was major-general of volunteers when killed September 14, 1862 at the battle of South Mountain.

*594. FRENCH, CAPT. THOMAS. Copies of parts of letters written by French to Mrs. Cooke, mother of Adjutant Cooke, as to Reno and DeRudio.

An extremely bitter attack on DeRudio by French, with a rather scathing comment on French by Fred Dustin.

*595. GHENT, W. J. Some notes on Theodore W. Goldin and W. J. Ghent by Fred Dustin.

*596. .... "Theodore W. Goldin and His Ride to Reno."

*597. .... Comments on Major James S. Brisbin's Letter to Capt. (General) Godfrey in a letter to Col. W. A. Graham, April 4, 1932, with notes on the same by Fred Dustin.

598. .... "When Custer Fought the Indians." A review of "Custer's Indian Battles" by Charles Francis Bates. *New York Sunday Times*, Nov. 8, 1936. Ghent was a rabid pro-Custer partisan and his "review" is in that spirit.

599. GILMAN, SAMUEL C. *The Conquest of the Sioux*. Indianapolis, Ind., 1926. With D. F. Barry pictures.

*600. GODFREY, LIEUT. EDWARD S. Letter to his wife after the Little Big Horn battle, dated July 4, 1876, from the camp on the Yellowstone. Typed copy. Informative and useful.

*601. . . . . Long letter to E. S. Paxson, of Butte, Mont.

Very informative as to clothing worn by Custer's officers, equipment, etc.; where the bodies of the officers were found; the condition of the dead and the burials. A valuable source-material paper written by Godfrey when his memory was clear. It was published in "Sources of Northwestern History," No. 39, Missoula, Mont. This typed copy was sent me with some accompanying useful notes, by Mr. James S. Hutchins, of Columbus, Ohio.

602. Goldin, Theodore W. See under Ghent.

*603. GIBSON, LIEUT. FRANCIS M. Letter to Edward S. Godfrey, as to the march of Benteen's battalion, June 25, 1876, dated Aug. 9, 1908. Typed copy.

Gibson gives what he claims or "understood" to have been Custer's reason for the movement, but in accordance with his former writings to others. He was not a witness at the Reno Court, and knew no more about what Custer's "reason" was than did Benteen or Godfrey; they, years later, also "understood" several things about the matter, that like Gibson's, were "post mortem," afterthoughts to fit theories, Typed copy.

*604. GRAHAM, WILLIAM A. Colors of the Seventh *at the Little Big Horn; Custer's Battle Flags*.

Two company guidons are in existence carried by men of Custer's battalion, one of which was noted in "The Custer Tragedy," by the compiler of this bibliography, and Col. Graham's story with its fine illustrations is an absorbing one. Autographed presentation copy, n.p., 1952.

*605. GRAHAM, WILLIAM A. *The Official Record of A Court of Inquiry Convened by the President of the United States at Chicago, Ill., January 13, 1879, By Request of Major Marcus A. Reno to investigate his conduct at the Battle of the Little Big Horn, June 25-26, 1876*. Pacific Palisades, Calif., 1951. Two large volumes, about 600 pages.

This monumental work has long been needed, and should be in the library of every large university or public library. A necessity for every serious student of that minutely dissected story of the Little Big Horn, sweeping away the all too numerous fictions of "feature writers" and partisan authors.

606. GRAHAM, COL. WILLIAM A. *The Story of the Little Big Horn*. Fourth Edition; The Stackpole Company, Harrisburg, Pa., 1952.

This book, first published in 1926 by The Century Company, New York, summarized the Little Big Horn fight, and added authoritative quotations directly from the proceedings of the Reno County of Inquiry, and while brief, filled a long-felt want among those to whom the "much in little" that it furnished was highly acceptable. The new editions contain more illustrations, and also the article, now practically unobtainable, by Col. Robert P. Hughes on Custer's disobedience of orders. This paper was originally published in the "Journal of The Military Service Institution," January, 1896, in reply to Gen. Fry's comments on Godfrey's *Century* story. We are thankful to Col. Graham for putting this authoritative analysis by Hughes again in print, for it is source material of great importance. Hughes was Aide to General Terry in the expedition which culminated in the disaster on the Little Big Horn.

*607. . . . . Prospectus of the Official Record of the Court of Inquiry above.

In this Prospectus, Colonel Graham gives a history of all previous copies of the Record and other pertinent matters in connection.

*608. JOHNSTON, CHARLES H. L. *Famous Cavalry Leaders*. I. C. Page & Co.

One of a series of books for boys, the last chapter being the Custer story. Well-written, but no new material, and follows the hero idea, although with moderation. As usual in this type of book, there are many errors, and it is to be regretted that so competent a writer was not able to stick to the factual story, which in itself contains all the charm of the heroic without the falsehoods of which I doubt that the author was aware, and it may be said that the restraint shown by him was admirable.

*609. KUHLMAN, CHARLES, PH.D. *Legend into History-The Custer Mystery*. The Stackpole Company, Harrisburg, Pa., 1951.

This remarkable work by Dr. Kuhlman is the result of years of study of the authorities, and days without number on the fields where Custer fought and died and Reno fought and lived. Much of the story, more especially, the fight of Custer with his five companies, is based on the author's deductions supplemented by accounts of a few enemy Sioux and Cheyennes, and of Curly the Crow scout.

Naturally, Dr. Kuhlman has met with some difficulties, but he has not been at a loss in finding his own solutions of the many problems. While some may disagree with a few of his conclusions, it must be said that no one yet has produced a work with the painstaking care necessary for such an effort in speculative deduction, and the book is of the greatest interest from cover to cover. There are six maps interpreting the text with several new illustrations.

*610. Lord, Dr. George W. Letter from V. P. McGillicuddy to Earl E. Brininstool as to.

*611. . . . . Dr. Lord's last letter to his wife. The copy of this letter is attached as an addenda to the Benteen-Goldin letters. It is of pathetic interest, and is informative.

612. MASTERS, JOSEPH G. *Shadows Fall Across the Little Big Horn*. Laramie, Wyo., 1951.

*613. McLAUGHLIN, JAMES. *My Friend the Indian: "Three heretofore unpublished Chapters."* Prefaced and edited by Ushur L. Burdick, Baltimore, Md., 1936.

*614. Pauling, Holmes O., Diary of, on the march of Gibbon's command, campaign of 1876.

Pauling was an army assistant-surgeon, the only medical man with Gibbon's column. In the whole account one is struck with the fact that he does not seem to commend a single person from Terry and Gibbon down. He entered the army late in 1874. His diary shows a woeful lack of ordinary judgment, and is one of the "choice" bits of anti-Reno and anti-Brisbin collected by W. J. Ghent. Has some value to the Custer student, but of a negative character. Typed copy.

615. Rain-In-The-Face. See under THOMAS, W. KENT.

*616. "RED HORSE, His Story of the Custer Fight." Tepee Book, 1926.

*617. Relics of the Little Big Horn. See "Mackenzie's Last Fight With the Cheyennes," *Winners*, Vol. VII, No. 5, Apr. 30, 1930.

618. Reno's Positions in the Valley, by Fred Dustin. In manuscript, 26 pages with map, June 1, 1952.

619. Reno, Old Fort. See under ELLISON, ROBERT S.

620. Reno Court of Inquiry. See under GRAHAM, WILLIAM A.

621. Reynolds, Charley. See under BRININSTOOL, EARL A.

622. Roe, Charles F. See Curley, A Crow Scout. No. 578.

*623. Siverton, John. His Story of the Little Big Horn. *Tepee Book*, 1926.

*624. SMITH, H. E. "Comanche Still Lives." In Robert Bruce's pamphlet, *Custer's Last Battle,* which see.

*625. Terry, Gen. Alfred H. Terry, Official Letter, signed.

626. THOMAS, W. KENT. "An Interview With Rain-in-the-Face." First published in the *Nickell Magazine,* December, 1896, and reprinted in *Outdoor Life,* March 1903.

This was the "heart-eating" story that has gained so many believers. It appears that Thomas and another young man got Rain-in-the-Face drunk at Coney Island, and concocted the ridiculous story, which was accepted by the Rev. Cyrus Townsend Brady, as completely worthy of credence. Brady repeats the story of the two fakirs in his book, "Indian Fights and Fighters," but a very casual analysis of the whole matter in P. E. Byrne's "The Red Man's Last Stand" is sufficient to demolish the whole story.

*627. VAN DE WATER, F. F. As to W. J. Ghent's "Varnum, Reno, and the Little Big Horn" which was published in *Winners of the West,* Vol. XII, No. 5, Apr. 30, 1936.

A scathing reply to Ghent's article. *Winners* refused to print. Manuscript copy.

*628. VARNUM, LIEUT. CHARLES A. Letter from, to his father, as to the Little Big Horn Fight. Printed in the Lowell, Mass., *Weekly Journal,* August, 1876, dated from camp on the Yellowstone, July 2, 1876.

A valuable contribution. Typed copy.

*629. WILBER, "JAMES, His Story of the Little Big Horn": *Tepee Book,* 1926.

630. *Yale University Library Gazette,* for which see ENGLISH, LIEUT. WILLIAM, No. 390; STURGIS, COL. SAMUEL D., No. 522; and TAYLOR, SERGEANT, No. 527.

*631. ZELLER, GERHARD D. Index to "My Life on the Plains," Custer.

WESTERN FORTS, PLACES, PERSONS, INDIANS

*632. BARRY, J. NEILSON. "Captain Bonneville." *Annals of Wyoming,* Vol. 8, No. 4, April, 1932.

*633. BRUCE, ROBERT. *Three Old Plainsmen and Other Western Stories.* New York, 1923.

The three old plainsmen were Ezra Meeker, Albert R. Baiseley, and William Francis Hooker.

*634. ELLISON, ROBERT S. "Fort Bridger, Wyoming." Historical Landmark Commission of Wyoming, Casper, Wyo., 1931.

Autographed Presentation copy to Major A. B. Ostrander, Dec. 25, 1931.

*635. .... *Casper, Wyoming, Development and History.* n.p. n.d. reprinted.

*636. .... *Historical Landmark Commission of Wyoming.* First Biennial Report, 1920 (Two copies).

*637. .... *Independence Rock, The Great Record of the Desert.* Casper, Wyo., 1930. Autographed Presentation copy to Major A. B. Ostrander, Aug. 4, 1930.

*638. Fox, George W., Diary of. Jan. 1, 1866 to Sept. 12, 1866. *Annals of Wyoming,* Vol. 8, No. 3, January, 1932.

Fox made the overland trip from Omaha, Neb., May 31, 1866 to Sept. 12, 1866, as far as Virginia City, a note at the close saying that he continued his diary to the end of the year, "but from September 12 on it was Montana history." Annals of Wyoming, Vol. 8, No. 3, January, 1932.

*639. Laramie, Fort, National Monument, Wyoming. Natl. Park Service, 1941 (?)

*640. Ostrander, Aison B., Diary of. Oct. 1, 1866 to May 15, 1867. *Wyoming Historical Dept., Quarterly Bulletin,* Cheyenne, Nov. 1, 1924.

*641. WILSON, RICHARD H. "The Indian Treaty of April, 1896." (With the Shoshones and Arapahos). *Annals of Wyoming,* Vol. 8, Oct., 1931.

INDEX

The following *name index* omits the three highly controversial figures of the Sioux War—General Custer, Major Reno and Captain Benteen, for their names appear on almost every page: nor was it thought desirable to index the names of the signers of the enlisted men's petition of 4 July 1876, which asked the President and the Congress to promote Reno and Benteen.